P9-DGW-484

Baltic Sea

Stralsund

Rostock

MECKLENBURG-
LOWER POMERANIA

Schwerin

MANY

Saxony-Anhalt
Pages 146–161

**Mecklenburg-
Lower Pomerania**
Pages 470–485

BERLIN

Potsdam

BRANDENBURG

Magdeburg

SAXONY-
ANHALT

EASTERN

Cottbus

GERMANY

Halle

Leipzig

SAXONY

Dresden

Berlin
Pages 66–123

Brandenburg
Pages 132–145

urt

Jena

THURINGIA

Chemnitz

Nürnberg

Thuringia
Pages 186–201

Saxony
Pages 162–185

ERN

ANY

Regensburg

BAVARIA

g

Munich

Munich
Pages 210–241

Bavaria
Pages 242–291

EYEWITNESS TRAVEL

GERMANY

EYEWITNESS TRAVEL

GERMANY

Main Contributors **Joanna Egert-Romanowska
and Małgorzata Omilanowska**

DK

LONDON, NEW YORK,
MELBOURNE, MUNICH AND DELHI
www.dk.com

Produced by Wydwnictwo Wiedza i Życie, Warsaw
Contributors Małgorzata Omilanowska, Marek Stańczyk, Tomasz Torbus,
Hanna Köster, Teresa Czerniewicz–Umer
Cartographers Kartographie Huber (Munich), Magdalena Polak, Dariusz Romanowski
Photographers Adam Hajder, Dorota and Mariusz Jarymowiczowie, Wojciech Mędrzak,
Tomasz Myśluk, Paweł Wójcik
Illustrators Lena Maminajszwili, Paweł Marczak, Andrzej Wielgosz, Bohdan Wróblewski,
Magdalena Żmudzińska
DTP Designers Paweł Pasternak, Paweł Kamiński
Editors Teresa Czerniewicz-Umer, Joanna Egert-Romanowska
Production Anna Kożurno-Królikowska
Designers Ewa Roguska, Piotr Kiedrowski

Dorling Kindersley Limited
Editors Sylvia Goulding, Irene Lyford
Translators Magda Hannay, Ian Wisniewski
DTP Designers Jason Little, Conrad Van Dyk
Production Marie Ingledew, Joanna Bull

Printed and bound by Vivar Printing Sdn Bhd, Malaysia

First American Edition 2001

14 15 16 17 10 9 8 7 6 5 4 3 2

Published in the United States by DK Publishing,
345 Hudson Street, New York, New York 10014

**Reprinted with revisions 2003, 2004, 2005, 2006, 2007, 2008,
2010, 2012, 2014**

Copyright 2001, 2014 © Dorling Kindersley Limited, London
A Penguin Random House Company

Published in Great Britain by Dorling Kindersley Ltd

A catalog record for this book is available from the Library of Congress.
ISSN 1542-1554
ISBN 978-1-4654-1152-5

Floors are referred to throughout in accordance with European usage;
ie the "first floor" is the floor above ground level.

Front cover main image: Fachwerk-style houses in the historic town of Freudenberg,
North Rhine-Westphalia

The information in every DK Eyewitness Travel Guide is checked regularly.
Every effort has been made to ensure that this book is as up to date as possible at
the time of going to press. Some details, however, such as telephone numbers,
opening hours, prices, gallery hanging arrangements and travel information are
liable to change. The publishers cannot accept responsibility for any consequences
arising from the use of this book, nor for any material on third party websites, and
cannot guarantee that any website address in this book will be a suitable source of
travel information. We value the views and suggestions of our readers very highly.
Please write to: Publisher, DK Eyewitness Travel Guides, Dorling Kindersley, 80 Strand,
London WC2R 0RL, Great Britain or email: travelguides@dk.com.

◀ St Sebastian's Church in Ramsau an der Ache, with the Eisberg (Reiter Alpe) mountain in the background

Contents

How to Use
This Guide **6**

Heraldic shield over the entrance to the
Nuremberg town hall

Introducing
Germany

Discovering Germany **10**

Putting Germany on
the Map **18**

A Portrait of Germany **22**

Germany Through
the Year **44**

The History of
Germany **50**

Berlin Area by
Area

Berlin at a Glance **68**

Eastern Centre **70**

Western Centre **86**

Further Afield **98**

Shopping in Berlin **110**

Entertainment in
Berlin **112**

Eastern Germany

Introducing Eastern
Germany **126**

Brandenburg **132**

Saxony-Anhalt **146**

Saxony **162**

Thuringia **186**

Southern Germany

Introducing Southern Germany **204**

Munich **210**

Shopping in Munich **234**

Entertainment in Munich **236**

Picturesque landscape in Mecklenburg

Statue of a dancing figure, Stadtmuseum in Munich *(see p218)*

Bavaria **242**

Baden-Wurttemberg **292**

Western Germany

Introducing Western Germany **334**

Rhineland-Palatinate and Saarland **340**

Hesse **364**

North Rhine-Westphalia **386**

Northern Germany

Introducing Northern Germany **422**

Lower Saxony, Hamburg and Bremen **428**

Schleswig-Holstein **458**

Mecklenburg-Lower Pomerania **470**

Travellers' Needs

Where to Stay **488**

Where to Eat and Drink **504**

Shopping in Germany **534**

Outdoor Activities and Specialist Holidays **536**

Survival Guide

Practical Information **542**

Travel Information **552**

General Index **560**

Acknowledgments **580**

Mainz Cathedral
(see pp354–5)

HOW TO USE THIS GUIDE

This guide will help you to get the most out of a visit to Germany, providing expert recommendations as well as thoroughly researched practical information. The first section, *Introducing Germany*, locates the country geographically and provides an invaluable historical and cultural context. Succeeding sections describe the main sights and attractions of the different regions and major cities. Feature spreads, with maps and photographs, focus on important sights. Information on accommodation and restaurants is provided in *Travellers' Needs*, while the *Survival Guide* has useful tips on everything you need to know from money to getting around.

Berlin

This section is divided into two parts: East and West. Sights outside the centre are described in the section *Around Berlin*. All sights are numbered and plotted on a map of the region. Detailed information for each sight is given in numerical order to make it easy to locate within the chapter.

Sights at a Glance describes, by category, buildings in a particular area: Historic Streets and Buildings, Museums and Galleries, Churches, Parks and Gardens.

Pages marked with red refer to Berlin.

A locator map shows where you are in relation to the city plan.

1 Area Map For easy reference the sights in each area are numbered.

2 Street-by-Street Map gives a bird's-eye view of each sightseeing area described in the section.

Stars indicate the sights that no visitor should miss.

A suggested route for a walk is marked with a broken red line.

3 Detailed Information All the sights of Berlin are described individually. Addresses, telephone numbers, opening hours, admission charges and information on how to get there are given for each sight. The key to symbols is shown on the back flap.

MUNICH

The capital of Bavaria, Munich is sometimes called "Germany's secret capital" Lying right at the heart of Europe, the city rapidly overshadowed once powerful neighbours, such as Regensburg, Augsburg and Nuremberg, to become southern Germany's main metropolis. With its vibrant cosmopolitan atmosphere, the buildings, museums and shops, it is one of the country's most popular tourist destinations.

The citizens of Munich have been known for centuries for their love of the arts. The masterpieces that were created here during the Baroque and Rococo periods were equal to Italian and French works.

In the 18th century, the town's development continued along New Classical lines, gaining for it the name of "Athens on Isar." Just how appropriate the name is can be seen when strolling along Ludwigstrasse or Königsplatz or visiting the Glyptothek, which houses Ludwig II's collection of Greek and Roman sculptures.

In the late 19th century the Art Academy of Fine Arts was amongst Europe's best art schools. Not many cities have as great a choice of world-class theatres, operas and museums as can be found here in Munich.

But it is not only art that gives Munich its unique charm. The country's biggest folk festival, the Oktoberfest, is held each year in Theresienwiese, where visitors to the town can join in the revelries or just sit and watch, ordering a plate of sauerkraut with sausages and washing it down with some of the excellent Bavarian beer.

When planning a shopping trip to Munich visitors can be sure that its shops are equal to those of Paris and Milan, not only in the breadth of their range but also in terms of their prices.

The town is also one of Germany's main centres of high-tech and media industries. Many TV stations and film studios, as well as over 300 book and newspaper publishers, have their main offices in Munich.

1 Introduction
The landscape, history and character of each region are described, showing how the area has changed through the ages. It also outlines the sights on offer for visitors.

Germany Area by Area

In this guide, Germany is divided into 13 areas, each of which is covered in a separate section. The most interesting cities, towns, villages and sights in the area are marked on the Area Map.

Exploring Saxony

When travelling in Saxony, a visit to Dresden is a must. Visitors should set aside several days to explore its historic sights and magnificent monuments. Dresden is also a convenient base for excursions to the attractive landscape of the Sächsische Schweiz ("Saxon Switzerland") and further afield – to Bautzen, Görlitz and Zittau, or to the Erzgebirge Mountains, towards Freiberg and Chemnitz. Another town worth visiting, at least for a day, is Leipzig with its historic sights, cultural events, trade fairs and exhibitions.

Getting Around

Leipzig and Dresden both have airports, as well as excellent train and coach connections with the rest of Germany. The A4 motorway runs west from Görlitz, through Dresden and Chemnitz; the A13 links Dresden with Berlin, and the A14 with Leipzig. Other roads, national and regional, are clearly signposted, and all the towns described in this guide can also be reached by local buses.

2 Regional Map
This shows the main roads and the general topography of the area. All sights are numbered, and there are also details on how to get there.

Boxes contain additional information about sights.

Colour coding at the edge of every page makes it easy to find each particular region.

3 Detailed Information
All major towns, places of interest and other tourist sights are listed in order and numbered according to the Regional Map. Each entry contains information on important sights.

A Visitors' Checklist for each of the main sights provides practical information to help you plan your visit.

Naumburg Dom

The impressive Cathedral of Saints Peter and Paul in Naumburg is one of the finest Gothic structures in Germany. The present cathedral is the second to be built on the same site; only a section of the eastern crypt survived of the earlier Romanesque church. Construction started before 1213, with the earliest parts including the late-Romanesque east choir, the transept and the main body. The early-Gothic west choir was built in the mid-13th century, the newer Gothic east choir c.1330. The northeast towers date from the 15th century; the southwest towers from 1894.

4 Major Sights
At least two pages are dedicated to each major sight. Historic buildings are dissected in order to show their interiors. Interesting towns or town centres have street maps with the main sights indicated and described.

INTRODUCING GERMANY

Discovering Germany   10–1

Putting Germany
  on the Map   18–21

A Portrait of Germany   22–43

Germany Through the Year   44–49

The History of Germany   50–65

DISCOVERING GERMANY

The following tours have been designed to take in as many of the country's highlights as possible, while keeping long-distance travel to a minimum. First, there are three two-day tours of Germany's most dynamic cities: Berlin, Hamburg and Munich. These itineraries can be combined to form a week-long tour; extra suggestions are supplied for those who want to extend their stay. Next come three five-day tours covering the north, centre and south of Germany. Add these tours together to create a superb two-week tour of the country. Finally, there are two themed itineraries tailored to specific interests. Pick, combine and follow your favourite tours, or simply dip in and out and be inspired.

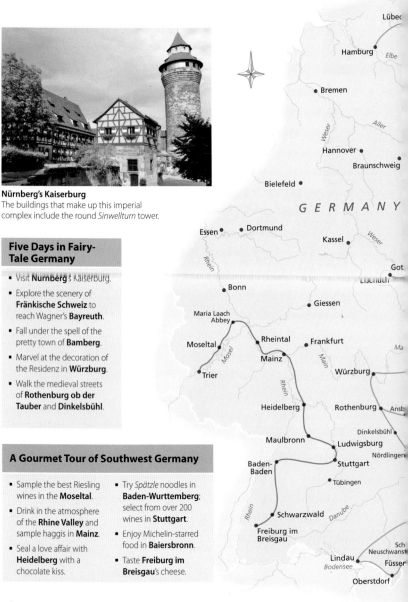

Nürnberg's Kaiserburg
The buildings that make up this imperial complex include the round *Sinwellturm* tower.

Five Days in Fairy-Tale Germany

- Visit **Nürnberg**'s Kaiserburg.
- Explore the scenery of **Fränkische Schweiz** to reach Wagner's **Bayreuth**.
- Fall under the spell of the pretty town of **Bamberg**.
- Marvel at the decoration of the Residenz in **Würzburg**.
- Walk the medieval streets of **Rothenburg ob der Tauber** and **Dinkelsbühl**.

A Gourmet Tour of Southwest Germany

- Sample the best Riesling wines in the **Moseltal**.
- Drink in the atmosphere of the **Rhine Valley** and sample haggis in **Mainz**.
- Seal a love affair with **Heidelberg** with a chocolate kiss.
- Try *Spätzle* noodles in **Baden-Wurttemberg**; select from over 200 wines in **Stuttgart**.
- Enjoy Michelin-starred food in **Baiersbronn**.
- Taste **Freiburg im Breisgau**'s cheese.

◀ View of Sendlinger-Tor-Platz in Munich as seen during the 1950s

View of Lübeck from across the River Trave
The city skyline is famous for its seven towers.

Key

=== Fairy-Tale Germany

=== Southwest Germany

=== Coastal Germany

=== East Germany

=== Bavarian Alps

0 kilometres/metres   100

0 miles/yards   100

Five Days around Coastal Germany

- Discover treasures of Baltic Gothic in **Lübeck**.

- Visit the magnificent ducal palace in **Schwerin**.

- Marvel at medieval **Wismar**; catch a steam train from **Bad Doberan** to the beach.

- Explore the medieval port of **Stralsund**.

- Enjoy the sea air and white cliffs of **Rügen** island.

A Cultural Tour of East Germany

- Learn how **Eisenach** shaped the life of Martin Luther.

- Visit **Weimar**, spiritual capital of German high culture.

- Enjoy a concert in Bach's Thomaskirche, in **Leipzig**.

- See how **Meissen** porcelain is created.

- Discover the architecture and art that made **Dresden** the "Florence on the Elbe".

Five Days in the Bavarian Alps

- Take a cablecar into the Alps from **Oberstdorf**.

- Visit King Ludwig II's iconic **Schloss Neuschwanstein**.

- Discover Ludwig's eccentricity in **Schloss Linderhof**.

- Reach **Herrenchiemsee Palace** by crossing the Chiemsee by ferry.

- Tour the alpine **Berchtesgadener Land** to see corkscrew peaks, deep lakes and rustic chapels.

Two Days in Berlin

Berlin is a rewarding city to explore, with a fascinating history and superb nightlife.

- **Arriving** Berlin has two airports. Tegel, 8 km (5 miles) from the city centre, can be reached by bus or taxi; buses also connect with the U-bahn service. Schönefeld is 20 km (12 miles) south of the city and well served by trains, S-bahn, and buses that link with the U-bahn.

The imposing steel-and-glass dome of the Reichstag in Berlin

Day 1
Morning Start at the icons of a reunified Germany: spiral up inside the glass dome of the **Reichstag** (p97), then circuit the **Brandenburger Tor** (p73). Beyond is **Unter den Linden** (pp74–5), the leafy promenade that reveals the swagger of 19th-century Prussia through monuments like the **Neue Wache** (p75), **Friedrichs-werdersche Kirche** (p75) and nearby **St-Hedwigs-Kathedrale** (p74). Friedrich the Great ordered the **Französischer Dom** (p76) to be built on an Italianate square – this is a lovely spot for lunch.

Afternoon The handsome **Schlossbrücke** (p76) hints at the cultural feast to be found on **Museum Island** (pp78–9). The **Pergamonmuseum** (pp80–81), with its 170 BC altar, holds a remarkable collection of antiquities. Stop in at the **Deutscher Dom** afterwards (p76), then take a quiet stroll into picturesque **Nikolaiviertel** to sense the capital's medieval roots (p84).

Day 2
Morning After exploring Berlin's historic core, the focus shifts to more recent history. **Checkpoint Charlie** (p84), the east–west border immortalized by many Cold War thrillers, is an essential stop. The darkest period in German history is chillingly laid bare in the **Jüdisches Museum** (pp84–5), while the wave-like **Holocaust Denkmal** (p74) represents the scale of the Jewish tragedy in stark sculptural form.

Afternoon Walk off lunch in the **Tiergarten** (p91), then pore over the Old Masters in the **Gemälde-galerie** (pp94–5) or crafts in the nearby **Kunstgewerbemuseum** (closed for renovation until 2014; p93). For more astonishing craftsmanship, take the U-Bahn west from **Potsdamer Platz** (p96) to reach beautiful **Schloss Charlottenburg** (pp102–3). Otherwise, admire the mosaics in the shattered **Kaiser-Wilhelm-Gedächtnis-Kirche** (p90), the symbol of West Berlin, on the city's retail high street, **Ku'damm** (p91) – time at last, for some shopping (pp110–11).

> **To extend your trip…**
> Wander through bohemian Berlin at **Prenzlauer Berg** (p105), or escape the city on the beaches of **Strandbad Wannsee** (p108) or the lovely **Park Sanssouci** (pp140–41), in **Potsdam**.

Two Days in Munich

Munich is a popular tourist destination and the gateway to Bavaria.

- **Arriving** Munich airport is served by the S-Bahn and various buses. Taxis are also available. From Munich there are good train connections with the rest of Europe.

Day 1
Morning There's no finer introduction to Munich than **Marienplatz** (pp214–15), boxed in by monuments of civic pride: the **Neues Rathaus** (p219), its façade a carnival of statues, the **Altes Rathaus** (pp218–19) and the **Michaelskirche** (p216). For a mid-morning snack of *Weisewurst*, head south to the **Viktualienmarkt** (p218). The icon on souvenir beer tankards is the soaring **Frauenkirche** (p217), unmissable because of its domed spires; however, the highlights of Munich's sacred architecture are the nearby **Bürgersaal** (p216) and the **Asamkirche** (p217), the latter the most enchanting example of Bavarian rococo you'll see.

Afternoon After the return walk via Marienplatz, stop for a beer at the **Hofbräuhaus** (p219), Munich's most famous beer hall and the site of Hitler's infamous Beer Hall Putsch. Suitably fortified, discover the head-spinning array of architecture, artwork and treasure on display

The entrance to Schloss Charlottenburg in Potsdam

in the **Residenz** (*pp220–21*). The former palace of Bavarian kings is so large it takes two tours just to see the half open to the public. Check if any seats are available for a night at its magical Cuvilliés-Theater.

Day 2
Morning The kings reveal their impeccable taste again through their gallery, hung in the **Alte Pinakothek** (*pp226–7*). You can easily lose the morning among its Old Masters, with the most comprehensive lesson in German art history you'll ever receive, or among more modern works in the neighbouring **Neue Pinakothek** (*p224*) and **Pinakothek der Moderne** (*p225*) galleries. Make time to walk to nearby Königsplatz, where the Neo-Classical **Glyptothek** (*p225*) and **Propyläen** (*p225*) reveal why Munich was nicknamed "Athens on Isar". The nearby **Staatliche Antikensammlungen** (*p225*) displays Ludwig I's antiquities.

Afternoon The **Deutsches Museum** (*pp232–3*) is unbeatable for rainy days, with 20,000 exhibits spread over seven floors dedicated to science and arts. Otherwise, escape the busy city streets and head to **Schloss Nymphenburg** (*pp228–9*), like Electress Henriette-Adelaide. Her portrait is not one of those in the Gallery of Beauties, one highlight of this Italianate garden palace. Others are the Festsaal, which tempers Rococo opulence with playful

The awe-inspiring interior of the Michaelskirche, Munich

The monumental organ in Hamburg's Michaeliskirche

detail, and the astonishingly ornate Amalienburg hunting lodge in the gardens.

> **To extend your trip…**
> Discover **Dachau** (*p268*), a pretty medieval town that is now synonymous with the Holocaust, or relax with a beer at **Andechs** (*p268*).

Two Days in Hamburg

Germany's second-largest city is full of attractive parks and varied architectural styles.

- **Arriving** The airport, 8 km (5 miles) from the city, is well served by buses, the S-Bahn and trains. There are also good train and ferry services.

Day 1
Morning Decorated with statues of local heroes and the trades that made Hamburg's fortune, the vast town hall on **Rathausmarkt** (*p438*) perfectly expresses the civic pride of this city-state. On Hamburg's shopping street, Mönckeberg-strasse, **St Petrikirche** (*p438*) and **Jakobikirche** (*pp438–9*) are eloquent about past wealth; chic boutique shops on Neuer Wall and Grosse Bleichen, north of the Rathaus, reveal current prosperity. Relax with a boat trip on the **Alster lakes** (*p438*).

Afternoon Walk around the Binnenalster lake to the **Kunsthalle** (*pp440–41*), which features paintings by German artists such as the medieval Master Bertram, Cranach and Caspar David Friedrich. There's modern art in the adjacent Galerie der Gegenwart, and arts and crafts in the Museum für Kunst und Gewerbe, on the south side of the train station.

Day 2
Morning The port that made Hamburg's fortune is at its most evocative in **Speicherstadt** (*p439*); merchants hoisted goods direct from its canals into the 19th-century warehouses, some converted to museums. Older wharves south are being transformed in a development known as Hafen City – the Elbphilharmonic concert hall is especially striking. Its waterside restaurants or those in the city's original merchant street, Deichstrasse, are ideal for lunch.

Afternoon Walk west along the **port** (*p442*), perhaps stopping to explore the museum ships *Rickmer Rickmers* and *Cap San Diego*. The goal is **Landungs-brücken** (*p442*), from where fascinating boat tours around Europe's second-largest harbour depart at regular intervals. Hamburg ships imported the tropical woods that were transformed into the Baroque fittings of the **Michaeliskirche** (*p442*), also worth a visit for the view of the port from its observation tower. By now the nightlife will be warming up in **St Pauli** (*pp442–3*), the former dockers' drinking quarter. Made famous by The Beatles and its red-light district, St Pauli has now been gentrified for tourist-friendly titillation.

Five Days in Fairy-Tale Germany

- **Airports** Arrive and depart from Nürnberg airport.
- **Transport** It is easy to make day trips to all destinations from Nürnberg. Trains connect the towns in an hour or so, except Frankische Schweiz. Dinkelsbühl requires a change on to a bus from Rothenburg.
- **Booking ahead** Residenz, Würzburg.

Day 1: Nürnberg
Albrecht-Dürer-Haus (p263), **Kirche St Sebald** (p262) and the wishing fountain on pretty **Hauptmarkt** (p262) all testify to Nürnberg's tradition for craftsmanship. For the best panoramic views, climb to the top of the 12th-century Sinwellturm, at the **Kaiserburg** (p263). For lunch, snack on Nürnberg's stubby *Bratwürste*, ordered three in a bun (*"Drei im Weckla"*) from the food stalls located on Hauptmarkt.

Day 2: Fränkische Schweiz to Bayreuth
A driving tour in the **Fränkische Schweiz** (p247) reveals scenery perfectly suited to *Snow White and the Seven Dwarfs*. Forchheim has a fine medieval core, tiny Tüchersfeld could double as a Disney film set, and Pottenstein boasts the region's oldest castle. **Bayreuth** (pp256–7) is synonymous with Wagnerian opera; however, the **Markgräfliches Opernhaus** (p256) pre-dates this composer by

two centuries and is still in use even though Wagner dismissed it as too small.

Day 3: Bamberg
UNESCO-listed **Bamberg** (pp252–5) is immediately striking: its symphony of superb artistry, beautiful buildings and small-town charm emerged unscathed from World War II. Must-sees here are the art on Domplatz – the **Cathedral** (pp254–5), plus the Neue Residenz und Staatsgalerie – and the Altes Rathaus, which leapfrogs the Regnitz river via an islet. Must-dos include having a glass of *Rauchbier* (smoked beer) at Schlenkerla.

Day 4: Würzburg
Unlike Bamberg, **Würzburg** (pp248–51) took a direct hit during World War II, but restoration has revived its UNESCO World Heritage Site, the prince-bishops' **Residenz** (pp250–51) by star architect Balthasar Neumann. Elegant and giddily opulent by turns, this 17th-century palace is fit for a ball.

Day 5: Rothenburg
Slip into a timewarp back to medieval Germany at **Rothenburg** (pp266–7). A local legend says the town was spared destruction in the Thirty Years' War because its mayor downed 3.25 litres (7 pints) of wine in one gulp. In summer, tour early or at dusk (when it's pure magic) to avoid the crowds. **Dinkelsbühl** (p258) is another gem, while **Nördlingen** (pp258–9) and **Ansbach** (p259) are also within reach by car.

Picturesque house on a bridge in Bamberg

A Week around Coastal Germany

- **Airports** Arrive at Hamburg Airport and depart from Lübeck, Hamburg or Berlin airports.
- **Transport** Trains connect the towns in an hour or so, except the Fischland, Darß and Zingst peninsula, for which you will need a car. Boats to Hiddensee run from Stralsund from April to October.

Day 1 and 2: Hamburg
See the city itinerary on p13.

Day 3: Lübeck
Whether you're after culture, architecture or simply small-town charm, **Lübeck** (pp466–9) is the place. The Backsteingotik brick architecture of its Hanseatic heyday set the blueprint for the entire region: highlights include the Holstentor, Rathaus and soaring Marienkirche, all expressions of civic pride. While you're in town, visit the St Annen-Museum for its altarpieces and sample delicious Lübeck marzipan from Niederegger patisserie.

Day 4: Schwerin and Ludwigslust
Encircled by lakes and well worth a diversion inland, **Schwerin** (pp474–5) is the capital of Mecklenburg-Lower Pomerania. Tour the fairy-tale Schloss, then discover the dukes' fine taste in art in the Staatliches Museum and the Dom. Before they built the castle here, the Mecklenburg

Panoramic view of the city of Würzburg, with the River Main flowing through it

For practical information on travelling around Germany, see pp552–9

The luxuriant gardens of Schloss Linderhof, dotted with statuary

dukes resided in **Ludwigslust** *(p476)*. Money was tight, which is why the stucco here is actually papier-mâché.

Day 5: Wismar and Bad Doberan

Maritime flavour returns in **Wismar** *(pp476–7)* – the size of the Markt and merchants' Georgenkirche testifies to the wealth of this medieval port. The Nikolaikirche retains Middle Age frescoes and altarpieces. Finer still are those of the Cistercian Münster in **Bad Doberan** *(p477)*, its interior a treasure trove. If there's time, embark for a jaunt to the beach on the "Molli" steam train.

Day 6: Rostock to Stralsund

Rostock *(p480)* feels gritty after the small towns before. Heavily bombed in 1942, this port town warrants a stop for its Rathaus and Marienkirche. The **Fischland, Darß and Zingst peninsula** *(p480)* offers a superb route west. Ahrenshoop, a former artists' village, is now a chic escape for city-slickers because of its fine beach and galleries. In UNESCO-listed **Stralsund** *(p481)*, go to the Alter Markt and compare the architecture with Lübeck.

Day 7: Rügen

Sea, sand, spa resorts and steam trains contribute to the holiday vibe of **Rügen** *(pp482–3)*. A popular resort since Caspar David Friedrich painted the white cliffs of the Jasmund Peninsula, today it is a national park. For a day on the beach, base yourself at Binz or slow down on Hiddensee, where transport is by bike or horse and cart.

A Week in the Bavarian Alps

- **Airports** Arrive and leave from Munich.

- **Transport** Füssen and Garmisch-Partenkirchen are accessible by train from Munich; other destinations are served by local bus. Chiemsee (Prien station) requires a return to Munich via train. Berchtesgaden requires a change at Freilassing.

- **Booking ahead** Schloss Neuschwanstein, Schloss Linderhof.

Day 1 and 2: Munich

See the city itinerary on *pp12–13*.

Day 3: Lindau and Oberstdorf

Lindau *(p288)*, on the Bodensee, is charming and uncomplicated. Stroll the harbour, guarded by lighthouses, gaze at the Alps on the horizon, then discover the only frescoes of Hans Holbein the Elder in the church of St Peter. For more fabulous alpine views, take a cablecar up Mount Nebelhorn, near **Oberstdorf** *(p289)*.

Day 4: Füssen to Oberammergau

Explore the cobbled lanes of **Füssen** *(p289)* before a visit to Bavarian King Ludwig II's **Schloss Neuschwanstein** *(pp286–7)*, the embodiment of fairy-tale Germany. You can't beat **Oberammergau** *(p284)* for postcard-pretty alpine charm. Famous for a passion

---

play that takes place every decade (the next one will be in 2020), it also appeals for wood carvings and colourful frescoes.

Day 5: Ettal to Garmisch-Partenkirchen

Tiny **Ettal** *(p284)* sits in awe of alpine peaks and a Benedictine abbey with a splendid Rococo interior. More theatrical still is the setting of **Schloss Linderhof** *(p285)*, where eccentric King Ludwig played out his Sun King fantasies. From here it's a short drive to Germany's most celebrated alpine resort, **Garmisch-Partenkirchen** *(p284)*, for a ride up Zugspitze, Germany's highest mountain.

Day 6: Chiemsee

Chiemsee *(pp282–3)*, Bavaria's largest lake, is a lovely place to while away a day. Take a boat to Herreninsel to discover the last of King Ludwig II's delusional monuments, Versailles-inspired **Herrenchiemsee Palace**, and to Fraueninsel for its Benedictine heritage. There are good walks and cycle rides on the lake shores, or spend an afternoon on the beach at Chieming.

Day 7: Berchtesgadener Land

Corkscrew peaks, deep lakes and rustic chapels create the splendid landscape of **Berchtesgadener Land** *(pp280–81)*. Take a boat trip on the Königsee to see the pilgrimage chapel of St Bartholomä, then visit the cosy village of Ramsau an der Ache. Finally, ascend to the Eagle's Nest, Hitler's mountain retreat; dedicated buses go from Obersalzberg.

A Cultural Tour of East Germany

- **Duration** 7 days – but can be extended to a 12-day tour with extra suggestions.

- **Airports** Arrive at Berlin, Erfurt Weimar or Dresden international airports and depart from Dresden International Airport.

- **Transport** Trains connect all destinations in the tour in 2 hours or less. This tour can also be done by car, but public transport will be easier. If you choose to start in Berlin, note that it's a train journey of approximately 3 hours and 30 minutes to Eisenach.

This route follows in the footsteps of giants of German culture through the sights and museums of Thuringia and Saxony. For background on Germany's cultural heroes, see *pp30–35*. If you want to extend your trip, spend a day or two in Berlin (*p12*) before heading to Eisenach.

Day 1: Eisenach
Meet three of this tour's figureheads in **Eisenach** (*pp190–91*). Excommunicated Martin Luther translated the New Testament in the Wartburg in 1521; Lucas Cranach the Elder painted his portrait, hung in its small museum; and Johann Sebastian Bach was born in a townhouse in the old town in 1685. The story of his life as a tetchy court composer is told in a museum.

Day 2: Gotha
Marvel at the power of Thuringia's ducal dynasties as you stroll around old-town **Gotha** (*p193*), laid at the feet of the majestic Schloss Friedenstein. The dukes expressed their court's magnificence through culture, gathering superb Old Masters, antiquities and treasures in a palace museum and building one of Europe's first Baroque court theatres. Leave time to discover the palace gardens.

To extend your trip…
The Thüringerwaldbahn tram pootles through pretty countryside before arriving at Friedrichroda, in the **Thuringian Forest** (*pp194–5*).

Day 3: Erfurt
Erfurt (*pp196–7*) is a historic town with a lively university. Admire the Romanesque and medieval artworks in the Dom St Marien and St Severi-Kirche, then browse the craftshops on the Krämerbrücke. Next, visit a monastic cell in the Augustinerkloster, where Martin Luther studied. The Angermuseum holds a collection of decorative arts and paintings.

To extend your trip…
An unknown young organist named Johann Sebastian Bach first shocked congregations with his fugal compositions in pretty **Arnstadt** (*p194*).

Day 4: Weimar
Weimar (*pp198–9*) is the birthplace of the Enlightenment and the spiritual capital of German culture. Discover its sophistication in the ducal Stadtschloss and the Herzogin-Anna-Amalia Bibliothek, then see its private face in the home of Goethe, who worked as a court adviser to Duke Carl August. Tour the houses of Schiller and Liszt, then see the last artwork by Cranach in the St Peter und St Paul church. Finally, relax with a stroll in Park an der Ilm.

The tower of Weimar's Stadtschloss

Day 5: Leipzig
The fast-paced city of **Leipzig** (*pp166–7*) has a mercantile zeal that overshadows its cultural weight as a former home of Bach, who is buried in the Thomaskirche (where he was chorister), and of Goethe, who immortalized the Auerbachs Keller restaurant in *Faust*. The Grassimuseum holds a world-class collection of decorative arts; alternatively, there's painting and sculpture in the Museum der Bildenden Künste.

Day 6: Meissen
In **Meissen** (*p171*), the tangled lanes in the old town are fun to get lost in; then, head up to the Albrechtsburg complex before visiting the porcelain factory for which the town is synonymous. The first china outside Asia was produced here in 1710. Learn how on factory tours, and see the extravagant 3.5-m (11.4-ft) high decoration that graced the dining table of Saxony Electors.

The imposing Schloss Friedenstein, in Gotha, located above the old town

Day 7: Dresden

Stroll around the Baroque buildings that earned **Dresden** *(pp172–81)* the moniker of "Florence on the Elbe": the Frauenkirche, Brühlsche Terrasse and Hofkirche. Finest of all is the **Zwinger** *(pp178–9)*. Saxony Elector Augustus the Strong held alfresco balls here; today there is an excellent gallery. For more of Augustus's glittering court, visit his Grünes Gewölbe treasury in the Residenzschloss.

To extend your trip…
The bizarre landscapes of **Sächsische Schweiz** *(pp182–3)* and **Schloss Moritzburg** *(p171)* are easily accessible on day trips.

A Gourmet Tour of Southwest Germany

- **Duration** 7 days – but can be extended to a 10-day tour with extra suggestions.
- **Airports** Arrive in and depart from either Frankfurt or Stuttgart airports.
- **Transport** This tour is most easily done by car. If you choose to arrive in Frankfurt Airport, you might want to spend two days in the city before hiring a car and driving to Trier.

This tour explores Rheinland-Palatinate and Baden-Wurttemberg, including the Schwarzwald, to uncover the food and wine of southwest Germany. If you are travelling in late summer/early autumn, look out for wine and harvest festivals in the region.

Day 1: Trier and Moseltal

The Romans left behind fine monuments in **Trier** *(pp344–7)* and a tradition of viticulture on the south-facing slopes of the **Moseltal** *(p349)*. Follow the river beneath vineyards that produce elegant Rieslings, pausing at the world's steepest vineyard, Bremmer Calmont (www.bremmer-calmont.de).

The statue of Emperor Wilhelm von Rumann on Karlsplatz, Stuttgart

Day 2: Maria Laach and the Rheintal

Stop by the **Maria Laach** abbey *(pp362–3)* before taking a trip down the **Rhine Valley** *(pp358–9)*, famous for its castles and white wines. Relax in a *Weinstube* (bar/tavern); those in **Bacharach** *(p359)* tend to be housed in old timbered buildings, whereas in **Mainz** *(pp352–5)* they're often in smarter venues. Try the regional delicacy of *Pfälzer Saumagen* (sow's stomach stuffed with sausage, potatoes and herbs).

To extend your trip…
Frankfurt *(pp378–83)* is renowned for its *Ebbelwoi* (cider). Enjoy it in a tavern in the Sachsenhausen district.

Day 3: Heidelberg

The must-see of the university town of **Heidelberg** *(pp300–3)* is its castle. Tour its romantic shell by day, then return at night for seasonal German fare at Schlossweinstube. Inbetween, enjoy a Studentenkuss (students' kiss), a chocolate praline made in Cafe Knösel on Haspelgasse since 1830.

Dresden's magnificent Frauenkirche

Day 4: Maulbronn, Ludwigsburg and Stuttgart

Tour the UNESCO-listed monastery in **Maulbronn** *(pp306–7)* or **Ludwigsburg** *(pp310–11)*, then enjoy the local specialities *Spätzle* noodles with cheese and *Maultaschen* (large ravioli). **Stuttgart** *(pp312–17)* is as synonymous with *Weinstüben* as Munich is with beer halls – Stetter (Rosenstrasse 32) serves 200 local wines.

Day 5: Baden-Baden

You can be sure of good-quality food in **Baden-Baden** *(p305)*, the "summer capital of Europe". This is also the queen of German spa resorts. Spend an afternoon in the health-giving waters of the Friedrichsbad, then treat yourself to a sumptuous meal.

To extend your trip…
Tübingen *(p320)* is a lovely university town and a gateway to **Schwäbische Alb** *(pp318–19)*.

Day 6: Schwarzwald

Schwarzwälder Schinken (local ham), trout and *Schwarzwälder Kirschtorte* (Black Forest gâteau laced with cherry liqueur) are the delicacies of the **Schwarzwald** *(pp330–31)*. Gourmets should visit the town of **Baiersbronn** (www.baiersbronn.de), home to three Michelin-starred restaurants.

Day 7: Freiburg im Breisgau

Kick back in pretty **Freiburg im Breisgau** *(pp328–9)*. See the Münster and either buy a cheese sandwich from a stall on Münsterplatz, or join students in the cafés of its cobbled lanes.

Putting Germany on the Map

Located in the centre of Europe, between the North and Baltic Seas and the Alps, Germany covers an area of nearly 360,000 sq km (139,000 sq miles). Its neighbouring countries are Poland and the Czech Republic to the east, Austria and Switzerland to the south, France, Belgium, Luxembourg and Holland to the west, and Denmark to the north. The capital is Berlin. Its largest river is the Rhine. Germany is inhabited by over 81 million people.

Key

— National border

= Motorway

— Major road

-- Ferry route

For map symbols *see back flap*

Germany: Region by Region

The Federal Republic of Germany is made up of
16 states. Bremen is the smallest state, with around
700,000 inhabitants; North Rhine-Westphalia is
the most densely populated state, with
18 million inhabitants. The largest state,
Bavaria, covers an area of 70,531
sq km (27,232 sq miles).
Berlin, Bremen and
Hamburg are
self-governing
city-states.

How to get there

Germany has an excellent
transport system. There are
14 international airports
with flights to all parts of
the world; a comprehensive
network of toll-free
motorways that make
travelling by car easy and
fast; and an efficient railway
system, with high-speed
InterCity Express (ICE) link
between major cities.

Key

- ═══ Motorway
- ▬▬▬ Major road
- ═══ Minor Road
- ──── Minor Railway

0 km   100

0 miles   100

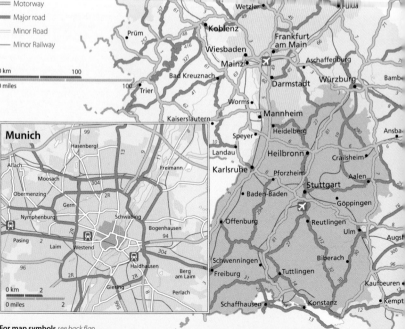

For map symbols *see back flap*

Berlin

Pankow
Reinickendorf
Weissensee
Wedding
Prenzlauer Berg
Tiergarten
Charlottenburg
Mitte
Friedrichshain
Kreuzberg
Wilmersdorf
Treptow
Schöneberg
Neukölln
Tempelhof
Steglitz

0 km   3
0 miles   3

Stralsund
Greifswald
Rostock
Wismar
Schwerin
Neubrandenburg
Neustrelitz
Pritzwalk
tenberge
Schwedt/Oder
Stendal
Rathenow
Oranienburg
BERLIN
see inset above
Potsdam
Magdeburg
Luckenwalde
Schönebeck
Lübbenau
Lutherstadt Wittenberg
Cottbus
Halle
Delitzsch
Leipzig
Hoyerswerda
Naumburg
Bautzen
Görlitz
Weimar
Döbeln
Dresden
Zeitz
Gera
Freiberg
Zwickau
Chemnitz
Annaberg-Buchholz
Hof
Cheb
Bayreuth
langen
Weiden
Nürnberg
Schwandorf
Cham
Regensburg
Deggendorf
Straubing
Passau
stadt
Landshut
MUNICH
see inset left
Rosenheim

Area Colours

◼ Berlin

Eastern Germany

◻ Brandenburg
◻ Saxony
◼ Saxony-Anhalt
◻ Thuringia

Southern Germany

◼ Munich
◻ Bavaria
◼ Baden-Wurttemberg

Western Germany

◻ Rhineland-Palatinate & Saarland
▦ Hesse
◻ North Rhine-Westphalia

Northern Germany

◻ Hamburg, Bremen, Lower Saxony
◻ Schleswig-Holstein
▦ Mecklenburg-Lower Pomerania

A PORTRAIT OF GERMANY

Germany is a wealthy country, whose people are generally regarded as hard-working, determined and efficient. This view stems from the country's industrial might and the smooth functioning of its economy, but it overlooks other important aspects of Germany. These include its important contributions to art and culture, its breathtaking scenery and excellent tourist facilities.

Contemporary Germany is far removed from the traditional, stereotyped view of the country. In the last 60 years, it has developed into a multi-ethnic, multi-cultural melting pot. Over 7 million of Germany's inhabitants are immigrants; the majority of these are Turks, with more recent guest workers arriving from the former Yugoslavia, Italy and Greece. In the city of Stuttgart, every third inhabitant is a foreigner; in Frankfurt it is one in four. Hamburg has more mosques than any other city in Europe and, in some schools in Berlin, German children are in the minority. Almost every town has a selection of Italian, Chinese, Greek and Turkish restaurants and cafés, testifying to the multi-ethnicity of its population.

History and Romance

For many, the river Rhine epitomizes tourist Germany, particularly the romantic stretch between Mainz and Cologne. The country has far more than this to offer in the way of scenery, however. There is the ever-changing Baltic coastline, the sandy islands of the North Sea, the lakes of Mecklenburg, lonely castles perched on crags in Baden and Thuringia, mountain ranges including the Alps, the vast Bodensee lake, medieval cities and fairy-tale villages. Not all of the latter are original, as countless towns were destroyed by bombs during World War II, but many have been meticulously rebuilt to the original plans, and now it is difficult to tell the difference between the old and the new.

Verdant Alpine meadow against a backdrop of majestic, snowy peaks

◀ A wintry Bavarian scene, with Neuschwanstein Castle in the background

Procession during the Plärrer Fest, a beer festival in Augsburg

Traditions

Today's German nation has evolved over the past thousand years, mainly from various Germanic tribes, notably the Franks, Saxons, Swabians and Bavarians. Traditions and dialects have developed within regional ethnic groups that emerged as a result of historical alliances. There is no such thing as a single German tradition. Even the assumption that Germany is a country of beer-drinkers is belied by the large numbers of wine lovers. These groups, along with consumers of stronger beverages, have given Germany a high position in the world league table for alcohol use. Nevertheless, drunks are rarely seen in Germany.

Various ethnic groups in the country are ascribed different characteristics. The people of Mecklenburg, for example, are seen as introspective, while Swabians are regarded as thrifty; the Saxons are seen as disciplined and cunning, while Bavarians are typified as a people bound by rustic traditions, quick to quarrel and fight. Indeed, one of the most popular Bavarian men's folk-dances ends with them slapping each other in the face.

A Bavarian dressed in regional costume

Bavaria, of course, is home to the traditional Oktoberfest, a beer festival that brings millions of people to Munich every year from virtually all over the world.

The people of the Rhineland have a reputation for enjoying life. Their favourite season is the Carnival period, and they spend practically the entire year preparing for this week-long event. It begins on the last Thursday before Lent, with "town soldiers", helped by the huge crowds, storming the town hall. The town councillors surrender and power passes to the masked revellers. On the Monday, the Carnival proceeds through the thronged streets of the towns on the Rhine, and the pubs are busy until the end of Shrovetide.

Carnival is rooted in ancient rituals marking the banishment of winter. This custom was most common in the south of Germany, but it also reached the Rhineland, the Palatinate and Hessen. When the German government moved back to Berlin from Bonn in the Rhineland in 1999, attempts were made to establish Carnival in the new capital, but it never really took root.

Art and Culture

Germany is a land of sagas and legends that tell of woodland spirits, beautiful princesses, magicians and sirens such as the Lorelei. These legends have had a strong influence on German art. An example is the German epic poem, the *Nibelungenlied,* which was written around 1200 on the basis of old legends. This poem was the inspiration for Richard Wagner's cycle of operas, *The Ring of the Nibelungen,* as well as for a trilogy of plays by Christian Friedrich Hebbel and a film by Fritz Lang.

Germans have won eight Nobel Prizes for Literature. The most recent prize-winner was Günter Grass, whose *Tin Drum* brought him world renown. More recently a film adaptation of the book was made by Volker Schlöndorff, which won the Golden Palm at the Cannes Film Festival. After a relatively stagnant period, the German film industry became revitalized around 1995 with a number of hits, albeit only at the national level. German cinemas are now always full and traditional cinemas are increasingly being replaced by multiplexes.

Germans read widely, even in today's age of television and the internet. Every year 70,000 new books are published in Germany and eight times that many titles are on sale. Germany is second only to the United States in the number of books published annually, while the number of bookshops per square kilometre is the highest in the world. The same applies to museums and art galleries.

Germany has over 2,000 national, provincial and local history museums, as well as numerous church museums, folk

The historical Frohnauer hammer forge near Annaberg in Saxony

museums and former royal palaces. This variety and choice owes much to the fact that, in the past, local dukes acquired collections of art in order to impress others and to demonstrate their wealth. The Bavarian dukes also built up extensive collections of machines, artisans' tools, musical instruments and minerals. As early as the 16th century, Munich was an international centre of the arts and the Grünes Gewölbe in 17th-century Dresden was one of the largest treasuries for storing fine art in Europe. Of the many art galleries to be found throughout Germany, the finest are in Cologne, Frankfurt, Stuttgart, Munich and Berlin.

Lorelei overlooking the Rhine

Music also flourishes in Germany. Most large cities have their own symphony orchestra and opera company and every year some 100 regional and local music festivals take place. Musical comedies are especially popular.

The imposing Schönburg Castle, near Oberwesel on the Rhine

Society and Politics

The scars of World War II are more evident in Eastern Germany, although they are gradually disappearing there, too. Görlitz, Bautzen, Leipzig and Weimar have now acquired a splendour that was previously hidden behind the grim façade of East Germany. The mental, social and political scars of the war and subsequent division of Germany have, however, left deeper scars. Although reunification took place on 3 October 1990, unity among the people themselves has been longer in coming. East Germans are the poor relations: the region has high unemployment rates and its people tend to regard their western counterparts as arrogant and self-assured. The latter, for their part, claim that the inhabitants of the "new states" are jealous and ungrateful despite the billions of marks and euros that have been poured into the region to equalize living standards.

Germany has almost always been divided regionally into states with fluctuating borders. The present-day states were, for the most part, created after 1945 while those in East Germany were not created until forty years later. In all cases, old territorial and historical ties were taken into account. That is the reason for their evocative names, such as the "Free State of Bavaria" or the "Free State of Saxony".

The Reichstag building, where the *Bundestag* sessions are held

There are now 16 federal states, or provinces. North Rhine-Westphalia, Baden-Wurttemberg and Bavaria are the largest and are like economically powerful countries. At the other end of the scale, the tiny province of Saarland has only 1.1 million inhabitants, while the Free Hanseatic City of Bremen has fewer than 700,000. The former East German states are also relatively small but all play an important role in the *Bundesrat*, or Federal Council, where they are instrumental in enacting legislation. All laws, apart from those relating to the Federation as a whole, such as defence or foreign policy, require the agreement of the *Bundesrat*, which is made up from current local governments. Depending on the number of inhabitants, each federal state has from four to six votes.

The skyline of Frankfurt am Main

A government with a majority in the *Bundestag* (parliament) cannot always count on support in the *Bundesrat,* even if it has a majority there. Each state looks after its own interests and often makes alliances with other states to achieve its own aims, without regard for party loyalty. The complex working of German federalism is based on the compromises that this system requires.

Bathers on the sandy beaches of Norddeich

Daily Life

The traditional image of German women used to be summed up in the "three Ks": *Küche, Kinder, Kirche* (kitchen, children, church). As in other Western European countries, however, this stereotype no longer holds true. Although cookery is fashionable and there are countless TV cookery programmes starring celebrity chefs, for everyday meals, ready-prepared dishes are eaten, either at the work canteen or from the supermarket. The German birthrate is declining, while the anti-authoritarian model of education that was introduced in the 1960s has to some extent relieved parents of many of the more onerous duties of child-rearing. As a result, many young people show little respect for their elders. The churches, for their part, are usually empty. Although the largest churches (Catholic and Protestant) have many adherents, the vast majority are not practising believers and limit themselves to payment of church dues.

Germans speak of themselves as a high-performance society *(Leistungsgesellschaft),* which gives the highest rewards to those who devote almost all their energies to their careers. As a result, stress is often a factor in people's lives, from schooldays onwards. In Germany today there are increasing

Participant in a parade marking the Reunification celebrations

numbers of people who live alone. Single-person households are most common in the cities and even young people regard their careers as of paramount importance. Large numbers say that they are not interested in having a family.

Nevertheless, Germans enjoy mass events such as public holidays and popular festivals. The country has the highest number of public holidays in Europe and German workers have the longest annual holidays. Its citizens are Europe's most enthusiastic travellers, each year spending more than 35 million euros on foreign holidays. When they return there is a tendency to long for the southern climes they have just visited – perhaps this explains why restaurants offering Mediterranean food are so popular.

The Bodensee, a popular tourist destination

Flora and Fauna

Germany is a vast country whose varied geography has given rise to a great diversity of flora and fauna. It is famous for its forests, many of mixed deciduous trees, including oak, beech and birch. Around 31 per cent of the country is forested. The Alpine regions have a rich variety of wild flowers, with meadow species a particular feature in spring and summer. On the northern peat moors, heaths and heathers are common. Germany is home to a wide range of wildlife, including wild boar, lynx and marmots. Many valuable wildlife areas have now been placed under protection.

German Wildlife

The fauna of Germany is typical of central Europe, with a variety of woodland, wetland and Alpine birds. Of the larger mammals, visitors are most likely to see deer, squirrels and foxes. Small **Alpine raven** populations of rarer species such as lynx and European beaver exist, but these are threatened with extinction.

Coastal Regions

Germany's coasts vary considerably: the North Sea coast is predominantly flat with drained land, dikes and islands; the Baltic Sea coast is hillier with sandy inlets and cliffs. Together with differences in tides and temperature, these variations determine the variety of species found along coastal regions.

Lakes

Most of Germany's lakes are grouped in the northern part of the country, mainly in the Mecklenburg region, where they are divided from the south by the mountain ranges, rifts and valleys of the Central Uplands. However, the largest lake in Germany – the Bodensee (Lake Constance) – is situated in the south, on the border with Austria and Switzerland.

Cross-leaved heath is a species of heath that is commonly found growing on the moors and peat bogs and in the damp coastal forests of northern Germany.

Yellow floating heart grows in shallow, fertile water. Its habitats are disappearing but it still survives in the Rhine basin and on the lower Elbe.

Sea lavender is one of the salt-tolerant species that grow along Germany's North Sea coast.

Sea holly is a beautiful thistle-like plant with an amethyst hue. It is commonly found growing in sand dunes.

The white water lily, with its elegant floating flowers and lush foliage, adorns lakes and reservoirs.

Yellow flag is a protected species of iris that is found amongst reeds and in damp woodlands, particularly in older, mixed species forests.

Wild boars are mammals of the pig family, living in boggy forests. They feed mainly on acorns, beechnuts and the small animals that live in the ground cover of the forest.

Deer live in leafy and mixed forests and are one of the most common mammals seen in Germany.

Marmots live on vegetation growing in the high Alpine meadows. Rodents of the squirrel family, they sleep in burrows at night and whistle loudly when anxious.

Lynx are distinguished by small tufts of hair on the tips of their ears. These mammals are becoming ever rarer.

Uplands

Upland landscapes dominate the southern part of Germany, including Bavaria. Here, the climate is mild, and forests cover nearly a third of the region. In this picturesque and popular part of the country, winter-sports centres and spa resorts are common.

Mountains

Mountain ranges in Germany vary both in age and in height above sea level. Older, not very high mountains covered with forests predominate. The Bavarian Alps are higher and more recent. Here sub-alpine plants grow, with alpine plants at higher altitudes.

Beech is one of the commonest trees found in Germany's forests of mixed deciduous species.

Gentian, with its intensely blue trumpet-like flowers, is one of the most impressive plants to be seen in the Alps. It is pollinated by bumblebees.

Holly, the symbol of Christmas with its glossy leaves and scarlet berries, is found in forests of beech or beech and fir in the west of the country.

Edelweiss is a small flowering plant with flat, white flowers and grey-green woolly leaves. It grows high up in the Alps.

Hepatica is a protected plant in Germany. It blooms in early spring and the seeds of the blue, star-like flowers are distributed by ants.

Rhododendron hirsutum is a low, dense variety of rhododendron, one of a group of plants that grow at sub-Alpine levels.

German Literature

The first known examples of written German date from the 8th century. German literature flourished in the Renaissance, although it was mainly later writers who entered the world's canon of great literature. Goethe and Schiller, who wrote many of their most famous works in the *Sturm und Drang* (Storm and Stress) era, in the late 18th century, count among the greatest. Germany also produced many dramatists, poets and novelists in the 19th and 20th centuries. German writers have won eight Nobel Prizes for literature, awarded to Nelly Sachs, Thomas Mann, Heinrich Böll and Günter Grass among others.

Gotthold Ephraim Lessing (1729–81), the most famous German writer of the Age of Enlightenment, wrote dramas such as *Nathan the Wise*, reviews of plays performed in Hamburg as well as essays on literary and cultural theory.

Erich Maria Remarque (1898–1970) emigrated from Germany in 1931. His pacifist writings, including *All Quiet on the Western Front* and *L'Arc de Triomphe*, brought him acclaim around the world.

The Brothers Grimm, Jacob Ludwig Karl (1785–1863) and Wilhelm Karl (1786–1859), were university professors and philologists, but better known as collectors and publishers of some of the world's favourite fairy-tales.

Friedrich Schiller (1759–1805) wrote about the concept of individual freedom in his great dramas, such as *The Robbers* and *Wallenstein*. He also wrote ballads and songs, including *Ode to Joy*.

Kiel

SCHLESWIG-HOLSTEIN

Bremerhaven

Hamburg

Bremen

LOWER SAXONY, HAMBURG AND BREMEN

Hannover

Bielefeld

Dortmund

Kassel

Düsseldorf

NORTH RHINE-WESTPHALIA

Bonn

HESSE

Frankfurt am Main

RHINELAND-PALATINATE AND SAARLAND

Saarbrücken

Stuttgart

BADEN-WÜRTTEMBERG

0 kilometres   75

0 miles   75

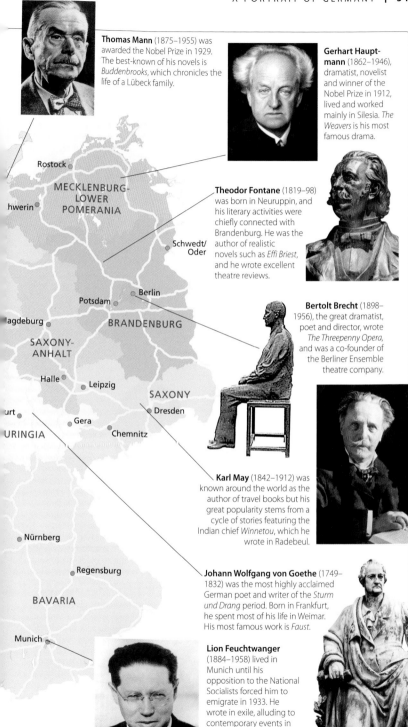

Thomas Mann (1875–1955) was awarded the Nobel Prize in 1929. The best-known of his novels is *Buddenbrooks*, which chronicles the life of a Lübeck family.

Gerhart Hauptmann (1862–1946), dramatist, novelist and winner of the Nobel Prize in 1912, lived and worked mainly in Silesia. *The Weavers* is his most famous drama.

Theodor Fontane (1819–98) was born in Neuruppin, and his literary activities were chiefly connected with Brandenburg. He was the author of realistic novels such as *Effi Briest*, and he wrote excellent theatre reviews.

Bertolt Brecht (1898–1956), the great dramatist, poet and director, wrote *The Threepenny Opera*, and was a co-founder of the Berliner Ensemble theatre company.

Karl May (1842–1912) was known around the world as the author of travel books but his great popularity stems from a cycle of stories featuring the Indian chief *Winnetou*, which he wrote in Radebeul.

Johann Wolfgang von Goethe (1749–1832) was the most highly acclaimed German poet and writer of the *Sturm und Drang* period. Born in Frankfurt, he spent most of his life in Weimar. His most famous work is *Faust*.

Lion Feuchtwanger (1884–1958) lived in Munich until his opposition to the National Socialists forced him to emigrate in 1933. He wrote in exile, alluding to contemporary events in his historical novels.

Rostock

MECKLENBURG-LOWER POMERANIA

hwerin

Schwedt/Oder

Potsdam

Berlin

agdeburg

BRANDENBURG

SAXONY-ANHALT

Halle

Leipzig

SAXONY

urt

Gera

Dresden

URINGIA

Chemnitz

Nürnberg

Regensburg

BAVARIA

Munich

Music in Germany

German composers have made an enormous contribution to the world's cultural heritage. Many great musical geniuses were born and worked here, including Johann Sebastian Bach and Ludwig van Beethoven. Today their work, and that of other German composers, continues to be performed to enthusiastic new generations of music-lovers in concert halls and opera houses around the world. In Germany, their work is celebrated regularly at hugely popular music festivals.

Renowned composer, Johann Sebastian Bach (1685–1750)

Early Music

During the early Middle Ages, music evolved in the courts and monasteries of Europe. The basis of sacred music was the Gregorian chant, which was introduced by Pope Gregory I in the late 6th century. An influential role in medieval court music was played by roving poets (*Minnesänger*), who sang love verses to a lute accompaniment. From the 14th century, German singing guilds known as *Meistersinger* emerged. Unlike the *Minnesänger,* these artistes adopted a settled lifestyle. In the succeeding centuries, both vocal and instrumental music continued to evolve, with many new forms appearing.

In the second half of the 17th century, interest in organ music developed and organ schools were established in many towns. One of the best was in Nuremberg. This was directed by Johann Pachelbel (c.1653–1706), who worked in Vienna, Stuttgart, Erfurt and Nuremberg as a church organist. He is best known for his organ work *Canon,* a set of variations on a theme.

The first German opera, *Dafne,* was composed by Heinrich Schütz (1585–1672). Completed in 1627, the opera has unfortunately been lost.

The 18th Century

A huge flowering of musical talent took place in Germany during the 18th century, when divisions both in German politics and religion led to the development of several important artistic and cultural centres. The most renowned figure in German music in the 18th century was undoubtedly

Georg Friedrich Händel (1685–1759)

Johann Sebastian Bach who, until 1717, was associated with the Weimar court. From 1723 until his death, he was associated with Leipzig, where he was the choir master at the church of St Thomas. Bach's output as a composer is vast and embraces most of the musical forms known at that time. His Passions are today performed in many countries during Holy Week, and his Brandenburg Concertos are among his most frequently performed works. His sons – Wilhelm Friedemann, Carl Philipp Emanuel, Johann Christoph Friedrich and Johann Christian – also became acclaimed composers and made significant contributions to German classical music.

Georg Friedrich Händel was another great composer of late Baroque music. Before forging a prestigious career in England, he began as the cathedral organist in Halle, from where he transferred to the opera house in Hamburg. A friend of Händel and another important composer, Georg Philipp Telemann (1681– 1767) was employed as conductor at many German courts. His work includes chamber music, operas and church music. Son of a court musician and arguably the greatest figure in classical music, Ludwig van Beethoven (1770–1827) was

The Bach festival in Leipzig's Church of St Thomas

Music Festivals

Germany is a country of musical festivals, which are usually held in the summer and early autumn. Among the most popular are the festivals dedicated to the works of a single composer, such as Wagner in Bayreuth, Bach in various cities of Thuringia, Händel in Halle and Beethoven in Bonn. Apart from these specialized festivals, opera festivals with a broader repertoire are also popular. These include the outdoor opera festival in Berlin and the Sommerfestspiele in Xanten.

born in Bonn, although he worked mainly in Vienna. Among his best-known works are his nine symphonies, as well as piano and violin concertos, two masses, various chamber works and the opera *Fidelio*.

The life of this great composer, is shrouded in legend. Succeeding generations have been fascinated not just by his music, but also by the fact that he began to lose his hearing at the age of 30. During his final years, when totally deaf, he composed from memory.

Statue of Ludwig van Beethoven

The 19th Century

Romanticism brought about the flowering of opera in Germany. One of the leading creators in this tradition was the composer Ernst Theodor Amadeus Hoffmann (1776–1822), whose opera *Undine* was staged for the first time in 1816 in Berlin. Carl Maria von Weber (1786–1826) rose to prominence following the success of his opera *Der Freischütz*, which was the first opera in the German Romantic tradition. Another major figure from this time was Felix Mendelssohn-Bartholdy,

Composer Felix Mendelssohn-Bartholdy (1809–47)

whose "Wedding March" from *A Midsummer Night's Dream* accompanies wedding celebrations around the world. As well as this famous piece of music, however, Mendelssohn left a legacy that includes five symphonies, piano music, chamber music and oratorios. In 1843, Mendelssohn founded Germany's first musical conservatory, in Leipzig.

The master of chamber music was Robert Schumann (1810–56), a poet and composer whose miniature works for piano, violin sonatas and song cycles all remain popular. The Hungarian composer Franz Liszt, who worked in Weimar from 1848 to 1861, also made a significant contribution to the evolution of German music.

In the second half of the 19th century, Richard Wagner was the major influence on German opera. During his early years, he composed traditional operas such as *Tannhäuser*. He later developed his own creative synthesis, integrating lyrics with the music. This found its finest expression in his Ring cycle, which was based on medieval sagas.

Wagner's ideas about musical theatre, including his use of *leitmotifs* (recurring phrases), were adopted by Richard Strauss (1864–1949), who composed many operas, symphonies and songs. The first bars of his symphonic poem *Zarathustra* became a guiding musical motif in Stanley Kubrick's 1968 film *2001: A Space Odyssey*. Johannes Brahms (1833–97) composed in traditional forms

Composer and pianist Johannes Brahms (1833–97)

and was unsympathetic to the progressive ideas of Wagner and Liszt. From 1872 to 1875, Brahms was the musical director of the *Gesellschaft der Musikfreunde* (Society of Friends of Music).

The 20th Century

During the 20th century, many contemporary composers continued the traditions of the earlier masters. One renowned figure was Paul Hindemith (1895–1963), whose work includes opera, ballet and concertos. His music was banned by the Nazis in 1933 and Hindemith emigrated to the USA in 1939.

Richard Wagner (1813–83)

Another important figure in German musical life was Carl Orff (1895–1982) whose best-known work is the oratorio *Carmina Burana*, based on 13th-century Latin and German poems found in a Benedictine monastery in Bavaria. The Austrian composer Arnold Schönberg (1874–1951) lived in Berlin during the 1920s and exerted great influence on German music.

Among the most important composers living and working in Germany today, mention should be made of Hans Werner Henze, Dieter Schnebel, Helmut Lachenmann, Moritz Eggert and Jörg Widmann.

German Painting

The diversity in German painting has its roots in the political and religious divisions that existed in the country in the past. The Old Masters working in the north, for example, were more likely to be influenced by the Netherlandish school, while artists working in the south leaned towards Italian styles. German art reached the peak of its individuality during the late-Gothic, late-Baroque and Expressionist periods – all periods when one of the chief characteristics of artistic style was strength of expression.

Emil Nolde (1867–1956), one of Germany's foremost Expressionists, painted landscapes of his native region. Pictured above is his *North Friesian Landscape*.

Kie

SCHLESW
HOLSTE

Master Francke (14th– 15th century) was the leading representative of the North German Late-Gothic style, working in Hamburg c.1410–24. He painted religious scenes and his works include *St Thomas's Altar*, of which this is a detail.

Bremerhaven
Hamburg

Bremen
LOWER SAXONY,
HAMBURG AND BREME

Hannover

Bielefeld

Dortmund
Düsseldorf NORTH RHINE-
WESTPHALIA
Kassel

Bonn
HESSE

RHINELAND-
PALATINE AND
SAARLAND
Frankfurt
am Main

Peter von Cornelius (1783–1867) joined the Nazarenes during the anti-academic rebellion. He later became director of the academy in Dusseldorf and others. He painted the picture *The Wise and Foolish Maidens* at that time.

Saarbrücken

Stuttgart

Adam Elsheimer (1578–1610) was born in Frankfurt am Main but spent most of his life in Rome. His poignant landscapes, such as *The Flight to Egypt* shown here, greatly influenced the development of 17th-century painting.

BADEN-
WÜRTTEMBERG

Freiburg

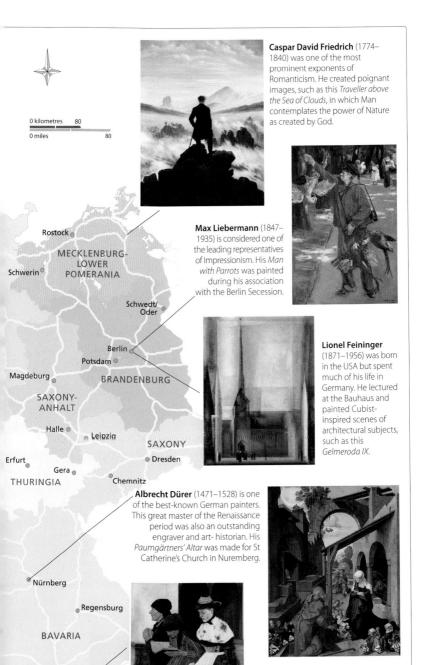

Caspar David Friedrich (1774–1840) was one of the most prominent exponents of Romanticism. He created poignant images, such as this *Traveller above the Sea of Clouds*, in which Man contemplates the power of Nature as created by God.

Max Liebermann (1847–1935) is considered one of the leading representatives of Impressionism. His *Man with Parrots* was painted during his association with the Berlin Secession.

Lionel Feininger (1871–1956) was born in the USA but spent much of his life in Germany. He lectured at the Bauhaus and painted Cubist-inspired scenes of architectural subjects, such as this *Gelmeroda IX*.

Albrecht Dürer (1471–1528) is one of the best-known German painters. This great master of the Renaissance period was also an outstanding engraver and art-historian. His *Paumgärtners' Altar* was made for St Catherine's Church in Nuremberg.

Wilhelm Leibl (1844–1900) painted this scene of women praying in a village church in Bavaria, *Three Women in a Church*, which is regarded as one of the outstanding works of German Realism.

0 kilometres   80

0 miles   80

Rostock

MECKLENBURG-LOWER POMERANIA

Schwerin

Schwedt/Oder

Berlin

Potsdam

BRANDENBURG

Magdeburg

SAXONY-ANHALT

Halle

Leipzig

SAXONY

Erfurt

Gera

Dresden

THURINGIA

Chemnitz

Nürnberg

Regensburg

BAVARIA

Munich

Castles in Germany

In a number of German regions, medieval castles are among the most characteristic features of the landscape. Some have survived only in the form of picturesque ruins, but many others, refurbished and modernized over the years, continue to be the main residence for the families for whom they were built. The most impressive grouping of great fortresses is to be found along the banks of the Mosel and the central Rhine, while, in the Münster area, you will see the most beautiful moated castles to have survived in the lowlands.

The Great Knights' Hall, where knights ate, drank and entertained, was a feature of every castle.

The 15th-century Michaels-kapelle

Marburg Castle is one of the best-preserved fortresses in Hesse. At its core is a 12th-century building, but the castle's current appearance is the result of work carried out between the 14th and 16th centuries *(see p373)*.

The Royal Room was an apartment specially designated for the use of important guests.

The Wartburg in Eisenach is one of the most important monuments in Thuringia, not only because of its excellently preserved architecture but also for its association with Martin Luther *(see pp190–91)*.

Heidelberg Castle has survived as a picturesque ruin. A Gothic- Renaissance structure of imposing proportions, it continues to captivate with its commanding position and fascinating architecture *(see pp302–3)*.

Gardens were laid out in the 19th century in an area between the castle walls and the site of the farm buildings.

Raesfeld is one of the most beautiful castles in Münsterland, a region of Westphalia that is renowned for its historic moated castles. The castle was extended in the mid-17th century for Alexandra II von Velen *(see p392)*.

19th-Century Castles

In the 19th century, many ruined castles in Germany were rebuilt in a wave of nostalgia for the Middle Ages. A number of completely new castles were built, which were modelled on medieval designs.

The Schwerin castle, originally built in the 16th century, was extensively reconstructed in 1843–57 – work inspired by French castles along the river Loire *(see p474)*.

Lichtenstein castle owes its fame to the novel *Lichtenstein* by Wilhelm Hauff and its beauty to the Romantic style of a new castle built in 1840–41 on the grounds of a pre-existing one *(see p319)*.

Evangelical Chapel

The main entrance to the castle leads through a gate house – here in the form of a tower.

Wernigerode's castle dominates the entire city. Despite later reconstruction work, it has retained a late-Gothic tower, a beautiful staircase dating from 1495 and some valuable furnishings *(see p150)*.

Burg Hohenzollern

The family seat of the Hohenzollern family, Burg Hohenzollern in Hechingen, is set on a clifftop in the Swabian Jura. The first building was established here in the 13th century and rebuilt many times over the years. The current medieval appearance is the result of work that was carried out in 1850–67 in the spirit of romantic historicism (see p318).

Burg Eltz, set high above the Mosel, is one of the most beautiful castles in Germany. Built between the 12th and 16th centuries, it has survived with very few alterations *(see p349)*.

German Scientists and Inventors

Germany is popularly regarded as a nation of practical people, so it is hardly surprising that the history books abound with the names of Germans who have made important contributions to technological progress and the development of science. They include Johann Gutenberg (c.1400–68), who invented printing with movable type, and Karl Benz (1844–1929) and Gottlieb Daimler (1834–1900) who developed the first petrol-driven car. In terms of Nobel Prize winners alone (and not counting those who received the prize for achievements in other fields), there is currently a total of 69 Germans. One of the most illustrious of these is physicist Albert Einstein (1879–1955).

1791 Alexander von Humboldt, a naturalist and geographer, discovers the presence of carbon dioxide in the air

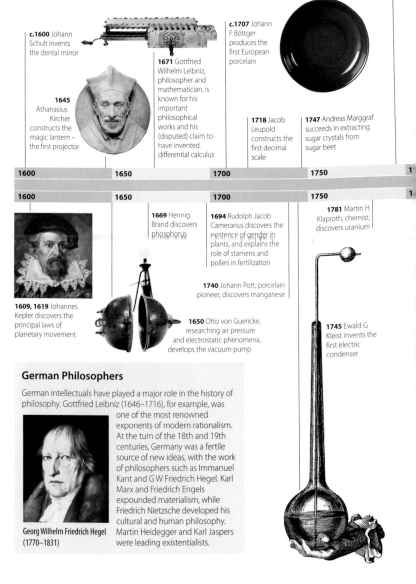

c.1600 Johann Schult invents the dental mirror

1645 Athanasius Kircher constructs the magic lantern – the first projector

1671 Gottfried Wilhelm Leibniz, philosopher and mathematician, is known for his important philosophical works and his (disputed) claim to have invented differential calculus

c.1707 Johann F Böttger produces the first European porcelain

1718 Jacob Leupold constructs the first decimal scale

1747 Andreas Marggraf succeeds in extracting sugar crystals from sugar beet

1600	1650	1700	1750	1

1600	1650	1700	1750	1

1669 Hennig Brand discovers phosphorus

1694 Rudolph Jacob Camerarius discovers the existence of gender in plants, and explains the role of stamens and pollen in fertilization

1781 Martin H Klaproth, chemist, discovers uranium

1740 Johann Pott, porcelain pioneer, discovers manganese

1609, 1619 Johannes Kepler discovers the principal laws of planetary movement

1650 Otto von Guericke, researching air pressure and electrostatic phenomena, develops the vacuum pump

1745 Ewald G Kleist invents the first electric condenser

German Philosophers

German intellectuals have played a major role in the history of philosophy. Gottfried Leibniz (1646–1716), for example, was one of the most renowned exponents of modern rationalism. At the turn of the 18th and 19th centuries, Germany was a fertile source of new ideas, with the work of philosophers such as Immanuel Kant and G W Friedrich Hegel. Karl Marx and Friedrich Engels expounded materialism, while Friedrich Nietzsche developed his cultural and human philosophy. Martin Heidegger and Karl Jaspers were leading existentialists.

Georg Wilhelm Friedrich Hegel (1770–1831)

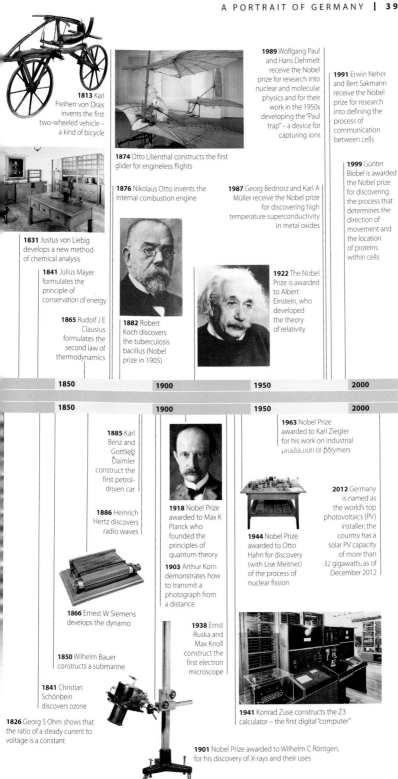

1813 Karl Freiherr von Drais invents the first two-wheeled vehicle – a kind of bicycle

1874 Otto Lilienthal constructs the first glider for engineless flights

1876 Nikolaus Otto invents the internal combustion engine

1831 Justus von Liebig develops a new method of chemical analysis

1841 Julius Mayer formulates the principle of conservation of energy

1865 Rudolf J E Clausius formulates the second law of thermodynamics

1882 Robert Koch discovers the tuberculosis bacillus (Nobel prize in 1905)

1989 Wolfgang Paul and Hans Dehmelt receive the Nobel prize for research into nuclear and molecular physics and for their work in the 1950s developing the "Paul trap" – a device for capturing ions

1987 Georg Bednorz and Karl A Müller receive the Nobel prize for discovering high temperature superconductivity in metal oxides

1922 The Nobel Prize is awarded to Albert Einstein, who developed the theory of relativity

1991 Erwin Neher and Bert Sakmann receive the Nobel prize for research into defining the process of communication between cells

1999 Günter Blobel is awarded the Nobel prize for discovering the process that determines the direction of movement and the location of proteins within cells

| 1850 | 1900 | 1950 | 2000 |

| 1850 | 1900 | 1950 | 2000 |

1885 Karl Benz and Gottlieb Daimler construct the first petrol-driven car

1886 Heinrich Hertz discovers radio waves

1866 Ernest W Siemens develops the dynamo

1850 Wilhelm Bauer constructs a submarine

1841 Christian Schönbein discovers ozone

1826 Georg S Ohm shows that the ratio of a steady current to voltage is a constant

1918 Nobel Prize awarded to Max K Planck who founded the principles of quantum theory

1903 Arthur Korn demonstrates how to transmit a photograph from a distance

1938 Ernst Ruska and Max Knoll construct the first electron microscope

1963 Nobel Prize awarded to Karl Ziegler for his work on industrial production of polymers

1944 Nobel Prize awarded to Otto Hahn for discovery (with Lise Meitner) of the process of nuclear fission

2012 Germany is named as the world's top photovoltaics (PV) installer; the country has a solar PV capacity of more than 32 gigawatts, as of December 2012

1941 Konrad Zuse constructs the Z3 calculator – the first digital "computer"

1901 Nobel Prize awarded to Wilhelm C Röntgen, for his discovery of X-rays and their uses

German Beer

Although fine wines are produced in Germany, beer is unquestionably the country's favourite alcoholic drink. Germans drink an average of 100 litres of beer annually and Bavarians lead the world in consumption, drinking an average of 215 litres each per annum. Beer is drunk on every occasion, but it tastes best in the summer when it is poured straight from a barrel at one of the numerous festivals or public holidays.

The mass is a tankard that is used to serve beer in Bavaria. It holds a litre, but waitresses are used to carrying eight or nine such tankards at a time.

Historic brewing facilities in Freising (see p255)

German Breweries

In Germany most towns and the larger villages have a brewery. The country's oldest brewery, established in 1040, is the Weihenstephan Benedictine monastery in Freising, which is believed to be the oldest working brewery in the world. Many large breweries and consortiums produce beer that is known throughout the world, but beers produced by small operators, which are available only in a few regional pubs, are in no way inferior. When visiting Germany, do try the produce of small local breweries as well as the beer produced by the giants, such as Paulaner and Löwenbrau.

Logo of the famous Munich brewery, Paulaner

Styles of Beer

One of the most popular styles of beer is *Pils* (short for *Pilsener*) a light, bottom-fermented beer of the lager type. Of the seasonal beers, it is worth trying spring beers such as *Maibock* or *Doppelbock*, and in autumn the strong beer that is brewed especially for the Oktoberfest. In the lower Rhine valley, *Altbier* is still produced; this is a top-fermented beer, prepared by traditional methods. In the south, *Weizenbier*, a wheat beer, is also produced. The Berlin version, *Berliner Weisse* (white beer), is served with fruit juice. Dark beers, such as *Dunkel* and *Schwarzbier*, also enjoy great popularity. Breweries have their own specialities. In Bamberg, they produce *Rauchbier*, which has a light smokiness; in Kulmbach it is *Eisbock*, which gains its thicker consistency through a freezing process.

Wheat beer, Berliner Weisse

Seasonal autumn beer, Bock

The largest pub in the world, created during the Oktoberfest

Drinking Beer

In Germany, beer is served with a head. Pouring lager from a barrel is supposed to take about 10 minutes, so the head sinks to the regulation level and has a thick consistency. A small beer is normally 0.3 litre, a large one 0.5 litre. In Bavaria, however, a large beer is served in a *Mass*, a tankard holding 1 litre. When travelling in Germany, order the brew of the local brewery, ideally in a *Bierkeller* or *Bierstube* (pub) and, in summer, in a *Biergarten* (beer garden). The largest gardens are in Bavaria – Munich's *Hirschgarten* caters for 8,000 beer drinkers. The Oktoberfest, which is celebrated each year in Munich (see p231), is the largest beer festival in the world.

How Beer is Brewed

The method of brewing beer that is now virtually standard dates from the 19th century, when Czech brewers first produced bottom-fermented beers at lower temperatures. The method was perfected by Gabriel Sedlmayr. Each brewery has its secrets, but the initial stages of production are the same.

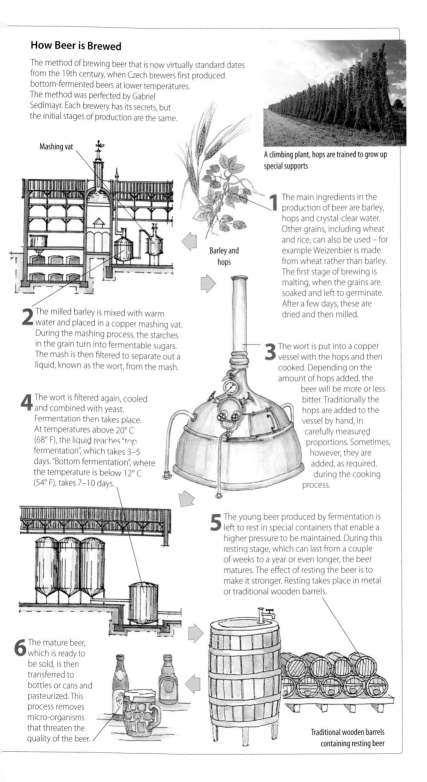

A climbing plant, hops are trained to grow up special supports

Mashing vat

Barley and hops

1 The main ingredients in the production of beer are barley, hops and crystal-clear water. Other grains, including wheat and rice, can also be used – for example Weizenbier is made from wheat rather than barley. The first stage of brewing is malting, when the grains are soaked and left to germinate. After a few days, these are dried and then milled.

2 The milled barley is mixed with warm water and placed in a copper mashing vat. During the mashing process, the starches in the grain turn into fermentable sugars. The mash is then filtered to separate out a liquid, known as the wort, from the mash.

3 The wort is put into a copper vessel with the hops and then cooked. Depending on the amount of hops added, the beer will be more or less bitter. Traditionally the hops are added to the vessel by hand, in carefully measured proportions. Sometimes, however, they are added, as required, during the cooking process.

4 The wort is filtered again, cooled and combined with yeast. Fermentation then takes place. At temperatures above 20° C (68° F), the liquid reaches "top fermentation", which takes 3–5 days. "Bottom fermentation", where the temperature is below 12° C (54° F), takes 7–10 days.

5 The young beer produced by fermentation is left to rest in special containers that enable a higher pressure to be maintained. During this resting stage, which can last from a couple of weeks to a year or even longer, the beer matures. The effect of resting the beer is to make it stronger. Resting takes place in metal or traditional wooden barrels.

6 The mature beer, which is ready to be sold, is then transferred to bottles or cans and pasteurized. This process removes micro-organisms that threaten the quality of the beer.

Traditional wooden barrels containing resting beer

Sport in Germany

Sport has long enjoyed a significant role in German life both for active participants and spectators. The country regularly produces world champions in a variety of activities, including football, tennis and motor racing. Excellent facilities exist throughout the country for taking part in sporting activities, including sailing, swimming, climbing and skiing as well as in field- or track-based events. Southern Germany plays host to a variety of winter sports and competitions.

The German Open in Hamburger Rothenbaum

Football

The largest sports organization in the country, the German Football Association has over 6 million registered members in some 25,000 clubs. The national team has won the World Cup three times – in 1954, 1974 and 1990 – and the European Cup in 1972, 1980 and 1996.

One of the outstanding figures in German football is Franz Beckenbauer, who was a member of the team that won the European Cup in 1972 and the World Cup in 1974. He trained the team that took second place in the 1986 World Cup and first place in 1990. Beckenbauer was twice named the best footballer in Europe.

The best-known club is Bayern München, which has won the German Cup a record 23 times. Matches between teams in the elite *Bundesliga* enjoy a great following. League matches are held on Saturday afternoons while European Cup games are usually held on Wednesday evenings. The club teams include a significant number of professionals from abroad. The 2006 World Cup was held in Germany.

Competing in Hamburg's annual Deutsches Spring Derby

Show-Jumping And Equestrian Events

Show-jumping is another sport at which Germany excels. Since its introduction to the Olympic Games in 1912, German riders have won more than 30 gold medals and many more have been awarded silver and bronze. Major equestrian events are held in Hamburg and Aachen in June. Hamburg's Derby Week is popular with racing fans.

Lawn Tennis

The German Tennis Association is the largest in the world with over 2 million members, belonging to some 10,200 clubs. From the mid-1980s, Germany became one of the world's most successful tennis nations thanks to some outstanding players. In 1985, aged 18, Boris Becker was the youngest player to win the Wimbledon championships. He repeated his achievement in 1986 and 1989 and was runner-up to fellow-German Michael Stich in 1991. From 1987–91 Steffi Graf was ranked number one among the world's female tennis players.

Athletics

During the Cold War period, East and West German athletes competed against each other for the glory of their rival political systems as much as for the love of their sport. The extraordinary achievements of the East German athletes during that time have since been tarnished by revelations of systematic drug abuse. Since reunification, some athletes have managed to maintain their reputations, but the majority have not.

Germany's most important event, the Internationales Stadionfest (DKB-ISTAF), is held each year in Berlin, as the climax of the season.

Football match between Borussia Moenchengladbach and SC Freiburg, Moenchengladbach

Formula One

Back in the 1930s, motor-racing was dominated by the famous "Silver Arrows", made by Mercedes-Benz. Formula One has been a decidedly German discipline since its beginnings in 1950. In all the events there have always been at least three German drivers taking part. The German Formula One Grand Prix is held each July at the Hockenheim-Ring, near Heidelberg. In most years there is a second Grand Prix at the Nürburgring circuit close to the Belgian border. This is dubbed the European Grand Prix or the Luxembourg Grand Prix.

Germany's leading Formula One driver, Michael Schumacher, won the World Championship in 1994 and 1995 and every year from 2000 to 2004.

The Hockenheim race track near Heidelberg

Markus Eberle during the slalom in Ofterschwang in the Allgäu

Skiing

Since 1953, the last week of December and the first week of January have been dominated by the Four Ski Jumps Championship for ski jumpers. This classic event, which is held in Oberstdorf and Garmisch-Partenkirchen in Germany, as well as in Innsbruck and Bischofshofen in Austria, attracts several thousand spectators and millions of television viewers. German athletes have gained first place in this competition 15 times over the years.

As well as in the German Alps, which have the most popular ski resorts, excellent conditions exist for downhill and cross-country skiing in the less glamorous and less expensive Black Forest and the Harz Mountains.

Cycling

Cycling enjoys a great following in Germany. The Tour de France is broadcast simultaneously by two television stations, and ever-increasing numbers of people are taking part in the sport, both for pleasure and competitively. Success on the cycle track has long been a German tradition, but Jan Ullrich exceeded expectations when he won gold in the long distance at the Sydney Olympics in 2000 and silver in the 2012 London Games.

Sailing

Kieler Woche is the most important regatta in the world, according to Paul Henderson, the President of the International Sailing Federation. On 1 September 1881, five officers of the Emperor's navy held a yachting race in the Bay of Kiel, as it was then called. The following year 20 yachts competed while thousands of spectators watched from the shore. The championship went on to become an international event, which gained in prestige as the Emperor took part in each race from 1894 until 1914.

Today it is traditional for the president of the German Federal Republic to formally open the regatta (in the last week of June) in which thousands of yachts from many countries take part.

Swimming

Swimming, more than any other sport in Germany, has seen a decline in success since reunification and the subsequent cessation of competition between East and West. At the 1988 Olympics in Seoul, for example, Kristin Otto won 6 gold medals. In 2000, the reunified German team returned from Sydney having gained only three bronze medals. Two figures who rose to the top in the past are Michael Gross, who was a member of the West German team, and Franziska van Almsick, a member of the East German team.

Franziska von Almsick during the German Swimming Championships

GERMANY THROUGH THE YEAR

Germans love to have fun and this is evident from the huge number of light-hearted events that are held throughout the year. Virtually every town has a calendar of festivals and fairs. These include folk festivals connected with local traditions – for example celebrating the asparagus or grape harvest. Many towns preserve the tradition of an annual fair– or Jahrmarkt – known in Westphalia as Kirmes and in Bavaria as Dult. Germany is also known for its music and film festivals, which attract an international audience, as well as for organizing major international trade fairs, such as the annual Frankfurt Book Fair.

Witches participating in the Walpurgisnacht celebrations in Thale

Spring

Spring is an idyllic time to arrive in Germany. In the high mountains, conditions are still ideal for skiing, while in the valleys everything is already in bloom. In April and May the first spring fairs and festivals are held. Spring is also time for the traditional solemn observance of Easter and its associated celebrations. May Day, which is also International Labour Day, is marked both by traditional festivities and, in some cities, by demonstrations.

March

Sommergewinn *(3 weekends before Easter)* Eisenach. The largest folk festival in Thuringia, linked with a fair.
CeBIT *(beginning of March)* Hanover. International trade fairs dedicated to information technology, telecommunications and automation.
Easter During Holy Week, Passion concerts are held throughout the country and colourful church services take place, particularly in rural Catholic areas. On Easter Sunday, in cities in the Luzyce region, horse races and a gala take place.
Leipziger Buchmesse *(mid-March)* Leipzig. International book fair with antiquarian books.

April

Thüringer Bach-Wochen *(April)*. Celebration of the life and works of Johann Sebastian Bach with concerts and lectures: held in Arnstadt, Eisenach, Erfurt, Gotha, Mühlhausen and Weimar.
Hannover Messe *(2nd half of April)* Hanover. International industrial trade fairs.

The International Dixieland Festival, held annually in Dresden in May

Hamburger Dom *(April, August and November)* Hamburg. The largest folk festival in northern Germany, held three times a year.
Walpurgisnacht *(30 April/1 May)*. On the witches' sabbath, witches gather on Brocken Mountain and in several other places in the Harz mountains.
Kurzfilmtage *(end April/ beginning of May)*. Oberhausen. The International Festival of Short Films has been held here since 1955.

May

Maibaumaufstellen *(1 May)*. In Bavarian villages, maypoles are decorated with highly ornamental wreaths.
Rhein in Flammen *(May September)*. Festivals with firework displays, in towns in the Rhine Valley.
Hafengeburtstag *(8–10 May)* Hamburg. A huge festival with fireworks, regatta and a parade of sailing boats.
Ruhrfestspiele *(May–June)* Recklinghausen. Cultural festival with a number of concerts and performances.
International Dixieland Festival *(2nd week of May)* Dresden. A traditional jazz festival has been held here since 1971.
Blutritt *(Friday after Ascension)* Weingarten. A horseback procession carrying religious relics around the town – held here for over 450 years.
Leineweber Markt *(end of May)* Bielefeld. Street theatre, jazz and folk concerts.

Summer

In Germany the summer is a time of great open-air festivals and other outdoor events and activities. Nearly every town and village has its festival with a parade, street shows, concerts and fairs. In many places there are colourful illuminations and firework displays. Banquets and knights' tournaments are held in historic castles, while concert series are organized in palaces and castles with the tourist particularly in mind. In June, a number of classical music festivals take place, while July is a popular month for water-related festivals.

A wedding couple during the Landshuter Hochzeit festival

Kieler Woche (3rd week in June) Kiel. Huge regatta with concerts and fairs.

Open-Air-Saison (4th week in June, beginning of July) Berlin. Opera festival held on outdoor stages.

Schützenfest (June). The traditional start of the hunting season. Celebrated in many north German cities.

July

Landshuter Hochzeit (every 4th summer: next in 2017) Landshut. Re-enactment of the wedding feast of Georg, son of Duke Ludwig the Rich and Polish Princess Jadwiga. Costumed wedding

procession and medieval tournament.

Lights of Cologne (early July) Cologne. Very popular, big fireworks event.

Schwörmontag (penultimate Monday) Ulm. Folk festival with a parade by the Danube.

Kinderzeche (3rd Monday) Dinkelsbühl. Ten-day folk festival commemorating the events of the Thirty Years' War (1618–48).

Richard-Wagner-Festspiele (last week July/August) Bayreuth. Festival dedicated to the works of Richard Wagner.

Wikingerfest (even years) Schleswig. Historical festival with costumed participants, tournaments and regattas.

Machseefest (late July) Hannover. Summer outdoor carnival on the shores of Lake Machsee.

August

Zissel (beginning of August) Kassel. Picturesque folk festival with parades, markets and concerts.

Mainfest. Frankfurt am Main. Feast of the river Main.

Gäubodenfest (mid-August) Straubing. Folk festival with a market and beer tasting.

Weindorf (end August) Stuttgart. Huge wine festival with wines served along with typical Swabian cuisine.

Yacht race during the annual Kieler Woche regatta in Kiel

June

Bachfest Leipzig (early June) Leipzig. International music competition dedicated to Johann Sebastian Bach.

Internationales Stadionfest (DKB-ISTAF), (2nd Sunday in June) Berlin. The largest athletics event of the season.

Luther's Wedding (second weekend in June) Wittenberg. A celebration of the marriage of Martin Luther to Katharina von Bora with music and a parade.

Spreewaldfest (June) Spreewald. Festivals are held throughout the summer in Lübben and other villages.

Fronleichnam. Observed in Catholic majority states. Processions in towns in Bavaria and in Cologne.

Christopher Street Day (mid-June). Gay and lesbian parades held in many cities, including Berlin and Köln.

Performance of *Tannhäuser* at Richard-Wagner-Festspiele, Bayreuth

Autumn

Autumn is an extremely popular time for tourism in Germany, especially September and early October when many cities, including Berlin and Munich, organize cultural events and important festivals. The autumn is also the time when the most significant trade fairs and great sporting events take place. At this time, also, conditions in the mountains and countryside continue to be ideal for outdoor activities such as walking and cycling.

September

Berliner Festwochen, Berlin. Lasting all month, this is a major series of cultural events, opera performances, exhibitions and various literary events.
Beethovenfestival, Bonn. A musical festival celebrating the works of Beethoven in the city where he was born.
Heilbronner Herbst *(1st Saturday)* Heilbronn. Popular wine festival, which also includes parades and firework displays.
Popkomm *(mid-September)* Berlin. One of the world's biggest music industry conferences, which also features public performances by up-and-coming bands and DJs.
Berlin-Marathon *(mid-late September)* Berlin. Marathon

Pumpkin race during Dorffest

through the streets of the city centre, taking in several notable landmarks, with runners in various age groups and the participation of the disabled in wheelchairs.
Oktoberfest *(last two weeks of September)* Munich. World-famous beer festival held over 16 days, beginning with a parade through the city's streets. Ceremonial removal of the bung from a new barrel of beer that has been brewed for the festival.
Plärrer *(May and September)* Augsburg. Two-week festival held twice a year, considered

one of the most important in Swabia.
Dorffest im Spreewald *(end of September)* Lehde. Folk festival.
Cannstatter Wasen *(end September/beginning October)* Stuttgart. The second largest beer festival in the world.

October

Tag der Deutschen Einheit *(3 October)*. National holiday, established after re-unification. Concerts, parades and meetings.
Frankfurter Buchmesse *(2nd week in October)* Frankfurt am Main. The world's largest book fair, which attracts publishers from around the world and also features talks by authors.
Freimarkt *(mid-October)* Bremen. Two-week folk festival beginning with a procession.
Liszt-Tage Weimar. Celebration of the life and work of Franz Liszt, with concerts at which world-class musicians are invited to perform.
Colmansfest *(2nd Sunday)* Schwangau. Religious festival featuring hundreds of horses and decorated carriages.
Kasseler Musiktage *(end of October)* Kassel. One of Europe's longest-established classical music festivals.

November

Weinfest *(1st weekend in November)* Cochem. Festival celebrating the removal of the bung from the first barrel of young Mosel wine.
Martinsfest *(11 November)*. St Martin's Day is celebrated in northern Baden and the Rhineland with fairs and the essential roast goose. In the Rhine Valley, St Martin's Day signifies the beginning of the Carnival season.
Internationales Film-festival *(2nd week in November)* Mannheim-Heidelberg. Annual festival of short, documentary and educational films.

The International Book Fair in Frankfurt am Main

Berlinale – the grand festival of world cinema

Winter

December is synonymous with Christmas festivities. Every city has fairs where you can buy Christmas-tree decorations, delicacies and presents. In December, shops have longer opening hours and the skiing season begins in the Alps. January and February are a time for parties and balls (the Carnival season), with enjoyment reaching a peak in the last few days of the season. Then the fun continues all weekend from Thursday, reaching a height on *Rosenmontag* then diminishing on the last Tuesday of Carnival.

December

Christkindelsmarkt and **Weihnachtsmarkt**. Christmas fairs are held from the beginning

The famous Christmas market in the city of Nuremberg

of the month until Christmas Eve. The most beautiful are in Baden-Wurttemberg and in Bavaria, while the most renowned is held in Nuremberg.
Christmas *(25/26 December)*. Traditionally celebrated throughout Germany. A Christmas tree is considered essential, together with presents and delicacies.
New Year's Eve *(31 December)*. The New Year is greeted at balls, opera galas, in restaurants, clubs, private houses and in the streets and squares of city centres.

January

Four Ski Jumps Tournament *(begins 1 January)*. Renowned tournament for ski-jumping held annually in Garmisch-Partenkirchen.
Sechs-Tage-Rennen *(early January)* Berlin. Spectacular cycle races with associated events, held in Berlin Velodrome.
Grüne Woche *(2nd week)* Berlin. International trade fairs dedicated to agriculture, animal breeding and the food processing industry. Producers from all over the world offer specialities from their own national cuisines.

February

Berlinale–Internationale Filmfestspiele *(2nd and 3rd weeks)* Berlin. International film festival in which major stars participate.

Fastnacht, also known as **Fasnet**, **Fasching** or **Karneval** (Shrovetide). Carnival is celebrated enthusiastically in virtually every region of Germany. The most interesting events are held in the Rhine Valley, and particularly in Cologne. *Karneval am Rhein*, which marks the lasts three days of the Carnival, begins on the Thursday of the week before Ash Wednesday with a women's parade, known as *Weiberfastnacht*. On the Monday there is a superb costume parade, known as *Rosenmontagsumzug*.

Costumed revellers on the streets of Cologne during Carnival

Public Holidays

Neujahr *New Year* (1 Jan).
Hl. Dreikönige *Three Kings* (6 Jan: Bavaria, Baden-Wurttemberg, Saxony-Anhalt).
Karfreitag *Good Friday*.
Ostern *Easter*.
Maifeiertag/Tag der Arbeit *Labour Day*.
Christi Himmelfahrt *Ascension*.
Pfingsten *Pentecost*.
Fronleichnam *Corpus Christi* (Bavaria, Baden-Wurttemberg, Hesse, North Rhine Valley-Westphalia, Rhine Valley-Palatinate and Saar).
Mariä Himmelfahrt *Assumption of the BVM* (15 Aug: Bavaria, Saar).
Nationalfeiertag *Reunification of Germany Day* (3 Oct).
Allerheiligen *All Saints* (1 Nov: Bavaria, Baden-Wurttemberg, North Rhine Valley-Westphalia, Rhine Valley-Palatinate).
Weihnachten *Christmas* (25/26 Dec).

The German Climate

Germany lies in a temperate climatic zone. In the north of the country, with marine influences predominating, summers tend to be quite cold and winters mild, with relatively high rainfall. In the eastern part of the country, however, the climate is more continental and this produces harsher winters and hotter summers. Germany's highest rainfall and the lowest temperatures are recorded in the Alps.

SCHLESWIG-HOLSTEIN

°C (F)	Jan	Apr	Jul	Oct
Average daily maximum temperature		10.5 (51)	20 (68)	13 (55)
	2.2 (36)	3 (37)	12 (54)	7 (45)
Average daily minimum temperature	0			
	-2 (28)			
Average daily amount of sunshine	1.3 hrs	5.5 hrs	7 hrs	3 hrs
Average monthly rainfall	80 mm	55 mm	92 mm	90 mm
month	Jan	Apr	Jul	Oct

BREMEN, HAMBURG, LOWER SAXONY

°C (F)	Jan	Apr	Jul	Oct
		12.5 (55)	22 (72)	14 (57)
	3.2 (38)	3.5 (38)	12 (54)	6 (43)
	0			
	-2 (28)			
☀	1.3 hrs	5 hrs	6 hrs	3 hrs
☂	56 mm	48 mm	69 mm	55 mm
month	Jan	Apr	Jul	Oct

NORTH RHINE-WESTPHALIA

°C (F)	Jan	Apr	Jul	Oct
		14 (57)	23 (73)	15 (59)
	4.5 (40)	3.6 (38)	12.5 (55)	6 (43)
	0			
	-1 (30)			
☀	1.5 hrs	5 hrs	6.5 hrs	3.7 hrs
☂	62 mm	54 mm	84 mm	55 mm
month	Jan	Apr	Jul	Oct

HESSE

°C (F)	Jan	Apr	Jul	Oct
		(57)	24 (75)	14 (57)
	3 (37)	4 (39)	13 (55)	6 (43)
	0			
	-2 (28)			
☀	1.3 hrs	5 hrs	7.4 hrs	3.3 hrs
☂	44 mm	51 mm	63 mm	50 mm
month	Jan	Apr	Jul	Oct

RHINELAND-PALATINATE, SAARLAND

°C (F)	Jan	Apr	Jul	Oct
		13 (55)	23 (73)	14 (57)
	3 (37)	4 (39)	12 (54)	7 (45)
	0			
	-1.5 (29)			
☀	1.3 hrs	5 hrs	7 hrs	3 hrs
☂	60 mm	53 mm	69 mm	65 mm
month	Jan	Apr	Jul	Oct

BADEN-WÜRTTEMBERG

°C (F)	Jan	Apr	Jul	Oct
		14 (57)	23 (73)	15 (59)
	4 (39)	5 (41)	13 (55)	7 (45)
	0			
	-1 (30)			
☀	1.7 hrs	5 hrs	8 hrs	4 hrs
☂	60 mm	80 mm	95 mm	66 mm
month	Jan	Apr	Jul	Oct

Average daily maximum temperature

Average daily minimum temperature

Average daily amount of sunshine

Average monthly rainfall

Flensburg
Schleswig
Hamb
Bremen
Nient
Hanove
Münster
Paderborn
Dortmund
Göttinge
Düsseldorf
Kassel
Aachen
Cologne
Siegen
Bonn
Marburg
Koblenz
Frankfurt am Main
Trier
Würzbu
Mainz
Mannheim
Saarbrücken
Heidelberg
Karlsruhe
Stuttgart
Ul
Freiburg im Breisgau
Konstar

0 km 100
0 miles 100

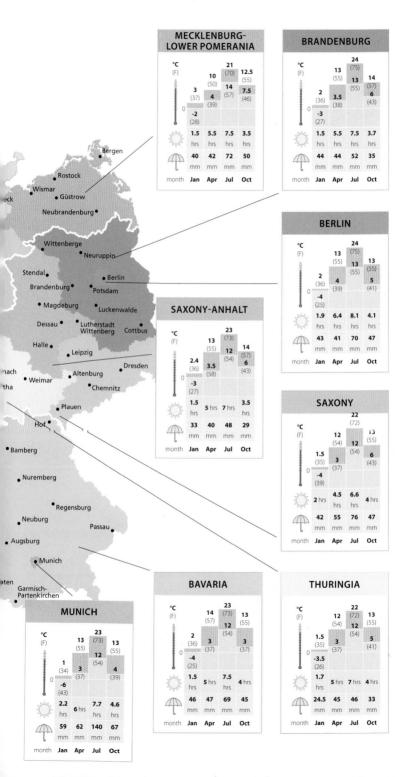

MECKLENBURG-LOWER POMERANIA

°C (F)			
		21 (70)	12.5 (55)
	10 (50)	14 (57)	7.5 (46)
3 (37)	4 (39)		
-2 (28)			

1.5 hrs	5.5 hrs	7.5 hrs	3.5 hrs
40 mm	42 mm	72 mm	50 mm

| month | Jan | Apr | Jul | Oct |

BRANDENBURG

°C (F)			
		24 (75)	
	13 (55)	13 (55)	14 (57)
2 (36)	3.5 (38)		6 (43)
-3 (27)			

1.5 hrs	5.5 hrs	7.5 hrs	3.7 hrs
44 mm	44 mm	52 mm	35 mm

| month | Jan | Apr | Jul | Oct |

BERLIN

°C (F)			
		24 (75)	
	13 (55)	13 (55)	13 (55)
2 (36)	4 (39)		5 (41)
-4 (25)			

1.9 hrs	6.4 hrs	8.1 hrs	4.1 hrs
43 mm	41 mm	70 mm	47 mm

| month | Jan | Apr | Jul | Oct |

SAXONY-ANHALT

°C (F)			
		23 (73)	
	13 (55)	12 (54)	14 (57)
2.4 (36)	3.5 (58)		6 (43)
-3 (27)			

1.5 hrs	5 hrs	7 hrs	3.5 hrs
33 mm	40 mm	48 mm	29 mm

| month | Jan | Apr | Jul | Oct |

SAXONY

°C (F)			
		22 (72)	
	12 (54)	12 (54)	13 (55)
1.5 (35)	3 (37)		6 (43)
-4 (39)			

2 hrs	4.5 hrs	6.6 hrs	4 hrs
42 mm	55 mm	76 mm	47 mm

| month | Jan | Apr | Jul | Oct |

MUNICH

°C (F)			
		23 (73)	
	13 (55)	12 (54)	13 (55)
1 (34)	3 (37)		4 (39)
-6 (43)			

2.2 hrs	6 hrs	7.7 hrs	4.6 hrs
59 mm	62 mm	140 mm	67 mm

| month | Jan | Apr | Jul | Oct |

BAVARIA

°C (F)			
		23 (73)	
	14 (57)	12 (54)	13 (55)
2 (36)	3 (37)		3 (37)
-4 (25)			

1.5 hrs	5 hrs	7.5 hrs	4 hrs
46 mm	47 mm	69 mm	45 mm

| month | Jan | Apr | Jul | Oct |

THURINGIA

°C (F)			
		22 (72)	
	12 (54)	12 (54)	13 (55)
1.5 (35)	3 (37)		5 (41)
-3.5 (26)			

1.7 hrs	5 hrs	7 hrs	4 hrs
24.5 mm	45 mm	46 mm	33 mm

| month | Jan | Apr | Jul | Oct |

Bergen · Rostock · Wismar · Güstrow · Neubrandenburg · Wittenberge · Neuruppin · Stendal · Brandenburg · Berlin · Potsdam · Magdeburg · Luckenwalde · Dessau · Lutherstadt Wittenberg · Cottbus · Halle · Leipzig · Dresden · Altenburg · Weimar · Chemnitz · Plauen · Hof · Bamberg · Nuremberg · Regensburg · Neuburg · Passau · Augsburg · Munich · Garmisch-Partenkirchen

THE HISTORY OF GERMANY

Germany is a country of cultural and religious contrasts Regional differences in culture, language and traditions arose from the historical division of the country into many small states. Such differences have been further accentuated by the recent experience of generations of Germans who, until 1990, grew up under two conflicting social systems: capitalism and communism.

Early History

In the 1st millennium BC, the basins of the Rhine, Danube and Main rivers were settled by Celts, who had been largely displaced by Germanic tribes by the 2nd century BC. In the 1st century BC the Roman legions waged wars with the Germans, and conquered the territories west of the Rhine. The settlements they founded there later developed into towns like Trier, Mainz, Cologne and Xanten. The Romans made numerous attempts to conquer the eastern regions between the Rhine and the Elbe rivers. They eventually reached the Elbe at the end of the 1st century BC, but the Germans, under the leadership of Arminius, also known as Germanus, defeated the Roman armies in the Teutoburg Forest in AD 9, and so ended their presence in this region. A system of fortifications, or *limes*, built in the 2nd century along the course of the Danube and the Rhine, divided the region into two: *Germania Romana*, the Roman province, and *Germania Libra*, free Germany. The free German tribes, notably the Goths, often entered into alliances with the Romans. In the 5th century, however, they took advantage of Rome's weakness to appropriate parts of the empire for themselves.

Early Middle Ages

After the collapse of the Roman Empire, the area between the Rhine and the Elbe was ruled by the Franks, who gradually converted to Christianity from the 6th century. One of the most important figures in this process was the 8th-century missionary, St Boniface. When Charlemagne was crowned Emperor in 800, the territory of present-day Germany became part of the Frankish Empire. The Empire was partitioned by the Treaty of Verdun in 843, with the eastern part going to Ludwig the German. In the 10th century the kingdom, which was made up of numerous tribal states, passed to the house of Liudolf. Otto I, son of Heinrich I and the first king from this Saxon family, was crowned Emperor in 962 after several political and military victories, in particular his defeat of the Magyars.

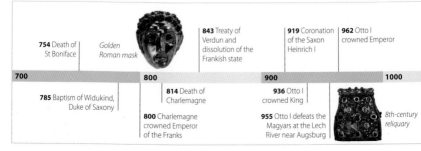

754 Death of St Boniface

Golden Roman mask

843 Treaty of Verdun and dissolution of the Frankish state

919 Coronation of the Saxon Heinrich I

962 Otto I crowned Emperor

700   **800**   **900**   **1000**

785 Baptism of Widukind, Duke of Saxony

814 Death of Charlemagne

800 Charlemagne crowned Emperor of the Franks

936 Otto I crowned King

955 Otto I defeats the Magyars at the Lech River near Augsburg

8th-century reliquary

◀ *Germany's Awakening*, a patriotic 19th-century work by Christian Köhler

Consolidating Power

With Otto being crowned emperor, the dynasty of the Saxon house of Liudolf acceded to power. It gave the country three further rulers – Otto II, Otto III and Heinrich II. In the year 925 Otto I annexed Lotharingia (present-day Lorraine). On the eastern frontier he created two "marks", the Nordmark and the Ostmark, as buffer states designed to subjugate the Slav-populated regions east of the Oder River. After Heinrich II's death, the house of the Salian Franks took the imperial throne and used their authority to limit the power of the local feudal dukes.

Stained-glass window in Augsburg cathedral

The Investiture Controversy

In the 11th century the empire came into conflict with the papacy. Matters came to a head in the so-called "investiture controversy". Pope Gregory VII asserted the church's right to appoint bishops. Emperor Heinrich IV meanwhile, who had been relying on the support of the clergy he had appointed, called his bishops together and asked the Pope to step down. Pope Gregory VII excommunicated Heinrich. The dukes of Saxony used the opportunity to appoint a king in opposition to Heinrich, and the Pope attempted to intervene in the dispute. Heinrich IV saw himself forced to march to Canossa in Italy, where the Pope had sought refuge, in order to stop his empire from falling apart. Doing penance in this way forced the Pope to withdraw his excommunication. However, the dispute did not end there, but continued for several years, finally ending with the Signing of the Concordat of Worms in 1122.

Enamelled Romanesque medallion, dating from c.1150

Hohenstaufens And Welfs

After the Salian dynasty died out in 1125 and the brief reign of Lothar III of the Saxon dynasty, another long drawn-out conflict broke out, between the houses of Hohenstaufen and Welf (known in Italian as Ghibellines and Guelphs). Imperial power went to the Hohenstaufens, while the greatest political victories were scored by Friedrich I Barbarossa (meaning "red beard"). He intended gradually to break up his subject principalities and to rule them under a feudal system. The 12th century also saw further expansion eastwards and northwards into areas inhabited by the

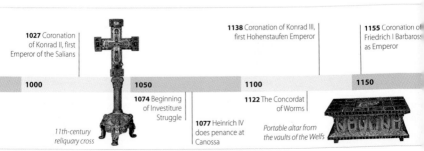

12th-century reliquary from the Welf family vaults

1027 Coronation of Konrad II, first Emperor of the Salians

1138 Coronation of Konrad III, first Hohenstaufen Emperor

1155 Coronation of Friedrich I Barbarossa as Emperor

1000 | **1050** | **1100** | **1150**

11th-century reliquary cross

1074 Beginning of Investiture Struggle

1077 Heinrich IV does penance at Canossa

1122 The Concordat of Worms

Portable altar from the vaults of the Welfs

northwestern Slavic tribes. From the start of the 13th century Barbarossa also conquered territories occupied by the Baltic peoples and the Estonians, which involved armed expeditions by the North German cities and orders of knights.

Friedrich II, crowned Emperor in 1220, was also King of Sicily and his Italian interests brought further conflict with the papacy. Ultimately his policies brought about the collapse of imperial power. After his death in 1250, his successor was unable to find any support, which led to the period known as the Great Interregnum.

Emperor Rudolf I of Habsburg

duchies. In the 13th century a system evolved by which only seven elector-dukes had the right to elect the emperor. These were the Margrave of Brandenburg, the Elector of Palatine (or the Bavarian dukes), the Duke of Saxony, the King of Bohemia and the Archbishops of Trier, Cologne and Mainz. Starting with Rudolf I of Habsburg, who was elected king of Germany in 1273, until 1438 the kings came from the rival houses of Habsburg, Wittelsbach and Luxemburg. After 1312, the same houses also competed for the title of Emperor. The most outstanding of the 14th-century rulers of Germany was Karl IV of Luxemburg, who resided permanently in Prague. In 1338 the electors had rejected the requirement for the Pope to confirm election results. In 1356 Karl IV issued the "Golden Bull" which underlined the federal nature of the state, and clarified the rules for electing its leader.

The Interregnum

The fall of the Hohenstaufens marked the end of the old imperial system. The absence of an overall ruler led to a breakdown in law and order, and resulted in the rise of the *Raubritter* (robber-barons). To protect their common interests, the trading cities set up alliances. The collapse of imperial power, and the decline in the power of the dukes thus gradually led to an increase in the power of the German cities.

From the beginning the imperial throne had been elective, with dukes electing the emperor from the male members of the dynasty. There was also no capital city, as the emperors moved from one city to another, thus spreading the costs of maintaining the imperial court among different

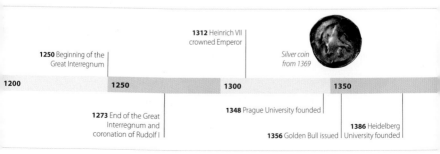

A "Minneteppich" – part of a medieval tapestry, depicting a variety of human traits and a griffin, the mythical beast

1250 Beginning of the Great Interregnum

1312 Heinrich VII crowned Emperor

Silver coin from 1369

1200   1250   1300   1350

1273 End of the Great Interregnum and coronation of Rudolf I

1348 Prague University founded

1356 Golden Bull issued

1386 Heidelberg University founded

The Hanseatic League

The German Hanseatic League, or Hanse, was only one of many guilds of traders or cities that existed in the Middle Ages, but its important historical role made it one of the best known. Established in the 13th century, it reached its peak in the 14th century and declined again in the 16th century. Over 160 cities, primarily the trading cities of northern Germany, but also including Baltic ports as far afield as Visby, Riga and Tallinn, joined the League. It exercised total control over trade from the Baltic in the east to England in the west. The Hanseatic cities were among the wealthiest in Europe, and crafts and the arts flourished there.

Madonna of the Roses
15th-century painting by Stefan Lochner of the Cologne School.

The Wise and Foolish Maidens
The flowering of art in the Hanseatic cities brought about works such as this portal of Magdeburg Cathedral.

Hanse ships, loaded with merchandise, entering the harbour

Revenue officials awaiting the cargo

Round wooden cranes with swivelling arms were used to unload ships. One example still survives in Lüneburg.

Crucifix in Lübeck Cathedral
This crucifix is one of only few painted wood-carvings made by Bernt Notke of Lübeck that have survived until today.

Cogs
Heavy, flat-bottomed sailing ships with limited manoeuvrability, cogs were fishermen's and merchants' boats or navy vessels in the North Sea and the Baltic from the 12th to the 14th centuries.

Panoramic view of Lübeck
The vast port town of Lübeck was the largest Hanseatic city. This 15th-century woodcut shows a view of the city with its numerous church spires.

The Hanseatic Cities

In the major Hanseatic cities, the most prominent buildings grew up around the *Markt* (market square) and along the streets that led to the port. The market square would contain the *Rathaus* (town hall), with its multi-functional interiors, and the equally splendid banqueting halls and ballrooms, such as the Gürzenich in Cologne. The main cathedrals in the cities were dedicated either to St Mary or St Nicholas. The gabled residential houses had narrow façades with distinctive portals. The townscape of the port areas was dominated by granaries, warehouses and numerous cranes. The cities were all enclosed and protected by solid fortifications.

Harbour officials in their offices

The Leichter was a harbour boat used to carry cargo from the ships to the warehouses.

Hamburg merchants

Russian merchants, recognizable by their distinctive clothing, are engrossed in intense negotiations.

The Port Of Hamburg
Hamburg, along with Bremen, Lübeck and Gdansk, was one of the leading Hanseatic cities. In the 14th century, it was the main centre for trade between the North Sea and the Baltic. This miniature, showing the port of Hamburg, dates from the 15th century.

The town hall in Brunswick, with its open upper arcades and statues of the Welfs, is one of the finest surviving Hanseatic secular buildings.

The Kröpeliner Tor in Rostock (see p480) is one of 22 towers on the defensive walls around the medieval city centre.

Jan Hus being burned at the stake

The Hussite Wars And The Habsburg Dynasty

The last king and emperor of the house of Luxemburg, Sigismund, brought an end to the "Great Schism" in the Western church that had persisted since 1378. The Council of Constance, which he called in 1414, led to the election of a single, rather than two rival popes. However, new religious controversy was provoked by the death sentence for heresy passed in 1415 on Jan Hus, a religious reformer from Bohemia. The ensuing Hussite Wars ravaged the northern and western regions of Germany.

From 1482 the imperial crown went to the Habsburgs, who

Title page of the first German edition of the Bible

retained it until 1740. Attempts at political reform in the second half of the 15th century failed. The most ambitious reformer was Maximilian I. He called an Imperial Tribunal in 1495 which set about transferring part of the king's authority to the judiciary; however, it did not result in any great practical changes, although it gave slightly more power to the *Reichstag*, the imperial parliament.

The Reformation

Lion-shaped water jug (1540)

Germany entered the 16th century as a country simmering with social conflict, gradually becoming steeped in the ideas of humanism, thanks to the writings of Erasmus of Rotterdam and others. The rise of Martin Luther, who in 1517 nailed his 95 Theses to the door of the Castle Church in Wittenberg, and who opposed the trade in indulgences conducted by the clergy, set the Reformation in motion *(see pp130–31)*. The idea of ecclesiastical reform propounded by Luther gained a growing following. His supporters included princes who hoped to profit from the secularization of church property, as well as other social classes that simply saw an opportunity to improve their lot. In 1519 Maximilian I died, and Karl V was elected to succeed him. Karl's interests were focused on Spain and the Netherlands,

1419–36 Hussite Wars

c.1450 The first printing press

Maximilian I

1517 Luther's Theses and the start of the Reformation

1540 The first stock exchanges are set up in Augsburg and Nürnberg

1400

1450

1500

1414–18 Council of Constance

1438 Coronation of Albrecht II, first Emperor of the House of Habsburg

1495 Edict banning the waging of private wars

1522 The Knights' War

1524–25 The Peasants' War

Urban life in Germany in the early 16th century, in a painting by Jörg Breu the Elder (c.1475–1537)

and he was unable to prevent the spread of Lutheranism. The unrest led to rebellions such as the Knights' War of 1522 and the Peasants' War of 1524, and these were followed by continuous religious conflict. In 1530 the Protestants set up the League of Schmalkalden, which was finally broken up by the Emperor in the war of 1546–7. These basically religious clashes ultimately led to the division of Germany into a northern Protestant part and a Catholic south, a situation that was sanctioned in 1555 by the Peace of Augsburg. This established the principle of *cuius regio, eius religio*, which meant that each ruler had the right to decide on the faith of the region, and the only option left for anyone of a different persuasion was to move elsewhere.

The Thirty Years' War

The second half of the 16th century was relatively stable for Germany, despite

the religious conflicts. However, the influence of the Counter-Reformation in the early 17th century ended this stability. The Protestant Union and Catholic League were established in 1608 and 1609 respectively. Unrest in Prague, where the states with a Protestant majority opposed the election of the Catholic Ferdinand II as king of Bohemia, began the Thirty Years' War. This religious war quickly spread throughout Germany, and also drew in Denmark, Spain, Sweden and France. Much of the country and many towns were laid waste, and vast numbers of people died. Finally, in 1648, the German states, France and Sweden signed the Peace of Westphalia in Münster, resulting in major losses of territory for Germany, mainly in the north. A new political system emerged, with the German princes enjoying complete political independence, under a weakened emperor and pope. The second half of the 17th century was marked by the rebuilding of towns and the hard work of restoring the ruined economic infrastructure.

A scene in the Thirty Years' War, in a painting by Wilhelm von Diez

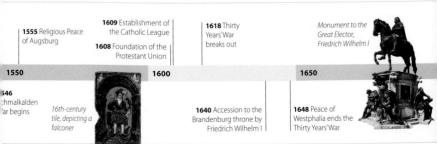
1555 Religious Peace of Augsburg
1609 Establishment of the Catholic League
1608 Foundation of the Protestant Union
1618 Thirty Years' War breaks out
Monument to the Great Elector, Friedrich Wilhelm I
1550
1600
1650
1546 Schmalkalden War begins
16th-century tile, depicting a falconer
1640 Accession to the Brandenburg throne by Friedrich Wilhelm I
1648 Peace of Westphalia ends the Thirty Years' War

Goethe in the Roman Campagna by Johann H. W. Tischbein (1787)

Absolutism and the Rise of Prussia

In the second half of the 17th century and throughout the 18th century, Germany was a loose federation of small, politically weak states in the west, and much more powerful states in the east and the south – Saxony, which was ruled by the house of Wettin, and Bavaria, ruled by the Wittelsbachs. However, the rising star was the state of Brandenburg, ruled by the house of Hohenzollern, which from 1657 also ruled Prussia. In 1701 the Elector Friedrich III crowned himself King of Prussia (as Friedrich I), and subsequently the name "Prussia" was applied to all areas ruled by the house of Hohenzollern. During the 18th century Prussia became the greatest rival to Habsburg Austria. In 1740, Friedrich II, also known as Frederick the Great, was crowned King of Prussia. Under his rule, Berlin became a major

Portrait of Frederick the Great as successor to the throne

European city and a centre of the Enlightenment. In 1740–42, in the Seven Years' War, Frederick the Great took Silesia from the Habsburgs without major losses. In 1772 he took part in the first partition of Poland.

In the second half of the 18th century Germany produced a succession of great poets and playwrights – figures such as Gotthold Ephraim Lessing, Friedrich Schiller and Johann Wolfgang von Goethe.

The Napoleonic Wars, Restoration and Revolution

From 1793 onwards the German states were involved in the Napoleonic Wars. After France's occupation of the lands west of the Rhine, a territorial reform was carried out by the Reichsdeputations Hauptschluss in 1803. This resulted in the secularization of most church property, and the total of 289 states and free cities was reduced to 112 larger states. States that gained from this supported Napoleon in his defeat of Austria in the war of 1805–7. In 1806 the Holy Roman Empire of German Nations was dissolved, and Bavaria, Saxony and Wurttemberg were given the status of kingdoms. Napoleon defeated Prussia at Jena and the country was occupied by France.

1701 The first king of Prussia is crowned

1702–14 Germany joins the War of Spanish Succession

1740–42 The Silesian War

Leopold Hermann von Boyen, Prussian army general

1813 Battle of the Nations at Leipzig

1700	**1730**	**1760**	**1790**

1710 Meißen porcelain factory opened

1700 Academy of Sciences founded in Berlin

1756–63 The Seven Years' War

1740 Frederick the Great crowned King of Prussia

1803 Territorial reform of the German states

1806 Dissolution of the Empire

1814–15 The Congress of Vienna

The tide turned for Germany at the Battle of Leipzig in 1813, when Russia, Austria and Prussia defeated the French. After Napoleon's final defeat at Waterloo in 1815, the Congress of Vienna established a German Confederation under Austrian control. Its supreme body was the Bundestag (federal parliament), which met at Frankfurt am Main.

Victory Report at the Battle of Leipzig by Johann Peter Krafft (1839)

Vase with portrait of Kaiser Wilhelm II

The wars of liberation against Napoleon had led to a growth in nationalism and democratic awareness, as well as a desire for unification. In 1848 the March Revolution broke out in Berlin. Its main driving force was the urban middle class, but the revolt was finally put down by Prussian troops in 1849.

In the 1820s and 1830s, Germany underwent rapid industrialization, and the establishment of the Zollverein (customs union) in 1834 marked the first step towards a united Germany. Uniting Germany was the main goal of the Prussian premier Otto von Bismarck. Prussia's victories over Austria in 1866 and France in 1871 resulted in the proclamation of a German Empire on 18 January 1871.

The Second Reich

The Second Reich was a federation of 25 states, and its first Chancellor was Otto von Bismarck. The unification of Germany led to a widespread confrontation between the state and the Catholic Church (known as the "Kulturkampf"). The economy, however, flourished, due to the boom in industry, in particular mining, metallurgy, electrical and chemical engineering. This led to the rise of a workers' movement, inspired by the ideas of Karl Marx. In 1875 the workers' parties united and formed the Social Democratic Party of Germany (SPD). Although the party was banned between 1878 and 1890, it rapidly gained support, and a system of social welfare for workers was gradually introduced.

At the beginning of the 20th century, Germany was a powerful state with overseas colonies. Imperialist tendencies grew, and increased tensions in European politics, particularly in the Balkans, led inevitably to war.

Fighting on the Barricades in May 1848, a fanciful picture of the revolution in Berlin by Julius Scholz

1834 German Customs Union (Zollverein) is established

1848 The Communist Manifesto is published

1848–49 The March Revolution

1871 Proclamation of the German Empire with Prussian king as Emperor Wilhelm I

1898 Construction of the German navy begins

1820 **1850** **1880** **1910**

1844 Silesian weavers' uprising

Neo-Gothic chalice designed by K.F. Schinkel

1870–71 Franco-Prussian War

1866 Prussian-Austrian War

1890 Fall of Bismarck

Abandoned, bas-relief by Ernst Barlach

Bismarck's Germany

The establishment of a Reich headed by the King of Prussia on 18 January 1871 ensured Prussia's prominent role over the following decades. The Chancellor was the Prussian Prime Minister Otto von Bismarck. Thanks to large reparations paid by France and a favourable economic situation, the economy flourished throughout the Reich. This in turn fostered the development of science and culture. The cities grew rapidly, and the housing shortage led to the development of huge *Mietskasernen*, blocks of apartments for renting.

Germany In 1871
▪ The Second German Reich

Kaiser Wilhelm I
Mosaics, depicting a procession of members of the house of Hohenzollern, decorate the vestibule of the Kaiser-Wilhelm Gedächtnichskirche (memorial church) in Berlin.

The Kaiser's Family Taking a Walk in Sanssouci Park
"Happy family" portraits such as this one were often painted for propaganda purposes.

The Reichstag
The monumental Reichstag (parliament building), was built in the centre of the capital, Berlin, by the architect Paul Wallot.

Members of Parliament

Heads of the federal states

A Steel Mill in Königshütte
Germany's economic progress was achieved through a high degree of industrialization. Adolf von Menzel's painting depicts a steel mill in Königshütte, Upper Silesia.

Officer's helmet
The characteristic spiked helmet worn by German soldiers was known as a *Pickelhaube*.

Ludwig II of Bavaria
The federal states, which made up the Reich, enjoyed complete autonomy. Their rulers, however, for instance King Ludwig II of Bavaria, patron of Richard Wagner and builder of "fantastic" castles and palaces, had little real political influence.

The Kaiser's wife, Augusta Victoria

Wilhelm, the heir to the throne

Mourning dress was worn by the women and black ribbons by the men as a mark of respect for the two previous Kaisers who had died in 1888 – the father and grandfather of Wilhelm II.

The Diplomatic Corps

Otto von Bismarck

Kaiser Wilhelm II

Inauguration of the Reichstag

This vast canvas by Anton von Werner (1893) shows the opening ceremony for the Reichstag after the coronation of Kaiser Wilhelm II on 25 June 1888 in the Kaiser's Palace in Berlin. The painter depicts the moment when the Kaiser delivers his speech.

Otto von Bismarck
Originating from a Pomeranian family of Junkers, the Prussian Premier and Chancellor of the Reich was one of the most prominent political figures of his time.

World War I

When Germany entered World War I in 1914, the Kaiser's generals hoped for a quick victory, but their invasion of France was halted on the Marne. The war dragged on for the next four years, devastating much of Europe, and ending in Germany's defeat. The Allied offensive in the summer of 1918 forced Germany to the negotiating table – it also led to the November revolution in Germany. Within days the state monarchs were toppled from power, Kaiser Wilhelm II abdicated, and on 9 November 1918 a republic was proclaimed. The form of government had not been decided, and at first the political advantage was held by the socialists. But the Workers' Uprising in Berlin in 1919 was defeated.

Ein Volk, ein Reich, ein Führer!

Propaganda poster for Adolf Hitler

The Weimar Republic

The Treaty of Versailles of 1919 imposed many unfavourable conditions on Germany. The country lost a great deal of her territory, mainly to Poland, France and Lithuania, and she was obliged to pay huge reparations, undergo partial demilitarization and limit arms production.

During the Weimar Republic, Germany was riddled with instability. The economy collapsed under the heavy burden of reparation payments and the onset of hyperinflation. Constant changes of government failed to stabilize the political situation, which led to the rise both of left-wing revolutionaries and of right-wing nationalists, and to a general dissatisfaction with the country's status after the humiliating Treaty of Versailles. It is perhaps remarkable that at this time German culture flourished. However, this was not sufficient to stave off the political disaster that led to the rise of the Nazi Party (the NSDAP or National Socialist German Workers' Party).

DURCH LICHT ZUR NACHT

Cover of a Socialist magazine attacking the book-burning

The Third Reich

Adolf Hitler was appointed Chancellor by President Hindenburg on 30 January 1933 and immediately started to get rid of potential opponents. A fire that burned down the Reichstag served as a pretext for persecuting the communists, while

A Berlin synagogue burning during Kristallnacht, 1938

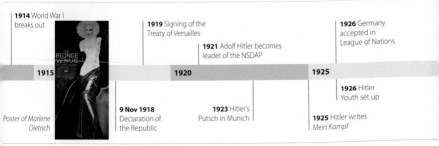

1914 World War I breaks out

1919 Signing of the Treaty of Versailles

1921 Adolf Hitler becomes leader of the NSDAP

1926 Germany accepted in League of Nations

1915

1920

1925

Poster of Marlene Dietrich

9 Nov 1918 Declaration of the Republic

1923 Hitler's Putsch in Munich

1925 Hitler writes *Mein Kampf*

1926 Hitler Youth set up

in April 1933 a boycott of Jewish businesses began. Trade unions were banned, as were all parties apart from the Nazis. Books by "impure" authors were burned, and the work of "degenerate" artists was exhibited as a warning, marking the start of the persecution of artists and scientists, many of whom decided to emigrate. At the same time, Hitler attempted to present to the world a face of openness and success, particularly with the Berlin Olympics of 1936. Germany broke almost all the demilitarization conditions of the Versailles Treaty. The growth in arms production brought with it an improved economic situation, increasing Hitler's popularity. All his opponents who had not managed to emigrate were either killed or sent to concentration camps.

In 1935 the Nuremberg Laws were passed, which officially sanctioned the persecution of Jews. During the *Kristallnacht* (crystal night) of 9 November 1938, synagogues throughout Germany were burned and Jewish shops and homes were looted, resulting in streets littered with broken glass. Hitler's plans to conquer Europe were realized in March 1938, with the "Anschluss" (annexation) of Austria, then in 1939 German forces occupied Czechoslovakia. After obtaining peace guarantees from the USSR, Germany invaded Poland on 1 September 1939, thus starting World War II.

Pieta, sculpture by Käthe Kollwitz (1937–8)

The centre of Dresden after Allied carpet-bombing

World War II

The first two years of World War II were marked by one victory after another for the German Army, which managed to occupy half of Europe. Great Britain was the only country that succeeded in fending off Hitler. In 1941 the Wehrmacht occupied large swathes of the Soviet Union. Terror and genocide were instigated in all occupied territories. The decision to exterminate all Jews in Europe was taken at the Wannsee Conference in Berlin in January 1942. Attempts to oppose Hitler in Germany were crushed. The course of the war did not change until 1943, when on 31 January Germany suffered a major defeat in the Battle of Stalingrad.

The Allied landings in Normandy and the creation of the second front helped bring the war to an end. When Soviet forces reached Berlin in 1945 the city lay in ruins and the populace was starving. During five and a half years, 55 million people had lost their lives.

1935 Enactment of law to build up army

1938 Anschluss with Austria; occupation of Czechoslovakia

1 Sep 1939 German invasion of Poland; the beginning of World War II

30 Jan 1933 Hitler appointed Chancellor of the Reich

9/10 Nov 1938 "Kristallnacht"

The Enigma Code machine

1935

1940

1945

1936 Berlin Olympics

Poster for the Berlin Olympics in 1936

1935 November laws sanction persecution of Jews

22 Jun 1941 Germany invades USSR

20 Jan 1942 Wannsee conference

30 Apr 1945 Hitler commits suicide as Soviet troops enter Berlin

Nazi war criminals on trial at Nuremberg

The Aftermath of World War II

Germany's unconditional surrender was signed on 8 May 1945, ending the bloodiest war in human history. Peace negotiations began which were to shape the new face of Europe for decades to come. In fact, discussions on Germany's future had already taken place at the Tehran and Yalta Conferences, where the leaders of the Big Three Powers met. But it was not until the Potsdam Conference that the terms were finally agreed.

Germany lost large parts of its territory to the east, displacing the German population there. It was decided to demilitarize Germany. The four Allied powers – the USA, the USSR, Britain and France – divided Germany into zones of occupation which they would rule until democratic structures were in place. The main perpetrators of war crimes were tried in Nuremberg and sentenced to death. Unfortunately, tensions increased between the Western powers and the Soviet Union, rapidly escalating in the "Cold War", which was largely played out in occupied Germany. In 1948 the three western zones introduced a new currency, which led the Soviets to blockade the western part of Berlin. Thanks to the Berlin Airlift, which supplied the population with food and fuel,

the blockade was abandoned. On 23 May 1949 the Federal Republic (Bundesrepublik) of Germany was established in the three western zones, and on 7 October 1949 the

Germany 1949–90
- Federal Republic
- DDR

German Democratic Republic (DDR) was set up in the Soviet zone. West Berlin became an enclave inside East Germany.

Germany Divided

The German Democratic Republic was democratic only in name. It became one of the satellites of the Soviet Union, and as the westernmost outpost of the Eastern Bloc it was subject to great restrictions. Attempted protests, such as the Workers' Uprising of 17 June 1953 in Berlin, were ruthlessly suppressed. For many people the only solution was to leave the country. As the exodus of skilled workers to the West continued, on 13 August 1961 a wall with barbed wire was built to contain them. Many attempts to cross the frontier ended in death. A highly efficient

Graffiti-covered section of the Berlin Wall

4–11 Feb 1945 Yalta Conference
8 May Germany capitulates
17 Jun 1953 Workers' uprising in East Berlin
13 Aug 1961 Building of the Berlin Wall
1968 Student riots
1973 West and East Germany accepted into UN
1982 Helmut Kohl becomes German Chancellor

1945 | **1950** | **1955** | **1960** | **1965** | **1970** | **1975** | **1980**

24 Jun 1948 Blockade of West Berlin starts
1949 Federal Republic and DDR established
1955 Federal Republic and German Democratic Republic gain sovereignty
Konrad Adenauer
1972 Official relations established between East and West Germany; Munich Olympics
The Trabant, a trade of East German inde

Reunification ceremony outside the Reichstag in Berlin in 1990

apparatus was set up in East Germany to watch over citizens' activities by the infamous Stasi secret police.

The first Chancellor of the Federal Republic of Germany, Konrad Adenauer, had Germany's integration into Western Europe as his main objective. Thanks to aid under the Marshall Plan, the economy rapidly recovered. Willy Brandt, first elected as Chancellor in 1969, pursued a policy of openness to the East, and recognized the German Democratic Republic.

Reunification

German reunification was made possible by a number of political events, in particular those going on in Eastern Europe. The Soviet premier Gorbachev's policy of *glasnost* led to the loosening of political constraints throughout the Eastern Bloc. Democratic changes in Poland set off a chain reaction. In 1989, people started to flee the German Democratic Republic en masse via its embassy in Prague and across the Austro-Hungarian border. Then, on 9 November 1989, the Berlin Wall fell due to protests in the East, and East Germans were free to leave. When, only three weeks later, Chancellor Helmut Kohl presented a ten-point plan for German reunification, few believed

that it would happen, but the country was officially reunified on 3 October 1990. Since then, Germany has been undergoing a process of integration.

Germany today

Since reunification Germany has increasingly shouldered responsibility in the international political and economic sphere. German troops take part in peacekeeping operations throughout the world and the country has become one of the world's strongest economic powers. With a highly regarded engineering industry producing and exporting a range of goods world-wide, including luxury cars and solar power technology, the country's financial growth continues to stand strong against the global economic downturn. Germany has also enjoyed a surge in tourism, making it one of Europe's most popular travel destinations.

Under the leadership of Federal Chancellor Angela Merkel since 2005, Germany has held a predominant position in the European Union. The country has been instrumental in helping to resolve the Euro debt crisis that continues to severely affect countries such as Greece and Spain.

Angela Merkel campaigning during the 2009 European General Elections

Helmut Kohl and Richard von Weizsäcker at the reunification ceremony

3 Oct 1990 Reunification of Germany

2002 Floods cause havoc across Germany

2006 Germany hosts FIFA World Cup

2011 Germany hosts the FIFA Women's World Cup

2013 Devastating floods in Germany and Eastern Europe are said to be the worst in over 400 years

| 1990 | 1995 | 2000 | 2005 | 2010 | 2015 | 2020 |

9 Nov 1989 Fall of the Berlin Wall

1994 Withdrawal of last Russian military units from Berlin

1998 Gerhard Schröder becomes Chancellor

2000 Expo 2000 World Fair in Hannover

2005 Ceremonial reopening of the reconstructed Fraueukirche in Dresden, a symbol of East-West efforts

2005 Angela Merkel is the first female chancellor in a "Grand Coalition" government

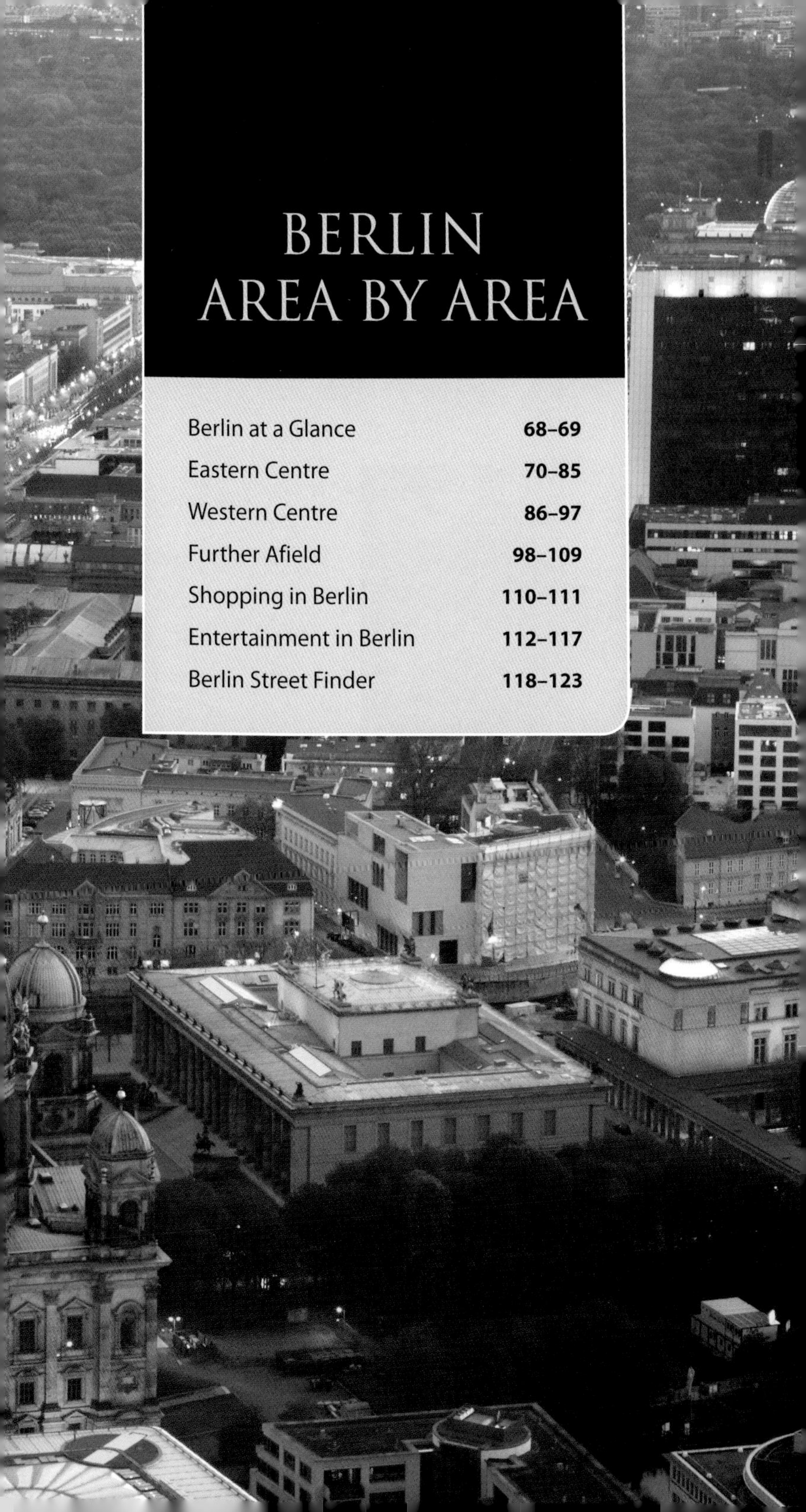

BERLIN
AREA · BY AREA

Berlin at a Glance   **68–69**

Eastern Centre   **70–85**

Western Centre   **86–97**

Further Afield   **98–109**

Shopping in Berlin   **110–111**

Entertainment in Berlin   **112–117**

Berlin Street Finder   **118–123**

Berlin at a Glance

Since the reunification of Germany in 1990, Berlin has become an increasingly popular destination for visitors. The following pages provide a useful guide to places of interest both in the town centre and the outskirts, including historic monuments such as Nikolaikirche *(see p84)*, museums, modern developments, such as the Potsdamer Platz, as well as places of recreation and amusement, such as the Botanical Gardens *(see p108)*. In the guide, we have divided central Berlin into two parts (east and west); these, however, do not correspond with the city's former partition into East and West Berlin.

LOCATOR MAP
See Street Finder pp118–23

Berlin

The Tiergarten was once a royal hunting estate but, after 1818, it was converted into a landscaped park by Peter Joseph Lenné *(see p91)* with lakes and streams.

WESTERN CENTRE
(See pp70–85)

GROSSER STERN

STRASSE DES 17 JUNI

Spree

Landwehrkanal

KURFÜRSTENSTR

KURFÜRSTENDAMM

The Gemäldegalerie *(see pp94–5)* houses an exceptional collection of European masters, including Hans Holbein's *Portrait of George Gisze (1532)*.

The Kaiser-Wilhelm-Gedächtnis-Kirche was almost totally destroyed by bombs during World War II. A new annex was built in 1963 to a design by Egon Eiermann *(see p90)*.

◀ Aerial view of Berlin

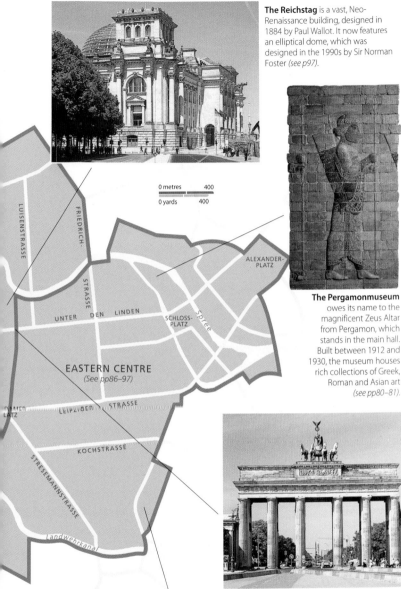

The Reichstag is a vast, Neo-Renaissance building, designed in 1884 by Paul Wallot. It now features an elliptical dome, which was designed in the 1990s by Sir Norman Foster *(see p97)*.

The Pergamonmuseum owes its name to the magnificent Zeus Altar from Pergamon, which stands in the main hall. Built between 1912 and 1930, the museum houses rich collections of Greek, Roman and Asian art *(see pp80–81)*.

0 metres	400
0 yards	400

ALEXANDER-PLATZ

LUISENSTRASSE

FRIEDRICH-STRASSE

UNTER DEN LINDEN

SCHLOSS-PLATZ

Spree

EASTERN CENTRE
(See pp86–97)

LEIPZIGER STRASSE

KOCHSTRASSE

STRESEMANNSTRASSE

Landwehrkanal

The imposing Neo-Classical Brandenburg Gate stands at the end of Unter den Linden. It is crowned with a 6-m (20-ft) high sculpture of the Roman Quadriga driven by Victoria, the goddess of victory *(see p73)*.

The Jüdisches Museum (Jewish Museum) is housed in a building designed by Daniel Libeskind. It features a symbolic projection of a broken Star of David *(see p84)*.

EASTERN CENTRE

This part of Berlin is the historic centre of the city, and includes the Mitte district and parts of Kreuzberg. Its beginnings date back to the 13th century when two settlements were established on the banks of the river Spree. One was the former Cölln, situated on an island, and the other its twin settlement, Berlin. Berlin's first church, the Nikolaikirche, survives to this day.

This part of the city features most of its historic buildings, which are located mainly along Unter den Linden. It also includes Museumsinsel, the location of the vast Berliner Dom as well as of the impressive collection of museums that gives the island its name. These include the Pergamonmuseum.

During the city's partition, Mitte belonged to East Berlin while Kreuzberg was in West Berlin.

Sights at a Glance

Museums and Galleries
- ⑧ Zeughaus
- ⑭ DDR Museum
- ⑯ Altes Museum
- ⑰ Neues Museum
- ⑱ Alte Nationalgalerie
- ⑲ Pergamonmuseum
- ⑳ Bode-Museum
- ㉖ Märkisches Museum
- ㉗ Checkpoint Charlie
- ㉘ Jüdisches Museum
- ㉙ Topographie des Terrors
- ㉚ Deutsches Technikmuseum Berlin

Streets and Squares
- ③ Bebelplatz
- ⑤ Unter den Linden
- ⑬ Schlossplatz
- ㉓ Alexanderplatz
- ㉕ Nikolaiviertel

Historic Buildings and Monuments
- ① Brandenburger Tor
- ② Holocaust Denkmal
- ④ Humboldt-Universität
- ⑦ Neue Wache
- ⑩ Konzerthaus
- ⑫ Schlossbrücke
- ㉒ Rotes Rathaus
- ㉔ Fernsehturm

Churches
- ⑥ St Hedwigs-Kathedrale
- ⑨ Französischer Dom
- ⑪ Deutscher Dom
- ⑮ Berliner Dom
- ㉑ Marienkirche

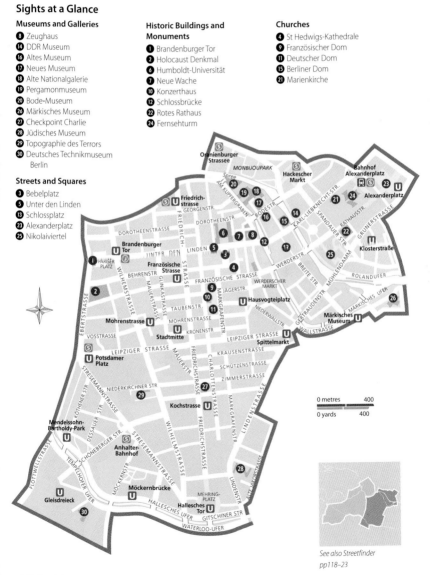

0 metres 400
0 yards 400

See also Streetfinder pp118–23

◀ The Brandenburg Gate at twilight

For map symbols *see back flap*

Street-by-Street: Around Bebelplatz

The section of Unter den Linden between
Schlossbrücke and Friedrichstrasse is one of the
most attractive areas in central Berlin. As well as
some magnificent Baroque and Neo-Classical
buildings, many of them designed by famous
architects, there are also some restored palaces
that are now used as public buildings. Of particular
interest is the beautiful Baroque building of the
Zeughaus (the former Arsenal), which now houses
the German History Museum.

❻ Humboldt University
The university courtyard
teems with life all year
round. Second-hand book-
sellers set up their stalls in
front of the gate.

**Equestrian statue of King
Friedrich II of Prussia**
This monument was erected
in 1851 to mark the 111th
anniversary of Friedrich II's
ascension to the Prussian throne.

0 metres   100
0 yards   100

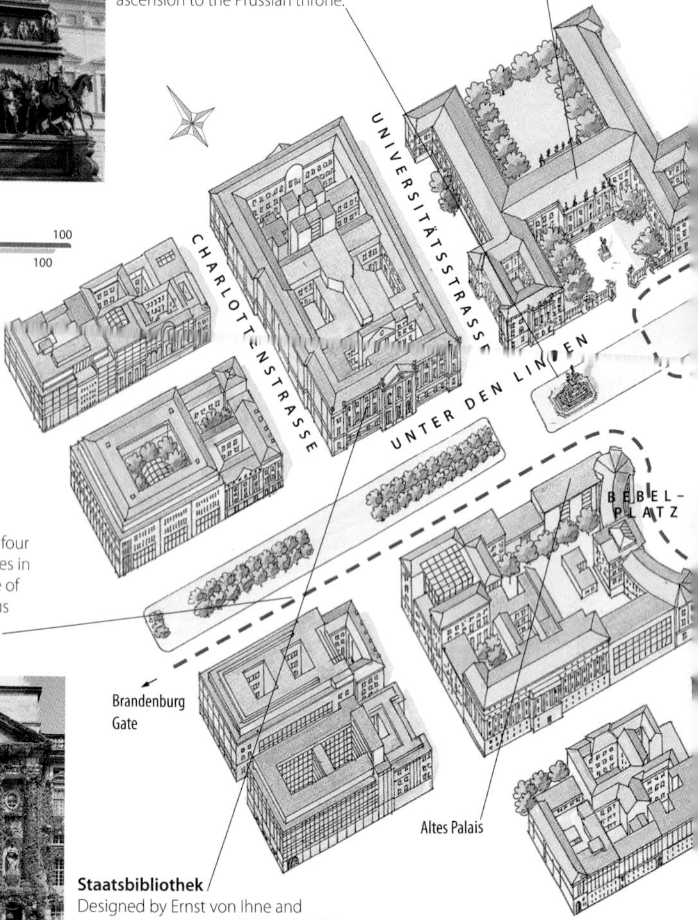

**❺ Unter den
Linden**
Replanted with four
rows of lime trees in
1946, this is one of
the most famous
streets in Berlin.

Brandenburg
Gate

Altes Palais

Staatsbibliothek
Designed by Ernst von Ihne and
constructed between 1903 and 1914,
this impressive building houses part of
the State Library collection.

Key
— Suggested route

❽ ★ Zeughaus (Deutsches Historisches Museum)
Minerva, goddess of wisdom, decorates this beautiful Baroque building, which has a wing designed by I M Pei.

Locator Map
See Street Finder maps 1, 4 & 5.

❼ ★ Neue Wache
Now serving as a memorial to all victims of war and dictatorship, this monument was designed by Karl Friedrich Schinkel.

Rotes Rathaus

UNTER DER KATH, KIRCHE

Staatsoper Unter den Linden

❹ St-Hedwigs-Kathedrale
Bas-reliefs (1837) by Theodore Wilhelm Achtermann adorn the cathedral's supports.

Kronprinzenpalais
A magnificent portal from the dismantled Bauakademie building can be found the rear of the palace.

❶ Brandenburger Tor
Brandenburg Gate

Pariser Platz. **Map** 4 A2, 15 A3. Ⓢ & Ⓤ Brandenburger Tor. 🚌 100.

The Brandenburg Gate is the quintessential symbol of Berlin. A magnificent Neo-Classical structure, modelled on the Athenian Propylaea (the entrance to the Acropolis), it was constructed between 1788 and 1791. Its sculptured decorations were completed in 1795. A pair of pavilions, once used by guards and customs officers, frames its powerful Doric colonnade and entablature. The bas-reliefs depict scenes from Greek mythology and the whole structure is crowned by Johann Gottfried Schadow's famous sculpture, *Quadriga*. In 1806, during the French occupation, the sculpture was dismantled, on Napoleon's orders, and taken to Paris. On its triumphal return in 1814, it was declared a symbol of victory, and the goddess received a staff bearing the Prussian eagle and an iron cross adorned with a laurel wreath. Throughout its history, the Brandenburg Gate has borne witness to many of Berlin's important events. Located in East Berlin, the gate was restored between 1956 and 1958, when the damaged *Quadriga* was rebuilt in West Berlin. Over the next 40 years it stood watch over the divided city, until 1989, when the first section of the Berlin Wall came down.

Frieze and sculpture, *Quadriga*, on the Brandenburg Gate

❷ Holocaust Denkmal

Map 4 A2. Ⓢ & Ⓤ Brandenburger Tor. 🚌 100, 200, M85.

Germany's national Holocaust memorial was designed by American architect Peter Eisenman. Completed in 2005, it is made up of a large field with dark grey steles of various heights that symbolize the six million Jews and others murdered by the Nazis in concentration camps between 1933 and 1945.

Visitors can walk their own route, and there is an information centre underneath the memorial.

There are also memorials in nearby Tiergarten to murdered homosexuals and murdered Sinti and Roma people.

The façade of St-Hedwigs-Kathedrale, with beautiful bas-relief sculptures

Relief on the façade of the Staatsoper (Opera House), Bebelplatz

❸ Bebelplatz

Map 4 C2. Ⓢ & Ⓤ Friedrichstraße. 🚌 100, 200, TXL.

Bebelplatz was intended to be the focal point of the Forum Fridericianum – an area designed to mirror the grandeur of ancient Rome. Although the plans were only partly implemented, many important buildings were eventually erected here.

In 1933, the square was the scene of the infamous book-burning act organized by the Nazis. Some 25,000 books, written by authors considered to be enemies of the Third Reich, were burned. Today, a monument in the square commemorates this dramatic event.

❹ St-Hedwigs-Kathedrale
St Hedwig's Cathedral

Bebelplatz. **Map** 4 C2. **Tel** (030) 203 48 10. Ⓢ & Ⓤ Friedrichstraße. 🚌 100, 147, 200, TXL. **Open** 10am–5pm Mon–Fri, 10am–4:30pm Sat, 1pm–5pm Sun & holy days.

This huge church is the Catholic Cathedral of the Roman Archdiocese of Berlin. The initial design was similar to the Roman Pantheon. Construction began in 1747, although work continued on and off until 1887.

It was damaged during World War II and rebuilt between 1952 and 1963. The building received a reinforced concrete dome and its interior was refurbished in a modern style. The crypt contains bishops' tombs and a 16th-century Madonna.

❺ Unter den Linden

Map 1 F4, 4 A2, B2, C2, 5 D2. Ⓢ & Ⓤ Brandenburger Tor. 🚌 100, 200, TXL.

One of the most famous streets in Berlin, Unter den Linden starts at Schlossplatz and runs down to Pariser Platz and the Brandenburg Gate. It was once the route to the royal hunting grounds, which were later transformed into the Tiergarten.

In the 17th century, the street was planted with lime trees, to which it owes its name. Although the original trees were removed around 1658, four rows of limes were planted in 1820.

During the 18th century, Unter den Linden became the main street of the westward-growing city and gradually came to be lined with

Wilhelm and Alexander von Humboldt

The Humboldt brothers rank among the most distinguished Berlin citizens. Wilhelm (1767–1835) was a lawyer and politician on whose initiative the Berlin University (later renamed Humboldt University) was founded in 1810. At the university, he conducted studies in comparative and historical linguistics. His brother Alexander (1769–1859), a professor at the university, researched natural science, including meteorology, oceanography and agricultural science.

Alexander von Humboldt

The 19th-century Neue Wache, now dedicated to the victims of war and dictatorship

prestigious buildings, which have been restored in the years following World War II.

Since the reunification of Germany in 1990, Unter den Linden has acquired several cafés and restaurants, as well as many smart shops. The street has also become the venue for interesting outdoor events. It is usually crowded with tourists and students browsing the bookstalls around the Humboldt Universität and the Staatsbibliothek (State Library).

❻ Humboldt Universität

Humboldt University

Unter den Linden 6. **Map** 4 C2. Ⓢ & Ⓤ Friedrichstraße. 100, 200, TXL.

The university building was constructed in 1753 for Prince Heinrich of Prussia. The overall design of the palace, with its main block and the courtyard enclosed within two wings, has been extended many times. Two marble statues by Paul Otto (1883) stand at the entrance; these represent Wilhelm and Alexander von Humboldt.

Many famous scientists have worked at the university, including physicians Rudolf Virchow and Robert Koch and physicists Max Planck and Albert Einstein. Among its graduates are Heinrich Heine, Karl Marx and Friedrich Engels.

After World War II, the university was in the Russian sector and the difficulties encountered by the students of the western zone led to the establishment in 1948 of the Freie Universität.

❼ Neue Wache

Unter den Linden 4. **Map** 7 A3, 16 E2. Ⓢ Hackescher Markt. 100, 200, TXL. **Open** 10am–6pm daily.

Designed by Karl Friedrich Schinkel and built between 1816 and 1818, this monument is considered to be one of the finest examples of Neo-Classical architecture in Berlin. The front of the monument is dominated by a huge Doric portico with a frieze made up of bas-reliefs depicting goddesses of victory.

In 1930–31 the building was turned into a monument to soldiers killed in World War I. Following its restoration in 1960, Neue Wache became the Memorial to the Victims of Fascism and Militarism. It was rededicated in 1993 to the memory of all victims of war and dictatorship. Inside is an eternal flame and a granite slab over the ashes of an unknown soldier, a resistance fighter and a concentration camp prisoner. In the roof opening is a copy of the sculpture *Mother with her Dead Son,* by Berlin artist Käthe Kollwitz.

❽ Zeughaus

Unter den Linden 2. **Map** 5 D2. **Tel** 20 30 40. Ⓢ Hackescher Markt. 100, 200, TXL. New wing: **Open** 10am–6pm daily.

This former arsenal was built in the Baroque style in 1706 under the guidance of Johann Arnold Nering, Martin Grünberg, Andreas Schlüter and Jean de Bodt. A magnificent structure, its wings surround an inner courtyard. Its exterior is decorated with Schlüter's sculptures, which include masks of dying warriors. Home to the German History Museum since 1952, it was renovated in 2005. A modern, glass and steel wing, designed by architect I M Pei, now houses temporary exhibits, and there is an extensive exhibition on German history.

Part of the façade of the Zeughaus on Unter den Linden

Side elevation of the Französischer Dom, built for Huguenot refugees

❾ Französischer Dom

French Cathedral

Gendarmenmarkt 5. **Map** 4 C2.
Tel (030) 206 49 922/3. 🆄 Stadtmitte or Französische Straße. Museum: **Open** noon–5pm Tue–Sat, 11am–5pm Sun. 🏛 Church: **Open** noon– 5pm Tue–Sun. ✝ Sun 10am.

Although the two churches standing on opposite sides of Schauspielhaus seem identical, their only common feature is their matching front towers. The French cathedral was built for the Huguenot community, who found refuge in protestant Berlin following their expulsion from France after the revocation of the Edict of Nantes in 1598. The modest church, built between 1701 and 1705 by Louis Cayart and Abraham Quesnay, was modelled on the Huguenot church in Charenton, France, which was destroyed in 1688. The interior features a late-Baroque organ from 1754.

The structure is dominated by a massive, cylindrical tower, which is encircled by Corinthian porticos at its base. The tower and porticos were designed by Carl von Gontard and added around 1785. It houses the Huguenot Museum, which charts the history of the Huguenot community in France and Brandenburg.

A viewing platform, which is 40 m (131 ft) above the ground, is the city's highest historic observation platform and offers stunning views of Berlin's skyline.

❿ Konzerthaus

Concert Hall

Gendarmenmarkt 2. **Map** 4 C2.
Tel (030) 203 09 21 01. 🆄 Stadtmitte.

A late Neo-Classical jewel, this magnificent theatre building, known until recently as the Schauspielhaus, is one of the greatest achievements of Berlin's best-known architect, Karl Friedrich Schinkel. It was built between 1818 and 1821 around the ruins of Langhans's National Theatre, destroyed by fire in 1817. The portico columns were retained in the new design. Following bomb damage in World War II, it was reconstructed as a concert hall and the exterior was restored to its former glory. The Konzerthaus is now home to the Berlin Symphony Orchestra.

The whole building is decorated with sculptures alluding to drama and music. The façade, which includes a huge Ionic portico with a set of stairs, is crowned with a sculpture of Apollo riding a chariot pulled by griffins.

In front of the theatre stands a shining white marble statue of Friedrich Schiller, which was sculpted by Reinhold Begas and erected in 1869. Removed by the Nazis during the 1930s, the

Interior of the Konzerthaus, formerly the Schauspielhaus

monument was returned to its rightful place in 1988. The statue is mounted on a high pedestal surrounded by allegorical figures representing Lyric Poetry, Drama, Philosophy and History.

⓫ Deutscher Dom

German Cathedral

Gendarmenmarkt 1. **Map** 4 C3.
Tel (030) 227 30431. 🆄 Stadtmitte or Französische Straße. Exhibition: **Open** 10am–6pm Tue–Sun (to 7pm May–Sep).

The cathedral at the southern end of the square is an old German Protestant-Reformed church. Based on a five-petal shape, it was designed by Martin Grünberg and built in 1708 by Giovanni Simonetti. In 1785 it acquired a dome-covered tower identical to that of the French cathedral.

Burned down in 1945, it was rebuilt in 1993, with its interior adapted as exhibition space. On display is the popular "Fragen an die Deutsche Geschichte" ("Questions on German History"), which was formerly on show in the Reichstag building.

Sculpture from Deutscher Dom

⓬ Schlossbrücke

Map 5 D2. Ⓢ Hackescher Markt. 🚌 100, 200, TXL.

This is one of the city's most beautiful bridges, connecting Schlossplatz with Unter den Linden. It was built in 1824 to a design by Karl Friedrich Schinkel. Statues were added to the top of the bridge's sparkling red-granite pillars in 1853. These figures, made of white Carrara marble, were also created by Schinkel. The statues depict tableaux from Greek mythology, such as Iris, Nike and Athena, training and looking after their favourite young warriors. The elaborate wrought-iron balustrade is decorated with intertwined sea creatures.

The surviving Stadtschloss portal fronting a government building

⓭ Schlossplatz

Map 5 D2. Ⓢ Hackescher Markt.
🚌 100, 147, 200, TXL.

This square was once the site of a huge residential complex known as Stadtschloss (City Castle). Built in 1451, it served as the main residence of the Brandenburg Electors. It was transformed from a castle to a palace in the mid-16th century when Elector Friedrich III (later King Friedrich I) ordered its reconstruction in the Baroque style. The main seat of the Hohenzollern family for almost 500 years until the end of the monarchy, the palace was partly burned during World War II but was provisionally restored and used as a museum.

In 1950–51, despite protests, the palace was demolished and the square was renamed Marx-Engels-Platz under the GDR.

Now all that remains is the triumphal-arch portal that once adorned the façade on the Lustgarten side. This is now incorporated into the wall of the former government building, the Staatsratgebäude, which was erected in 1964 on the square's south side. The building's decor features the remaining original sculptures, including the magnificent atlantes by the famous Dresden sculptor, Balthasar Permoser. Their inclusion was due to their propaganda value: it was from the balcony of the portal that in 1918 Karl

Liebknecht proclaimed the birth of the Socialist Republic.

In 1989 the square reverted to its original name and a former GDR government building was torn down. A palace-like building, the Humboldt-Forum, will be an international and cultural centre when complete in 2018.

⓮ DDR Museum

Karl-Liebknecht Str. 1. **Map** 5 D2. **Tel** (030) 847 123 731. Ⓢ & Ⓤ Alexanderplatz. 🚌 100, 200, TXL. **Open** 10am–8pm Mon–Sun (to 10pm Sat).

This small, privately run museum provides a fascinating, interactive insight into daily life in the former East Germany. Visit a reconstructed apartment and take a simulated ride in an old Trabant car through a concrete housing estate.

⓯ Berliner Dom

Am Lustgarten. **Map** 5 D1. **Tel** (030) 20 26 91 36. Ⓢ Hackescher Markt. 🚌 100, 200, TXL **Open** Apr–Sep: 9am–8pm Mon–Sat, noon–8pm Sun; Oct–Mar: 9am–7pm Mon– Sat, noon–7pm Sun. 🎧 🚻 10am, 6pm Sun.

The original Berliner Dom was based on a modest Baroque

design by Johann Boumann. Built between 1747 and 1750, the cathedral included the original crypt of the Hohenzollern family, one of the largest of its kind in Europe. The present Neo-Baroque structure is the work of Julius Raschdorff and dates from 1894 to 1905. Following severe World War II damage, the cathedral has been restored in a simplified form. The Hohenzollern memorial chapel, which adjoined the northern walls, has been dismantled.

The Neo-Baroque interior of the Berliner Dom

Berlin's Bridges

Despite wartime damage, Berlin's bridges are still well worth seeing. The Spree river and the city's canals have some fine, exemplary architecture on their banks, while many of the bridges were designed and decorated by famous architects and sculptors. Probably the most renowned bridge is the Schlossbrücke designed by Karl Friedrich Schinkel. Further south along the Kupfergrabenkanal, the Schleusenbrücke, dating from c.1914, is decorated with reliefs of the early history of the city's bridges and sluices. The next bridge, heading south, is the Jungfernbrücke (1798), which is the last drawbridge in Berlin. The next bridge along is the Gertraudenbrücke. Where Friedrichstrasse crosses the Spree river is the Weidendammer Brücke, built originally in 1695–7 and subsequently rebuilt in 1923, with an eagle motif adorning its balustrade. On the Spree near the Regierungsviertel is the magnificent Moltkebrücke (1886–91). The bridge is guarded by a huge griffin wielding a shield adorned with the Prussian eagle, while cherubs dressed in a military fashion hold up lamps. On the arches of the bridges are portraits of leaders, designed by Karl Begas.

Ornamental feature of a bear on the Liebknechtbrücke

Street-by-Street: Museum Island

The long island that nestles in the tributaries of the Spree river is the cradle of Berlin's history. It was here that the first settlements appeared at the beginning of the 13th century: Cölln is mentioned in documents dating back to 1237, and its twin settlement, Berlin, is mentioned a few years later, in 1244. The island's character was transformed by the construction of the Brandenburg Electors' palace, which served as their residence from 1470. Although it was razed to the ground in 1950, some interesting buildings on the north side of the island have survived, including the Berliner Dom (Berlin Cathedral) and the impressive collection of museums that give the island its name, Museuminsel.

Locator Map
See Street Finder maps 4 & 5

⑳ Bode-Museum
A rounded corner of the building, crowned with a dome, provides a magnificent end-piece to the tip of the island.

⑰ ★ Neues Museum
This museum houses exhibitions on antiquities and ancient Egyptian art.

⑱ Alte Nationalgalerie
The equestrian statue of King Friedrich Wilhelm IV in front of the building is the work of Alexander Calandrelli.

⑯ ★ Altes Museum
The corners of the central building feature the figures of Castor and Pollux, heroes of Greek mythology.

0 metres 100
0 yards 100

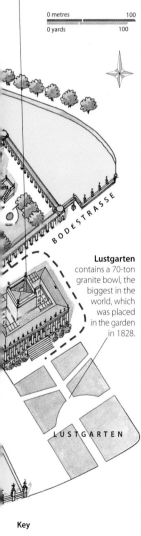

Lustgarten
contains a 70-ton granite bowl, the biggest in the world, which was placed in the garden in 1828.

LUSTGARTEN

Key
— Suggested route

⑯ Altes Museum
Old Museum

Am Lustgarten (Bodestraße 1–3). **Map** 5 D1. **Tel** (030) 20 90 55 77. Ⓢ Hackescher Markt. 🚌 100, 200, TXL. **Open** 10am–6pm Mon–Wed & Fri–Sun, 10am–10pm Thu. 🚻

Designed by Karl Friedrich Schinkel, this museum building is one of the world's most beautiful Neo-Classical structures, with an impressive 87-m (285-ft) high portico supported by 18 Ionic columns. Officially opened in 1830, the museum was purpose-built to house the royal collection of art and antiquities.

Following World War II, the building was used only for temporary exhibitions. It now houses the Antikensammlung, with a magnificent collection of Greek, Roman and Etruscan antiquities.

⑰ Neues Museum
New Museum

Bodestraße 1–3. **Map** 5 D1. Ⓢ Hackescher Markt or Friedrichstraße. 🚌 100, 200, TXL. 🚊 M1, M4, M5. **Open** 10am–6pm daily (to 8pm Thu). 🚻

The Neues Museum was built on Museum Island between 1841 and 1855 to a design by Friedrich August Stüler. Until World War II, it housed a collection of antiquities, mainly ancient Egyptian art. The rooms in the museum building were decorated specifically to complement the exhibitions they contained, while wall paintings by Wilhelm von Kaulbach depicted key events in world history. The building was damaged in 1945 and the museum closed. It reopened in October 2009 after reconstruction and once again houses the Egyptian Museum as well as the Museum of Prehistory and Early History.

Many sculptures, sarcophagi, murals and architectural fragments of various eras are on display, including the famous

Pericles' Head

bust of Nefertiti. Most popular is the collection from 19th-century archaeological digs by Richard Lepsius and Johann Ludwig Burckhardt at Tell al-Amarna, Egypt. Tell al-Amarna was the capital founded by Pharaoh Amenhotep IV in the 14th century BC. In a break with tradition, Amenhotep and his wife, Nefertiti, are depicted in a more naturalistic manner.

⑱ Alte Nationalgalerie
Old National Gallery

Bodestraße 1–3. **Map** 5 D1. **Tel** (030) 20 90 55 77. Ⓢ Hackescher Markt. 🚌 100, 200, TXL. 🚊 M1, M4, M5. **Open** 10am–6pm Tue–Sun, 10am–10pm Thu.

The old Nationalgalerie building, designed by Friedrich August Stüler, was erected between 1866 and 1876. It was originally intended to house the collection of modern art that had been on display in the Akademie der Künste (Art Academy). After World War II, however, the collection was split up into several sections and part of it was shown in West Berlin, where the Neue Nationalgalerie was specifically erected for this purpose (see p92). This building was then renamed Alte Nationalgalerie.

Following the reunification of Germany, the modern art collections were merged again. Two new exhibition halls now show paintings from the German Romantic era, including work by Caspar David Friedrich and Karl Friedrich Schinkel. The famous 19th-century marble sculpture of the two Prussian princesses by Johann Gottfried Schadow is also on display, as is a significant collection of works by Adolph Menzel, including his most famous painting, *The Balcony Room*.

⓳ Pergamonmuseum

The Pergamonmuseum was built between 1912 and 1930 to a design by Alfred Messels and Ludwig Hoffmann. It houses one of the most famous collections of antiquities in Europe and owes its name to the famous Pergamon Altar, which takes pride of place in the main hall (closed until 2019). Its collections are the result of intensive archaeological excavations by German expeditions to the Near and Middle East. Major renovation until after 2025 means a selection of the museum's treasures are shown in the south wing, while most of the Museum of Antiquities' pieces are displayed in Altes Museum.

★ **Pergamon Altar** (170 BC)
This scene, featuring the goddess Athena, appears on the large frieze illustrating a battle between the gods and the giants.

Roman Mosaic
(3rd or 4th century AD) This ancient mosaic was found at Jerash, Jordan. A second part of it is in the collection of the Stark Museum of Art, Texas.

Non-exhibition rooms

First floor

The Goddesss Athena
This enchanting Hellenistic sculpture of the goddess Athena is one of many displayed in the museum.

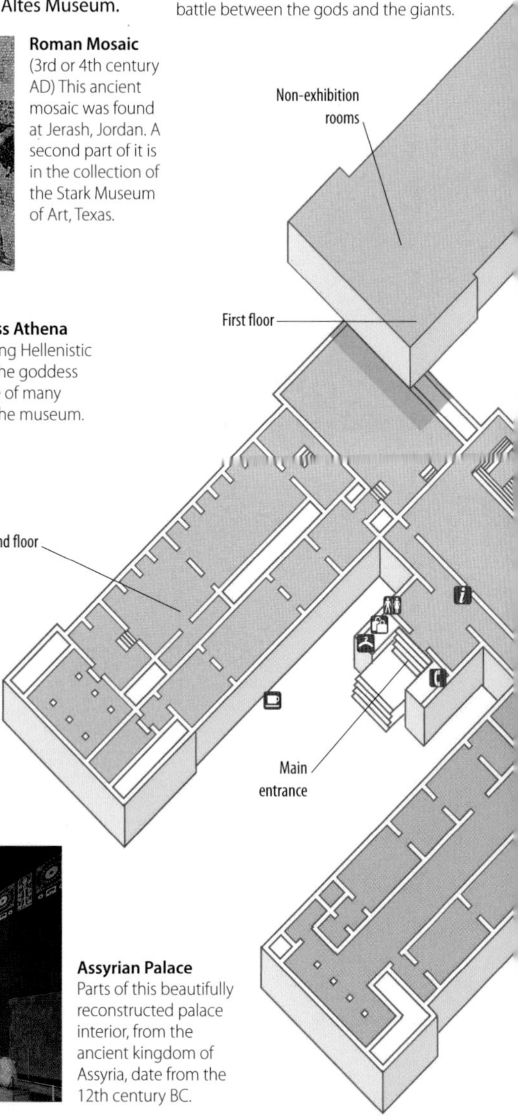

Ground floor

Main entrance

Assyrian Palace
Parts of this beautifully reconstructed palace interior, from the ancient kingdom of Assyria, date from the 12th century BC.

Façade of the Mshatta Palace (AD 744)
This fragment is from the southern façade of the Jordanian Mshatta Palace, presented to Wilhelm II by Sultan Abdul Hamid of Ottoman in 1903.

VISITORS' CHECKLIST

Practical Information
Bodestraße 1–3.
Map 4 C1, 5 D1.
Tel (030) 20 90 55 77.
Open 10am–6pm daily (to 8pm Thu).
smb.museum.de

Transport
Friedrichstraße or Hackescher Markt. 100, 200, TXL.

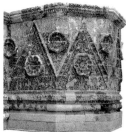

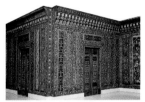

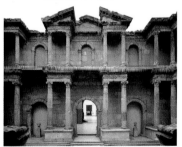

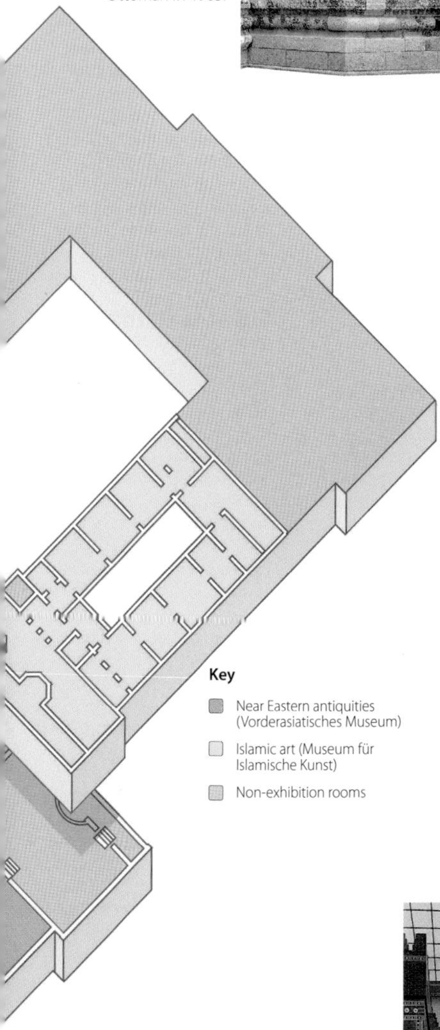

Key
Near Eastern antiquities (Vorderasiatisches Museum)
Islamic art (Museum für Islamische Kunst)
Non-exhibition rooms

Aleppo Zimmer (c.1603)
This magnificent panelled room comes from a merchant's house in the Syrian city of Aleppo.

★ **Market Gate from Miletus** (c.120 AD)
Measuring over 16 m (52 ft) in height, this gate opened onto the southern market of Miletus, a Roman town in Asia Minor.

Gallery Guide

The right wing houses the Museum of Near Eastern Antiquities; the first floor of the right wing houses the Museum of Islamic Art. The left wing will be closed until 2019.

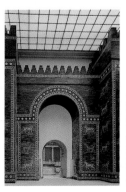

★ **Ishtar Gate from Babylon**
(6th century BC)
Original glazed bricks decorate both the huge Ishtar gate and the impressive Processional Way that leads up to it.

The Bode-Museum designed by Ernst von Ihne

⓴ Bode-Museum

Monbijoubrücke (Bodestraße 1–3).
Map 4 C1. **Tel** (030) 20 90 56 01. Ⓢ
Hackescher Markt or Friedrichstraße.
Open 10am–6pm daily (to 10pm Thu).
🚊 M1, M4, M5, 12.

The fourth museum building on
Museuminsel was constructed
between 1897 and 1904. It was
designed by Ernst von Ihne
to fit the wedge-shaped
northwestern end of the island.
The interior was designed with
the help of an art historian,
Wilhelm von Bode, who was
the director of the Berlin state
museums at the time.

The museum displayed a
rather mixed collection that
included some old masters. Its
original name, Kaiser Friedrich
Museum, was changed after
World War II. Following the
reassembling of the Berlin
collections, all the paintings
were rehoused in the
Kulturforum (see pp88–9),
while the Egyptian art and the
papyrus collection were moved
to the Ägyptisches Museum
(Egyptian Museum) at the
Neues Museum (see p79).

Following its refurbishment,
the building once again houses
a collection of over 50,000 coins,
plus medals and Byzantine art.
It is also home to an extensive
collection of sculptures, which
includes the works of Tilman
Riemenschneider, Donatello,
Gianlorenzo Bernini and
Antonio Canova. A copy of
the magnificent equestrian
statue of the Great Elector,
Friedrich Wilhelm, by Andreas
Schlüter, has also taken its
place in the old hall.

㉑ Marienkirche

Karl-Liebknecht-Straße 8. **Map** 5 E1.
Tel (030) 242 44 67. Ⓢ Hackescher
Markt. 🚌 100, 200, TXL. **Open** Apr–
Oct: 10am–9pm daily; Nov–Mar:
10am–6pm daily. ✝ 10:30am Sun.

St Mary's Church, or the
Marienkirche, was first
established as a parish church
in the second half of the 13th
century. Started around 1280,
construction was completed
early in the 14th century. During
reconstruction works in 1380,
following a fire, the church was
altered slightly, but its overall
shape changed only in the
15th century when it acquired
the front tower. In 1790, the
tower was crowned with a
dome, designed by Carl
Gotthard Langhans, which
includes both Baroque and
Neo-Gothic elements.

The Marienkirche was once
hemmed in by buildings, but
today it stands alone in the
shadow of the Fernsehturm
(Television Tower). The early

Baroque altar in the Marienkirche,
designed by Andreas Krüger

Gothic hall design and the
lavish decorative touches make
this church one of the most
interesting in Berlin. An
alabaster pulpit by Andreas
Schlüter, dating from 1703, is
decorated with bas-reliefs of St
John the Baptist and the
personifications of the Virtues.

The Baroque main altar was
designed by Andreas Krüger
around 1762. The paintings
with which it is adorned include
three works by Christian
Bernhard Rode.

A Gothic font, dating from
1437, is supported by three
black dragons and decorated
with the figures of Jesus Christ,
Mary and the Apostles.

㉒ Rotes Rathaus

Red Town Hall

Rathausstraße 15. **Map** 5 E2. Ⓤ &
Ⓢ Alexanderplatz. Ⓤ Klosterstraße,
🚌 TXL, 248.

This impressive structure is
Berlin's main town hall. Its
predecessor was a much more
modest structure that, by the
end of the 19th century, was
inadequate to meet the needs
of the growing metropolis.

The present building was
designed by Hermann Friedrich
Waesemann, and the
construction works went on
from 1861 until 1869. The
architect took his main inspiration
from Italian Renaissance
municipal buildings, but the
tower is reminiscent of Laon
cathedral in France. The walls
are made from red brick and it
was this, rather than the political
orientation of the mayors, that
gave the town hall its name.

The whole building has a
continuous frieze known as
the "stone chronicle", which
was added in 1879. The frieze
features scenes and figures from
the city's history and traces the
development of its economy
and science.

The Rotes Rathaus was
severely damaged during
World War II but, following its
reconstruction between 1951
and 1958, it became the seat
of the East Berlin authorities.
The West Berlin magistrate

㉔ Fernsehturm

The television tower, called by the locals *Telespargel*, or toothpick, remains to this day the city's tallest structure at 368 m (1,207 ft). It is also the second-tallest structure in Europe. The tower was built in 1969 to a design by a team of architects including Fritz Dieter and Günter Franke, with the help of Swedish experts. However, the idea for the tower originated much earlier from Hermann Henselmann (creator of the Karl-Marx-Allee development) in the Socialist-Realist style.

VISITORS' CHECKLIST

Practical Information
Panoramastrasse 1a.
Map 5 E1. **Tel** (030) 242 33 33.
Open Mar–Oct: 9am–midnight daily; Nov–Feb: 10am–midnight daily.

Transport
Ⓢ & Ⓤ Alexanderplatz. 🚌 100, 200, TXL.

View from the Tower
On a clear day the viewing platform offers a full view of Berlin. Visibility can reach up to 40 km (25 miles).

The television antenna is visible all over Berlin.

Transmitter aerial

The metal sphere is covered with steel cladding.

Tele-Café
One of the attractions of the tower is the revolving café. A full rotation takes about half an hour, so it is possible to get a bird's-eye view of the whole city while sipping a cup of coffee.

Concrete structure rising to 250 m (820 ft)

The concrete shaft contains two elevators that carry passengers to the café and viewing platform.

The monumental, red-brick town hall, known as the Rotes Rathaus

was housed in the Schöneberg town hall (*see p107*). Following the reunification of Germany in 1990, the Rotes Rathaus became the centre of authority, housing the offices of the mayor and the Berlin cabinet.

The forecourt sculptures by Fritz Kremer, which depict Berliners helping to rebuild the city, were added in 1958.

㉓ Alexanderplatz

Map 5 E1, F1. Ⓤ & Ⓢ Alexanderplatz. 🚌 100, 200, TXL.

Alexanderplatz, or "Alex" as it is called locally, has a long history, although it would be hard now to find any visible traces of the past. Once known as Ochsenmarkt (oxen market), it was the site of a cattle and wool market. It was later renamed after Tsar Alexander I who visited Berlin in 1805. At that time, the square boasted a magnificent monumental colonnade, which was designed by Carl von Gontard.

In time, houses and shops sprang up around the square and a market hall and urban train line were built nearby. "Alex" became one of the

city's busiest spots. Its frenzied atmosphere was captured by Alfred Döblin (1878–1957) in his novel *Berlin Alexanderplatz*.

In 1929, attempts were made to develop the square, though only two office buildings were added – the Alexanderhaus and the Berolinahaus, both by designed Peter Behrens.

World War II erased most of the square's buildings and they were replaced by characterless 1960s edifices, including the Park Inn Hotel (formerly Hotel Stadt Berlin) and the Fernsehturm. However, the area has been redeveloped and is home to several shopping plazas and cinemas, as well as open-air markets during the holidays.

Riverside buildings of the Nikolaiviertel

❺ Nikolaiviertel

Map 5 E2. **U** & **S** Alexanderplatz.
U Klosterstraße. 🚌 100, 147, 200, 248, M48.

This small area on the bank of the Spree is a favourite place for both Berliners and tourists. Some of Berlin's oldest houses stood here until they were destroyed in World War II. The redevelopment of the area, which was carried out by the GDR government between 1979 and 1987, was an interesting attempt to recreate a medieval town. Now, with the exception of one or two restored buildings, the Nikolaiviertel consists entirely of newly built replicas of historic buildings.

The **Nikolaikirche** was destroyed by bombing in 1945 and rebuilt in 1987. All that remains of the original structure, which was probably built around 1230, is the base of the two-tower façade of the present church, which dates from around 1300.

The only Baroque building in Nikolaiviertel to escape damage during World War II was the **Knoblauchhaus**, a small townhouse built in 1759 for the Knoblauch family. The current appearance of the building is the result of work carried out in 1835 when the façade was given a Neo-Classical look.

Ephraim-Palais was built in 1766 for Nathan Veitel Heinrich Ephraim, Frederick the Great's mint master and court jeweller. Parts of the original structure, which were saved from demolition, were used in the reconstruction.

❻ Märkisches Museum

Am Köllnischen Park 5. **Map** 5 F2.
Tel (030) 30 86 62 15. **U** Märkisches Museum. **S** Jannowitzbrücke.
🚌 147, 265. **Open** 10am–6pm Tue, Thu–Sun, noon–8pm Wed. 📷 (free 1st Wed of month). Presentation of mechanical instruments 3pm Sun.

Built between 1901 and 1908, this complex of red brick buildings was inspired by the brick-Gothic style popular in the Brandenburg region. The museum, founded in 1874, is dedicated to the cultural history of Berlin from the first settlements to today. The department "Berliner Kunst" (art), for example, presents a remarkable collection of paintings, sculpture, textiles, faiences, glass and porcelain. The main hall features the original Gothic portal from the sculpture *Quadriga*, which once crowned the Brandenburg Gate *(see p73)*. A further collection is devoted to the Berlin theatre from 1730 to 1933. One of the galleries houses some old-time mechanical musical instruments.

Surrounding the museum is the Köllnischer Park, home to three brown bears – the city mascots.

❼ Checkpoint Charlie

Friedrichstraße 43–45. **Map** 4 C4.
Tel (030) 253 72 50. **U** Kochstraße.
🚌 M29. Haus am Checkpoint Charlie:
Open 9am–10pm daily. 📷

The name of this notorious border crossing between the American and Soviet sectors comes from the word that signifies the letter C in the international phonetic alphabet: Alpha, Bravo, Charlie.

Between 1961 and 1990, Checkpoint Charlie was the only crossing for foreigners between East and West Berlin. It came to represent a symbol of both freedom and separation for the many East Germans trying to escape Soviet communism.

Today, a single watchtower is all that remains. Next to it is a museum – **Haus am Checkpoint Charlie**. Its rich collection details the years of the Cold War in Berlin.

❽ Jüdisches Museum

Lindenstraße 14. **Map** 4 C5. **Tel** (030) 25 99 33 00. **U** Hallesches Tor or Kochstraße. 🚌 M29, M41, 265.
Open 10am–10pm Mon, 10am–8pm Tue–Sun.

The building housing the city's Jewish Museum is an exciting and imaginative example of 20th-century architecture. Designed by a Polish-Jewish architect based in the United States, Daniel Libeskind, the plan, shape, style and interior

The exterior of the Märkisches Museum, echoing a medieval monastery

and exterior arrangement of the building are part of a profoundly complicated philosophical programme. The museum's architecture itself is intended to convey something of the tragic history of the millions of Jews who perished in the Holocaust. For example, the zig-zag layout recalls a torn Star of David.

The interior arrangement is dominated by a gigantic empty crack, which cuts a swathe through the building. Several corridors lead to a windowless Holocaust tower.

The collection focuses on Jewish history and art. Also on display are artifacts that were once part of everyday Jewish life in Berlin.

The museum is accessible only through an underground passageway in the former Berlin-Museum building next door.

The austere, steel-clad walls of the Jüdisches Museum

❷ Topographie des Terrors

Niederkirchnerstraße 8. Map 4 B4. Tel (030) 25 45 09 50. ◼ & ◼ Potsdamer Platz, Anhalter Bahnhof. @ M29. Open May–Sep: 10am–8pm daily; Oct–Apr: 10am–6pm daily.

During the Third Reich, Prinz-Albrecht-Straße (Niederkirch-nerstraße) was probably the most frightening address in Berlin: here, three of the most terrifying Nazi political depart-ments had their headquarters. The Neo-Classical Prinz-Albrecht

palace, which stood at Wilhelmstraße No. 102, became the headquarters of Reinhard Heydrich and the Third Reich's security service. The school of arts and crafts at Prinz-Albrecht-Straße No. 8 was occupied by the head of the Gestapo, Heinrich Müller, while the Hotel Prinz Albrecht at No. 9 became headquarters of the Schutzstaffel or SS.

After World War II, the bomb-damaged buildings were pulled down and, in 1987, a hall was built to house an exhibition on the history of the site. The museum houses the permanent exhibition 'Topography of Terror' alongside temporary displays.

❸⓪ Deutsches Technikmuseum Berlin

Trebbiner Straße 9. **Map** 4 A5. **Tel** (030) 90 25 40. ◻ Gleisdreieck. ▣ 140. **Open** 9am–5:30pm Tue–Fri, 10am–6pm Sat & Sun. ♿ 📷

The Technical Museum was first established in 1982 with the intention of grouping more than 100 smaller, specialized collections under one roof. The current collection is arranged on the site of the former trade hall, the size of which allows many of the museum's exhibits,

The stark exterior of the Topographie des Terrors

such as locomotives, water towers and storerooms, to be displayed full-size and in their original condition.

Of particular interest in the collection are the dozens of locomotives and railway carriages from different eras, as well as vintage cars. There are also exhibitions dedicated to flying, the history of paper manufacture, printing, weaving, electro-technology and computer technology. There are also two windmills, a brewery and an old forge. The section called Spectrum is especially popular with children as it allows them to try the "hands-on" experiments. One hall is dedicated to the display of aircraft and aircraft engines.

A special attraction of the Technical Museum is the Historical Brewery. The building was once used by the brewery Tucker Bräu for storing beer, but it was destroyed in World War II. Decades later, the brewery was rebuilt on four levels. Some visitors claim they can smell roasted malt.

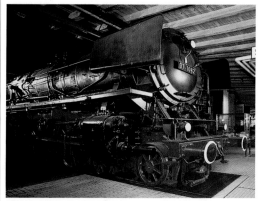

One of dozens of locomotives displayed in the Deutsches Technikmuseum

WESTERN CENTRE

This part of Berlin includes the areas of Tiergarten, Charlottenburg and parts of Kreuzberg, as well as a small section of Mitte, which used to belong to East Berlin.

Tiergarten, which was once a royal hunting estate, became a park in the 18th century. It survives as a park to this day, although in an altered form.

To the south of Tiergarten is the Kulturforum – a large centre of museums and other cultural establishments, which was created after World War II. The neighbouring Potsdamer Platz is now an ultra-modern development, built on the wasteland that formerly divided East and West Berlin.

Although the eastern part of Charlottenburg does not feature a great number of historic buildings, it is one of the city's most attractive districts, which, after World War II, became the commercial and cultural centre of West Berlin. Kreuzberg is a lively area that is now populated by immigrants, artists and affluent young professionals.

Sights at a Glance

Museums and Galleries

3 Käthe-Kollwitz-Museum
7 Bauhaus-Archiv
8 Bendlerblock
9 Gemäldegalerie
10 Kupferstichkabinett und Kunstbibliothek
11 Neue Nationalgalerie
12 Kunstgewerbemuseum
14 Musikinstrumenten-Museum
17 Regierungsviertel i Hamburger Bahnhof
19 Museum für Naturkunde

Streets and Squares

2 Kurfürstendamm (Ku'damm)
4 Zoologischer Garten
5 Tiergarten
15 Potsdamer Platz

Churches

1 Kaiser-Wilhelm-Gedächtniskirche

Historic Buildings and Monuments

6 Siegessäule
13 Philharmonie
16 Reichstag

See also Streetfinder maps
pp119–122

Street-by-Street: Kulturforum

The idea of creating a new cultural centre in West Berlin was first mooted in 1956. The first building to go up was the Berlin Philharmonic concert hall, built from 1960 to 1963 to an innovative design by Hans Scharoun. Most other elements of the Kulturforum were realized between 1961 and 1987, and came from such famous architects as Ludwig Mies van der Rohe. The area is now a major cultural centre that attracts millions of visitors every year.

⓬ ★ Kunstgewerbemuseum
Among the collection at the Museum of Arts and Crafts you can see this intricately carved silver and ivory tankard, made in an Augsburg workshop around 1640.

⓾ Kupferstichkabinett
The large collection of prints and drawings owned by this gallery includes this portrait of Albrecht Dürer's mother.

⓽ ★ Gemäldegalerie
Among the most important works of the old masters exhibited in this gallery of fine art is this *Madonna in Church* by Jan van Eyck (c.1425).

Kunstbibliothek
The Art Library that boasts a rich collection of books, graphic art and drawings.

REICHPIETSCHUFER

LANDWEHRKANAL

⓫ Neue Nationalgalerie
Sculptures by Henry Moore and Alexander Calder stand outside this streamlined building, designed by Ludwig Mies van der Rohe.

0 metres 50
0 yards 50

Key

— Suggested route

⓭ ★ Philharmonie
Its exterior covered in a layer of golden aluminium, the Berlin Philharmonic concert hall is known all over the world for its superb acoustics.

Locator Map
See Street Finder maps 1 & 3

SCHAROUNSTRASSE

POTSDAMER STRASSE

MATTHÄIKIRCH PLATZ

ISMUNDSTRASSE

POTSDAMER STRASSE

⓮ Musikinstrumenten-Museum
This harpsichord is part of a collection of musical instruments dating from the 16th to the 20th century.

St-Matthäus-Kirche
This 19th-century church stands out among the modern buildings of the Kulturforum.

Neue Staatsbibliothek
Hans Scharoun designed this public lending and research library built in 1978.

❶ Kaiser-Wilhelm-Gedächtnis-Kirche

This church-monument is one of Berlin's most famous landmarks. The vast Neo-Romanesque church was designed by Franz Schwechten. It was consecrated in 1895 and destroyed by bombs in 1943. After the war the ruins were removed, leaving only the front tower, at the base of which the Gedenkhalle (Memorial Hall) is situated. This hall documents the church's history and contains some original ceiling mosaics, marble reliefs and liturgical objects. In 1963, Egon Eiermann designed a new octagonal church in blue glass and a new freestanding bell tower.

VISITORS' CHECKLIST

Practical Information
Breitscheidplatz.
Map 2 B4. **Tel** (030) 218 50 23.
Open Church: 9am–7pm daily.
Gedenkhalle: 10am–6pm Mon–
Sat (to 5:30pm Sat), noon–5:30pm
Sun. 🕙 10am & 6pm Sun. 🅰 🆆
gedaechtniskirche-berlin.de

Transport
🆂 & 🆄 Zoologischer Garten or
🆄 Kurfürstendamm. 🚌 100,
200, X-9.

Tower Ruins
The damaged roof of the former church has become one of the best-known symbols of Berlin.

Tower Clock

★ **Kaiser's Mosaic**
Kaiser Heinrich I, seated on his throne, is depicted in this elaborate mosaic.

Main Altar
The massive figure of Christ on the Cross is the work of Karl Hemmeter.

Main entrance

Figure of Christ
This vast sculpture by Hermann Schaper once decorated the church altar. It survived World War II damage.

❷ Ku'damm

Plan 2 A5, 2 B4. **U** Kurfürstendamm.
🚌 109, 110, X10, M19, M29, M46.

The eastern area of the
Charlottenburg region, around
the boulevard known as
Kurfürstendamm (the Ku'damm),
was developed in the 19th
century. Luxurious buildings were
constructed along the Ku'damm,
while the areas of Breitscheidplatz
and Wittenbergplatz filled up
with hotels and department
stores. After World War II, with
the old centre (Mitte) situated
in East Berlin, Charlottenburg
became the centre of West
Berlin. After the war the area
was transformed into the
heart of West Berlin, with
dozens of new company
headquarters and trade centres
being built. It is now Berlin's
main shopping street.

Mother and Child, from the Käthe-Kollwitz-
Museum

❸ Käthe-Kollwitz-Museum

Fasanenstraße 24. **Map** 2 A5. **Tel** (030)
882 52 10. **U** Uhlandstraße or
Kurfürstendamm. 🚌 109, 110, X10,
M19, M29, 249. **Open** 11am–6pm
daily. 🚗 📷 **W** kaethe-kollwitz.de

This small private museum
provides a unique opportunity
to become acquainted with the
work of Käthe Kollwitz (1867–
1945). Born in Königsberg, the
artist settled in Berlin where she
married a doctor who worked in
Prenzlauer Berg, a working-class
district. Her drawings and
sculptures portrayed the social

A tranquil area within the Tiergarten

problems of the poor, as well as
human suffering.
This museum displays the
work of Käthe Kollwitz and
includes posters, drawings and
sculptures as well as documents,
such as letters and photographs.

❹ Zoologischer Garten

Zoological Garden

Hardenbergplatz 8 / Budapester Str.
34. **Map** 2 B3, C3, 2 B4, C4. **Tel** (030) 25
40 10. **S** & **U** Zoologischer Garten.
🚌 M46, X9, X10, X34, 100, 109, 149,
200, 245, 249. **Open** spring & summer:
9am–6:30pm, autumn: 9am–5:30pm,
winter: 9am–4:30pm. 🚗 **W** zoo-
berlin.de

The zoological garden is
actually part of the Tiergarten
and dates from 1844, making
this one of the oldest zoos in
Germany. The main attraction
is its family of polar bears.
A monkey house contains a
family of gorillas, and there is a
specially darkened pavilion
for observing nocturnal
animals. A glazed wall in the
hippopotamus pool enables
visitors to observe these
enormous animals moving
through the water. The large
aquarium contains sharks,
piranhas and unusual
animals from coral reefs.
There is also a huge
terrarium with an overgrown
jungle that is home to a
group of crocodiles. Just to
the west of the zoological
garden on Jebenstraße
is the **Newton-
Sammlung**. This
gallery houses
photographs by
Helmut Newton.

❺ Tiergarten

Map 2 C3, 3 D3, E3, F3.
S Tiergarten or Bellevue.
🚌 100, 187, 341.

Once a forest used as
the Elector's hunting
reserve, the Tiergarten
was transformed into a
landscaped park by Peter
Joseph Lenné in the 1830s.
A Triumphal Avenue,
lined with statues of the
country's rulers and
statesmen, was built in the
eastern section at the end
of the 19th century.
World War II inflicted huge
damage, but replanting has
restored the Tiergarten and
its avenues are bordered
with statues of figures such as
Johann Wolfgang von Goethe
and Richard Wagner.
Near the lake and the
Landwehrkanal are memorials
to Karl Liebknecht and Rosa
Luxemburg, the leaders of the
Spartakus movement who were
assassinated in 1918.

❻ Siegessäule

Triumphal Column

Großer Stern. **Map** 3 D2. **U**
Hansaplatz **S** Bellevue. 🚌 100, 187,
106. **Open** Apr–Oct: 9:30am–6:30pm
Mon–Fri, 9:30am–7pm Sat & Sun;
Nov–Mar: 10am–5pm Mon–Fri,
10am–5:30pm Sat & Sun.

This column, based on a design
by Johann Heinrich Strack,
was built to commemorate
victory in the Prusso-Danish
war of 1864. After further
Prussian victories in wars
against Austria (1866) and
France (1871), a gilded figure
representing Victory, known
as the "Goldelse", was added
to the top. It originally stood
in front of the Reichstag
building but was moved to its
present location by the Nazi
government in 1938. The base
is decorated with bas-reliefs
commemorating battles, while
higher up a mosaic frieze
depicts the founding of
the German Empire in
1871. An observation
terrace offers
magnificent views.

Siegessäule (Triumphal
Column)

The captivating, streamlined buildings of the Bauhaus-Archiv

❼ Bauhaus-Archiv

Klingelhöferstraße 14. **Map** 3 D4, E4.
Tel (030) 254 00 20. Ⓤ Nollendorf-
platz. 🚌 100, 187, M29. **Open** 10am–
5pm Wed–Mon. 🚶 Library: 9am–
1pm Mon–Fri. 🚻 🌐 **bauhaus.de**

The Bauhaus school of art, started
by Walter Gropius in 1919, was
one of the most influential art
institutions of the 20th century.
Originally based in Weimar, it
inspired many artists and
architects. Staff and students
included Mies van der Rohe,
Paul Klee and Wassily Kandinsky.
The school moved to Berlin in
1932 from Dessau, but was
closed by the Nazis in 1933.

After the war, the Bauhaus-
Archiv was relocated to
Darmstadt. In 1964 Walter
Gropius designed a building to
house the collection but, in 1971,
the archive was moved to Berlin
and the design was adapted to
the new site. As Gropius had died
in 1969, Alexander Cvijanovic
took over the project. Built
between 1976 and 1979 the
gleaming white building with its
glass-panelled gables houses
the archive, library and
exhibition halls.

❽ Bendlerblock (Gedenkstätte Deutscher Widerstand)

Stauffenbergstraße 13–14. **Map** 3
E4, F4. **Tel** (030) 26 99 50 00.
Ⓤ Mendelssohn-Bartholdy-Park.
🚌 M29, M48. **Open** 9am–6pm Mon–
Fri (to 8pm Thu), 10am–6pm Sat &
Sun. **Closed** 1 Jan, 24, 25 & 31 Dec.

The collection of buildings
known as the Bendlerblock

built during the Third Reich as
an extension to the German
State Naval Offices. During World
War II they were the headquarters
of the Wehrmacht (German
Army). It was here that a group
of officers planned their assassination attempt on Hitler on 20
July 1944. When the attempt led
by Claus Schenk von Stauffenberg
failed, he and his fellow
conspirators were arrested and
death sentences passed.
Stauffenberg, Friedrich Olbricht,
Werner von Haeften, and Ritter
Mertz von Quirnheim were shot
in the Bendlerblock courtyard. A
monument commemorating
this event, designed by Richard
Scheibe in 1953, stands where
the executions were carried out.

On the upper floor of the building there is an exhibition which
documents the history of the
German anti-Nazi movements.

❾ Gemäldegalerie

See pp94–5.

❿ Kupferstich-kabinett und Kunstbibliothek

Matthäikirchplatz 8. **Map** 3 F3.
Tel (030) 266 20 02. Ⓢ & Ⓤ
Potsdamer Platz or Ⓤ Mendelssohn-
Bartholdy-Park. 🚌 M48, M85, 200,
M29, M41. Kupferstichkabinett
Exhibitions: 10am–6pm Tue–Fri,
11am–6pm Sat & Sun. Studio gallery:
9am–4pm Tue–Fri. Kunstbibliothek
Exhibits: 10am–6pm Tue–Fri,
11am–6pm Sat & Sun. Library: 2–8pm
Mon, 9am– 8pm Tue–Fri. 🚶 🚻 ♿

The print collections of galleries
in the former East and West

Berlin were united in 1994 in
the Kupferstichkabinett (Print
Gallery), whose collection
includes around 2,000
engraver's plates, over 520,000
prints and 80,000 drawings
and watercolours.

The **Kunstbibliothek** (Art
Library) is not only a library with
a range of publications about
the arts; it is also a museum
with an extensive collection of
posters, advertisements and
other practical forms of design.

Munch's lithograph *Girl on a Beach*,
Kupferstichkabinett

⓫ Neue Nationalgalerie

Potsdamer Straße 50. **Map** 3 F4.
Tel (030) 266 26 51. Ⓤ & Ⓢ
Potsdamer Platz or Ⓤ Mendelssohn-
Bartholdy-Park. 🚌 M48, M85, 200,
M29, M41. **Open** 10am–6pm Tue &
Wed, 10am–10pm Thu, 11am–6pm
Sat & Sun. 🚶 🚻

After World War II, when this
magnificent collection of
modern art ended up in West
Berlin, the commission to
design a suitable building to
house it was given to Mies van
der Rohe. The result is a striking
building with a flat steel roof
over a glass hall, which is
supported only by six slender
interior struts.

The collection comprises
largely 20th-century art, but
begins with artists of the late
19th century, such as Edvard
Munch. German art is well
represented: as well as the
Bauhaus movement, the gallery
shows works by exponents of a
crass realism, such as Otto Dix.

Karl Schmidt-Rottluff's *Farm in Daugart* (1910), Neue Nationalgalerie

concept for concert hall interiors, with a podium occupying the central section of the pentagonal hall, around which are galleries for the public. The exterior is reminiscent of a circus tent. The gilded exterior was added between 1978 and 1981.

Between the years 1984 to 1987 the Kammermusiksaal, which was designed by Edgar Wisniewski on the basis of sketches by Scharoun, was added to the Philharmonie. This building consolidates the aesthetics of the earlier structure by featuring a central multi-sided space covered by a fanciful tent-like roof.

The most celebrated artists of other European countries are included, as are examples of post-World War II art.

⓬ Kunstgewerbe-museum

Tiergarten-Str. 6. **Map** 3 F3. **Tel** (030) 266 2902. Ⓢ Potsdamer Platz. Ⓤ Potsdamer Platz or Mendelssohn-Bartholdy-Park. 🚌 100, 123, 148, 200, M29, M41. **Closed** for ongoing renovation in 2014. 🖼 ♿ ♿

This museum holds a rich collection embracing many genres of craft and decorative art, from the early Middle Ages to the modern day. Goldwork is especially well represented, as are metal items from the Middle Ages. Among the most valuable exhibits is a collection of medieval goldwork from the church treasures of Enger and the Guelph treasury from Brunswick. The museum also takes great pride in its collection

of late Gothic and Renaissance silver from the civic treasury in the town of Lüneberg. In addition, there are fine examples of Italian majolica, and 18th- and 19th-century German, French and Italian glass, porcelain and furniture.

⓭ Philharmonie

Philharmonic and Chamber Music Hall

Herbert-von-Karajan-Straße 1. **Map** 3 F3. **Tel** (030) 25 48 80. Ⓢ & Ⓤ Potsdamer Platz or Ⓤ Mendelssohn-Bartholdy-Park. 🚌 200, M29 M41.

Home to one of the most renowned orchestras in Europe, this unusual building is among the finest postwar architectural achievements in Europe. Built between 1960 and 1963 to a design by Hans Scharoun, the Philharmonie pioneered a new

⓮ Musikinstru-menten-Museum

Tiergartenstraße 1. **Map** 1 D5. **Tel** (030) 25 48 10. Ⓢ & Ⓤ Potsdamer Platz. 🚌 200. **Open** 9am–5pm Tue–Fri (to 10pm Thu), 10am–5pm Sat & Sun. Wurlitzer Organ demonstration: noon, first Sat of the month. 🖼 ♿

Behind the Philharmonie, in a small building designed by Edgar Wisniewski and Hans Scharoun between 1979 and 1984, the fascinating Museum of Musical Instruments houses a collection dating from 1888. Intriguing displays trace the development of each instrument from the 16th century to the present day. Most spectacular of all is a working Wurlitzer cinema organ dating from 1929. Saturday demonstrations of its impressive sounds attract enthusiastic crowds. There is also an archive and a library.

The tent-like gilded exterior of the Philharmonie and Kammermusiksaal

❾ Gemäldegalerie

The Gemäldegalerie collection is exceptional in the consistently high quality of its paintings. Unlike those in other collections, they were chosen by specialists who, from the end of the 18th century, systematically acquired pictures to represent all the major European schools. Originally displayed in the Altes Museum building (see p79), the paintings achieved independent status in 1904 when they were moved to what is now the Bode-Museum (see p82). After the division of Berlin in 1945, part of the collection was kept in the Bode-Museum, while the majority ended up in the Dahlem Museum (see p108). Following reunification, and with the building of a new home as part of the Kulturforum development, this unique collection has finally been united again.

★ **Cupid Victorious** (1602)
Inspired by Virgil's *Omnia vincit Amor*, Caravaggio depicted a playful god trampling over the symbols of Culture, Fame, Knowledge and Power.

Madonna with Child and Angels (c.1477)
A frequent subject of Sandro Botticelli, the Madonna and Child are depicted surrounded by angels holding lilies to symbolize purity.

Birth of Christ (c.1480)
This beautiful religious painting is one of the few surviving paintings on wood by Martin Schongauer.

Circular lobby leading to the galleries

Portrait of Hieronymus Holzschuher (1526)
Albrecht Dürer painted this affectionate portrait of his friend, who was the mayor of Nuremberg.

Main entrance

The Glass of Wine
(1661/62)
Jan Vermeer's carefully composed picture of a young woman drinking wine with a young man gently hints at the relationship developing between them.

VISITORS' CHECKLIST

Practical Information
Matthäikirchplatz.
 Map 3 F3. **Tel** (030) 266 42 30 40.
 Open 10am–6pm Tue–Sun (to 8pm Thu). **Closed** 24 & 31 Dec.
🚼 🏛 👪 👍 📷 🏠
 w smb.museum.de

Transport
Ⓢ & Ⓤ Potsdamer Platz.
Ⓤ Mendelssohn-Bartholdy-Park.
🚌 M29, M41, 200.

Love in the French Theatre
This picture has a companion piece called *Love in the Italian Theatre*. Both are by French painter, Jean-Antoine Watteau (1684–1721).

★ Portrait of Hendrickje Stoffels
(1656–57)
Rembrandt's portrait of his lover, Hendrickje Stoffels, is typical of his work in the way it focuses on the subject and ignores the background.

Key

- 🔲 13th–16th-century German painting
- 🔲 14th–16th-century Dutch and French painting
- ⬜ 17th-century Flemish and Dutch painting
- 🔲 18th-century French, English and German painting
- 🔲 17th–18th-century Italian painting, 17th-century German, French and Spanish painting
- 🔲 13th–16th-century Italian painting
- 🔲 16th–18th-century miniatures

Gallery Guide
The main gallery contains over 900 masterpieces grouped by period and country of origin. These are complemented by around 400 works in the gallery on the lower floor.

★ Netherlandish Proverbs (1559)
Pieter Brueghel managed to illustrate more than 100 proverbs in this painting.

⑮ Potsdamer Platz

In the short space of a few years a modern financial and business district sprang up on the vast empty wasteland surrounding the Potsdamer Platz. It boasts splendid constructions designed by Renzo Piano, Arata Isozaki and Helmut Jahn. As well as office blocks, the area has many public buildings, including cinemas and a theatre, as well as a huge shopping centre – the Arkaden, plus luxury hotels, restaurants and several bars.

The Sony Tower, designed by Helmut Jahn, is the most modern building in Potsdamer Platz and is curved on one side and flat on the other.

The Beisheim Center has a mix of exclusive apartments and international hotels.

The Sony Center

POTSDAMER PLATZ

ENTLASTUNGSSTRASSE

This office building, the tallest in Potsdamer Platz, has an observation terrace and café on the 24th and 25th floors.

Arkaden, opened in autumn 1998, immediately became one of the city's favourite shopping centres.

Theater am Potsdamer Platz, designed by Italian architect Renzo Piano, hosts musicals throughout the year and is the main location for Berlinale, the annual film festival.

The Debis House, designed by Italian architect Renzo Piano.

LANDWEHRKANAL

| 0 metres | 100 |
| 0 yards | 100 |

The Reichstag, crowned by a dome designed by Sir Norman Foster

⓰ Reichstag

Platz der Republik. **Map** 1 E4, 4 A1, A2. **Tel** (030) 22 73 21 52. Ⓤ Bundestag. Ⓢ Brandenburger Tor. 100, M85. Dome: **Open** by appointment only. Assembly Hall: **Open** Apr–Oct: 9am–6pm Mon–Fri, 9am–5pm Sat–Sun. Nov–Mar: 9am– 5pm Mon–Fri, 10am–4pm Sat & Sun.

Built to house the German Parliament, the Reichstag was constructed between 1884 and 1894 to a New-Renaissance design by Paul Wallot.

In February 1933, a fire destroyed the main hall, and the impending world war delayed rebuilding work for decades. Between 1957 and 1972, the reconstructed Reichstag was the meeting-place for the lower house of the German Parliament as well as a spectacular backdrop for festivals and rock concerts.

After German reunification in 1990, the Reichstag was the first meeting place of a newly elected Bundestag. The most recent update, by Sir Norman Foster, transformed the Reichstag into a meeting hall.

⓱ Regierungs-viertel

Government Quarter

Map 1 D3, D4 ,E3, E4; 4, 4 A1, A2. Ⓤ Bundestag. Ⓢ Brandenburger Tor. 100, M85.

Located in the bend of the river Spree, the new government quarter was built between 1993 and 2003 to accomodate the relocation of the German government from Bonn in 1999.

Most of the buildings offer limited access to the public, however, several art and political exhibitions are open daily and art and architecture tours run at weekends.

⓲ Hamburger Bahnhof

Invalidenstraße 50/51. **Map** 1 D2, B2. **Tel** (030) 397 834-11. Ⓤ Zinnowitzer straße. Ⓢ Hauptbahnhof. M41, TXL, 120, 123, 147, 245. M6, M8, 12. **Open** 10am– 6pm Tue–Fri, 11am–8pm Sat, 11am–6pm Sun. **Closed** Mon, 24 & 31 Dec.

This museum is situated in a Neo-Renaissance building, formerly the Hamburg Railway station, which dates from 1847. It stood vacant after World War II but, following refurbishment by Josef Paul Kleihues, it was opened to the public in 1996. The neon installation surrounding the façade is the work of Dan Flavin. The museum houses a magnificent collection of contemporary art, including the work of Erich Marx and, from 2004, the world-renowned Flick collection. The result is one of the best modern art museums to be found in Europe, which features not only art, but also film, video, music and design.

Jeff and Ilona (1991), Hamburger Bahnhof

⓳ Museum für Naturkunde

Natural History Museum

Invalidenstraße 43. **Map** 1 E2. **Tel** (030) 20 93 85 91. Ⓤ Naturkunde-museum. 147, 245. M6, M8, 12. **Open** 9:30am–5pm Tue–Fri, 10am–6pm Sat & Sun. **Closed** 24, 25 & 31 Dec.

Occupying a purpose-built Neo-Renaissance building constructed between 1883 and 1889, this is one of the biggest natural history museums in the world, with a collection containing over 60 million exhibits. Although it has undergone several periods of extension and renovation, it has maintained its unique old-fashioned atmosphere.

The highlight of the museum is the world's largest dinosaur skeleton, which is housed in the glass-covered courtyard. The colossal brachiosaurus measures 23 m (75 ft) long and 12 m (39 ft) high. It was discovered in Tanzania, in 1909, by a German fossil-hunting expedition.

The adjacent rooms feature collections of colourful shells and butterflies, as well as stuffed birds and mammals. A favourite with children is Bobby the Gorilla, who lived in Berlin Zoo from 1928 until 1935. The museum also boasts an impressive collection of minerals and meteorites.

Brachiosaurus skeleton in the Museum für Naturkunde

FURTHER AFIELD

Berlin is a huge city with a unique character that has been shaped by the events in its history. Until 1920 the city consisted only of the districts that now comprise mainly Mitte, Tiergarten, Wedding, Prenzlauer Berg, Friedrichshain and Kreuzberg. At that time the city was surrounded by satellite towns and villages that had been evolving independently over many centuries.

In 1920, as part of great administrative reform, seven towns, 59 parishes and 27 country estates were incorporated into the city, thus creating an entirely new city covering nearly 900 sq km (350 sq miles), with a population of 3.8 million. This metropolis extended to small towns of medieval origin, such as Spandau, as well as to private manor houses and palaces, towns and smart suburban districts. Although the 20th century has changed the face of many of these places, their unique characters have remained undiminished. Because of this diversity, a trip to Berlin is like exploring many different towns simultaneously.

Sights at a Glance

Museums and Galleries
1 Bröhan-Museum
2 Sammlung Berggruen
4 Langhansbau
9 Gedenkstätte Plötzensee
12 Brecht-Haus
13 Anne Frank Zentrum
16 Gedenkstätte Berlin-
   Hohenschönhausen
17 Stasi-Museum
25 Brücke-Museum

Places of Interest
7 Olympiastadion
14 Prenzlauer Berg
18 Köpenick
20 Old Flughafen Tempelhof

23 Museumszentrum Dahlem
26 Strandbad Wannsee
27 Pfaueninsel
28 Nikolskoe
29 Klein Glienicke

Streets, Squares and Parks
3 Schlosspark
15 Karl-Marx-Allee
19 Treptower Park
21 Victoriapark

Historic Buildings and Monuments
5 Schloss Charlottenburg
6 Messegelände
8 Zitadelle Spandau

10 Schloss Tegel
11 Neue Synagoge
22 Rathaus Schöneberg
24 Jagdschloss Grunewald

Key
■ Central Berlin
□ Outskirts of Berlin
═ Motorway
▬ Main road
═ Secondary road
— Railway line

0 kilometres 5

0 miles 5

Map of Greater Berlin

◀ Equestrian statue of "The Great Elector" outside Schloss Charlottenburg   **For additional map symbols** *see back flap*

Pablo Picasso's *Woman in a Hat* (1939), Sammlung Berggruen

❶ Bröhan-Museum

Schlossstraße 1a. **Tel** (030) 32 69 06 00.
Ⓤ Richard-Wagner-Platz & Sophie-Charlotte-Platz. Ⓢ Westend. 🚌 109,
M45. **Open** 10am–6pm Tue–Sun.
Closed 24 & 31 Dec. 🎫 (free 1st Wed).

Located in a late-Neo-Classical building is this interesting, small museum. The collection was amassed by Karl H Bröhan who, from 1966, collected works of art from the Art Nouveau (Jugendstil or Secessionist) and Art Deco styles. The paintings of artists who were particularly connected with the Berlin Secessionist movement are especially well represented. Alongside the paintings are fine examples of other media and crafts including furniture, ceramics, glassware, silverwork and textiles.

Each of the main halls features an individual artist, often employing an array of media. There is also a display of furniture by Hector Guimard, Eugène Gaillard, Henri van de Velde and Joseph Hoffmann, glasswork by Emile Gallé, and porcelain from the best European manufacturers.

❷ Sammlung Berggruen

Schlossstraße 1. **Tel** (030) 326 95 815.
Ⓤ Richard-Wagner-Platz & Sophie-Charlotte-Platz. Ⓢ Westend. 🚌 109,
309, M45. **Open** 10am–6pm Tue–Sun.
🎫 (free 4–8pm Thu.) 📷 ♿

Heinz Berggruen assembled this tasteful collection of art dating from the late 19th and first half of the 20th century. Born and educated in Berlin, he emigrated to the US in 1936, spent most of his life in Paris, but finally entrusted his collection "Picasso and his Time" to the city of his birth. The

museum opened in what was once the west pavilion of the barracks, using the space freed up by moving the Antikensammlung to Museum Island *(see p78)*. The exhibition halls were modified according to the designs of Hilmer and Sattler, who also designed the layout of the Gemäldegalerie.

The Sammlung Berggruen is well known for its large collection of paintings, drawings and gouaches by Pablo Picasso. In addition to these, the museum displays more than 20 works by Paul Klee and paintings by other major artists – Matisse, Braque and Cézanne. The exhibition is supplemented by some excellent sculptures, particularly those of Henri Laurens and Alberto Giacometti.

❸ Schlosspark
Palace Park

Luisenplatz (Schloss Charlottenburg).
Ⓤ Richard-Wagner-Platz & Sophie-Charlotte-Platz. Ⓢ Westend. 🚌 109,
309, M45. Neuer Pavillon: **Tel** (030) 32 09 14 43. Mausoleum: **Tel** (030) 32 09 14 46. **Open** Apr–Oct: 10am–6pm Tue–Sun, Nov–Mar: noon–4pm.
Belvedere: **Tel** (030) 32 09 14 45.
Open Apr–Oct: 10am–8pm Tue–Sun;
Nov–Mar: noon–4pm Tue–Sun.

This extensive royal park surrounding Schloss Charlottenburg is a favourite place for Berliners to stroll. The park is largely the result of work carried out after World War II, when 18th-century prints were used to help reconstruct the layout of the original grounds. Just behind Schloss

French-style garden in the Schloss Charlottenburg park

Charlottenburg is a French-style Baroque garden, constructed to a strict geometrical design with a vibrant patchwork of flower beds, carefully trimmed shrubs and ornate fountains adorned with replicas of antique sculptures. Beyond the curved carp lake is a less formal English-style landscaped park, the original layout of which was created between 1819 and 1828 under the direction of the renowned royal gardener, Peter Joseph Lenné.

Designed by Karl Friedrich Schinkel and completed in 1825, the Neo-Classical **Neuer Pavillon** is a charming two-storey building with rooms ranged around a central staircase. A cast-iron balcony encircles the entire structure.

The **Mausoleum** in which Queen Luise, wife of Friedrich Wilhelm III, was laid to rest, was designed by Karl Friedrich Schinkel in the style of a Doric portico-fronted temple. After the death of the king in 1840, the mausoleum was refurbished to create room for his tomb. The tombs of the king's second wife and those of Kaiser Wilhelm I and his wife were added later.

Built as a summerhouse for Friedrich Wilhelm II, with a mixture of Baroque and Neo-Classical elements, the **Belvedere** now houses the Royal Porcelain Collection, with pieces ranging from the Rococo period up to late Biedermeier.

➍ Langhansbau

Luisenplatz (Schloss Charlottenburg). **Tel** (030) 32 67 48 40. Ⓤ Richard-Wagner-Platz. 🚌 109, 309, M45. **Open** 9am–5pm Tue–Fri, 10am–5pm Sat & Sun. ♿ 📷

This Neo-Classical pavilion was designed by Carl Gotthard Langhans and added to the orangery wing of the Schloss Charlottenburg (see pp102–3) between 1787 and 1791. It was originally used as the court theatre and for many years housed a museum which documents cultures and civilizations from the Stone Age up to medieval times. The collection is now housed in the reconstructed Neues Museum on Museum Island (see p79).

➎ Schloss Charlottenburg

See pp102–3.

The Funkturm (radio tower) in Berlin's Messegelände

➏ Messegelände

Hammarskjöldplatz. Ⓢ Messe Nord/ICC. Ⓤ Kaiserdamm. 🚌 139, 218, X49.

The pavilions of the vast exhibition and trade halls south of Hammarskjöldplatz cover more than 160,000 sq m (1,700,000 sq ft). The original exhibition halls were built before World War I, but nothing of these buildings remains. The oldest part is the Funkturm and the pavilions surrounding it. The building at the front (Ehrenhalle) was built in 1936 to a design by Richard Ermisch, and is one of the few surviving buildings in Berlin designed in a Fascist architectural style.

The straight motorway at the rear of the halls is the famous Avus, the first German autobahn, built in 1921. At one point adapted as a car-racing track, it now forms part of the autobahn system.

➐ Olympiastadion

Olympischer Platz. 🚉 & Ⓤ Olympia-Stadion. **Tel** (030) 30 68 81 00. **Open** late Mar–May: 9am–7pm daily; Jun–mid-Sep: 9am–8pm daily, mid-Sep–Oct: 9–7pm daily; Nov–late Mar: 9am–4pm daily. ♿ 📷 🌐 olympiastadion-berlin.de

Olympiastadion, originally known as Reichssportfeld, was built for the 1936 Olympic Games in Berlin. It was designed by Werner March in the Nazi architectural style and was inspired by the architecture of ancient Rome. To the west of the stadium lie the Maifeld and what is now called the Waldbühne. The former is an enormous assembly ground surrounded by grandstands and fronted by the Glockenturm, a 77 m (250 ft) tower, while the latter is an open-air amphi-theatre. A four-year high-tech modernization project on the stadium was completed in 2004. It now features a sweeping, illuminated roof.

Newly modernized and ever impressive Olympiastadion

❺ Schloss Charlottenburg

The palace in Charlottenburg was intended as a summer home for Sophie Charlotte, the wife of Elector Friedrich III. Construction began in 1695 to a design by Johann Arnold Nering. Johann Eosander Göthe enlarged the palace between 1701 and 1713, adding the orangery wing. Further extensions were undertaken between 1740 and 1746 by Frederick the Great (Friedrich II) who added the new wing.

The palace was restored to its former elegance after World War II and its richly decorated interiors are unequalled in Berlin.

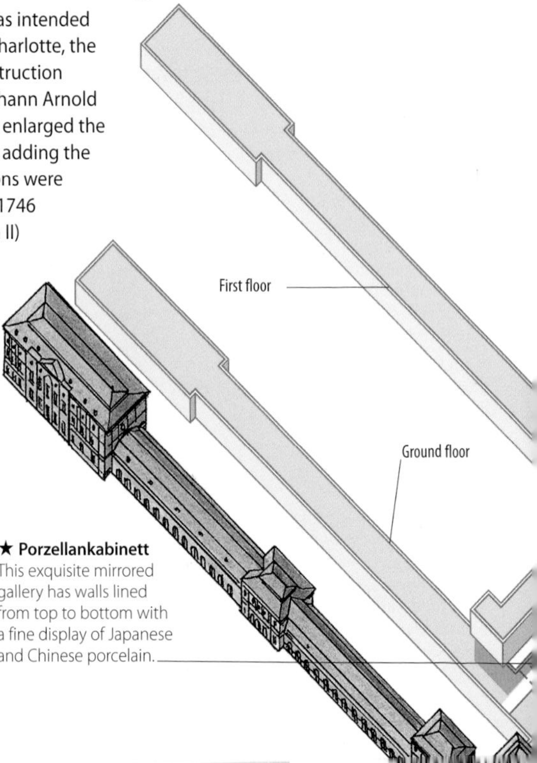

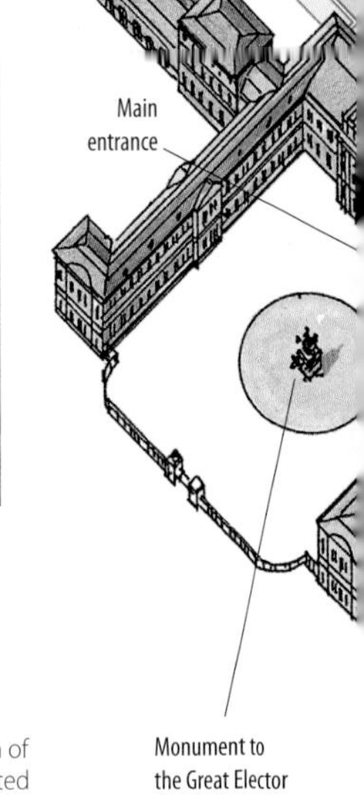

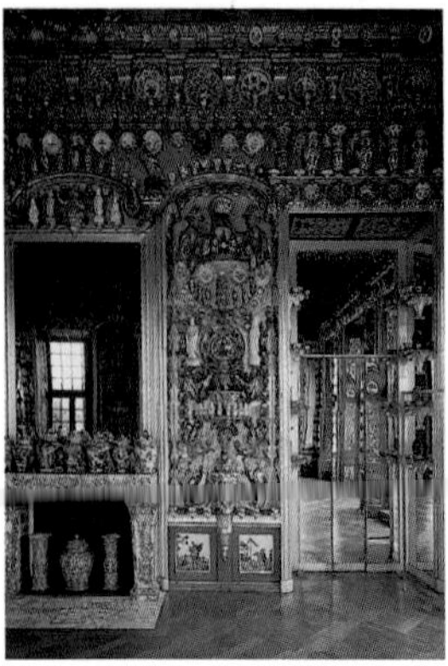

First floor

Ground floor

★ Porzellankabinett
This exquisite mirrored gallery has walls lined from top to bottom with a fine display of Japanese and Chinese porcelain.

Main entrance

Schlosskapelle
Only the pulpit in the court chapel is original. All the remaining furniture and fittings, including the splendid royal box, are reconstructions.

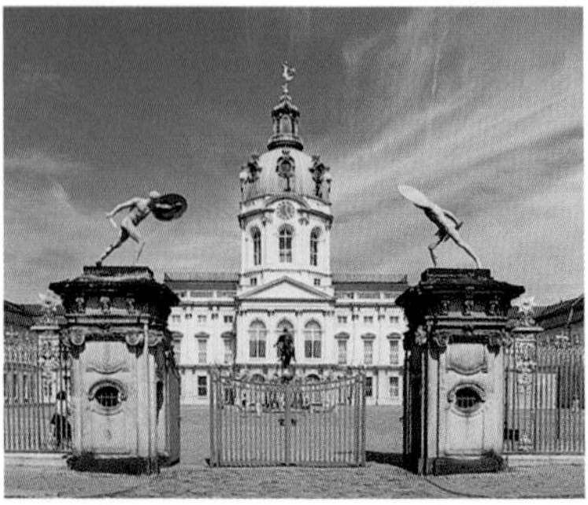

Palace Façade
The central section of the palace, decorated with Corinthian pilasters and topped with a decorative cornice, is the oldest part of the building. It is the work of Johann Arnold Nering.

Monument to the Great Elector

Fortuna
This sculpture by Richard Scheibe crowns the palace, replacing the original statue destroyed during World War II.

VISITORS' CHECKLIST

Practical Information
Spandauer Damm 20–24.
Tel (030) 32 09 10.
Altes Schloss: **Open** 10am–6pm Tue–Sun (Nov–Mar: to 5pm).
Neuer Flügel: **Open** 10am–6pm Wed–Mon (Nov–Mar: to 5pm).

Transport
U Richard-Wagner-Platz & Sophie-Charlotte-Platz.
S Jungfernheide & Westend.
M45, 109, 309.

Friedrich Wilhelm IV's Apartments
This oval hall, decorated with mirrors and offering a delightful garden view, was the king's dining quarters and ballroom.

Key

- Official reception rooms
- Sophie-Charlotte's apartments
- Neuer Flügel or Knobelsdorff-Flügel exhibition space
- Friedrich Wilhelm II's apartments
- Mecklenburg apartments
- Friedrich Wilhelm IV's apartments
- Friedrich Wilhelm II's apartments
- Frederick the Great's apartments
- Non-exhibition space

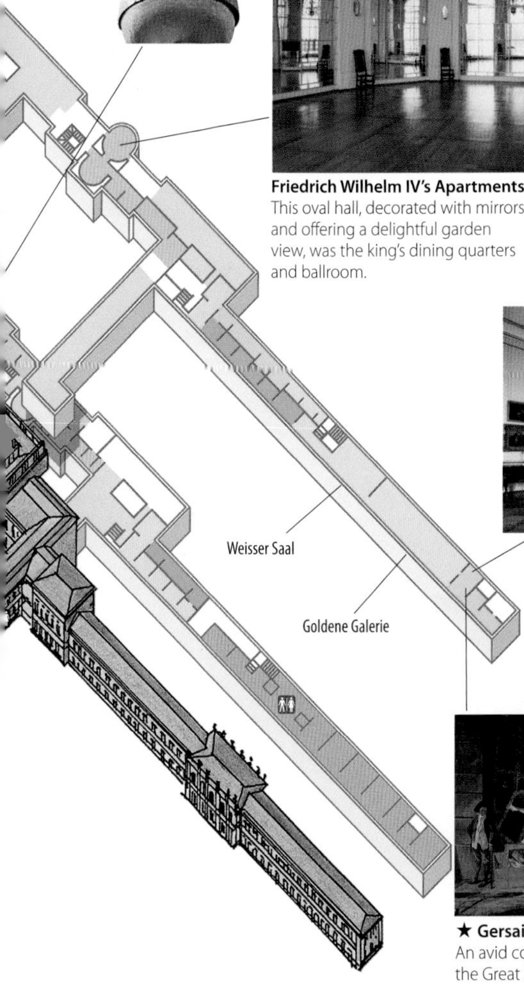

Weisser Saal

Goldene Galerie

Frederick the Great's Apartments
Located on the upper floor of the new wing, this concert room was part of the elegant living quarters of Frederick the Great.

★ **Gersaint's Shop Sign** (1720)
An avid collector of French painting, Frederick the Great bought this and other fine canvases by Antoine Watteau for his collection.

Hohenzollern coat of arms above the main gate of Spandau's citadel

❽ Spandau

Zitadelle Spandau: Am Juliusturm 64.
Tel (030) 354 94 40. 🚇 Zitadelle.
🚌 X33. **Open** 10am–5pm daily. 🏛
🌐 **zitadelle-spandau.de**

Spandau is one of the oldest towns within the area of greater Berlin, and it has managed to retain its own distinctive character. Although the town of Spandau was only granted a charter in 1232, evidence of the earliest settlement here dates back to the 8th century.

The area was spared the worst of the World War II bombing, so there are still some interesting sights to visit. The heart of the town is a network of medieval streets with a picturesque market square and a number of the original timber-framed houses. In the north of Spandau, sections of the town wall dating from the 15th century are still standing.

In the centre of town is the magnificent Gothic St-Nikolai-Kirche, dating from the 15th century. The church holds many valuable ecclesiastical furnishings, such as a splendid Renaissance stone altar from the end of the 16th century, a Baroque pulpit from around 1700 that came from a royal palace in Potsdam, a Gothic baptismal font and many epitaphs.

A castle was first built on the site of the Zitadelle Spandau (citadel) in the 12th century, but today only the 36 m (120 ft) Juliusturm (tower) remains. In 1560 the building of a fort was begun here, to a design by

Francesco Chiaramella da Gandino. It took 30 years to complete and most of the work was supervised by architect Rochus Graf von Lynar. Although the citadel had a jail, the town's most infamous resident, Rudolf Hess, was incarcerated a short distance away in a military prison after the 1946 Nuremberg trials. In 1987, when the former deputy leader of the Nazi party died, the prison was torn down.

❾ Gedenkstätte Plötzensee

Plötzensee Memorial

Hüttigpfad 16. **Tel** (030) 26 99 50 00.
🚇 Jakob-Kaiser-Platz, then 🚌 123, 126. **Open** Mar–Oct: 9am–5pm; Nov–Feb: 9am–4pm.

A narrow street leads from Saatwinkler Damm to the site where nearly 2,500 people convicted of crimes against the

Memorial to concentration camp victims at Gedenkstätte Plötzensee

Third Reich were hanged. The Gedenkstätte Plötzensee is a simple memorial in a brick hut, which still retains the iron hooks from which the victims were suspended.

Claus Schenk von Stauffenberg and the other main figures in the assassination attempt against Hitler on 20 July 1944 were executed in the Bendlerblock *(see p92)*, but the rest of the conspirators were executed here at the Plötzensee prison.

Count Helmut James von Moltke, one of the leaders of the German resistance movement, was also killed here. He was responsible for organizing the Kreisauer Kreis – a political movement that gathered and united German opposition to Hitler.

❿ Schloss Tegel

Adelheidallee 19–21. **Tel** (030) 434 31 56. 🚇 Alt Tegel. 🚌 124, 133, 222.
Open May–Sep: 10am, 11am, 3pm, 4pm. 🎧 compulsory.

Schloss Tegel is one of the most interesting palace complexes in Berlin. The site was occupied in the 16th century by a manor house. In the second half of the 17th century, this was rebuilt into a hunting lodge for the Elector Friedrich Wilhelm. In 1766 the ownership of the property passed to the Humboldt family and, between 1820 and 1824, Karl Friedrich Schinkel thoroughly rebuilt the palace, giving it its current style.

Decorating the elevations on the top floor of the towers are tiled bas-reliefs designed by Christian Daniel Rauch, depicting the ancient wind gods. Some of Schinkel's marvellous interiors have survived, along with several items from what was once a large collection of sculptures. The palace is still privately owned by descendants of the Humboldt family, but guided tours are offered on Mondays.

It is also worth visiting the park in which the palace stands. On the western limits of the park lies the Humboldt family tomb, also designed by

The elegant Neo-Classical façade of Schloss Tegel

Schinkel. The tomb contains a copy of a splendid sculpture by Bertel Thorwaldsen. The original piece stands inside the Schloss Tegel.

The Neue Synagogue with its splendidly reconstructed dome

⓫ Neue Synagoge
New Synagogue

Oranienburger Straße 30. **Tel** (030) 880 28 300. Ⓢ Oranienburger Straße. 🚋 M1, M6. **Open** daily. 🗺 📷

Construction of the New Synagogue, begun in 1859 by architect Eduard Knoblauch, was completed in 1866. The design was a response to the asymmetrical shape of the plot of land, with a narrow façade flanked by a pair of towers and crowned with a dome containing a round vestibule.

With its gilded dome, this was Berlin's largest synagogue until it was partially destroyed during the infamous *Kristallnacht* in 1938. The building was damaged further by Allied bombing in 1943 and was eventually demolished in 1958. Reconstruction began in 1988 and was completed in 1995. Public exhibitions by the Centrum Judaicum are held in the front of the building.

⓬ Brecht-Weigel-Gedenkstätte
Brecht-Weigel Memorial

Chausseestraße 125. **Tel** (030) 200 57 18 44. Ⓤ Naturkunde Museum or Oranienburger Tor. 🚌 340. 🚋 M6, 12. 📷 compulsory. Every half hour (every hour on Sun). 10am–3:30pm Tue, 10am–11:30pm Wed, Fri; 10am–6:30pm Thu; 10am–3:30pm Sat, 11am–6pm Sun. **Closed** Mon, public holidays. 🗺

Playwright Bertolt Brecht was associated with Berlin from 1920, but emigrated in 1933. After the war, his left-wing views made him an attractive potential resident of the newly created German socialist state. Lured by the promise of his own theatre, he returned to Berlin in 1948 with his wife, the actress Helene Weigel.

In 1953, Brecht moved into Chausseestraße 125 and lived there until his death in 1956. His wife founded an archive of his work, which is located on the second floor.

Bertolt Brecht's study in his former apartment

⓭ Anne Frank Zentrum

Rosenthalestraße 39. **Tel** (030) 288 86 56 00. Ⓤ Weinmeisterstraße. Ⓢ Hackescher Markt. **Open** 10am–6pm Tue–Sun. 🗺 🌐 annefrank.de

Anne Frank's short life and her diary are at the heart of this interactive exhibition, which connects history to the present day. Visitors are encouraged to reflect on their own views through listening to young people from Berlin discussing the issues that occupied Anne Frank, such as identity, values, war and discrimination.

⓮ Prenzlauer Berg

Sammlung Industrielle Gestaltung: Kulturbrauerei entrance, Knaackstraße 97. **Tel** (030) 473 77 79 40. Ⓤ Senefelderplatz or Eberswalderstraße. **Open** phone ahead to check.

Towards the end of the 19th century, this was one of the most impoverished, densely populated districts of Berlin, which became a centre for anti-Communist opposition.

After 1989, however, artists, professionals and students began to gather here from all parts of Germany and Europe, creating a colourful, vibrant community.

Schönhauser Allee is the main thoroughfare of Prenzlauer Berg. A former old brew-ery was transformed into the "Kulturbrauerei", a centre for cultural events. It also houses a museum – **Sammlung Industrielle Gestaltung** – with a collection of industrial designs from East Germany.

Heading along Sredzkistraße you reach Husemannstraße. This beautifully renovated street complete with shops and inns gives the impression of Berlin around the year 1900. Amid the greenery around Belforter Straße is a water tower built in the mid-19th century. Near-by, on Schönhauser Allee, there is an old Jewish cemetery dating from 1827. Among those buried here is the renowned painter Max Liebermann.

Fragment of Socialist Realist decoration from Karl-Marx-Allee

⑮ Karl-Marx-Allee

Map 5 F1. Ⓤ Strausberger Platz or Weberwiese.

The section of Karl-Marx-Allee between Strausberger Platz and Frankfurter Tor is effectively a huge open-air museum of Socialist Realist architecture. The route to the east was named Stalinallee in 1949 and chosen as the site for the showpiece of the new German Democratic Republic. The avenue was widened to 90 m (300 ft) and, over the next ten years, huge residential tower blocks and a row of shops were built. The designers, led by Hermann Henselmann, succeeded in combining three sets of architectural guidelines. They used the Soviet wedding cake style according to the precept: "nationalistic in form but socialist in content", and linked the whole work to Berlin's own traditions. Hence there are motifs taken from famous Berlin architects Schinkel and Gontard, as well as from the renowned Meissen porcelain.

The buildings on this street, renamed Karl-Marx-Allee in 1961, are now considered historic monuments.

⑯ Gedenkstätte Berlin-Hohen-schönhausen

Genslerstraße 66. **Tel** (030) 9860 82 30. Ⓢ Landsberger Allee, then 🚋 M5, M6. 🚌 256. **Open** 11am–3pm Mon–Fri, 10am–4pm Sat & Sun. 📷 English tour 2:30pm daily, public tours 2pm Sat. 📷

This museum was established in 1995 within the former Stasi

detention centre. The building was part of a huge complex built in 1938. In May 1945, the occupying Russian authorities created a special transit camp here, in which they interned war criminals and anyone under political suspicion. From 1946 the buildings were refashioned into the custody area for the KGB; in 1951, it was given over to the Stasi.

The prisoners' cells and interrogation rooms are on view, two of which have no windows and are lined with rubber. Housed in the cellars was the "submarine" – a series of cells without daylight to which the most "dangerous" suspects were brought.

⑰ Forschungs- und Gedenkstätte Normannenstraße (Stasi-Museum)

Ruschestraße 103 (Haus 1). **Tel** (030) 553 68 54. Ⓤ Magdalenenstraße. **Open** 11am–6pm Mon–Fri, 2–6pm Sat–Sun. 📷 🌐 **stasimuseum.de**

Under the German Democratic Republic, this huge complex of buildings at Ruschestrasse housed the Ministry of the Interior. It was here that the infamous Stasi (GDR secret service) had its headquarters.

Office of the infamous Stasi chief Erich Mielke at the Stasi Museum

The Stasi's "achievements" in infiltrating its own community were without equal in the Eastern block.

Since 1990 one of the buildings has housed a museum that displays photographs and documents depicting the activities of the Stasi. Here, you can see a model of the headquarters, and equipment that was used for bugging and spying on citizens suspected of holding unfavourable political views. You can also walk around the office of infamous Stasi chief Erich Mielke.

⑱ Köpenick

Ⓢ Spindlersfeld, then 🚌 167 or Ⓢ Köpenick, then 🚌 164, 167. 🚋 27, 60, 61, 62, 68. Kunstgewerbemuseum: Schloss Köpenick, Schlossinsel. **Tel** (030) 6566 17 49. **Open** 10am–5pm Thu–Sun.

Köpenick is much older than Berlin. In the 9th century AD, this island contained a fortified settlement known as Kopanica. In about 1240 a castle was built on the island, around which a town began to evolve. Craftsmen settled here and, after 1685, a large colony of Huguenots also settled.

In the 19th century Köpenick recreated itself as an industrial town. Despite wartime devastation it has retained its historic character and, though there are no longer any 13th-century churches, it is worth strolling around the old town. By the old market square and in the neighbouring streets, modest houses have survived that recall the 18th century, alongside buildings from the end of the 19th century.

At Alt Köpenick No. 21 is a vast brick town hall built in the style of the Brandenburg Neo-Renaissance. In 1906, a famous swindle took place here and the event became the inspiration for a popular comedy by Carl Zuckmayer, *The Captain from Köpenick*. Köpenick's greatest attraction is a three-storey

A reconstructed drawing room from 1548 in the Kunstgewerbemuseum

Baroque palace, built between 1677 and 1681 for the heir to the throne Friedrich (later King Friedrich I), to a design by the Dutch architect Rutger van Langfeld. In 2003, the **Kunstgewerbemuseum** *(see p92)* opened a suite of Renaissance and Baroque rooms to the public in the Köpenick Palace.

Gigantic wreath commemorating the Red Army in Treptower Park

⓳ Treptower Park

Archenhold-Sternwarte, Alt-Treptow. Ⓢ Treptower Park. 🚌 166, 167, 265. Archenhold Sternwarte: **Tel** (030) 536 06 37 19. 📷 compulsory; 2–4:30pm Wed–Sun. 🌐 **sdtp.de**

The vast park in Treptow was laid out in the 1860s on the initiative and design of Johann Gustav Meyer. In 1919 it was where revolutionaries Karl Liebknecht, Wilhelm Pieck and Rosa Luxemburg assembled 150,000 striking workers.

The park is best known for the colossal monument to the Red Army. Built between 1946 and 1949, it stands on the grave of 5,000 Soviet soldiers killed in the battle for Berlin in 1945. The gateway, which leads to the mausoleum, is marked by a vast granite sculpture of a grieving Russian Motherland surrounded by statues of Red Army soldiers.

In the farthest section of the park is the astronomical observatory, **Archenhold Sternwarte**, which was built for a decorative arts exhibition in 1896. Given a permanent site in 1909, the observatory was used by Albert Einstein for a lecture on the Theory of Relativity in 1915. It is also home to the longest reflecting telescope in the world (21 m or 70 ft), and a small planetarium.

Beyond Treptower Park lies another park, Plänterwald.

⓴ Old Flughafen Tempelhof

Platz der Luftbrücke. Ⓤ Platz der Luftbrücke. 🚌 104, 184.

Tempelhof was once Germany's largest airport. Built in 1923, the structure is typical of Third Reich architecture. Additions to the original structure were completed in 1939.

In 1951, a monument was added in front of the airport. Designed by Edward Ludwig, it commemorates the airlifts of the Berlin Blockade. The names of those who lost their lives appear on the plinth.

After a long public debate, Tempelhof was decommissoned as a functioning airport in 2008. It has been turned into a public park and exhibition venue.

㉑ Viktoriapark

Ⓤ Platz der Luftbrücke. 🚌 104, 140.

This rambling park, with several artificial waterfalls, short trails and a small hill, was designed by Hermann Mächtig and built between 1884 and 1894. The Neo-Gothic Memorial to the Wars of Liberation at the summit of the hill is the work of Karl Friedrich Schinkel and was constructed between 1817 and 1821. The monument commemorates the Prussian victory against Napoleon's army in the Wars of Liberation. The monument's cast-iron tower is well ornamented.

In the niches of the lower section are 12 allegorical figures by Christian Daniel Rauch, Friedrich Tieck and Ludwig Wichmann. Each figure symbolizes a battle and is linked to a historic figure – either a military leader or a member of the royal family.

㉒ Rathaus Schöneberg

Schöneberg Town Hall

John-F-Kennedy-Platz. Ⓤ Rathaus Schöneberg.

The Schöneberg town hall is a gigantic building with an imposing tower, which was built between 1911 and 1914. From 1948 to 1990 it was used as the main town hall of West Berlin, and it was outside here, on 26 June 1963, that US President John F Kennedy gave his famous speech. More than 300,000 Berliners assembled to hear the young president say *"Ich bin ein Berliner"* – "I am a Berliner", intended as an expression of solidarity from the democratic world to a city defending its right to freedom.

While Kennedy's meaning was undoubtedly clear, pedants were quick to point out that what he actually said was "I am a small doughnut".

Japanese woodcut from the Museum für Ostasiatische Kunst

㉓ Museumszentrum Dahlem

Lansstraße 8, Dahlem. **Tel** (830) 14 38.
Ⓤ Dahlem Dorf. X111, X83.
Museum für Asiatische Kunst
(Museum of Asian Art), Museum
Europäischer Kultures (Museum of
European Cultures), Ethnologisches
Museum (Museum of Mankind): **Open**
10am–6pm Tue–Fri, 11am–6pm Sat &
Sun. smb.spk-berlin.de

Dahlem's first museums were
built between 1914 and 1923,
but the district was confirmed
as a major cultural and
education centre after World
War II with the establishment
of the Freie Universität and
completion of the museum
complex. With many of
Berlin's collections fragmented,
a miscellany of art and
artifacts was put on display
here. In the 1960s the museums
were extended and the
Museumszentrum was
created to rival East Berlin's
Museum Island.

German reunification in 1990
meant that the collections
could once again be reunited
and reorganized. Paintings were
moved to the Kulturforum (*see
pp88–9*), and sculptures to the
Bodemuseum *see p82*.

Three museums are now
housed at Dahlem: the
Ethnologisches Museum, which
focuses on pre-industrial
societies from around the world;
the Museum für Asiatische
Kunst, one of the largest

musems of Asian art in the
world and the Museum
Europäischer Kultures.

Highlights include bronzes
from Benin and gold Inca
jewellery at the Museum of
Mankind and Japanese woodcuts
from Chinese Turkestan at the
Museum of Asian Art. The
Exhibition of Native North
American Cultures, part of the
Museum of Mankind, opened in
1999, includes a collection of
600 ceremonial objects.

㉔ Jagdschloss Grunewald

Am Grunewaldsee 29. **Tel** (030) 813 35
97. 115, X10. **Open** Apr–Oct:
10am–6pm Tue–Sun; Nov–Mar: tours
only, 11am, 1pm, 3pm Sat & Sun.
spsg.de

Jagdschloss Grunewald is one
of the oldest surviving civic
buildings in Berlin. Built for
the Elector Joachim II in 1542,
it was rebuilt around 1700 in
a Baroque style.

In this small palace on the
edge of the Grunewaldsee
is Berlin's only surviving
Renaissance hall, which
currently houses a collection
of paintings that include a
range of canvases by Rubens
and van Dyck, among others.

In the east wing is the small
Waldmuseum, which has a
collection of illustrations
depicting forest life and the
history of forestry. Opposite
the Jagdschloss, a hunting
museum (Jagdmuseum)
houses a collection of historic
weapons and equipment.

㉕ Brücke-Museum

Bussardsteig 9, Dahlem. **Tel** (030) 831
20 29. 115. **Open** 11am–5pm
Wed–Mon. bruecke-museum.de

This elegant Functionalist
building hosts a collection of
German Expressionist painting
linked to the Die Brücke group.
It is based on almost 80 works
by Schmidt-Rottluff bequeathed
to the town of Dahlem in 1964.
In addition to other works of art
contemporary to Die Brücke,
there are paintings from the
later creative periods of these
artists, as well as works of other
closely associated artists.
Nearby lie the foundation's
headquarters, established in the
former studio of the sculptor
Bernhard Heliger.

㉖ Strandbad Wannsee

Wannseebadweg. Ⓢ Nikolassee.
112, 218.

The vast lake Wannsee, on
the edge of Grunewald, is
a popular destination for
Berliners seeking recreation.
The most developed part is the
southeastern corner where
there are yachting marinas
and harbours. Further north
is one of the largest inland
beaches in Europe, Strandbad
Wannsee, which was developed
between 1929 and 1930 by
the construction of shops,
cafés and changing rooms
on man-made terraces. It is
also pleasant to walk around
Schwanenwerder island,
with its many elegant villas.

Boarding point for lake cruises on the Wannsee

The Schloss Pfaueninsel designed by Johann Brendel

Pfaueninsel

Pfaueninsel. **Tel** (030) 805 86 830. Ⓢ Wannsee, then take 🚌 218. 🚢 Schloss Pfaueninsel. **Open** Apr–Oct: 10am–5pm Tue–Sun. 🎫

This picturesque island, named for the peacocks that inhabit it, is now a nature reserve, reached by ferry across the Havel river. It was laid out in 1795 according to a design by Johann August Eyserbeck. Its final form, which you see today, is the work of the landscape architect Peter Joseph Lenné.

One of the most interesting sights on the island is the small romantic palace of **Schloss Pfaueninsel**. Dating from 1794, it was designed by Johann Gottlieb Brendel for Friedrich Wilhelm II and his mistress Wilhelmine Encke (the future Countess Lichtenau). The palace was built of wood, with a façade fashioned in the form of a ruined medieval castle. The cast-iron bridge that links the towers was built in 1807. The palace is open to the public in the summer months, when you can see the 18th- and 19th-century furnishings.

Other sights worth visiting include **Jakobsbrunnen** (James's Well), which was built to resemble an ancient ruin. Towards the northeast corner of the island is the **Luisentempel** in the form of a Greek temple. Its sandstone portico was relocated to the island from the mausoleum in Schlosspark Charlottenburg *(see pp102–3)* in 1829. Nearby is a stone commemorating Johannes

Kunckel, an alchemist who lived on Pfaueninsel in the 17th century. During his quest to discover how to make gold, he discovered a method of producing ruby-coloured glass. Near the **Aviary**, home to multicoloured parrots and pheasants, is a tall fountain that was designed by Martin Friedrich Rabe in 1824.

Nikolskoe

Nikolskoer Weg. Ⓢ Wannsee, then take 🚌 316.

Across the river from Pfaueninsel (Peacock Island) is Nikolskoe. Here you'll find the Blockhaus Nikolskoe, a Russian-style *dacha* (country house) that was built in 1819 for the future Tsar Nicholas I and his wife, the daughter of King Friedrich Wilhelm III.

The house was built by the German military architect Captain Snethlage, who was responsible for the Alexandrowka estate in Potsdam *(see p138)*. Following a fire in 1985, the *dacha* was reconstructed. It currently houses a restaurant.

Guests on the terrace of the Blockhaus Nikolskoe in summer

Close by is the church of St Peter and Paul, which was built between 1834 and 1837, to a design by Friedrich August Stüler. The body of the church is completed by a tower crowned by an onion-shaped dome, reflecting the style of Russian Orthodox sacral architecture.

Klein Glienicke

Königstr. 36. 🚌 316. **Tel** (0331) 96 94 200. **Open** Apr–Oct: 10am–6pm Tue–Sun; Nov–Mar: 10am–5pm Sat & Sun. 🎫

The palace in the palace-park of Klein Glienicke was built in 1825 according to a design by Karl Friedrich Schinkel for Prince Karl of Prussia. The charming parkin which it is located was created by Peter Joseph Lenné. Beyond the Neo-Classical palace extends an irregular cluster of buildings, grouped around a courtyard, including a pergola and staff cottages. Passing by the palace, you approach the **Coach House**, also designed by Schinkel and now housing a restaurant. Nearby are an orangery and greenhouses designed by Ludwig Persius. Also by Persius is the **Klosterhof**, a mock monastery with pavilions, on whose walls are many Byzantine and Romanesque architectural elements from Italy. Towards the lake is the **Grosse Neugierde**, a circular pavilion based on the Athenian monument to Lysikrates from the 4th century BC. From here there are beautiful views across the Havel river and **Glienicker Brücke** (known under the East German regime as the bridge of unity). The border with West Berlin ran across this bridge where, during the Cold War, the exchange of spies was conducted.

Karl Friedrich Schinkel's Neo-Classical Schloss Klein Glienicke

SHOPPING IN BERLIN

With a shopping centre in every district, each selling a variety of merchandise, Berlin is a place where almost anything can be bought, so long as you know where to shop. The most popular areas are Kurfürstendamm and Friedrichstrasse, but the smaller shops in Wedding, Friedrichshain, Schöneberg and the Tiergarten are also worth a visit. Small boutiques selling flamboyant Berlin-style clothes crop up in unexpected courtyards, while the top fashion houses offer the latest in European elegance. Early on Saturday morning is often the best time to visit the city's various markets, the most popular of which – with their colourful stalls full of hats, bags and belts – can be found on Museum Island and near the Tiergarten. The Galeries Lafayette, KaDeWe and any of the city's numerous bookshops all make ideal venues for a pleasant afternoon's window shopping.

A shop-floor display in the lobby of KaDeWe

Practical Information

The majority of shops are open Monday to Saturday from 10am to 8pm. Before Christmas, many shops are open on Sundays. Some smaller stores do not accept credit cards, so be sure to have some cash.

Department Stores and Shopping Centres

The **Alexa Centre**, a large shopping mall located at Alexanderplatz, houses most of the major fashion chains. Kaufhaus Des Westens, better known as **KaDeWe** at Wittenbergplatz, is undoubtedly the biggest and the best department store in Berlin, while **Galeries Lafayette** on Friedrichstrasse is nothing less than a slice of Paris in the heart of Berlin. Perfumes, domestic accessories and clothing attract an enormous clientele.

Another very popular store is **Karstadt** on the Ku'damm.

Although the outfits sold here are less haute couture than at Galeries Lafayette, there is still an enormous choice and the top-floor restaurant offers excellent views over the city.

One of the newest shopping centres is the **Potsdamer Platz Arkaden**, which is a very popular meeting place. On a slightly smaller scale is **Das Schloss** in Steglitz, and the **Gesundbrunnencenter** is the biggest shopping passage in Berlin with stalls full of bargains. **Europa-Center** is the most visually stunning with its beautiful sculpted fountains.

Fashion

The Ku'damm and Friedrichstrasse areas play host to all the best known high street names and department stores, as well as most of the top fashion houses in Berlin. **Escada** is one of the best known of the German designers, but Berlin also has a wealth of young designers and their lines are mainly to be seen in the northern part of the Mitte area. **NIX**, for example, offers timeless clothes made from heavy, dark fabrics, while **Department Store Quartier 206** sells everything from evening dresses to casual wear and accessories. It offers only top international designer wear and many unique pieces. An exciting designer is **Antonia Goy**, who creates stunning dresses and accessories for women.

For men's fashions, once again the Ku'damm area is the place to look. **Patrick Hellmann** is certainly worth a visit with its wide choice of the best designer labels around.

The spacious Karstadt department store on Kurfürstendamm

September and top orchestras and performers come from all over the world to put on classical music concerts around the city.

Also in September, pop fans will love **Berliner Clubnacht**, which offers an opportunity to dance on 60 floors in 44 Berlin clubs.

Jazzfest Berlin takes place in July and tends to attract lovers of more traditional styles of jazz, but it also focuses on the more experimental and innovative styles of the genre in its accompanying Total Music Meeting.

Traditional jazz music at Berlin's Jazzfest

Rock, Pop & Jazz

Whether it is a major event by a world-famous band or a small-scale evening of jazz improvisation, you need not look too far to find what you want. The biggest concerts tend to take place in sports halls and stadiums, like **O₂ World** and the **Olympiastadion** (see p101), whilst smaller venues like **SO 36** play host to the best new talent in popular music. In addition, a lot of the action tends to take place in the city's many bars, discos and clubs or, if you are looking for particularly atmospheric concerts, you might try those put on at the **Passionskirche**, a converted church in Kreuzberg.

Jazz clubs abound in Berlin, as the style remains very popular amongst locals. The **A-Trane** and **b-flat** are classical jazz bars where you can listen to small

bands just about every night of the week, and **Quasimodo** is renowned for its schedule of local and touring jazz, soul and world music performers.

Apart from the typical classical jazz clubs, jazz can also be heard in many of the city's smaller bars, like **Schlot**. If it is a mixture of soul, rap and jazz you want to listen to, then head for the **Junction Bar** in Kreuzberg. The small bebop jazz club in Kreuzberg is a good choice for meeting locals, and the **Badenscher Hof Jazzclub** is always a good bet.

World Music

Berlin is home to a wide variety of world music. The Haus der Kulturen der Welt organizes all kinds of concerts at its own **Café Global** and **Kulturbrauerei** has become the main venue for world-class artists.

Latin American discos are becoming ever more popular

and **Havanna** in Schöneberg is one of the city's best.

Irish music is also well represented in Berlin's pubs – **Wild at Heart** is very popular, although it does not play Irish music all the time.

Rosa's Dance Co. at the "Tanz" dance festival, organized by the Hebbel Am Ufer (HAU)

Classical and Modern Dance

There are three major ballet groups in Berlin and they work within Berlin's opera houses. The Komische Oper has a modern repertoire, whilst the Staatsoper Unter den Linden focuses on more classical work.

The **Hebbel Am Ufer (HAU)** stages avant-garde pieces and welcomes troupes from all over the world and also organizes the dance festival "Tanz" every August. The seating at all three theatres is rather limited, so you need to book well in advance.

Tanzfabrik, based on Möckernstrasse in Kreuzberg, is an excellent stage for all kinds of modern dance and it also organizes dance work-shops as well as popular body-work courses.

One of the many concerts at Berlin's annual Popkomm festival

Nightlife

Among its many artistic claims, Berlin is also the techno capital of Europe, with over a million devotees celebrating the genre at a number of annual festivals.

One of the best clubs for techno lovers is **Tresor**, situated in a former power plant. The best DJs in town can be heard here.

Columbia Club is a concert venue featuring touring rock bands, so the look and style of the place changes with each performance.

If it is a good old-fashioned disco you are looking for, with happy tunes and a little less techno, the **Far Out** is the place to go.

There is also a new generation of clubs offering a sleek combination of restaurant, lounge, dance floor and event centre. Each night there is a different, often themed, party, or simply a relaxed lounge occasion. The top two locations are **40seconds**, set in an old high-rise with a great view of the night-lit city, and the exclusive **Spindler + Klatt**. Other clubs, such as **Felix**, welcome a well-to-do clientele to contemporary pop music. By contrast, **White Trash** and **Café Moskau** attract a more alternative, hip and young urban crowd.

During the summer, you can dance to pop music in the open air at **Golgatha** in Kreuzberg's Viktoriapark. **Delicious Doughnuts** is one of the best places in town for ambient, house and acid-jazz, while lovers of soul and reggae should head for the lively **Hoppetosse**. For anyone looking for something a little more intimate, the romantic atmosphere of **Sophienclub** might be worth investigating.

Those who enjoy dancing should head for **Ballhaus** in Mitte, which offers a different style each evening, either salsa, tango, swing, cha-cha or disco.

The city also has a vibrant gay and lesbian scene.

The reconstructed medieval settlement at the Museumdorf Düppel

SchwuZ, **Berghain** and **Ackerkeller** are among the best gay venues in Berlin.

Spectator Sports

As a rule, Berlin's sports teams tend to be among the country's best, and rank highly in each of their respective leagues. Hertha BSC's football matches take place in the **Olympiastadion** and Alba Berlin's basketball games are on at the O$_2$ Arena. For international events it is usually best to book in advance.

Lovers of horse racing have two tracks to choose from in Berlin. **Trabrennbahn** in Mariendorf is open all year and the races held here are strictly commercial. **Galopprennbahn Hoppegarten**, on the other hand, has a much more friendly, approachable feel.

Children's Activities

People of all ages are catered for in Berlin, and children are no exception. **Visit Berlin** can offer

Flamingos in the beautiful Zoologischer Garten

details of special children's discounts for many different activities. The **Zoologischer Garten** is very popular, with its playgrounds and many animal enclosures. Small children will love the **Kinderbauernhof Görlitzer Bauernhof**, which has a collection of domestic animals. In addition, Berlin's museums are well set up for children. The **Deutsches Technikmuseum** *(see p85)* allows children to take part in all kinds of experiments, while the **Ethnologisches Museum** prepares special exhibitions for children. A visit to the **Museumsdorf Düppel** is an excellent way to show a child life in a medieval village and the **Puppentheatermuseum** offers a chance for children to take part in minor performances.

Another option is one of the city's many lively circuses, such as **Circus Cabuwazi**, or, if it is sport that your child enjoys, it is possible to swim in many rivers, lakes and, of course, swimming pools (the **Berliner Bäder-betriebe** hotline offers useful information). Also, each district has its own ice-skating rink, but the **Eisstadion Berlin Wilmers-dorf** is by far the best, whilst **FEZ Wuhlheide** offers a special daily programme for kids.

The Story of Berlin is a fun way to experience the history of Berlin in a multi-media exhibit, and the **Berliner Gruselkabinett** (Room of Fear) is suitably scary.

The **Zeiss-Planetarium** or the Planetarium... kids the opportunity to explore the universe in a fun, yet educational, way.

DIRECTORY

Practical Information

Hekticket Theaterkassen
Hardenbergstraße 29d.
Map 2 B4.
Karl Liebknechtstraße 12.
Map 5 D1. **Tel** 230 99 30.
W hekticket.de

Classical Music

Deutsche Oper
Bismarckstraße 34–37.
Tel 34 38 43 43.

Komische Oper
Behrenstraße 55–57.
Map 1 F4. **Tel** 47 99 74 00.

Konzerthaus Berlin
Gendarmenmarkt 2. **Map** 4 C2. **Tel** 203 09 21 01/02.

Philharmonie & Kammermusiksaal
Herbert-von-Karajan-Str. 1.
Map 3 F3. **Tel** 25 48 89 99.

Staatsoper Unter den Linden
Temporarily at Schiller-theater, Bismarckstraße 110.
Tel 20 35 44 38.

Music Festivals

Berliner Clubnacht
W berlin-clubnacht.de

Berliner Festspiele
Schaperstraße 4.
Map 2 B5. **Tel** 25 48 90.

Jazzfest Berlin
Schaperstraße 24.
Tel 25 48 90.

Rock, Pop & Jazz

A-trane
Pestalozzistraße 105.
Map 2 A3. **Tel** 313 25 50.

b-flat
Rosenthaler Straße 13.
Map 5 D4.
Tel 283 31 23.

Badenscher Hof Jazzclub
Badensche Straße 29.
Tel 861 00 80.

Junction Bar
Gniesenaustraße 18.
Tel 694 66 02.

O₂ World
Mühlenstraße 12–30/
O₂-Platz-1.
Tel 20 60 70 80.

Passionskirche
Marheineckeplatz.
Tel 69 40 12 41.

Privatclub
Skalitzer Straße 85-86,
Kreuzberg.
Tel 61 67 59 62.

Quasimodo
Kanstr. 12a. **Map** 2 B4.
Tel 312 80 86.

Schlot
Chausseestraße 18 (enter via Schlegelstraße).
Tel 448 21 60.

SO 36
Oranienstraße 190.
Tel 61 40 13 06.

World Music

Café Global
John-Foster-Dulles-Allee 10. **Map** 3 F2.
Tel 39 78 71 75.

Havanna
Hauptstraße 30.
Tel 784 8565.

Kulturbraueri
Schönhauser Allee 36,
Prenzlaverberg.
Tel 44 35 260.

Wild at Heart
Wiener Stra. 20, Kreuzberg.
Tel 610 74701.

Classical and Modern Dance

Hebbel Am Ufer
Hau Eins: Stresemann-straße 29; Hau Zwei:
Hallesches Ufer 32; Hau Drei: Tempelhofer Ufer 10.
Map 4 B5. **Tel** 259 00 40.

Tanzfabrik
Möckernstraße 68.
Tel 786 58 61.

Nightlife

40seconds
Potsdamer Str. 58.
Tel 89 06 42 41.

Ackerkeller
Bergstraße 68.
Tel 364 61356.

Ballhaus
Auguststraße 24, Mitte.
Tel 282 92 95.

Berghain
Am Wriezener Bahnhof,
Frederichshain.
Tel 364 61356.

Café Moskau
Karl-Marx-Allee.
Tel 24 63 16 26.

Columbia Club
Columbiadamm 9–11,
Kreuzberg.

Delicious Doughnuts
Rosenthaler Straße 9.
Map 5 D1. **Tel** 28 09 92 74.

Far Out
Joachimstalerstraße 15.
Map 2 B5. **Tel** 32 00 07 23.

Felix
Behrenstr. 72.
Map 4 A2.
Tel 301 117 152.

Golgatha
Dudenstraße 48–64.
Tel 785 24 53.

Hoppetosse
Eichenstraße 4.
Tel 533 203 40.

SchwuZ
Mehringdamm 61.
Tel 629 0880.

Sophienclub
Sophienstraße 6.
Tel 282 45 52.

Spindler + Klatt
Köpenicker Str. 16–17.
Map 5 F3.
Tel 319 88 1860.

Tresor
Köpenicker Str. 59–73.
Tel 24 72 49 82.

White Trash
Schönhauser Allee 167.
Tel 50 34 86 68.

Spectator Sports

Galopprennbahn Hoppegarten
Goetheallee 1.
Tel (03342) 389 30.

Olympiastadion
Olympischer Platz.
Tel 306 88 100.

Trabrennbahn
Mariendorfer Damm 222,
Tempelhof.
Tel 740 12 12.

Children's Activities

Berliner Bäderbetriebe
Tel (01803) 10 20 20.

Berliner Grusselkabinett
Schöneberger Straße 23a.
Tel 26 55 55 46.

Circus Cabuwazi
Tel (030) 611 92 75.
W cabuwazi.de

Deutsches Technikmuseum
Trebbiner Straße 9.
Tel 90 25 40.

Eisstadion Berlin Wilmersdorf
Fritz-Wildung-Straße 9.
Tel 824 10 12.

Ethnologisches Museum
Lansstraße 8.
Tel 83 01 438.

FEZ Wuhlheide
An der Wuhlheide 197,
Köpenick. **Tel** 53 07 10.

Kinderbauernhof Görlitzer Bauernhof
Wiener Straße 59b.
Tel 611 74 24.

Museumsdorf Düppel
Clauertstraße 11.
Tel 802 66 71.

Planetarium am Insulaner
Munsterdamm 90.
Tel 790 09 30.

Puppentheater-museum
Karl-Marx-Straße 135.
Tel 687 81 32.

The Story of Berlin
Kurfürstendamm 207–208. **Tel** 88 72 01 00.

Visit Berlin
Tel (030) 25 00 25.
W visitberlin.de

Zeiss-Planetarium
Prenzlauer Allee 80.
Tel 42 18 45 12.

Zoologischer Garten
Hardenbergplatz 9,
Charlottenburg.
Tel 25 40 10.

Theatre and Cinema

Berlin can lay many claims to being a centre for artistic greatness, but possibly its most valid claims lie in the areas of theatre and cinema. Berlin has been the capital of German cinema since brothers Emil and Max Skladanowsky showed a series of short films to a spellbound German public in 1896. By 1918 there were already some 251 cinemas in Berlin and by 1925, the number of people involved in the film industry was nearly 50,000. At the same time, Berlin was fast becoming a landmark in European theatre thanks mainly to Reinhardt and Brecht. During the years of Nazi rule, many theatre people were killed or forced to emigrate as the stage became a propaganda machine, but after World War II a revival spread through Berlin's theatres. The popularity of theatre and cinema continues today, perpetuated by the annual Film Festival.

A Berlin International Film Festival poster from 1960

Ticket and Price Information

Tickets for both cinema and theatre are usually reasonably priced in Berlin, but there are a few tips which are useful to remember if you are planning to visit either.

Students and senior citizens do not always receive a discount at the cinema, but often Tuesday or Wednesday is declared Cinema Day, when some tickets are €1–2 cheaper. It is worth knowing that most ticket offices do not accept credit cards, so take cash.

For theatres, it is usually possible to pre-book tickets at least two weeks before a performance. You can buy them directly from the box office of the theatre, online or by telephone. Independent ticket vendors usually charge a commission of between 15 and 22 per cent.

Hekticket Theaterkassen specializes in last-minute tickets, so check with them on the day for special deals.

Major Stages

The **Deutsches Theater** and its small hall **Kammerspiele** on Schumannstrasse are top-class theatres and offer a varied repertoire of productions. At **Volksbühne** you can see interesting performances of classical plays in modern settings and new plays by young authors.

The **Berliner Ensemble (BE)** was once managed by Bertolt Brecht and Heiner Müller. The spectacles created by these two are still performed today.

Other major venues include the **Maxim Gorki Theater**, the **Renaissance-Theater** and the **Schaubühne**.

Alternative Theatre

There are a number of alternative theatres in Berlin. The three-theatre company **Hebbel am Ufer (HAU)** is devoted to avant-garde theatre and considered the city's best alternative stage. The smaller boulevard theatres like **Theater am Kurfürstendamm** offer different, and somewhat lighter programmes.

Other notable venues include **Bat-Studiotheater** and the **Kleines Theater**.

Musicals, Reviews and Cabarets

There are three main musical theatres in Berlin, in addition to the many small venues which fit musicals into their more general repertoire. **Friedrichstadt-Palast** and **Admiralspalast**, in the eastern part of the city, stage many of the new major shows, while the **Theater des Westens** in Charlottenburg tends to be more traditional. In addition to these is the **Theater am Potsdamer Platz**, a modern theatre that was established in the Potsdamer Platz in 1999 and shows contemporary musical hits.

As for cabaret, there are probably as many acts in Berlin today as there were in the 1920s. **Distel**, in Friedrichstrasse, continues its success from GDR times, and **Die Stachelschweine** celebrates its popularity in western Berlin.

Other great venues for lively musicals, reviews and cabarets include **Bar jeder Vernunft**, **Chamäleon Variété**, **Scheinbar**, **Wintergarten Variété** and **Wühlmäuse**.

Big Screens and Big Films

After the fall of the Berlin Wall, many multiplex cinemas

The retro façade of Friedrichstadtpalast in the east of Berlin

were built, the biggest being the **CinemaxX Potsdamer Platz** and the **Cinestar Sony Center**, which show films in the original language. In most cinemas, mainstream Anglo-American movies tend to be dubbed rather than subtitled.

For a breathtaking experience, try the **IMAX** at the Sony Centre, with its huge 3-D screen.

Studio Cinema

For those who like their movies a little less mainstream, there are plenty of small studio cinemas scattered across town that show a large number of recently released independent films. **Hackesche Höfe Kino** or **Central**, situated near Hackescher Markt, offer a pleasant break from city life and have bars of their own.

The **Arsenal**, on Potsdamer Platz, shows German film classics; if you are interested in original language films, Berlin has various options. **Cinéma Paris** in Charlottenburg is the place to go for French films, while the **Odeon** in Schöneberg specializes in English and American films.

Open-Air Cinema

Open-air cinemas start operating as soon as the weather allows. The biggest is **Waldbühne** – a concert hall that seats an audience of 20,000. Others can be found in Hasenheide, Künstler Haus Bethanien garden in Friedrichshain or at Potsdamer Platz. The films shown are a mixture of new releases and old classics, and showings tend to start at around 9pm.

DIRECTORY

Ticket and Price Information

Hekticket Theaterkassen
Hardenbergstraße 29d.
Map 2 B4.
Tel 230 99 30.
W hekticket.de

Major Stages

Berliner Ensemble (BE)
Bertolt-Brecht-Platz 1.
Map 1 F3.
Tel 28 408 155.
W berliner-ensemble.de

Deutsches Theater
Schumannstraße 13.
Map 1 F3.
Tel 28 44 12 25.
W deutschestheater.de

Kammerspiele
Schumannstraße 13a.
Map 1 F3.
Tel 28 44 12 22.
W deutschestheater.de

Maxim Gorki Theater
Am Festungsgraben 2.
Map 4 C2.
Tel 20 22 11 29.
W gorki.de

Renaissance-Theater
Hardenbergstraße 6.
Map 2 A3.
Tel 312 42 02.
W renaissance-theater.de

Schaubühne
Kurfürstendamm 153.
Tel 89 00 20.
W schaubuehne.de

Volksbühne
Rosa-Luxembourg-Platz.
Tel 240 655.

Alternative Theatre

Bat-Studiotheater
Belforter Straße 15.
Tel 755 41 7777.
W bat-berlin.de

Kleines Theater
Südwestkorso 64.
Tel 821 20 21.
W kleines-theater-de

Hebbel am Ufer (HAU)
Hallesches Ufer 32.
Tel 25 90 04 27.

Theater am Kurfürstendamm
Kurfürstendamm 206.
Map 2 A5.
Tel 88 59 11 88.

Musicals, Reviews and Cabarets

Admiralspalast
Friedrichstrasse 101.
Map 4 C1.
Tel 47 99 74 99.
W admiralspalast.de

Bar jeder Vernunft
Schaperstraße 24.
Map 2 B5.
Tel 883 15 82.

Chamäleon Varieté
Rosenthaler Straße 40–41.
Map 5 D4.
Tel 4000 590.
W chamaeleon berlin.de

Die Stachelschweine
Europa-Center.
Map 2 C4.
Tel 261 47 95.
W die-stachel schweine.de

Distel
Friedrichstraße 101.
Map 1 F3.
Tel 204 47 04.

Friedrichstadt-Palast
Friedrichstraße 107.
Map 1 F3.
Tel 23 26 23 26.
W friedrichstadt palast.de

Scheinbar
Monumentenstraße 9.
Tel 784 55 39.

Theater am Potsdamer Platz
Marlene-Dietrich-Platz 1.
Map 4 A3.
Tel 259 244 555.
W stage-entertainment.de

Theater des Westens
Kantstraße 12.
Tel 259 244 555.
W stage-entertainment.de

Wintergarten Varieté
Potsdamer Straße 96.
Map 3 F4.
Tel 25 00 88 88.
W wintergarten-variete.de

Wühlmäuse
Pommernallee 2–4.
Tel 306 73011.
W wuehlmaeuse.de

Big Screens and Big Films

CinemaxX Potsdamer Platz
Potsdamer Straße 1–19.
Map 4 A3.
Tel (0180) 524 63 62 99.
W cinemaxx.de

Cinestar Sony Center & Imax
Potsdamer Straße 4.
Map 4 A3.
Tel 01805 118811.

Studio Cinema

Arsenal
Potsdamer Straße 2.
Map 4 A3.
Tel 26 95 51 00.

Central
Rosenthaler Straße 39.
Map 5 D1.
Tel 28 59 99 73.

Cinéma Paris
Kurfürstendamm 211.
Tel 881 31 19.

Hackescher Höfe Kino
Rosenthaler Straße 40–41.
Map 5 D1.
Tel 283 46 03.

Odeon
Hauptstraße 115.
Tel 78 70 40 19.

Open-Air Cinema

Waldbühne
Glockenturmstraße 1.
Tel 74 73 75 00.

BERLIN STREET FINDER

Map references given for historic buildings, hotels, restaurants, bars, shops and entertainment venues refer to the maps included in this section of the guidebook. The key map below shows the area of Berlin covered by the Street Finder. The maps include all major sightseeing areas, historic attractions, railway stations, bus stations, U-Bahn stations and the suburban stations of the S-Bahn. The names of the streets and squares in the index and maps are given in German. The word Straße (or STRASSE, Str) indicates a street, Allee an avenue, Platz a square, Brücke a bridge and Bahnhofa railway station.

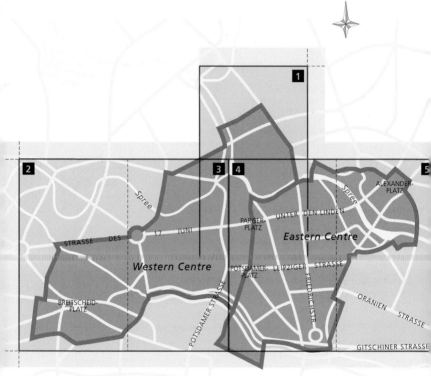

Key

Major sight

Place of interest

Other building

Ⓢ S-Bahn station

Ⓤ U-Bahn station

🚉 Railway station

🚌 Bus sttion

🚊 Tram stop

✚ Hospital with emergency dept.

🏤 Police station

ℹ Tourist information

✝ Church

✡ Synagogue

Railway line

Pedestrian-only street

0 km ——————— 1
0 miles ——————— 1

Scale of Maps 1–5

0 metres ——————— 250
0 yards ——————— 250   1:15 000

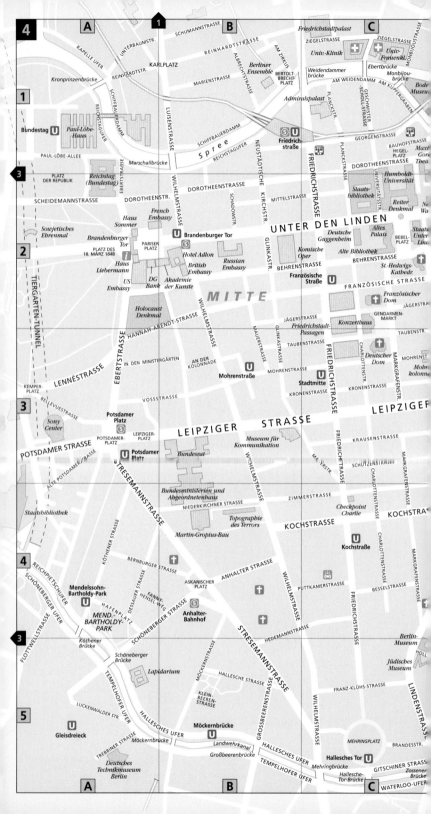

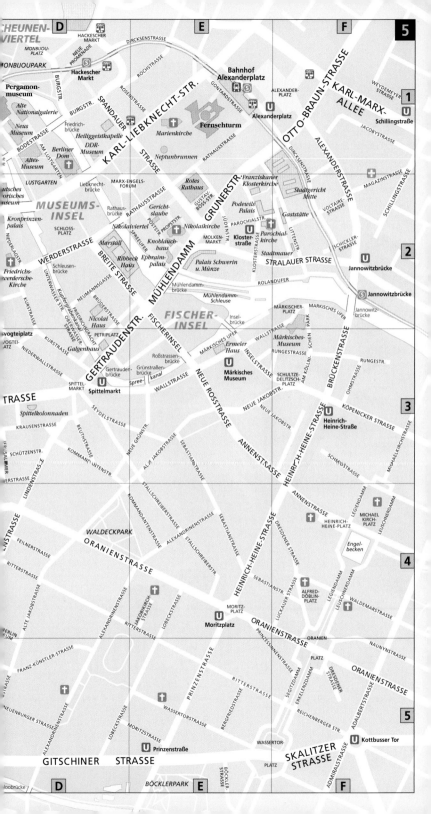

EASTERN GERMANY

Introducing Eastern
  Germany   126–131
Brandenburg   132–145
Saxony-Anhalt   146–161
Saxony   162–183
Thuringia   186–201

Eastern Germany at a Glance

The eastern region of Germany is immensely rich in tourist attractions. The imposing valley of the Elbe River, the beautiful lake district of Lower Brandenburg, attractive trails in the Harz Mountains of Saxony-Anhalt, the Thuringian Forest as well as the Erzgebirge and the Lusatian Mountains in Saxony all invite the visitor with their dramatic scenery and excellent recreational facilities.

Eastern Germany is rich in historic sights, too, ranging from the Baroque residences of Potsdam in Brandenburg to the grand architecture of Dresden and Leipzig in Saxony and the important cultural centre of Weimar in Thuringia. The most rewarding destinations in the region are featured here.

The Magdeburg Reiter, in the market square, is the copy of one of Thuringia's most famous sights. The identity of the rider is not certain.

Naumburg Dom is a huge, well preserved Gothic cathedral *(see pp154–5)*, one of Germany's greatest buildings. Splendid statues of its founders, Ekkehart and Uta, adorn the walls of the presbytery.

Erfurt Dom dominates the townscape. A massive Gothic structure, the cathedral's three towers were built on the Romanesque foundations of an earlier church.

Pritzw

Witte

Ster

Magde

Schö

Halberstadt

SAXONY-ANHALT
(See pp146–61)

Nordhausen

Halle

Mühlhausen

Naumburg

Eisenach

Weimar

Gotha

Erfurt

Jena

G

THURINGIA
(See pp184–201)

Suhl

Saalfeld

Weimar, with its picturesque market square *(see pp198–9)* and historic buildings, was an important cultural centre for many centuries. Friedrich Schiller, Johann Wolfgang von Goethe and Johann Sebastian Bach all lived here.

◀ A statue of Greek goddess Minerva in front of the main façade of Schloss Sanssouci

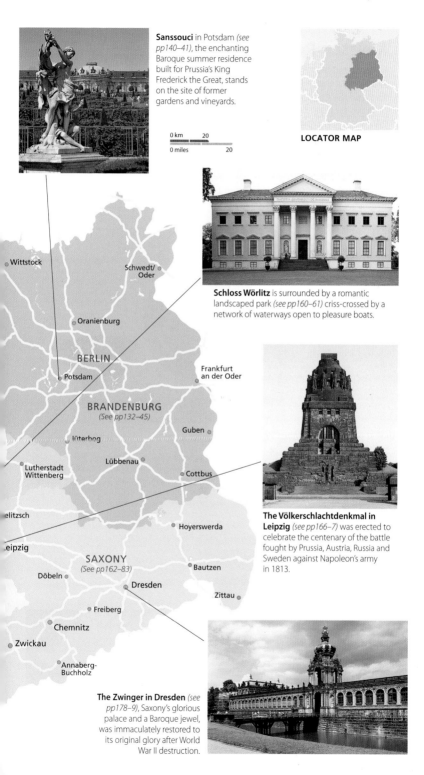

Sanssouci in Potsdam *(see pp140–41)*, the enchanting Baroque summer residence built for Prussia's King Frederick the Great, stands on the site of former gardens and vineyards.

0 km 20
0 miles 20

LOCATOR MAP

Schloss Wörlitz is surrounded by a romantic landscaped park *(see pp160–61)* criss-crossed by a network of waterways open to pleasure boats.

Wittstock

Schwedt/ Oder

Oranienburg

BERLIN

Potsdam

Frankfurt an der Oder

BRANDENBURG
(See pp132–45)

Jüterbog

Guben

Lübbenau

Lutherstadt Wittenberg

Cottbus

elitzsch

Hoyerswerda

eipzig

SAXONY
(See pp162–83)

Döbeln

Bautzen

Dresden

Zittau

Freiberg

Chemnitz

Zwickau

Annaberg-Buchholz

The Völkerschlachtdenkmal in Leipzig *(see pp166–7)* was erected to celebrate the centenary of the battle fought by Prussia, Austria, Russia and Sweden against Napoleon's army in 1813.

The Zwinger in Dresden *(see pp178–9)*, Saxony's glorious palace and a Baroque jewel, was immaculately restored to its original glory after World War II destruction.

Meissen Porcelain

Until the early 18th century the only porcelain known in Europe was that imported from the Far East, and the Chinese jealously guarded the secrets of its production. Finally, in 1707, Johann Friedrich Böttger and Ehrenfried Walther von Tschirnhaus succeeded in developing a recipe that made it possible to produce genuine porcelain. A factory was set up in Meissen, and from 1713 it began to export its products to the entire European continent. Its first famous designers were Johann Joachim Kändler and Johann Gregor Höroldt.

The Porcelain Museum, opened in 1906, holds exhibitions and demonstrations illustrating the various stages in the manufacture of porcelain. The museum also runs courses on porcelain-making.

Böttger Stoneware

Johann Friedrich Böttger's first success in recreating Chinese ceramics came in 1707 when, with the assistance of Ehrenfried Walther von Tschirnhaus, he managed to produce stoneware almost identical to that produced in Yi Hsing. The stoneware was dark, varying in colour from red to brown.

These plates and bowls are typical examples of Böttger stoneware; its plain and simple lines were modelled on Far-Eastern designs.

The dark colour of the dishes is due to the use of red clays.

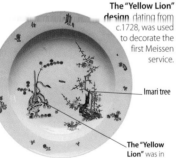

The **"Yellow Lion" design**, dating from c.1728, was used to decorate the first Meissen service.

Imari tree

The "Yellow Lion" was in reality a tiger.

Far-Eastern Motifs

Until the 17th century the only porcelain known in Europe came from the Far East, and the first items made from Saxon hard porcelain were initially strongly influenced by the Asian products. In Meissen, Chinese figurines and dishes were copied, adapting "European" shapes, but using Japanese or Chinese motifs for decoration. Special designs were created to adorn the services intended for the royal court. The oldest among these include the "Yellow Lion" and the "Red Dragon". New designs, inspired by European art, began to appear after 1738, and gradually replaced the Asian patterns.

Production Process

The process of porcelain production has not changed significantly over the centuries. The formula for "hard-paste" porcelain contains kaolin, quartz and feldspar. Each product is dried and fired, with glazed products being fired twice. The decoration can be applied before or after the glazing process. Hand-painted and gilded items are the most expensive.

Demonstration of the intricate art of hand-painting porcelain at the Meissen factory

Tableware

In the second half of the 18th and in the 19th centuries, porcelain manufacturers developed their own designs. This proved so popular that some remain in production to this day. The best-known Meißen designs are the "vine-leaves" and the "onion" patterns, first introduced in the 18th century. Customers can thus still replace items in the services that have graced their family tables for generations.

This coffee pot and cup is decorated with the cobalt "onion" pattern, depicting stylized pomegranate fruits.

Fine-Art Motifs

A new type of decoration, which became popular in the second half of the 18th century, involved the accurate copying of famous paintings or etchings onto a vase, a pot or a plate. This type of decoration proved particularly popular during the Classicist period.

Decorator copying an etching onto a vessel

Vase decorated with a miniature of a painting by Antoine Watteau

Services and Figurines

Several outstanding sculptors and painters were employed in the Meißsen porcelain manufacture to design unique services and figurines for the royal courts. The most famous among them are the services designed by Johann Joachim Kändler. He also created sets of figurines to adorn dining tables, vases and censers (containers for burning incense) for decorating the home, and large religious compositions for churches.

"Swan" Service Tureen

Figurine of August III

Europa, a figure from the "Four Continents" series, designed by J. J. Kändler

Marks on Meissen Porcelain

All porcelain manufacturers mark their products with their own symbols. The symbols are generally applied under the glaze, at the bottom of the piece. The Meissen factory initially used marks that imitated Japanese or Chinese writing; later, for a short time, letters were used, and from 1724 blue trademarks in the shape of crossed swords became the standard mark. The last three symbols below identify the respective court for which each piece of porcelain was produced.

K.P.F.

Königliche Porzellan-Fabrik, trademark used in 1723

K.P.M.

Königliche Porzellan-Manufaktur, trademark used in 1723–4

Trademarks used from 1724

Augustus Rex, the initials of King August

K.H.K

Königliche Hof-Küche

K.H.C.W.

Königliche Hof-Conditorei Warschau

Luther and the Reformation

In 1517, on the eve of All Souls' Day (31 October), Martin Luther nailed his 95 "theses" to the doors of the castle church in Wittenberg, condemning the practice of indulgences. His subsequent pronouncements, in which he criticized many aspects of the Church's teaching, made him the "father" of the Reformation movement in Germany and other countries. Luther's teaching gained the support of many of the princes, who in 1531 formed the Schmalkalden Union and started to introduce a new administration to the Church. This led to religious wars which finally ended with the Augsburg Peace Treaty, signed in 1555, which confirmed the religious division of Germany.

The Bible, translated into German by Luther, was first published in one volume in 1534. One year later an illustrated, two-volume luxury version was published in Augsburg.

The baptism of a child is performed by Philipp Melanchthon.

The Schlosskapelle in Hartenfels Castle, in Torgau (see p168), was built in 1543–4 and consecrated by Martin Luther. It is generally considered to be the first church built specifically for the Lutheran community.

The Last Supper, at the centre of the altar, stresses the importance attached by Lutherans to the sacrament of communion. The figures of the Apostles are portraits of the main church reformers.

This group of faithful, listening to the sermon, includes members of Luther's family.

Martin Luther, the great theologian and religious reformer, initiator of Church reform and founder of Lutheranism, is depicted in this portrait by Lucas Cranach the Elder (1520).

Luther's Room (Lutherstube), shown here, is part of Luther's House in Wittenberg *(see p158)*. The famous reformer lived here with his wife and family.

Philipp Melanchthon, an associate of Luther's and the co-founder of Lutheranism, initiated a great educational reform. He was also known as *praeceptor Germaniae*, Germany's teacher.

Reformation Altar

The main altar of St Mary's Church in Wittenberg (see pp158–9) is one of the most important works of art of the Reformation period. The central picture was painted by Lucas Cranach the Elder (c.1539), the wings by his son, Lucas Cranach the Younger, before 1547.

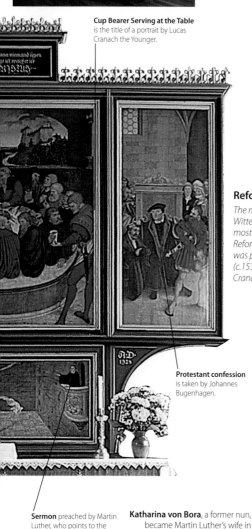

Cup Bearer Serving at the Table is the title of a portrait by Lucas Cranach the Younger.

Protestant confession is taken by Johannes Bugenhagen.

Sermon preached by Martin Luther, who points to the figure of the crucified Christ.

Katharina von Bora, a former nun, became Martin Luther's wife in 1525. She lies buried in the Marienkirche in Torgau *(see p168)*, in a tomb which survives to this day.

BRANDENBURG

The province of Brandenburg is a lowland region criss-crossed by a dense network of rivers, canals and lakes. Quiet in part, it is also crossed by some of the main tourist routes to Berlin. Its most popular attractions are the historic sights of its capital city, Potsdam, and the Spreewald, where all day can be spent boating on the waterways of the Lusatian forests and villages.

In early medieval times, the area that was to become present-day Brandenburg was the scene of violent conflict between various Germanic tribes. The latter conquered the region, and in 1157 created the margravate of Brandenburg. Its first ruler was Albrecht der Bär (Albert the Bear), from the house of Ascan. From 1415, Brandenburg was ruled by the Hohenzollern dynasty. It was quick to embrace the Reformation, which was officially adopted here as early as 1538. In 1618, Brandenburg merged with the duchy of Prussia through personal union. The region became entangled in the Thirty Years' War and suffered devastating losses; depopulated and plundered, it took Brandenburg many years to rise from the ashes. In 1701, the Great Elector, Frederick III, crowned himself King Frederick I, and the whole region now assumed the name of Prussia.

While Berlin remained the seat of power and a strong industrial and cultural centre, 18th-century Potsdam also played an important role: it was, after all, the favourite haunt of Frederick the Great. Other towns in the region were less significant – Brandenburg was, and still is, a fairly rural region. Reunification in 1990, however, has opened up the newly created land to Berliners and tourists alike.

Travellers in Brandenburg will encounter ancient tree-lined avenues that stretch to the horizon. The Spreewald, Brandenburg's lake district, is an oasis of tranquillity, ideal for boating and cycling. Brandenburg also has grand castles in Oranienburg, Branitz just outside Cottbus and Rheinsberg, Gothic churches and monasteries in Lehnin and Chorin and the towns of Brandenburg/Havel and Potsdam.

Baroque palace in Rheinsberg, on the shores of the Grienericksee

◄ Sculptures and statues outside the Neues Palais, Potsdam

Exploring Brandenburg

Brandenburg is ideally suited for gentle exploration by
bicycle or car, and its proximity to Berlin allows the visitor
to make a one-day excursion to the capital. A whole day
should be allocated for visiting Potsdam and the castle of
Sanssouci, and another day for a boat trip in the
Spreewald. A visit to Cottbus can be
combined with an excursion to
Frankfurt an der Oder. The best
time for a visit to Chorin is
the summer when
concerts are held there
in the ruined
monastery.

Cecilienhof, the summer residence of the Hohenzollern
family in Potsdam

Schloss Branitz in Cottbus

For additional map symbols *see back flap*

Key

▬▬ Motorway

▬▬ Major road

▬▬ Minor road

▬▬ Main railway

▬▬ Minor railway

▬▬ International border

▬▬ Regional border

Tourist boats on the Spreewald canals, near Lehde

Getting Around

There are many flights to Berlin. Brandenburg has an extensive network of motorways – the circular Berliner Ring joins with the motorways A11 from Stettin, A24 from Hamburg, Schwerin and Rostock, A2 from Hanover, A9 from Munich and Nuremberg, A12 from Frankfurt an der Oder and A13 from Cottbus and Dresden. Local roads and country lanes in Brandenburg are often narrow and twisting. The outskirts of Berlin are well served by the local train network, which provides frequent links with many small towns. There are also numerous local bus services.

0 kilometres 20
0 miles 20

Sights at a Glance

1 Elbtalaue
2 Wittstock
3 Neuruppin
4 Oranienburg
5 Brandenburg/Havel
6 Lehnin
7 *Potsdam pp138–43*
8 Chorin
9 Frankfurt an der Oder
10 Cottbus
11 Spreewald
12 Jüterbog

For hotels and restaurants in this area see pp492–503 and pp510–33

❶ Elbtalaue

Road map D2. 🚉 to Wittenberge or Bad Wilsnack. 🛈 Am Markt 5, Bad Wilsnack (038791-26 20). 🌐 **bad-wilsnack.de**

The Elbe valley in the western part of Prignitz is an area of gentle rolling hills and unspoiled nature. Storks, increasingly rare in Germany, still nest here. When travelling around this parkland it is worth stopping at **Pritzwalk** to admire the late-Gothic Nikolaikirche (St Nicholas church). Another place of interest is **Perleberg** with its picturesque market square featuring an original 1515 timber-frame building, a sandstone statue of the knight Roland (1546), now standing by the 1850 Town Hall, and the town's star attraction – the 15th-century Gothic Jakobskirche (church of St Jacob).

Bad Wilsnack owes its fame to the discovery of the therapeutic properties of the iron oxide-rich mud found in the surrounding marshes. Already known in medieval times, the town was an important place of pilgrimage. After a church fire, in 1384, three hosts displaying the blood of Christ were found untouched on the altar. The Gothic **Nikolaikirche** (church of St Nicholas), which survives to this day, was built soon after for the pilgrims.

Plattenburg Castle, in a scenic situation on an island, is also worth a visit. Combining late-Gothic and Renaissance architecture, it is used as a venue for concerts.

Chapel of the Holy Sepulchre in Heiligengrabe, near Wittstock

❷ Wittstock

Road map E2. 🚹 13,700. 🚌 🛈 Walter-Shulz-Pl. 1, Wittstock/Dosse (03394-43 34 42). 🌐 **wittstock.de**

The small town of Wittstock was first awarded its municipal status in 1284. From the 13th century to the Reformation, Wittstock was the see of the Havelberg bishops. Although much of the town was destroyed, the original city walls remained almost completely intact, with one surviving gate – the **Gröper Tor**. All that remains of the former bishop's castle is the gate tower, which now houses a small museum. The town's star attraction is the Gothic **Marienkirche** with its late-Gothic reredos depicting the crowning of St Mary. It originated in the wood carving workshop of Claus Berg, probably after 1532. Other interesting features include the 1516 sacrarium and the late-Renaissance pulpit.

Environs
Ten km (6 miles) to the west lies **Heiligengrabe**, with its Gothic Cistercian Abbey. One of its many highlights is the 1512

Chapel of the Holy Sepulchre with an intricately sculpted gable and some charming timber-frame cloister buildings.

❸ Neuruppin

Road map E2. 🚹 27,300. 🚌 🛈 Karl-Marx-Str. 1 (03391-454 60). 🌐 **neuruppin.de.**

The town of Neuruppin, in a scenic location on the shores of a large lake, the Ruppiner See, is mainly Neo-Classical in style, having been rebuilt to the design of Bernhard Matthias Brasch after the great fire of 1787. The only older buildings are the Gothic post-Dominican church and two small hospital chapels. Neuruppin is the birthplace of the architect **Karl Friedrich Schinkel** and the novelist **Theodor Fontane** (see p31).

Environs
The beautifully restored palace of **Rheinsberg**, 25 km (16 miles) to the north, was converted from 16th-century Renaissance castle in 1734–7. In 1734–40 it was the residence of the Crown Prince, who later became Frederick the Great, King of Prussia. Some 30 km (19 miles) northeast of Rheinsberg is the site of the former National Socialist concentration camp **Ravensbrück**, for women and children. It is now a place of remembrance.

Schinkel monument

❹ Oranienburg

Road map E3. 🚹 30,000. 🚉 🚌 🛈 Bernauer Str. 52 (033 01-70 48 33). 🌐 **tourismus-or.de**

The star attraction of the town is **Schloss Oranienburg,** the Baroque residence built for Louisa Henrietta von Nassau-Oranien, wife of the Great Elector Friedrich Wilhelm.

The Gothic-Renaissance Plattenburg Castle, in the Elbtalaue

Designed by Johann Gregor Memhardt and Michael Matthias Smids, it was built in 1651–5 and later extended to reach its present H-shape.

🏛 Schloss Oranienburg
Schlossplatz 1. **Tel** (03301) 53 74 37.
Open Apr–Oct: 10am–6pm Tue–Sun;
Nov–Mar: 10am–5pm Sat & Sun.

Environs
Sachsenhausen, which is located northeast of Oranienburg, is now a place of remembrance and a museum. Opened in 1936 by the National Socialists, this concentration camp claimed the lives of 100,000 inmates.

🏛 Sachsenhausen
Tel (03301) 20 00. **Open** mid-Mar–mid-Oct: 8:30am–6pm daily; mid-Oct–mid-Mar: 8:30am–4:30pm daily.
W gedenkstaette-sachsenhausen.de

❺ Brandenburg/ Havel

Road map E3. 🗺 87,700. 🚉 🚌
🅸 Neustädtischer Markt 3 (03381-796 360). 🎭 Havelfestspiele (Jun).
W stadt-brandenburg.de

Brandenburg is the oldest town of the region. It was settled by Slavs as early as the 6th century, and a mission episcopate was established here in 948. Scenically sited on the Havel River, it has preserved historic centres on three islands, despite wartime destruction. The oldest island is the **Dominsel**, with its

Baroque palace in Caputh, north of Lehnin

Romanesque **Dom St Peter und St Paul**. This cathedral was constructed from 1165 to the mid-13th century. In the 14th century it was raised and given new vaultings. It contains numerous valuable Gothic objects, including the **"Czech" altar** (c.1375), the present main altar (from Lehnin, 1518) and the sacrarium of the same year. The most valuable treasures are on display in the **Dommuseum**.

Other sights worth visiting are the huge, 15th-century **Katharinenkirche** built by Hinrich Brunsberg, the **Gotthardkirche**, in the Altstadt ("old town"), with its Romanesque façade and Gothic interior, the Gothic Rathaus (Town Hall), with a statue of Roland from 1474, and the **Stadtmuseum**, a museum of local history.

🏛 Dommuseum
Burghof 10. **Tel** (03381) 211 2221.
Open 10am–5pm daily, 12:30–5pm Sun. 🅿 **W** brandenburg-dom.de

🏛 Stadtmuseum
Ritterstr. 96. **Tel** (03381) 58 45 01.
Open 9am–5pm Tue–Fri, 10am–5pm Sat & Sun. 🅿

❻ Lehnin

Road map E3. 🗺 3,100. 🚌
🅸 Markgrafenplatz (03382 704 480).

Visitors mainly come to see the huge Klosterkirche (abbey) founded for the Cistercian order of Otto I, son of Albert the Bear. The church was built from the late 12th to the late 13th century, originally in Romanesque, then in early-Gothic style. Following the dissolution of the monastery, in 1542, the buildings fell into disrepair, but much of the abbey has survived.

🏛 Klosterkirche
Klosterkirchplatz. **Tel** (03382) 76 80 10.
Open Apr–Oct: 10am–4pm Mon–Fri, 10am–5pm Sat, 1–5pm Sun; Nov–Mar: 10:30am–3:30pm Mon–Sat, 1–4pm Sun. **W** klosterkirche-lehnin.de

Environs
Caputh, situated 23 km (14 miles) to the north, has an early-Baroque **Palace** built during the second half of the 17th century, as summer residence for the wives of the Great Electors. The interior has many original features.

The Gothic "Czech" altar in the Dom St Peter und St Paul in Brandenburg

❼ Potsdam

An independent city close to Berlin, Potsdam, with over 150,000 inhabitants, is also the capital of Brandenburg. The first documented reference to Potsdam dates back to AD 993; it was later granted municipal rights in 1317. The town blossomed during the times of the Great Electors and then again in the 18th century. Potsdam suffered very badly during World War II, particularly on the night of 14–15 April 1945 when Allied planes bombed the town centre.

A sculpture on display in Park Sanssouci

Sightseeing in Potsdam

Potsdam remains one of Germany's most attractive towns. Tourists flock to see the magnificent royal summer residence, Schloss Sanssouci, to stroll around Neuer Garten (new garden) with its Marmorpalais (marble palace) and Cecilienhof, to visit the old city centre and the Russian colony of Alexandrowka, to be entertained in the film studios of Babelsberg and to take a walk around the parks of Schloss Babelsberg.

✚ Cecilienhof

Am Neuen Garten (Neuer Garten). **Tel** (0331) 969 42 44. 🚌 695. **Open** Apr–Oct: 10am–6pm Tue–Sun; Nov–Mar: 10am–5pm Tue–Sun.

The Cecilienhof residence played a brief but important role in history, when it served as the venue for the 1945 Potsdam Conference (see p143). Built between 1913 and 1917, the palace is the most recent of all Hohenzollern dynasty buildings. Designed by Paul Schultze-Naumburg in the style of an English country manor, Cecilienhof is a sprawling, asymmetrical, timber-frame building with inner courtyards and irregular breaks.

The palace remained a residence of the Hohenzollern family after they had lost the crown – the family stayed in Potsdam until February 1945. Today the palace is a hotel, where visitors interested in history are

able to relax amid green shrubs. The large, scenic park remains open to the public even when the rooms used during the Potsdam Conference are closed to visitors.

✚ Marmorpalais

Am Neuen Garten (Neuer Garten). **Tel** (0331) 969 42 46. 🚌 695. **Open** Apr: 10am–6pm Sat & Sun; May–Oct: 10am–6pm Tue–Sun.

This small palace, situated on the edge of the lake, is a beautiful example of early Neo-Classical architecture. The palace is named after the Silesian marble used on its façade. The main part of it was built between 1787 and 1791 by Carl von Gontard to a design and under the direction of Carl Gotthard Langhans, on the initiative of King Friedrich Wilhelm II.

🚊 Alexandrowka

Russische Kolonie Allee/Puschkinallee. 🚋 92, 95. 🚌 603, 609, 638, 639.

A visit to Alexandrowka takes the visitor into the world of Pushkin's fairy tales. Wooden log cabins with intricate carvings, set in their own gardens, create a charming residential estate. They were constructed in 1826 under the direction of the German architect Snethlage, for 12 singers of a Russian choir that was established in 1812.

🚊 Holländisches Viertel

Friedrich-Ebert-Str, Kurfürstenstr., Hebbelstr., Gutenbergstr. 🚌 138, 601–604, 606–612. 🚋 92, 95.

Just as amazing as the Russian colony of Alexandrowka is the Holländisches Viertel (Dutch quarter), part of a Baroque town built in the middle of Germany.

A view of the Baroque Dutch district known as Holländisches Viertel

Dutch workers arrived in Potsdam in the early 18th century and, between 1733 and 1742, a settlement was built for them on the orders of Friedrich Wilhelm I to plans by Johann Boumann the Elder. It comprised 134 gabled houses arranged in four groups. The houses were built from small red bricks and finished with stone and plaster details.

Nikolaikirche

Alter Markt. **Tel** (0331) 270 86 02. 601, 603, 692, 694, 91, 92, 95, 96, 99. **Open** Apr–Oct: 9am–7pm daily; Nov–Mar: 9am–5pm daily.

This imposing church built in the late Neo-Classical style, is

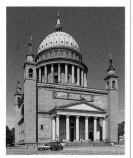

The Nikolaikirche, with its dome resting on a colonnaded wall

indisputably the most beautiful church in Potsdam. It was built on the site of an earlier, Baroque church, which burned down in 1795. It was designed during 1828–30 by Karl Friedrich Schinkel and the building work was supervised by Ludwig Persius. The interior decoration and furnishings of the church date from the 1850s, but were mostly based on the earlier designs by Schinkel.

Marstall

Breitestr. 1a. **Tel** (0331) 271 81 12. 601, 603, 692, 694. 91, 92, 93, 95, 96, 98. **Open** 10am–6pm daily.

This long Baroque pavilion, once used as royal stables, is the only remaining building of a royal residence. It was constructed in 1714 and currently houses a film museum devoted to the history and work of the nearby Babelsberg Film Studio.

Bildergalerie

Zur Historischen Mühle. **Tel** (0331) 969 41 81. 612, 614, 695. **Open** 15 May– 15 Oct: 10am–5pm Tue–Sun.

Baroque paintings once owned by Frederick the Great, including Caravaggio's *Doubting Thomas*, Guido Reni's *Cleopatra's Death*,

as well as paintings by Rubens and van Dyck, are on show in the picture gallery situated next to Schloss Sanssouci.

Caravaggio's *Doubting Thomas*, on show in the Bildergalerie

Potsdam

① Cecilienhof
② Marmorpalais
③ Alexandrowka
④ Holländisches Viertel
⑤ Nikolaikirche
⑥ Marstall
⑦ Bildergalerie
⑧ Park Sanssouci

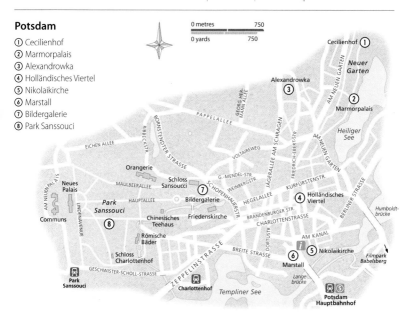

For additional map symbols *see back flap*

Park Sanssouci

The enormous Park Sanssouci, which occupies an area of 287 hectares (700 acres), is one of the most beautiful palace complexes in Europe. The first building to be constructed on the site was Schloss Sanssouci, built as the summer palace of Frederick the Great. It was erected in 1747, on the site of a former orchard. Over the years, Park Sanssouci was expanded considerably and other palaces and pavilions added. To enjoy the park fully, allow at least a whole day.

★ Neues Palais
Constructed between 1763 and 1769, the monumental building of the Neues Palais is crowned by a massive dome.

Römische Bäder
Shaded by pergolas overgrown with greenery, the Roman baths include a Renaissance-style villa.

KEY

① **Communs**, situated next to a pretty courtyard, has an unusually elegant character. It is now used to house palace staff.

② **Orangerie** is a large Neo-Renaissance palace. It was built in the mid-19th century to house foreign royalty and other guests.

③ **Bildergalerie**, built between 1755 and 1764, is Germany's oldest purpose-built museum building. The Baroque pavilion houses an art gallery.

Schloss Charlottenhof
This Neo-Classical palace gained its name from Charlotte von Gentzkow, the former owner of the land on which the palace was built.

Lustgarten
The extensive parkland is made up of several gardens. The Lustgarten (pleasure garden) is nearest to the Orangerie.

VISITORS' CHECKLIST

Practical Information
Historic Windmill, An Der Orangerie 1 & New Palace, Am Neuen Palais 3. **Tel** (0331) 969 42 00. **Open** 8:30am–6pm Tue–Sun (Nov–Mar: to 5pm). (free access to park). **spsg.de**

Transport
606, 695.

Neue Kammern
Once the orangerie of the Sanssouci Palace, this Rococo pavilion was later rebuilt as a guest house.

★ Schloss Sanssouci
A beautifully terraced vineyard creates a grand approach to Schloss Sanssouci, the oldest building in the complex.

Friedenskirche
The Neo-Romanesque Church of Peace is modelled on the Basilica of San Clemente in Rome.

Chinesisches Teehaus
An exhibition of exquisite Oriental porcelain is housed in the small, Rococo-style Chinese Tea House.

0 metres 200
0 yards 200

Paintings in the music room, in Schloss Sanssouci

🏛 Schloss Sanssouci

Zur Historischen Mühle. **Tel** (0331)
969 40. **Open** Apr–Oct: 10am–6pm
Tue–Sun; Nov–Mar: 10am–5pm Tue–
Sun. Damenflügel: **Open** May–Oct:
10am–6pm Sat & Sun. Schlossküche:
Open Apr–Oct: 10am–6pm
Tue–Sun. 🧺

This Rococo palace was built in
1745–7 by Georg Wenzeslaus
von Knobelsdorff to sketches by
Frederick the Great. Knobelsdorff
and Johann August Nahl
designed the interior. *Sanssouci*
("carefree") was the perfect
name for the enchanting castle.
The Damenflügel, the castle's
west wing which was added in
1840 to house ladies and
gentlemen of the court, and the
Schlossküche (castle kitchen)
can also be visited.

🏛 Schloss Neue Kammern

Zur Historischen Mühle (Lustgarten).
Tel (0331) 969 42 06. **Open** Apr: 10am–
6pm Wed–Mon; May–Oct: 10am–6pm
Tue–Sun. 🎧 obligatory. 🧺

The Neue Kammern (new
chambers) adjoin Schloss
Sanssouci in the west, like the
Bildergalerie in the east. As part
of this ensemble it was originally
built in 1747 as an orangery, to a
design by Georg Wenzeslaus
von Knobelsdorff who gave it its
elegant Baroque forms. The
building has an attractive roof
with sloping ends and sides. In
1777 Frederick the Great ordered
the building to be transformed
into guest accommodation. The
architect, Georg Christian Unger,
left the exterior of the orangery
largely untouched but converted
the interior into sumptuous

suites and four elegant halls.
The Rococo décor has been
maintained, similar to that of
other palaces and pavilions
of Sanssouci.

🏛 Orangerieschloss

Maulbeerallee. (Nordischer Garten).
Tel (0331) 969 42 80. **Open** Apr:
10am–6pm Sat & Sun; May–Oct:
10am–6pm Tue–Sun. Viewing terrace:
Open Apr–May: 10am–5pm Sat &
Sun; late May–Oct: 10am–5pm
Tue–Sun.

Above the park towers the
Orangerie, designed in Italian
Renaissance style and crowned
by a colonnade. It
was built to house
guests, not
plants, and
served as
guest
residence for
Tsar Nicolas and his wife,
King Friedrich Wilhelm
IV's sister. The
Orangerie was
constructed in
1852–60 for the king
by Friedrich August
Stüler, with the final
design partly based on plans
by Ludwig Persius. Modelled on
the Regia Hall in the Vatican,
the rooms were grouped
around the Raphael Hall and
decorated with replicas of this
great Italian master's works.
The observation terrace offers
a good view over Potsdam.

🏛 Chinesisches Teehaus

Ökonomieweg (Rehgarten). **Tel** (0331)
969 42 22. **Open** 15 May–15 Oct:
10am–5pm Tue–Sun.

Figure on the roof of
Chinesisches Teehaus

The lustrous, gilded pavilion that
can be seen glistening between
the trees from a distance is the
Chinese Teahouse. Chinese art
was very popular during the
Rococo period – people wore
Chinese silk, wallpapered their
rooms with Chinese designs,
lacquered their furniture, drank
tea from Chinese porcelain and
built Chinese pavilions in their
gardens. The one in Sanssouci
was built in 1754–56 to a design
by Johann Gottfried Büring.
Circular in shape, it has a
centrally located main hall
surrounded by three studies.
Between these are pretty *trompe
l'oeil* porticos. The structure is
covered with a tent roof and
topped with a lantern. Gilded
ornaments, columns and
Chinese figures surround the
pavilion. Originally a tea room
and summer dining house, it
houses today a collection of
18th-century porcelain.

🏛 Römische Bäder

Lenné-Str. (Park Charlottenhof).
Tel (0331) 969 42 25. 📧 606. 🚇 91.
Open May–Oct: 10am–6pm Tue–Sun.

The Roman baths, situated by
the edge of a lake, form a
picturesque group of pavilions
which served as accommodation
for the king's guests. They were
designed in 1829–40 by Karl
Friedrich Schinkel, with
the help of Ludwig Persius.
The gardener's house
at the front stands
next to a low,
asymmetrical
tower, built in the
style of an Italian
Renaissance villa.
In the background,
to the left, extends
the former bathing
pavilion, which is currently used
for temporary exhibitions. The
pavilions are grouped around a
garden planted with colourful
shrubs and vegetables.

🏛 Schloss Charlottenhof

Geschwister-Scholl-Straße. (Park
Charlottenhof). **Tel** (0331) 969 42 02.
🚇 91. **Open** May–Oct: 10am–5pm
Tue–Sun. 🎧 obligatory.

This small Neo-Classical palace
stands at the southern end of
Park Sanssouci, known as Park

Charlottenhof. Built in 1826–9 for the heir to the throne, the future King Friedrich Wilhelm IV, this small, single-storey building was designed by Karl Friedrich Schinkel in the style of a Roman villa. Some of the wall paintings, designed by Schinkel in the so-called Pompeiian style, are still in place. There is also a collection of Italian engravings. The most interesting part of the interior is the Humboldt Room. The palace is surrounded by a landscaped park designed by Peter Joseph Lenné.

🏛 Neues Palais

Am Neuen Palais. **Tel** (0331) 969 42 02. **Open** Apr–Oct: 10am–6pm Wed–Mon; Nov–Mar: 9am–5pm Wed–Mon. 📷 💿 obligatory.

One of Germany's most beautiful palaces, this imposing Baroque structure, on the main avenue in Park Sanssouci, was built for Frederick the Great to initial plans by Georg Wenzeslaus von Knobelsdorff in 1750. Its construction, to designs by Johan Gottfried Büring, Jean Laurent Le Geay and Carl von Gontard, was delayed until 1763–9, after the Seven Years' War. The vast, three-wing structure comprises over 200 richly adorned rooms and has many interesting sculptures.

The Potsdam Conference

Towards the end of World War II, the leaders of the Allies – Winston Churchill, Franklin Roosevelt, and Joseph Stalin – met in Schloss Cecilienhof in Potsdam. The aim of this conference, which lasted from 17 July until 2 August 1945, was to resolve the problems arising at the end of the war. The main participants changed, however, before it was concluded. Churchill was replaced by newly elected Clement Attlee, and Harry S. Truman took over after President Roosevelt died. The conference set up the occupation zones, the demilitarization and monitoring of Germany, the punishment of war criminals and the reparations. It also revised the German borders. These decisions established the political balance of power in Europe, which continued for 45 years.

Attlee, Truman and Stalin in Potsdam

The south wing houses the kings' quarters.

🏛 Schloss Babelsberg

Park Babelsberg 10. **Tel** (0331) 969 42 50. **Closed** until 2015.

Built in 1833–5 for Prince Wilhelm (Kaiser Wilhelm I), by Karl Friedrich Schinkel, this extravagant castle ranks as one of his finest works. An irregular building with many towers and bay windows, built in the spirit of English Neo-Gothic, with allusions to Windsor Castle and Tudor style, it now holds the Museum of Pre-History.

🎬 Filmpark Babelsberg

Großbeerenstraße. **Tel** (0331) 721 27 38. **Open** 15 Apr–31 Oct: 10am–6pm daily. 📷 🖥 **filmpark.de**

This amazing film park was laid out on the site where Germany's first films were produced in 1912. From 1917 the studio belonged to Universum-Film-AG (UFA), which produced some of the most famous films of the silent era, including Fritz Lang's *Metropolis* and some films with Greta Garbo. The *Blue Angel*, with Marlene Dietrich, was also shot at Babelsberg, but subsequently, the studios were used to film Nazi propaganda. The studio is still operational, and the public can admire some of the old sets, the creation of special effects and stuntmen in action.

🖥 Einsteinturm

Albert-Einstein-Strraße. **Open** Oct–Mar: visits daily by arrangement with the Urania Society (0331 291 741). 🚌 694.

This tower, built in 1920–21 by Erich Mendelssohn, is one of the finest examples of German Expressionist architecture. Its fantasy forms were to demonstrate the qualities of reinforced concrete to spectacular effect. However, the cost of formwork, assembled by boat builders, limited the use of the material to the first storey, while the upper floors are plastered brickwork.

The impressive Marble Hall in the Baroque Neues Palais

❽ Chorin

Road map E2. 🚂 510. 🚌 Kloster
Chorin, Amt 11A. **Tel** (033366) 703 77.
Open Apr–Oct: 9am–6pm daily;
Nov–Mar: 9am–4pm daily. 🎭
🎵 Choriner Musiksommer.

On the edge of the vast
Schorfheide forest, which has
been listed as a World Biosphere
Reserve by UNESCO, stands one
of Brandenburg's most beautiful
Gothic buildings – the
Cistercian **Kloster** (abbey) of
Chorin. The Cistercians arrived
here in 1258, but work on the
present Gothic abbey did not
start until 1270. The church is a
triple-nave, transeptal basilica,
with a magnificent façade.
Preserved to this day are two
wings of the monastic quarters
plus several domestic buildings.
Following the dissolution of the
monastery in 1542, the entire
complex fell into disrepair.
Today the church, deprived of
its traditional furnishings, is used
as a venue for classical concerts.
The park established by Peter
Joseph Lenné is conducive to
pleasant strolls.

Environs

For visitors to Niederfinow, the
giant **Schiffshebewerk** (barge-
lift) is a definite must. This
wonder of technology was
designed for lifting and
lowering ships from one canal
to another. Commissioned in
1934, it is 60 m (197 ft) tall and
capable of lifting barges laden
with 1,000 tonnes or more.

Portal of the St Marienkirche in Frankfurt
an der Oder

❾ Frankfurt an der Oder

Road map F3. 🚂 87,900. 🚌 🚏
ℹ️ Karl-Marx-Str. 1. (0335-32 52 16).
🎭 Frankfurter Musikfesttage (Mar);
Hansefest (Jul); Kleist-Tage (Oct).

Frankfurt, on the banks of the
river Oder, was granted municipal rights in 1253, prospered in
the 13th century and joined
the Hanseatic league in 1368.
In 1945, the right bank was
ceded to Poland and is now
known as Słubice.
  Viadrina University, founded
in 1506, was reopened in 1991
and now educates both German
and Polish students. The town's
most famous son is playwright
and writer Heinrich von Kleist

(1777–1811); the Kleist-Museum,
devoted to his life and work, is in
the former garrison school. The
Gothic **Rathaus** (town hall) in the
centre escaped destruction in
World War II and now houses an
art gallery. The main church,
Marienkirche (church of St
Mary), is a vast, five-nave Gothic
hall which has stood in ruins
since 1945. Some of the Gothic
furnishings were rescued and can
now be seen in **St Gertraud**
(church of St Gertrude) which
dates back to 1368. The main
altar from 1489 and the huge,
5m- (16ft-) tall candelabrum from
1376 are particularly valuable.
Another Gothic church, originally
built for the Franciscans in 1270,
has been transformed into the
C.P.E. Bach Konzerthalle
(concert hall), named after Carl
Philipp Emmanuel Bach, son of
Johann Sebastian.

Environs

Neuzelle, 36 km (23 miles) to
the south, has a magnificent
former Cistercian Abbey,
with an impressive Baroque
relief façade.

❿ Cottbus

Road map F3. 🚂 121,000.
🚌 Bahnhofstr. 🚏 ℹ️ Berliner Platz
6 (0335-754 20). 🎭 Karnevalsumzug
(Feb); Cottbuser Musik-Herbst (Oct).
🌐 **cottbus.de**

Tourists rarely visit Cottbus,
despite the many attractions
offered by the town. Its

The Baroque Schloss Branitz in Cottbus

enchanting town square is surrounded by impressive Baroque buildings. The house at No. 24 is the quaint Löwen-apotheke (lion's pharmacy), which now houses a small pharmaceutical museum, the **Brandenburgisches Apothekenmuseum**, with displays of historical interiors. Nearby, the Gothic **Oberkirche St Nikolai** features an unusual original late-Gothic mesh vaulting. Another interesting Gothic structure, the **Wendenkirche** (Sorbian church), is a former Franciscan church, from the 14th–15th centuries.

Other attractions of the town include the remains of the medieval city walls with three preserved towers. Perhaps the most attractive building in Cottbus is the **Staatstheater** (state theatre) designed in Jugendstil (Art Nouveau style) by Bernhard Sehring and built in 1908.

The **Wendisches Museum** is devoted to the culture of the Sorbs which is experiencing a revival *(see p185)*.

Schloss Branitz is a late-Baroque palace, originally built in the 18th century, at the southeastern edge of town. It became the residence of Prince Hermann von Pückler-Muskau in 1845, who had its interior redesigned by Gottfried Semper. Today, the palace houses the **Fürst-Pückler-Museum**, which exhibits paintings by Karl Blechen, a local artist from Cottbus. The star attraction of the palace is its **Park**, which was designed by Prince Pückler-Muskau himself. This vast landscaped garden includes a lake with an island on which stands a grass-covered mock-Egyptian earth pyramid containing the tomb of the extravagant and eccentric Prince.

🏛 **Schloss Branitz and Fürst-Pückler-Museum**
Kastanienalle 11. **Tel** (0355) 751 50. **Open** Apr–Oct: 10am–6pm daily; Nov–Mar: 11am–5pm Tue–Sun. 📷

🏛 **Wendisches Museum**
Mühlenstr. 12. **Tel** (0355) 79 49 30.

Boats and canoes in the Spreewald, near Lübben

Open 10am–5pm Tue–Fri, 1–5pm Sat & Sun and bank holidays.

🏛 **Brandenburgisches Apothekenmuseum**
Altmark 24. **Tel** (0355) 239 97. **Open** visits possible with guide 11am–2pm Tue–Fri; 2pm & 3pm Sat & Sun. 📷

⓫ Spreewald

Road map F3. 🚉 Lübben.
ℹ️ Raddusch, Lindenstr. 1 (035433-722 99), Lübbenau, Ehm-Welk-Str. 15 (03542-36 68). 🚉 🎭 Spreewaldfest in Lübbenau (Jul); Lübben (Sep).
🌐 **spreewald.de**

Designated as one of the World Biosphere Reserves, this marshy region, criss-crossed by hundreds of small rivers and canals, attracts large numbers of tourists each year. An all-day trip by **Kahn** (boat) or canoe, which is best started in **Lübben** or **Lübbenau**, can prove to be an unforgettable experience. The splendour of nature, numerous water birds and the endless chain of small restaurants which serve meals straight from the jetty, ensure an exciting day for the visitor. Do not miss the local speciality, pickled gherkins.

Lübben has an original Gothic church and a Baroque palace, rebuilt in the 19th century. Lübbenau features a small Baroque church and the Neo-Classical house of the von Lynar family. In **Lehde** the small open-air museum and the private collection of the **Bauernhaus-und Gurkenmuseum** – the only gherkin museum in Germany – are highly recommended.

Environs
Luckau, 18 km (11 miles) west of Lübben, has a lovely town square, surrounded by attractive Baroque houses with stucco façades, and the ornamented, 14th-century Gothic Nikolaikirche.

⓬ Jüterbog

Road map E3. 🚉 13,000. 🚉 🚌 ℹ️ Markt 21 (03372-46 31 13).

Jüterbog is a small, picturesque town featuring many Gothic structures including some well-preserved sections of three city walls with gates and towers, dating back to the 15th century. It also boasts a beautiful town hall with arcades and three churches. **Nikolaikirche** (church of St Nicholas), the largest of them, is a magnificent hall church, with a twin-tower façade, built in several stages. The so-called New Sacristy features a set of medieval wall paintings, while the naves contain many Gothic furnishings.

Environs
Five km (3 miles) to the north of Jüterbog stands **Kloster Zinna**, a former Cistercian Abbey with an early-Gothic stone church. It features 16th-century stained-glass windows depicting the saints Bernhard and Benedikt.

The early-Gothic ex-Cistercian Kloster Zinna, near Jüterbog

SAXONY-ANHALT

The scenic Harz mountains, a popular recreation area with fascinating rock formations and pleasant walks, are the best known attraction of Saxony-Anhalt. Yet this state also boasts a number of interesting towns, such as Lutherstadt Wittenberg and Magdeburg, steeped in history and blessed with magnificent historic remains, which range from Romanesque churches and abbeys to medieval castles.

This province consists of the areas of the former Duchy of Anhalt and the Prussian province of Saxony, that part of the Kingdom of Saxony which was incorporated into Prussia after the Congress of Vienna (1815) as punishment for supporting Napoleon.

The landscape in this region is highly varied. Its northern part, the Altmark, is a largely flat area of farmland and heath. The gentle hills of the Harz Mountains in the southwest, although not especially high (their highest peak, the Brocken, rises to only 1142 m/3747 ft), are picturesque and fairly well provided with tourist facilities. The eastern, flat part of the region is more industrialized. It also includes two very important towns: the small town of Wittenberg, where Martin Luther proclaimed his theses in 1517, thus launching the Reformation, and Dessau, the former capital of the Duchy of Anhalt and from 1925 to 1932 the seat of the Bauhaus Art School. The southern part of the province, with its interesting and varied landscape, features one of the land's most impressive historic buildings – the gigantic Naumburg Cathedral.

After World War II Saxony-Anhalt was occupied by the Soviets, and in 1949 it was incorporated into the GDR. It underwent major industrial development, mainly due to lignite mining. The state of Saxony-Anhalt was first created in 1947, only to be abolished five years later. It was finally re-established as a federal state in 1990, with Magdeburg as its capital.

Timber-frame houses in Quedlinburg

◀ Interior of the Schlosskirche in Lutherstadt Wittenberg

Exploring Saxony–Anhalt

Touring Saxony-Anhalt can be an unforgettable experience, especially for admirers of Romanesque art, as this region abounds in churches and abbeys of that period. A visit to Wörlitz provides the opportunity to see one of Germany's most beautiful landscaped gardens. Nature lovers, hill-walkers and, in the winter, cross-country skiers should include a few days in the romantic Harz Mountains in their schedule. An added attraction here is a ride on the narrow-gauge railway drawn by a steam engine which, today as in years gone by, still links some of the most interesting places of the region.

Interior of the Gothic cathedral in Havelberg

Zoo-Park in Dessau

For additional map symbols *see back flap*

0 kilometres   15

0 miles   15

Listening to a summer water concert, in Wörlitz Park

Getting Around

The A2 motorway from Hanover to Berlin runs through Magdeburg to the northern part of the region. Another motorway, the A9 which links Berlin and Munich, provides easy access to Dessau and Halle, which is also served by the recently constructed A14 motorway from Leipzig to Magdeburg. Other major and minor roads, well signposted, provide access to smaller towns and villages. Larger towns are easily accessed by rail or local bus services. In the Harz Mountains the narrow-gauge train is an alternative form of transport.

Key

═══ Motorway

─── Major road

─── Minor road

= = Under construction

─── Scenic route

⚊⚊ Main railway

─── Minor railway

─── Regional border

△ Summit

Sights at a Glance

❶ Halberstadt
❷ Wernigerode
❹ Quedlinburg
❺ Bernburg
❻ Halle
❼ Merseburg
❽ Querfurt
❾ *Naumburg pp154–5*
❿ *Magdeburg p156*
⓫ Stendal
⓬ Havelberg
⓭ Tangermünde
⓮ Dessau
⓯ *Lutherstadt Wittenberg pp158–9*
⓰ *Wörlitz Park pp160–61*

Tours

❸ The Harz Mountain Trail

Interior of the Gothic Cathedral of Halberstadt

❶ Halberstadt

Road map D3. 🏛 42,000. 🚍 🚌
ℹ Hinter dem Rathause 6 (03941-
55 18 15). 🌐 **halberstadt.de**

Halberstadt enjoys a
picturesque location in the
foothills of the Harz
Mountains. Its history
goes back to the
9th century, when it
became a seat of a
mission episcopate.
Once an important
town, Halberstadt
had 80 per cent
of its buildings
destroyed during
World War II. Fortunately, many
of its beautiful historic buildings
have been restored to their
former glory.

The vast **St Stephans Dom** is
the fourth successive church
built on the same site. Construction began in the 13th century
and the church was consecrated
in 1491. The two-tower transeptal basilica ranks as one of
the most beautiful pure Gothic
forms in Germany. Its oldest part
is the 12th-century font. Also
notable are the Romanesque
Crucifixion group (c.1220), set
above the choir screen, and
several examples of Gothic
sculpture. Stained-glass windows
from around 1330 have survived
in the Marian Chapel, and
15th-century windows can be
found along the cloisters and in
the presbytery.

The adjoining chapter buildings contain one of Germany's

Romanesque Crucifixion group
in the Dom, Halberstadt

richest cathedral treasuries – the
Domschatz, with precious 12th-
century tapestries, numerous
sculptures and liturgical vessels.

Other interesting churches to
have survived in the old town
district include the Romanesque 12th-century
Liebfrauenkirche
and the Gothic
**Marktkirche St.
Martini** with a
statue of Roland,
symbolizing the
freedom of the
city. Remaining
timber-frame
houses can be seen
in Gröper- and Taubenstrasse.

🏛 Domschatz
Tel 03941 24237. ⏰ Apr–Oct:
10am–5:30pm daily (from 11am Sun);
Nov–Mar: 10am–4pm Tue–Sun.
📷 obligatory. 🌐 **dom-und-
domschatz.de**

Environs
An original 12th-century
Benedictine church stands in
Huysburg, 11 km (7 miles) to
the northwest.

❷ Wernigerode

Road map D3. 🏛 36,000. 🚍 🚌
ℹ Marktplatz 10 (03943-55 37 835).
🎭 Rathausfest (Jun); Schlossfestspiele
(Jul & Aug). 🌐 **wernigerode.de**

Wernigerode is attractively
situated at a confluence of two
rivers. Timber-frame houses lean
across its steep, winding streets,

and a massive castle rises above
the town. The **Harzquerbahn**, a
narrow-gauge railway which
links the small towns and villages
in the Harz Mountains, between
Wernigerode and Nordhausen,
provides another popular tourist
attraction. The Brockenbahn
runs between Wernigerode and
the Brocken mountain.

Strolling around the Old Town
it is well worth stepping into
St John's Church, featuring a
Romanesque west tower. It
contains some late-Gothic
features, including the font and
the altar. The variety of
ornaments adorning the houses
in Wernigerode is truly
staggering. Particularly interesting
are the houses along **Breite
Straße**, the town's main shopping
street which is closed to traffic.

🏰 Schloss Wernigerode
Am Schloss 1. **Tel** 03943-55 30 30.
⏰ May–Oct: 10am–6pm; Nov–Apr:
10am–5pm Tue–Fri, 10am–6pm Sat &
Sun. 🅿

The fairy-tale castle, spiked
with z the years 1861–83 on
the site of an older fortress.
Now a museum, it houses the
Stolberg-Wernigerode family
art collection. The castle
ramparts afford a fantastic
view of the town and the
nearby Harz mountains.

Environs
The small town of **Osterwieck**,
22 km (14 miles) to the north,
has over 400 timber-frame
buildings, dating mainly from
the 16th and
17th centuries.

The romantic façade of Schloss
Wernigerode, now a museum

❸ The Harz Mountain Trail

The tourist trail across the Harz Mountains leads through charming historic towns and villages, as well as past the other attractions of the region including some fascinating caves and unusual rock formations.

Tips for Drivers

Length: 55 km (34 miles).
Stopping places: there are many attractive restaurants all along the trail, in every town.
Walpurgisnacht, Thale: 30 Apr.

① The Rübeland Caves
Rübeland's main attractions are the Hermannshöhle and Baumannshöhle, two caves with amazing stalactites and stalagmites.

② Blankenburg
This charming mountain town is overlooked by an 18th-century castle. The Teufelsmauer, a spectacular 4-km (2-mile) long sandstone cliff, attracts many climbers.

③ Thale
Many mountain walks start in Thale, including one to the Hexentanzplatz, a platform suspended above a cliff, from where witches fly to Sabbath celebrations in the Walpurgis Night.

⑦ Harzgerode
The town has charming timber-frame houses in the Old Town, and a 16th-century castle.

⑥ Burg Falkenstein
This huge castle, built in the 12th century and extended many times, is now a museum. From the castle, the visitor can enjoy a splendid view over the surrounding Harz Mountains.

④ Gernrode
The star attraction in this town is the 10th-century church of St Cyriacus. Its interior is devoid of ornaments, yet enchantingly pure in form.

⑤ Ballenstedt
The former home of the von Anhalt-Bemburg family enchants visitors to this day with its imaginative design, including the Baroque castle set in a park.

Key

▬ Tour route
▭ Other road
═ Scenic route

```
0 km          2
0 miles       2
```

The Renaissance portal of Quedlinburg Schloss

❹ Quedlinburg

Road map D3. 🏛 26,000. 🚌 🚊
ℹ Markt 2 (03946-90 56 24 and 90 56 25). 🎷 Musiksommer (Jun–Sep).

The rise of the small town of Quedlinburg was closely connected with its convent, established in 936 by Emperor Otto I and his mother, St Mathilde. On the hill above the town stands the vast Romanesque structure of the **Stiftskirche St Servatius** (Collegiate Church of St Servatius), built between 1017 and 1129. Its old crypt, the Huysburg which belonged to the previous church, features Romanesque wall paintings and contains tombs of the prioresses and of the Emperor Henry and his wife Mathilde. An exhibition of treasures is shown in the arms of the transept, including the Romanesque reliquary of St Servatius and the remaining fragments of the 12th-century Knüpfteppich (tapestry). The **Quedlinburg Schloss**, a Renaissance palace surrounded by gardens, occupies the other side of the hill.

Both Old and New Town of Quedlinburg have valuable examples of timber-frame architecture. The buildings date from various times – the modest house at **Wordgasse 3**, from around 1400, is the oldest surviving timber-frame building in Germany. Also noteworthy are the numerous churches, including the 10th-century **Norbertinenkirche**, the **Wippertikirche** with its early-Romanesque crypt, and the 15th-century, late-Gothic **Marktkirche St Benedicti**.

❺ Bernburg

Road map D4. 🏛 36,000. 🚌 🚊 ℹ
Lindenplatz 9 (03471 346 9311). 🎷
Walpurgisnacht (May). 🖥 **bernberg.de**

Once the capital of one of Anhalt's Duchies, Bernburg enjoys a picturesque location on the banks of the Saale River. It has a **Bergstadt** (upper town) and a **Talstadt** (lower town), and its attractions include the Gothic parish churches and the town square with its Baroque buildings. The most important historic building is the **Bernburg Schloss**, a castle built on a rock. It owes its present appearance to refurbishments (1540–70), yet many features of this multi-wing structure are much older, including the 12th-century Romanesque chapels and Gothic towers.

Burg Giebichenstein, in Halle, with the Arts and Crafts College

❻ Halle

Road map D4. 🏛 232,300. 🚌 🚊
ℹ Marktplatz 13 (0345 122 99 84).
🎷 Händel-Festspiele (Jun); Hallesche Musiktage (Nov). 🖥 **halle.de**

Halle is an old town with a rich history in commerce and trade, its wealth founded on the production and sale of salt. Later, the town was turned into a centre for the chemical industry. Halle has preserved most of its historic heritage. On the **Marktplatz** (town square) stands an interesting church, **Unser Lieben Frauen** (Our Lady), whose late-Gothic main body (1530–54) was positioned between two pairs of towers that had remained intact

The impressive Bernburg Schloss, built on a rock

Renaissance residence in Merseburg

from previous Romanesque churches. Nearby is the **Roter Turm** (Red Tower), an 84-m (276 ft) tall belfry, built in 1418–1506. The house at Nikolaistraße 5, the birthplace of Georg Friedrich Händel, now houses a small museum, the **Händel-Haus**. In Domplatz stands the early-Gothic **Dom**, built in 1280–1331 by the Dominicans and restored between 1525 and 1530 in Renaissance style.

Halle has some other medieval churches, including the late-Gothic **Moritzkirche** built in the latter part of the 14th century. It is also worth visiting the **Kunststiftung des Landes Sachen-Anhalt**, housed in the refurbished Citadel building known as **Moritzburg** and built during 1484-1503. On the outskirts of town stands **Burg Giebichenstein**, the former castle residence of the Magdeburg bishops. The upper part of the castle remains in ruins, while the lower part houses an Arts & Crafts College.

The **Landesmuseum für Vorgeschichte** (State Museum of Prehistory) has more than 11 million exhibits. Its centrepiece is the Nebra Sky Disc, a 3,600-year-old bronze disc recognized by UNESCO as the earliest known image of the night sky.

Kunststiftung des Landes Sachen-Anhalt
Friedemann-Bach-Platz 5. **Tel** (0345) 21 25 90. **Open** 10am–6pm Tue–Sun. free last Sun of month.

Landesmuseum für Vorgeschichte
Richard-Wagner-Str. 9. **Tel** (0345) 52 47 30. **Open** Tue–Sun.

7 Merseburg

Road map D4. 40,000.
Burgstr. 5 (03461-21 41 70)
Schlossfest (Jun). **merseburg.de**

The first sight visitors see as they arrive in Merseburg is the **Domburg** – a vast complex of buildings spiked with towers, consisting of a cathedral and residences. The cathedral is not uniform in style; it includes some Romanesque elements (the eastern section and twin towers in the west) erected in the 11th and 12th centuries, and the late-Gothic triple-nave main body, which was built in 1510–17. All that remains of the older, early-Romanesque structure is the crypt, underneath the presbytery. The cathedral contains remarkable Gothic and Renaissance features, as well as numerous sarcophagi of bishops, such as that of Thilo von Troth (1470). The chapter buildings house a library with precious manuscripts, including the **Merseburg Bible** (c. 1200). Adjacent to the cathedral is a three-wing Renaissance-style **Schloss**. Magnificent portals and an attractive oriel in the castle's west wing are noteworthy.

8 Querfurt

Road map D4. 11,000.
Markt 14 (034771-237 99)
Brunnenfest (Jun). **querfurt.de**

The narrow streets of Querfurt are crammed with timber-frame houses, and the giant **Schloss** towers over the town square with its Renaissance town hall. The castle's present form is the result of Renaissance refurbishments, but it maintains many Romanesque features, such as the 11th-century donjon (keep), known as **Dicker Heinrich** (Fat Henry) and a 12th-century church. Also worth seeing is the burial chapel, the Baroque **Fürstenhaus** (ducal house) and a small museum, situated in the former armoury and granary.

9 Naumburg

Road map D4. 30,500.
Markt 12 (03445-27 31 25).
Hussiten-Kirsch-Fest (Jun).
naumburg-tourismus.de

The town's star attraction is the **Dom** (cathedral of Saints Peter and Paul *see pp154–5*). There is a late-Gothic **Rathaus** (town hall), restored in Renaissance style, and the main square is surrounded by quaint houses. Further attractions include the **Marientor** gate (1455–6) with the puppet theatre, and the Gothic **Stadtkirche St. Wenzel** (Church of St Wenceslas). The latter has two paintings by Lucas Cranach the Elder as well as the 18th-century organ that Johann Sebastian Bach played on. Friedrich Nietzsche, the philosopher, spent his childhood at No. 18 Weingarten, now a small museum.

Gothic stone retable of the main altar in Naumburg Dom

Naumburg Dom

The impressive Cathedral of Saints Peter and Paul in Naumburg is one of the finest Gothic structures in Germany. The present cathedral is the second to be built on the same site; only a section of the eastern crypt survived of the earlier Romanesque church. Construction started before 1213, with the earliest parts including the late-Romanesque east choir, the transept and the main body. The early-Gothic west choir was built in the mid-13th century, the newer Gothic east choir c.1330. The northeast towers date from the 15th century, the southwest towers from 1894.

Stained-Glass Windows in the Presbytery
The stained-glass windows depict scenes of the apostles of virtue and sin. Some sections are original 13th-century work, but two were completed in the 19th century.

★ Founders' Statues
The statues of Margrave Ekkehard and his wife, Uta, are true masterpieces – the artist succeeded marvellously in capturing the beauty and sensitivity of his subjects.

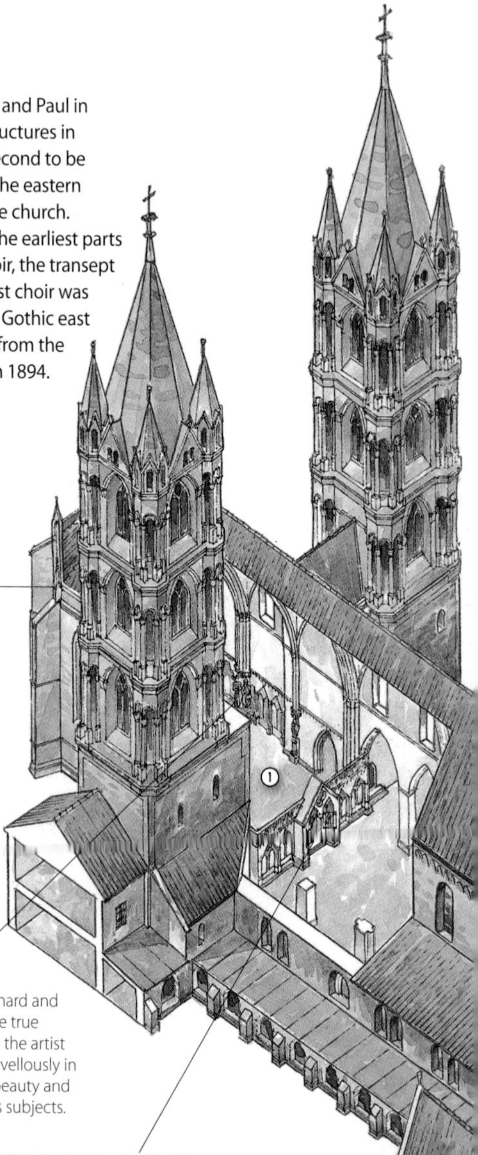

KEY

① West choir

② Sarcophagus of Bishop Dietrich II

③ East choir

④ **The Main Altar**, built in the mid-14th century, is a stone retable depicting the Crucifixion with the saints which was transferred from another altar.

★ Portal of the West Reading Room
The Gothic twin portal depicts the Crucifixion, a moving and highly expressive group sculpture by the brilliant "Naumburger Meister" whose identity remains unknown.

Pulpit
The richly ornamented pulpit basket, from 1466, and the adjoining stairs have been renovated.

VISITORS' CHECKLIST

Practical Information
Domplatz 16–17.
Tel (03445) 23 01 10.
Open Mar–Oct: 9am–6pm Mon–Sat, noon–6pm Sun; Nov–Feb: 10am–4pm Mon–Sat, noon–4pm Sun.

★ Main Portal
The late-Romanesque, 13th-century portal is decorated on the left side with eagles. The tympanum features Christ in a mandorla (almond-shaped area) supported by angels.

East Choir Altar
This Gothic altar features the Virgin Mary with the Infant Jesus, surrounded by the figures of the saints.

St Mary's Altar
This late-Gothic triptych (c.1510) depicts the Virgin Mary with the Infant, framed by Saints Barbara and Catherine, with the Apostles in the wings.

Interior of the Gothic presbytery in the Magdeburg Dom

❿ Magdeburg

Road map D3. 🏛 235,000. 🚊 🚌
ℹ️ Ernst-Reuter-Allee 12 (0391-838
0405). 🎷 Jazzfestival (Jun), Klassik-
Open Air (Jul). 🌐 magdeburg
tourist.de

The large-scale development of
Magdeburg, today the capital of
Saxony-Anhalt and a port on the
river Elbe, began in the 10th
century when Emperor Otto I
established his main residence
here. In medieval times the town
became a political and cultural
centre. After the abolition of the
archbishopric and the destruction wrought by the Thirty Years'
War, it lost its political importance.
About 80 per cent was destroyed
during World War II, but it is still
worth a visit since many historic
buildings have been reconstructed in the Old Town.

🏛 Dom St Mauritius und
St Katharina

Domplatz. **Tel** (0391) 541 04 36.
Open May–Sep: 10am–6pm; Apr & Oct:
10am–5pm; Nov–Mar: 10am–4pm.

The vast Magdeburg cathedral is
one of the most important
Gothic churches in Germany. Its
construction, which started in
1209 on the site of an earlier
Romanesque church, was
completed in 1520, although
much of it was built by the mid-
14th century. The result is a lofty,
aisled basilica with transept,
cloisters, a ring of chapels
surrounding the presbytery and
a vast twin-tower façade. The
cathedral has several
magnificent, original
sculptures. Other notable
features include the tomb of
Emperor Otto I, as well as the
12th-century bronze tomb
plaques of archbishops
Friedrich von Wettin and
Wichmann.
The memorial for the
dead of World War I is the
work of Ernst Barlach,
dating from 1929. Visitors
to the cathedral
may notice several
elements that were
preserved from
ancient structures
and have been
incorporated into
the walls or used as
ornaments inside
the building.

🏛 Kulturhistorisches
Museum

Otto-von-Guericke-Str. 68–73.
Tel (0391) 540 35 01. **Open** 10am–
5pm Tue–Sun. 🖼 .

This museum contains works
of art, archaeological finds and
historic documents of the town.
Its most valuable exhibit is the
Magdeburger Reiter (Magdeburg
Rider), a sculpture dating from
around 1240 of an unknown
ruler on a horse (probably Otto I).

⛪ Kloster Unser
Lieben Frauen

Regierungsstr. 4–6. Kunstmuseum
Tel (0391) 56 50 20. **Open** 10am–5pm
Tue–Sun. 🖼

This Austere Romanesque
church, Magdeburg's oldest
building, was built for the
Norbertine order during the
second half of the 11th and the
early 12th centuries. Stripped of
all its ornaments, it now serves
as a concert hall. The adjacent
Romanesque abbey is a museum
with medieval and modern
sculptures (Barlach, Rodin).

⛪ Halle an der Buttergasse

Alter Markt. Weinkeller Buttergasse.

The basement of a late-
Romanesque market hall from
c.1200 was rediscovered in 1948,
and is used today as a wine cellar.

🏛 Rathaus

Alter Markt.

The present Baroque town hall,
built in 1691–8 on the site of
an earlier, late-Romanesque
town hall, was restored after
World War II.

⛪ Pfarrkirche St
Johannis

Am Johannisberg 1.
Viewing tower:
Tel (0391) 59 34 50.
Open Mar–Oct:
10am–6pm Tue–Sun;
Nov–Feb: 10–5pm. 🖼

Near the market
square is the
Gothic church of St
John, destroyed
during World War II
and later rebuilt. In
1524 Martin Luther
preached here.
Today it is used as
a concert hall.

Kloster Unser Lieben
Frauen in Magdeburg

⓫ Stendal

Road map D3. 🔼 39,600. 🚊 🚌
ℹ️ Kornmarkt 8 (03931-65 11 90).
Rolandfest (early Jul). 🔳 **stendal.de**

In medieval times Stendal was one of the richest towns of the Brandenburg margravate, and its most valuable historical remains date from that period. The late-Gothic **St Nikolai** cathedral was built in 1423–67, on the foundations of a Romanesque Augustinian church. Its star attractions are 15th-century stained-glass windows in the presbytery and the transept.

The late-Gothic, 15th-century church **St Marien** (St Mary) has some original Gothic elements, and the oldest parts of the **Rathaus** (town hall) date back to the 14th century. Other attractions include the remains of the town walls, with a beautiful tower, **Uenglinger Torturm**.

Gothic traceries of the cloisters in the Dom, Havelberg

⓬ Havelberg

Road map D3. 🔼 7,000. 🚌
ℹ️ Uferstr. 1. (039387-79 091).
🔳 **havelberg.de**

Havelberg played an important role in the Christianization of this region, with a mission episcopate established here as early as the mid-10th century. The present cathedral – **Dom St Marien** – was built in 1150–70, and although redesigned in the early 14th century, it nevertheless maintained its Romanesque character. Its most interesting features include

Back of the Gothic Rathaus in the market square in Tangermünde

huge stone candelabra taken from the former reading room, dating back to around 1300, and the present reading room, which is decorated with reliefs carved in the workshop of the Parler family, in Prague, between 1396 and 1411.

⓭ Tangermünde

Road map D3. 🔼 10,000. 🚊 🚌
ℹ️ Markt 2 (039322-223 93).
🔳 **tourismus-tangermuende.de**

Situated at the confluence of the Tanger and Elbe rivers, this town grew rapidly during medieval times. For centuries it remained the seat of the Brandenburg margraves, and King Charles IV chose it as his second residence. The town joined the Hanseatic League, and grew in status thanks to its trade links.

The **Rathaus** (town hall) has timber-frame architecture and houses the municipal museum.

The only remains of the old castle are its main tower and the **Kanzlei** (chancellery). In 1377, King Charles IV brought the Augustinian monks to town and had the **St Stephanskirche** (church of St Stephen) built for them. Construction continued until the end of the 15th century. This magnificent, late-Gothic hall church with transept and cloister contains interesting features: a 1624 organ made in

the Hamburg workshop of Hans Scherer the Younger, the 1619 pulpit created by Christopher Dehne and a font dating from 1508, the work of Heinrich Mente.

The east wing of the beautiful Gothic **Rathaus** (town hall) dates back to 1430 and is the work of Heinrich Brunsberg, its richly ornamented spire being typical of his work. The west wing with its arcades was added around 1480, and the external stairs date from the 19th century.

Tangermünde has retained some remains of the city walls, dating from around 1300 and including a magnificent late-Gothic gate, the **Neustädter Tor**, whose tall, cylindrical tower has intricate, lacy ceramic ornaments.

🏛️ **Rathaus (Stadtgeschichtliches Museum)**
Am Markt. **Tel** (039322) 42 153.
Open 10am–5pm Tue–Sun.

Environs
A Romanesque **Klosterkirche** (abbey) in Jerichow, 10 km (6 miles) north of Tangermünde, is the earliest brick structure of the region. It was built in the 1150s, for Norbertine monks. The west towers were completed during the 15th century. Its austere, triple-nave vaulted interior is impressive. There are also many remains of the former abbey.

Interior of the former Norbertinenkirche, in Jerichow, north of Tangermünde

⑭ Dessau

Road map E3. 🚶 84,400. 🚗 🚌
ℹ️ Zerbster Str. 2c (0340-204 14 42).
🎭 Kurt-Weill-Fest (late Feb–Mar),
Elbmusikfest (Jun). 🌐 **dessau.de**

Dessau, once a magnificent city and the capital of the duchy of Anhalt-Dessau, is less attractive today, yet it has some excellent historic sights. In the town centre are some interesting Baroque churches and the **Johannbau**, the remains of a Renaissance ducal residence.

Dessau is also known for the **Bauhaus** complex. Built in 1925 to a design by Walter Gropius, it is the home of the famous art school, which moved here from Weimar. The **Bauhausmuseum** is housed in one of its wings. Nearby, in Friedrich-Ebert-Allee, five of the so-called **Meisterhäuser** – master houses for the Art College professors – have survived World War II. The houses of Lyonel Feininger and Paul Klee are open to the public. Wassily Kandinsky was also a former resident. The **Kornhaus**, on Elballee, restored in 1996, contains a restaurant, café and dance hall.

Many splendid residences set in landscaped gardens were built in 18th- and 19th-century Dessau. In the town centre stands a Neo-Classical palace, **Schloss Georgium**, built in 1780 to a design by Friedrich Wilhelm von Erdmannsdorff. Today it houses a collection of old masters, including works by Rubens, Hals and Cranach.

🏛 Bauhausmuseum
Gropiusallee 38. **Tel** (0340) 65 080.
Open 10am–6pm daily. 🚫

🏰 Schloss Georgium
Puschkinallee 100. **Tel** (0340) 61 38 74.
Open 10am–5pm Tue–Sun. 🚫

Environs
Haldeburg, which is situated on the outskirts of Dessau, has a Neo-Gothic hunting lodge built in 1782–3, and Mosigkau boasts **Schloss Mosigkau**, Princess Anna Wilhelmina's Baroque residence, designed by Christian Friedrich Damm. It contains some excellent examples of 17th-century painting.

In **Oranienbaum**, 12 km (7 miles) east of Dessau, stands a late-17th-century, early-Baroque palace that was built for Princess Henrietta Katharine of Orange by the Dutch architect Cornelius Ryckwaert.

🏰 Schloss Mosigkau
Knobelsdorffallee 2. **Tel** (0340) 50 255 721. **Open** Apr, Oct: 10am–5pm Sat & Sun; May–Sep: 10am–6pm Tue–Sun. **Closed** Dec–Mar. 🎫 🚫

⑮ Lutherstadt Wittenberg

Road map E3. 🚶 55,000. 🚗 🚌
ℹ️ Schlossplatz 2 (03491-41 48 48).
🎭 Wittenberger Stadtfest & Luthers Hochzeit (Jun). 🌐 **wittenberg.de**

This small town, named after its most famous resident, Martin Luther, enjoys a scenic position on the banks of the Elbe River.

Its main development took place during the 16th century, under the Great Elector, Frederick the Wise. Wittenberg became the capital of the Reformation thanks to the work of Martin Luther and Philipp Melanchthon, and as such it attracts many visitors. Another famous resident of that period was the painter Lucas Cranach the Elder.

🏰 Schloss Wittenberg
Schlossplatz. Museum für Naturkunde und Völkerkunde (Museum of Natural History and Ethnography):
Tel (03491) 43 34 920. **Open** 9am–5pm Tue–Sun. 🚫

Built for Frederick the Wise in 1489–1525, the castle was greatly altered during reconstruction following fire and wartime damage. A museum is housed in the west wing.

The tomb of Frederick the Wise, in Schlosskirche

⛪ Schlosskirche
Schlossplatz. **Tel** (03491) 40 25 85.
Open May–Oct: 10am–6pm Mon–Sat, 11:30–6pm Sun; Nov–Apr:10am–4pm Mon–Sat, 11:30am–4pm Sun.

Built after 1497, this church was made famous by Martin Luther, who allegedly posted his theses on its door in 1517. The original door no longer exists, but the church contains many interesting tombs, including that of Frederick the Wise, created in 1527 in the workshop of Hans Vischer, as well as modest tombs of Martin Luther and Melanchthon.

Schloss Georgium in Dessau

🏛 Cranachhaus

Markt 4. **Tel** (03491) 420 19 11.
Open 10am–5pm Mon–Sat (from
1pm Sun). **Closed** Nov–Apr: Mon.

This beautiful, early
16th-century Renaissance
house once belonged to
Lucas Cranach the Elder and
was the birthplace of his son,
Lucas Cranach the Younger.
His studio was located at
No. 1 Schlossstraße.

🏛 Rathaus

Markt 26. **Open** 10am–5pm Tue–Sun.

The Renaissance town hall
was built in 1523–35, and later
twice extended in the 16th
century. In its forecourt are two
19th-century monuments: to
Martin Luther by Gottfried
Schadow and to Philipp Melanchthon by Friedrich Drake.

🏛 Marienkirche

Kirchplatz. **Tel** (03491) 40 44 15.
Open Easter–Oct: 10am–6pm daily
(Sun from 11:30am); Nov–Easter:
10am–5pm daily (Sun from 11:30am).

The Gothic church of St Mary
with its twin-tower façade
was built between the 13th
and 15th centuries. Luther

The market square with Baroque fountain, in Lutherstadt Wittenberg

was married to Katharina von
Bora in this church where
he also preached, and six of
their children were baptised.
Inside there is a magnificent
Reformation altar (constructed
in 1547), the work of father
and son Cranach, as well as
interesting tombs and epitaphs.

🏛 Melanchthonhaus

Collegienstr. 60. **Tel** (03491) 40 32 79.
Open Apr–Oct: 10am–6pm daily;
Nov–Mar: 10am–5pm Tue–Sun.

This museum is devoted to
Luther's closest ally, Philipp

Schwarzerd, generally known
as Melanchthon.

🏛 Lutherhaus

Collegienstr. 54.
Tel (03491) 42 030. **Open** same as
Melanchthonhaus.

The museum, which is in
the former residence of Martin
Luther and his family, also
chronicles the work of Lucas
Cranach the Elder. It has a
large number of documents
relating to the Reformation
and Luther's translation
of the Bible.

Lutherstadt Wittenberg Town Centre

① Schloss Wittenberg
② Schlosskirche
③ Cranachhaus
④ Rathaus
⑤ Marienkirche
⑥ Melanchthonhaus
⑦ Lutherhaus

For keys to symbols *see back flap*

⑯ Wörlitz Park

Wörlitz is a charming, English-style landscaped garden, the first of its kind in continental Europe. It was established in stages, commencing in 1764, for Prince Leopold III, Frederick Franz of Anhalt-Dessau. Many famous gardeners worked in Wörlitz, including Johann Christian Neumark and Johann Leopold Ludwig Schoch, as well as the architect Friedrich Wilhelm von Erdmannsdorff. The country house (1769–1773), the first building in the Classical style in Germany, houses a valuable collection of sculpture, furniture and paintings. Another interesting collection, including Swiss glass pictures, can be admired in the Gotisches Haus.

Floratempel
Modelled on an ancient temple with columns, this Neo-Classical temple served as a music pavilion.

★ **Gotisches Haus**
This house, built in stages, is one of the earliest examples of German Neo-Gothic style. On display inside is a unique collection of Swiss glass pictures.

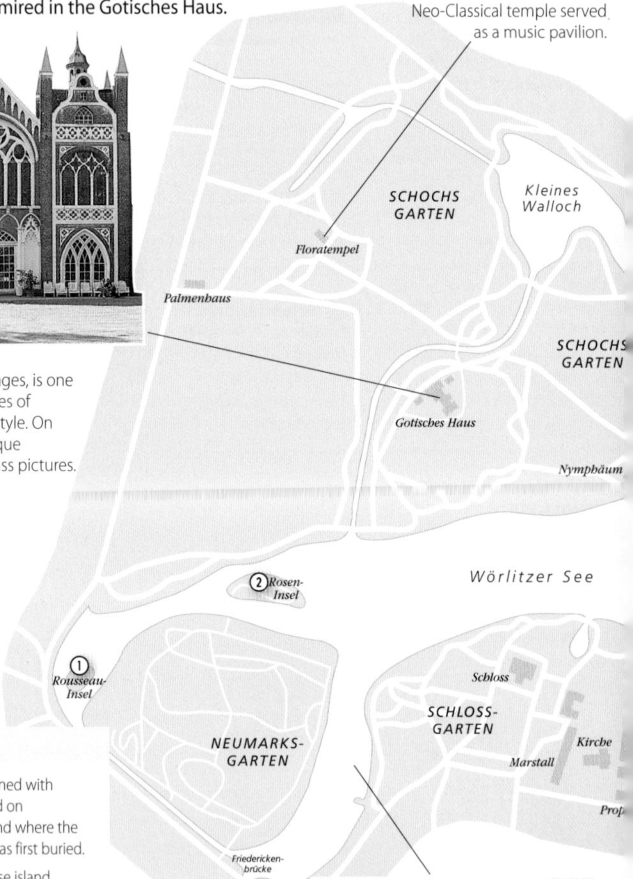

SCHOCHS GARTEN

Kleines Walloch

Floratempel

Palmenbaus

SCHOCHS GARTEN

Gotisches Haus

Nymphäum

② Rosen-Insel

Wörlitzer See

① Rousseau-Insel

Schloss

SCHLOSS-GARTEN

Kirche

NEUMARKS-GARTEN

Marstall

Prop

Friedericken-brücke

KEY

① **Rousseau-Insel**, lined with poplars, was modelled on Ermenonville, the island where the French philosopher was first buried.

② **Rosen-Insel**, or rose island, was created as one of several artificial islands in the part of the garden designed by Johann Christian Neumark.

③ **The Pantheon**, built in 1795–6, houses a collection of antique sculptures.

④ **Stein** (Rock Island) is a working artificial volcano modelled on Mount Vesuvius in Italy.

Gondolas on the Lake
Romantic gondolas wait by the jetties to take tourists across the lake.

Lake Concert
Classical concerts are held on Wörlitz Lake in the evening during the summer season. The audience is all afloat in boats.

VISITORS' CHECKLIST

Practical Information
ℹ️ Förstergasse 26 (34905 310 09). 🗑 woerlitz-information.de Schloss: **Open** Apr & Oct: 11am–5pm Tue–Fri; 10am–5pm Sat & Sun. 📷 📶

Transport
🚌 🚏

Amalien-Insel
In keeping with the fashion of the day, this artificial island, on Großes Walloch lake, has a grotto, which provides a cool resting place.

③ *Pantheon*

WEIDEN-HEGER

Herderinsel

Großes Walloch

Amalien-Insel

NEUE ANLAGEN

Wörlitzer See
The largest of the three lakes, which are all joined by canals, this is prettiest when the water lilies are in bloom.

④ *Stein*

★ **Synagogue**
Built in 1790 and modelled on the Vesta Temple in Rome, the synagogue was gutted by the National Socialists in 1938 and now shows a Jewish history exhibit.

| 0 metres | | 500 |
| 0 yards | | 500 |

SAXONY

Saxony has a long history and is rich in historic sites. Its capital city, Dresden, ranks among the most beautiful and interesting towns in Germany, despite the devastation it suffered during World War II. The region also boasts the enchanting Erzgebirge Mountains and the glorious scenery of "Saxon Switzerland", where the mighty Elbe river runs amid fantastic rock formations.

In the 10th century, Emperor Otto I created an eastern border province (margravate) in the area presently known as Saxony. It quickly grew in size as it expanded into neighbouring territories inhabited by the Polabian Slavs. It was divided and part became the Meissen Margravate, ruled by the powerful house of Wettin from 1089. This dynasty's political power increased when it acquired the Saxon Electorate in 1423; subsequently the entire region under their rule became known as "Saxony".

From 1697 until 1763 Saxony was united with Poland, and the Saxon Great Electors, Frederick Augustus the Strong and his son Frederick Augustus II, were also kings of Poland. During this period Saxony flourished, and Dresden became a major centre of the arts and culture until the Seven Years' War (1756–63) put an end to the region's prosperity. In 1806, Saxony declared itself on the side of Napoleon, and the Great Elector acquired the title of King. But Saxony paid a heavy price for supporting Napoleon – following the Congress of Vienna (1815), the kingdom lost the northern half of its territory to Prussia, and in 1871 it was incorporated into the German Empire.

At the end of World War II Saxony was in the Soviet-occupied zone and became part of the GDR in 1949. Since 1990 it has been a state in the Federal Republic of Germany. Saxony is densely populated and in some parts heavily industrialized, but it also has many interesting and unspoiled towns.

The scenic Bastei rocks in Saxon Switzerland

◀ Night-time view of Dresden's Brühlsche Terrace

Exploring Saxony

When travelling in Saxony, a visit to Dresden is a must. Visitors should set aside several days to explore its historic sights and magnificent museums. Dresden is also a convenient base for excursions to the attractive landscapes of the Sächsische Schweiz ("Saxon Switzerland") and further afield – to Bautzen, Görlitz and Zittau, or to the Erzgebirge Mountains, towards Freiberg and Chemnitz. Another town worth visiting, at least for a day, is Leipzig with its historic sights, cultural events, trade fairs and exhibitions.

The Old Town of Bautzen, situated high above the banks of the Spree River

Sights at a Glance

1 *Leipzig pp166–7*
2 Torgau
3 Mulde Valley
4 Zwickau
5 Chemnitz
6 Augustusburg
8 Freiberg
9 Meißen
10 Moritzburg
11 *Dresden pp172–81*
12 Pirna
14 Kamenz
15 Bautzen
16 Bad Muskau
17 Görlitz
18 Zittau

Tours

7 Sächsische Silberstraße
13 Sächsische Schweiz

For additional map symbols *see back flap*

Lutherstadt Wittenberg

Bad Düben

Delitzsch

Halle

Rackwitz

2 TORGA

Eilenburg

LEIPZIG 1

Wurzen

Osch

Markkleeberg

Zwenkau

Colditz

Leisnig

Rochlitz

Burg Kriebse

Wechselburg

3

Rochsburg

Mittweida

Hainic

Meerane

Erfurt

AUGUSTUSB

5

CHEMNITZ

Neukirchen

4 ZWICKAU

Reichenbach

Schneeberg

SÄCHSISCHE SILBERSTR

Plauen

Auerbach

Auersberg 1019m △

7

Annabe Buchho

Oberwiesenthal

Fichtelberg 1214m

Oelsnitz

Vogtland

Nurnberg

Key

▬▬▬	Motorway
▬▬▬	Major road
▬▬▬	Minor road
▬▬▬	Scenic route
▬▬▬	Main railway
▬▬▬	Minor railway
▬▬▬	Country border
▬▬▬	International border
△	Summit

The giant castle and cathedral complex in Meissen

Getting Around

Leipzig and Dresden both have airports, as well as excellent train and road connections with the rest of Germany. The A6 motorway runs west from Görlitz, through Dresden and Chemnitz; the A13 links Dresden with Berlin, and the A14 with Leipzig. Other roads, national and regional, are clearly signposted, and all the towns described in this guide can also be reached by local buses.

Saddle horses grazing on paddocks near Kamenz

0 kilometres 20

0 miles 20

Young musicians in the Barockgarten,
in Großsedlitz, near Dresden

For hotels and restaurants in this area see pp492–503 and pp510–33

❶ Leipzig

Granted town status in 1165, Leipzig is not only one of Germany's leading commercial towns, but also a centre of culture and learning, with a university founded in 1409. An important centre for the German publishing and book trade, it is the home of the Deutsche Bücherei, the German national library established in 1912. During the various trade fairs, such as the Book Fair in spring, it receives a great number of visitors, and it has much to offer in terms of entertainment, including concerts by the renowned Gewandhaus symphony orchestra and the Thomanerchor boys' choir, which boasts Johann Sebastian Bach as a past choirmaster.

Impressively lofty interior of the Neo-Classical Nikolaikirche

Exploring Leipzig

Most of the interesting sights can be found in the old town encircled by the Ring road, which includes Europe's biggest railway station, the **Hauptbahnhof**, built in 1902–15 to a design by William Lossow and Max Hans Kühne. The heart of musical Leipzig beats in the eastern part of the old town, around Augustusplatz. Here stands the **Neues Gewandhaus** (built 1977– 81) and the **Opernhaus** (built 1959– 60). The University Tower nearby is being redesigned.

In Nikolaikirchhof stands the **Nikolaikirche** (church of St Nicholas). The present church was built during the 16th century, although the lower sections of its north tower date from the 12th century. It has Neo-Classical furnishings. The **Alte Handelsbörse** (old stock exchange) in Naschmarkt is an early-Baroque building,

designed by Johann Georg Starcke. Built in 1678–87 and reconstructed almost from the ground after World War II, it is now a concert hall. In front of the building stands a monument (1903) to Goethe showing him as a student.

In the market square, near the beautiful Renaissance town hall, is the **Alte Waage**, the old municipal weigh-house, a Renaissance work by Hieronymus Lotter. It was built in 1555 and reconstructed in 1964 following damage in World War II.

The area to the south of the town square is taken up by a block of trade fair buildings. The most interesting are the beautifully restored **Specks Hof** (Reichestraße/Nikolaistraße), the oldest arcade in Leipzig with three enclosed courts built between 1908 and 1929, and **Mädlerpassage**, built in 1912–14, a Modernist commercial building with a three-tier passageway connecting Grimmaische Straße and Naschmarkt. Beneath it is the **Auerbachs Keller**, magnificent, 16th-century vaults, immortalized by Goethe in *Faust* and featuring a room that bears his name. The **Commerzbank** (Klostergasse/Thomasgasse) and the **Riquet Café**, a fine Viennese-style coffee house, are attractive Art Nouveau buildings.

Lovers of Johann Sebastian Bach's music will wish to visit **Thomaskirche**, the magnificent late-Gothic church of St Thomas, built in 1482–96, where Bach was the choirmaster from 1723. It now

contains the composer's tomb. Worth noting are the beautiful Renaissance galleries built by Hieronymus Lotter, in 1570. The famous Thomanerchor choir still sings at services on Friday evenings and Saturday afternoons, and organ concerts are held in the churches of St Thomas and St Nicholas during the summer months. Bach is also commemorated with a monument in front of the church (1908). Nearby, the **Bosehaus**, a Baroque 17th-century building, is the home of the Bachmuseum, devoted to the composer.

🏛 Grassimuseum

Johannisplatz 5–11. Museum für Völkerkunde: **Tel** (0341) 97 31 900. Museum für Angewandte Kunst: **Tel** (0341) 22 29 100. Museum für Musikinstrumente: **Tel** (0341) 97 30 750. **Open** Library and museum shop with workshops and lectures. Exhibitions: 10am–6pm Tue–Sun.
W **grassimuseum.de**

The Grassimuseum is one of Germany's greatest museum complexes, housing three fascinating collections: the Museum für Völkerkunde (ethnography) with exhibits from around the world; the Museum für Musikinstrumente (musical instruments) with a magnificent collection, including the world's oldest surviving clavichord, and the Museum für Angewandte (decorative arts) with its stunning gold and ivory ornaments, as well as the valuable town treasury.

🏛 Deutsches Buch- und Schriftmuseum

Deutscher Platz 1. **Tel** (0341) 227 13 24. **Open** 9am–4pm Mon–Sat.

The early-Baroque pavilion of the Alte Handelsbörse, the old stock exchange

The Russische Kirche, a pastiche of the churches in Novgorod

This museum is devoted to the history of German literature. It contains rare manuscripts and old prints.

🏛 Museum der Bildenden Künste

Katharinenstr. 10 (Sachsenplatz). **Tel** (0341) 216 999 20. **Open** 10am–6pm Tue & Thu–Sun, noon–8pm Wed.

This museum has an excellent collection of German masters, including Lucas Cranach the Elder, Martin Schongauer and Caspar David Friedrich, as well as other magnificent European paintings. There are canvases by Jan van Eyck, Rubens, Frans Hals, Tintoretto and

sculptures by Balthasar Permoser, Antonio Canova and Auguste Rodin.

🏛 Russische Kirche

Philipp-Rosenthal-Str. 51a. **Tel** (0341) 878 14 53. **Open** 10am–5pm daily (to 4pm in winter).

The Russian Orthodox Church of St Alexius was built in 1912–13 to commemorate the 22,000 Russian soldiers who died in 1813, in the Battle of the Nations. The architect, Vladimir Pokrowski, based his design on the churches of Novgorod in Russia.

🏛 Völkerschlachtdenkmal

Prager Str. **Tel** (0341) 241 68 70. **Open** Apr–Oct: 10am–6pm daily, Nov–Mar: 10am–4pm daily.

This giant, Teutonic-style monument is the work of architect Bruno Schmitz. Completed for the centenary of the 1813 Battle of the Nations, which pitched the combined Prussian, Austrian and Russian armies against Napoleon, it now houses a small museum.

🏛 Altes Rathaus

Markt 1. **Tel** (0341) 261 77 60. Museum für Geschichte der Stadt Leipzig: **Open** 10am–6pm Tue–Sun.

VISITORS' CHECKLIST

Practical Information
Road map E4.
Tel (0341) 224 11 55 & 22 40.
ℹ Richard-Wagner-Str. 1 (0341-710 42 60). 🎭 Leipziger Buchmesse (Mar); Leipziger Orgelsommer (Jul–Aug); Internationaler Johann-Sebastian-Bach Wettbewerb (Jul); Leipziger Jazztage (Oct). **w leipzig.de**

Transport
✈ Flughafen Leipzig–Halle.
🚉 Willy-Brandt-Platz.

The grand Renaissance town hall, built in 1556 to a design by Hieronymus Lotter, is now the home of the municipal museum. One room is devoted to Felix Mendelssohn-Bartholdy, who conducted the symphony orchestra from 1835 until his death in 1847.

🏛 Bacharchive und Bachmuseum

Thomaskirchhof 15–16. **Tel** (0341) 913 72 202. **Open** 10am–6pm daily.

This museum houses archives and documents relating to the life and works of the composer J. S. Bach.

Leipzig City Centre

① Opernhaus
② Gewandhaus
③ Nikolaikirche
④ Alte Handelsbörse
⑤ Alte Waage
⑥ Altes Rathaus
⑦ Mädlerpassage
⑧ Thomaskirche

0 metres 200
0 yards 200

For map symbols see back flap

Doorway of Schloss Hartenfels, with its coat of arms, in Torgau

❷ Torgau

Road map E3. ▦ 23,000. 🚂 🚌 *i* Markt 1 (03421-70 140). ☗ Torgauer Auszugsfest (May). 🅦 **torgau.eu**

This small town, with its scenic location on the Elbe, was once the favourite residence of the Saxon Electors. Its main square is surrounded by attractive houses of various styles, in particular Renaissance. The Renaissance **Rathaus** (town hall), built in 1561–77, has a lovely semicircular oriel. Other old town attractions include the **Marienkirche**, a late-Gothic church with an extended Romanesque west section. The interior has many original features, including a painting by Lucas Cranach the Elder, *The Fourteen Helpers*, and the tomb of Luther's wife, Katharina von Bora, who died in Torgau.

The main historic building in Torgau is the Renaissance **Schloss Hartenfels**, built on the site of a 10th-century castle. Its courtyard is surrounded by clusters of residential wings, including the late-Gothic Albrechtspalast built in 1470–85, the Johann-Friedrich-Bau (1533–6) with its beautiful external spiral staircase and the early-Baroque west wing (1616–23). The **Schlosskapelle** (castle chapel), which was consecrated by Martin Luther in 1544, is considered to be one of the oldest churches built for Protestants.

❸ Muldetal

Road map E4.

Several magnificent old castles nestle in the scenic hills at the confluence of two rivers – the Zwickauer Mulde and the Freiberger Mulde. In the small town of **Colditz**, with its timber-frame houses, lovely Renaissance town hall and Gothic church of St Egidien, stands a huge Gothic castle built in 1578–91 on the site of an 11th-century castle. During World War II it was a famous prisoner-of-war camp known as Oflag IVC.

In **Rochlitz**, 11 km (7 miles) south of Colditz, stands another large castle, built in stages from the 12th to the 16th centuries. Travelling further south you will encounter other castles: the **Wechselburg**, a reconstructed Baroque castle featuring a late-Romanesque collegiate church, as well as the Renaissance castle in **Rochsburg**. In the neighbouring Zschopau valley stands the magnificent, oval **Burg Kriebstein**, built in stages and completed in the late 14th century. This fortress houses a small museum and concert hall, and medieval music concerts are held here during the summer.

❹ Zwickau

Road map E4.
▦ 120,000. 🚂 🚌
i Hauptstr. 6 (0375-27 13 240). ☗ Robert-Schumann-Tage (Jun); TrabiTreffen (Jun).
🅦 **zwickau.de**

An old commercial town, Zwickau flourished in the 15th and 16th centuries. Today it is known for the Trabant cars that were produced here during the GDR era. Almost all the town's attractions can be found in the old town, on the banks of the Zwickauer

Mulde river. The most important historic building in the town is the **Dom St Marien** (cathedral of St Mary), a magnificent late-Gothic hall-church built 1453–1537. Preserved to this day are its original main altar dating from 1479, the work of Michael Wolgemut, the grand architectural Holy Tomb of Michael Heuffner, dating from 1507, as well as a Renaissance font and a pulpit of 1538, both by Paul Speck.

Also worth visiting in the old town are the **Old Pharmacy**, the **Schumann-Haus**, the composer's birthplace (1810), and the Renaissance **Gewandhaus** (cloth house), once the seat of the Drapers' Guild and now a theatre and museum.

❺ Chemnitz

Road map E4. ▦ 260,000.
🚂 Georgstr. 🚌 Markt. *i* Markt 1 (0371-690 680/ 0371-19 433).
🅦 **chemnitz-tourismus.de**

After World War II, when 90 per cent of its buildings had been reduced to rubble, the town was rebuilt in the Socialist-

Gate of the Renaissance pulpit in the Dom St Marien, in Zwickau

Lew Kerbel's monument to Karl Marx at the Stadthalle in Chemnitz

Realist style and renamed Karl-Marx-Stadt. Only a handful of historic buildings escaped destruction. The most interesting is the **Schlosskirche**, the former Benedictine abbey church St Maria, built at the turn of the 15th and 16th centuries.

Sights in the town centre include the reconstructed **Altes Rathaus** (old town hall), the Gothic **Roter Turm** (red tower) and remains of fortifications. In the main square is the reconstructed Baroque **Siegertsches Haus**, originally built in 1737–41 to a design by Johann Christoph Naumann. The new town centre is dominated by the vast **Stadthalle** (city hall) with Lew Kerbel's 1971 monument to Karl Marx. The **König-Albert-Kunstsammlungen** has a museum of natural history and a fine arts collection, including works by Karl Schmidt-Rottluff.

🏛 **Kunstsammlungen Chemnitz**
Theaterplatz 1. **Tel** (0371) 488 44 24. **Open** 11am–6pm Tue–Sun. Bibliothek: 1–6pm Wed. 🖼

❻ Augustusburg

Road map E4. 🔼 5,000 🚌
ℹ Marienberger Str. 24 (037291-395 50). Schloss: **Open** Apr–Oct: 9:30am–6pm daily; Nov–Mar: 10am–5pm daily. 🆆 augustusburg.de

The small town is insignificant compared with the vast palace complex bearing the same name. The best way to get there is by cable car, from Erdmannsdorf. This Renaissance hunting palace was built for the Great Elector, Augustus, in 1567–72, on the site of the former Schloss Schellenberg, which had been destroyed by fire. Constructed under Hieronymus Lotter and Erhard van der Meer, it is a symmetrical, square building with towered pavilions at each corner, joined by galleries, gates and a chapel to the east, with an altar by Lucas Cranach the Younger. Today the palace houses several museums devoted to motorcycles, coaches and hunting.

❼ Sächsische Silberstraße

See pp170–71.

❽ Freiberg

Road map E4. 🔼 45,000. 🚃 🚌
ℹ Burgstr. 1 (03731-419 5190). 🎭 Bergstadtfest (Jun), Silbermann-Tage (Sep). 🆆 freiberg.de

Development of this mining town was due to the discovery of silver deposits, and Freiberg was granted town status in 1186. It escaped World War II with remarkably little damage.

Today its attractions include the reconstructed old town and many historic buildings, the gem among them being the **Dom St Marien** (cathedral). This late-Gothic hall-church, erected at the end of the 15th century, features a magnificent main portal, the Goldene Pforte, dating from 1225–30. Inside are many original items, such as a tulip-shaped pulpit (1505), two Baroque organs by Gottfried Silbermann and many sculptures and epitaphs.

When visiting nearby Untermarkt, it is worth going to the **Stadt- und Bergbaumuseum** (municipal and mining museum) which explains the history of mining in the area, as well as the collection of minerals at the **Mineralien- und Lagerstätten sammlung der Bergakademie**. A stroll along the winding streets will take the visitor to **Obermarkt**, where the 15th-century Gothic town hall, a fountain with the statue of the town's founder and attractive houses can be seen.

Otto of Meissen, founder of Freiberg

🏛 **Dom St Marien**
Untermarkt 1. Goldene Pforte: **Tel** (03731) 225 98. 🕐 May–Oct: 10am–noon, 2–5pm daily; Nov–Apr: 11am–noon, 2–4pm daily. Organ presentation: 11:30am Sun.

🏛 **Stadt- und Bergbaumuseum**
Am Dom 1. **Tel** (03731) 202 50. **Open** 10am–5pm Tue–Sun. 🖼

🏛 **Mineralien- und Lagerstättensammlung der Bergakademie**
Brennhausgasse 14. **Tel** (03731) 39 22 64. **Open** 9am–noon & 1–4pm Wed–Fri, 9am–4pm Sat.

Façade of the Renaissance Schloss Augustusburg

❼ Sächsische Silberstraße

The Saxon silver route, through the Erzgebirge (mineral ore mountains), takes the visitor to some of the most interesting and scenic places of the region. Silver was mined here from the 12th century, and mining traditions have been preserved to this day. Small towns entice visitors with their interesting parish churches, former mining settlements, museums and disued mines.

① **Schneeberg** A small mining town, which to this day cultivates its art and crafts traditions, Schneeberg is also famous for the St Wolfgangkirche, with an altar masterpiece by Lucas Cranach the Elder.

② **Oberwiesenthal** This important wintersports resort, close to the Czech border and at the foot of the Fichtelberg, offers a ski-jump, downhill ski runs and toboggan runs.

③ **Annaberg-Buchholz**
Although the town enjoyed only a brief spell of prosperity in the 16th century, its church from that period, St Annen, ranks among the most beautiful examples of late-Gothic architecture in Saxony.

```
0 km        5
0 miles     5
```

Wolkenstein

Ehrenfrie-dersdorf

Obernhau

Aue

Lauter

Schwarzenberg

⑥ **Marienberg** This small town, with its wonderful Renaissance town hall, is known mainly for the production of furniture.

Key

▬ Suggested route
═ Other road
▬ Scenic route
–·– State boundary
🌄 Viewpoint

⑤ **Greifensteine** Fantastic, craggy rock formations in the north of the region, shaped like an amphitheatre, attract rock-climbers and hill-walkers.

④ **Frohnau** The biggest attraction of this town is its old forge, featuring the Frohnauer Hammer, a huge original hammer that remained in use until 1904.

Tips for Drivers

Length of the route: 55 km (34 miles).
Stopping points: inns and restaurants in every town.

⑨ Meissen

Road map 4E. 🚶 36,000. 🚇 🚌 _i_
Markt 3 (03521-419 40). 🎭 Stadt- und
Weinfest (Sep). **W** **stadt-meissen.de**

Meissen is famous for its porcelain manufacture. Its history began in 929, when Henry I made it the bridgehead for his expansion to the east, into Slav territories. In 966 Meissen became the capital of the newly established Meissen Margravate, and in 968 a bishopric.

This town has retained much of its charm. In the town square is the late-Gothic **Rathaus** (town hall), built in 1472–8, some beautiful Renaissance houses and the **Frauenkirche**, a late-Gothic, 15th-century church boasting the world's oldest porcelain carillon, which was hung here in 1929. It is also worth taking a stroll to St Afra's church, built in the 13th century for the Augustian monks.

🏛 Albrechtsburg

Domplatz 1. **Tel** (03521) 47 070.
Open Mar–Oct: 10am–6pm daily;
Nov–Feb: 10am–5pm daily.
Closed 24, 25, 31 Dec. 🚻

The Albrechtsburg is a vast, fortified hilltop complex with a cathedral and an Elector's palace. The latter was built in 1471–89 for the Wettin brothers, Ernst and Albrecht. Designed by Arnold von Westfalen, its special feature is the magnificent external spiral staircase. From 1710 the palace was used as a porcelain factory. It was restored to its former glory in 1864. Huge wall paintings of this period,

showing historical scenes, are the work of Wilhelm Römann. The cathedral church of St John the Evangelist and St Donat, built from the mid-13th century to the early 15th century, has some splendid early-Gothic sculptures, an altar by Lucas Cranach the Elder in the Georgskapelle and ducal tombs in the Fürstenkapelle.

🏭 Staatliche Porzellan-Manufaktur

Talstraße 9. **Tel** (03521) 46 87 00.
Open May–Oct: 9am–6pm daily;
Nov–Apr: 9am–5pm daily.
W **meissen.com**

The first porcelain factory in Europe was set up in 1710 in the castle and moved to its present premises in 1865. Documents relating to the history of the factory and many interesting examples of its products are on display in the exhibition rooms. Guided tours and demonstrations take the visitor through all the stages of the porcelain manufacturing process.

The Baroque hunting lodge in Moritzburg

⑩ Moritzburg

Road map 4E. 🚇 _i_ Schlossallee
3b (035207-85 40). 🎭 Kammer-
musikfestival (Aug); Fischzug (Oct).

The first hunting lodge in this marshy region was built in the mid-16th century, for Moritz of Saxony. The present **Schloss Moritzburg** is the result of extensive alterations ordered by Augustus the Strong, directed by Matthäus Daniel Pöppelmann, and carried out in 1723–26. The result is a square building, with four cylindrical corner towers. Much of the interior has survived, including period furnishings and hunting trophies.

Also open to visitors is the 17th-century castle chapel decorated with splendid stucco ornaments. Augustus the Strong ordered the marshes to be drained, and the newly available land to be transformed into landscaped gardens and lakes. The **Fasanenschlösschen** (little pheasant castle) in the eastern part of the gardens features several interesting Rococo interiors, and also houses a zoological exhibition.

At the end of World War II, the German artist Käthe Kollwitz spent the last years of her life in Moritzburg. The house in which she lived and worked is now the **Käthe-Kollwitz-Gedenkstätte**.

🏛 Schloss Moritzburg

Tel (035207) 8730. **Open** Feb–Mar:
10am–4pm Sat & Sun; Apr–Oct:
10am–5:30pm daily; Nov–Dec:
10am–4pm Tue–Sun. 🚻

🏛 Fasanenschlösschen

Open as above. 📷 compulsory.

The late-Gothic Rathaus in Meissen

For hotels and restaurants in this area see pp492–503 and pp510–33

⓫ Dresden

One of Germany's most beautiful cities, Dresden first gained its pre-eminence in the year 1485, when the Albertine Wettins decided to establish their residence here. The town blossomed during the 18th century when it became a cultural centre and acquired many magnificent buildings. Almost all of these, however, were completely destroyed during the night of 13/14 February 1945, when British and American air forces mounted a vast carpet-bombing raid on the city. Today, meticulous restoration work is in progress to return the historic city centre to its former glory, now with renewed effort because of the damage caused by flooding in 2002.

Roof top view of Frauenkirche's dome

Statue of the Saxon King Johann, in front of the Sächsische Staatsoper

🏛 Sächsische Staatsoper

Theaterplatz 2. **Tel** (0351) 49 110.
Tours Tel (0351) 79 66 305.

The imposing, Neo-Renaissance building of the Saxon state opera is one of Dresden's landmarks. It is also known as Semperoper after its creator, the famous architect Gottfried Semper, who designed it twice: the first building, erected in 1838–41, burned down in 1869, the second one was completed in 1878. Reconstruction after World War II dragged on until 1985. The opera house was the venue for many world premieres, including *Tannhäuser* and *The Flying Dutchman* by Richard Wagner, as well as many works by Richard Strauss.

In front of the opera, in Theaterplatz, is a monument to the Saxon King Johann, by Johannes Schilling.

🏛 Schinkelwache

Theaterplatz. **Tel** (0351) 49 11 705 (box office). **Open** 10am– 6pm Mon–Fri, 10am–1pm Sat & Sun.

This small Neo-Classical building, with its sophisticated lines and its immaculate proportions, is the work of the famous Berlin architect, Karl Friedrich Schinkel. It was built between 1830 and 1832.

🏛 Hofkirche

Theaterplatz. (Entrance on Schlossplatz). **Open** daily.

This monumental Baroque royal church has served as the Catholic Dom (cathedral church) of the Dresden-Meißen Diocese since 1980. The presence of this Catholic church in staunchly Protestant Saxony was dictated by political necessity: in his struggle for the Polish crown, the Elector, Augustus the Strong, was forced to convert to Catholicism. The church was designed by an Italian architect, Gaetano Chiaveri, and built in 1738–51.

The church's interior has two-tier passageways which run from the main nave to the side naves. Rebuilt after World War II, it features a magnificent Rococo pulpit by Balthasar Permoser, a painting by Anton Raphael Mengus entitled *Assumption* in the main altar, and the vast organ – the last work of Gottfried Silbermann.

🏛 Frauenkirche

An der Frauenkirche. **Tel** (0351) 65 60 656. **Open** 10am–noon, 1pm–6pm daily.

This giant church, designed by Georg Bähr and built in 1726–43, has been restored to its former glory. Once again, the shining, giant dome dominates the city's skyline. Completely destroyed in 1945 by Allied bombing, its shell survived intact, only to collapse later. Reconstruction began in 1993 and is now complete. Notable features include an elegant cupola and, inside, a colourful dome.

🏛 Residenzschloss

Taschenberg 2. **Grünes Gewölbe Tel** (0351) 49 142 000. **Open** 10am–6pm Wed–Mon. **Hausmannsturm Open** 10am–6pm Wed–Mon.

Façade of a wing of the Residenzschloss, with *sgraffito* decoration

This former residence of the Wettin family was built in stages from the late 15th to the 17th centuries. It houses some of the most beautiful art collections in East Germany, including the world famous Grünes Gewölbe (Green Vaults), a vast collection of royal jewels, gems and table decorations. Book in advance for the ground-floor "vault". The Hausmannsturm, which is a tall tower, affords a great view of the Dresden skyline.

🏛 Fürstenzug
Augustusstr.

Langer Gang (long walk) is a long building, erected in 1586–91, which connects the castle with the Johanneum. The elegant façade facing the courtyard is decorated with *sgraffito* and has shady arcades supported by slim columns. It provided an excellent backdrop for tournaments and parades. The wall facing the street features the so-called Fürstenzug (procession of dukes) – a magnificent, 102 m (111 yd)-long frieze depicting the procession of many Saxon rulers. The frieze was originally created by Wilhelm Walther in 1872–6 using the *sgraffito* technique, but it was replaced in 1907 by 24,000 Meissen porcelain tiles.

🏛 Verkehrsmuseum (Johanneum)
Augustusstr. 1. **Tel** (0351) 86 440.
Open 10am–5pm Tue–Sun.

VISITORS' CHECKLIST

Practical Information
Road map E4. 🗺 480,000.
ℹ Prager Str. 10–11 (0351-49 12 00); Schinkelwache, Theaterplatz.
🎫 Flotten-parade der Sächs. Dampfschiffahrt (May); Elbhangfest (Jun); Stadtfest (Aug); Weihnachtsmarkt (Nov–Dec).
🌐 **dresden.de**

Transport
✈ Dresden-Klotzsche 15 km (9 miles) from centre.
🚉 Hauptbahnhof, Wiener Platz (0351-461 37 10).
⛴ Sächsische Dampfschiffahrt, Radebeul, Hertha-Lindner-Str. 10. (0351) 86 60 90.

This late 16th-century Renaissance building, originally designed as royal stables by Paul Buchner, was refurbished in the mid-18th century and housed first a gallery of paintings, later an armoury and a porcelain collection. Since 1956 it has been a museum of transport, with old trams, locomotives, a collection of vintage cars and models of famous German ships.

Fragment of the Fürstenzug, outside Langer Gang

Dresden City Centre

① Zwinger
② Sächsische Staatsoper
③ Schinkelwache
④ Hofkirche
⑤ Residenzschloss
⑥ Fürstenzug
⑦ Johanneum
⑧ Frauenkirche
⑨ Brühlsche Terrasse
⑩ Albertinum
⑪ Stadtmuseum Dresden
⑫ Kreuzkirche
⑬ Neues Rathaus
⑭ Museum f. Sächs. Volkskunst
⑮ Goldener Reiter
⑯ Japanisches Palais

0 metres 100
0 yards 100

For map symbols *see back flap*

🏛 Brühlsche Terrasse
Brühlsche Terrasse.

Once part of the town's fortifications, this attractive terrace subsequently lost its military importance and was transformed into magnificent gardens by the diplomat and patron of arts Heinrich von Brühl, after whom it is named. Offering splendid views over the River Elbe, it was known as "the balcony of Europe". There are several great buildings on the terraces – the first one, seen from Schlossplatz, is the Neo-Renaissance **Landtag** (parliament building); next to it is a small Neo-Baroque building, the **Secundogenitur** library built for the second generation of Brühls, now a popular café; this is followed by the **Kunstakademie** (art academy), known as Zitronenpresse (lemon squeezer) because of its ribbed glass dome. Among the statues and monuments on the terrace are works by the sculptor Ernst Rietschel, the architect Gottfried Semper and the painter Caspar David Friedrich.

🏛 Albertinum
Brühlsche Terrasse. **Tel** (0351) 491 45 90. Galerie Neue Meister. **Open** 10am–6pm Tue–Sun. **W** skd-dresden.de

Originally a royal arsenal, the Albertinum was rebuilt in its current Neo-Renaissance style in the 1880s by Carl Adolf Canzler. Forty years earlier, Bernhard von Lindenau had donated his considerable fortune to the city to set up a collection of contemporary art, which was then displayed in the Albertinum. Today, the building houses two magnificent collections. That of the **Galerie Neue Meister**, which was established in the mid-19th

Two Women on Tahiti, Paul Gauguin, 1892, in the Albertinum

century, contains paintings from the 19th and 20th centuries, including works by the German Impressionists Lovis Corinth and Max Liebermann, landscapes by Caspar David Friedrich, canvases by the Nazarene group of painters and works by European masters such as Edgar Degas, Paul Gauguin, Vincent van Gogh, Édouard Manet and Claude Monet.

The Albertinum's other collection, the **Skulpturensammlung**, is a small collection of sculptures, including remarkable late Baroque and early Rococo works by Balthasar Permoser.

🏛 Kreuzkirche
An der Kreuzkirche 6. **Tel** (0351) 439 39 20. **Open** Summer: 10am–6pm Mon–Fri; winter: 10am–4pm Mon–Fri. Tower: 10am–5pm daily.

The present Baroque/Neo-Classical church was built in 1764–92 to a design by Johann Georg Schmidt. To commemorate the shelling in World War II, the interior has not been fully restored. The Cross of Nails from the ruins of Coventry Cathedral in England creates a powerful symbolic link between the two countries.

🏛 Goldener Reiter
Neustädter Markt.

The **Neustadt** (new town), on the right bank of the Elbe, lost much of its former glory through destruction in World War II. Visitors may therefore be surprised to come across this glistening, gilded equestrian statue of Augustus the Strong in the middle of a square, at the end of the plane tree-lined Hauptstraße. The monument, which was erected in 1736, is the work of Jean Joseph Vinache, court sculptor to Augustus.

The Goldener Reiter in the new town

🏛 Neues Rathaus
Dr.-Külz-Ring.

The giant Neo-Renaissance new town hall, in the southwest of the old town, was erected in 1905–1910. Its round tower (70 m/230 ft), crowned with a gilded statue of Hercules, offers a good view of the old city centre. In the foyer is a large model of the city as planned for 2015.

🏛 Museum für Sächsische Volkskunst (Jägerhof)
Köpckestr. 1. **Tel** (0351) 49 14 20 00. **Open** 10am–6pm Tue–Sun.

This Renaissance hunting lodge on the north bank of the Elbe was built between 1568 and 1613. Its west wing – the only part that escaped destruction – now houses a museum of ethnography with collections of

Secundogenitur library on Brühlsche Terrasse

◀ Moritzburg Castle and its reflected façade, Saxony

Saxon culture and traditions, especially from the Erzgebirge Mountains.

🏛 Japanisches Palais

Palaisplatz II. **Tel** (0351) 81 44 08 41. Museum für Völkerkunde (Museum of Ethnography): **Open** 10am–6pm Tue–Sun. Landesmuseum für Vorgeschichte (State Museum of Prehistory): **Open** 10am–6pm Tue–Sun. Senckenberg Naturhistorische Sammlungen: **Open** 10am–6pm Tue–Sun.

The Baroque Schloss Pillnitz, Augustus the Strong's summer residence

Originally the Dutch Palais, this three-wing structure was built in 1715. It was extended in 1729–31, by Zacharias Longuelune, for Augustus the Strong's Japanese porcelain collection, at which time the palace changed its name. For years the palace served as a library; today it holds spectacular exhibitions run by the above-mentioned museums.

🏛 Pfunds Molkerei

Bautzner Str. 79. **Tel** (0351) 80 80 80. **Open** 10am–6pm Mon–Sat, 10am–3pm Sun.

In the 19th-century part of the Neustadt, with its many bars, galleries, pubs and fringe theatres, stands this old dairy founded by Paul Pfund. Its interior is lined with dazzling, multi coloured tiles, showing Neo-Renaissance motifs relating to the dairy's products. Today there is a shop which offers hundreds of dairy products, as well as a small bar, where visitors can sample the specialities.

🏛 Kraszewski-Museum

Nordstr. 28. **Tel** (0351) 804 44 50. **Open** 1–6pm Wed–Sun.

This small museum is devoted to the life of the Polish writer Józef Ignacy Kraszewski who, having escaped arrest in Warsaw, settled in Dresden in 1853. Inspired by the town's history, several of his novels (for example *Hrabina*

Cosel, Brühl) are set during the time of Augustus the Strong.

🌳 Großer Garten

City centre.

The history of this great garden goes back to the 17th century, although it has been redesigned several times since. At the park's centre stands an early Baroque palace built in 1678–83 to a design by Johann Georg Starcke. A miniature railway takes visitors to Carolasee, a boating lake. It also stops at the botanical gardens in the northwest section of the park, and at the zoo. The Mosaik-brunnen (mosaic fountain) nearby was designed by Hans Poelzig and built in 1926.

🏛 Blaues Wunder

Loschwitz/Blasewitzer Brücke.

The suspension bridge which spans the River Elbe in the eastern part of the town is painted blue and nicknamed "blue wonder". Built in 1891–3, its main span is 141.5 m (464 ft) long. The bridge leads to Loschwitz, a neighbourhood in a picturesque location amidst hills, which has many attractive villas and small palaces built in the 19th century.

🏛 Schloss Pillnitz

Tel (0351) 261 30. Kunstgewerbemuseum Bergpalais: **Open** May–Oct: 10am–6pm Tue–Sun.

Wasserpalais: **Open** May–Oct: 10am–6pm Wed–Mon.

This charming summer residence, on the banks of the Elbe, was built in 1720–23 by Augustus the Strong and designed by Matthäus Daniel Pöppelmann. There are two parallel palaces: the Berg-palais (mountain palace) and the Wasserpalais (water palace); the latter can be reached by stairs directly from the river jetty. Between 1818 and 1826 the two palaces were joined by a third one, the Neues Palais. Today the Bergpalais houses a fascinating museum of decorative art. The main attraction, however, is the park, laid out in English and Chinese styles, with an orangery and pavilions.

🏛 Karl-May-Museum

Radebeul, Karl-May-Str. 5. **Tel** (0351) 837 30 10. **Open** Mar–Oct: 9am–6pm; Nov–Feb: 10am–4pm Tue–Sun. **Closed** 1 Jan, 24, 25, 31 Dec.

Radebeul, 5 km (3 miles) northwest of Dresden, is much visited by the fans of Winnteou, a fictional Indian chief, and his friend Old Shatterhand. A museum is devoted to the life and work of the author, Karl May, who lived and died in Radebeul. It also displays May's large collection of Native American costumes and other items.

The suspension bridge across the Elbe River, nicknamed "Blaues Wunder"

For hotels and restaurants in this area see pp492–503 and pp510–33

The Zwinger

The most famous building in Dresden is the Zwinger, a beautiful Baroque structure. Its name means "intermural", and it was built in the space between the former town fortifications. Commissioned by Augustus the Strong, it was constructed in 1709–32 to a design by Matthäus Daniel Pöppelmann, with the help of the sculptor Balthasar Permoser. Its spacious courtyard, once used to stage tournaments, festivals and firework displays, is completely surrounded by galleries into which are set pavilions and gates. Today it houses several art collections.

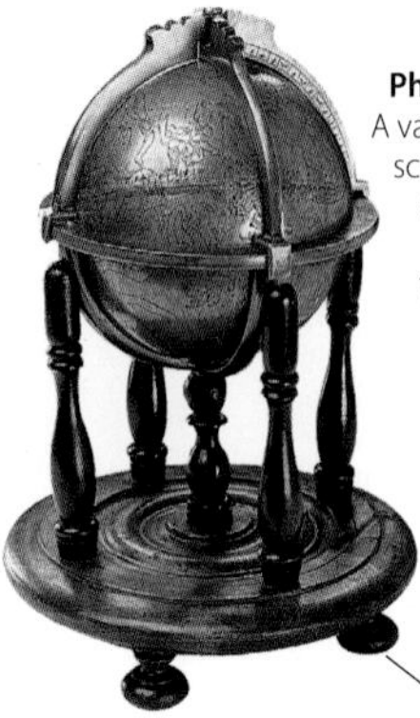

Mathematisch-Physikalischer Salon
A valuable collection of scientific instruments, clocks, sextants and globes, including a 13th-century Arabic globe of the sky.

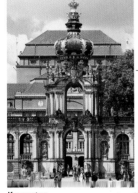

Kronentor
This gate owes its name (crown gate) to the crown positioned on top of its dome.

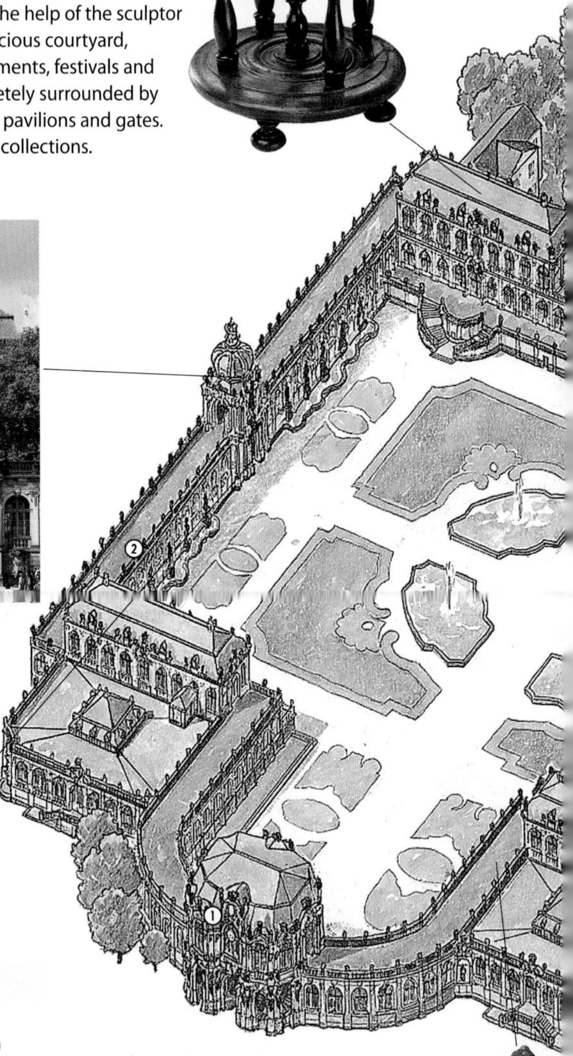

Main entrance
2
1

KEY

① **Glockenspielpavillon** was formerly known as Stadtpavillon (town pavilion). However, the name was changed to carillon pavilion when it acquired a carillon with Meissen porcelain bells, in 1924–36.

② **Allegorical figures** crown the balustrades.

③ **Courtyard**

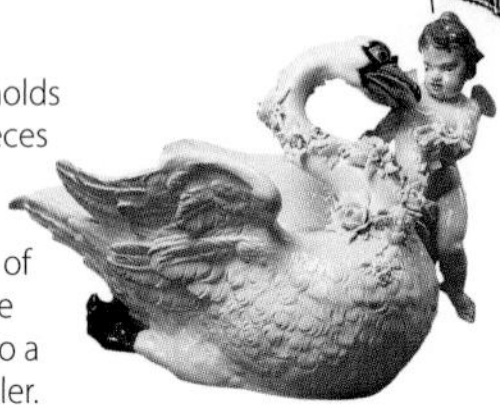

★ Porzellansammlung
The porcelain collection holds Japanese and Chinese pieces but its centrepiece is a collection of Meissen porcelain, including parts of the stunning Swan Service made for Heinrich Brühl, to a design by Joachim Kaendler.

For hotels and restaurants in this area see pp492–503 and pp510–33

Wallpavillon
A stunning marriage of architecture and sculpture, this Baroque masterpiece is crowned by a statue of Hercules, symbolizing the Elector, Augustus the Strong.

★ Nymphenbad
This fountain features tritons and nymphs, sculptures, and grottoes, which were popular in the Baroque era.

Galerie Alte Meister
This gallery of old masters occupies the wing which was added by Gottfried Semper (see pp180–81).

★ Rüstkammer
Exhibited in the armoury are magnificent arms, with the best examples dating from the 16th century, including a suit of armour made for Erik XIV by Eliseus Libaerts in 1562–4.

Gemäldegalerie Alte Meister

The Dresden gallery of old masters contains what is considered to be one of Europe's finest art collections. Its core consists of the canvases collected by the Wettin family from the 16th century, but the majority of exhibits were purchased at the order of King Augustus II the Strong and his son Augustus III. It was during that time that the gallery was moved to its own premises – first to the Johanneum and later to its present home in the Zwinger, built by Gottfried Semper in 1847–55.

Gallery Guide

Until 2015, during an overhaul of the gallery building, the ground floor has works by Raphael, Dürer and Giorgione; the 1st floor, Rembrandt, van Eyck, Velázquez and Titian; and the 2nd floor, paintings by Vermeer, Liotard and Watteau.

2nd floor

1st floor

Dresden landscapes and portraits

Ground floor

Main entrance

Portrait of a Man (c.1633)
This highly expressive portrait, by Diego Rodríguez de Silva y Velázquez, remained unfinished, yet it still captivates with its powerful imagery.

Key

- 15th–17th-century Italian painting
- 15th–16th-century German painting
- Canaletto and scenes of Dresden
- 17th-century Dutch and Flemish painting
- 17th-century French painting
- Spanish painting
- 18th-century Italian and French painting
- German, Czech, Austrian, English and Swiss painting
- Non-exhibition space

★ Self-Portrait with Saskia
(c.1635) This magnificent painting depicting Rembrandt with his wife, Saskia, is considered by some to be a representation of the Prodigal Son of the Bible.

Girl Reading a Letter
(c.1659) This exquisite painting, of a lone woman by the window reading a letter, is among the finest works by Jan Vermeer van Delft.

VISITORS' CHECKLIST

Practical Information
Theaterplatz 1. **Tel** (0351) 491 42000. **Open** 10am–6pm Tue–Sun. 🏛 👫 📷 🚗 ♿
W skd.museum

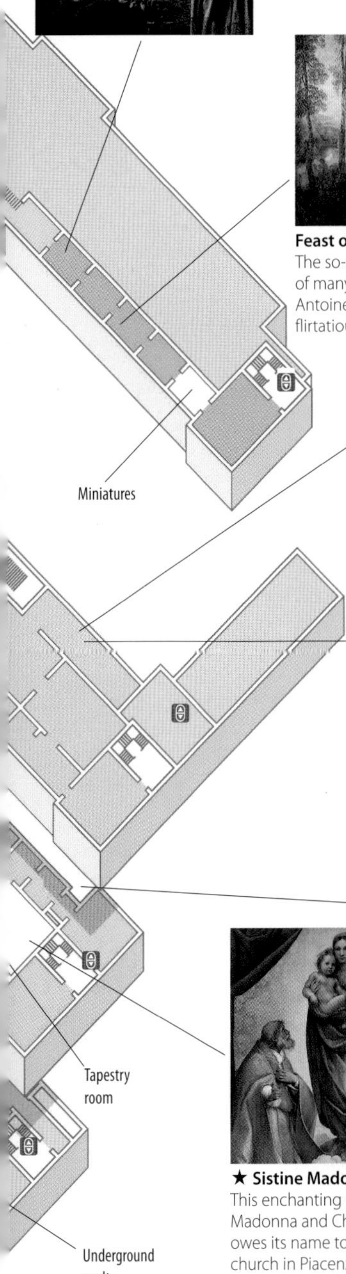

Feast of Love (c.1717)
The so-called fête galante is one of many splendid paintings by Antoine Watteau, depicting a flirtatious group in a park.

Tribute Money (c.1516)
Titian depicts the theme of this popular New Testament parable in an unusual way, zooming in on the figures of Christ and a Pharisee who shows him a coin.

Miniatures

Madonna and Infant Triptych (1437)
This superb small triptych depicting the Virgin Mary with the Holy Infant, St Catherine and the Archangel St Michael, is one of very few works signed by its creator, Jan van Eyck.

Tapestry room

★ Sistine Madonna (1512/13)
This enchanting picture of the Madonna and Child by Raphael owes its name to St Sixtus's church in Piacenza, for which Pope Julius II had commissioned it.

Sleeping Venus (c.1508–10)
This famous nude was probably painted by Giorgione, but when he died of the plague in 1510, his friend, Titian, completed the work.

Underground vaults

Market square with Renaissance Rathaus (town hall) in Pirna

⑫ Pirna

Road map F4. 🚇 38,000. 🚉 🚍
ℹ️ Am Markt 7 (03501-55 64 47).
📅 Stadtfest (Jun). 🌐 pirna.de

In the old town, on the banks of the River Elbe, Pirna has preserved an amazingly regular, chequerboard pattern of streets. Time has been kind to the many historic buildings in this town. Its greatest attraction is the **Marienkirche**, a late-Gothic hall-church with fanciful vaulting designed by Peter Ulrich von Pirna and painted by Jobst Dorndorff, in 1519–0. Inside, an original late-Gothic font and a Renaissance main altar can be seen.

Other interesting buildings are the mid-16th century **Rathaus** (town hall) with its Gothic portals, the beautiful houses in the town square and the ex-Dominican, Gothic church of St Heinrich. **Schloss Sonnenstein**, extended during the 17th and 18th centuries, towers above the old town.

Environs
10 km (6 miles) southwest of Pirna is the picturesque **Schloss Weesenstein**, much altered from its Gothic origins until the 19th century. It houses a small museum with an interesting collection of wallpapers.

🏛 **Museum Schloss Weesenstein**
Müglitztal, Am Schlossberg 1.
Tel (035027) 6260. **Open** Apr–Oct: 9am–6pm; Nov–Mar: 10am–5pm Tue–Sun.

⑬ Sächsische Schweiz

Saxon Switzerland, the wonderfully wild region around the gorge cut into the Lusatian mountains by the River Elbe, features stunningly bizarre rock formations and several formidable castles. The best way to explore the area is on foot as many places are inaccessible to cars. Alternatively you can admire the spectacular scenery from a boat, on the Elbe.

① **Großsedlitz** This vast Baroque park, established after 1719 to a design by Johann Christoph Knöffel, continues to delight visitors to this day with its flower beds and numerous sculptures.

⑦ **Stolpen** The 35-year-old Countess Cosel, one of Augustus II the Strong's mistresses, was imprisoned in this castle, built on rock.

⑥ **Bastei** The "bastion" comprises so-called inselbergs – bizarre, tall rock formations that rise abruptly. Connected by foot-bridges, they offer splendid views.

Weissig

Heidenau

Pirna • Elba

Teplice

② Festung Königstein
This powerful fortress was built in the second half of the 16th century on the site of a medieval castle, and altered in subsequent centuries. Spectacular views have made it a popular tourist destination.

③ Lilienstein
This tall rock, which has to be climbed on foot, rewards the visitor with splendid views of Festung Königstein.

④ Burg Hohnstein
The castle, which holds within its walls a medieval building, is now a museum and one of Germany's largest youth hostels.

Bautzen

Bischofswerda •

6

Gr. Röder

7

ürröhrsdorf

Polenz

ELBSANDSTEIN-GEBIRGE

⑤

⑥

③

Elba

172

②

④

Schmilka

SÄCHSISCHE SCHWEIZ

⑤ Bad Schandau A small spa that is popular as a base for walking tours into the surrounding mountains. A small railway, the Kirnitzschtalbahn, takes visitors to a scenic waterfall, the Lichtenhainer Wasserfall.

Tips for Visitors

Length of tour: 41 km (25 miles).
Stopping places: inns and restaurants in every town.
Suggestions: walk from the railway at the Lichtenhainer Waterfalls to the Kuhstall (cow stable) and Barbarine needle rocks.

Key

▬ Tour route
= Road
▬ Scenic route

0 km   4
0 miles   4

Gothic altar from 1513 in St Annen church, in Kamenz

⓮ Kamenz

Road map F4. 16,800.
Pulsnitzer Str. 11 (03578 379 205).
Hutbergfest (May). **kamenz.de**

The best time for a visit to Kamenz is the end of May or June, when the rhododendrons that cover the Hutberg (294 m/965 ft high) are in flower. The poet, Gotthold Ephraim Lessing, was born in Kamenz in 1729. Although his house no longer exists, the **Lessingmuseum**, founded in 1929, is devoted to his work.

A great fire destroyed much of the town in 1842, but it spared the late-Gothic **St Marien** church, a four-nave 15th-century structure with Gothic altars and other interesting features. Equally noteworthy for their furnishings are the Gothic ex-Franciscan **St Annen** church and the unusual hall-church **Katechismuskirche**. Originally part of the town's fortification system, it has a row of loopholes on its upper storey. The old cemetery and the Gothic funereal church **Begräbniskirche St Just** are also worth a visit. As is the **Museum der Westlausitz**, a museum of the local region.

Lessingmuseum
Lessingplatz 1–3. **Tel** (03578) 380 50. **Open** 9am–5pm Tue–Fri, 1pm–5pm Sat & Sun.

⓯ Bautzen

Road map F4. 44,000.
Hauptmarkt 1 (03591-4 20 16).
Vogelhochzeit (Jan); Lausitzer Fischwochen (Oct). **bautzen.de**

This town is scenically situated on a high rock overhanging the Spree River valley. Known mainly for its top-security jail for political prisoners during the GDR era, today it enchants visitors with its beautifully reconstructed old town. Many signs are bilingual, German and Sorbian, reflecting the fact that Bautzen is the cultural capital of the Sorbs. The winding streets with their original houses, the city walls, the curiously crooked **Reichenturm** tower and the Baroque town hall in the town square form a very attractive complex. It is also worth climbing the 15th-century **Alte Wasserkunst**, a tower that pumped Spree water up to the town. It is the symbol of Bautzen and offers splendid views.

The cathedral **Dom St Peter** is now used jointly by Catholics (choir) and Protestants (nave). The late-Gothic **Schloss Ortenburg** houses the **Sorbisches Museum**, devoted to Sorbian history and culture.

Sorbisches Museum
Ortenburg 3. **Tel** (03591) 42 403. **Open** Apr–Oct: 10am–5pm Tue–Sun; Nov–Mar: 10am–4pm Tue–Sun.

Impressive Baroque entrance to the Domstift in Bautzen

Doorway of the Neo-Renaissance palace in Bad Muskau

⓰ Bad Muskau

Road map F4. 4,170.
Schlossstr. 6 (035771-504 92).
badmuskau.de

Bad Muskau, a small town and spa, boasts one of Saxony's most beautiful parks, which has been included in the UNESCO Cultural Heritage list. It was created in 1815–45 by the writer Prince Hermann von Pückler-Muskau. The Neo-Renaissance palace at its centre was destroyed in World War II and reopened after reconstruction in 2008. The English-style landscaped park surrounding it, a nature reserve since 1952, is well worth visiting. Its main part, on the northern shores of the Lusatian Neisse River, is in Poland. A joint Polish-German programme has opened the entire area to visitors from both sides of the border.

Baroque Neptune fountain in Untermarkt, in Görlitz

⑰ Görlitz

Road map F4. 🚹 66,000. 🚇 🚌
ℹ Obermarkt 32 (03581-475 70).
🎭 Kultursommer (May– Sep);
Sommertheater (Jul); Straßentheater-
festival (Aug). 🔲 **goerlitz.de**

This border town, whose eastern part, Zgorzelec, has belonged to Poland since 1945, boasts a long history. Its oldest records date back to 1071. Founded in 1210–20, the town flourished in the 15th and 16th centuries. In 1990 an extensive restoration plan was begun, and now visitors can see its historic buildings in their former glory.

The charming houses in **Obermarkt** (upper market), the Renaissance portals and decorations on houses in Brüderstraße and the fascinating **Untermarkt** (lower market), with its vast town hall complex, enchant everyone. The older wing of the town hall, the work of Wendel Roskopf, has an amazing external staircase with Renaissance ornaments, and winds around the statue of Justice.

One of the most remarkable churches is the imposing five-nave, 15th-century **Haupt-stadtpfarrkirche St Peter und St Paul** whose Baroque furnish-ings are among the finest in Saxony. Also noteworthy is the **Oberkirche**, with an original Gothic main altar and 15th-century wall paintings in the side nave. One of Görlitz's curiosities is the **Heiliges Grab** (Holy tomb), built in 1481–1504, a group of three chapels that are replicas of churches in Jerusalem. Görlitz still has remains of its medieval town fortifications with original towers and gates, including the **Kaisertrutz**, a 15th-century barbican, extended in the 19th century and now home to the town's art collection.

Environs
The small town of **Ostritz**, 16 km (10 miles) to the south, has a charming original Cistercian abbey, St Marienthal (1230). Its red-and-white buildings are to this day inhabited by nuns, who show visitors around and serve food and home-brewed beer.

⑱ Zittau

Road map F4. 🚹 28,000. 🚇 🚌
ℹ Markt 1 (03583-75 22 00).
🎭 Klosterfest (Ascension) (May); Fest
am Dreiländereck (Jun); Stadtfest (Jul).
🔲 **zittau.eu**

Zittau is an excellent starting point for excursions into the Zittau Mountains, a paradise for rock-climbers, walkers and nature lovers. The town itself is splendidly preserved, with many historic buildings, such as the beautiful, Baroque **Noacksches Haus** (Markt 2). The Neo-Renaissance **Rathaus** (town hall) was built in 1840–45, to a design by Carl Augustus Schramm. The **Johanniskirche**, by Karl Friedrich Schinkel, combines elements of Neo-Classical and Neo-Gothic styles and is an excellent example of Historicist architecture.

Environs
The charming spa town of **Oybin**, 9 km (6 miles) south of Zittau, can be reached by narrow-gauge railway. Its attractions include the hilltop ruins of a Gothic abbey, immortalized by Caspar David Friedrich. It is worth timing your visit for a Saturday evening in summer, when you can witness the procession of torch-bearing monks or listen to a concert.

Fountain with a statue of Roland, the French knight, in Zittau

The Sorbs

The Sorbs, also known as the Lusatians or Wends, are an indigenous Slav minority who live in the eastern regions of Saxony and Brandenburg. Their ancestors, the Lusatian Slavs, were conquered by Germans in the 10th century. Although condemned to extermination by the National Socialists, today they enjoy complete cultural autonomy. The revival of their language and traditions is apparent in the bilingual signs in towns.

THURINGIA

Thuringia is a beautiful state, with much to entice the visitor. The Thuringian Forest, in the south, is a highland area densely covered with spruce, beech and oak forests, inviting visitors to ramble along its enchanted trails, while the area's medieval abbeys, castles and charming small towns are popular destinations with those who are interested in art and history.

The Kingdom of Thuring, as it was known in the 5th century, was conquered by the Franks in the following century. The demise of the Thuringian land-graves, who had ruled here for hundreds of years, resulted in the outbreak of the Thuringian War of Secession. It ended in 1264, with most of Thuringia falling into the hands of the Wettin dynasty.

Split into several smaller principalities, the region lost its political might, but driven by the ambitions of many of its rulers, magnificent castles, churches and abbeys were built everywhere. Thanks to enlightened royal sponsors many towns became important cultural centres, such as 18th-century Weimar, whose residents at one time included Johann Wolfgang von Goethe, Friedrich Schiller, Johann Gottfried Herder and Christoph Martin Wieland.

After World War II, Thuringia was initially occupied by the US Army, but it soon passed into the Soviet sphere of influence, and in 1949 it became part of the GDR. In 1952 Thuringia lost its status as a federal state, but this was later restored in the reunited Federal Republic of Germany, in 1990.

The majority of tourist attractions can be found in the southern part of the state. The Thuringian Forest has many popular health resorts and wintersport centres, such as Oberhof. This highland area, cut with deep river gullies, is littered with medieval castles built on steep crags. Many of these are now no more than picturesque ruins, but others, such as the Wartburg, have been completely restored to their former glory, and today delight visitors with their magnificent interiors.

Schloss Belvedere, the royal summer residence in Weimar

◄ A stream running through the beautiful Thüringer Wald (Thuringian Forest)

Exploring Thuringia

A visit to Thuringia is most enjoyable in late summer, when
the magnificent forests of the Thuringian Mountains are set
ablaze with all the hues of red and yellow as the leaves turn
colour, or in spring when verdant green cloaks the trees.
Allow at least one day to explore Erfurt, the state's capital city,
with a further two days in Weimar. Eisenach, with its
magnificent Wartburg castle, is also a must.

Street vendor selling hand-painted
Easter eggs in Erfurt

Sights at a Glance

1. Eisenach-Wartburg pp190–91
2. Heiligenstadt
3. Mühlhausen
4. Sondershausen
5. Kyffhäuser Mountains
6. Gotha
8. Erfurt pp196–7
9. Weimar pp198–9

10. Jena
11. Rudolstadt
12. Saalfeld
13. Gera
14. Altenburg

Walks

7. Thüringer Wald
   (Thuringian Forest)

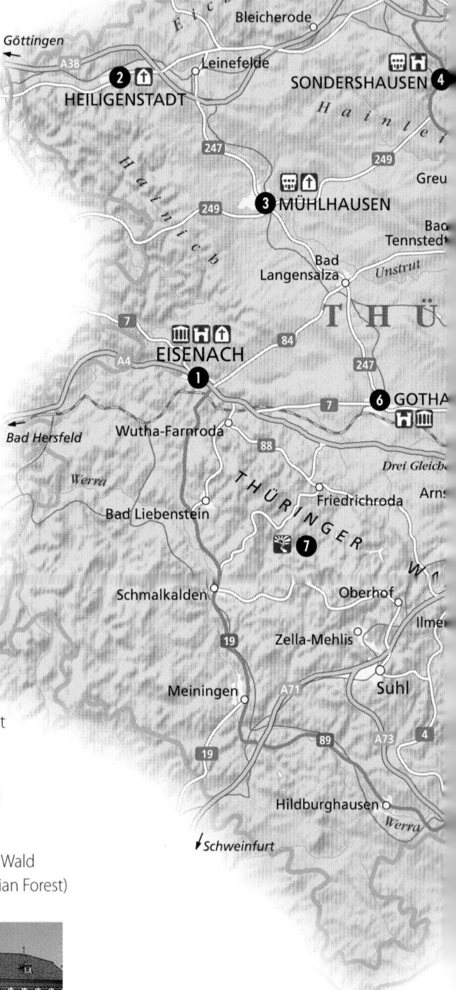

Petersburg fortress in Erfurt

For additional map symbols see back flap

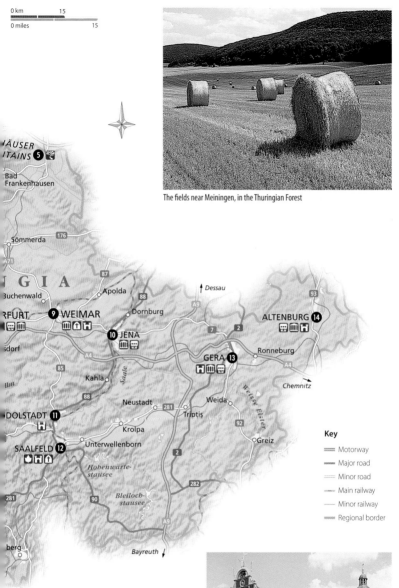

The fields near Meiningen, in the Thuringian Forest

Key

═══ Motorway

─── Major road

═══ Minor road

-·-· Main railway

─── Minor railway

═══ Regional border

Getting Around

Erfurt has an airport. The A4 motorway running through Thuringia links Gera with Jena, Weimar, Erfurt, Gotha and Eisenach. Other towns can be reached by local roads, which are clearly signposted. When touring the Thuringian Forest it is well worth following one of the marked tourist routes, such as Klassikerstraße (the route of the classics) or Porzellanstraße (porcelain street).

The Renaissance town hall in Gotha

❶ Eisenach – Wartburg

The mighty fortress towering above the town is the legendary castle which was probably founded by Ludwig the Jumper, in the late 11th century. Reputedly, it was the setting for the singing contest immortalized by Wagner in his opera *Tannhäuser*. Between 1211 and 1228 the castle was the home of Saint Elizabeth of Thuringia, and from 4 May 1521 until March 1522 Martin Luther found refuge here while he translated the New Testament into German. Major reconstruction in the 19th century gave the castle its old-time romantic character.

Festsaal
The impressive and ornate Festival Hall extends over the entire length and width of the Romanesque Palas. Today, it is the venue for a number of events.

★ Elisabethkemenate
The mosaics adorning the walls of St Elizabeth's rooms illustrate the story of the saint's life. They were designed by August Oetken and placed in 1902–06.

Landgrafenzimmer
In 1854 the landgraves' chambers in the oldest part of the castle, the Palas, were decorated with paintings depicting the castle's history, by Moritz von Schwind.

KEY

① **Neue Kemenate**, the "new chambers", were added during the mid-19th century. Today they house an art collection with beautiful sculptures from Tilman Riemenschneider's workshop.

② **Bergfried** is a vast, square tower crowned with a cross, beautifully restored in the 19th-century.

Vogtei
In 1872 this building acquired an original oriel window (c.1475), brought here from the Harsdörffersches House in Nuremberg.

VISITORS' CHECKLIST

Practical Information
Road map C/D4. 🏘 44,000.
ℹ Markt 9 (03691-79 23-0).
🎻 Thüringer Bachwochen (Mar–Apr). Wartburg: **Tel** (03691) 25 00;
🌐 **wartburg-eisenach.de**
Open guided tours Apr–Oct: 8.30am–5pm daily (gate closes 8pm); Nov–Mar: 9am–3:30pm daily (gate closes 5pm). 🚫 📷

Transport
🚆 🚌

★ Lutherstube
The room where Martin Luther lived and worked for ten months is very plainly furnished and has simple wood-panelling on the walls.

Entrance gate

Exploring Eisenach
The town, at the foot of the castle hill, was founded in the middle of the 12th century and played an important political role in medieval times. There are interesting remains of fortifications, dating from the late 12th century, which include a Romanesque gate, the Nikolaitor. The Nikolaikirche nearby, also Romanesque in style, once belonged to the Benedictine Sisters. In the market square is a 16th-century town hall, and in Lutherplatz stands the house where Martin Luther once lived; it is now a small museum of his work.

⌂ Predigerkirche
Predigerplatz 4. **Tel** (03691) 78 46 78.
Open 11am–5pm Tue–Sun. 🚫
This church, built in honour of Elisabeth von Thüringen shortly after she had been canonized, is part of the Thüringer Museum and has been used for changing exhibitions since 1899. It also houses a permanent exhibition, "Medieval Art in Thuringia".

🏛 Automobile Welt Eisenach
F. Naumanstr. 10. **Tel** (03691) 77 21 2.
Open 11am–5pm Tue–Sun.
This car museum celebrates the local car manufacturing industry in Eisenach. Its collection includes old BMWs and Wartburgs.

🏛 Bachhaus
Frauenplan 21. **Tel** (03691) 7 93 40.
Open 10am–6pm daily. 🚫
🌐 **bachaus.de**
Johann Sebastian Bach, the famous composer, was born in Eisenach in 1685. His birthplace is now demolished, but this small museum nearby is devoted to his life and work.

The Bachhaus and museum, surrounded by a garden

❷ Heiligenstadt

Road map C4. ☷ 17,500. ☐ ☷
ℹ Wilhelmstr. 50 (03606-67 71 41).
Ⓦ **heilbad-heiligenstadt.de**

This pleasant spa and health resort, well placed for visiting the gardens of Eichsfeld, is worth an extended stop. Heiligenstadt is the birthplace of Tilman Riemenschneider, an outstanding sculptor of the Gothic era; it is also the place where the poet and writer Heinrich Heine was baptized in 1825, at the age of 28.

Heiligenstadt has several churches worth visiting, including the Gothic **Pfarrkirche St Marien** with its original wall paintings dating from around 1500. Not far from the church stands the **Friedhofskapelle St Annen**, an octagonal Gothic cemetery chapel. The town's most interesting church, however, is the **Stiftskirche St Martin**, dating back to the 14th–15th centuries. It has a well-preserved Romanesque crypt and an amusing Gothic pulpit, made in the shape of a book-holding chorister.

❸ Mühlhausen

Road map D4. ☷ 38,000. ☐ ☷
ℹ Ratsstr. 20 (03601-40 47 70).
🎭 Mühlhauser Stadtkirmes (Aug).
Ⓦ **muehlhausen.de**

Mühlhausen is one of Thuringia's older towns, with its earliest records dating back to AD 967. In medieval times it enjoyed the status of an imperial free town, which could explain why it became the centre of political activities during the 1525 Peasants' War, led by Thomas Müntzer, a local clergyman. In

Part of the well-preserved town walls surrounding Mühlhausen

1975, on the 450th anniversary of the revolt, the town underwent restoration, and it delights visitors to this day with its beautifully preserved old town surrounded by **city walls**, including gates and towers, which have survived almost intact.

Mühlhausen's streets are lined with charming timber-frame houses. It is also worth stepping into one of the six Gothic churches in this area. The **Pfarrkirche Divi Blasii**, built for the Teutonic Knights, has 14th-century stained-glass windows in the presbytery. The ex-Franciscan **Barfüßerklosterkirche** (on the Kornmarkt) houses a museum devoted to the Peasants' War. The huge five-nave 14th-century **Marienkirche**, a hall-church, is one of Thuringia's largest sacral buildings. It has a magnificent main portal and late-Gothic altars. Another interesting historic structure is the **Rathaus** (town hall), in a narrow street between the old and the new town. This vast complex was enlarged several times, from medieval times until the 18th century.

❹ Sondershausen

Road map D4. ☷ 23,000. ☷
ℹ Markt 9 (03632-78 81 11).
🎭 Residenzfest (Jun), Schlossfestspiele (Jul). Ⓦ **sondershausen.de**

Sondershausen was the capital city of the small principality of Schwarzburg-Sondershausen. The town's main attraction is the **Schloss** (ducal palace), a sprawling building built in stages from the 16th to the 19th century. The palace features some interesting original interiors. Particularly noteworthy are the **Am Wendelstein** rooms, decorated with 17th-century stucco ornaments, as well as the Neo-Classical Liebhabertheater (connoisseurs' theatre, c.1835) and the Baroque Riesensaal (giants' hall), a ballroom with 16 enormous statues of ancient gods. When strolling around the palace gardens it is worth looking at the **Karussell**, an octagonal building dating from 1700.

The most interesting Neo-Classical building complex in town can be found around **Marktplatz** (market square).

Environs
In the **Hainleite** hills, 4.5 km (3 miles) south of Sondershausen, stands the Jagdschloss Zum Possen, once an 18th-century hunting lodge, now an inn. The timber-frame observation tower nearby, dating from 1781, affords beautiful views of the district. **Nordhausen**, situated 20 km (12 miles) to the north, is worth visiting for its attractive timber-frame houses and its 14th-century cathedral, Dom zum Heiligen Kreuz, with a Romanesque crypt.

The extensive façade of the ducal palace in Sondershausen

Monument to Wilhelm I in the Kyffhäuser Mountains

❺ Kyffhäuser Mountains

Road map D4. **ⓘ** Bad Frankenhausen, Anger 14 (034671-71 717).

This small mountain range along the border between Thuringia and Saxony-Anhalt is not only picturesque but is also shrouded in legends and associated with important historic events.

According to one legend, the Emperor Frederick I Barbarossa found his final resting place in one of the caves. Allegedly, he did not drown during the Crusades, as historic records would have us believe, but is waiting here, in the company of six knights. As soon as his beard is long enough to wind three times around the table, it is said, he will return to save Germany from oppression. On the site of the former imperial palace now stands a giant monument with a figure of Barbarossa and an equestrian statue of Emperor Wilhelm I – the work of Bruno Schmitz, erected in 1891–6.

A small health resort, **Bad Frankenhausen**, nestles at the foot of the mountains. It has a number of Gothic churches, including Oberkirche, famed for its leaning tower, and a Renaissance palace, now home to a small museum. Nearby, on the **Schlachtberg** (slaughter mountain), the decisive battle in the Peasants' War took place. The **Pavilion Museum** there holds a vast panoramic picture of the battle, painted in 1971–5.

❻ Gotha

Road map D4. **🗺** 48,000. **🚉 🚌 ⓘ** Hauptmarkt 33 (03621-50 78 57 12). **🎭** Gothardusfest (May). **🌐 gotha.de**

From 1640 the old commercial town of Gotha was the capital of Saxe-Gotha and later of Saxe-Coburg-Gotha Duchy, the dynasty from which Prince Albert, Queen Victoria's husband, descended. The vast ducal palace, **Schloss Friedenstein**, built in 1643–55, towers above the city. This mighty rectangular structure was the first Baroque building in Thuringia. Particularly noteworthy are the ballroom, the palace chapel with the ducal sarcophagi in the crypt and the court theatre, built in 1683. The palace museum houses an art collection including works by famous artists such as Peter Paul Rubens, Anton van Dyck, Frans Hals and Jan van Goyen. The palace garden is also worth a visit. To the south of the palace stands a Neo-Renaissance building, which was purpose-built for the ducal art collection. Now it houses the **Museum der Natur**, a natural history museum. The Renaissance town hall (1567–77) in the old town is surrounded by a number of interesting houses.

Gotha played an important role in the German workers' movement: the Socialist Workers' Party (today's SPD), was founded here in 1875. The conference hall has been reconstructed and houses the **Gedenkstätte der Deutschen Arbeiterbewegung** (memorial to the German workers' movement).

🏛 Schloss Friedenstein
Tel 03621-8234 51. **Open** May–Oct: 10am–5pm Tue–Sun; Nov–Apr: 10am–4pm Tue–Sun.

🏛 Gedenkstätte der Deutschen Arbeiterbewegung
Am Tivoli 3. **Tel** (03621) 70 41 27. **Open** only by prior arrangement.

Doorway of the Renaissance town hall on the Hauptmarkt, in Gotha

❼ Thüringer Wald (Thuringian Forest)

Narrow, winding roads lead through the mountains, which are densely covered with spruce forests. Small towns, charming spas and wintersports resorts nestle in the valleys, while the ruins of once fearsome castles occupy the hilltops. This is prime walking country, and Gotha is the best starting point for a walking holiday. For a longer hike, stop in Ilmenau, and from there follow the upward trail marked G, to a hunters' shelter and a foresters' lodge.

① Friedrichroda
The Neo-Gothic Reinhardsbrunn castle in Friedrichroda was the place where Queen Victoria met her fiancé, Prince Albert von Sachsen-Coburg-Gotha, in 1840.

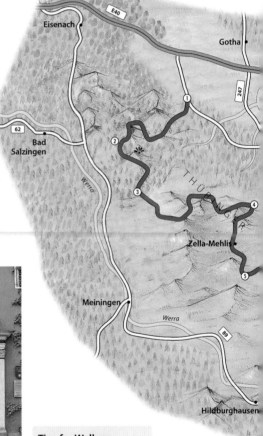

⑨ Drei Gleichen
This name, meaning "three of the same", refers to three castles – Mühlburg and Burg Gleichen have stood in ruins for centuries, but the third castle, Wachsenburg, has survived and now serves as a hotel.

⑧ Arnstadt
This picturesque town, once the home of Johann Sebastian Bach, features a town hall in the Mannerist style, dating from the late 16th century. Other places of interest are an early-Gothic church and a Baroque palace that is now home to a wax museum.

Tips for Walkers

Length: 150 km (90 miles).
Stopping places: inns and restaurants in every town.
Suggestions: walk along the Goethe-Wanderweg trail, from Ilmenau. Train journey by Thüringerwaldbahn, from Gotha via Friedrichroda to Tabarz.

② Trusetal

The magnificent waterfall in Trusetal, the work of human hands, was built in the mid-19th century. Another site worth visiting is the nearby Marienglashöhle in Friedrichroda, an unusual crystal grotto.

③ Schmalkalden

This charming little town, packed with timber-frame houses, attracts visitors to the Wilhelmsburg, its Renaissance palace, and to Neue Hütte, an interesting old smelting plant dating from 1835.

④ Oberhof

This is a popular wintersports resort, with excellent ski-jumps. In the summer it is worth visiting the Rennsteiggarten, the town's botanical gardens with a vast collection of alpine plants.

⑤ Suhl

Famous from the 16th century as a centre of arms manufacture, Suhl's history can today be gleaned in the local Waffenmuseum (armaments museum).

⑥ Ilmenau

This small university town, teeming with life, is the starting point of the so-called Goethe-Wanderweg, a walking trail leading to all the places where the famous poet once stayed.

⑦ Paulinzelle

The 12th-century Romanesque abbey, now in ruins, was once a home for Benedictine monks, but it was later abandoned during the Reformation.

Key

═══ Suggested route

▬▬ Other road

── Scenic route

---

0 km　　　10
0 miles　　10

Erfurt
Weimar
E40
Gera
8
4
B85
Rudolstadt
7
Bad Blankenburg
6
Schwarza
281
Eisfeld

❽ Erfurt

The Thuringian capital, Erfurt, is also the oldest town in the region – its earliest historic records date from AD729, and in AD742 a bishopric was founded here. As an important trading post between east and west, the town grew quickly. Erfurt University was founded in 1392; it became a stronghold for radical thought, and Martin Luther was one of its pupils. Until the 17th century, Erfurt was famous for its red dyes extracted from the madder root; in the 18th century the town became a horticultural centre, and to this day it hosts an impressive garden show in one of Germany's largest parks.

Picturesque half-timbered houses, lining the Krämerbrücke

Exploring Erfurt

The town, on the banks of the river Gera, is dominated by two hills. On the higher one, Petersberg, stands a huge fortress surrounding a Romanesque church, while the lower **Domberg** has two churches, the **Dom St Marien** and the **St Severikirche**. From the Domplatz, at the foot of the hill, a row of narrow streets leads to Fischmarkt. If you cross the river here, you will get to Erfurt's old commercial district and its market square, the Anger.

⛪ Dom St Marien

Domberg. **Tel** (0361) 646 12 65.
Open Apr–Oct: 9am–6pm Mon–Sat, 1–6pm Sun; Nov–Mar: 10am–5pm Mon–Sat, 1–5pm Sun.

The wide stairs leading from Domplatz to the main entrance of the cathedral provide a good view over the 14th-century Gothic presbytery, which is supported by a massive vaulted substructure, known as the Kavaten. The main body of the cathedral dates from the 15th century, but its huge towers are the remains of an earlier Romanesque building. **Maria Gloriosa**, a huge bell 2.5 m (8 ft) in diameter, hangs in the centre tower. Cast by Gerhard Wou in 1497, it is one of the largest bells in the world. The church interior has well preserved Gothic decorations and rich furnishings. Particularly valuable are the 14th- and 15th-century stained-glass windows, the Gothic stalls (c.1370) and Wolfram, a Romanesque

Rich furnishings in the Gothic interior of Dom St Marien

bronze candelabra, (c.1160), shaped like a man.

⛪ St Severi-Kirche

Domberg. **Tel** (0361) 57 69 60.
Open Apr–Oct: 9am–6pm Mon–Sat, 1–6pm Sun; Nov–Mar: 10am–5pm Mon–Sat, 1–5pm Sun.

This five-nave Gothic hall-church, next to the cathedral, dates from the late 13th and early 14th century. Inside it has the Gothic sarcophagus of St Severus, from about 1365, a huge font of 1467 and interesting Gothic altars.

🏛 Fischmarkt

This small market square, with its Neo-Gothic town hall (1870–74), is surrounded by houses dating from various periods, including the 16th-century Renaissance buildings **Zum Breiten Herd** (No. 13, To the Wide Hearth) and **Zum Roten Ochsen** (No. 7, To the Red Ox). On the streets off the market square are three Gothic churches: Michaeliskirche, opposite the ruins of the late-Gothic university buildings, the twin-nave Ilerheiligenkirche (late 13th to early 14th century), and the ex-Dominican Predigerkirche.

🏛 Krämerbrücke

The "merchant bridge" which spans the River Gera is one of Erfurt's most interesting structures. The present stone bridge was built around 1325. It is lined by 32 houses with shops, dating mainly from the 17th to 19th centuries, which replaced its 60 original medieval houses. On its eastern viaduct stands Ägidienkirche, a 14th-century Gothic church.

⛪ Augustinerkloster–Augustinerkirche

Augustinerstr. 10. **Tel** (0361) 576 60 10.
10am–4pm daily.

This early Gothic church was built for Augustinian monks at the end of the 13th century. Particularly noteworthy are its original Gothic stained-glass windows. In the neighbouring monastery, the reconstructed cell where Martin Luther lived as a monk can be admired.

Fischmarkt, surrounded by houses from various periods

🏛 Stadtmuseum

Johannesstr. 169. **Tel** (0361) 655 56 51. **Open** 10am–6pm Tue–Sun.

Erfurt's history museum is housed in a beautiful, late-Renaissance building called **Zum Stockfisch** (To the Dried Cod), built in 1607.

🚏 Anger

Now pedestrianized, this is a market square and Erfurt's main shopping street, lined with attractive 19th-century mansions and commercial premises. There are two Gothic churches: **Kaufmanns-kirche** and **Reglerkirche**, with a huge Gothic altar dating from around 1470. At Nos. 37 and 38 there is the **Dacherödensches Haus**, a complex of beautiful Renaissance buildings.

🏛 Angermuseum

Anger 18. **Tel** (0361) 55 45 615. **Open** 10am–6pm Tue–Sun. Barfüßerkirche: Barfüßerstr. 20. **Tel** (0361) 55 45 615. **Open** Mar–Nov: 10am–6pm Tue–Sun. 📷

The museum, housed in a Baroque building, has a collection of decorative and sacred arts including paintings by Lucas Cranach the Elder, and 19th- and 20th-century German works. One of its rooms is decorated with Expressionist murals (1923–4) by Erich Heckel. The medieval section is in the presbytery of the **Barfüßer-kirche**, a former Franciscan church that was destroyed during World War II.

🏛 EGA and Gartenbaumuseum

Cyriaksburg, Gothaer Str. 38. **Tel** (0361) 223 22 0. **Open** 10am–4pm daily (to 8pm May–Oct). Museum: **Tel** (0361) 22 39 90. **Open** 10am–6pm Tue–Sun. **Closed** Jan & Feb. 📷

On the hill around Erfurt's ruined castle (c.1480) are the grounds of the International Garden Show (*Erfurter Gartenausstellung*). As well as exhibition halls, show gardens and a butterfly house, there is a museum of horticulture and beekeeping.

Environs
Molsdorf, 10 km (6 miles) to the southeast, has a lovely 16th-century Baroque palace set in landscaped parkland, with a museum.

Erfurt City Centre

1. Dom St. Marien
2. St Severi-Kirche
3. Fischmarkt
4. Krämerbrücke
5. Augustinerkirche
6. Stadtmuseum
7. Anger
8. Angermuseum

0 metres 300
0 yards 300

For additional map symbols *see back flap*

❾ Weimar

Had it not been for the enlightened sponsorship of its rulers, Weimar would have become just another residential town in Thuringia. The town flourished, particularly under Duke Carl Augustus and his wife Anna Amalia, when Goethe, Schiller and Herder lived here. Famous 19th- and 20th-century residents included Franz Liszt, Richard Strauss, Friedrich Nietzsche and many distinguished writers and artists associated with the Bauhaus School, which was founded here in 1919. It also gave its name to the Weimar Republic, the democratic German State, lasting from World War I to 1933.

Exploring Weimar

Weimar is relatively small and most of its tourist attractions are near the town centre, on the left bank of the Ilm River. In the north of the centre are the Neues Museum and the Stadtmuseum (municipal museum). Many interesting buildings can be found around Theaterplatz, from where you proceed towards the Markt to visit the ducal palace. In the south of the centre are the former homes of Goethe and Liszt.

St Peter und St Paul, also known as the Herderkirche

🏛 Neues Museum

Weimarplatz 5. **Tel** (03643) 545 400.
Open Apr–Oct: 11am–6pm Tue–Sun; Nov–Mar: 11am–4pm Tue–Sun.

This Neo-Renaissance building, once the Landesmuseum (regional museum), was transformed into a gallery in 1999. It displays changing exhibits of modern art, with an emphasis on colour.

🏛 Stadtmuseum

Karl-Liebknecht-Str. 5–9. **Tel** (03643) 826 00. **Open** 11am–5pm Tue–Sun.

This museum is devoted to the history of Weimar, but it also holds an interesting natural history collection. It is housed in a Neo-Classical house, which was built in the late 18th century for the publisher Justin Bertuch.

🎭 Deutsches Nationaltheater

Theaterplatz 2. **Tel** (03643) 75 50.
The present Neo-Classical building, built in 1906–7 to a design by Heilmann & Littmann, is the third theatre to stand on this site. Famous conductors who worked here include Franz Liszt and Richard Strauss, and it was also the venue for the world premiere of Wagner's *Lohengrin*. In 1919 the National Congress sat in the National-theater and passed the new constitution for the Weimar Republic. In front of the theatre is a monument to Goethe (who founded the theatre) and Schiller, by the sculptor Ernst Rietschel (1857).

🏛 Bauhaus-Museum

Theaterplatz 4. **Tel** (03643) 545 400.
Open 10am–6pm daily.
This museum is devoted to the famous art school, which was founded in Weimar in 1919, moved to Dessau in 1925 *(see p158)* and later, in 1933, to Berlin *(see p92)*.

🏛 Wittumspalais

Theaterplatz. **Tel** (03643) 545 401.
Open Apr–Oct: 10am–6pm Wed–Mon; Nov–Mar: 10am–4pm Wed–Mon.

The Dowager Duchess Anna Amalia lived in this Baroque palace, designed by Johann Gottfried Schlegel and built in 1767–9. Visitors can admire fine interiors and mementoes of the Enlightenment figure Christoph-Martin Wieland.

🏛 Schillerhaus

Schillerstr. 12. **Tel** (03643) 545 401.
Open Apr–Sep: 9am–6pm Tue–Fri & Sun (to 7pm Sat); Oct: 9am–6pm Tue–Sun; Nov–Mar: 9am–4pm Tue–Sun.

The museum is in the house where Friedrich Schiller wrote *Wilhelm Tell* (1804) and spent the last years of his life.

⛪ St Peter und St Paul

Herderplatz. **Tel** (03643) 85 15 18.
Open Apr–Oct: 10am–6pm Mon–Fri, 10am–noon & 2–4pm Sat; Nov–Mar: 11am–noon & 2–4pm daily.

This late-Gothic hall-church has Baroque furnishings and an original altar painted by the Cranachs. It is also known as the Herderkirche, after the poet who preached here.

🏛 Kirms-Krackow-Haus

Jakobstr. 10. **Tel** (03643) 545 401.
Open Apr–Oct: 10am–6pm Tue–Sun.
Closed Nov–Apr.

This Renaissance house, which was extended in the late 18th century, illustrates how people lived in Goethe's time.

⛪ Stadtschloss

Burgplatz 4. Schlossmuseum:
Tel (03643) 54 59 60. **Open** Apr–Oct: 10am–6pm Tue–Sun; Nov–Mar: 10am–4pm Tue–Sun.

This vast ducal castle was rebuilt in the Neo-Classical style for Duke Carl August. It has original interiors and fine paintings from the Weimar Art School, and a gallery devoted to Lucas Cranach.

The Stadtschloss in Burgplatz, with its tall Renaissance tower

For hotels and restaurants in this area see pp492–503 and pp510–33

Picturesque Baroque summer residence known as Schloss Belvedere

🏛 Herzogin-Anna-Amalia Bibliothek

Platz der Demokratie 4. **Tel** (03643) 54 52 00. **Open** 9:30am– 2:30pm Tue–Sun.

This former Mannerist palace, also known as Grünes Schloss (green castle), became the duchess' library in 1761–6. Its oval Rococo interior is one of the finest of its type in Europe.

🏛 Schloss Belvedere

Tel (03643) 545 400. **Open** Apr–Oct: 10am–6pm Tue–Sun. 🧷

This ducal summer residence, which was built between 1724 and 1732 in Belvedere Park, has a fine collection of decorative art from the Rococo period and a wonderful park.

🏛 Goethes Wohnhaus and National Museum

Frauenplan 1. Tel (03643) 54 53 00.

Open Apr–Oct: 9am–6pm, Nov–Mar: 9am–4pm. Closed Mon. 🧷

This house was presented to Goethe by the Duke Carl Augustus. Here the writer wrote his most famous work, *Faust*. Today the museum shows items associated with Goethe and other Enlightenment poets from Weimar.

🏛 Goethes Gartenhaus

Park an der Ilm. **Open** Apr–Oct: 10am–6pm Wed–Mon; Nov–Mar: 10am–6pm Wed–Mon. 🧷

Goethe's first home in Weimar, this small villa is in the pleasant park alongside the River Ilm which Goethe helped design.

🏛 Liszt Museum

Marienstr. 17. **Tel** (03643) 54 54 01. **Open** Apr–Dec: 10am–6pm Tue–Sun. **Closed** Jan–Mar. 🧷

VISITORS' CHECKLIST

Practical Information
Road map D4. 🅰 62,000.
ℹ Markt 10 (03643-74 50).
🎭 Thüringer Bach-Wochen (Mar), Spiegelzelt (May/Jun), Kunstfest (Aug/Sep), Fest an Goethes Geburtstag 28 Aug), Liszt-Tage (Oct), Zwiebelmarkt (Oct).
🌐 weimar-tourist.de

Transport
🚉 Schopenhauerstr.
🚌 Washingtonstr.

Franz Liszt lived here in 1869–86, while he composed the *Hungarian Rhapsody*. His apartment and the room in which he worked have been preserved to this day.

Environs

Buchenwald, 8 km (5 miles) north of Weimar, was the site of a concentration camp set up by the Nazis. During the period 1937 to 1945, over 54,000 people were killed here. It is now a place of remembrance, a museum and a documentation centre.

🏛 Buchenwald

Tel (03643) 430 100. **Open** Apr–Oct: 10am–6pm Tue–Sun; Nov–Mar: 10am–4pm Tue–Sun.

Weimar City Centre

① Stadtmuseum
② Deutsches Nationaltheater
③ Bauhaus-Museum
④ Wittumspalais
⑤ Schillerhaus
⑥ St Peter und St Paul
⑦ Krims-Krackow-Haus
⑧ Stadtschloss
⑨ Grünes Schloss
⑩ Goethe-Museum

0 metres 300
0 yards 300

Key to Symbols *see back flap*

The modest Gothic town hall on Marktplatz, in Jena

⑩ Jena

Road map D4. 🚊 100,000. 🚍 🚌
ℹ️ Markt 16 (03641-49 80 50).
🎭 Altstadtfest (Sep). 🖥️ **jena.de**

Jena is famous for the world-renowned Carl-Zeiss–Jena Optical Works and its university, founded in 1558. One of the most important schools in Germany, its former tutors included Schiller, Fichte and Hegel. The oldest university building is the **Collegium Jenense**. The main building was built by Theodor Fischer in 1905–8. The complex includes a 120-m (394-ft) cylindrical tower block, completed in 1972 and known as the "phallus Jenensis".

In the town's main square, Marktplatz, stands the late-Gothic **Rathaus** (town hall), dating from the early 15th century. Once every hour, a figure known as the Schnapphans tries to catch a ball, a symbol of the human soul. The Gothic church of **St. Michael** nearby was built in the 15th and the 16th centuries. The **Stadtmusem Alte Göhre** has an interesting collection of regional history. In Unterer Markt the **Romantikerhaus** is worth a visit; formerly the home of Johann Gottlieb Fichte, it now houses a museum devoted to the Romantic period.

Also worth visiting are the fascinating **Optisches Museum** on the history of the Carl Zeiss Works and the **Zeiss-Planetarium**, the world's oldest of its type. In the north is the **Goethe-Gedenkstätte**, a museum that is devoted to Goethe's work as poet, politician and scientist.

🏛️ **Stadtmuseum Göhre**
Markt 7. **Tel** (03641) 498 261. **Open** 10am–5pm Tue–Sun, 3–10pm Thu.

🏛️ **Romantikerhaus**
Unterer Markt 12A. **Tel** (03641) 49 82 49. **Open** 10am–5pm Tue–Sun.

🏛️ **Optisches Museum**
Carl-Zeiss-Platz 12. **Tel** (03641) 44 31 65. **Open** 10am–4:30pm Tue–Fri, 11am–5pm Sat.

Historical Zeiss-Workshop
🎭 11:30am Sat.

Environs
Dornburg, 12 km (8 miles) to the northeast, has three palaces: the Altes Schloss, a Gothic castle transformed in the Renaissance; the Renaissanceschloss (1539–47) and the charming Rokokoschloss (1736–41).

⑪ Rudolstadt

Road map D4. 🚊 28,000. 🚍 🚌
ℹ️ Marktstr. 57 (03672-48 64 40).
🎭 Tanz-und Folk Fest (Jul).
🖥️ **rudolstadt.de**

Although Rudolstadt has the Gothic-Renaissance St Andreas church, a fascinating 16th-century town hall and some historic houses, tourists come here mainly to see majestic **Schloss Heidecksburg**, a vast palace perched on a hill. Its present form is mainly the result of reconstruction work carried out in the mid-18th century by Johann Christoph Knöffel and Gottfried Heinrich Krone. Inside

Baroque Schloss Heidecksburg towering over Rudolstadt

are some beautifully arranged Rococo state rooms. The museum also has a splendid porcelain collection, a gallery of paintings and the so-called Schiller's Room. From the castle there are fantastic views of the Schwarza valley.

🏰 **Schloss Heidecksburg**
Schlossbezirk 1. **Tel** (03672) 42 900. **Open** Apr–Oct: 10am–6pm Tue–Sun; Nov–Mar: 10am–5pm Tue–Sun.

Entrance gate to the 11th-century Schloss Ranis, near Saalfeld

⑫ Saalfeld

Road map D4. 🚊 34,000. 🚍
🚌 ℹ️ Am Markt 6 (03671-339 50).
🎭 Zunftmarkt (Jun).

Saalfeld flourished in the 14th–16th centuries. From 1680 it was the seat of the Duchy of Sachsen–Saalfeld, and the magnificent Baroque **Schloss**, built between 1676 and 1720, dates from this period. The former palace chapel, now used as a concert hall, is particularly noteworthy. Also worth visiting is the **Johanniskirche**, a late-Gothic hall-church with interesting furnishings, a valuable Gothic Holy Tomb and the sculpted life-size figure of John the Baptist, carved by Hans Gottwalt, a student of Tilman Riemenschneider.

Another interesting building in Saalfeld is the early-Renaissance **Rathaus** (town hall), built in 1529–37. The town also has well preserved medieval town fortifications with gates and towers. In the southern part of the town stands the **Hoher Schwarm**, ruins of a 13th-century Gothic castle. In Garnsdorf, on the outskirts of Saalfeld, are the **Feengrotten**, grottoes created by both natural and human activity. From the mid-16th century until 1846 alum slate was mined in this cave, called "Jeremiasglück" (Jeremiah's good fortune). It was finally closed due to humidity, but the dripping water has created some astonishingly colourful stalagmites and stalactites.

🔵 Feengrotten Grottoneum
Feengrottenweg 2. **Tel** (03671) 550 40. **Open** Apr–Oct: 9:30am–5pm daily; Nov–Mar: 10:30am–3:30pm daily.

Environs
From Saalfeld it is worth taking a trip to the Hohenwarte-Talsperre, an artificial lake and paradise for watersports enthusiasts. **Burg Ranis**, a scenic hill-top castle, was probably built in the 11th century for an emperor. Later it became the seat of the Thuringian landgraves, Meißen margraves and the counts of Schwarzburg. Now it houses a museum of the region's natural history.

🔵 Gera

Road map D4. 🚗 121,000. 🚊 🚌
ℹ️ Heinrich Str. 35 (0365-830 44 80).
🎭 International Open Air Theatre Festival (Jun), Geraer Höhlerfest (Sep).

The second largest town in Thuringia, Gera is not impressive at first sight, but it has many attractions, including a picturesque **Rathaus** (town hall) whose oldest, Renaissance part dates from 1573–6. The Geraer Elleblon, on the right-hand side of the entrance, is a unit of measurement equal to 57 cm (22 in). A short distance from the market square, in Nikolaiberg, you will find the **Salvatorkirche**. This Baroque church got its Secession-style interior in 1903, after a fire. The theatre (1900–02) was designed in the same style, by Heinrich Seeling. The Küchengarten (kitchen garden) surrounds the

Picturesque Altenburg Castle complex

ruins of **Schloss Osterstein** of which only the Baroque orangerie remains. It now houses the **Kunstsammlung**, with paintings by Lucas Cranach the Elder, Max Liebermann and others.

Otto Dix, a leading artist of the *Neue Sachlichkeit*, was born in Gera, and his birthplace has been turned into the **Otto-Dix-Haus**.

🔵 Kunstsammlung
Küchengartenallee 4. **Tel** (0365) 838 42 50. **Open** 11am–6pm Tue–Sun.

🔟 Otto-Dix-Haus
Mohrenplatz 4. **Tel** (0365) 832 49 27. **Open** 11am–6pm Tue–Sun.

The multi-coloured Renaissance doorway of the Rathaus in Gera

🔵 Altenburg

Road map E4. 🚗 45,000. 🚊 🚌
ℹ️ Moritzstr. 21 (03447-55 18 38).
🎭 Prinzenraubfest (Jul); Altstadtfest (Aug). 🌐 altenburg-tourismus.de

In Germany, Altenburg is known as "Skatstadt", the town of skat, a traditional and very popular card game. Altenburg also has some fascinating historic remains. The **Schloss** (ducal castle), which towers over the old town, has a 10th-century tower, reconstructed mainly in the Baroque style. Today the castle houses the **Spielkartenmuseum** (museum of playing cards). The late-Gothic castle church is also worth seeing. It has rich Baroque furnishings and an organ that was played by the composer Bach. Next to the castle gardens is the **Lindenau-Museum**, with Augustus von Lindenau's collection of 16th–20th century paintings and sculptures, including works by Simone Martini, Fra Angelico, Auguste Rodin, Ernst Barlach and Max Liebermann. The old town, at the foot of the hill, has a beautiful Renaissance town hall with an enormous octagonal tower. In Brühl Platz is a fountain and the figures of skat players, as well as the Baroque **Seckendorffsche Palais** and the Renaissance chancellery.

🔟 Schloss und Spielkartenmuseum
Schloss 2–4. **Tel** (03447) 51 27 12. **Open** 10am–5pm Tue–Sun.

🔟 Lindenau-Museum
Gabelentzstraße 5. **Tel** (03447) 895 53. **Open** noon–6pm Tue–Fri, 10am–6pm Sat, Sun.

SOUTHERN GERMANY

Introducing
  Southern Germany   **204–209**

Munich   **210–233**

Shopping in Munich   **234–235**

Entertainment in Munich   **236–237**

Bavaria   **242–291**

Baden-Wurttemberg   **292–331**

Southern Germany at a Glance

The southern regions of Germany, with their wealth of natural beauty, historic sights and folk culture, are particularly attractive to tourists. This part of the country includes two *Länder*: Bavaria, famous for its Alps, beer and the fairytale castle of Ludwig II at Neuschwanstein, and Baden-Wurttemberg, whose highlights include the Bodensee lake, Heidelberg and taking a trip on the scenic Schwarzwaldbahn railway line between Offenburg and Villingen.

Locator Map

Würzburg Residenz
Set in a magnificent park on the eastern outskirts of the town, this imposing bishop's palace was built between 1720 and 1744, to a design by Balthasar Neumann. The palace is constructed in a U-shape, with a central pavilion flanked by four two-storey courts.

Aschaffenburg

W

Mannheim

Heidelberg

Karlsruhe

Heilbronn

Baden-Baden

Pforzheim

Aalen

Stuttgart

Offenburg

Reutlingen

Ulm

BADEN-WURTTEMBERG
(See pp292–331)

Bibera

Freiburg
in Breisgau

Tuttlingen

Schaffhausen

Konstanz

Kem

Heidelberg Castle is one of Germany's finest examples of a Gothic-Renaissance fortress. Its origins go back to the 13th century, but new buildings sprang up around the inner courtyard during the 16th century as the castle gained importance as a royal residence.

Maulbronn Abbey, founded in the heart of the Stromberg region in 1147, is one of the best-preserved abbeys in Europe. It was established by Cistercian monks with the bequest of a knight named Walter von Lomersheim and provides a graphic account of the austere life led by the monks.

◀ Neuschwanstein Castle, near Füssen

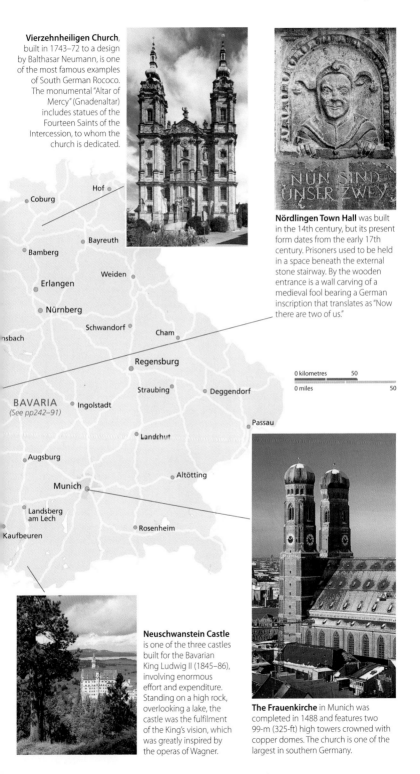

Vierzehnheiligen Church, built in 1743–72 to a design by Balthasar Neumann, is one of the most famous examples of South German Rococo. The monumental "Altar of Mercy" (Gnadenaltar) includes statues of the Fourteen Saints of the Intercession, to whom the church is dedicated.

Nördlingen Town Hall was built in the 14th century, but its present form dates from the early 17th century. Prisoners used to be held in a space beneath the external stone stairway. By the wooden entrance is a wall carving of a medieval fool bearing a German inscription that translates as "Now there are two of us."

Hof

Coburg

Bayreuth

Bamberg

Weiden

Erlangen

Nürnberg

Schwandorf

Cham

nsbach

Regensburg

0 kilometres   50

0 miles   50

Straubing   Deggendorf

BAVARIA
(See pp242–91)   Ingolstadt

Passau

Landshut

Augsburg

Altötting

Munich

Landsberg
am Lech

Rosenheim

Kaufbeuren

Neuschwanstein Castle is one of the three castles built for the Bavarian King Ludwig II (1845–86), involving enormous effort and expenditure. Standing on a high rock, overlooking a lake, the castle was the fulfilment of the King's vision, which was greatly inspired by the operas of Wagner.

The Frauenkirche in Munich was completed in 1488 and features two 99-m (325-ft) high towers crowned with copper domes. The church is one of the largest in southern Germany.

The Baroque in Southern Germany

Because of religious conflicts and the Thirty Years' War (1618–48), the Baroque style did not flourish in Germany until the 18th century. Then it did so most lavishly in the southern, Catholic regions of the country. Here, influenced by Italian architecture, the Baroque reached new heights of flamboyance: the impressive spaciousness of religious buildings provided the setting for dynamic compositions in sculpture, fine stuccowork and vividly coloured *trompe l'oeil* paintings. Southern Germany's major artists of the 18th century included Balthasar Neumann, François Cuvilliés and the Asam brothers.

The main altar in Rohr, which was created by Egid Quirin Asam in 1723, is in the form of a proscenium (stage) with wings. The sculptural group depicts the Assumption of the Virgin Mary into Heaven.

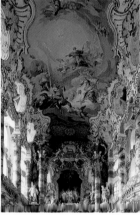

Ceiling frescos were a basic element of the Baroque interior. This example by Johann Baptist Zimmermann in the Wieskirche in Steingaden, presents a glowing vision of the afterlife.

Galleries with curved balustrades add vitality to the interior.

Light plays a vital role in enlivening the interior decoration.

Figures of saints clad in flowing, dynamic robes and standing in curving, asymmetrical poses, complement the rich iconography and complex composition of the altars.

18th-century monasteries in southern Germany, like this one in Ottobeuren with its imposing stairway, are reminiscent of royal residences.

Late Baroque church façades, such as that of the Theatinerkirche in Munich, have a "rippled" design that creates an unusual effect of light and shadow.

Baroque Residences

South German Baroque was not limited solely to religious architecture. As well as the magnificent monasteries and pilgrimage churches, it was also the inspiration for the impressive residences that were built by abbots, as well as by bishops. As in the rest of Europe, these were modelled on the French royal palace in Versailles with its imposing grandeur, striking interiors and breathtaking gardens.

Vaults with fine painting and exquisite stuccowork round off the architectural elements.

The Monstrance in Passau is a fine example of the art of 18th-century goldsmiths, who created these receptacles for the consecrated Host.

The Baroque vestibule in the Neues Schloss in Schleißheim *(see pp268–9)* is decorated with exquisite stuccowork and frescos.

Baroque Interiors

Although they may seem over-elaborate, the late Baroque interiors of southern German churches are carefully planned compositions intended to have a powerful effect. Their magnificent combination of architecture, sculpture and painting, and often organ music, resulted in "Gesamtkunstwerk" – a homogenous work that combines all the arts.

Schloss Nymphenburg was a summer residence of the rulers of Bavaria. It has a grand driveway and a park *(see pp228–9).*

The pulpit and other furnishings are designed to blend harmoniously with the decoration.

Stuccowork fills every interior space that is not decorated with paintings. Sometimes gilded, sometimes white, it may depict complex scenes or, in some cases, be adorned with ornamental designs.

Schloss Favorite is a small palace that forms part of a huge Baroque-style residence in Ludwigsburg *(see pp310–11).*

The German Alps

Part of Germany extends into a fairly moderate section of the Alps, Europe's highest mountain range. They stretch from the Bodensee (Lake Constance) to Berchtesgaden. A section of the northern calcareous Alps belonging to the Eastern Alps of Allgäu, Bavaria and Salzburg falls within Germany. The mountains are a holidaymaker's paradise all year round. In the summer mountain walks can be enjoyed, with well-marked trails, as well as climbing, hang-gliding and paragliding; in the winter skiing is possible in superbly equipped resorts.

Alpine meadows are rich pasture lands, providing premium quality hay. They are also home to a rich variety of wildflowers.

Mountain streams have, over the years, cut a path through the rocks to create picturesque ravines. One of the most beautiful is this one at Wimbachklamm.

Mountain peaks with their breathtaking jagged rocks.

Local architecture blends happily into the landscape.

The Alpine Lakes

A melting glacier created many lakes in Bavaria. Their clear, unpolluted waters attract all kinds of watersports enthusiasts, while the picturesque surroundings are equally popular with other recreational users.

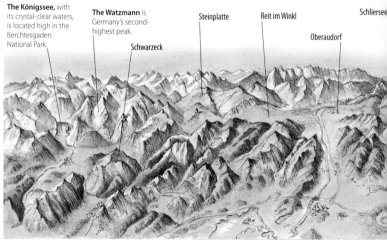

The Königssee, with its crystal-clear waters, is located high in the Berchtesgaden National Park.

The Watzmann is Germany's second-highest peak.

Schwarzeck

Steinplatte

Reit im Winkl

Schliersee

Oberaudorf

The Zugspitze, at 2,962m (9,700 ft), is the highest peak in all of Germany.

Alpine Flora and Fauna

Alpine vegetation varies according to height above sea level. On the lower slopes are mixed deciduous forests. Higher up are Alpine forests, generally coniferous. Above the tree line, dwarf mountain pine grow and higher still are stretches of high-altitude meadows. Beyond this is bare rock. Wild goats are found above the tree line and chamois in the foothills.

The Alpine ibex lives only in the Italian and Swiss Alps. This wild goat with long, backward-curving horns is a rare sight.

The mouflon is a wild sheep with large horns. It is also found in Corsica and Sardinia.

Alpine rock jasmine forms carpets of colour on the mountain slopes.

The Alpine pasqueflower is a white variant of the species that tolerates the harsh soil and climatic conditions of its Alpine habitat.

The peacock butterfly is a common Eurasian species that has adapted successfully to the harsh Alpine environment.

Alpine thrift, with its round heads of pink and purple flowers, is a delightful sight.

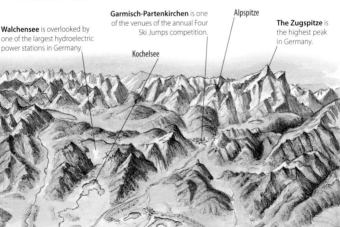

Tegernsee

Walchensee is overlooked by one of the largest hydroelectric power stations in Germany.

Garmisch-Partenkirchen is one of the venues of the annual Four Ski Jumps competition.

Kochelsee

Alpspitze

The Zugspitze is the highest peak in Germany.

MUNICH

The capital of Bavaria, Munich is sometimes called "Germany's secret capital". Lying right at the heart of Europe, the city rapidly overshadowed once powerful neighbours, such as Ingolstadt, Augsburg and Nuremberg, to become southern Germany's main metropolis. With its vibrant cosmopolitan atmosphere, fine buildings, museums and shops, it is one of the country's most popular tourist destinations.

The citizens of Munich have been known for centuries for their love of the arts. The masterpieces that were created here during the Baroque and Rococo periods were equal to Italian and French works.

In the 19th century, the town's development continued along Neo-Classical lines, gaining for it the name of "Athens on Isar". Just how appropriate the name is can be seen when strolling along Ludwigstrasse or Königsplatz or visiting the Glyptothek, which houses Ludwig I's collection of Greek and Roman sculptures.

In the late 19th century the Munich Academy of Fine Arts was amongst Europe's best art schools. Not many cities have as great a choice of world-class theatres, operas and museums as can be found here in Munich.

But it is not only art that gives Munich its unique charm. The country's biggest folk festival, the Oktoberfest, is held each year in Theresienwiese, where visitors to the town can join in the revelries or just sit and watch, ordering a plate of sauerkraut with sausages and washing it down with some of the excellent Bavarian beer.

When planning a shopping trip to Munich visitors can be sure that its shops are equal to those of Paris and Milan, not only in the breadth of their range but also in terms of their prices.

The town is also one of Germany's main centres of high-tech and media industries. Many TV stations and film studios, as well as over 300 book and newspaper publishers, have their main offices in Munich.

The Neo-Gothic Rathaus in Marienplatz, Munich's central square

◄ Interior and ceiling of the Antiquarium Hall in the Residenz Museum

Exploring Munich

Munich, the capital of Bavaria, is exceptionally rich in
interesting museums, churches and historic sights. This
urban conurbation of about 1.4 million inhabitants
increasingly swallows up the neighbouring areas.
Many tourist attractions are located outside the town
centre but, thanks to excellent public transport,
it is easy to visit them. It is worth taking a trip
to Nymphenburg to visit the famous palace
and gardens there. Another interesting
excursion is a stroll along Leopoldstraße
or Theresienwiese, where the huge,
annual Oktoberfest is held.

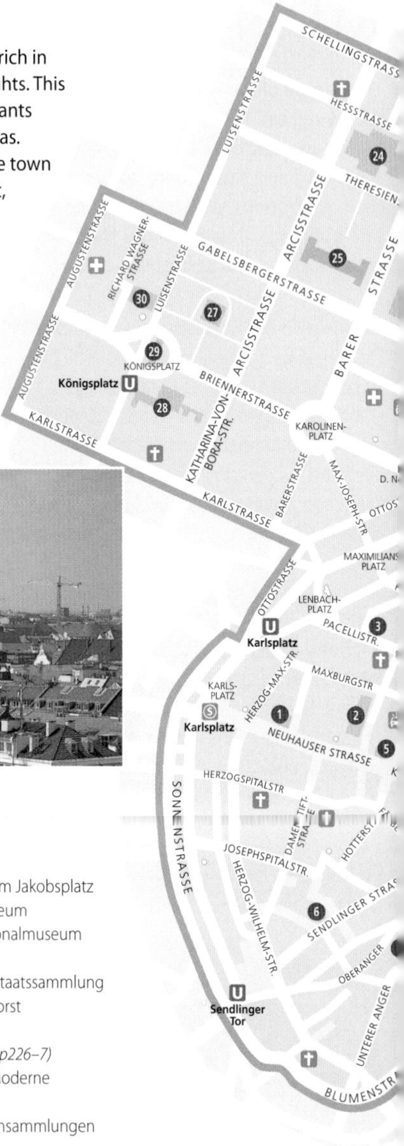

The distinctive towers of Munich's skyline

Sights at a glance

Churches

1. Bürgersaal
2. Michaelskirche
3. Dreifaltigkeitskirche
4. Frauenkirche
6. Asamkirche
16. Theatinerkirche (St Cajetan)
22. Ludwigskirche

Buildings

10. Altes Rathaus
11. Neues Rathaus
14. *Residenz (pp220–21)*
15. Feldherrnhalle
21. Bayerische Staatsbibliothek
29. Propyläen
31. *Schloss Nymphenburg (pp228–9)*
35. Villa Stuck

Museums and Galleries

5. Deutsches Jagd- und Fischereimuseum
7. Stadtmuseum
8. Jüdisches Zentrum Jakobsplatz
12. Völkerkundemuseum
18. Bayerisches Nationalmuseum
19. Schack-Galerie
20. Archäologische Staatssammlung
23. Museum Brandhorst
24. Neue Pinakothek
25. *Alte Pinakothek (pp226–7)*
26. Pinakothek der Moderne
27. Glyptothek
28. Staatliche Antikensammlungen
30. Lenbachhaus
34. *Deutsches Museum (pp232–3)*

Other Attractions

9. Viktualienmarkt
13. Hofbräuhaus
32. Olympiapark
33. Englischer Garten
36. Bavaria-Filmstadt
37. Theresienwiese

Getting there

Munich is an important railway
junction and has its own
international airport. It also has
motorway connections with all the
major towns and cities in Germany.

Television Tower in Olympiapark

Street-by-Street: Around Marienplatz

In medieval times, Marienplatz was Munich's salt- and corn-market. The origins of Munich itself lie with a handful of monks who built their abbey here, giving the place its name (from the word for 'monks') and its heraldic arms. In 1175 town status was officially bestowed on Munich and in 1180 the town was allocated to the Wittelsbachs, who soon established a residence here. During the Reformation, Munich became a bastion of Catholicism and an important centre of the Counter-Reformation. Its magnificent churches, the Altes Rathaus (old town hall) and the Residenz all bear witness to that era.

Karlstor
Known as the Karl's Gate, the west entrance to the old town was part of the medieval fortifications. It was given its present name in 1791, in honour of Elector Karl Theodore.

Augustinerbräu
The oldest and most celebrated brewery in Munich was founded by Augustinian monks in 1328. It currently occupies two 19th-century houses with picturesque façades.

0 metres 50
0 yards 50

❶ ★ **Bürgersaal**
Bürgersaal was built in 1709–10 for a Marian congregation (followers of the Virgin Mary), as a place of meeting and worship. It includes an upper and lower church. Rupert Mayer, an opponent of Nazism, is buried in the crypt. He was beatified in 1987.

❷ **Michaelskirche**
The interior of St Michael's Church is surprisingly large. The massive barrel vaulting over the nave is the second largest after St Peter's Basilica in Rome.

Key

— Suggested route

5 Deutsches Jagd- und Fischereimuseum
A huge collection of hunting and fishing exhibits is housed in the Augustinerkirche. The deconsecrated church, which has an ornate Rococo interior, once belonged to the Augustinian order.

Locator Map
See Street Finder maps pp238–41.

4 ★ Frauenkirche
Partially demolished in 1944–45, this imposing church, with its landmark dome-topped towers, has been rebuilt along Gothic lines.

10 ★ Neues Rathaus
The ornate façade of the new town hall includes figures from Bavarian legend and history. The bronze statue at the top is the "Münchner Kindl" – a character that features in the city's heraldic arms.

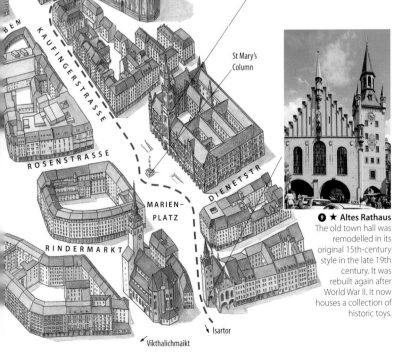

St Mary's Column

STSTRASSE

BEN

KAUFINGERSTRASSE

ROSENSTRASSE

MARIEN-PLATZ

RINDERMARKT

DIENETSTR

↘ Isartor

↙ Vikthalichmaikt

9 ★ Altes Rathaus
The old town hall was remodelled in its original 15th-century style in the late 19th century. It was rebuilt again after World War II. It now houses a collection of historic toys.

Interior of the Bürgersaal, featuring original 19th-century frescoes

❶ Bürgersaal

Neuhauser Straße 14. **Map** 1 F4.
Tel (089) 219 97 20. **U** or **S** Karlsplatz.
🚋 18, 19, 20, 21, 27. Lower church
hall: **Open** 8:30am–7pm daily. Upper
church hall: **Open** 10:30am–noon daily.

This church belonging to the
Marian congregation was
designed by Giovanni Antonio
Viscardi and built by Johann
Georg Ettenhofer in 1709–10.
(The Marian congregation,
founded in 1563, is linked to the
Jesuit order.)

The church was damaged
during World War II, but still
features original frescos. In the
oratory is a figure of the
Guardian Angel by Ignaz
Günther (1770), a fine example
of south-Bavarian Rococo.
Rupert Mayer, parish priest
during World War II and
Munich's leading opponent of
Nazism, is buried in the crypt.

❷ Michaelskirche

St Michael's Church

Neuhauser Straße 6. **Map** 2 A4.
U or **S** Karlsplatz. 🚋 18, 19, 20,
21, 27. **Open** 8am–7pm Tue–Thu &
Sat; 10am–7pm Mon & Fri; 7am–
9:30pm Sun.

The monumental St Michael's
Church was built by Duke
Wilhelm V for the Jesuits who
arrived here in 1559. The
foundation stone was laid in
1585 and initial building work
on the first church, which was
smaller than the present one,
commenced in 1588. However,
the tower in front of the
presbytery collapsed, demolish-
ing a large part of the building.
A transept and new presbytery
were added to the remaining
part of the building and the
church – which was the first
Jesuit church in northern Europe
– was consecrated in 1597. The

Statue of St Michael at the entrance
to Michaelskirche

interior of Michaelskirche is
awe-inspiring, with its wide, well-
proportioned nave, three pairs
of shallow chapels on either side,
a short transept and an elongated
presbytery. It is not certain who
was the architect of the project,
but it is believed that Wolfgang
Müller created the main body of
the church and Wendel Dietrich
the Mannerist façade. Later
extensions are thought to be
the work of a Dutch architect,
Friedrich Sustris.

In the church crypt, which is
open to the public, are the
tombs of many members of the
Wittelsbach dynasty, including
King Ludwig II.

❸ Dreifaltigkeits-
kirche

Holy Trinity Church

Pacellistraße 6. **Map** 2 A3. 🚋 19.
Open 7:30am–7pm daily.

The Baroque church of the
Holy Trinity is one of the few
historic buildings in the city
that avoided bomb damage in
World War II. The church was
built as a votive gift from the
city's aristocracy and clergy
in the hope of averting the
dangers threatened by the
War of the Spanish Succession
(1702–14). The foundation
stone was laid in 1711 and

the church was consecrated seven years later. The royal architect, Giovanni Antonio Viscardi, assisted by Enrico Zucalli and Georg Ettenhofer, created a building that is one of the most beautiful examples of Italian Baroque in Munich. The church's original features include the dome fresco by Cosmas Damian Asam, *The Adoration of the Trinity*.

❹ Frauenkirche

Frauenplatz 1. **Map** 2 B4. Ⓤ or Ⓢ Karlsplatz & Marienplatz. 🚊 19. Church: **Open** 7am–7pm Sat–Thu, 7am–6pm Fri. Tower: **Open** Apr–Oct: 10am–5pm Mon–Sat (7am–8:30pm Thu). **Closed** Sun & holidays.

The site of the Frauenkirche was originally occupied by a Marian chapel, built in the 13th century. Some two hundred years later, Prince Sigismund ordered a new, much bigger church to be built on the site. Its architects were Jörg von Halspach and Lukas Rottaler. The Frauenkirche was completed in 1488, though the distinctive copper onion-domes were not added to its towers until 1525. The church is one of southern Germany's biggest Gothic structures, which can accommodate a congregation of about 2,000.

A triple-nave hall with no transept features rows of side chapels, a gallery surrounding the choir and a monumental western tower. The whole huge structure measures over 100 m (330 ft) in length and almost 40 m (130 ft) wide.

The church treasures that escaped destruction during World War II include a Marian painting, dating from around 1500, by Jan Polak; the altar of St Andrew in St Sebastian's chapel, with statues by Meister von Rabenden and paintings by Jan Polak, dating from 1510; and the monumental tomb of Emperor Ludwig IV of Bavaria, the work of Hans Krumpper (1619–22).

❺ Deutsches Jagd- und Fischerei- museum

German Museum of Hunting and Fishing

Neuhauser Straße 2. **Map** 2 A4. **Tel** (089) 22 05 22. Ⓤ or Ⓢ Marienplatz. 🚊 18, 19, 20, 21, 27. **Open** 9:30am–5pm Mon–Wed, Fri– Sun, 9:30am–9pm Thu. 🅿

Immediately adjacent to St Michael's Church is the Augustinerkloster, the former Augustinian church, which now houses the Museum of Hunting and Fishing. The original building dates from around 1300 (the first Augustinian monks arrived here in 1294). It was rebuilt in the mid-15th century and then remodelled in the Baroque style in 1620–21. The church was deconsecrated in 1803.

Since 1966, the building's ornate Rococo interior has housed a very interesting museum, with a collection of weapons dating from the Renaissance, Baroque and Rococo periods, as well as hunting trophies and related paintings, prints and dioramas. Artists

Carving on main Frauenkirche portal

represented in the museum's collection include several great names such as Rubens, Snyders and Antonio Pisanello.

❻ Asamkirche

Asams' Church

Sendlinger Straße 32. **Map** 2 A5. Ⓤ Sendlinger Tor. 🚊 16, 17, 18, 27. 🚌 52, 152. **Open** 8am–7:30pm daily. ⛪ 5pm Tue, Thu, Fri; 10am Sun. 📷 noon Sat (7 May–24 Sep).

Officially known as St Johann-Nepomuk, this gem of Rococo architecture stands in Sendlingerstrasse and is part of a complex built by the Asam brothers in the mid-18th century. In 1729–30, the sculptor and stuccoist Egid Quirin Asam acquired two properties that he intended to convert into a family home for himself. He subsequently acquired a plot adjacent to these properties, where he wished to build a church devoted to the newly canonized St Nepomuk, a Bohemian monk who had drowned in the Danube. Above the entrance to the church is a statue of the saint.

At the same time, Cosmas Damian, the brother of Egid Quirin Asam, bought a plot on which he built the presbytery. The church building adjoins the residential house of Egid Quirin. The two buildings were joined by a corridor and from one of his bedroom windows the artist could see the main altar.

In this small but unique church, the Asam brothers achieved a rare and striking unity of style. In the dimly lit interior, with its dynamically shaped single nave, no surface is left unembellished. The eye is drawn to the altar, which features a sculpted group of the Holy Trinity.

Pulpit in the Rococo-style Asamkirche

A Wilhelm von Kaulbach painting (1847) in the Stadtmuseum

❼ Stadtmuseum
Town Museum

St Jakobsplatz 1. **Map** 2 A5. **Tel** (089) 23 32 23 70. Ⓤ or Ⓢ Marienplatz. Ⓤ Sendlinger Tor. **Open** 10am–6pm Tue–Sun.

A few steps away from the Viktualienmarkt, on St Jakobsplatz, stands the Town Museum. Its rich collection has been housed since 1880 in the former arsenal building, which was built in 1491–93 by Lucas Rottaler. It is one of Munich's most fascinating museums, with exhibits such as *Typisch München!* (Typical Munich!) illustrating the everyday lives of the city's citizens from the Middle Ages to the present day.

Its greatest treasures are the famous ten dancing Moors by Erasmus Grasser (1480), carved in lime wood and originally numbering 18. Also on the ground floor, in the Waffenhalle, is a splendid collection of arms. Other displays include furniture (in styles ranging from Baroque to Art Deco), photographs, film, brewing equipment and musical instruments. There is also a large and fascinating doll collection, which includes a variety of original puppets, and a collection of paintings and prints.

The museum regularly stages special exhibitions. A cinema, the *Filmmuseum*, puts on nightly showings of English-language films.

❽ Jüdisches Zentrum Jakobsplatz
Jewish Centre Jakobsplatz

St Jakobsplatz 16. **Map** 2 A5. Ⓤ or Ⓢ Marienplatz. **Tel** 23 39 60 96. Jewish Museum: **Open** 10am–6pm Tue–Sun. 🅆 juedisches-museum-muenchen.de

The Jewish Museum, the Jewish Community Centre of Munich and Upper Bavaria, and the main synagogue, Ohel Jakob, together constitute a prestigious modern centre for Munich's Jewish community.

The museum is housed in a cube-shaped building. Three floors of exhibitions, plus a library and a learning centre, all provide extensive information on Jewish culture and history and highlight important aspects of contemporary Jewish life.

The synagogue is crowned by a light-flooded roof. The community centre contains the administrative department, the rabbinate, conference rooms, a kindergarten, a public full-time school, a youth and arts centre and a kosher restaurant.

❾ Viktualienmarkt

Peterplatz-Frauenstraße. **Map** 2 B5. Ⓤ or Ⓢ Marienplatz. 52.

Right at the heart of the city is the Viktualienmarkt, a large square that has been the city's main marketplace for over 200 years. Apart from stalls selling vegetables and fruit brought in daily from suburban orchards or village gardens, the local beer

Colourfully laden market stalls in Munich's Viktualienmarkt

garden provides a welcome retreat for a beer or snack.

One of the features of the square is a statue of famous Munich actor and comedian Karl Valentin (1882–1948), also commemorated in the nearby Valentin Karlstadt Musäum.

An impressive view over the market can be enjoyed from the tower of Peterskirche (St Peter's Church), alongside the square.

Signs of the Zodiac adorning the clock face on the Altes Rathaus

❿ Altes Rathaus
Old Town Hall

Marienplatz 15. **Map** 2 B4. Ⓤ or Ⓢ Marienplatz. **Closed** to visitors. Spielzeugmuseum: **Tel** (089) 29 40 01. **Open** 10am–5:30pm daily. 🅆 spielzeugmuseum-muenchen.de

Munich's old town hall stands in the eastern part of Marienplatz, immediately next to the new town hall. The original building, which has been remodelled several times, was built in 1470–75 by Jörg von Halspach, who also designed the Marian church.

The building's present Neo-Gothic look is the result of remodelling work carried out between 1877 and 1934, when the nearby dual carriageway ring road was being built.

The interior of the building, which was restored following World War II bomb damage, features the Dance Hall with a wooden cradle vault. It is adorned with an old frieze featuring 87 (originally 99) heraldic arms painted by Ulrich Füetrer in 1478, and a further seven carved by Erasmus Grasser in 1477. The figures standing by the walls are copies of the famous dancing Moors, whose originals by Erasmus

Grasser (1480) are kept in the Town Museum (Stadtmuseum).

The lofty tower rising above the old city gate (Talbrucktor) was remade in 1975 based on pictures dating from 1493. Since 1983, the tower has housed the toy collection of the Spielzeugmuseum.

⓫ Neues Rathaus

New Town Hall

Marienplatz 8. **Map** 2 B4. **Tel** (089) 233 00. U or S Marienplatz. **Open** Town Hall and Tower: May–Oct: 10am–7pm daily; Nov–Apr: 10am–5pm Mon–Fri. Carillons: Mar–Oct: 11am, noon, 5pm daily; Nov–Feb: 11am, noon daily.

The Neo-Gothic new town hall standing in Marienplatz was built by Georg Hauberrisser in 1867–1909. Its 100-m (330-ft) high façade features a fascinating set of statues depicting Bavarian dukes, kings and electors, saints, mythical and allegorical figures as well as a variety of gargoyles inspired by medieval bestiaries. The central façade features an 80-m (260-ft) high clock tower, known as Glockenspiele. Each day, at 11am and 5pm, the bells ring out a carillon, while mechanical knights fight a tournament and a crowd dances. The latter is a reenactment of the first coopers' dance, which was held in 1517 to boost the morale of citizens when the town was beset by the plague. Other mechanical figures appear in the windows on the seventh floor in the evenings (9:30pm in summer, 7:30pm in winter). These are flanked by figures of the town guardsman carrying a lantern and the Guardian Angel blessing a Munich child, the *"Münchner Kindl"*.

Statue on façade of Neues Rathaus

Richly decorated entrance to the Völkerkundemuseum

⓬ Völkerkunde-museum

State Museum of Ethnography

Maximilianstraße 42. **Map** 2 D4. **Tel** (089) 210 136 100. 19. **Open** 9:30am–5:30pm, Tue–Sun.

On the opposite side of the ring road from the Maxi-milianeum (the Upper Bavaria Government building) is the State Museum of Ethnography. Built in 1858–65, to a design by E Riedel, its façade is decorated with eight figures personifying the virtues of the Bavarian people: patriotism, diligence, magnanimity, piety, loyalty, justice, courage and wisdom. Originally intended to house the Bavarian National Museum (now in Prinzregentenstraße), the building has been home to the State Museum of Ethnography since 1925. It is the second largest (after Berlin) ethnographic museum in Germany.

The origins of the museum's collection go back to 1782, when curios taken from the treasures of various Bavarian rulers were exhibited in a gallery in the gardens of the residence. Attention began to focus on ethnography after expansion of the collection in 1868. The museum currently houses some 300,000 exhibits depicting the art and culture of non-European nations, with a particular emphasis on the Far East (China and Japan), South America and Eastern and Central Africa. The collection is presented in a series of changing exhibitions.

⓭ Hofbräuhaus

Platzl 9. **Map** 2 C4. **Tel** (089) 290 136 100. U or S Marienplatz. **Open** 9am–11:30pm daily. W **hofbraeuhaus.de**

The Hofbräuhaus is the most popular beer hall in Munich and a great tourist attraction. Established as a court brewery in 1589 by Wilhelm V, it was originally housed in Alter Hof, but moved to Platzl in 1654. In 1830 permission was granted to build an inn where beer could be sold to the public.

The Neo-Renaissance form of the building dates from 1896. The Schwemme, on the ground floor, is a large hall with painted ceiling and room for about 1,000 guests. The Festall, on the first floor, has a barrel-shaped vault and can accommodate 1,300 guests.

In a courtyard, surrounded by chestnut trees, is the beer garden, which is always very popular during the summer.

Guests enjoying a drink in the beer garden of the Hofbräuhaus

⑭ Residenz

This former residence of Bavarian kings has housed a museum since 1920. Over the years, the original Wittelsbachs' castle, which had stood on the site since the 14th century, was gradually extended. Major work in the 17th century included new surroundings for the Brunnenhof and the construction of buildings around the imperial courtyard, Hofkapelle and Reiche Kapelle. Königsbau and Festsaalbau were added in the first half of the 19th century. The Renaissance façade includes two magnificent portals and features a statue of the Holy Virgin as Patroness of Bavaria (Patrona Boiariae).

Hofkapelle
This imposing chapel, dating from the early 17th century, was modelled on St Michael's Church. Vault decorations date from 1614.

Reiche Kapelle
This was the private chapel of Maximilian I. Though smaller than the Residenz's other chapel, it is richly furnished.

Grottenhof
In the eastern section of this courtyard is this grotto lined with crystal, coloured shells and tufa.

★ **Nibelungensäle**
Built by Leo von Klenze, Königsbau features five Halls of the Nibelungs. The rooms owe their name to the wall paintings, which depict scenes from the famous German medieval epic Nibelungenlied.

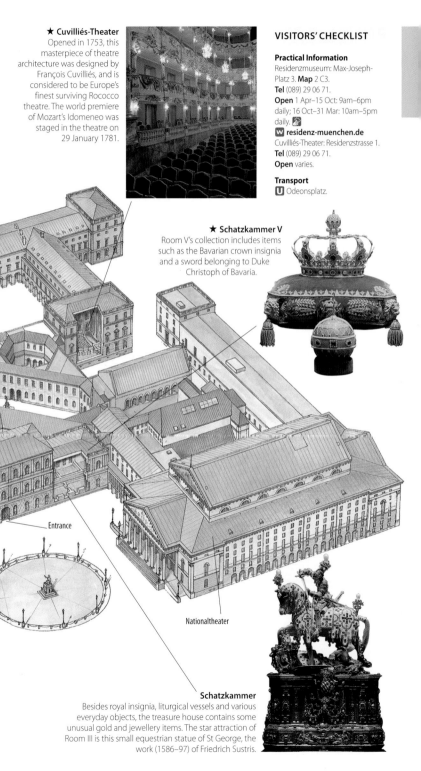

★ Cuvilliés-Theater
Opened in 1753, this masterpiece of theatre architecture was designed by François Cuvilliés, and is considered to be Europe's finest surviving Rococo theatre. The world premiere of Mozart's Idomeneo was staged in the theatre on 29 January 1781.

VISITORS' CHECKLIST

Practical Information
Residenzmuseum: Max-Joseph-Platz 3. **Map** 2 C3.
Tel (089) 29 06 71.
Open 1 Apr–15 Oct: 9am–6pm daily; 16 Oct–31 Mar: 10am–5pm daily.
w **residenz-muenchen.de**
Cuvilliés-Theater: Residenzstrasse 1.
Tel (089) 29 06 71.
Open varies.

Transport
U Odeonsplatz.

★ Schatzkammer V
Room V's collection includes items such as the Bavarian crown insignia and a sword belonging to Duke Christoph of Bavaria.

Entrance

Nationaltheater

Schatzkammer
Besides royal insignia, liturgical vessels and various everyday objects, the treasure house contains some unusual gold and jewellery items. The star attraction of Room III is this small equestrian statue of St George, the work (1586–97) of Friedrich Sustris.

⓯ Feldherrnhalle

Odeonsplatz. **Map** 2 B3.
Ⓤ Odeonsplatz. 🚋 19. 🚌 100.
Open daily.

Until 1816, the site of this monumental building was occupied by a Gothic town gate – Schwabinger Tor. In the early 19th century, however, when Kings Maximilian I Joseph and Ludwig I decided to expand Munich northwards and westwards, their chief architect, Leo von Klenze, ordered the gate to be pulled down, as it stood in the way of the prestigious thoroughfare (Ludwigstrasse) that he intended to build.

Built in 1841–44, the Feldherrnhalle was designed by Friedrich von Gärtner, who modelled it on the Loggia dei Lanzi in Florence. Intended as a monument to the heroes of Bavaria, the interior contains statues of two great military leaders, Johann Tilly and Karl Philipp von Wrede by Ludwig Schwanthaler.

The central carved composition devoted to the heroes of the 1870–71 Franco-Prussian War is much newer, dating from 1882. It was designed by Ferdinand von Miller

The Feldherrnhalle was the scene of Hitler's unsuccessful "Beer-hall Putsch", after which he was arrested. This resulted in the loggia acquiring a certain cult status in Nazi propaganda.

Hitler and the Feldherrnhalle

On the evening of 8 November 1923, Adolf Hitler announced the start of the "people's revolution" in the Bürgerbräukeller and ordered the takeover of the central districts of Munich. On 9 November a march of some 2,000 people acting on his orders was stopped by a police cordon outside the Feldherrnhalle in Residenzstraße. Four policemen and 16 of Hitler's supporters were shot. The marchers were dispersed, and Hitler fled to Uffing am Starnberger See, but was arrested and imprisoned. When Hitler finally came to power in 1933, he turned what became known as the Hitler-Putsch into a central element of the Nazi cult.

The accused in the trial against the participants in the Hitler-Putsch of 1923

⓰ Theatinerkirche (St Cajetan)
St Cajetan's Church

Theatinerstraße 22. **Map** 2 B3. Ⓤ or Ⓢ Marienplatz. 🚋 19. **Open** 7am–8pm daily.

In Odeonsplatz, next to Feldherrnhalle, stands one of the most magnificent churches in Munich, St Cajetan's Church. When Henrietta Adelaide of Savoy presented the Elector Ferdinand with his long awaited heir, Maximilian, the happy parents vowed to build an abbey in commemoration. The project was given to an Italian architect, Agostino Baralli, who based his design on St Andrea della Valle, in Rome.

Although construction work on the church ended in 1690, the façade – designed by François de Cuvilliés – was not completed until 1765–68. The interior of the church is adorned with stuccos by Giovanni Antonio Viscardi and furnished in rich Baroque style. Its twin towers and copper dome are dominant features on the Munich skyline.

⓱ Haus der Kunst
Arts House

Prinzregentenstraße 1. **Map** 3 D2.
Tel (089) 21 12 71 13. 🚌 100.
Open 10am–8pm daily (to10pm Thu).

Built between 1933 and 1937, the Neo-Classical building is the work of a Nazi architect, Paul Ludwig Trost. It opened its doors in 1937 with a display of propaganda art, which was proclaimed by the Nazis as "truly German".

Since 1945 the building has become a dynamic centre of modern art that is famous for its temporary exhibitions.

Its central hall, the former Ehrenhalle (Hall of Honour), which was subdivided into smaller spaces, was reopened in stages, each stage accompanied by a special exhibition. In 2006 the hall once again became the centre of the building and is used as a space for events and temporary installations. In the

Pediment on the gable of Theatinerkirche, with copper dome behind

foyer is a permanent exhibition documenting the history of the building.

In 2002 the National Collection of Modern and Contemporary Arts, which was housed in the west wing, moved to the Pinakothek der Moderne (see p225).

⓲ Bayerisches Nationalmuseum
Bavarian National Museum

Prinzregentenstraße 3. **Map** 3 E3. **Tel** (089) 211 24 01. 🚊 17. 🚌 100. **Open** 10am–5pm Tue–Wed, Fri–Sun, 10am–8pm Thu. **Closed** Mon. Ⓦ bayerisches-nationalmuseum.de

The Bavarian National Museum was founded in 1855 by King Maximilian II. Between 1894 and 1900 it acquired a new building in Prinzregentenstrasse, designed by Gabriel von Seidel; this building alone is worth a closer look. The complex structure consists of wings representing various architectural styles, while the ground floor features halls that are built in styles that are appropriate to their exhibits. This means that the visitor can see Romanesque and Gothic art in Neo-Romanesque and Neo-Gothic rooms, Renaissance art in Neo-Renaissance rooms and Baroque in Neo-Baroque rooms. The individual rooms have been arranged in subject groups, with paintings and sculptures supplemented by superb collections of decorative art and everyday objects, including furniture. The exhibits include a beautiful sculpture of the Madonna by Tilman Riemenschneider.

The first-floor collections are arranged thematically and include German porcelain, clocks, glass paintings, ivory

Conrad Meit's *Judith* (1515), Bavarian National Museum

carvings, textiles and gold items. Particularly interesting is a collection of small oil sketches, painted by artists when designing some large-scale compositions, such as an altar or a ceiling painting.

A special annex houses the Bollert Collection, which contains sculptures from the late-Gothic period.

Poster advertising an exhibition at the Schack-Galerie

⓳ Schack-Galerie

Prinzregentenstraße 9. **Map** 3 E3. **Tel** (089) 23 80 52 24. **Open** 10am–6pm Wed–Sun (1st & 3rd Wed of month: to 8pm). 🚌 100. 🚊 17. 🚶

The magnificent collection of German paintings on display in this gallery come from the private collection of Adolf Friedrich von Schack. They are housed in this elegant building built in 1907 by Max Littmann for use by the Prussian Legation.

As Schack's main interest was in 19th-century painting, the gallery features works that represent the Romantic period, including Leo von Klenze and Carl Spitzweg, as well as witty, fairy-tale works by Moritz von Schwind. Particularly notable are his *Morning*, *In the Woods* and *Rübezahl* – in which the mythical Guardian of the Riesengebirge

Mountains wanders through an enchanted forest. Late 19th-century painters are represented by Franz von Lenbach, Anselm Feuerbach and, above all, by Arnold Bocklin. Bocklin's Romantic works, which are full of symbolism, include *Villa on the Coast* and *Man Scaring a Deer*. The gallery has a large collection of landscapes, including interesting sun-soaked Italian scenes by German masters, as well as a valuable collection of paintings devoted to historic themes.

⓴ Archäologische Staatssammlung
Prehistory Museum

Lerchenfeldstraße 2. **Map** 3 E2. **Tel** (089) 211 24 02. 🚊 17. 🚌 100. **Open** 9:30am–5pm Tue–Sun. 🚶 ♿ Ⓦ archaeologie-bayern.de

Immediately adjacent to the Bavarian National Museum is the Prehistory Museum, which was founded in 1885 by King Ludwig II. Since 1976, this spacious building has housed a rich collection of artifacts from various parts of Bavaria. The oldest items in the collection date from the Palaeolithic era while later exhibits illustrate the region's early history. The collection includes Bronze Age, Roman and early Medieval treasures.

A 3rd-century mosaic floor from a Roman villa, on display in the Prehistory Museum

㉑ Bayerische Staatsbibliothek
Bavarian National Library

Ludwigstraße 16. **Map** 2 C1, C2.
Tel (089) 286 38 23 22. Ⓤ Odeonsplatz, Universität. **Open** times vary.
🚻 (telephone bookings required).
🆆 bsb-muenchen.de

The monumental Bavarian
national library was designed by
Friedrich von Gärtner, who took
over, in 1827, from Leo von
Klenze as the main architect on
the prestigious Ludwigstrasse
project – commissioned by
King Ludwig I. Gärtner was
also responsible for the
Feldherrnhalle, Siegestor, St
Ludwig's Church, and the
University building.

This massive structure, in a
style reminiscent of the Italian
Renaissance, was erected
between 1832 and 1843. Its
external staircase is adorned
with the seated figures of
Thucydides, Hippocrates,
Homer and Aristotle, by Ludwig
von Schwanthaler.

Equally impressive are the
stairs leading to the main
rooms, which are modelled on
the Scala dei Gianti of the Doge
Palace in Venice. With its
collection of 5 million volumes,
the library is on a par with the
Berlin Staatsbibliothek *(see p72)*
as the biggest in Germany.

A statue of Hippocrates at the Bavarian
National Library

The imposing twin-tower façade of
Munich's Ludwigskirche

㉒ Ludwigskirche
St Ludwig's Church

Ludwigstraße 20. **Map** 2 C1.
Ⓤ Universität. **Open** 8am–8pm daily
(to 8:45pm Tue; 7pm Sat).

Inspired by the Romanesque
churches of Lombardy, Friedrich
von Gärtner built this monumental basilica between 1829
and 1844.

The vast interior features
magnificent frescos designed by
the main exponent of the Nazarene style, Peter von Cornelius,
and painted by his associates.
Von Cornelius himself painted
the massive choir fresco, *The Last
Judgement*. One of the biggest
in the world, it rivals in size
Michelangelo's *Last Judgement*.

㉓ Museum Brandhorst

Theresienstr. 35a. **Map** 2 B2. **Tel** (089)
23 80 53 45. Ⓤ Köningsplatz. 🚌 100,
154. 🚊 27.**Open** 10am–6pm Tue–
Sun, 10am–8pm Thu. 🚻
🆆 museum-brandhorst.de

Museum Brandhorst features
the modern and contemporary
art of the Udo and Anette
Brandhorst collection. It
comprises over 700 works,
including more than 60 works
by Cy Twombly, and an
impressively large collection
of Andy Warhol's works. Other
artists represented include

Joseph Beuys, Damien Hirst,
Jean-Michel Basquiat, Sigmar
Polke and Mike Kelley.

Original editions of over a
hundred books illustrated by
Picasso are also on display.

㉔ Neue Pinakothek
The New Pinakothek

Barerstraße 29. **Map** 2 A1. **Tel** (089) 23
80 51 95. Ⓤ Theresienstraße. 🚊 2.
🚌 27. **Open** 10am–6pm Thu–Mon,
10am–8pm Wed. 🚻
🆆 neue-pinakothek.de

This building, designed by
architect Alexander von Branca
from 1975–1981, features a
representative collection of
German works. This includes
Neo-Classicism through
Romanticism, the "Nazarenes",
German and Austrian
Biedermeier, Realism, Historicism,
Impressionism, Pointillism and
Secession paintings.

It also includes works by
renowned French Realists,
Impressionists, Post-
Impressionists and Symbolists,
purchased in 1909–11, when
the gallery's director was the art
historian Hugo von Tschudi. The
space between the Old
and New Pinakothek is a
sculpture park that features a
work by Henry Moore.

Goya's *Marquesa de Caballero* in the Neue
Pinakothek

㉕ Alte Pinakothek
The Old Pinakothek

See pp226–7.

Façade of the Glyptothek, with its central column portico

㉖ Pinakothek der Moderne

Barer Straße 40. **Map** 2 A2. **Tel** (089) 23 80 53 60. Ⓤ Königsplatz. 🚌 53. 🚊 27. **Open** 10am–6pm Tue–Wed & Fri–Sun, 10am–8pm Thu. 🅿 ♿ ▯
🆆 pinakothek-der-moderne.de

Designed by the German architect Stephan Braunfels, this gallery was built to complement the collections in the Alte and Neue Pinakoheks nearby. The modern building brings together the worlds of art, design, graphics, jewellery and architecture under one roof.

Highlights of the collection include Cubist works by Picasso and Georges Braque, and paintings by Matisse, Giorgio De Chirico and Max Beckmann. Pop Art, Minimal Art and photo realism are also represented. The international design collection is outstanding.

㉗ Glyptothek
Glyptotheca

Königsplatz 3. **Map** 1 F2. **Tel** (089) 28 61 00. Ⓤ Königsplatz. **Open** 10am–5pm Tue–Sun, 10am–8pm Thu.

The Königsplatz complex, including Glyptothek and Propylaeum, was the work of Leo von Klenze. It was built in 1816–34 to house Ludwig I's collection of Greek and Roman sculptures and was the first public museum to be devoted to a single art discipline.

The most famous pieces in the museum's collection are the ancient statue of a young man, *Apollo of Terentia* (560 BC), the tomb stele of Mnesareta (380 BC) and sculptures from the front of the Aphaia temple of Aegina.

㉘ Staatliche Antiken-sammlungen
The National Collection of Antiquities

Königsplatz 1. **Map** 1 F2. **Tel** (089) 59 98 88 30. Ⓤ Königsplatz. **Open** 10am–5pm Tue–Sun, 10am–8pm Wed. 🅿

Built in 1838–48 by Georg Friedrich Ziebland, this building is on the south side of the Königsplatz. Since 1967, it has housed one of the world's finest collections of antique vases from the 5th and 6th centuries BC. There are also many other masterpieces of Greek, Roman and Etruscan ornamental art, jewellery and small statues. Among the famous exhibits is a golden Greek necklace from the 4th century BC.

㉙ Propyläen

Königsplatz. **Map** 1 F2. Ⓤ Königsplatz.

Derived from the Propylaea to the Athenian Acropolis, this magnificent Neo-Classical structure stands at the end of Brienner Strasse and is visible from as far as Karolinenplatz. Built by Leo von Klenze in 1846–62, its austere form, featuring Doric porticos, provides an excellent final touch to the composition of Königsplatz by linking together the National Collection of Antiquities and the Glyptotheca.

The Propyläen is also a symbolic gateway to the new parts of the city. It was funded by the private foundation of King Ludwig I, although built after his abdication.

The carved decorations depict scenes from the Greek War of Liberation against Turkey (1821–29), led by King Otto I, son of Ludwig I.

㉚ Lenbachhaus

Luisenstraße 33. **Map** 1 F2. **Tel** (089) 23 33 20 00. Ⓤ Königsplatz. Kunstbau: **Open** 10am–10pm Tue–Sun. 🆆 lenbachhaus.de

This Italian-style villa was built between 1887 and 1891 by Gabriel von Seidl for painter Franz von Lenbach.

Since 1929, it has housed the Municipal Art Gallery. As well as masterpieces such as *Portrait of a Man* by Jan Polak (c.1500), it also has the world's biggest collection of works by the *Der Blaue Reiter* (The Blue Rider) artists. Kandinsky was a leading proponent of this movement.

The Kunstbau, part of Lenbachhaus, is in a subway station under Königsplatz. It features temporary exhibitions.

Fountain in the beautiful front garden of the Lenbachhaus

㉕ Alte Pinakothek

Construction work on the Alte Pinakothek, one of the world's most famous art galleries, began in 1826 and was completed 10 years later. Leo von Klenze designed the Italian Renaissance-style building. The history of princely collections goes back to the Renaissance period, when Wilhelm IV the Steadfast (ruled 1508–50) decided to adorn his residence with historic paintings. His successors were equally keen art collectors and, by the 18th century, an outstanding collection of 14th- to 18th-century paintings had been amassed.

St Luke Painting the Madonna (c.1484)
This is one of the most frequently copied masterpieces by the Dutch painter Roger van der Weyden.

★ Four Apostles (1526)
These two panels were painted by Albrecht Dürer, a founding figure of the German school of art. They were acquired in 1627 by Maximilian I from the town of Nuremberg.

Emperor Charles V (1548)
This portrait was painted by the Venetian artist Titian during the Emperor's visit to the Reich's Parliament in Augsburg.

Main entrance

Key

 Flemish and Dutch paintings

German paintings

Italian paintings

French paintings

Spanish paintings

Temporary exhibitions

Non-exhibition space

Adoration of the Magi (1504)
The depiction of the adoration is just one small part of the most important altarpiece by Hans Holbein the Elder.

Rape of the Daughters of Leukippos (1618)
A highlight of the museum is the Rubens collection, which includes his depiction of the abduction of Hilaeria and Phoibe by Castor and Pollux.

VISITORS' CHECKLIST

Practical Information
Barer Straße 27. **Road map** 2 A1.
Tel (089) 23 80 52 16.
Open 10am–6pm Wed–Sun,
10am–8pm Tue. (admission
free to children under 8.)
w alte-pinakothek.de

Transport
53. 27. Königsplatz.

Gallery Guide

The ground-floor rooms of the gallery are devoted to the works of German old masters dating from the 16th and 17th centuries. On the first floor are works by Dutch, Flemish, French, German, Italian and Spanish artists.

First floor

★ **Descent from the Cross** (1633)
Rembrandt's dramatic vision of the Saviour's sacrifice emotively depicts Christ's passion.

Disrobing of Christ (c.1583–84)
The gallery's small but interesting collection of Spanish paintings includes this work by El Greco, one of his three most important compositions.

★ **Land of Cockaigne** (1567)
In this vividly detailed painting by Pieter Brueghel the Elder, the Flemish artist depicts the mythical land of plenty. The work is an ironic condemnation of gluttony and laziness, themes that are depicted in its many humorous scenes.

Ground floor

㉛ Schloss Nymphenburg

One of Europe's most beautiful palaces, Schloss Nymphenburg grew up around an Italianate villa built in 1663–64 for the Electress Henriette-Adelaide to a design by Agostino Barelli. The palace was dedicated to the pastoral goddess Flora and her nymphs, hence the name. Several additions were made over the years, including four pavilions. These were designed by Joseph Effner and Enrico Zuccalli who directed works from 1715. Built to the side of the original villa, these were connected by arcaded passageways.

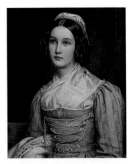

★ Gallery of Beauties
Portraits of royal favourites include this one of Helene Sedlmayr, a 17-year-old girl from Munich.

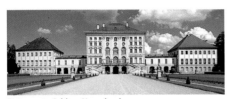

Entrance to Schloss Nymphenburg
Seen in this view are the original Italianate villa and two of the side pavilions that were added later.

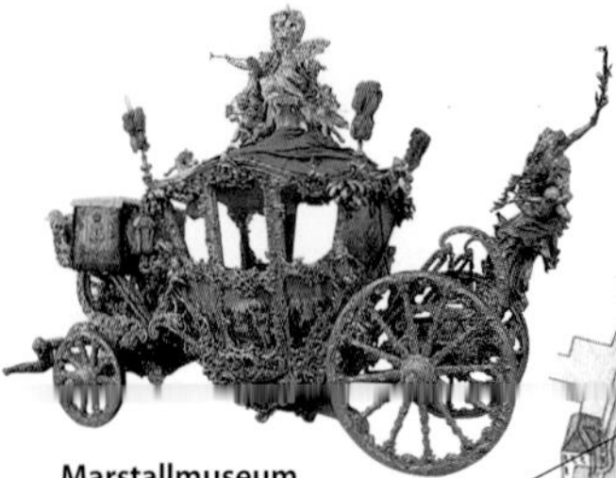

Marstallmuseum
The former stables house a collection of carriages that once belonged to Bavarian rulers. They include the magnificent carriages of Ludwig II.

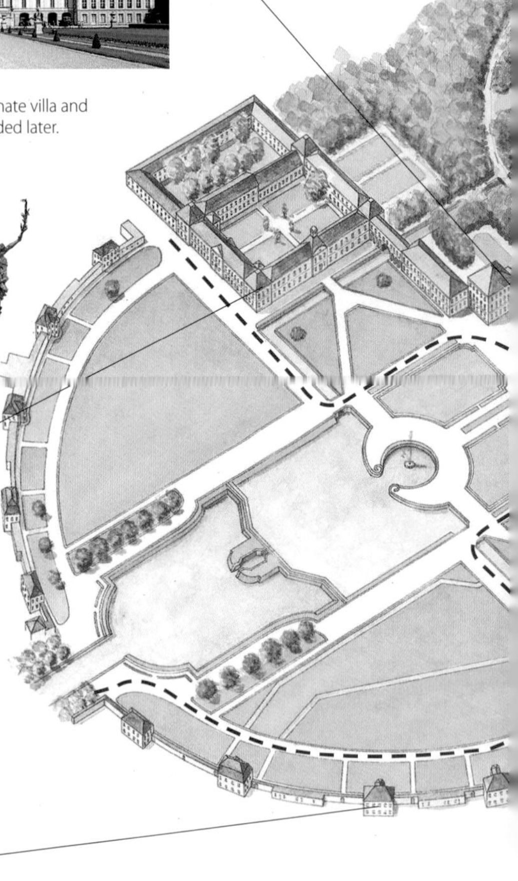

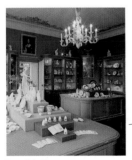

Porcelain Factory
Established in 1747 by Franz Anton Bustelli and transferred to Nymphenburg in 1761, this is one of the oldest porcelain factories in Europe.

Key

▬ Suggested route

KEY

① **Museum Mensch und Natur** is devoted to the research of geology and human biology.

For hotels and restaurants in this area see pp492–503 and pp510–33

★ Amalienburg
The interior of this hunting lodge in the Schlosspark is a superb example of Rococo style by François Cuvilliés.

Magdalenenklause
After a lifetime of revels, Maximilian Emanuel commissioned a hermitage where he could pray and meditate. It was completed in 1725.

Badenburg →

Pagodenburg ↗

Lackkabinett
This small 17th-century cabinet owes its name to its panels of black and red Chinese lacquer.

Botanical Garden
A collection of botanical specimens, including many rare plants, is featured in this fascinating garden.

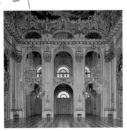

★ Festsaal (Steinernen Saal)
Featuring decorations devoted to the goddess Flora, this vast Rococo ballroom is the work of father and son Johann Baptist and Franz Zimmermann.

View from the platform of the television tower in Olympiapark

❷ Olympiapark

Tel (089) 30 67 24 14. Ⓤ Olympia-zentrum. 🚋 20, 21. 🚌 173. Television tower: **Open** 9am–midnight daily.

Built for the 1972 Olympic Games, this vast sports stadium can be spotted from almost anywhere in Munich, as it is the site of a 290-m (950-ft) high television tower, the Olympiaturm. At the top of the tower there is a viewing platform that affords visitors amazing views, and also a restaurant.

The stadium has three main facilities: the Olympic Stadium, which seats 62,000 spectators, the Olympic Hall and the Swimming Hall. In what is one of the most original constructions of 20th-century German architecture, all three are covered by a vast transparent canopy, stretched between a series of tall masts to form an irregular tent.

The stadium includes many other facilities, such as an indoor skating rink, a cycle racing track and tennis courts.

The sports complex is located beside the park's artificial lake.

Apart from sporting events, the Olympiapark hosts many popular events, including fireworks displays and regular open-air rock and pop concerts in the summer months.

Next to the park are the BMW Museum and BMW Welt, featuring the world's largest permanent BMW collection.

❸ Englischer Garten

Ⓤ Giselastraße. 🚌 54.

The idea of creating this garden, which would be open to all the inhabitants of Munich and not only to its aristocracy, came from Count von Rumford, an American-born chemist and physicist who lived in Bavaria from 1784. As the region's Minister of War, he was responsible for reorganizing the Bavarian army. His idea of creating a garden of this size – the garden covers an area of 5 sq km (1,235 acres) – right in the centre of a large city, was quite unique in Germany. In 1789, taking advantage of his influential position, he persuaded Karl Theodor to put his plans into action.

The project leader was Friedrich Ludwig von Sckell. He was brought to Munich from Schwetzingen by the Elector to create the garden on an area of former marshland. Opened in 1808, the

Chinese Tower in the Englischer Garten

Karl-Theodor-Park is today known simply as the Englischer Garten (English Garden). It is a popular place for long walks, jogging or just lying on the grass in the cool shade of a spreading old tree.

There are some interesting old buildings in the park, such as the Monopteros, a Neo-Classical temple by Leo von Klenze (1837), and the Chinese Tower (1789–90), which is similar to the pagoda in London's Kew Gardens. The Tower stands in one of the park's beer gardens.

It is also worth dropping in to the Japanese Teahouse, where the gentle art of tea brewing is demonstrated.

❹ Deutsches Museum

See pp232–3.

Franz von Stuck's *Die Sünde*, on display in the Villa Stuck

❺ Villa Stuck

Prinzregentenstraße 60. **Tel** (089) 45 55 51 0. 🚋 18. 🚌 100. **Open** 11am–6pm Tue–Sun.

This villa was the home of the famous painter Franz von Stuck, the co-founder of the Munich Secession school of painting. As well as numerous portraits, nudes and sculptures, Von Stuck was the creator of many mythological and allegorical scenes, all painted in dark colours and full of eroticism.

Submarine used in the film *Das Boot*, displayed in Bavaria-Filmstadt

These include eight variations (1893) on the theme of sin. His *Amazon* (1897) stands in front of the villa.

Franz von Stuck built the villa in 1897–98, to his own design, decorating it with his own paintings and sculptures. Since 1968, it has housed a museum. A permanent exhibition of Stuck's work is displayed in the magnificent music room on the ground floor, while the second-floor rooms are used for temporary exhibitions devoted mainly to early 20th-century art.

㊱ Bavaria-Filmstadt

Bavariafilmplatz 7. **Tel** (089) 64 99 20 00. 🚋 25. **Open** mid-Apr–Oct: 9am–4pm daily; Nov: 10am–3pm daily. 🎦 only; in English at 1pm daily. 🅿 🆆 filmstadt.de

Commonly known as Holly-wood on Isar, this vast site in the southern suburb of Geiselgasteig covers an area of over 3.5 sq km (865 acres).

Since 1919 the world's greatest cinema stars have worked here, including Orson Welles and Billy Wilder. The British film director Alfred Hitchcock made his first films here (*The Pleasure Garden*, 1925 and *The Mountain Eagle*, 1926). Elizabeth Taylor, Gina Lollobrigida and Romy Schneider have all stood in front of the cameras here.

Strolling visitors to the site will often come across some well-known characters who have appeared in films such as *E.T.* or *The Neverending Story*, which were filmed here. The sets of other films made here, including

Enemy Mine and *Cabaret*, can also be seen. You can also peep into the submarine that was reconstructed for Wolfgang Petersen's classic film *Das Boot* (1981) – the film follows the voyage of one such boat during World War II. The Bullyversum (named after "Bully" Herbig, a German comedian, actor and director) is an interactive 3-D adventure.

VIP tours of the Filmstadt include fascinating demonstrations of many technical film-making tricks and techniques. A special attraction is the cinema called Showscan, whose seats move according to the story on the screen, giving visitors the sensation of a trip through the universe or of flying through the tunnels of an old silver mine.

㊲ Theresienwiese

Theresienhöhe. 🆄 Theresienwiese. 🎡 Oktoberfest (Sep–Oct).

For most of the year this is simply a vast oval meadow encircled by the Bavariaring. Theresienwiese comes into its own once a year, however, during the Oktoberfest. Then it turns into a gigantic, boisterous beer-drinking venue, with stalls, marquees, funfair and loud music.

Towering above the meadow is a monumental 18-m (59-ft) high statue, symbol of the state of Bavaria. Made in 1844–50, the statue is the work of Ludwig Schwanthaler. It incorporates an internal staircase leading to the figure's head, where there is a viewing platform.

Bavaria statue in Theresienwiese

Just behind the statue is the Ruhmeshalle, a Neo-Classical building surrounded by a colonnade. Designed by Leo von Klenze and built in 1843–53, the building contains numerous busts of eminent Bavarians.

Oktoberfest

Munich's Oktoberfest is one of the biggest folk fairs in Europe. In 1810 the site on which it is held was the venue for a horse race, held to celebrate the marriage of Ludwig (later King of Bavaria) and Thérèse von Saxe-Hildburghausen. A few years later it became the venue for an autumn fair that has grown into an enormous event over the years. Chief amongst the attractions is beer, drunk in vast quantities, in marquees erected by the breweries. The festival starts in late September with a huge procession through the town

Revellers at the annual Oktoberfest in Theresienwiese

and the ceremonial opening of the first barrel of beer. It finishes, 16 days later, on the first Sunday of October.

❹ Deutsches Museum

The Deutsches Museum, one of the oldest and largest museum of technology and engineering in the world, draws over 1.4 million visitors each year. It was founded in 1903 by Oskar von Miller, an engineer. The building in which it is housed, located on the Museum Island, was designed by Gabriel von Seidl in 1925. The collections cover most aspects of technology, from its history to its greatest achievements. The museum also houses one of the world's largest libraries of technology.

Exterior of the Museum
The building combines Neo-Baroque, Neo-Classical and modern elements.

Decorative Arts
This plate with the portrait of a lady from Ludwig I's "gallery of beauty" is an example of reproduction techniques applied to porcelain. The ceramics section illustrates the development of faience, stoneware and porcelain.

Second floor

★ **Physics**
Galileo's workshop features a large collection of the scientific equipment used by the famous astronomer and physicist to establish the basic laws of mechanics.

First floor

★ **Pharmaceutics**
Among the exhibits in this section is a model of a human cell magnified 350,000 times and graphically illustrating how it functions.

Main entrance

Museum Guide

The museum's 20,000 exhibits are displayed over seven floors. While those on the lower floors include heavy vehicles and sections on chemistry, physics, scientific instruments and aeronautics, those on the middle floors relate to the decorative arts. The upper floors are devoted to astronomy, computers and microelectronics.

Ground floor

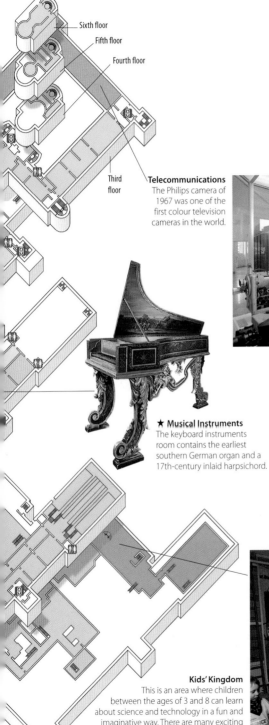

Sixth floor

Fifth floor

Fourth floor

Third floor

Telecommunications
The Philips camera of 1967 was one of the first colour television cameras in the world.

★ Musical Instruments
The keyboard instruments room contains the earliest southern German organ and a 17th-century inlaid harpsichord.

Key to Floorplan

▢ Design and Technology
▢ Centre for New Technology
▢ Kids' Kingdom
▢ Physics and Chemistry
▢ Musical Instruments
▢ Decorative Arts
▢ Time, Weights and Measures
▢ Automation, Microelectronics and Telecommunications
▢ Astronomy
▢ Agriculture and Geodesy
▢ Miscellaneous

Kids' Kingdom
This is an area where children between the ages of 3 and 8 can learn about science and technology in a fun and imaginative way. There are many exciting exhibits, including a giant guitar, a fire engine and an electric light cinema.

SHOPPING IN MUNICH

Munich often claims to be Germany's richest and most sophisticated city, and so when it comes to shopping you are sure not to be disappointed. The key shopping areas are dotted around the centre of the city. You can conveniently walk around the pedestrianized central area, with numerous options for taking a break for lunch or a coffee. Not to be missed is the visual and gourmet treat of the Viktualienmarkt food market, the classic department store Ludwig Beck and some of the smaller speciality stores tucked away in side streets. In the less commercial shopping streets, stores tend to open late morning or in the afternoon only.

Main Shopping Areas

Munich's key luxury shopping street is Maximilianstraße and those streets connected to it, Theatinerstraße, Briennerstraße and Residenzstraße. Here you will find all the top international brands and jewellery stores. For more affordable shops head to the central pedestrianized area between Kaufingerstraße, Neuhauserstraße and Marienplatz. Here you will find family stores, large chains, mid-market fashion, souvenirs and department stores. For less conventional areas with small specialist boutiques and local designers seek out the Glockenbachviertel around Hans-Sachs Straße, or streets radiating out from Gärtnerplatz, home to the Art Nouveau State Theatre and relaxed cafés. Schwabing is the young Bohemian area with a variety of casualwear and jeanswear stores, plus fashion boutiques and plenty of laid-back bistros and coffee bars.

Department Stores and Shopping Centres

The most famous department store in Munich is **Ludwig Beck**, which has a particularly impressive Christmas decorations department in December. **Galeria Kaufhof** is another large national department store chain offering several floors of goods. Shopping Centres (*Einkaufspassagen*) are also aplenty. **Fünf Höfe** ("the five courtyards") is central and upmarket. It sits between Theatiner, Maffei, Kardinal-Faulhaber and Salvator streets and mixes shopping, art and culture with cafés including a great restaurant/café attached to the Kunsthalle art museum. Munich has three other large shopping malls. **Olympia Einkaufszentrum** (OEZ) is vast with over 140 stores on two levels. **Perlacher Einkaufspassage (PEP)** shopping mall (PEP) has over 110 stores. The **Riem Arcaden** is home to the largest branch of H&M, a huge Lego store, C&A and Ludwig Beck Fashion.

Pedestrianized shopping area in central Munich

Fashion

Munich has a wide variety of shops for clothes and accessories. Try the following boutiques to find Munich-style chic. **Theresa** has the best choice of designer fashion and accessories, while **Trachten Angermaier** sells Bavarian folk costumes, including dirndls, and **Off & Co** in Schwabing has fashion items for men and women. Hohenzollernstraße in Schwabing is a good place to shop for youthful street fashion and trainers. For traditional Bavarian Loden costumes take a look in **Lodenfrey**.

Children's Shops

Munich is a stylish and expensive city and parents love to dress their children accordingly. This means there are some good shopping opportunities for kids' clothing and toys, mainly in the department stores and C&A. A large central store for mother, baby and toys is **Schlichting**, as well as **Thierchen Kindermode**

The exclusive shopping centre, Fünf Höfe

One of the city's regularly held flea markets

for original handmade clothing. **Noemi & Friends** is a kids' beauty salon cum accessories shop, a haven for little and big girls. **Die Puppenstube** is also good for old-fashioned toys and gifts.

Flea Markets

Flea markets are popular, especially at the weekends. Most take place on Saturday, some every two weeks and most only from spring to late autumn. The key ones around Munich are **Zenith Flohmarkt** and **Antik Palast** flea market at Lilienthallee, every weekend, and **Flohmarkt**

Riem, the largest flea market in Bavaria, at the trade show grounds.

Food Shopping

Viktualienmarkt *(see p218)* is a huge produce market, selling fruit, vegetables, spices, meat, poultry, fish, preserves and flowers. It is a feast for all the senses and a permanent fixture – open daily. *Bio* is the German word for organic and Germans have always been enthusiastic about organic produce.

Basic Bio is a good organic supermarket in the city centre. For a selection of gourmet treats head to **Dallmayr** or **Käfer**, the city's top

delicatessens, while butchers' shops sell the famous Bavarian white sausages.

Christmas Market

Munich holds a traditional Christmas market *(Christkindlmarkt)* from the first week of Advent until Christmas Eve. The market is a great tourist attraction and special trips are organized from all over Europe. Wooden stalls sell a huge variety of handcrafted decorations, in particular wooden mangers and tree decorations, all delicately carved, in addition to candles, ornaments, food and mulled wine.

Christkindlmarkt, Munich's Christmas market

DIRECTORY

Department Stores and Shopping Centres

Fünf Höfe
Theatinerstraße.
Map 2 B4.
w fuenfhoefe.de

Galeria Kaufhof
Kaufingerstraße 1–5.
Map 2 B4.
Tel (089) 231851.
w galeria-kaufhof.de

Ludwig Beck
Marienplatz 11.
Map 2 B4.
Tel (089) 236910.
w ludwigbeck.de

Olympia-Einkaufszentrum
Hanauer Straße 68.
w olympia-einkaufszentrum.de

Perlacher Einkaufs-passage (PEP)
Thomas-Dehler-Straße 12.
w einkaufscenter-neuperlach.de

Riem Arcaden
Willy-Brandt-Platz 5.
w riem-arcaden.de

Fashion

Lodenfrey
Maffeistraße 7. **Map** 2 B4.
w lodenfrey.com

Off & Co
Belgradstraße 1.
w offandco.com

Theresa
Maffeistraße 3. **Map** 2 B4.
w mytheresa.com

Trachten Angermaier
Rosental 11 and
Landsberger Str. 101–103.
w trachten-angermaier.de

Children's Shops

Die Puppenstube
Luisenstraße 68.
Tel (089) 2723267.

Noemi & Friends
Marktstraße 13,
Schwabing.
w noemiandfriends.de

Schlichting
Weinstraße 8.
Map 2 B4.
w schlichting.de

Thierchen Kindermode
Hans-Sachs-Straße 15.
w thierchen.net

Flea Markets

Antik Palast
Lilienthallee 29.
w antikpalast muenchen.de

Flohmarkt Riem
Am Messeturm.
Tel (089) 960 51632.
w flohmarkt-riem.com

Zenith Flohmarkt
Lilienthallee.
Tel 0173 683 5152.
w flohmarkt-freimann.de

Food Shopping

Basic Bio
Westenriederstraße 35.
Map 2 B4.
Tel (089) 242 0890.
w basic-ag.de

Dallmayr
Dienerstraße 14–15.
Map 2 B4.
w dallmayr.de

Käfer
Prinzregentenstraße 73.
w feinkost-kaefer.de

Viktualienmarkt
Petersplatz-Frauenstraße.
Map 2 B4.

ENTERTAINMENT IN MUNICH

Munich is best known for the Oktoberfest, the Olympic grounds and Hofbräuhaus, but it also has an international reputation as a city of culture. There are 56 theatres, three large orchestras and one opera house. Munich has the rich and the powerful of its past to thank for creating and preserving its many splendid venues. This cultured metropolis on the Isar caters to all tastes, from traditional to modern, whether in theatre, music or film. There are several festivals during the year, as well as various sporting events, when the city comes alive, attracting visitors from all over the world.

Entertainment Guides and Tickets

Munich Found is the best events magazine and the **Munich Tourist Board** has comprehensive listings of events happening all over Munich. Also, check the Thursday edition of *Süddeutsche Zeitung* and the daily *Münchner Merkur*.

You can book tickets direct from box offices by phone or in person. There are also two **Zentraler Kartenverkauf** ticket kiosks in Marienplatz underground concourse, or use the **Abendzeitung Schalterhalle** (kiosk).

Theatre, Opera and Classical Music

State theatres are subsidized and so tickets are very reasonably priced. The Bavarian State Orchestra, Opera and Ballet all perform at the **Nationaltheater**. The **Deutsches Theater** offers musicals and shows, while the **Prinzregententheater** has the Bavarian State Opera and a concert hall. The Art Nouveau **Staatstheater am Gärtnerplatz** (closed for renovation until 2015) presents opera, ballet, operetta, musicals and the Symphony Orchestra. **Gasteig Culture Center** is a world-class concert hall, home to the Munich Philharmonic Orchestra. The city also hosts an opera festival in July.

Music and Dance

The **Pasinger Fabrik** offers a good programme of jazz, chansons and café theatre. There are numerous dance events and dance clubs. Big name artists, such as James Blunt, Massive Attack and the Rolling Stones, tend to perform at the **Circus Krone Bau**, **Zenith Kulturhalle**, Gasteig Culture Center, **Olympiahalle** and the **Olympic Stadium**.

Film

As the centre of the German film industry Munich offers 76 cinemas, the **Bavaria Film Studios** and a college for film and television. Try the English tour of the studios daily at 1pm.

Munich's world-famous Oktoberfest

The **Munich Film Festival** in July boasts over 200 films on 15 screens, almost all of them German, European or world premieres.

Festivals

Munich's most famous festival is the **Oktoberfest**. For the whole of September it takes over a dedicated fairground, Theresienwiese, with beer tents, traditional Bavarian brass bands, people dressed in traditional Bavarian costume *(Trachten)*, fairground rides and the famous iced gingerbread hearts, *Lebkuchen*. There is also the **Tollwood Festival** in July and December, which has music, food, a circus, performances in tents, family fun and a craft fair. Munich also celebrates the *Dult* on three occasions throughout the year. *Dult* is the old word for street fair or market and there are traditional stalls and merry-go-rounds. Carnival or *Fasching* is celebrated throughout Munich with parties, processions and dressing up, but it is not as important here as in other cities.

Sport

Most Münchners love the outdoors. Many make regular

The imposing Nationaltheater on Max-Joseph-Platz

Munich's ultra-modern Allianz Arena

trips to the not too distant Alps. Running, skiing, rollerblading, cycling, Nordic walking and football are all very popular. The English Garden in the city centre is a huge park where people rollerblade, cycle, run or just meet up with friends.

Munich has two football teams: FC Bayern and TSV 1860 München, also known as "the Lions" because they are sponsored by the Löwenbräu Munich brewery with a lion as its coat of arms. The **Allianz Arena** is the fantastic stadium built for the 2006 World Cup. It is an architectural marvel which lights up in various colours

For Bayern Munich merchandise head to the **FC Bayern Shop** in the Arena. The shop website gives details of other stores located at Central Station and the Hofbräuhaus.

Other key sporting events are the Bavariasn International Tennis Championships (ATP tournament), the BMW International Golf Open and Munich Blade Night, Monday evenings from April to September, when rollerbladers take over the streets. Runners will enjoy the Media Marathon and also the Münchner Stadtlauf (city run). A sport unique to Munich is surfing on the River Isar at the weirs

Kids' Entertainment

Children will love Kids' Kingdom – **Kinderreich** – in the Deutsches Museum. The area is designated for children and has giant interactive games and water games, plus a real fire engine. Adults can only enter with their kids. Several playgrounds can be found along the River Isar in the city centre, but the best is **Westpark Spielzone Ost**, which can be reached by the underground. The new **Sea Life Olympiapark** centre also provides an excellent outing, as does the zoo at **Tierpark Hellabrunn**.

Sea life exhibit at Olympiapark, Munich

DIRECTORY

Entertainment Guides and Tickets

Abendzeitung Schalterhalle
Sendlingerstr. 10.
Map 2 A5.
Tel (089) 267024.

Munich Tourist Board
W muenchen.de

Zentraler Kartenverkauf
Tel (0180) 54818181.
W muenchenticket.de

Theatre, Opera and Classical Music

Deutsches Theater
Schwanthalerstr. 13. **Map**
1 E4. **Tel** (089) 552 340.

Gasteig Culture Center
Rosenheimer Str. 5.
Tel (089) 54 818181.

Nationaltheater
Max-Joseph-Platz.
Map 2 B4.
Tel (089) 21851920.

Prinzregententheater
Prinzregentenstr. 12.
Map 3 D3.
Tel (089) 21852899.

Staatstheater am Gärtnerplatz
Gärtnerplatz 3.
Tel (089) 202411.

Music and Dance

Circus Krone Bau
Marsstraße 43.
Map 1 E3.
Tel (085) 545 8000.
W circus-krone.de

Olympiahalle and Olympic Stadium
Spiridon-Louis-Ring 21.
Tel (089) 54 818181
(tickets).

W olympiapark-muenchen.de

Pasinger Fabrik
August-Exter-Str. 1.
Tel (089) 82929079.

Zenith Kulturhalle
Lilienthalallee 29.
W zenith-die-kulturhalle.de

Film

Bavaria Film Studios
W filmstadt.de

Munich Film Festival
W filmfest-muenchen.de

Festivals

Oktoberfest
W oktoberfest.de

Tollwood Festival
W tollwood.de

Sport

Allianz Arena
W allianz-arena.de

FC Bayern Shop
W shop.fcbayern.de

Kids' Entertainment

Kinderreich
Deutsches Museum,
Museumsinsel 1. **Tel** (089)
21791. W deutsches-museum.de

Westpark Spielzone Ost
Pressburger Straße.

Sea Life Olympiapark
Willi-Daume-Platz 1.
Tel (089) 45 00 00.
W sealifeeurope.com

Tierpark Hellabrunn
Tierparkstr. 30. **Tel** (089) 625
080. W zoo-munich.de

MUNICH STREET FINDER

Map references given in this chapter for sights (and in the Munich hotel and restaurant listings at the back of the book) refer to the maps here. The key map below shows the area of Munich covered by the *Street Finder*. The maps include the major

sightseeing areas, historic attractions, railway stations, bus stations, U-Bahn and S-Bahn stations and train stations. The word Straße (Str.) indicates a street, Platz a square, Brücke a bridge and Bahnhof a railway station.

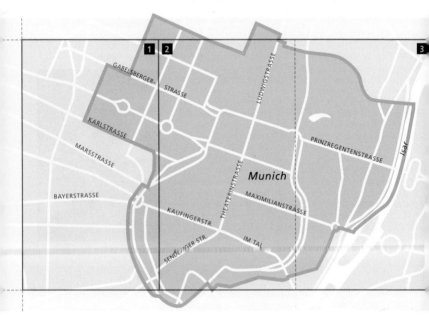

Key to the Munich Street Finder

◼ Major sight		🛈 Tourist information	
◼ Place of interest		✚ Hospital with casualty unit	
◻ Other building		🚓 Police station	
Ⓢ S-Bahn station		✝ Church	
Ⓤ U-Bahn station		═ Railway line	
🚉 Railway station		Pedestrianized street	

Scale of Maps 1–3

0 metres		200
0 yards		200

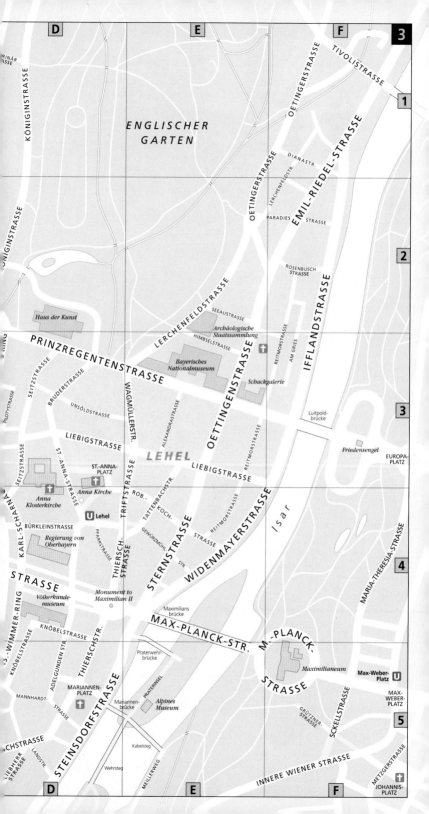

BAVARIA

Bavaria is the biggest federal state in the Federal Republic of Germany. It is made up of regions that, in the past, were either independent secular territories or bishoprics. It includes former free towns of the Holy Roman Empire, such as Nördlingen, Rothenburg ob der Tauber, Dinkelsbühl, Nuremberg and Augsburg, which lost their independence to Bavaria only in the early 19th century.

The area that is now known as Bavaria was inhabited in early times by Celts and Romans. The German Baiovarii, which gave the territory its name, arrived here during the 5th and 6th centuries. In the second half of the 6th century, the area was conquered by the Franks then, from 1180 until 1918, Bavaria was ruled by the Wittelsbach dynasty. During Medieval times, this split into the Upper Bavarian line (Straubing, Ingolstadt and Munich) and the Lower Bavarian line (Landshut). In 1505, separate provinces were once again combined into a single country. During the 16th and 17th centuries the duchy of Bavaria was the bulwark of Roman Catholicism within the Holy Roman Empire and during the reign of Maximilian I, Bavaria fought against the Protestant

Union in the Thirty Years' War. For his loyalty to Rome, Maximilian I was rewarded in 1623 with the title of Elector, which meant that he could vote in elections for the Emperor. Following the fall of the Holy Roman Empire, Bavaria became a kingdom and remained as such until 1918.

Bavaria's turbulent history has left behind a rich architectural and cultural heritage. In addition to Roman antiquities, Baroque fortresses and fairy-tale castles, the region also has more than its share of glorious Alpine scenery, beer halls and colourful festivals, all of which make this one of the most popular parts of Germany for tourists. The capital, Munich, is a lively cosmopolitan city of wide boulevards and leafy squares with a wide choice of shops, restaurants, cinemas and theatres.

Girls dressed in national costume celebrating St Leonard's Festival

◀ Clock face of the brick Gothic Frauenkirche, or Church of Our Lady, in Nuremberg

Exploring Bavaria

Bavaria is a paradise for tourists. Its beautiful lakes attract lovers of water sports, while the mountainous regions of the Bavarian Forest offer the unspoiled charms of nature. The Alps, with their charming mountain hostels and numerous ski-lifts, provide endless possibilities for enjoyment. Towns and villages feature magnificent historic sights and the capital, Munich, combines the advantages of a lively metropolis with a peaceful atmosphere that is not often found in large cities.

The façade and central rotunda of Bayreuth's Eremitage

Sights at a Glance

1. Aschaffenburg
2. Pommersfelden
3. Coburg
4. Vierzehnheiligen
5. Fränkische Schweiz
6. *Würzburg pp248–9*
7. *Bamberg pp252–3*
8. *Bayreuth pp256–7*
9. Berching
10. Amberg
11. Dinkelsbühl
12. Nördlingen
13. Ansbach
14. Eichstätt
15. Donaustauf
16. *Nürnberg (Nuremberg) pp260–61*
17. *Rothenburg ob der Tauber pp266–7*
18. Andechs
19. Landsberg am Lech
20. Dachau
21. Schleißheim
22. Freising
23. Ingolstadt
24. Neuburg an der Donau
25. Landshut
26. Dingolfing
27. Straubing
28. *Regensburg (Ratisbon) pp272–3*
29. Altötting
30. Burghausen
31. Bayerischer Wald
32. *Passau pp278–9*
33. *Berchtesgadener Land pp280–81*
34. *Chiemsee pp282–3*
35. Garmisch-Partenkirchen
36. Oberammergau
37. Ettal
38. Linderhof
39. *Schloss Neuschwanstein pp286–7*
40. Hohenschwangau
41. Kempten
42. Lindau
43. Oberstdorf
44. Füssen
45. Ottobeuren
46. *Augsburg pp290–91*

0 kilometres 30

0 miles 30

The beautiful riverside town of Passau

Key

═══ Motorway

━━━ Major road

┉┉┉ Minor road

──── Main railway

──── Minor railway

▬▬▬ International border

▬▬▬ Regional border

△ Summit

Map labels:

Leipzig ↑
Chemnitz →
Hof
OBURG
ichtenfels
Kulmbach
Entenbühl 936m
VIERZEHN-HEILIGEN
Hollfeld
FRÄNKISCHE SCHWEIZ
8 BAYREUTH
mannstadt
5
Pottenstein
Forchheim
Weiden in der Oberpfalz
Prague
ngen
Wernberg-Köblitz
Signalberg 886m
NÜRNBERG (NUREMBERG)
10 AMBERG
abach
Neumarkt in der Oberpfalz
Schwandorf
Schwarzach
BAYERN
Cham
Roding
Großer Arber 1456m
RCHING 9
REGENSBURG 28 15 DONAUSTAUF
Zwiesel
Großer Rachel 1453m
Finsterau
Oberalteich
BAYERISCHER WALD
14 EICHSTÄTT
Aufhausen
27 STRAUBING
Grafenau
Freyung
12
LSTADT 23
Deggendorf
JBURG AN R DONAU
15
DINGOLFING
Landau an der Isar
24
26
Schrobenhausen
Moosburg
25 LANDSHUT
Arnstorf
ACHAU 20
FREISING 22
Pfarrkirchen
Pocking
32 PASSAU
21 SCHLEISSHEIM
Erding
mering
12
ALTÖTTING
Bad Füssing
18
München (Munich)
29
BURGHAUSEN 30
Inn
DECHS
Wolfratshausen
Wasserburg am Inn
304
CHIEMSEE
ger See
Rosenheim
34
Salzburg
Chieming
A8
Bad Reichenhall
ERAMMERGAU
Berchtesgaden
ERHOF
Bavarian Alps
Innsbruck ↓
33
ETTAL
BERCHTESGADENER LAND
GARMISCH-PARTENKIRCHEN

Getting Around

Munich, Nuremberg and Augsburg are all served by international airports, while fast train services operate throughout the region. The main motorways are the A93 linking Saxony with Ratisbon, the A9 between Thuringia and Munich, the A3 between Frankfurt and Passau and the A8, which runs between Stuttgart and Salzburg.

Nuremberg's imposing Kaiserburg, overlooking the city

For additional map symbols *see back flap*

Red sandstone exterior of Schloss Johannisburg, Aschaffenburg

❶ Aschaffenburg

Road map C5. ⚑ 41,000. ⛉
ℹ️ Schlossplatz 1 (06021-39 58 00).

Situated in Lower Franconia, Aschaffenburg enjoys a scenic position on the hilly right bank of the river Main. The town became the second seat of the Mainz bishops in the 13th century, the first being Mainz.

The northwest part of the old town features a majestic, red sandstone riverside castle, **Schloss Johannisburg**, which was once occupied by the Mainz bishops-electors.

The castle gallery holds a fine collection of European paintings, dating from the 15th to the 18th centuries. It includes works by Hans Baldung Grien and the most important collection of Lucas Cranach canvases in Europe. In the castle library are valuable medieval codices, such as the 10th-century *Book of Gospel Readings (Evangelarium)* from Fulda.

Occupying a scenic position above a vineyard a short distance to the northwest of the castle is Pompejanum. The Bavarian king Ludwig I was so fascinated with the discovery of Pompeii that he ordered a replica of the Castor and Pollux villa *(Casa di Castore e Polluce)* to be built. This he filled with his rich collection of antiquities.

After undergoing restoration work to repair war damage, the museum opened its doors to the public again in 1994.

🏛 **Schloss Johannisburg**
Schlossplatz 4. **Tel** (06021) 38 65 70.
⏱ Apr–Sep: 9am–6pm Tue–Sun; Oct–Mar: 10am–4pm Tue–Sun. 🎧

❷ Pommersfelden

Road map D5. ℹ️ Hauptstraße 11 (09548-922 00).

On the edge of the Steigerwald – a popular hiking area – is the small village of Pommersfelden, which is dominated by its magnificent Baroque palace, **Schloss Weißenstein**. The palace was commissioned by the Mainz Archbishop and Elector and the Prince-Bishop of Bamberg, Lothar Franz von Schönborn. It was built, in only five years (1711–16), to a design by the famous architect, Johann Dientzenhofer.

This masterpiece of secular Baroque architecture is worth visiting for several reasons. Particularly interesting is the three-storey-high ornamental ceiling by Johann Rudolf Byss. The most spectacular room is the Marble Hall, which features paintings by Michael Rottmayr. The well-preserved interior of the palace houses a gallery, a library, and a valuable collection of furniture. After visiting the palace, you can take a stroll around its gardens, which were created by Maximilian

von Welsch in 1715, in what was the then fashionable, geometric French style. It is now laid out in English-garden style.

🏛 **Schloss Weißenstein**
Tel (09548) 98180. **Open** Apr–Oct: 10am–5pm daily. 🎧 every hour. (Short tour: 11:30am and 4:30pm.) 🎧

❸ Coburg

Road map D5. ⚑ 41,000. ⛉
ℹ️ Herrngasse 4 (09561-89 8000).

Former residence of the Wettin family, Coburg is situated on the bank of the river Itz. It is dominated by a massive fortress, the **Veste Coburg**, which is one of the largest in Germany. Coburg's origins go back to the 11th century, but its present-day appearance is mainly the result of remodelling that was carried out in the 16th and the 17th centuries.

The fortress consists of a number of buildings clustered around several courtyards and surrounded by a triple line of walls. The complex is now a museum, housing various collections, including prints and drawings, arms and armour.

In 1530, the fortress provided refuge to Martin Luther who, as an outlaw, hid here from April until October. The room in which he hid is furnished with antique furniture and features a portrait of Luther,

Ornate entrance to Coburg's Stadthaus

painted by Lucas Cranach the Younger.

Among the most important buildings in the old town are the late-Gothic church of St Maurice and a beautiful Renaissance college building that was founded by Prince Johann Casimir in 1605. On the opposite side of the market square is the town hall, originally built in 1577–79 and remodelled in the 18th century.

Interior of the monumental, Baroque Vierzehnheiligen church

Further along is the town castle, **Schloss Ehrenburg**, which was built in the 16th century on the site of a dissolved Franciscan monastery. The castle burned down in 1693 and was subsequently rebuilt. The façade facing the square was remodelled by Karl Friedrich Schinkel in Neo-Gothic style.

The castle has some fine interiors, including the Baroque Riesensaal and Weisser Saal and a chapel with rich stucco decorations.

🏠 Veste Coburg

Tel (09561) 87 979. **Open** Apr–Oct: 9:30am–5pm Tue–Sun; Nov–Mar: 1–4pm Tue–Sun. 🅿

🏠 Schloss Ehrenburg

Schlossplatz 1. **Tel** (09561) 808 832. **Open** Apr–Sep: 9am–5pm Tue–Sun; Oct–Mar: 10am–3pm Tue–Sun. 🎫 every hour. 🅿

❹ Vierzehnheiligen

Staffelstein. **Road map** D5. **Tel** (09571) 950 80. **Open** Apr–Oct: 8am–7:30pm; Nov–Mar: 8am–6:30pm.
🌐 vierzehnheiligen.de

High above the river Main is Banz Abbey, a Benedictine monastery built in 1695 by Johann Leonhard and Leonhard Dientzenhofer. Opposite is the pilgrimage church of the Fourteen Saints of Intercession. The first two chapels, built in the 15th and 16th centuries, became too small to accommodate the growing numbers of pilgrims so, in 1741, the foundation stone was laid for the monumental new church, designed by Balthasar Neumann. Built in 1743–72, this is one of the most famous masterpieces of South German Baroque, with magnificent Rococo furnishings. The building is a cross-shaped basilica, with a monumental twin-tower façade.

The interior has an exceptionally dynamic style, achieved by combining the longitudinal and central planes: the three ovals laid along the main axis join with the two circles of the transept. The centrepiece of the nave is the "Altar of Mercy", which stands at the spot where, according to a 1446 legend, a shepherd had visions of the infant Christ with the fourteen Saints of Intercession. The altar features statues of the fourteen saints, and are the work of F X Feuchtmayr (1763). The rich stucco decorations and frescoes were crafted by Giuseppe Appiani.

❺ Fränkische Schweiz

Road map D5. **Tel** (09191) 861 054.

The area popularly known as Franconian Switzerland (*Fränkische Schweiz*) covers the area between Nuremberg, Bamberg and Bayreuth. One of Germany's most beautiful tourist regions, it offers its visitors picturesque green meadows, magnificent highlands covered with cornfields, imposing castles perched on top of high rocks, fabulous dolomite rocks and deep caves with stalactites. Its towns and villages, with their charming inns and timber-frame houses, look like a setting for *Snow White and Seven Dwarfs*.

The main routes across the area run alongside its rivers – the Wiesent, Leinleiter, Püttlach and Trubach. The Wiesent, which is ideal for canoeing, cuts across the region from east to west, joining the river Regnitz near the town of Forchheim. The town features many timber-frame houses, including the old town hall dating from the 14th to the 16th century. Near Forchheim, in **Ebermannstadt**, is a Marian church with a fine Madonna. The federal route B470 leads to the picturesque village of Tüchersfeld, which is built into the rocks. A good base for exploring this area is the village of Pottenstein. St Elizabeth of Thuringia is said to have stayed here in 1227. To the east of the castle is a cave with impressive stalactites.

Madonna from Marienkapelle in Ebermannstadt

Schloss Greifenstein in Heiligenstadt, in Fränkische Schweiz

❻ Würzburg

The bombing raid on Würzburg on 16 March 1945 lasted for about 20 minutes and destroyed over 80 per cent of the town's buildings. It seemed that Würzburg, which occupies a picturesque position on the banks of the river Main, had been erased from the face of the earth. Like Dresden, however, the town rose from the ashes and once again it enchants visitors with its rich heritage of historic sights. As well as being a popular tourist destination, Würzburg is also an important commercial and cultural centre for Lower Franconia and home of the excellent Franconian wine.

View over Würzburg, with Dom St Kilian in the foreground

▦ Residenz

See pp250–51.

⬆ Dom St Kilian

Domplatz. **Tel** (0931) 53 691.
Open 10am–5pm Mon– Sat,
1–6pm Sun and holidays.

Next to the great cathedral churches of Mainz, Speyer and Worms, this is Germany's fourth largest Romanesque church. It was built in 1045–1188, its patron saint an Irish monk who came to Würzburg in AD 686.

The church is a three-nave basilica with a transept and a twin-tower façade. Inside, the Romanesque main nave with its flat roof contrasts sharply with the Baroque stucco embellishments of the choir.

In the north nave is an interesting group of bishops' tombs, including two that are the work of Tilman Riemen-schneider. At the end of the north transept is a chapel, which was built by Balthasar Neumann for the bishops of the House of Schönborn.

⬆ Neumünster

St-Kilians-Platz.

Just north of the cathedral, the Neumünster church was built in the 11th century at the burial site of St Kilian and his fellow Irish martyrs, St Kolonat and St Totnan. The church's imposing Baroque dome and its red sandstone façade date from the 18th century. Featured in the interior are numerous works of art, including a late 15th-century *Madonna* and the *Man of Sorrow* by the 15th-century

The beautiful red sandstone façade of Neumünster-Kirche

German sculptor Tilman Riemenschneider. The north door leads to a lovely small courtyard; the remains of the cloister date from the Hohenstauf period. Under a lime tree is the resting place of a famous medieval minstrel Walther von der Vogelweide.

A procession is held each year on St Kilian's day (8 July) when theological students carry the skulls of the martyrs, contained in a transparent box, from the west crypt to the cathedral where they are put on public display.

✚ Bürgerspital

Theaterstraße.
The Bürgerspital was founded in 1319 by Johann von Steren. Hospitals like this originally provided charitable care for the old as well as the infirm, and today this institution provides care for over one hundred elderly residents of Würzburg. It operates as a self-financing foundation, its main source of income being from vine-growing. Residents are given a quarter of a litre (½ pint) of an excellent home-produced wine each day, with double the ration on Sundays. Visitors can also sample various vintages.

✚ Juliusspital

Juliuspromenade. **Tel** (0931) 393 14
00. **Open** Apr–mid-Nov: guided tours by appointment.
Founded in 1576 by Julius Echter, Juliusspital was remodelled in the 17th and the 18th centuries. The Rococo pharmacy (1760–65) in the hospital arcades has survived intact and is well worth a visit.

▦ Rathaus

Rueckermainstraße.
Würzburg's picturesque town hall was built in several stages. Begun in the 13th century, it was subsequently extended in the 15th and 16th centuries. Particularly noteworthy are the beautiful 16th-century paintings on the façade and the late-Renaissance tower, Roter Turm, which dates from around 1660.

▦ Alte Mainbrücke

Connecting the old town and Festung Marienberg, this

An old crane near Alte Mainbrücke over the river Main

here and, in 1201, work commenced on a fortress that served as the residence of the prince-bishops until 1719. Within its fortifications stands the first original donjon church dating from the 13th century, and the Renaissance-Baroque palace. The museum exhibits illustrate the 1,200-year history of the town. The former arsenal now houses the Franconian Museum with its valuable collection of sculptures by Tilman Riemenschneider.

🏛 Käppele

Mergentheimer Strasse.
Standing at the top of a hill at the southwestern end of the

VISITORS' CHECKLIST

Practical Information
Road map C5. 🏛 128,000.
i Falkenhaus am Markt (0931-372398). 🎭 Afrikafestival (May), Würzburger Weindorf (May/Jun), Mozartfest (Jun), Kilianifest (Jul), Bachtage (Nov–Dec).

Transport
✈ 7 km (4½ miles) west.
🚉 Hauptbahnhof.

city, this twin-towered Baroque chapel is the work of Balthasar Neumann (1747–50). Its interior is lavishly decorated with beautiful wall paintings by Matthias Günther.

beautiful bridge was built in 1473–1543. It is the oldest bridge over the Main.

🏛 Festung Marienberg

Fürstenbau-Museum: **Tel** (0931) 355 170. **Open** 16 Mar–Oct: 9am–6pm Tue–Sun. **Close**: Nov–Mar. 🅿
Mainfränkisches Museum: **Tel** (0931) 205 940. **Open** Apr–Oct: 10am–5pm Tue–Sun; Nov–Mar: 10am–4pm Tue–Sun. 🅿 Burgführungen: 🕐 16 Mar–Oct: 11am, 2pm, 3pm, 4pm Tue–Fri; 10am, 11am, 1pm, 2pm, 3pm, 4pm Sat & Sun.

Built on the site of an old Celtic stronghold, the Marienberg Fortress towers above the town. In AD 707 a church was built

Festung Marienberg, built on a hill overlooking the river Main

Wurzburg City Centre

① Residenz
② Dom St Kilian
③ Neumünster
④ Bürgerspital
⑤ Juliusspital
⑥ Rathaus
⑦ Alte Mainbrücke
⑧ Festung Marienberg

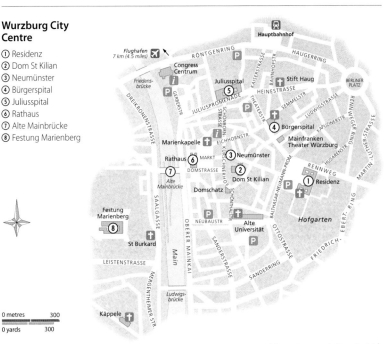

0 metres 300
0 yards 300

For additional map symbols see back flap

Residenz in Würzburg

This vast complex was commissioned by two prince-bishops, the brothers Johann Philipp Franz and Friedrich Karl von Schönborn. Its construction between 1720 and 1744 was supervised by several architects, including Johann Lukas von Hildebrandt and Maximilian von Welsch. However, the Residenz (which is on UNESCO's World Heritage list) is mainly associated with the architect Balthasar Neumann, who was responsible for the overall design.

★ Treppenhaus
The work of the Venetian artist Giovanni Battista Tiepolo, the largest fresco in the world adorns the vault of the staircase.

Main entra

Frankonia-Brunnen
This fountain, designed by Ferdinand von Miller, was constructed in the parade square in front of the Residenz. It was funded by donations from the inhabitants of Würzburg.

The Coat of Arms of the Patron
The richly carved coat of arms are by Johann Wolfgang von der Auwery and are the personal arms of Friedrich Karl von Schönborn, Prince-Bishop of Bamberg and Würzburg.

Martin-von-Wagner-Museum entrance

KEY

 Napoleon's bedroom

★ Kaisersaal
The centrepiece of the palace, the sumptuous emperor's chamber, testifies to the close relationship between Würzburg and the Holy Roman Empire. There are Tiepolo frescoes here too.

Garden Hall
This vast, low hall has Rococo stucco works by Antonio Bossi, dating from 1749. There is also a painting on the vaulting by Johan Zick dating from 1750, depicting *The Feast of the Gods* and *Diana Resting*.

Venetian Room
This room is named after three tapestries depicting the Venetian carnival. Further ornaments include decorative panels with paintings by Johann Thalhofer, a pupil of Rudolph Byss.

★ Hofkirche
The church interior is richly decorated with paintings, sculptures and stucco ornaments. The side altars were designed by Johann Lukas von Hildebrandt and feature paintings by Giovanni Battista Tiepolo.

❼ Bamberg

Situated on seven hills like ancient Rome, Bamberg features a splendidly preserved old town, encircled by the branches of the river Regnitz. The town is famous not only for its exceptional artistic heritage but also for its excellent beer, produced by one of the nine breweries that operate here. Its long history goes back to AD 902, when the Babenberg family established their residence here. The town grew and prospered in the wake of the Thirty Years' War. In 1993, Bamberg became a UNESCO World Heritage Site.

Beautiful rose garden at the rear of the Neue Residenz

Exploring Bamberg

A good place to start sight seeing is the Domplatz, one of Germany's loveliest squares, with its magnificent cathedral church and the old bishop's palace. After visiting the Neue Residenz you can go down to the river, where you will find the water palace, Concordia. The old town is reached by crossing one of two bridges – Untere or Obere Brücke.

⌂ Dom
See pp254–5.

▦ Alte Hofhaltung Historisches Museum
Domplatz 7. **Tel** (0951) 871 142. **Open** May–Oct: 9am–5pm Tue–Sun.

On the west side of Domplatz stands a magnificent portal, with statues of the imperial couple Heinrich II and Kunigunde. This is the gate to the former bishop's residence, built at the turn of the 15th and 16th centuries in place of an old fortress of Heinrich II. Within the building's wings is a pleasant courtyard. Inside is a museum that focuses on the history of the region.

▦ Neue Residenz und Staatsgalerie
Domplatz 8. **Tel** (0951) 519 390. **Open** Apr–Sep: 9am–6pm daily; Oct–Mar: 10–4pm daily. **w** schloesser-bayern.de

The Neue Residenz, with its richly decorated apartments and the Emperor's Room, was built in 1695–1704 and is the work of Johann Leonhard Dientzenhofer.

Its walls are adorned with magnificent frescos painted by the Tyrolean artist Melchior Steidl. The walls and pillars feature the Habsburg family tree, while 16 statues represent Emperors of the Holy Roman Empire. The Neue Residenz houses a collection of old German masters, including *The Flood* by Hans Baldung Grien and three canvases by Lucas Cranach the Elder.

⌂ Karmelitenkloster
Kreuzgang. **Open** 9–11.30am, 2:30–5:30pm daily.

The hospital-abbey complex of St Theodore was founded in the late 12th century by Bishop Eberhard. Since 1589 the church and abbey have belonged to the Carmelite order. The south tower and Romanesque portal are the remains of the massive 12th-century basilica. The interior of the church was redesigned in the late 17th and early 18th centuries so the altar is now situated at its western end, while the entrance is on the site of the previous presbytery. The layout of the cloisters on the south side of the church is typical of Cistercian designs.

⌂ Wasserschloss Concordia
Concordiastrasse. **Closed** to the public.

This magnificent Baroque palace, which enjoys a scenic position on the water's edge, was built for Counsellor Böttinger between 1716 and 1722, to a design by Johann Dientzenhofer. The building now houses a science institute.

The Baroque palace Concordia on the bank of the river Regnitz

Picturesque fishermen's cottages in Klein-Venedig

VISITORS' CHECKLIST

Practical Information
Road map D5. 71,000.
Geyerswörthstraße 5 (0951-297 62 00). Calderon-Festspiele (Jun), Sandkirchweih (Aug). **bamberg.info**

Transport
8 km (5 miles) to the southeast.

Altes Rathaus

The Baroque lower bridge, Untere Brücke, provides a magnificent view over the upper bridge, Obere Brücke, with its fabulous town hall. This originally Gothic seat of the municipal authorities was remodelled in 1744–56 by Jakob Michael Küchel. The half-timbered structure of the Rottmeisterhaus, which seems to be gliding over the waves of the river Regnitz, was added in 1688.

Klein-Venedig

"Little Venice" is a district of fishermen's cottages, their picturesque façades adorned with pots of geraniums. Visitors come here for a glass of Rauchbier – a local beer with a smoky flavour – while they enjoy the view.

Grüner Markt

With its historic houses and adjacent Maximilianplatz, Grüner Markt lies at the heart of the old town. It features the magnificent Baroque St Martin's Church, built in 1686–91 by the Dientzenhofer brothers. Also notable is the late-Baroque St Catherine Hospital and Seminary, built by Balthasar Neumann, which now serves as the town hall.

Kirche St Michael

Michaelsberg. Fränkisches Brauereimuseum: **Open:** Apr–Oct: 1–5pm Wed–Fri, 11am–5pm Sat & Sun.

The Benedictine abbey that stood on this site was founded in 1015. The surviving church was built after 1121 and later remodelled in the 16th and 17th centuries. On the ceiling of the church, nicknamed the "Botanical Gardens", are paintings depicting almost 600 species of medicinal plants. The abbey's Baroque buildings date from the 17th and 18th centuries and are the work of Johann Dientzenhofer and Balthasar Neumann. The abbey's brewery now houses a museum.

Schloss Seehof

Memmelsdorf. **Tel** (0951) 409 570. **Open** Apr–Oct: 9am–6pm Tue–Sun.

Built and designed by Antonio Petrini in 1686, this was originally the summer residence of the prince-bishops of Bamberg. The nine magnificent state rooms have been beautifully restored.

Façade of Schloss Seehof in Memmelsdorf

Bamberg City Centre

1. Dom
2. Alte Hofhaltung
3. Neue Residenz und Staatsgalerie
4. Karmeliterkloster
5. Wasserschloss Concordia
6. Altes Rathaus
7. Klein-Venedig

For map symbols see back flap

0 metres 300
0 yards 300

Bamberg Cathedral

Bamberg's skyline is dominated by the cathedral of St Peter and St George, which combines the late Romanesque and early French-Gothic styles. It was founded in 1004 and consecrated in 1012, and again in 1237 after being demolished by fire and then rebuilt. This is a triple-nave basilica with two choirs, whose apses are flanked by two pairs of towers. The cloisters were built between 1399 and 1457, while the monumental sculptures adorning the portals date from the 13th century. The western choir holds the only papal grave in Germany, that of Pope Clement II, who had been the local bishop.

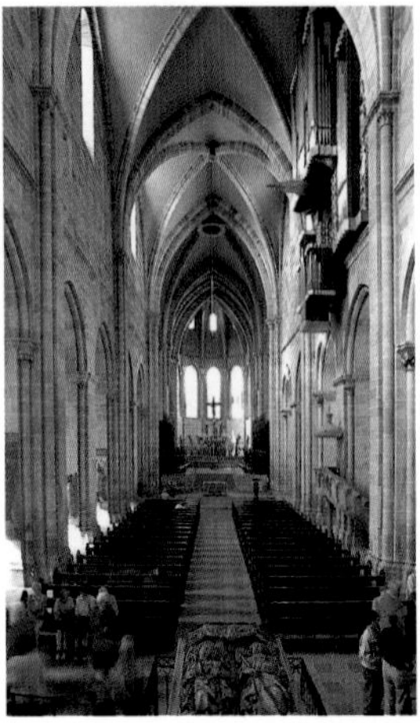

Interior
The illuminated main nave features a graceful, early Gothic, cross-ribbed vault.

★ Bamberger Reiter
By the northwestern pillar of the eastern choir stands the famous equestrian statue of the "Bamberg Rider", dating from about 1230. Many scholars have puzzled over the identity of the rider, but the riddle remains unsolved.

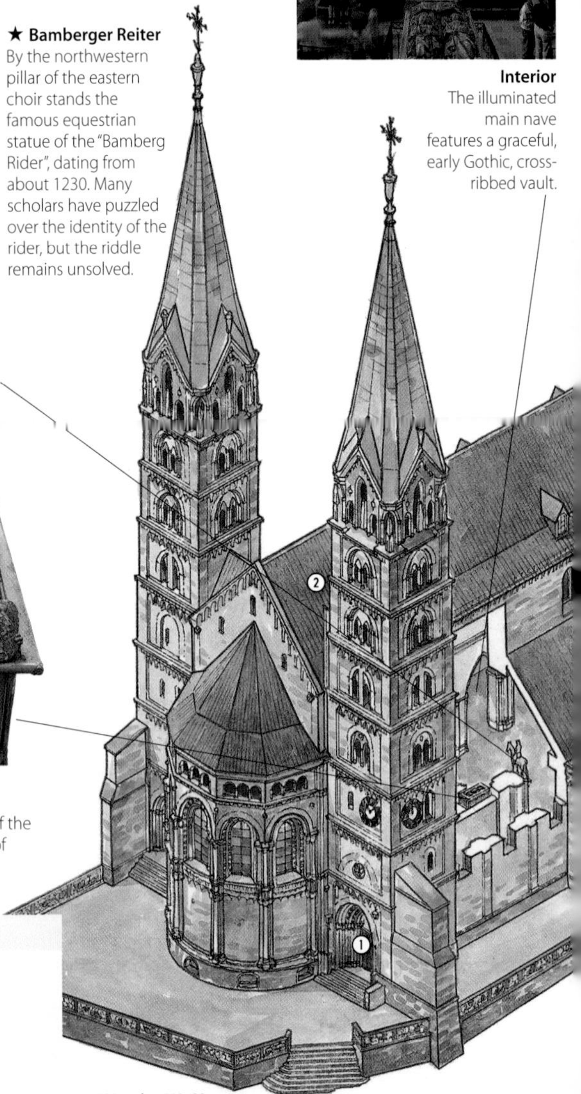

★ Tomb of Heinrich II and Kunigunde
This beautiful sarcophagus of the imperial couple is the work of Tilman Riemenschneider, completed in 1513.

KEY

① Marienpforte

② St George's Choir

③ St Peter's Choir

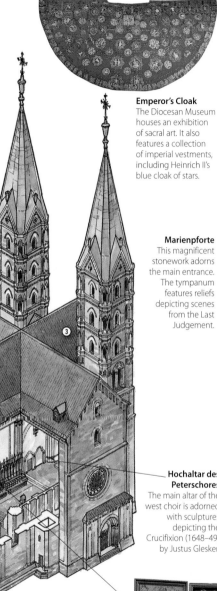

VISITORS' CHECKLIST

Practical Information
Domplatz 5. **Tel** (0951) 50 23
30. **Open** Apr–Oct: 9:30am–
6pm daily; Nov–Mar: 9:30am–
5pm daily.
Diözesanmuseum: **Tel** (0951)
50 23 16. **Open** 10am–5pm Tue–
Sun. **Closed** Good Friday, 25, 31
Dec.

Emperor's Cloak
The Diocesan Museum houses an exhibition of sacral art. It also features a collection of imperial vestments, including Heinrich II's blue cloak of stars.

Marienpforte
This magnificent stonework adorns the main entrance. The tympanum features reliefs depicting scenes from the Last Judgement.

Hochaltar des Peterschores
The main altar of the west choir is adorned with sculptures depicting the Crucifixion (1648–49) by Justus Glesker.

★ Marian Altar by Veit Stoß
Veit Stoß was commissioned to create this altar by his son, Andrew Stoß, who was a Carmelite prior in Nürnberg at the time. After the victory of the Reformation in Nürnberg, however, he moved to Bamberg in 1543.

⑧ Bayreuth

Lovers of German music associate this town with the composer Richard Wagner (1813–83), who took up residence here in 1872. Established in 1231, Bayreuth originally belonged to the family of Count von Andechs-Meran; in 1248 it passed to the Margraves of Nuremberg (von Zollern) and, since 1806, Franconian Bayreuth has belonged to Bavaria. The town flourished during the 17th and 18th centuries when it was the residence of the Margraves, particularly during the time of Margravine Wilhelmine, sister of the Prussian King Frederick the Great and wife of Margrave Frederick.

Extraordinary Baroque interior of the Markgräfliches Opernhaus

🏛 Markgräfliches Opernhaus
Opernstraße 14. **Tel** (0921) 759 69 22.
Closed for renovation. 🎫

One of the finest theatres in Europe, the Markgräfliches Opera House was built in the 1740s by Joseph Saint-Pierre. Its ornate Baroque interior was designed by Giuseppe Galli Bibiena and his son Carlo, who came from a famous Bolognese family of theatre architects.

🏰 Neues Schloss
Ludwigstraße 21. **Tel** (0921) 759 690.

Open Apr–Sep: 9am–6pm daily; Oct–Mar: 10am–4pm daily. 🎫

The Neues Schloss (New Castle) was commissioned by Margravine Wilhelmine and built by Joseph Saint-Pierre. The elongated, three-storey structure combines classical lines with a rustic ground floor. The Italian wing was added in 1759. To this day nearly all the rooms have retained their original Baroque and Rococo decor. The park is arranged in a typically English style.

🖼 Villa Wahnfried
Richard-Wagner-Museum: Richard-Wagner-Straße 48. **Tel** (0921) 75 72 816. **Open** Apr–Oct: 9am–5pm daily (to 8pm Tue & Thu); Nov–Mar: 10am–5pm daily. 🎫
Closed Easter Sunday.

On the northeast side of the castle garden is Villa Wahnfried. Built for Wagner by Carl Wölfel, the villa was destroyed during World War II but was restored in the 1970s. In the garden is Wagner's tomb and that of his wife Cosima, the daughter of Franz Liszt.

🏛 Franz-Liszt-Museum
Wahnfriedstraße 9. **Tel** (0921) 516 64 88. **Open** Sep–Jun: 10am–noon, 2–5pm daily; Jul–Aug: 10am–5pm daily. 🎫

A short distance from Villa Wahnfried, at the junction of Wahnfriedstrasse and Lisztstrasse, stands the house in which Hungarian composer Franz Liszt died in 1886. It is now a museum dedicated to the composer.

🖼 Eremitage
4 km (2.5 miles) northeast of town. **Tel** (0921) 759 69 37. Castle: **Open** Apr–Sep: 9am–6pm daily; 1 Oct–15 Oct: 10am–4pm. **Closed** 16 Oct–Mar. 🎫 Park: **Open** daily.

In 1715–18, following the example of the French king Louis XIV and the fashion among the nobility for playing at ascetism, Margrave Georg Wilhelm ordered the building of the Eremitage complex as a retreat. With its horseshoe-shaped orangery, the hermitage (or Altes Schloss) was given to Margravine Wilhelmine as a birthday present. She then set about transforming it into a pleasure palace.

Richard Wagner (1813–1883)

The German composer is inseparably linked with Bayreuth, where he enjoyed his greatest artistic triumphs. His career, which did not run smoothly in early days, began in Magdeburg, Königsberg and Riga. From there he had to flee, via London to Paris, from his pursuing creditors. His reputation was firmly established by successful performances of his romantic operas *The Flying Dutchman* (1843) and *Tannhäuser* (1845) in Dresden. Wagner's long-time sponsor was the eccentric Bavarian king, Ludwig II. From 1872 Wagner lived in Bayreuth, where Festspielhaus was built specifically for the operas.

Bust of Wagner by Arno Breker (1939)

Tomb of Wagner and his wife in the garden of Villa Wahnfried

Festspielhaus, specially designed venue for the annual Wagner Festival

🎭 Festspielhaus

Festspielhügel. **Tel** (0921) 787 80.
⏰ Sep–Oct: 10am, 11am, 2pm, 3pm
daily; Nov: 2pm Sat; Dec–Apr 10am,
2pm daily.

Each July and August, Wagner
festivals are held in this theatre,
built 1872–75 to a design by
Gottfried Semper. The world
premiere of *The Ring of the
Nibelung* played here in 1876.

Environs

Approximately 20 km (12 miles)
to the northwest of Bayreuth is
the town of **Kulmbach**. Famous
for its countless breweries, the
town hosts a big beer festival

each year, in July and August. Its
town hall has a beautiful, Rococo
façade dating from 1752. From
here you can walk to the castle
hill to visit the Plassenburg
Fortress, which has belonged to
the Hohenzollern family since
1340. Until 1604, this was the
seat of the von Brandenburg-
Kulmbach Margraves. This vast
structure was built in 1560–70.
The gem in its crown is the
Renaissance courtyard with
arcades (Schöner Hof). The castle
houses a vast collection of tin
figurines, with some 30,000
items. In **Ködnitz**, to the
southeast of Kulmbach, is the

VISITORS' CHECKLIST

Road map D5. 👥 75,000.
ℹ️ Luitpoldplatz 9 (0921-885 88).
🎪 Musica Bayreuth (May),
Fränkische Festwoche (May),
Richard-Wagner-Festspiele (Jul–
Aug), Bayreuther Barock (Sep).

Transport
✈️ Nuremberg, 86 km (53 miles).
🚉 Hauptbahnhof.

Upper Franconian Village School
Museum. Based on the original
school furnishings and various
old photographs, the exhibition
illustrates the teaching methods
that were used in this region
more than a hundred years ago.

Some 25 km (16 miles) from
Bayreuth, in Sanspareil Park near
Hollfeld, is the **Felsentheater** –
an unusual 80-seat theatre set
in a natural grotto.

Felsentheater, in a natural grotto in
Sanspareil Park near Bayreuth

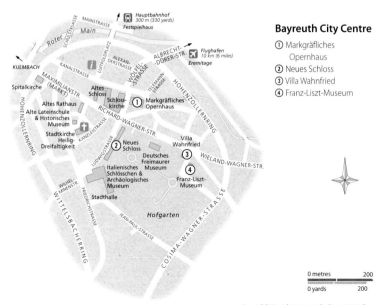

Bayreuth City Centre

① Markgräfliches
  Opernhaus
② Neues Schloss
③ Villa Wahnfried
④ Franz-Liszt-Museum

0 metres 200
0 yards 200

For additional map symbols *see back flap*

❾ Berching

Map D6. ⛰ 7,500. 🛈 Petten-koferplatz 12 (08462-205 13).

This charming little town, situated in the valley of the river Sulz, boasts a history that stretches back to the 9th century. To this day it retains the complete enclosure of its medieval city walls, including towers and gates with old oak doors. The most beautiful of the towers is the *Chinesische Turm* (the Chinese Tower).

The regional museum is well worth visiting, as are some of the local churches. These include an early Gothic church, Mariae Himmelfahrt, remodelled after 1756 by M Seybold and featuring some beautiful Rococo stucco ornaments. The Baroque St Lorenz, with its 13th century tower and original late-Gothic altar, is also noteworthy.

❿ Amberg

Map D5. ⛰ 43,000. 🛈 Hallplatz 2 (09621-102 39).

Situated at the edge of the Franconian Jura, on the banks of the river Vils, Amberg owes its development to local iron ore deposits and the steel industry. The well-preserved, oval-shaped old town is still encircled by medieval walls. At the centre is an enchanting market square with the vast 15th-century late-Gothic hall-church, Pfarrkirche St Martin, and Gothic town hall (1356), both still with their original interiors.

The symbol of Amberg is the bridge named "the town spectacles"

Amberg was once the residential town of the Rhine palatines, whose Renaissance palace and chancellery have survived to the present day.

The symbol of Amberg is the Stadtbrille, the bridge spanning the river Vils, whose arches reflected in the river resemble a pair of spectacles – hence its nickname "the town's spectacles".

The late-Gothic main altar in St George's Church, Dinkelsbühl

⓫ Dinkelsbühl

Map D6. ⛰ 11,000. 🚉 🛈 Altrathausplatz 14, (09851-902 440). 🎭 Kinderzeche (mid-Jul).

This old Franconian town is one of the best-preserved medieval urban complexes in Germany. The walls surrounding the city include four towers – Wörnitzer, Nördlinger, Seringer and Rothenburger Tor – which are all almost intact. The residential district of the town consists mainly of timber-framed houses.

The finest example of these is the Deutsches Haus, which stands opposite St George's Church. Dating from the late 15th to the early 16th century, the house once belonged to the Drechsel-Deufstetten family and is now a hotel-restaurant.

The late-Gothic Church of St George is a triple-nave hall-church with no transept. Together with the presbytery, it forms one large interior crowned with magnificent network vaults. The most valuable items of the interior furnishings include the pulpit, the font – which dates from around 1500 – and the Crucifixion in the main altar, which is attributed to Michael Wolgemut. A fine view of the town can be obtained from the church tower.

In Turmgasse stands the Baroque palace of the Teutonic Order, built in 1760–64 by Mathias Binder.

⓬ Nördlingen

Map D6. ⛰ 20,000. 🚉 🛈 Marktplatz 2 (09081-841 16). 🎭 Stabenfest (May), Nördlinger Pfingstmesse Scharlachrennen (Jun), Sommerfestspiele (Jul), Historisches Stadtmauerfest (every third year in Sep; next in 2016).

The town is situated in the Ries Basin, which is an immense and well-preserved crater that was formed millions of years ago by a meteor strike.

During the Middle Ages Nördlingen was a free town of the Holy Roman Empire and an important trade centre. The fortification walls that surround the city include five gates and 12 towers (dating from the 14th to the 15th centuries) that have survived intact to this day.

The late-Gothic church of St George was built by Nikolaus Eseler, who also built the St George Church in Dinkelsbühl. The church is a triple-nave hall-church with round pillars and network vaults. Its imposing west tower, known as the Daniel Tower, offers a magnificent panoramic view of the town and its environs.

The St Salvator's Church features original Gothic altars and a portal that has the scene of the *Last Judgement* in the tympanum. The former hospital of the Holy Spirit is now home to an interesting **Stadtmuseum**. The 14th-century town hall features a striking external stone stairway (1618).

Statue from the Tanzhaus façade

⟐ Stadtmuseum
Vordere Gerbergasse 1. **Tel** (09081-273 82 30). **Open** Mar–Oct: 1:30–4:30pm Tue–Sun. Nov–Feb: open only to guided tours (reserve a place in advance by telephone).

⓭ Ansbach

Map D6. 40,000. Johann-Sebastian-Bach-Platz 1 (0981-512 43 or 194 33. Ansbacher Frühlingsfest (May), Bach-Woche (every two years in Jul: the next one is in 2015), Ansbacher Rokokospiele (Jul), Heimatfest (Jul).

The town, situated west of Nuremberg, began its history in AD 748 with the foundation of a Benedictine Abbey by a man named Gumbert. A settlement called Onoldsbach, which sprang up nearby, is now called Ansbach. From 1460 until 1791 Ansbach was the home of the von Brandenburg-Ansbach Margraves and in 1791 it was incorporated into Prussia; after 1806 it passed into Bavaria. The Markgräfliche

residence is situated in the north-eastern part of the Old Town. Remodelled several times it is now a Baroque Neo-Classical structure. Its 27 original state apartments include the Mirror Room, Mirror Gallery, Dining Room and Audience Room. It now houses the Museum of Faience and Porcelain. The nearby Hofgarten has a 102-m (335-ft) long Orangery. It also houses a Kaspar Hauser Collection.

⟐ Markgrafenmuseum
Kaspar-Hauser-Platz 1. **Tel** (0981) 977 50 56. **Open** 10am–5pm Tue–Sun.

⟐ Markgräfliche Residenz "Ansbacher Fayence und Porzellan"
Promenade 27. **Tel** (0981) 953 83 90. **Open** Apr–Sep: 9am–6pm Tue–Sun; Oct–Mar: 10am–4pm Tue–Sun. hourly.

⓮ Eichstätt

Map D6. 15,000. Domplatz 8 (08421-600 1400).

Willibald, a close companion and compatriot of the Anglo-Saxon missionary Boniface, established a missionary-abbey (Eihstat) here. Soon afterwards Eichstätt became an episcopal town. In 1634 a fire ripped through the town, destroying four-fifths of its houses and four churches; after this the town was rebuilt in Baroque style.

Eichstätt is home to the country's only Catholic university, established in 1980. On the outskirts of town, on a hill overlooking the River

Majestic Walhalla near Donaustauf

Altmühl, stands the picturesque Willibald Castle, which until the 18th century was the residence of prince-bishops. Now it houses an interesting museum of artifacts from the Jurassic era, where visitors can see a very well preserved skeleton of *archaeopteryx*.

A new bishop's residence was built nearby from 1702 until 1768. Its west wing features a magnificent staircase and the Mirror Room, in which the works of Mauritio Pedetti, Johann Jakob Berg and Michael Franz are displayed.

⓯ Donaustauf

Walhalla. **Tel** (09403) 96 16 80. **Open** Apr–Sep: 9am–5:45pm; Oct: 9am–4:45pm; Nov–Mar: 10am–11:45am & 1–3:45pm.

In 1830–41 Leo von Klenze built the Walhalla *(see above)*. This monument to the national glory occupies a scenic location on the River Danube. The building stands on a raised terrace and has the form of a Neo-Classical columned temple (similar to the Parthenon in Athens). It is adorned with 121 marble busts of artists and scientists.

Orangery of the Markgräfliche residence, in Ansbach

⑯ Nürnberg (Nuremberg)

Situated on the river Pegnitz, Nuremberg is not only a paradise for lovers of its famous gingerbread and sausages but is also the symbol of Germany's history. The earliest records of the town, the second largest in Bavaria, date from 1050 when it was a trading settlement. From 1219 Nuremberg, a free town of the Holy Roman Empire, was an important centre of craft and commerce. Its most rapid development took place in the 15th and 16th centuries, when many prominent artists, craftsmen and intellectuals worked here, making Nuremberg one of the cultural centres of Europe.

Sights at a Glance

① Frauentor
② Marthakirche
③ Mauthalle
④ Germanisches Nationalmuseum
⑤ St Lorenz-Kirche
⑥ Lorenzer Platz
⑦ Heilig-Geist-Spital
⑧ Hauptmarkt
⑨ Frauenkirche
⑩ Rathaus
⑪ Spielzeugmuseum
⑫ Kirche St Sebald
⑬ Egidienkirche
⑭ Kaiserburg
⑮ Albrecht-Dürer-Haus

Picturesque alley near Frauentor

Exploring Lorenzer Alstadt

The southern part of the old town, known as Lorenzer Alstadt, is separated from the northern part by the river Pegnitz and encircled to the south by the city walls. Many of the area's historic treasures were carefully reconstructed following severe bomb damage during World War II.

🔲 Frauentor

Frauentorgraben.
Frauentor is one of the most attractive gates into the old town. It is installed in the massive city walls that were constructed during the 15th and 16th centuries. The vast tower, Dicker Turm, was erected nearby in the 15th century. Königstor, a magnificent gate that once stood to the right of Dicker Turm, was dismantled in the 19th century. Beyond Frauentor are a number of alleys with half-timbered houses, shops and cafés, built after the war.

🔲 Marthakirche

Königstraße 74–78.
Dating from the 14th century, the small hospital church of St Martha is tucked between the surrounding houses. Though its interior is virtually devoid of furnishing, it features some magnificent Gothic stained-glass windows, which date from around 1390.

🔲 Mauthalle

Hallplatz 2.
The massive structure that dominates Königstrasse is a Gothic granary built in 1498–1502 by Hans Beheim the Elder. It originally housed the town's municipal scales and the customs office. In the 19th century, the building was converted into a department store and continues in that role today, following post-war reconstruction.

🏛 Germanisches Nationalmuseum

See pp264–5.

🔲 St Lorenz-Kirche

Lorenzer Platz.
One of the most important buildings in Nuremberg is the

Panoramic view over the rooftops of Nuremberg

Impressive Mauthalle dominating Königstraße

crucifix within the main altar and the magnificent statue of the Archangel Michael standing by the second pillar of the main nave. There are also several Gothic altars and some magnificent 15th-century stained-glass windows (1493–95). The pillars of the nave are adorned with a number of fascinating statues of

Gothic original. Diagonally across the square is the Nassauer Haus, a Gothic mansion whose lower storeys were built in the 13th century. The upper floors were added in the 15th century.

A short distance from the square, in Karolinenstraße, is a fine sculpture by Henry Moore.

✠ Heilig-Geist-Spital

In the centre of town, on the banks of the river Pegnitz, stands the Hospital of the Holy Spirit. Founded in 1332, this is one of the largest hospitals built in the Middle Ages and features a lovely inner courtyard with wooden galleries. The wing that spans the river was built during extension works in 1488–1527. Lepers were kept at some distance from the other patients, in a separate half-timbered building that was specially erected for the purpose. From 1424 until 1796, the insignia of the Holy Roman Empire were kept here rather than in the castle.

The Heilig-Geist-Spital now houses a retirement home and a restaurant. The entrance to the building is on the northern side of the river.

Gothic church of St Lorenz, whose basilica-style main body was built around 1270–1350. The vast hall presbytery was added much later, in 1439–77. On entering the church it is worth taking a look at the magnificent main portal, which is adorned with sculptures. In the main nave of the church, suspended from the ceiling above the altar, is a superb group sculpture, *Annunciation*, the work of Veit Stoß (1519). He was also the creator of the

the Apostles, dating from the late 14th century.

🏛 Lorenzer Platz

Overlooked by the church of St Lorenz, Lorenzer Platz is a popular meeting place for the citizens of Nuremberg and visitors alike. Outside the church is the Fountain of the Virtues, *Tugendbrunnen* (1589), with water cascading from the breasts of its seven Virtues. Nearby is a statue of St Lorenz, which is a copy of the 1350

Heilig-Geist-Spital reflected in the waters of the river Pegnitz

For map symbols see back flap

Exploring Nürnberg (Nuremberg)

Nuremberg was once an important publishing centre. Schedel's *Liber Chronicarum* was published here in 1493 and, in 1543 – following the town's official adoption of the Reformation in 1525 – *The Revolutions of the Celestial Spheres* by Copernicus was published. The Thirty Years' War ended the town's development but, during the 19th century, it became the focus for the Pan-German movement. In 1945–49 the town was the scene of the trials for war crimes of Nazi leaders.

Detail of *Schöner Brunnen*, in Hauptmarkt

Hauptmarkt

Each year the Hauptmarkt provides a picturesque setting for the town's famous Christkindlesmarkt, which goes on throughout Advent. At this famous market you can buy gingerbread, enjoy the taste of German sausages, warm yourself with a glass of mulled wine spiced with cloves and buy locally made souvenirs.

Nuremberg's star attraction is the Gothic *Schöner Brunnen* (Beautiful Fountain), which was probably erected around 1385 but replaced in the early 20th century with a replica. It consists of a

19-metre (62-ft) high, finely carved spire standing at the centre of an octagonal pool. The pool is surrounded by a Renaissance grille that includes the famous golden ring: the local tradition is that if you turn the ring three times, your wishes will come true. The pool is adorned with the statues of philosophers, evangelists and church fathers, while the spire is decorated with the statues of Electors and of Jewish and Christian heroes. Features and details of the original fountain are kept in the **Germanisches Nationalmuseum** *(see pp264–5).*

Frauenkirche

Hauptmarkt. **Open** 9am–6pm Mon–Sat, 12:30pm–7pm Sun.

Commissioned by Emperor Charles IV, this Gothic hall-church dates from 1352–58. Over its richly decorated vestibule is the oriel of the west choir. Its gable contains a clock from Männleinlaufen, installed in 1509. Each day at noon the clock displays a procession of Electors paying homage to the Emperor. Also noteworthy is the Gothic altar *(Tucher Altar)*, which dates from 1445.

Rathaus

Rathausplatz.

The present town hall consists of several sections. Facing the Rathausplatz is the oldest, Gothic part, built in 1332–40 and remodelled in the early 15th century. Behind, facing Hauptmarkt, is the Renaissance part, built in 1616–22 by Jakob Wolff. Its magnificent portals are decorated with heraldic motifs. The courtyard features a fountain dating from 1557.

Spielzeugmuseum

Karlstraße 13–15. **Tel** (0911) 231 31 64. **Open** 10am–5pm Tue–Fri, 10am–6pm Sat & Sun. **Closed** Good Friday, 24, 25, 26, 31 Dec.

This enchanting toy museum, established in 1971, houses a magnificent collection of tin soldiers and a huge collection of dolls and puppets. Its greatest attraction, however, is a collection of antique dolls' houses, filled with miniature furniture and equipment.

Kirche St Sebald

Winklerstraße 26. **Open** year-round: 11am–6pm Sun; Jan–Mar: 9:30am–4pm Mon–Sat; Apr–May & Oct–Dec: 9:30am–6pm Mon–Sat; Jun–Sep: 9:30am–8pm Mon–Sat.

The oldest of Nuremberg's churches, Kirche St Sebaldus was built in 1230–73 as a Romanesque, two-choir basilica. During remodelling in the 14th century, it was given two side naves and a soaring western hall-choir. The Gothic towers were completed in the late 15th century. At the centre of the presbytery is the magnificent tomb of St Sebald. This cast bronze structure was made by Peter Vischer the Elder. It houses a silver coffin (1397) containing relics of the saint. The church features some splendid carvings by Veit Stoß, including a magnificent statue of St Andrew (1505), which stands in the ambulatory around the presbytery, the Volckamersche Passion (1499) and the Crucifixion scene in the main altar (1520). Also noteworthy is the magnificent Gothic font and the Tucher family epitaph by Hans von Kulmbach (1513).

Heraldic arms adorning the tympanum of the town hall portal

For hotels and restaurants in this area see pp492–503 and pp510–33

The timber-frame building of the Albrecht-Dürer-Haus

⚐ Egidienkirche

Egidienplatz.

Egidienkirche is the only surviving Baroque church in Nuremberg. Its façade, built after the fire of 1696, hides a building containing elements of the previous Romanesque-Gothic Benedictine church. The older chapels, including the Euchariuskapelle, Tetzelkapellethe and Wolfgang-kapelle, survive to this day.

⚐ Kaiserburg

Kaiserburg-Museum: Innerer Burghof.
Tel (0911) 200 95 40. **Open** Apr–Sep: 9am–6pm daily; Oct–Mar: 10am–4pm daily. ⚐

The three castles that tower over Nuremberg include the central burgraves' castle, with the Free Reich's buildings to the east, and the Imperial castle (whose origins go back to the 12th century) to the west. When climbing up the Burgstrasse you will first reach the Fünfeckturm (Pentagonal Tower), which dates from 1040. The oldest building in town, it is an architectural relic of the von Zollern burgraves' castle. At its foot are the Kaiserstallung

(Emperor's stables), which now houses a youth hostel. A continued climb will bring you, on the left, to the courtyard of the imperial palace, which features a round tower (Sinwellturm) dating from the 12th century, and a deep well – the Tiefe Brunnen. Passing through the inner gate of the castle you will finally reach its heart, the residential building.

⚐ Albrecht-Dürer-Haus

Albrecht-Dürer-Straße 39. **Tel** (0911) 231 25 68. **Open** Jul–Sep & during Christkindlesmarkt: 10am–5pm daily, 10am–8pm Thu; Oct–Jun: 10am–5pm Tue–Sun, 10am–8pm Thu. ⚐ ⚐

Spending much of his childhood in a house on the corner of Burgstrasse and Obere Schmiedgasse, the renowned artist and engraver Albrecht Dürer lived in this house from 1509 until his death in 1528. On the three-hundredth anniversary of his death, the building was bought by the town and many rooms have since been reconstructed. The third-floor room now contains a printing press dating from Dürer's time. Copies of his

pictures provide a useful insight into the work of this famous Nuremberg citizen.

⚐ St-Johannis-Friedhof

Am Johannisfriedhof.

The St John's Cemetery is one of the best preserved and most important in Europe. Established in 1518, it has provided a resting place for many famous people, including Albrecht Dürer (No. 649), the sculptor Veit Stoß (No. 268), the goldsmith Wenzel Jamnitzer (No. 664) and the painter Anselm Feuerbach (No. 715). The cemetery also contains a rich array of tombs from the 16th, 17th and 18th centuries.

⚐ Dokumentationszentrum Reichsparteitagsgelände

Bayernstr. 110. **Tel** (0911) 231 56 66.
Open 9am–6pm Mon–Fri, 10am–6pm Sat & Sun.

This vast, unfinished building complex in the southern part of town dates from the Nazi era, built for National Party gather-ings. The building now houses a historical exhibition and archive, reminding and educating visitors of its horrifying past.

The buildings of the Kaiserburg, towering over the town

Nuremberg: Germanisches Nationalmuseum

This museum, which was officially opened in 1852, was founded by a Franconian aristocrat named Hans von Aufsess. It houses a unique collection of antiquities from the German-speaking world. In 1945, towards the end of World War II, the buildings that had originally housed the museum were bombed. The architecture of the modern building, which was completed in 1993, cleverly incorporates the remaining fragments of a former Carthusian abbey. Among the most valuable items in the museum's collection are works by Tilman Riemenschneider, Konrad Witz, Lucas Cranach the Elder, Albrecht Altdorfer, Albrecht Dürer and Hans Baldung Grien.

Madonna with Child Crowned by Angels
This picture was painted by Hans Holbein the Elder (c.1465–1524) who created many festive altarpieces using warm colours.

★ Archangel (1516)
This enchanting wood-carving of the archangel Raphaël is one of many works produced by Veit Stoss after his return from Cracow.

Cloisters

Former Carthusian church

Ground floor

Entrance to study collections and library

Brooch from Domagnano
This Ostrogothic buckle from the 5th century AD, shaped like an eagle, was discovered in the late 19th century in Domagnano, in San Marino. It probably belonged to a rich Ostrogothic aristocrat.

★ Cover of the Codex Aureus
The richly ornamented cover of the *Codex Aureus*, also known as the Golden Gospel Book of Echternach, was produced in Trier in the 10th century.

Gallery Guide

The exhibits have been arranged in sections, ranging from prehistory to the Middle Ages, and are located on the ground and first floors. Twentieth-century art is on the second floor and the toy collection is housed separately.

VISITORS' CHECKLIST

Practical Information
Kartäusergasse 1. **Tel** (0911) 133 10. **Open** 10am–6pm Tue–Sun (to 9pm Wed). **Closed** Shrove Tue, 24, 25, 31 Dec. 🧒
W **gnm.de**

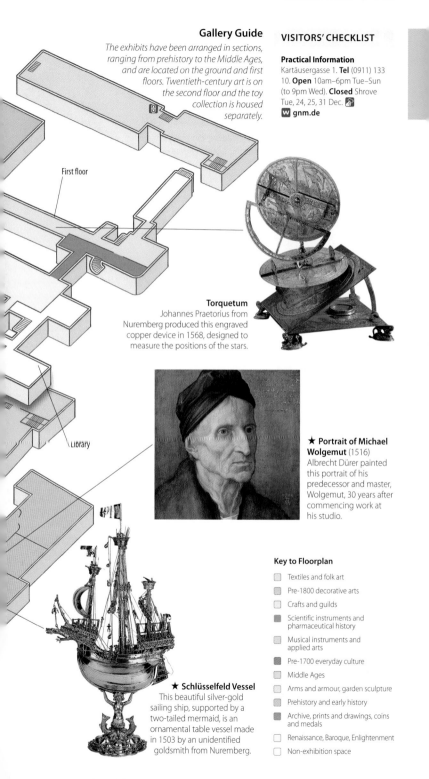

First floor

Library

Torquetum
Johannes Praetorius from Nuremberg produced this engraved copper device in 1568, designed to measure the positions of the stars.

★ **Portrait of Michael Wolgemut** (1516)
Albrecht Dürer painted this portrait of his predecessor and master, Wolgemut, 30 years after commencing work at his studio.

★ **Schlüsselfeld Vessel**
This beautiful silver-gold sailing ship, supported by a two-tailed mermaid, is an ornamental table vessel made in 1503 by an unidentified goldsmith from Nuremberg.

Key to Floorplan

- ☐ Textiles and folk art
- ☐ Pre-1800 decorative arts
- ☐ Crafts and guilds
- ■ Scientific instruments and pharmaceutical history
- ☐ Musical instruments and applied arts
- ■ Pre-1700 everyday culture
- ☐ Middle Ages
- ☐ Arms and armour, garden sculpture
- ☐ Prehistory and early history
- ■ Archive, prints and drawings, coins and medals
- ☐ Renaissance, Baroque, Enlightenment
- ☐ Non-exhibition space

⑰ Street-by-Street: Rothenburg ob der Tauber

If you want to sample the atmosphere of the Middle Ages, visit Rothenburg on the river Tauber, whose origins go back to the 12th century. Rothenburg was granted the status of a free town within the Holy Roman Empire in 1274 but its major growth took place in the 15th century. During the Thirty Years' War (1618–48) the town, which fought on the Protestant side, was captured by the Emperor's army. Little has changed since that time and the city walls still surround Gothic cathedrals and an array of gabled houses.

Reichsstadtmuseum
The former Dominican abbey now houses a museum devoted to the town's history. The abbey kitchen – the oldest surviving kitchen in Germany – is also open to visitors.

Franziskanerkirche
In this Gothic church is a retable depicting *The Stigmatization of St Francis*, believed to be an early work by Tilman Riemenschneider.

★ St Jakobs Kirche
In the Gothic church of St Jakob (built between 1311 and 1485) is the superb Zwölfbotenaltar by Friedrich Herlin.

★ Mittelalterliches Kriminalmuseum
Many blood-curdling exhibits are on display at this museum, which houses a collection of instruments of torture and punishment.

For hotels and restaurants in this area see pp492–503 and pp510–33

View from Burggarten
The castle garden (Burggarten) is reached through Burgtor, the tallest of the town's gates. The garden, which during the Middle Ages was the site of the Hohenstaufen family castle, provides a magnificent view over the town and the river valley.

Galgentor
Galgentor, an old execution place, is also known as Würzburger Tor, since it is the gate leading to Würzburg.

Rödertor
The best preserved segments of the old city walls are around the Rödertor gate, which dates from the late 14th century.

★ Rathaus
The town hall consists of the surviving Gothic section with a tower, and the later Renaissance structure with Baroque arcades.

Key
— Suggested route

⑱ Andechs

Road map D7. ℹ Andechser Straße 16 (08152-932 50).

The village of Andechs, at the summit of the 700-m (2,300-ft) high Holy Mountain of the same name, is not only the destination of pilgrimages to the local church, but also of many less spiritual trips to the *Bräustüberl*, where visitors can refresh themselves with a glass or two of the excellent beer brewed by local monks.

The present triple-nave Gothic hall-church was built in 1420–25. Its Rococo interior dates from 1755. The lower tier of the main altar contains the famous *Miraculous Statue of the Mother of God* (1468), while the upper tier features the *Immaculata* by Hans Degler (1609). On selected feast days, holy relics are displayed on the altar gallery.

Ammersee near the Holy Mountain of Andechs

⑲ Landsberg am Lech

Road map D7. 🚊 24,000. 🚍 ℹ Hauptplatz 152 (08191-12 82 46).

The history of Landsberg goes back to 1160 when Henry the Lion built his castle here, on the right bank of the river Lech. During the 13th century, the surrounding settlement grew into a town, which soon became a major trading centre. Religious conflicts, culminating in the Thirty Years'War, put an end to the town's development but, in the late 17th century, the town once again became an important commercial and cultural centre. Adolf Hitler wrote *Mein Kampf* here, while serving a prison term for his unsuccessful coup attempt in Munich.

At the heart of Landsberg is the Hauptplatz with its Baroque town hall and the intricately carved 14th-century tower, Schmalztor.

In Ludwigstrasse is the late-Gothic parish church, Stadtpfarrkirche Mariä Himmelfahrt, whose Baroque-style interior features a statue of the *Madonna and Child* by Hans Multscher. Bayertor, the original town gate, is in the eastern part of the old town.

The town's **Neues Stadt-museum** is a useful source of information on local history.

🏛 **Neues Stadtmuseum**
Von-Helfenstein-Gasse 426. **Tel** (08191) 12 83 60. **Open** 2–5pm Tue–Sun, 10am–5pm Sat & Sun. 📷

⑳ Dachau

Road map D6. 🚊 35,000. 🚍 ℹ Konrad-Adenauer-Straße 1 (08131-75286 or 75287).

For most people the name Dachau is inextricably linked with the concentration camp that was built here by the Nazis in 1933. Since 1965, the whole site has been designated as a memorial, **KZ-Gedenkstätte Dachau**, to over 40,000 prisoners who died there, with a perma-nent exhibition in the former domestic quarters of the camp.

Dachau is a beautiful town with many historic buildings. On the southwestern edge of the old town stands **Schloss Dachau**, summer residence of the Wittelsbachs. The palace that stands here today was created in the 18th century from the western wing of an earlier castle, the work of Joseph Effner.

In the early 19th century the area surrounding the castle housed a colony of artists who

Relief from the church façade in Landsberg

had tired of city life. They were known as *Malschule Neu-Dachau*. Some even built their own villas. Even earlier, however, the beauty of the surrounding countryside had been discovered by the impressionist painter Max Liebermann (1847–1935). The **Dachauer Gemäldegalerie** contains works of art inspired by local scenery, including one by Liebermann.

🏛 **Dachauer Gemäldegalerie**
Konrad-Adenauer-Straße 3. **Tel** (08131) 56 750. **Open** 11am– 5pm Tue–Fri, 1–5pm Sat & Sun. 📷

🏰 **Schloss Dachau**
Schlossstraße 2. **Tel** (08131) 879 23. **Open** 10am–7pm Tue–Sun. **Closed** 1 Jan; Shrove Tue; 24, 25 & 31 Dec. 📷

🏛 **KZ-Gedenkstätte Dachau**
Alte Römerstraße 75. **Tel** (08131) 66 99 70. **Open** 9am–5pm daily. **Closed** 24 Dec.

㉑ Schleißheim

Road map D6. Oberschleißheim.

Schleißheim is situated barely 14 km (9 miles) from Munich, making it within easy reach for an afternoon visit to its Baroque palace and park.

Surrounded by canals and now somewhat neglected, the park was established in the 17th and 18th centuries and includes

Baroque façade of the Wittelsbach palace, Schloss Dachau

three palaces. The modest **Altes Schloss** was built in 1623 for Prince Wilhelm V. Now it houses an exhibition of religious folk art.

Schloss Lustheim is a small, Baroque, hermitage-type palace, built in 1684–87 by Enrico Zucalli for the Elector Max Emanuel. As well as its beautiful interiors and stunning frescoes, it boasts a magnificent collection of Meissen porcelain, which is displayed in the **Museum Meißener Porzellan**.

The newest building is the **Neues Schloss**, designed by Enrico Zucalli. Work began in 1701 but was not completed until the second half of the 18th century. Despite wartime damage, it retains many original features. It now houses exhibits belonging to the Bavarian State Museum.

🔒 **Altes Schloss**
Tel (089) 315 87 20. **Open** as Neues Schloss.

🔒 **Neues Schloss**
Tel (089) 315 87 20. **Open** Apr–Sep: 9am–6pm Tue–Sun; Oct–Mar: 10am–4pm Tue–Sun. **Closed** Mon.

🔒 **Schloss Lustheim**
Tel (089) 315 87 20. **Open** Apr–Sep: 9am–6pm Tue–Sun; Oct–Mar: 10am–4pm Tue–Sun.

Museum Meißener Porzellan
Tel (089) 315 87 242. **Open** Apr–Sep: 9am–6pm Tue–Sun; Oct–Mar: 10am–4pm Tue–Sun.

🟫 Freising

Road map D6. 🏙 40,000. 🚃
ℹ Marienplatz 7 (08161-541 22).

Situated on the banks of the river Isar, just 20 minutes by train from Munich, is the old town of Freising. Its history is closely connected with St Korbinian, who founded the bishopric here in the early 8th century. Korbinian died around AD 725 and his remains still lie in the crypt of the Dom – the Cathedral Church of the Birth of the Virgin Mary and St Korbinian (1159–1205). This is a five-nave basilica, without transept, with an elongated choir and a massive twin-tower western façade. Its interior was remodelled in Baroque style by

The imposing bulk of the Neues Schloss in Ingolstadt

the Asam brothers, in 1724–25. The four-nave Romanesque crypt features a famous column, which is decorated with carvings of fantastic animals *(Bestiensäule)*. Nearby is the **Diözesanmuseum,** whose vast ecclesiastical collection includes two paintings by Rubens.

At the southwestern end of the old town is a former monastery, Weihenstephan, home to the world's longest-established brewery and a botanical garden.

🏛 **Diözesanmuseum**
Domberg 21. **Tel** (08161) 487 90.
Open 10am–5pm Tue–Sun.

🟫 Ingolstadt

Road map D6. 🏙 130,000. 🚃
ℹ Rathausplatz 2 (0841-305 30 30).

Lying on the river Danube, this former seat of the Wittelsbach family features many important historic buildings dating from the Middle Ages and the Renaissance and Baroque periods. Among the most

outstanding is the Church of the Virgin Mary, a triple-nave hall structure with circular pillars, chapels and choir with an ambulatory. Inside is the original Gothic-Renaissance main altar dating from 1572.

Another notable building is the Neues Schloss, built between the 15th and 18th centuries, with its stately rooms and Gothic chapel. It now houses the **Bayerisches Armeemuseum**.

A true gem of Bavarian architecture is the **Church of St Maria Victoria**, the work of Cosmas Damian Asam.

The **Deutsches Medizin-historisches Museum** exhibits medical instruments and has a garden with medicinal plants.

🏛 **Bayerisches Armeemuseum**
Neues Schloss, Paradeplatz 4. **Tel** (0841) 937 70. **Open** 9am–5:30pm Tue–Fri, 10am–5:30pm Sat & Sun.

🏛 **Deutsches Medizin-historisches Museum**
Anatomiestraße 18–20. **Tel** (0841) 305 28 60. **Open** 10am–5pm Tue–Sun.

Striking Baroque interior of the Church of St Maria Victoria, Ingolstadt

Arcaded courtyard of Neuburg Castle

㉔ Neuburg an der Donau

Road map D6. 🚊 25,000. 🚉 *i*
Ottheinrichplatz A118 (08431-552 40).

Perched on a promontory overlooking the river Danube, Neuburg is one of Bavaria's loveliest towns. During the Middle Ages, it changed hands frequently but was eventually ruled by Ottheinrich the Magnanimous, under whom the town grew and prospered on an unprecedented scale. He was the founder of the castle, built between 1534 and 1665, whose massive round towers still dominate the town. Its earliest part is the east wing. The courtyard, which is surrounded by arcades, features beautiful frescos by Hans Schroer. In the tower is a staircase adorned with paintings. The castle chapel, completed in 1543, is one of the oldest, purpose-built Protestant churches in Germany.

In Amalienstraße, leading down towards the town, stands the former Jesuits' College and the Court Church (Hofkirche). Work on the church began in the late 16th century and was completed in 1627. It was intended to be a Protestant church, but the ruling family converted back to Catholicism during its construction and it was taken over by the Jesuits who turned it into a counter-reformation Marian church. The

Heraldic crest on Neuberg Castle

triple-nave hall-structure has an exquisite interior decorated in gold, white and grey.

Among many old buildings that survive in the town centre are the Graf-Veri-Haus and the Baron-von-Hartman-Haus in Herrenstrasse. To the east of town stands the Grünau Castle (Jagdschloss), built for Ottheinrich in 1530–55.

Environs

18 km (11 miles) to the south, Schrobenhausen is the birthplace of the painter Franz von Lenbach, who was born in 1836. A museum in Ulrich-Peisser-Gasse is devoted to his life and work. While there, it is worth visiting St Jacob's Church, to see the fine 15th-century wall painting there.

🏛 **Schlossmuseum Neuburg**
Residenzstraße 2. **Tel** (08431) 88 97.
Open Apr–Sep: 9am–6pm Tue–Sun; Oct–Mar: 10am–4pm Tue–Sun. 🅿

㉕ Landshut

Road map E6. 🚊 57,000. 🚉
i Altstadt 315 (0871-92 20 50).
🎭 Fürstenhochzeit (every 4 years, next in 2017), Hofmusiktage (every 2 years, next in 2014), Frühjahrsdult (Apr–May), Bartlmädult (Aug), Haferlmarkt (Sep).

The earliest records of Landshut date from 1150. One hundred years later this was already a town and the main centre of power of the Dukes of Lower

Bavaria. In 1475 the town was the scene of a lavish medieval wedding, when Duke Georg of the House of Wittelsbach married the Polish Princess Jadwiga. Since 1903 the town has held regular re-enactments of the wedding feast (Landshuter Fürstenhochzeit).

Landshut has preserved its medieval urban layout, with two wide parallel streets, Altstadt and Neustadt, with clusters of historic 15th–16th century buildings. Opposite the town hall in Alstadt is the **Stadtresidenz**, a town house modelled on the Palazzo del Tè in Mantua. Sometimes known as the "Italian House", this was the first Renaissance palace to be built in Germany.

The vast brick church of St Martin (1385–1500) is a triple-nave, narrow hall-church featuring a presbytery, network vaults (1459) and the tallest church tower in Bavaria.

Landshut is dominated by the fortified 13th–16th century **Burg Trausnitz**, featuring a medieval tower, a Renaissance palace (1568–78) and the **Kunst- und Wunderkammer** ("room of arts and wonder"), a branch of the Bayerisches Nationalmuseum *(see p223)*.

Environs

From Landshut, it is worth taking a trip to Moosburg, situated 14 km (9 miles) to the

Stained-glass window in Landshut depicting Duke Georg and Jadwiga

west. Its early 13th-century Church of St Castulus features a 14-m (46-ft) high Marian altar by Hans Leinberger (1514).

🏰 Burg Trausnitz & Kunst- und Wunderkammer
Tel (0871) 92 41 10. **Open** Apr–Sep: 9am–6pm daily; Oct–Mar: 10am–4:30pm. 🎧

🏰 Stadtresidenz
Altstadt 79. **Tel** (0871) 92 41 10. **Open** Apr–Sep: 9am–6pm Tue–Sun; Oct–Mar: 10am–4pm Tue–Sun. 🎫 obligatory. 🎧

Interior of St George's Chapel in Burg Trausnitz

㊌ Dingolfing
Road map E6. 🏘 15,400. 🚉 Im Bruckstadel, Fischerei 9 (08731) 32 71 00.

The main tourist attraction in this small town on the banks of the river Isar is its Gothic castle. Built in the 15th century by the Bavarian dukes, this vast edifice now houses the Regional Museum. It is also worth taking a stroll to see Pfarrkirche St Johannes, a late-Gothic brick building dating from the late 15th century. Although what remains of its furnishings are merely the poor remnants of its former glory, nevertheless the church is still considered one of the most beautiful Gothic buildings in Bavaria.

Environs
In Landau an der Isar, situated 13 km (8 miles) to the east of Dingolfing, stands the picturesque Baroque church of Mariä Himmelfahrt, dating from the first half of the 18th century. There is also an interesting small

church, the Steinfelskirche (c.1700) inside a natural rock cave. In Arnstorf, 30 km (19 miles) to the east, is one of the few remaining Bavarian castles on water. Known as the Oberes Schloß, the castle was probably built in the 15th century and remodelled during the 17th and 18th centuries.

㊗ Straubing
Road map E6. 🏘 45,000. 🚉 ℹ Theresienplatz 2 (09421-19 433). 🎭 Agnes-Bernauer-Festspiel (Jul, every four years, next in 2015), Gäubodenvolksfest (Aug).

This market town enjoys a picturesque setting on the river Danube. The 600-m (1,970-ft) long market square is arranged into two sections, Theresien-platz and Ludwigplatz, and is part of the former trade route that led to Prague. The area is lined with historic buildings in Baroque, Neo-Classical and Secession styles.

At the centre of the market square stands the landmark 14th-century municipal tower, which offers a splendid view over the towns of the Bavarian Forest. At Ludwigplatz 23 is the "Lion's Pharmacy", where the famous Biedermeier painter Karl Spitzweg worked as an apprentice in 1828–30.

Turning from Theresienplatz into Seminargasse or Jakobs-gasse, you will reach the monumental brick structure of the parish church of St Jakob (1400–1590). This triple-nave hall-church, crowned with a network vault, retains many original features, including stained-glass windows in the chapels of Maria-Hilf-Kapelle (1420) and St Bartholomew. The so-called Moses' Window in the Chapel of St Joseph was made in 1490 in Nuremberg, based on a sketch provided by Wilhelm Playdenwurff. In the Cobbler's Chapel (Schusterkapelle) hangs a painting of *Madonna and Child*, by Hans

Holbein (c.1500). Overlooking the Danube is a 14th–15th-century castle, formerly a ducal residence. The Agnes-Bernauer Festival, held every four years, takes place in the courtyard of the castle. The Gäuboden-volksfest is the second largest folk festival in Bavaria after the Munich Oktoberfest. The **Gäuboden-museum** has a magnificent collection of Roman artifacts.

Environs
In the tiny village of Aufhausen, 21 km (12 miles) to the west, is the beautiful late-Baroque pilgrimage church of Maria Schnee. Built by Johann Michael Fischer in 1736–51, it includes magnificent wall paintings by the Asam brothers and a statue of the Madonna. Commissioned by Duke Wilhelm V of Bavaria, the Gnadenmadonna is believed to pardon sins.

In Oberalteich, some 10 km (6 miles) to the east, is the beautiful church of St Peter and St Paul built in the early 17th century for the Benedictine order. Inside, an unusual hanging staircase leads to the galleries, while the vestibule is decorated with stucco ornaments, depicting bird motifs.

In Windberg, 22 km (14 miles) east of Oberalteich, is a Romanesque Marian church whose main portal (c.1220) features an image of the Madonna in the tympanum.

🏛 Gäubodenmuseum
Fraunhoferstraße. **Tel** (09421) 974 110. **Open** 10am–4pm Tue–Sun. 🎧

Main altar in Ursulinenkirche, Straubing

㉘ Regensburg (Ratisbon)

Regensburg was once a Celtic settlement and later a campsite of the Roman legions. The outline of the Roman camp is still visible around St Peter's Cathedral. In the early 6th century, Regensburg was the seat of the Agilolfa ruling family, and in AD 739, a monk named Boniface established a bishopric here. From AD 843, Regensburg was the seat of the Eastern Frankish ruler, Ludwig the German. From 1245 it was a free town of the Holy Roman Empire and throughout the Middle Ages remained South Germany's fastest growing commercial and cultural centre. The city centre is a UNESCO World Heritage Site.

Picturesque Steinere Brücke leading to the old town of Regensburg

🔭 Steinerne Brücke
An outstanding example of medieval engineering, this 310-m (1,000-ft) long bridge over the Danube was built in 1135–46. It provides the best panoramic view of Regensburg. Near the bridge gate, Brückentor, stands an enormous salt warehouse topped with a vast five-storey roof.

🔭 Wurstküche (Wurstkuchel)
Thundorferstraße. **Open** 8am–7pm daily.

Immediately behind the salt warehouse is the famous *Wurstküche* (sausage kitchen), which has probably occupied this site since as early as the 12th century and may have served as a canteen for the builders of the bridge. Its Regensburger sausages are definitely worth trying.

🔭 Altes Rathaus
Rathausplatz. 🗓 Mon–Sat. Reichstagsmuseum. **Tel** (0941) 507 34 40. 🗓 Jan & Feb: 10am, 11:30am, 1:30pm, 3pm daily; Mar, Nov, Dec: 10am, 11:30am, 1:30pm, 3pm, 3:30pm daily; (every 30 mins) Apr–Oct: 9:30am–noon, 1:30–4pm daily (English tours 3pm). 🗓

In Rathausplatz stands an old 15th-century town hall with a 13th-century town tower. It contains a splendid, richly decorated hall – *Reichssaal* – where the Perpetual Imperial Diet (the first parliament of the Holy Roman Empire) sat between 1663 and 1806. Benches in the chamber were coloured to indicate who could sit where: for example, red benches for Electors. The adjoining new town hall dates

Late-Gothic oriel on the side elevation of the Altes Rathaus

from the late 17th–early 18th century.

🔭 Dom St Peter
Domschatzmuseum
Krauterermarkt 3. **Tel** (0941) 57 645. **Open** Apr–Oct: 10am–5pm Tue–Sat, noon–5pm Sun; Dec–6 Jan: 10am–4pm Sun; 7 Jan–Mar: 10am–4pm Fri & Sat, noon–4pm Sun. **Closed** Nov. 🗓

Towering above the city, on the site of the former Roman military camp, is the massive brick structure of St Peter's Cathedral. Built between 1250 and 1525, its imposing western towers were added only in 1859–69. The master architect, Ludwig, modelled his design for the building on French examples (the Rayonnant style). The stained-glass windows of the choir date from the early 14th century. The **Domschatzmuseum** has a collection of ecclesiastical vestments.

19th-century spires on the Gothic
St Peter's Cathedral

Sights at a Glance

① Steinerne Brücke
② Wurstküche
③ Altes Rathaus
④ Dom St Peter
⑤ Alte Kapelle
⑥ Schloss Thurn und Taxis
⑦ St Jakob Kirche

🏛 Alte Kapelle

Alter Kornmarkt.

The Old Chapel is really a Marian collegiate church. It stands on the foundations of an older, early Romanesque chapel dating from the Carolingian period. The building has been remodelled several times and contains some beautiful Rococo stuccoes by Anton Landes.

🏰 Schloss Thurn und Taxis

Emmeramsplatz 5. **Tel** (0941) 504 81 33. **Open** daily. **Closed** 1–12 Jan. 🗓 23 Mar–3 Nov: 10:30am–4:30pm (hourly) daily; 4 Nov–22 Mar: 10:30am–3:30pm (hourly exc 12:30pm) daily. 🎫

In the south end of the town you will find the buildings and churches of the former St Emmeram Abbey, which have been tastefully incorporated into the palace complex of the ducal family von Thurn und Taxis. These include a Gothic cloister dating from the 12th–14th centuries, a library

Enchanting Rococo interior of Alte Kapelle

with magnificent frescos by Cosmas Damian Asam and the burial chapel. In 1998, the Bavarian State Museum opened a branch here, the Schatzkammer, which has valuable collections of decorative art.

🏛 Baumburger Turm

Watmarkt.

Regensburg has many unique ancestral palaces dating from the 14th–15th centuries, with high towers modelled on Northern Italian architecture. Some 20 of the original 60 towers have survived. One of the most beautiful is the residential tower, Baumburger Turm. Nearby, at Watmarkt 5, stands the equally beautiful Goliathhaus, where Oskar Schindler lived for a time in 1945. A commemorative plaque has been placed at the rear of the building.

Gothic portals of St Emmeram Abbey in Schloss Thurn und Taxis

For map symbols see back flap

Winter view of Gnadenkapelle complex, from Altötting

㉙ Altötting

Road map E6. 📷 11,000.
🛈 Kapellplatz 2a (08671-50 62 19).
🚌 📅 pilgrimages to Altötting
(Whitsun). 🔷 altoetting.de

Altötting is renowned as the
earliest destination of pilgrimages
to the "Miraculous Statue" of the
Virgin Mary (1330). The statue
stands in the Wallfahrtskapelle
St Maria, which consists of two
parts. The central, octagonal
chapel, **Gnadenkapelle** (c.AD
750) was once the baptistery.
The external chapel was built in
1494 and the ambulatory in
1517. It also houses the so-called
"Silver Prince", representing the
miraculously cured son of the
Prince-Elector, Karl Albrecht.
Many Bavarian kings and princes
wished to be buried here.

Nearby is the interesting
Romanesque-Gothic church of
St Philip and St Jacob (1228–30
and 1499–1520). Its Neo-Classical
interior contains many
tombstones, while a separate
chapel, Tillykapelle, is the burial
place of Johann Tserclaes von
Tilly, a hero of the Thirty Years'
War and the Emperor's general.

The **Schatzkammer** (Treasury)
was housed in the former sacristy,
but after Pope Benedict XVI
turned it into a chapel in 2006
a new Schatzkammer and
Wallfahrtsmuseum (Pilgrimage
Museum) were built. The
collection includes an exquisite
example of French enamel and
gold artwork, the *Goldenes Rössl*
(Golden Steed), which dates from
around 1400. Despite its name,
the theme of this work is the
Adoration of the Magi. It was
commissioned by Isobel of

Bavaria as a New Year gift for her
husband, Charles VI of France.

**🏛 Neue Schatzkammer
and Wallfahrtsmuseum**
Kapellplatz 4. **Tel** (08671) 924 2015.
Open 10am–4pm Tue–Sun.
Closed Nov–mid-Mar. 📷

Walkway around Gnadenkapelle, in
Altötting, filled with offerings

㉚ Burghausen

Road map E6. 📷 19,500. 🛈
Stadtplatz 112 (08677-887 140). 🚌

The very picturesque town of
Burghausen is situated on the
river Salzach. Towering over the
town, the river and the lake is
Burghausen Castle, the world's
longest castle, built on a high
ridge stretching for 1,050 m

(1,150 yds). Work on the castle
started in 1253, but most of
the buildings were erected
during the reign of King George
the Rich and therefore have
magnificent, late-Gothic
forms. The king's wife, Jadwiga
Jagiellon, whom he married in
grand style in Landshut *(see
p270)*, was later rejected by him
and she spent her final days in
the fortress of Burghausen.

The castle consists of two
main parts: the main castle,
with tower, the residential
quarters, the courtyard and
domestic buildings; and the
castle approach (Vorburg).
The residential building has some
fine 15th- and 16th-century
paintings. A special door links
the Prince's quarters with the
"internal" Chapel of St Elizabeth.
Next to the chapel is the mid-
13th-century Dürnitz, which
served originally served as a
ballroom and banqueting hall.

The castle approach consists
of five courtyards (Vorhof). In the
fourth courtyard is the "external"
Chapel of St Jadwiga (Aussere
Burgkapelle St Hedwig) – the
work of Wolfgang Wiesinger, a
native of Salzburg (1489). This
has numerous original buildings,
including the town hall, which
was created by combining
three burgher houses dating
from the 14th–15th centuries
The parish church of St Jakob
(1353–1513) in Burghausen is
a three-nave basilica.

🏰 Burghausen Castle
Tel (08677) 887 140.

🏛 Museum
Open Apr–Sep: 9am–6pm daily; Oct–
Mar: 10am–4pm daily.

Panoramic view of Burghausen, with its vast castle complex on the hill

For hotels and restaurants in this area see pp492–503 and pp510–33

㉛ Bayerischer Wald

The Bavarian forest stretches north to the Danube, between Regensburg and Passau. It is part of Central Europe's largest woodland and provides idyllic grounds for a variety of outdoor pursuits. The local rocks contain large quantities of quartz, which contributed to the early development of the glass industry here. To this day, the region produces some fine, blown-glass artifacts. The region also hosts a number of popular festivals throughout the year.

① Zwiesel
In the old glassworks, which survive to this day, you can watch workers using blow irons to produce vases, jugs and other objects made of glass.

② Frauenau
Along with Zwiesel, this is the oldest centre of glass production in the area. The local museum illustrates the town's history.

③ Spiegelau
Spiegelau is one of the most popular starting points for tourists planning hiking trips into the mountains.

④ Grafenau
The main attractions of this small town are its snuff and furniture museums and the old town hall.

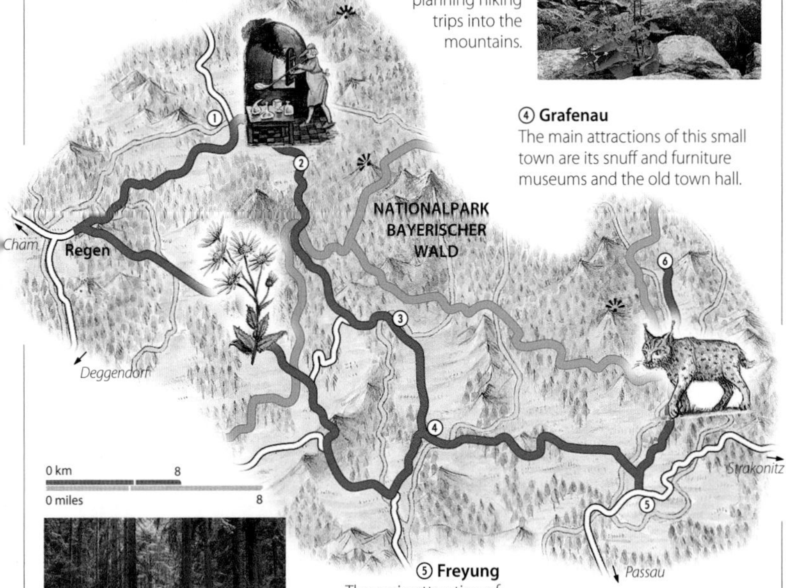

NATIONALPARK BAYERISCHER WALD

Cham   Regen

Deggendorf

0 km   8
0 miles   8

Strakonitz

Passau

⑤ Freyung
The main attraction of the town is the Schloss (Castle) Wolfstein, which now houses a museum of hunting and fishing.

⑥ Finsterau
Situated close to a vast artificial lake, Finsterau has an interesting open-air museum that displays examples of the local building trade.

Key

▬ Suggested route
— Other road
▬ Scenic route
🌟 Viewpoint

Tips For Walkers

Starting point: Zwiesel.
Distance: 82 km (51 miles).
Getting there: train to Frauenau, on the Zwiesel-Granau line; or Bodenmais, terminus of another branch line from Zwiesel.

㉒ Street-by-Street: Passau

Passau, whose long history goes back to Roman times, lies on a peninsula between the rivers Danube and Inn, near the Austrian border. During the second half of the 5th century, St Severinus established a monastery in Passau as well as several more nearby. In 739, an Irish monk called Boniface, known as "Germany's Apostle", founded a bishopric here and for many years this was the largest diocese of the Holy Roman Empire. Large parts of the town were destroyed by fires in 1662 and 1680. Reconstruction was carried out by Italian artists, who gave the town its Baroque, Rococo and Neo-Classical façades. However Passau retains a medieval feel in its narrow alleys and archways.

Passauer Glasmuseum
Opposite the old town hall is the beautiful patrician Hotel Wilder Mann, which now houses the Glasmuseum. The museum's vast collection includes valuable examples of Bohemian, Austrian and Bavarian glasswork.

★ **Dom St Stephan**
St Stephan's Cathedral is a true masterpiece of Italian Baroque, built by Italian architect Carlo Lurago to replace the original Gothic structure, which was largely destroyed by fire in the 17th century.

Deggendorf

ANGER STR

ST-ROID-GASSE

GROSSE MESSERGASSE

Passau-Hauptbahnhof

DOMPLATZ

University

INNKAI

MARIEN-BRÜCKE

★ **Altes Rathaus**
Dating from the 14th–15th century, the old town hall was created by combining eight patrician houses. The structure features a Neo-Gothic tower.

Neue Bischofsresidenz
Built by Domenico d'Angeli and Antonio Beduzzi in 1713–30, the Neue Residenz has a pilaster façade with protruding balconies and roof balustrade.

◄ The entrance to the harbour Lindau on Lake Constance

★ Veste Oberhaus
This former castle of the
prince-bishops now houses
the Oberhaus-Museum,
with displays on local and
regional history and the
work of local artists.

Schaiblingsturm
On the bank of the river Inn are
the remains of Passau's Gothic
town walls. They include this
tower, built in 1250.

PRINZREGENT
LUITPOLD BRÜCKE

ORT

| 0 metres | 100 |
| 0 yards | 100 |

**★ Wallfahrtskirche
Mariahilf**
High above the banks of
the river Inn stands this
early-Baroque abbey
complex dating from
1627–30. It includes a
pretty twin-towered
pilgrimage church.

Key
— Suggested route

For hotels and restaurants in this area see pp492–503 and pp510–33

㉝ Berchtesgadener Land

Berchtesgadener Land is one of the most beautiful regions, not just in Germany, but in the whole of Europe. It occupies the area of the Berchtesgadener Alps whose boundaries are defined by the river Saalach to the west, the river Salzach to the east, the "Stony Sea" (*Steinernes Meer*) to the south and, to the north, Untersberg, which is 1,972 m (7,500 ft) above sea level. To the south of Berchtesgaden village lies the National Park (Nationalpark Berchtesgaden).

★ Ramsau an der Ache
Set in an enchanting location in the Ramsau Valley, this village is a popular base for visitors to the area. Spectacular views of the mountains can be enjoyed from the small parish church.

Hintersee
This scenic lake has given its name to a picturesque hamlet nearby. A walk around the lake takes about one hour.

LATTEI

GEBIRG

REITER ALPE

HINTERSEE Ramsau

Wimbachkla

NATIONAL-

PARK

BERCHTESGADEN

①

Kehlsteinhaus

Standing on the summit of Kehlstein, this stone building resembling a mountain shelter is known as the Adlerhorst (Eagle's Nest). It was given to Hitler as a birthday present in 1939 by one of his closest allies, Martin Bormann, and it became one of the Führer's favourite residences. The approach to the building is a true engineering masterpiece: the initial section, the Kehlsteinstrasse, is a scenic mountain road, which passes through five tunnels and offers some breathtaking views. The final ascent is via a lift. The whole project took 13 months to complete. After the war, the

Eagle's Nest fell into the hands of the Americans, then, in 1960, it passed into private hands. The building now houses a restaurant that is very popular with tourists, not only because of its history but also for the spectacular views that it provides over part of the Alps.

KEY

① **Nationalpark Berchtesgaden**, is home to many rare species of plants and animals. You can visit this magnificent nation park by joining organized tours between May and October.

Berchtesgaden

The capital of the region features many historic buildings. The Schloss, originally an Augustinian priory, now houses the art treasures collected by Crown Prince Ruprecht. The local salt mine has been a source of wealth since the 16th century.

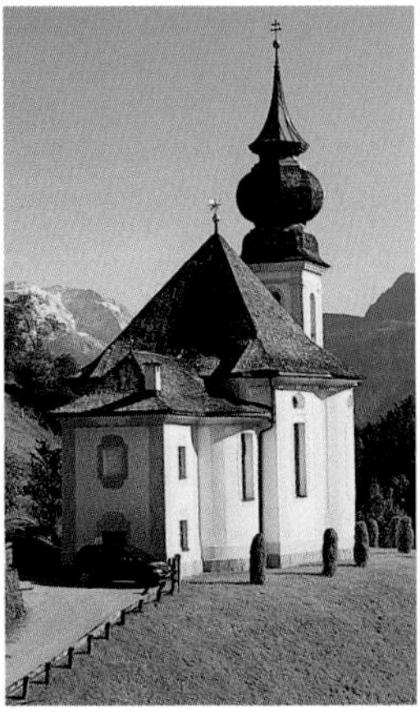

Wallfahrtskirche Maria Gern

One of the loveliest Baroque buildings in the region, the pilgrimage church of Maria Gern was built in 1709 in this idyllic location.

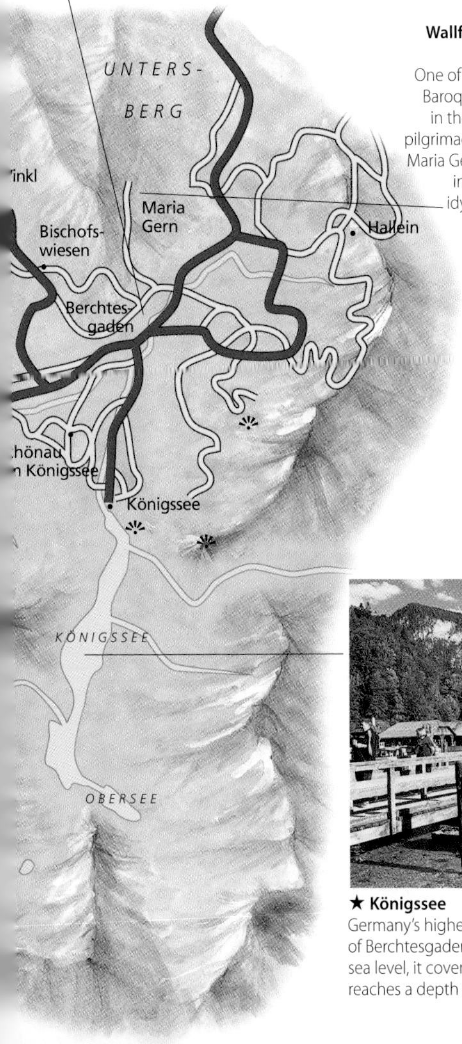

UNTERS-BERG

ïnkl

Maria Gern

Bischofs-wiesen

Berchtes-gaden

Hallein

hönau
n Königssee

Königssee

KÖNIGSSEE

OBERSEE

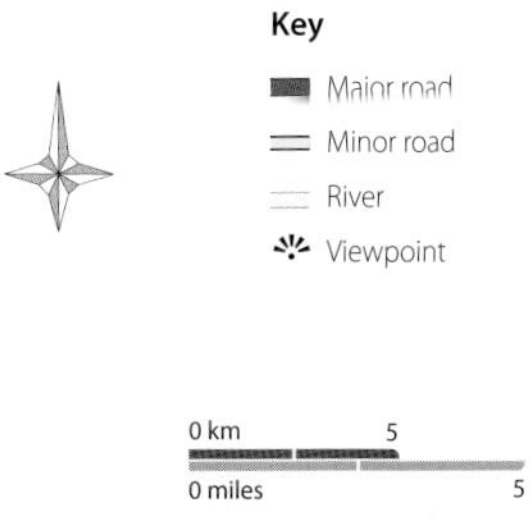

Key

━━ Major road

═══ Minor road

──── River

☀ Viewpoint

0 km   5

0 miles   5

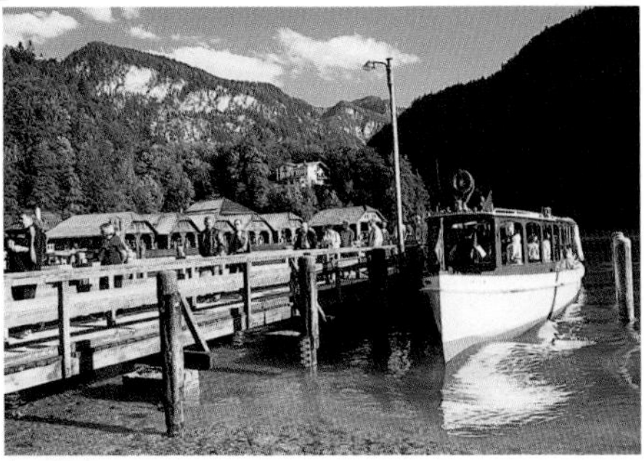

★ Königsee

Germany's highest lake, Königssee is the focal point of Berchtesgadener Land. Lying 600 m (2,000 ft) above sea level, it covers an area of 5.5 sq km (1,360 acres) and reaches a depth of 188 m (616 ft).

🔢 Touring Chiemsee

Bavaria's largest lake, Chiemsee is a real paradise for watersports enthusiasts, with sailors, water-skiers, swimmers and divers all enjoying the opportunities it offers. The lake is set amidst magnificent Alpine scenery in the region known as the Chiemgau, which stretches eastwards from Rosenheim to the border with Austria along the river Salzach. Chiemsee is surrounded by numerous small towns and villages and dotted with islands, some of which feature fascinating historic buildings. Excellent land, water and rail transport facilities ensure trouble-free travel to all destinations in the area.

Fraueninsel
Like its neighbour Herreninsel, this island is rich in art treasures. Its abbey (Klosterkirche) was founded in 766 and taken over by Benedictine nuns in the mid-9th century.

Stock
The harbour town of Stock is connected by narrow-gauge steam railway to the Chiemsee's main resort of Prien. The railway, the Chiemseebahn, is over one hundred years old.

Urschalling
The 12th-century church of St Jakobus features magnificent wall paintings dating from the 13th and 14th centuries.

Map labels

Obing
Hinzing
Halfing
HARTSEE
Eggstätt
Bad Endorf
LANGBÜRGNER SEE
SIMSSEE
Stock
Prien
Harras
Urschalling
Bernau

Key

▬ Motorway
▬ Major road
▬ Minor road
▭ River
✺ Viewpoint

Herrenchiemsee Palace
In 1873, King Ludwig II bought Herreninsel, with the intention of building a replica of the Palace of Versailles here. Funds ran out and the project was not completed, but the magnificent central section and park are well worth visiting.

For hotels and restaurants in this area see pp492–503 and pp510–33

Seeon Abbey

This post-Benedictine abbey, surrounded by the waters of Klostersee, was built in stages during the 11th and 12th centuries. It was remodelled in 1428–33 by Konrad Pürkel, a master-builder from Burghausen.

VISITORS' CHECKLIST

Practical Information
Road map E7.
[i] Tourismusverband Chiemsee, Alte Rathausstraße 11, 83209 Prien am Chiemsee (08051-690 50).
[w] mychiemsee.de

Castle in the Rock

One of the most interesting curiosities of this region is the "Höhlenburg" – a castle carved into a rock on the bank of the river Traun, some 30 m (98 ft) above water level. Visits are allowed only with a guide.

Chieming

Chieming lies on the eastern shore of the lake. Its 6-km (4-mile) long beach is an ideal place for sunbathing and swimming in the waters of the lake.

| 0 km | 4 |
| 0 miles | 4 |

Chiemsee

Lying at an altitude of 518 m (1,700 ft), the lake covers an area of 80 sq km (20,000 acres) with a depth of 70 m (230 ft). Its size makes it popular with sailing enthusiasts.

Colourful Alpine inn, dating from 1612, in Oberammergau

⑤ Garmisch-Partenkirchen

Road map D7. 27,000. 🚗 🚺
Richard-Strauss-Platz 2 (08821-18 07
00). 🎿 Neujahrs-Springen (1 Jan);
Hornschlitten-Rennen (6 Jan); Ski
World Cup Races; Richard-Strauss-
Tage (Jun). **W** gapa.de

Lying in the valley of the river
Loisach, Garmisch-Parten-
kirchen is the best-known resort
in the Bavarian Alps. To say that
it offers ideal skiing conditions
would be to state the
obvious. In 1936, it
hosted the Winter
Olympic Games and,
in 1978, the World
Skiing Championships.
From Garmisch-
Partenkirchen,
Germany's highest
peak, Zugspitze (2964
m/9,720 ft), can be
reached by taking the
narrow-gauge railway
to Zugspitzblatt and
from there a cable
car, which reaches
the summit in a few
minutes. Garmisch-
Partenkirchen's parish church of
St Martin (Alte Pfarrkirche St
Martin) is worth a visit. It was
built in the 13th century and
extended in the 15th century
and features some well-
preserved Gothic wall paintings
and net vaulting. The
Werdenfels Museum shows
how people in this region lived
in the past, with a collection of
furniture, clothing and room
reconstructions.

Oriel window in
Garmisch-Partenkirchen

🏛 Werdenfels Museum
Ludwigstraße 47. **Tel** (08821) 21 34.
Open Dec–Oct: 10am–5pm
Tue–Sun. 🚫

⑥ Oberammergau

Road map D7. 🚉 5,200. 🚺 Eugen-
Papst-Straße 9A (08822-922 740).
🎿 König-Ludwig-Lauf (Feb);
Oberammergauer Passionsspiele (May–
Oct, every ten years: 2020); König-
Ludwig-Feuer (24 Aug).

Situated some 20 km (12 miles)
north of Garmisch-
Partenkirchen, and standing on
the site of a 9th-century Welfs'
fort, Oberammergau is world
famous for its folk art and
passion plays. The Thirty
Years' War (1618–48)
and the plague of
1632 came close to
wiping out the
entire population of
the village. Its
surviving inhabitants
pledged that if they
were saved from
extinction they
would stage for ever
more a play about
Christ's Passion. No
further deaths
occurred and, to this
day, the villagers have
kept their pledge.
Every ten years (the next is in
2020), some 2,500 people take
part in the six-hour-long
spectacle, in which they
transform themselves from
Bavarians into Jews and Romans
from the time of Christ. About
one hundred performances
are staged between mid-May
and mid-October in the
huge Passionsspielhaus.

Among the buildings worth
seeing in Oberammergau are
the Rococo church of Saint
Peter and Saint Paul (1735–40)
and the famous *Pilatushaus*,
with its illusionist painting of
Christ before Pilate on the
façade. The **Oberammergau
Museum** has a notable
collection of wooden cribs.

🏛 Oberammergau Museum
Dorfstraße 8. **Tel** (08822) 922 740.
Open 10am–5pm Tue–Sun.
Closed Feb, Mar, Nov. 🚫

⑦ Ettal

Road map D7. 🚉 974.

About 4 km (2.5 miles) from
Oberammergau is the tiny resort
of Ettal, which is best known for
its Benedictine abbey, founded
by Emperor Ludwig IV of Bavaria.
The abbey's foundation stone
was laid in 1330, while the Church
of the Virgin Mary and the
convent were consecrated in
1370. The church building is a
Gothic structure but, in 1710–52,
Josef Enrico Zuccalli and Franz
Schmuzer carried out major
remodelling work in the
Baroque style. The church
interior is decorated with rich
Rococo stuccowork by Johann
Baptist and Johann Georg
Ubelhör, and wall paintings
by Martin Knoller.

The monastery produces fine
fruit, hay and honey liqueurs,
flavoured brandies and beer.

The Baroque Benedictine abbey in Ettal

⊕ Linderhof

In the early 1850s, Linderhof was bought by the Bavarian King Maximilian II. This remote mountain district had great appeal to the young heir to the throne, Ludwig, later to become the eccentric King Ludwig II. In 1874, work started on remodelling the existing *Königshäuschen* (royal cottage) in the Neo-Rococo style. The palace is surrounded by a delightful garden, which is dotted with romantic little buildings, including *Schwanenweiher* (Swan Lake), *Venusgrotte* (Venus grotto) and the *Marokkanisches Haus* (Moroccan house).

VISITORS' CHECKLIST

Practical Information
Road map D7.
Schloss Linderhof.
Tel (08822) 920 30. **Open** Apr–15 Oct: 9am–6pm daily; 16 Oct–Mar: 10am–4pm daily.

Tapestry Room
The walls of this room are painted in a style that is reminiscent of tapestry work, with depictions of pastoral scenes.

Reception Room
Although the palace was intended as a private residence, King Ludwig II insisted on the provision of a suitably ornate and regal reception room.

Dining Room
Designed by Christian Jank, the dining room was completed in 1872. It features gilded panelling by Phillip Perron and stuccowork by Theobald Behler.

Mirror Hall
The design of Linderhof's Mirror Hall was based on the Mirror Room of the royal residence in Munich (*see pp216–17*).

Terraces
Terraces in front of the palace are adorned with sculptures and include a pool with a fountain.

㊴ Schloss Neuschwanstein

Set amidst magnificent mountain scenery high above Forggensee, Alpsee and Schwansee, this fairy-tale castle was built in 1869–86 for the eccentric Bavarian King Ludwig II, to a design by the theatre designer Christian Jank. When deciding to build this imposing residence, the king was undoubtedly inspired by Wartburg Castle in Thuringia *(see pp190–91)*, which he visited in 1867. The pale grey limestone castle, which draws on a variety of historical styles, is a steep 30-minute walk from the nearby village of Hohenschwangau and offers spectacular views of the surrounding scenery.

★ Singers' Hall
The Sängersaal was modelled on the singing room of the Wartburg castle in Eisenach.

Vestibule
The walls of the vestibule and of other rooms in the castle are lavishly covered with paintings depicting scenes from old German myths and legends.

★ Throne Room
The gilded interior of the throne room reminds one of Byzantine temples and the palace church of All Saints (Hofkirche) in the Residenz *(see pp220–21)* in Munich.

KEY

① **Study**

② **Two-storey arcades** surround the castle courtyard.

③ **Gatehouse** provided the king with temporary accommodation during the castle's construction, completed in 1872.

Dining Room
Like other rooms in the palace, the dining room includes fabulous pictures, intricately carved panels and beautifully decorated furniture, all bearing witness to the skill and artistry of the 19th-century craftsmen.

★ **Castle Building**
Schloss Neuschwanstein is the archetypal fairy-tale castle and has provided the inspiration for countless toy models, book illustrations and film sets.

VISITORS' CHECKLIST

Practical Information
Road map D7. Schloss Linderhof. Neuschwansteinstrasse 20.
Tel (08362) 93 08 30. **Open** Apr–15 Oct: 9am–6pm daily; 16 Oct–Mar: 10am–4pm daily. **Closed** 1 Jan & 24, 25, 31 Dec. 🏞 🚗 ♿ (limited access). 🏞 🖥 🏠 ℹ
Ticket centre in Hohenschwangau.

Courtyard
The heart of the castle was supposed to have been a mighty 90-m (295-ft) high tower with a Gothic castle church. It was never built, but in 1988 its planned position was marked in white stone.

② ③ Main entrance

⑳ Hohen-schwangau

Road map D7. 🚗 Schwangau 3,818. ℹ Schwangau, Münchenerstr. 2 (08362-819 80). Ticket service: Hohenschwangau Alpseestr. 12 (08362-930 830).

The skyline of Schwangau is dominated by two castles, Schloss Neuschwanstein (left) and the majestic **Schloss Hohenschwangau**. The fortified castle that occupied this site in the Middle Ages was remodelled in 1538–47 and, in 1567, it passed into the hands of the Wittelsbach family. It was destroyed during the Tyrolean War but in 1832 the heir to the throne (later Maximilian II) ordered the ruins to be rebuilt in Neo-Gothic style. The plans were prepared by the painter Domenico Quaglio; after his death, work on the castle was continued by the architects Georg Friedrich Ziebland and Joseph Daniel Ohlmüller.

This four-storey building, standing on medieval foundations, is flanked by angular towers. The wall paintings that decorate the rooms of the castle date from 1835–36. Their iconographic content, which is based on old Germanic sagas, is the work of Moritz von Schwind. A walk around the castle provides an excellent opportunity to study the Wittelsbach family history and to see the mid-19th century furnishings. There are magnificent views of the surroundings from the castle's lovely terraced gardens.

🏰 **Schloss Hohenschwangau**
Tel (08362) 930 830. **Open** Apr–Sep: 9am–6pm daily; Oct–Mar: 10am–4pm daily. **Closed** 24 Dec. 🏞

Neo-Gothic castle of Maximilian II in Hohenschwangau

The Rococo Throne Room in the Kempten Residenz.

❶ Kempten

Road map C7. 🚶 65,000. 🚍
ℹ️ Rathausplatz 24 (0831-252 52 37).
🎭 Allgäuer Festwochen (Aug).
🌐 kempten.de

Kempten lies at the centre of one of Germany's most attractive tourist regions, the Allgäu, which stretches from Bodensee lake to the west and the river Lech to the east. The town, which boasts a history of over 2,000 years, was first mentioned by the Greek geographer and historian Strabon as a Celtic settlement, Kambodunon. Later, the Romans established Cambodunum on the right bank of the river Iller. Along with Augusta Vindelicorum (Augsburg) and Castra Regina (Regensburg), this was one of the most important towns in the Roman province of Raetia.

Medieval Kempten grew around a Benedictine Abbey, founded in 752. In the north-western part of town, near the former abbots' residence, is the church of St Lorenz. A triple-nave, galleried basilica with an octagonal cupola and a twin-tower façade, this is the work of Michael Beer and Johann Serro. The town's parish church of St Mang dates from the 15th century. In the Rathausplatz is an attractive town hall dating from 1474 and other historic buildings, including the Londoner Hof with its Rococo façade (1764). The **Allgäu-Museum** details the history of Kempten. On the right bank of the river Iller is the **Archäologischer Park**, with excavated remains of Roman Cambodunum. The 13th-century Erasmuskapelle chapel is also worth visiting.

🏛 Allgäu-Museum
Kornhaus, Großer Kornhausplatz 1. **Tel** (0831) 540 21 20. **Open** 10am–4pm Tue–Sun. 🖼

🏛 Archäologischer Park Cambodunum
Cambodunumweg 3. **Tel** (0831) 252 369. **Open** May–Oct: 10am–5pm Tue–Sun; Nov–Apr: 10am–4:30pm Tue–Sun. **Closed** mid-Dec–mid-Mar.

Epitaph of the family of Andreas Bertsch, in the Stadtmuseum Lindau

❷ Lindau

Road map C7. 🚶 24,000. 🚍
ℹ️ Ludwigstraße 68 (08382-26 00 30 or 19 433). 🎭 Lindauer Kinderfest (Jul).

In Roman times Lindau was a fishing settlement, which used to lie over three islands. The first historic records of the town date from 882. On the south side of the old-town island lies the harbour with its 13th-century lighthouse (Mangturm). The new lighthouse (Neuer Leuchtturm), built in 1856, stands on the neighbouring pier and offers a splendid view over the lake and the Alps. The marble Lion of Bavaria opposite is the symbol of Lindau.

The old town features many historic buildings, such as the Gothic-Renaissance town hall in Reichsplatz, which was built in 1422–36 and later remodelled in 1578. The picturesque Maximilianstrasse is lined with the houses of rich patricians; their shady arcades (Brodlauben) are typical of Lindau architecture.

In Schrannenplatz, in the northwest area of the town, stands the church of St Peter. Since 1928 this has been the war memorial chapel for World War I victims. Its eastern section dates from the mid-12th century while the bigger, western section was built between 1425 and 1480. The interior contains many wall paintings, including some by Hans Holbein the Elder dating from 1485–90. Nearby stands the *Diebsturm* (Thief's Tower) of 1380. The **Stadtmuseum** (town museum) is housed in Haus zum Cavazzen (1729) in Marktplatz, which also features a lovely Neptune fountain.

On the south side of the Market Square stands the Protestant Church of St Stephen, which dates from the 12th century and was remodelled in Baroque style in 1782. The Catholic Church of St Mary, built in 1748–52, has a lovely Rococo interior.

🏛 Stadtmuseum Lindau
Marktplatz 6. **Tel** (08382) 94 40 73. **Open** Apr–Oct: 11am–5pm Tue–Fri & Sun, 2pm–5pm Sat.

For hotels and restaurants in this area see pp492–503 and pp510–33

㊽ Oberstdorf

Road map C7. ⚐ 10,000. ⊞
ℹ Prinzregenten-Platz 1 (08322-70 00).

Oberstdorf lies in the valley of the River Iller. The ideal skiing conditions and the mild all-year-round climate make this one of the most popular health resorts and winter sports centres in Germany. Nearby is the skiing stadium (Schattenberg-Skistadion) with its famous ski-jump, where the annual "four ski-jump" tournament starts each year.

Although the fire of 1865 destroyed large sections of the settlement here, some of the most important historic buildings escaped. These include Seelenkapelle, whose façade is decorated with a 16th-century wall painting typical of the region, and two chapels, Lorettokapelle and Josephskapelle, which were joined together in 1707. Just to the east of Oberstdorf is the 2,224-m (7,300-ft) Mount Nebelhorn, whose summit can be reached in a few minutes by cable car. This offers a spectacular view over the majestic Allgäuer Alps as well as providing an excellent starting point for mountain hiking.

Ski-jump complex in Oberstdorf

㊼ Füssen

Road map D7. ⚐ 16,000. ⊞
ℹ Kaiser-Maximilian-Platz 1 (08362-938 50).

Situated conveniently on an important trade route, Füssen experienced its most rapid growth in the late Middle Ages, as witnessed by many of the buildings in Reichenstrasse and the remains of the town fortifications, which include Sebastiantor and sections of the walls with five turrets.

Perched on a rock, high above the town, stands the palace of the Augsburg prince-bishops. Started in 1291 by the Bavarian Prince Ludwig II the Severe, construction was continued in 1490–1503 by the Augsburg bishops. The residential buildings of the palace range around a courtyard whose walls are decorated with trompe l'oeil door and window frames.

Madonna in the Church of St Mang, in Füssen

At the foot of the castle stands the former Benedictine Abbey (Kloster St Mang), which was erected in the 9th century at the burial site of St Magnus, the "Apostle of the Allgäu". The only surviving part of the abbey is the late 10th-century crypt with the remains of wall paintings.

Late-Baroque interior of the Abbey Library, in Ottobeuren

㊼ Ottobeuren

Road map D7. ⚐ 8,000.
ℹ Marktplatz 14 (08332-92 19 50).

Situated 13 km (8 miles) from Memmingen, the small health resort of Ottobeuren is the site of one of Germany's most famous Benedictine abbeys. Founded in 764, the abbey is still a place of prayer and work for the monks who live here, having withstood even the radical secularization of 1803. In the 18th century the abbey was remodelled by the Abbot Rupert II. The foundation stone for the building complex was laid in 1717 and work began under the direction of Simpert Kraemer. The new buildings were completed in 1731. The richly decorated interiors, with stuccoes by Andrea Maini, still survive. A new abbey church was built between 1737 and 1766 with construction supervised initially by Simpert Kramer. In 1748, this was taken over by Johann Michael Fischer, who was responsible for its final appearance.

The interior of the church has a magnificent unity of style: Rococo stuccoes by Johann Michael Feuchtmayr are in perfect harmony with the vault frescos by Johann Jakob Zeiller as well as the splendid altars and stalls by Martin Hörmann and Johann Zeiller's brother Franz Anton Zeiller. The abbey's three organs, which are particularly beautiful, can be heard at regularly held recitals.

⓪ Augsburg

Situated at the confluence of the Lech and Wertach rivers, Augsburg is the third largest town in Bavaria and one of the oldest in Germany. As early as 15 BC this was the site of a Roman camp, which later became a town known as Augusta Vindelicorum. Until the end of the 13th century, the town was ruled by powerful bishops. From 1316, as a Free Imperial City of the Holy Roman Empire, Augsburg grew to become one of the richest and most powerful cities in Germany. The Thirty Years' War (1618–48), however, put an end to the town's prosperity.

Augustusbrunnen
Incorporating a statue of the Emperor Augustus, the fountain was created in the workshop of Dutchman Hubert Gerhard in 1594.

Church of St Anna
The star attraction of this unassuming ex-Carmelite church is the Renaissance memorial chapel endowed by the brothers Ulrich and Jacob Fugger in 1509.

Maximilianmuseum
Set in a Renaissance patrician mansion, the museum has a splendid collection of work by local gold- and silversmiths.

Zeughaus
A bronze group by Hans Reichle, *St Michael Overcoming Satan* (1607), adorns the façade of the former arsenal building by Elias Holl, the most important early Baroque architect.

For hotels and restaurants in this area see pp492–503 and pp510–33

★ Rathaus
The town hall, built by Elias Holl in
1615–20, is widely considered the
most significant secular Renaissance building north of the Alps.

★ Maximilianstraße
Augsburg's main thoroughfare is the most
beautiful street in southern Germany, with
notable fountains by Adrian de Vries.

★ Fuggerhäuser
Commissioned by Jacob
II Fugger (1459–1525)
for himself and his
family, this Italian-
style building,
with two arcaded
courtyards, was
built in 1512–15.

St Ulrich-
und-Afra

St Moritz Kirche

Key
— Suggested route

View of the monumental Gothic Dom
of the Holy Virgin

⬆️ Dom of the Holy Virgin
(Dom Unserer Lieben Frau)
Frauentorstr. 1. **Open** 9am–5:30pm.
Originally a Romanesque twin-
choir, pillared basilica with crypt,
western transept and two towers,
dating from 994–1065, the
structure was remodelled
between 1331 and 1431 along
Gothic lines. The church was
given two further side aisles, a
choir with an ambulatory and
a French-style ring of chapels.
Original features include the
richly carved portals and the
famous Romanesque bronze
door with 35 panels depicting
allegorical figures. There are
some unique stained-glass
windows, dating from 1140.

🏛️ Fuggerei
Fuggerei-Museum, Mittlere Gasse14.
Tel (0821) 319 88 10. **Open** Apr–Oct:
8am–8pm daily; Nov–Mar: 9am–6pm
daily. **Closed** 24 Dec–28 Feb. 🎫

The Fuggerei, in Augsburg's
Jakobervorstadt (Jacob's Suburb),
is Europe's oldest social housing
estate. It was founded in 1516
by Jacob Fugger, a member of
what was then the richest family
in Europe. The intention was to
provide homes for the town's
poorest citizens, particularly
families with children. Today,
however, it has evolved into
a home for retired citizens.
   The 52 houses in Fuggerei
were built in 1516–25 and line
six streets. They are surrounded
by gardens. One of the
buildings houses the **Fuggerei-
Museum**, which is devoted to
the history of the estate and
has a fascinating shop, the
Himmlisches Fuggereilädle.

BADEN-WURTTEMBERG

This German state, which includes territories of the former Grand Duchy of Baden, is one of the country's most popular tourist destinations. Its charming old university towns, such as Tübingen and Heidelberg, historic castles, luxurious resorts and the magnificent recreation areas of the Schwarzwald (Black Forest) and Bodensee (Lake Constance) guarantee enjoyable and memorable holidays.

This region's turbulent history, which has been ruled over the years by Palatinate electors, counts and finally kings of Wurttemberg, as well as by margraves and Grand Dukes of Baden, has given the province its cultural and religious diversity.

This southwestern area of Germany was the cradle of two great dynasties that played a significant part in German and European history and culture. The Hohenstaufen family – which originated from Swabia – produced kings and emperors who ruled during the most magnificent period of the German Middle Ages (1138–1254). These included Frederick I Barbarossa and Frederick II. The Hohenzollern family, also from Swabia, produced Brandenburg dukes, Prussian kings including Frederick the Great and German emperors from 1871–1918.

In Heidelberg the enlightened elector Ruprecht I founded the first university in Germany in 1386 and shortly after this epoch-making event, further universities were established in Tübingen and Freiburg im Breisgau. Many towns and villages in the region can boast a history going back to Roman times. The Romans used to grow vines in the area of Baden-Wurttemberg and now wines from the region are renowned worldwide for their high quality.

Baden-Wurttemberg, however, does not only represent an illustrious past, but also an impressive present. Unemployment figures for the region are the lowest in Germany, and many companies that are known and respected throughout the world – such as Bosch, Daimler, Porsche and the software company SAP – have their production plants here.

Magnificent French-style garden in front of the palace in Ludwigsburg

◀ The façade of a building within the walls of Heidelberg Castle

Baden-Württemberg

With its magnificent castles, luxurious resorts and the beautiful recreation areas of the Schwarzwald (Black Forest), Baden-Württemberg is one of Germany's most popular tourist destinations. In addition, the region's long and turbulent history has given it a rich cultural and religious diversity. The southwest region of Germany was the cradle of two dynasties that played important roles in German and European history and culture – the Hohenstaufen and Hohenzollern families. The great number of urban centres in the state is due to the influence of these two families. Baden-Württemberg also has more universities than any other state in Germany, the oldest being located at Heidelberg, Tübingen and Freiburg im Breisgau.

The picturesque castle in Sigmaringen, in the region of Schwäbische Alb

Key

═══ Motorway

─── Major road

⋯⋯⋯ Minor road

─·─· Main railway

─── Minor railway

▬▬▬ International border

▬▬▬ Regional border

△ Summit

Weinheim

MANNHE 6

SCHWETZINGEN 7

HEIDELBERG 9

BRUCHSAL 8

MAULBRO

KARLSRUHE 10

Ettlingen

Rastatt

Pforzheim

Gaggenau

BADEN-BADEN 11

Hornisgrinde 1164m

Strasbourg

Offenburg

Freudenstadt

Lahr

Gutach

ROTTWEIL 23

Emmendingen

Villingen-Schwenningen

Lemberg 1015m

Trossing

Kandel 1242m

Furtwangen

Tuttlingen

FREIBURG IM BREISGAU 29

30

Donaueschingen

Bad Krozingen

Feldberg 1493m

31

Blumberg

Müllheim

315

Todtmoos

St Blasien

Schopfheim

Lörrach

Waldshut-Tiengen

34

Basel

BADEN

SCHWARZWALD

The Gothic town hall in Ulm

For additional map symbols *see back flap*

| 0 kilometres | 20 |
| 0 miles | 20 |

Getting Around

The main communication centres of the area are Stuttgart, which has an international airport, and Mannheim. Main motorways include the A5 from Frankfurt to Basle, via Heidelberg, Karlsruhe, Baden-Baden and Freiburg; the A81 from Würzburg to Constance, via Tauberbischofsheim, Heilbronn, Stuttgart and Schwäbische Alb; the A6 from Mannheim to Ansbach, via Heilbronn and Crailsheim; and the A8 from Karlsruhe to Ulm, via Stuttgart.

Sights at a Glance

1 Wertheim
2 Tauberbischofsheim
3 Bad Mergentheim
4 Weikersheim
5 Creglingen
6 Mannheim
7 Schwetzingen
8 Bruchsal
9 *Heidelberg pp300–1*
10 Karlsruhe
11 Baden-Baden
12 *Maulbronn pp306–7*
13 Heilbronn
14 Schwäbisch Hall
15 Schwäbisch Gmünd
16 Bad Wimpfen
17 Marbach
18 Esslingen
19 *Ludwigsburg pp310–11*
20 *Stuttgart pp312–13*
21 Schwäbische Alb
22 Tübingen
23 Rottweil
24 Ulm
25 Ravensburg
26 Weingarten
27 Salem
28 *Bodensee pp324–25*
29 *Freiburg im Breisgau pp328–9*
30 *Schwarzwald (Black Forest) pp330–31*

Palace façade in Bruchsal

❶ Wertheim

Road map C5. 🗺 24,500. 🚆
ℹ Spitzen Turm (09342-935 090). 🎭
Altstadtfest (Jul), Burgweinfest (Aug).

The rivers Tauber and Main meet at Wertheim, whose historic records date from 1183. A gunpowder explosion in 1619 plus the destruction caused by the Thirty Years' War turned the **Wertheimer Burg** into a romantic ruin. Its tall watch-tower offers great views.

Wertheim's market square is lined with half-timbered houses, while the Baroque Protestant church nearby, dating from the 15th–18th centuries, has tombs of the von Wertheim family. The most spectacular is the tomb of Count Ludwig II von Löwenstein-Wertheim and his wife. Also worth visiting are the **Glasmuseum** (exhibits range from glass jewellery to scientific instruments), **Grafschaftsmuseum Wertheim** (local fairy tales feature in the museum's permanent collections) and **Museum Schlösschen im Hofgarten** (the "castle in the courtyard" houses romantic paintings and Parisian porcelain).

🏛 **Glasmuseum**
Mühlenstraße 24. **Tel** (09342) 68 66. **Open** Apr–Oct & Dec–6 Jan: 10am–5pm Tue–Thu, 1–6pm Fri–Sun & hols.

🏛 **Grafschaftsmuseum Wertheim**
Rathausgaße 6–10. **Tel** (09342) 30 15 11. **Open** 10am–noon, 2:30–4:30pm Tue–Sat (Sat: pm only), 2–5pm Sun. 🎭

🏛 **Museum Schlösschen im Hofgarten**
Würzburger Straße 30. **Tel** (09342) 301 511. **Open** Apr–Oct: 2–5pm Wed–Sat, noon–6pm Sun & hols.

Scenic castle ruins in Wertheim

Half-timbered houses and tower, Tauberbischofsheim

❷ Tauberbischofsheim

Road map C5. 🗺 13,000. 🚆
ℹ Marktplatz 8 (09341-8030).

Boniface, the Anglo-Saxon missionary to the German tribes, established Germany's first nunnery in AD 735. Its first prioress, Lioba, who was related to Boniface, gave her name to the Baroque church that stands in Tauberbischofsheim's market square.

The town, which enjoys a picturesque location in the valley of the river Tauber, still has a group of original half-timbered houses. On the market square is the Baroque Rehhof (1702) and the old "Star Pharmacy" in a house once occupied by Georg Michael Franck, grandfather of the Romantic poets Clemens and Bettina Brentano.

In the eastern section of Hauptstraße stands Haus Mackert – a Baroque mansion built in 1744 for a wealthy wine merchant. In Schlossplatz is the Kurmainzisches Schloss, an imposing edifice built in the 15th–16th centuries, that now houses the **Landschaftsmuseum**.

🏛 **Landschaftsmuseum Kurmainzisches Schloss**
Tel (09341) 37 60. **Open** Palm Sunday–Oct: 2–4:30pm Tue–Sat, 10am–noon & 2–4:30pm Sun. 🎭

❸ Bad Mergentheim

Road map C5. 🗺 25,000. 🚆
ℹ Marktplatz 1 (07931-574 815). 🎭 Markelsheimer Weinfest (after Whitsun).

Lying in a charming spot on the river Tauber, Bad Mergentheim was, from 1525 until 1809, the seat of the Grand Masters of the religious order of the "House of the Hospitallers of Saint Mary of the Teutons in Jerusalem", more commonly known as the Teutonic Knights. When three Hohenlohe brothers entered the Order in 1220, they contributed to it their share of their father's estate. This laid the foundations for one of the most powerful Teutonic commands at the heart of the Holy Roman Empire. From 1244 until 1250 Heinrich von Hohenlohe held the office of Grand Master.

The former Hohenlohe's castle, built in the 12th–13th centuries, was remodelled in Renaissance style in 1565–74 by Michael Bronner and Blasius Berwart. They gave the castle its winding stairs and the opulent decor of the staircase. The Baroque-Rococo Schlosskirche dominates the complex. Its interior was designed by François Cuvilliés,

Heraldic crest from the castle in Bad Mergentheim

For hotels and restaurants in this area see pp492–503 and pp510–33

while the ceiling fresco *(The Victorious Cross)* is the work of Nicolaus Stuber. The castle is now the home of a very interesting museum, the **Deutschordensmuseum**.

Many of the town's historic buildings survive to this day, including the 13th-century Church of the Knights of St John of Jerusalem and the Dominican church containing the epitaph of the Grand Master Walther von Cronberg. The **Pfarrkirche** (Parish church) in the Stuppach district contains a masterpiece by Grünewald (1519), known as the *Madonna of Stuppach*.

🔼 Pfarrkirche in Stuppach
Kapellenpflege. **Tel** (07931) 26 05. **Open** May–Oct: 8:30am–6:30pm daily; Mar, Apr & Nov: 11am–4pm. 🖼

🏛 Deutschordensmuseum
Schloss. **Tel** (07931) 522 12. **Open** Apr–Oct: 10:30am–5pm Tue–Sun; Nov–Mar: 2–5pm Tue–Sat, 10:30am–5pm Sun. 🖼

❹ Weikersheim

Road map C5. 🖼 8,000. 🖼 Am Marktplatz 7 (07934-102 55).

Eleven kilometres (7 miles) east of Bad Mergentheim is the picturesque little town of Weikersheim. A Rococo fountain from 1768 is at the centre of the market square while the late-Gothic parish church is on the north side. The latter is a triple-nave hall-church with a single-tower western façade and two towers by the choir. Inside are many tombs of the von Hohenlohe family. Also on the market square stands the **Tauberländer Dorfmuseum**, which charts the history of rural life in Franconia. In the western part of town stands the very well preserved **Schloss Weikersheim**, the palace complex of the Counts von Hohenlohe,

Figure of drummer in Weikersheim's Hofgarten

which dates from the 16th–18th centuries. Its highlight is undoubtedly the vast Rittersaal, a sumptuous banqueting hall that measures 35 m (115 ft) long x 12 m (39 ft) wide x 9 m (29 ft) high. The counts and their aristocratic guests used to enter this room on horseback. Its very rare, original furnishings include paintings and reliefs depicting hunting scenes.

A true rarity is the original Baroque Hofgarten (palace garden), designed by Daniel Matthieu and built in 1709.

🏛 Schloss Weikersheim
Tel (07934) 8364. **Open** Apr–Oct: 9am–6pm daily; Nov–Mar: 10am–noon & 1:30–5pm daily. 🖼

🏛 Tauberländer Dorfmuseum
Marktplatz. **Tel** (07934) 12 09. **Open** Apr–Oct: 2–5pm Wed, Fri, Sat, Sun. 🖼

❺ Creglingen

Road map C5. 🖼 5,000. 🖼 07933-6 31.

Upstream from Weikersheim, on the Bavarian border, is the small town of Creglingen. Here, sometime in the distant past, a ploughman found a luminous holy wafer in a clod of earth and within a few years, the **Herrgottskirche** was built, where the host was put on display for visiting pilgrims. Between 1502 and 1506 Tilman Riemenschneider carved an

Altar by Tilman Riemenschneider, in Creglingen's Herrgottskirche

altar for the church. The main theme of the polyptych is the *Assumption of the Virgin Mary*, considered to be the artist's masterpiece.

The town is also home to the esoteric collection of the famous **Fingerhutmuseum** (Thimble Museum).

🔼 Herrgottskirche
Kohlersmühle. **Tel** (07933) 338 or 508. **Open** Feb–Mar & Nov–Dec: 1–4pm Tue–Sun; Apr–Oct: 9:15am–6pm daily.

🏛 Fingerhutmuseum
Kohlersmühle. **Tel** (07933) 370. **Open** Apr–Oct: 10am–12:30pm & 2–5pm Tue–Sun; Nov–Mar: 1–4pm Tue–Sun. **Closed** Jan. 🖼

Teutonic Order

The Order of the Hospital of St Mary of the German House in Jerusalem was officially founded in Acre (Akkon) in 1190. Its aim was to care for sick pilgrims or Crusaders wounded in fights with the Saracens. In 1231–83, the Teutonic Knights took over all of Prussia and, in 1308–09 all Eastern Pomerania around Danzig, and they moved their headquarters from Venice to Marienburg on the river Nogat. In 1525 the Grand Master, Albrecht von Hohenzollern-Ansbach, converted to Lutheranism and secularized Teutonic Prussia. However, the Order remained in existence in the Holy Roman Empire: its German Master, Walter von Cronberg, who had his residence in Mergentheim, became *de facto* Grand Master. Napoleon abolished the Order in 1809, but it still exists today, with its headquarters based in Vienna since 1848.

The Wasserturm (Water Tower) in Friedrichsplatz, Mannheim

❻ Mannheim

Road map B5. 🚹 326,000. 🚉
ℹ️ Willy-Brandt-Platz 3 (0621-29 38 700). 🎬 Mannheim-Heidelberger Filmfestival (mid-Oct). 🌐 **tourist-mannheim.de**

Mannheim existed as a fishing hamlet as far back as 766. In 1606, Elector Frederick IV the Righteous ordered a fortress to be built on the site, at the junction of the rivers Rhine and Neckar. A trading settlement sprang up nearby and was soon granted town status. Having been repeatedly destroyed through the years, the town was finally rebuilt in Baroque style during the reign of the Elector Johann Wilhelm.

The town-centre layout follows the regular Baroque pattern of the early 18th century, when the town was divided into 136 regular squares. In 1720, when Elector Charles III Philip decided to move his residence from Heidelberg to Mannheim, the foundation stone for a Baroque palace was laid in the grounds of a former citadel.

With over 400 rooms, this became one of the largest and most opulent of all German palaces. Like the residences of many European rulers at that time, it was modelled on Versailles. The main palace has a horseshoe layout, and its symmetry is emphasized by a central projecting entrance. Building work was done by Johann Clemens Froimont, Alessandro Galli da Bibiena, Nicolas de Pigage and Guillaume d'Hauberat.

The second largest town of the region, Mannheim boasts many other historic buildings, including the post-Jesuit Church of St Ignatius and St Francis Xavier, designed by Alessandro Galli da Bibiena and built in 1733–60. Original wall-paintings by Egid Quirin Asam no longer exist, but the altars have survived to this day. These include JI Saler's *Silver Madonna in Radiant Glory* (1747). Also worth visiting are the Baroque Altes Rathaus (1701–23) and Secessionist buildings in Friedrichsplatz such as the Kunsthalle and Wasserturm – the symbol of Mannheim.

The town has several interesting museums: the **Kunsthalle Mannheim** has a large collection of 19th- and 20th-century art, including Francis Bacon's *Study After Velasquez's Portrait of Pope Innocent X*. The museum is renowned for its major temporary exhibitions. The **Reiss-Engelhorn-Museen** has a fine collection of 18th-century Dutch paintings and sections devoted to early history and ethnography. Another big attraction in Mannheim is the **TECHNOSEUM** (Museum of Technology and Labour). Opened in 1990, this houses a

Statue of Elector Karl Theodor in Mannheim's Jesuitenkirche

collection of historic machinery. Mannheim saw the first official demonstration of many inventions that have now become part of everyday life. In 1817, Baron Karl Friedrich von Sauerbronn demonstrated his first bicycle in the town and, in 1886, Carl Friedrich Benz unveiled his first automobile, produced at the nearby factory.

🏛 **Kunsthalle Mannheim**
Friedrichsplatz 4. **Tel** (0621) 293 64 52. **Open** 11am–6pm Tue–Sun (to 8pm Wed). **Closed** Carnival, 1 May, 24, 31 Dec. ♿

🏛 **TECHNOSEUM**
Museumsstraße 1. **Tel** (0621) 429 89. **Open** 9am–5pm daily. **Closed** Good Friday, 24, 31 Dec. ♿

🏛 **Reiss-Engelhorn-Museen**
Quadrat D5 and C5. **Tel** (0621) 293 31 50. **Open** 11am–6pm Tue–Sun. ♿
🌐 **rem-mannheim.de**

Paul Cézanne's *Pipe Smoker* (c.1890), in the Städtische Kunsthalle, Mannheim

❼ Schwetzingen

Road map B5. 🚹 21,500.
ℹ️ Dreikönigstr. 3 (06202-94 58 75). 🎬 Schwetzinger Festspiele (May), Mozartkonzerte (Sep).

Schwetzingen's Baroque-Renaissance palace was built during the reign of the Electors Johann Wilhelm, Charles II Philip and Karl Theodor as their summer residence. Erected on the site of a medieval castle that was later converted into a hunting lodge, it is one of the best known palace complexes of 18th-century Europe. The

Baroque Schwetzingen Palace, set amid beautiful gardens

conversion of the 16th-century hunting lodge was carried out by J A Breuning and the side wings were built by Alessandro Galli da Bibiena. The magnificent Rococo theatre, designed by Nicolas de Pigage, was built in 1752, while the palace garden is the work of Johann Ludwig Petri, who designed it in the French style. The garden includes a mosque with two minarets and a bathhouse. In 1776 Friedrich Ludwig von Sckell converted it into an English-style garden.

Heraldic insignia from Bruchsal Palace

palace to be built for himself and his court. The foundation stone of **Schloss Bruchsal** was laid in 1722 and the building works were carried out by Maximilian von Welsch, who was responsible for the right wing, and Michael Rohrer, who built the left wing between 1723 and 1728. The main body, preceded by a ceremonial courtyard, was designed by Baron Anselm von Grünsten. The central part of the palace is occupied by a magnificent staircase built by the great

Balthasar Neumann, with stuccowork by Johann Michael Feuchtmayer and paintings by Johann and Januarius Zick. The palace suffered severe bomb damage in 1945, but its major part was reconstructed between 1964 and 1975.

St Peter's church was built in 1740–49 by Johann Georg to Balthasar Neumann's 1736 design. The church features magnificent Baroque tombs of Schönborn and his successor Cardinal Franz Christoph von Hutten. The palace garden was designed in the French style by Johann Scheer.

This former residence of prince-bishops now houses a section of the Karlsruhe Museum, which features the largest collection of Flemish and French tapestries in Germany. It is also home to the **Deutsches Musikautomaten Museum**, which includes 500 mechanical musical instruments. Short demonstrations are given on these throughout the day.

Tel (07251) 74 26 61. **Open** 10am–5pm Tue–Sun & hols. 🕐 hourly. **Closed** 24, 25, 31 Dec. 🚫 Deutsches Musikautomaten Museum: **Open** 10am–5pm Tue–Sun. 🕐 11am, 2pm, 3:30pm. **Closed** Shrove Tuesday, 24, 25, 31 Dec. 🚫

🏠 Schloss Schwetzingen

Tel (06202) 12 88 28. Schloss: **Open** Apr–Oct: 11am–4pm Tue–Sun; Nov–Mar: 2pm Fri, 11am, 2pm, 3pm Sat & Sun. 🕐 obligatory. Garden: **Open** Apr–Sep: 8am–8pm daily; Oct & Mar: 9am–6pm daily; Nov–Feb: 9am–5pm daily.

❶ Bruchsal

Road map: B6. 🚇 43,000. 🚉 🛈 Am Alten Schloss 2 (07251-505 94 60).

Bruchsal belonged to the Bishops of Speyer from 1056 until 1803, since when it has been part of Baden. The town rose to prominence in the 17th century, when the Prince-Bishop of Speyer, Damian Hugo von Schönborn moved his residence from Speyer to Bruchsal. He not only initiated the town's development but, most importantly, ordered a

Central façade of the Baroque Schloss Bruchsal

❾ Street-by-Street: Heidelberg

Situated on the banks of the river Neckar, Heidelberg is one of Germany's most beautiful towns. For centuries it was a centre of political power, with a lively and influential cultural life. In 1386, Germany's first university was established here by the Elector Ruprecht I. Building of the palace began during his reign, continuing until the mid-17th century. However, in the late 17th century, French incursions totally destroyed medieval Heidelberg, including the castle. The town was subsequently rebuilt in the early 18th century in Baroque style.

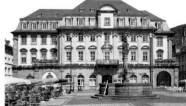

Marktplatz
Now adorned with the Neptune Fountain, the market square was, in the past, the site of executions and the burning of witches and heretics.

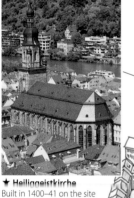

★ Heiliggeistkirche
Built in 1400–41 on the site of a late-Romanesque basilica, the Church of the Holy Spirit is the town's oldest sanctuary.

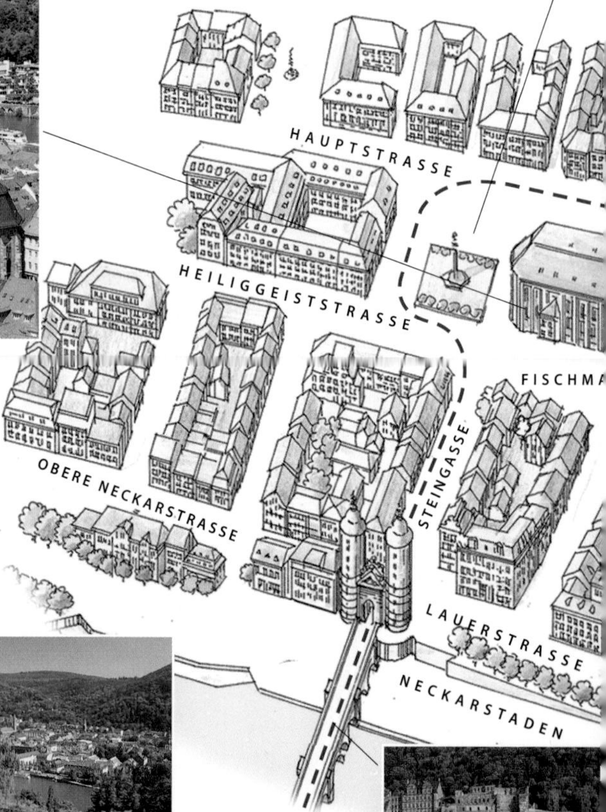

HAUPTSTRASSE
HEILIGGEISTSTRASSE
FISCHMA
STEINGASSE
OBERE NECKARSTRASSE
LAUERSTRASSE
NECKARSTADEN

0 metres 60
0 yards 60

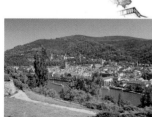

Philosophenweg
Built in 1817 on the slopes of Heiligenberg, at an altitude of 200 m (650 ft), the "Philosophers' Walk" offers magnificent views of Heidelberg and its castle.

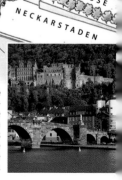

★ Alte Brücke
This imposing, nine-span bridge over the river Neckar was built in 1786–88 by Mathias Maier. In the background is the Heidelberger Schloss.

For hotels and restaurants in this area see pp492–503 and pp510–33

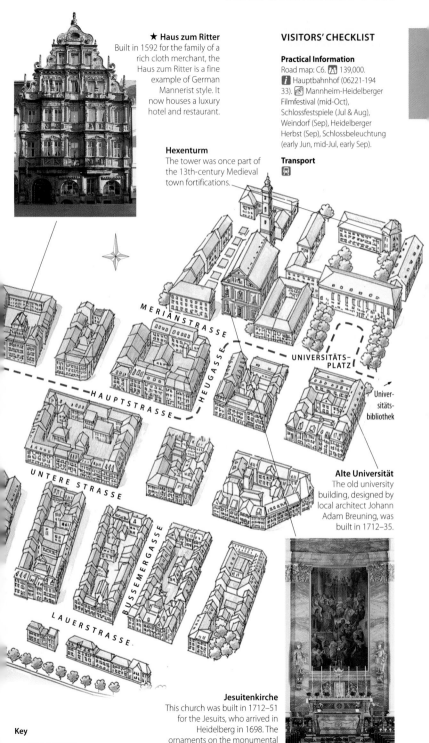

★ Haus zum Ritter
Built in 1592 for the family of a rich cloth merchant, the Haus zum Ritter is a fine example of German Mannerist style. It now houses a luxury hotel and restaurant.

Hexenturm
The tower was once part of the 13th-century Medieval town fortifications.

VISITORS' CHECKLIST

Practical Information
Road map: C6. 139,000. Hauptbahnhof (06221-194 33). Mannheim-Heidelberger Filmfestival (mid-Oct), Schlossfestspiele (Jul & Aug), Weindorf (Sep), Heidelberger Herbst (Sep), Schlossbeleuchtung (early Jun, mid-Jul, early Sep).

Transport

MERIANSTRASSE

HEUGASSE

UNIVERSITÄTS-PLATZ

Universitäts-bibliothek

HAUPTSTRASSE

UNTERE STRASSE

BUSSEMERGASSE

LAUERSTRASSE

Alte Universität
The old university building, designed by local architect Johann Adam Breuning, was built in 1712–35.

Jesuitenkirche
This church was built in 1712–51 for the Jesuits, who arrived in Heidelberg in 1698. The ornaments on the monumental façade were carved by Paul Egell.

Key
— Suggested route

Heidelberg Castle

Towering over the town, the majestic castle is really a vast residential complex that was built and repeatedly extended between the 13th and 17th centuries. Originally a supremely well-fortified Gothic castle, but now mostly in ruins, this was the seat of the House of Wittelsbach palatines. After remodelling in the 16th century, the castle became one of Germany's most beautiful Renaissance residences. However, its splendour was extinguished by the Thirty Years' War and the 1689 war with France, during which most of the structure was destroyed.

★ Ottheinrichsbau
The Deutsches Apothekenmuseum is housed within the shell of this Renaissance building. It features Baroque and Rococo workshops and a travelling pharmacy.

★ Friedrichsbau
One of the latest parts of the castle is Friedrich's Palace, which dates from 1601–07. On the façade are statues of the Wittelsbach dynasty, including Charles the Great.

Englischer Bau
These imposing ruins in the castle complex are the remains of a 17th-century building that Friedrich V built for his wife Elizabeth Stuart.

KEY

① **Castle moat**

② **The bell tower**, which was erected in the early 15th century, was remodelled frequently in subsequent years.

③ **Brunnenhalle** is a Gothic loggia that features early-Romanesque columns taken from the palace of Charles the Great in Ingelheim.

④ **Torturm**

VISITORS' CHECKLIST

Practical Information
Schlossberg. **Tel** (06221) 53 84 31.
Open 8am–6pm daily. Großes
Fass: **Open** 8am–5:30pm daily.
 w **schloss-heidelberg.de**
Deutsches Apothekenmuseum:
Tel (06221) 258 80. **Open** 10am–
5:30pm. **Closed** 1 Jan, 31 Dec.
w **deutsches-apotheken-
museum.de**

Pulverturm
Built during the reign of the
Elector Ruprecht, this
14th-century tower once formed
part of the castle defences.

Main entrance

★ **Ruprechtsbau**
Built around 1400 by a master
builder from Frankfurt, this is the
oldest surviving part of the castle.

Alte Universität
Grabengasse 1. **Tel** (06221) 54 21 52.
Universitätsmuseum: **Open** Apr–Sep:
10am–6pm Tue–Sun; Oct: 10am–4pm
Tue–Sun; Nov–Mar: 10am–4pm Tue–
Sat.

Designed by Mainz architect
Johann Adam Breuning, the
university was built in 1712–35.
On the north wall and ceiling
are allegorical paintings by
Ferdinand Keller. In front of the
building is a fountain crowned
by a sculpture in the form of the
heraldic Palatinate lion.

Universitätsbibliothek
Plöck 107–109. **Tel** (06221) 54 23 80.
Ausstellungsraum: **Open** 10am–6pm
Mon–Sat.

The monumental building of
the university library, designed
by Joseph Durm of Karlsruhe,
was erected in 1901–05 near
the church of St Peter. The
Heidelberg library, with over
2 million volumes, is one of the
largest in Germany. The
exhibition rooms hold many
precious manuscripts and old
prints, including the famous
Codex Manesse, illustrated with
137 beautiful miniatures.

Kurpfälzisches Museum
Hauptstraße 97. **Tel** (06221) 58 34 020.
Open 10am–6pm Tue–Sun.

The French Count Charles de
Graimberg spent the bulk of his
considerable fortune on building
up an extensive collection of
fine drawings, paintings, arms
and various curios associated
with the history of the Palatinate
and the castle of Heidelberg. In
1879, his collection became the
property of the town and forms
the core of this very interesting
museum, which also includes a
fascinating archaeology section.

Heiliggeistkirche
Hauptstraße.

This collegiate church, whose
Baroque dome is a city landmark, was built in 1400–41. The
canons of the college were also
university scholars and therefore
the church aisle features special
galleries for the extensive collections of library books – *Bibliotheca
Palatina*. The choir features a
tombstone of Ruprecht III and his
wife, Elisabeth von Hohenzollern.

⑩ Karlsruhe

Road map B6. 🏔 269,000. 🚉
ℹ️ Bahnhofsplatz 6 (0721 194 33).
🌐 **karlsruhe-tourismus.de**
🎭 Internationales Trachten-und-
Folklorefest (Jun). 🌐 **karlsruhe.de**

Karlsruhe, which is one of the
"youngest" towns in Germany,
flourished during the 19th
century as a centre for science
and art. In 1945, it lost its status as
a regional capital, but is now the
seat of the Bundesverfassungsge-
richt – the highest courts of the
Federal Republic.

The town originated in 1715
when the margrave of Baden,
Karl Wilhelm von Baden-Durlach,
ordered a lodge to be built in the
middle of his favourite hunting
grounds. Karl liked the area and
the lodge so much that he decided to move his residence here
and live the remainder of his days
in peace – hence the town's
name, meaning "Karl's rest". The
original Baroque-style design was
expanded during the reign of his
successor, Karl Friedrich.

The palace, which forms the
hub of 32 streets, was designed
by Leopoldo Retti, Mauritio
Pedetti, Balthasar Neumann,
Philippe de la Gaupière and
others, and built in 1749–81. The
town is based on a fan-like plan,
spreading from a base formed by
the open-sided wings of the
palace. The rest of the circle,
whose centre is marked by the
octagonal palace tower (1715), is
filled with green areas, including
the palace garden. In the early
19th century, the town was
remodelled along Neo-Classical
lines. The main architect of this

A pyramid containing the tomb of Karl Wilhelm
von Baden-Durlach in Karlsruhe

large-scale project was Friedrich
Weinbrenner, who created this
masterpiece of urban design. The
equilateral market square is
positioned along the palace axis.
It is filled with similar but not
identical buildings and features a
central pyramid containing Karl
Wilhelm's tomb. South of
Marktplatz is the circular
Rondellplatz. Weinbrenner's
other works include the
monumental town hall (1811–
25), the Protestant town church
and the Catholic parish church of
St Stephen.

Karlsruhe has some very
interesting museums. The
Badisches Landesmuseum in the
castle features a large collection
of antiquities, decorative arts,
sculpture, porcelain and furniture,
from the Middle Ages to the
present day. In a Neo-
Renaissance building (1843–46)
is the **Staatliche Kunsthalle**, with

its large collection of
mainly German and
Dutch paintings from
the 16th–19th
centuries. These
include the famous
Crucifixion by
Grünewald (1523).

Entirely different
in character are the
collections of the
Zentrum für Kunst
und Medientech-
nologie (ZKM) – an
establishment that
has combined the
role of art college and
museum since 1997.
It occupies a former
ammunitions factory
in the western part of
the town. Its core is the **Museum
für Neue Kunst**, featuring
installations, computer art and
videos and other work by
contemporary artists. The
**Stadtmuseum im Prinz-Max-
Palais**, based in a mansion
named after the last chancellor
of the Kaiserreich, contains
the local history museum.

🏛 **Staatliche Kunsthalle**
Hans-Thoma-Straße 2–6.
Tel (0721) 9 26 33 59. **Open** 10am–
8pm Tue–Sun. 🔲

🏛 **Museum für Neue Kunst**
Lorenzstraße 19.
Tel (0721) 81 000.
Open 10am–6pm Wed–Fri,
11am–6pm Sat & Sun. 🔲

🏛 **Stadtmuseum im
Prinz-Max-Palais**
Karlstraße 10. **Tel** (0721) 1 33 42 31.
Open 10am–6pm Tue, Fri & Sun,
10am–7pm Thu, 2–6pm Sat.

The Baroque residence of the Dukes of Baden in Karlsruhe

⑪ Baden–Baden

Road map B6. 🚈 50,000. ✈ Baden Airport (5 km/3 miles northwest of town). 🚉 🛈 Schwarzwaldstraße 52 & "i-Punkt" in der Trinkhalle (07221-27 52 00) . 🆆 **baden-baden.de**

Known as the "summer capital of Europe", this elegant spa resort is one of the oldest towns in Germany and was once the favourite destination of European aristocracy from Russia to Portugal. Even before the Romans built their camp here around AD 80, the site was occupied by a Celtic settlement of the Latenian period.

In the early years of the modern era, *Civitas Aurelia Aquensis* – known simply as Aquae – was already known in Italy for the therapeutic properties of its waters. In the 3rd century AD, Aquae was conquered by the Germanic tribe of Alamains and in the 6th century AD by the Francs, who built a fortress in the town. The Margrave Hermann II, known as "Marchio de Baduon", was the first important ruler of Baden.

During the horrific Black Death, the qualities of the local waters were once again recognized as beneficial to health. During the Palatinate War of Succession, Baden-Baden was almost totally destroyed but, by the end of the 18th century, it had become one of Europe's most fashionable resorts.

The old town of Baden-Baden lies at the foot of the Schlossberg (castle hill). The oldest surviving building in the town is the Gothic collegiate church, built during the 13th–15th centuries and then remodelled in the 18th century. It contains several valuable epitaphs. To the south of the church is the bathing hall – Friedrichsbad – which was built in Neo-Renaissance style in 1877. Nearby stands the magnificent New Palace, which was the residence of margraves

Baden-Baden's casino, set in the elegant Kurhaus

from the 15th century onwards. It was remodelled along German Renaissance lines in the 16th century by Kaspar Weinhart. The interiors are decorated with paintings by Tobias Stimmer.

Most of the spa buildings are the work of Friedrich Weinbrenner. His elegant Kurhaus in Werderstraße has been used as a casino since 1838. The most famous gamester at the casino was Fyodor Dostoevsky, who was not always lucky at roulette. His novel *The Gambler* (1866) is supposedly set in Baden-Baden. Nearby is the Trinkhalle (pump room), with its mineral water fountains. Built in 1839–42, it is decorated with wall paintings illustrating Schwarzwald (Black Forest) legends.

Rising behind the spa area is the last project completed by Leo von Klenze before his death – the Orthodox burial chapel of

a Romanian aristocratic family, the Stourdza Mausoleum. In Schillerstraße is the villa built in 1867 for the Russian writer, Ivan Turgenev, who lived here until 1872.

🏛 Brahmshaus

Maximilianstraße 85. **Tel** (07221) 99872. **Open** 3–5pm Mon, Wed, Fri, 10am–1pm Sun (10am–1pm daily during Brahmstage). 🛈

The exhibition displayed in this house is devoted to the life and works of the German composer Johannes Brahms who lived here from 1865 until 1874.

⛪ Kloster Lichtenthal

Hauptstraße 40. **Tel** (07221) 50 49 10. **Open** 3pm Wed, Sat, Sun. 🛈 Group tours (minimum 7 persons), advance telephone booking required. 🛈

This Cistercian nuns' abbey, situated on the outskirts of town, has a church dating from the 14th–15th centuries. Its ducal chapel contains many epitaphs of the Baden margraves. The abbey also has an interesting museum.

🏛 Staatliche Kunsthalle Baden-Baden

Lichtentaler Allee 8a. **Tel** (07221) 300 76400. **Open** 10am–6pm Tue–Sun. 🆆 **kunsthalle-baden-baden.de**

The Staatliche Kunsthalle Baden-Baden is an exhibition venue that specializes in modern and contemporary art.

🏛 Stadtmuseum

Lichtentaler Allee 10. **Tel** (07221) 93 22 72. **Open** 10am–6pm Tue–Sun.

The Stadtmuseum includes sections on glass, porcelain and paintings, as well as some old gambling equipment.

The Neo-Renaissance Trinkhalle (pump room) in Baden-Baden

⑫ Maulbronn

Situated on the edge of the Stromberg region, Maulbronn grew up around a Cistercian monastery, which was founded in 1147 in the valley of the river Salzach by monks who came here from Alsace. The church, built in 1147–78, is an elongated, triple-nave basilica with a transept and a chancel. The early Gothic porch in front of the church was added in 1220. Outside the enclosure are domestic buildings, such as a former mill, a forge, a bakery and a guest house. Defence walls with turrets and a gate tower encircle the entire complex, which was designated a UNESCO World Heritage Site in 1993.

Cloisters
In the Middle Ages, monks meditated as they walked around the cloisters, which gave them protection from bad weather. Talking was strictly forbidden.

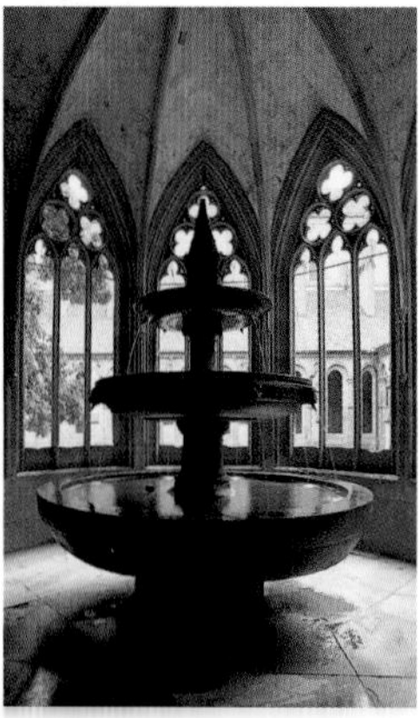

★ **Brunnenkapelle**
Built opposite the entrance to the refectory, the Well Chapel, with its intricate Gothic forms, is where the monks used to wash their hands before meals.

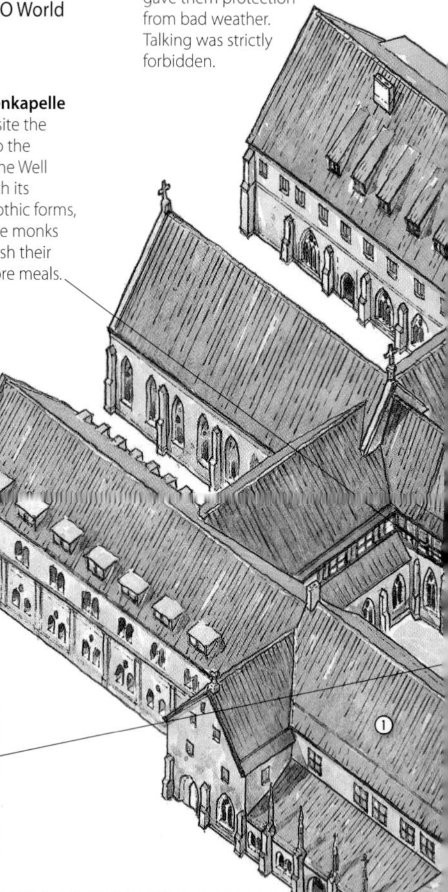

Inner Courtyard
Once a garden, the monastery's inner courtyard is surrounded by cloisters. It is a place that inspires contemplation.

The Porch
The porch, also known as "Paradise", was built onto the church façade in the early 13th century.

KEY

① Cloisters

★ **Chapter House**
The monks assembled in this Gothic hall to discuss affairs affecting the monastery. The hall has two naves, which are supported by three pillars.

VISITORS' CHECKLIST

Practical Information
Road map: C6. 🚇 6,400. 🛈 Stadt-verwaltung Maulbronn, Klosterhof 31 (07043-10 30). 🌐 **kloster-maulbronn.de** Infozentrum: Klosterhof 5. **Tel** (07043) 92 66 10. **Open** Mar–Oct: 9am–5:30pm daily; Nov–Feb: 9:30am–5pm Tue–Sun. 🎟 11:15am, 3pm. ♿

Church Interior
Originally the church had a wooden ceiling. In 1424 it was replaced with a network vault, which stands in stark contrast to the plain walls.

★ **Mourning**
This Gothic relief, made in around 1390 in the Parler family workshop, was part of an altar, which no longer exists. Today, it can be seen on the chancel in the monastery's choir.

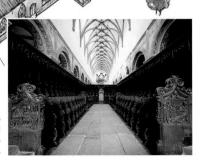

★ **Stalls**
Richly decorated with carved ornaments, the late-Gothic stalls date from around 1450.

⑬ Heilbronn

Road map C6. 🚹 119,000. 🚉
ℹ️ Kaiserstraße 17 (07131-56 22 70).
🎭 Pferdemarkt (Feb), Neckarfest (Jun).

Heilbronn's earliest records date from the 8th century, when the town was known as "Helibrunna". By the late 19th century, Heilbronn had become Wurttemberg's main industrial centre, with a large port on the river Neckar. Having suffered major destruction during World War II, the town's surviving buildings include the church of St Kilian, a Gothic basilica from the second half of the 13th century, with a triple-nave hall-choir flanked by two towers. The western tower was built in 1508–29. The magnificent altarpiece is an original late-Gothic polyptych, the work of Hans Seyffer (1498). Near the 15th–16th-century Rathaus (town hall) is a house reputed to have been the home of Käthchen, a character in Heinrich von Kleist's play *Das Käthchen von Heilbronn*. Near the rebuilt church of St Peter and St Paul (originally the church of the Teutonic Order) stands the former Teutonic convent – the Deutschhof.

Heilbronn is also one of Germany's largest wine-producing towns.

Isaak Habrecht's astronomical clock on Heilbronn town hall

Half-timbered houses on the bank of the river Kocher, in Schwäbisch Hall

⑭ Schwäbisch Hall

Road map C6. 🚹 35,000. 🚉
ℹ️ Am Markt 9 (0791-75 12 46).
🎭 Kuchen und Brunnenfest der Haller Salzsieder (Whitsun).

Archaeological excavations in 1939 proved the existence of a Celtic settlement on this site as early as 500 BC. The town features a great number of historic buildings from various periods, including many half-timbered 15th–16th-century houses, Baroque town houses, and a Rococo town hall and town palace (Keckenburg). The most interesting building is the hall-church of St Michael, whose Gothic main body was built in 1427–56. The Romanesque tower on the western façade, however, dates from the 12th century. The late-Gothic hall-choir (1495–1527) is famous for its decorative network vaults. Original furnishings include the main altar, the stalls and the Holy Sepulchre.

⑮ Schwäbisch Gmünd

Road map C6. 🚹 63,400. 🚉
ℹ️ Marktplatz 37/1 (07171-60 34 250). 🎭 Internationales Schatten-theater Festival (Jun), European Church Music (Jul).

This town – the birthplace of the architect Peter Parler and painters Hans Baldung Grien and Jörg Ratgeb – was

Madonna with Child, in Marktplatz, Schwäbisch Gmünd

once renowned throughout Europe for the magnificent goods produced by its goldsmiths. It has many great historic buildings, mainly churches, such as the late-Romanesque church of St John, which dates from around 1220, but was subsequently remodelled. The church of St Cross is famous not only for being the first Gothic hall-church in southern Germany, but also the first major work of the famous family of architects – the Parlers. This triple-nave hall with a hall-choir, featuring an ambulatory and a ring of side chapels, was built in several stages, between 1320 and 1521. Its western façade has a high triangular top with blind windows. Inside the church are many valuable historic relics, such as the Holy Sepulchre (1400), the stalls, which date from around 1550, and the organ gallery (1688). Other interesting structures in the town include the town fortifications and several half-timbered houses.

⑯ Bad Wimpfen

Road map C6. 🚹 6,676. 🚉 ℹ️ Carl-Ulrich-Straße 1 (07063-9 72 00). 🎭 Talmarkt (Jun/Jul), Zunftmarkt (Aug), Weihnachtsmarkt (Dec).

The town of Bad Wimpfen was created out of two settlements, Bad Wimpfen am Berg and Bad Wimpfen im Tal, which remain distinct to this day. The settlement on top of the hill grew around the Hohenstauf family palace, whose chapel and well-preserved arcade windows, resting on pairs of decorated columns, can still be seen. Built at the order of Frederick I

Barbarossa in 1165–75, this was the main and the biggest imperial palace (Kaiserpfalz) of the Holy Roman Empire. One of the surviving towers offers a spectacular view over the Neckar valley.

Set in a picturesque location, Bad Wimpfen features many half-timbered houses dating from the 16th–18th centuries.

Bad Wimpfen im Tal is built around the former collegiate church of St Peter and St Paul. This is a triple-nave basilica with transept, two eastern towers and cloister, dating from the 13th–15th centuries. The south façade of the transept and the portal are richly decorated with carvings, which are probably the work of Erwin von Steinbach, one of the builders of Strasbourg Cathedral. The church interior features many original carved statues and stalls.

⑰ Marbach

Road map C6. 🚗 1,450. 🚉
i Marktstraße 23 (07144-10 20).

This small town would probably never merit an entry in any guidebook were it not for the fact that the great writer Friedrich Schiller was born here in 1759. The modest, half-timbered house, in which the famous poet spent his childhood, has survived to this day and is now a small museum – the **Schiller-Geburtshaus**. The town also possesses a vast museum of literature (**Schiller-Nationalmuseum**), which is housed in a Neo-Baroque palace. Its collection is not limited to the life and work of Schiller, but also includes many documents relating to German literature.

Other attractions in Marbach include some of the original half-timbered houses and the remains of the town walls and town gates in the old town. The late-Gothic Alexanderkirche is also worth a visit. Built in the second half of the 12th century by Aberlin Jörg, it features interesting network vaulting covered with ornamental paintings.

🏠 **Schiller-Geburtshaus**
Niklastorstraße 31.
Tel (07144) 175 67.
Open 9am–5pm daily.
Closed 24, 25, 26, 31 Dec. 🏠

🏛 **Schiller-Nationalmuseum**
Schillerhöhe 8–10. **Tel** (07144) 84 80 10. **Open** 10am–6pm Tue–Sun.
Closed 24, 25, 26, 31 Dec. 🏠

⑱ Esslingen

Road map C6. 🚗 92,000.
i Marktplatz 2 (0711-39 69 39 69).

Set among vineyards on the banks of the river Neckar, the beautiful town of Esslingen is famous for its sparkling wines. The town's historic buildings were fortunate in surviving intact the ravages of World War II. A walk through the winding streets and narrow alleys of the old centre will yield many interesting sights, while a climb to the top of the hill affords a splendid view of the town and the Neckar valley, as well as the amazing **Innere Brücke**, a 14th-century bridge. From there visitors can descend towards the market square, stopping on the way to visit Frauenkirche, a Gothic hall-church dating from the 14th century. Its front tower, the work of Ulrich and Matthäus von Ensingen, was added later. In the market square is the Stadtkirche St Dionysius, the oldest church in town, built in the 13th century on the site of an earlier, 8th-century building. Inside are magnificent early-Gothic stained-glass windows and late-15th-century Gothic furnishings, including the choir partition, the sacrarium and the font. The nearby church of St Paul, built in the mid-13th century for the Dominicans, is the oldest surviving Dominican church in Germany. In neighbouring Rathausplatz stands the half-timbered old town hall, Altes Rathaus, with its beautiful Renaissance façade, and the Baroque new town hall. Designed as a palace for Gottlieb von Palm by Gottlieb David Kandlers, the Neues Rathaus was built between 1748 and 1751.

Friedrich Schiller statue in Marbach

The picturesque houses and chapel of Esslingen's 14th-century Innere Brücke

⑲ Ludwigsburg

Situated near Stuttgart and known as the "Versailles of Swabia", Ludwigsburg was founded in 1704 on the initiative of Eberhard Ludwig, Duke of Württemberg. At the heart of the town is the vast palace complex, which the Duke ordered to be built for his mistress, Countess Wilhelmine von Grävenitz. The construction of the palace, which was carried out between 1704 and 1733, involved many outstanding architects and interior decorators, including Philipp Jenisch, Johann Nette, Donato Frisoni and Diego Carlone.

Northern Garden
This magnificent Baroque park is the venue for a flower show ("Blooming Baroque") that is held here during the summer.

★ Western Gallery
The gallery features opulent stucco ornaments by Ricardo Retti and Diego Carlone (1712–15).

★ Marble Hall
This vast hall in the new wing of the palace was remodelled in 1816, but still retains some of its Baroque interior decor.

★ Queen's Library
The library is housed in the east wing of the palace, in the apartments arranged for Queen Charlotte Mathilde.

★ **Schloss Favorite**
The "Favorite" hunting lodge was built between 1716 and 1723, but its interior has been remodelled in Neo-Classical style.

VISITORS' CHECKLIST

Practical Information
Road map: C6. ⊞ 80,000.
🛈 Arsenalstraße 2 (07141-910 28 61). Residenzschloss: Schlosstraße 30. **Tel** (07141) 18 20 04.
🕐 10am–5pm (75 mins). In English: mid-Mar–Nov: 1:30pm Mon–Fri, 11am, 1:30pm, 3:15pm Sat & Sun. Dec–mid-Mar: 1:30pm. Mode-, Keramik-museums, Barockgalerie: **Open** 10am–5pm daily. 🅿

Transport
🚉

Märchengarten
The landscaped section of the park includes the "Fairy-tale Garden", which contains figures and models from German fairy-tales.

Emichsburg
This romantic castle, built in 1798–1802, was named after the founder of the Wurttemberg dynasty.

KEY

① **The new wing** of the palace houses a museum devoted to court art of the Neo-Classical period.

② **The old wing** contains the palace's oldest apartments.

③ **The upper fruit garden** attracts visitors with its picturesque paths, which are lined with apple trees and grapevines.

④ **Restaurant and café**

⑳ Stuttgart

The capital of Baden-Wurttemberg, Stuttgart is one of the largest and most important towns of the Federal Republic. It grew from a 10th-century stud farm, known as Stutengarten, to become the ducal (1321) and later the royal (1806) capital of Wurttemberg. Beautifully situated among picturesque hills, the town is a major industrial centre with many important manufacturing plants. It is also a well-known publishing and cultural centre, with a world-famous ballet company, chamber orchestra and splendid art collections.

Exploring Stuttgart

Start your tour of Stuttgart at Schlossplatz, continuing along Königstraße towards the Palace Gardens, with their many interesting buildings, and stopping to pay a visit to the Staatsgalerie, whose extension was designed by the British architect James Stirling. From there you can return via Konrad-Adenauer-Strasse, heading towards Karlsplatz, then to Schillerplatz and Marktplatz with its magnificent town hall, finally ending the walk at Hegelhaus museum.

🏛 Schlossplatz

At the centre of the square stands the **Jubiläumssäule** – a column erected in 1842–46 to celebrate the 25-year reign of Wilhelm I. The square also features sculptures by many famous artists, including Alexander Calder and Alfred Hrdlicka. The east side of the square features a huge palace complex, **Neues Schloss**, built in 1746–1807, while on the opposite side stands **Königsbau**, a Neo-Classical structure erected in 1856–60.

Neo-Classical façade of Stuttgart's Staatstheater

🏛 Kunstmuseum Stuttgart

Kleiner Schlossplatz 1. **Tel** (0711) 216 21 88. **Open** 10am–6pm Tue–Sun (to 9pm Wed). 🖼 🖼 🖼
🌐 kunstmuseum-stuttgart.de

The spectacular glass cube of the Kunstmuseum Stuttgart was designed by the Berlin architects Hascher & Jehle. It houses the Municipal Art Collection, which includes works by such artists as Adolf Hölzel, Joseph Kosuth, Dieter Krieg, Dieter Roth, the Swabian Impressionists and has an outstanding collection of Otto Dix's work.

🌳 Schlossgarten

The magnificent gardens stretching north of the Neues Schloss were established in the early 19th century. They have maintained, to this day, much of their original charm, with neat avenues and interesting sculptures. The attractions include the **Carl-Zeiss-Planetarium**, which runs an excellent science programme, using equipment made by the famous optics company.

On the edge of the park stands a vast Neo-Classical theatre building, the **Württembergisches Staatstheater**, built in 1909–12 by Max Littmann. In 1982–3 it was given a new, dome-covered wing, the Theaterpavilion, designed by Gottfried Böhm.

🏛 Staatsgalerie

See pp316–17.

🏰 Altes Schloss

Landesmuseum Württemberg
Schillerplatz 6. **Tel** (0 711) 895 3511.
Open 10am–5pm Tue–Sun. 🖼

When Württemberg castle burned down in 1311, it was decided to move the family seat to Stuttgart. In 1325, the existing small castle was extended, creating Dütnitzbau. This wing has survived and can be seen from Karlsplatz. A large-scale Renaissance remodelling project, designed by Aberlin Tresch and carried out in 1553–78, gave the castle its square layout, with three-storey arcaded cloisters encircling the inner courtyard. The southwestern wing contains the Schlosskapelle (chapel), the first sacral building in Stuttgart built especially for the Protestants. The castle now houses the **Landesmuseum Württemberg**, which includes

The façade of Stuttgart's Neues Schloss, combining Baroque and Neo-Classical elements

Cloistered courtyard of the Renaissance Altes Schloss

vast collections of decorative art, including those displaying the ducal and royal insignia of Württemberg. The prehistory section includes jewellery from the Frankish period and the preserved tomb of a Celtic nobleman from Hochdorf.

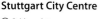 Schillerplatz

This is undoubtedly one of Stuttgart's most beautiful areas. It is here that the stud farm that gave Stuttgart its name is said to have stood. Today, a pensive statue of Friedrich Schiller, the work of the Danish sculptor Bertel Thorwaldsen (1839), occupies the centre of the square.

Schillerplatz is surrounded by historic buildings: the **Old Chancellery**, built in 1542–44 and extended upwards in 1566,

now houses a restaurant, the Prinzenbau (1605–78), and the Stiftsfruchtkasten, an attractive gabled granary (1578), now home to a museum of musical instruments.

⛪ Stiftskirche (Hl. Kreuz)

Stiftstraße 12.
From the south side of Schillerplatz there is a view of the presbytery of the collegiate church of the Holy Cross. This Gothic church, the work of Hänslin and Aberlin Jörg, was built in the 15th century and incorporated the walls of the previous, early-Gothic church. Despite World War II damage, this renovated church still has the original stone gallery of the dukes of Württemberg, built in 1576–84 by Simon Schlör to a design by Johann Steiner, as well as Gothic furnishings.

🏛️ Hegel-Haus

Eberhardstraße 53. **Tel** (0711) 216 67 33. **Open** 10am–5:30pm Mon–Fri, 10am–6:30pm Thu, 10am–4pm Sat.

Georg Wilhelm Friedrich Hegel – the creator of one of the most important modern philosophical systems – was born in this house on 27 August 1770. The house is now a museum, which houses an exhibition devoted to the life and work of the famous philosopher.

Figures of saints adorning the façade of the Stiftskirche

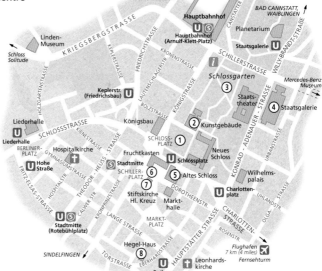

Stuttgart City Centre

① Schlossplatz
② Kunstmuseum Stuttgart
③ Schlossgarten
④ Staatsgalerie
⑤ Altes Schloss
⑥ Schillerplatz
⑦ Stiftskirche Hl. Kreuz
⑧ Hegel-Haus

0 metres 300
0 yards 300

For additional map symbols see back flap

🏛 Linden-Museum/ Staatl. Museum für Völkerkunde

Hegelplatz 1. **Tel** (0711) 2 02 23. **Open** 10am–5pm Tue, Thu–Sat, 10am–8pm Wed, 10am–6pm Sun. 🖼

The Linden Museum is one of Germany's finest ethnology museums. It was founded by Count Karl von Linden, who was also its director from 1889 until 1910. The museum contains many fascinating exhibits from all over the world, including figures from the Indonesian theatre of shadows, a Tibetan sand mandala, a 6th–8th-century mask from Peru in South America and a full-size reproduction of an Islamic bazaar.

Peruvian mask in the Linden-Museum

🏛 Weißenhofsiedlung

Weissenhofmuseum im Haus Le Corbusier, Rathenaustr. 1–3. **Tel** (0711) 2 57 91 87. **Open** 11am–6pm Tue–Fri, 10am–6pm Sat & Sun. Architektur-Galerie: **Tel** (0711) 257 14 34. **Open** 2–6pm Tue–Sat, noon–5pm Sun.

A building exhibition held in 1927 in Stuttgart had housing as its main theme. It left behind an estate that still exists today, although it was badly bombed during World War II. Most of the houses represent functionalism, which was being promoted at the time by the Bauhaus. The estate, which was to serve as an example to others, has some interesting houses, including works by Mies van der Rohe (Am Weißenhof 14–29), Le Corbusier (Rathenaustraße 1–3), Peter Behrens (Hölzelweg 3–5) and Hans Scharoun (Hölzelweg 1).

🏛 Liederhalle

Berliner Platz 1.

A must for all lovers of modern architecture, Liederhalle, in the centre of Stuttgart, is a successful synthesis of tradition and modernism. Built in 1955–56 by Adolf Abel and Rolf Gutbrod, this fine cultural and congress centre, with three concert halls clustered around an irregular hall, is still impressive today.

🏛 Mercedes-Benz Museum

Mercedesstraße 100. **Tel** (0711) 173 00 00. **Open** 9am–6pm Tue–Sun. **Closed** public holidays.

To the east of the town centre, in the Obertürkheim district, is the famous Mercedes-Benz Museum. Its splendid collection illustrates the development of motorcar production, from the earliest models to today's state-of-the-art, computerized products. Set up to celebrate the centenary of their inventions, the museum features over 70 historic vehicles, all in immaculate condition. The collection includes the world's two oldest automobiles, Gottlieb Daimler's horseless carriage and

Some of the models on display in the Mercedes-Benz Museum

Carl Benz's three-wheeled automobile from 1886. Also on display is a hand-made limousine that was built in the 1930s for the Emperor of Japan and the first "Popemobile", which was built for Pope Paul VI.

Another interesting exhibit is the famous 1950s racing car, *Silberpfeil* (Silver Arrow), as well as models that were built for attempts on world speed records. Also on display are scores of the latest models that have been produced by the company. The visitor can also learn the history of Daimler-Benz AG, which was created by the merger in 1926 of Daimler-Motoren-Gesellschaft and Benz & Cie., Rhein. The company's subsequent 1999 merger with Chrysler created one of the world's largest car manufacturing concerns, Daimler-Chrysler.

📺 Fernsehturm

Closed until further notice.

Built between 1954 and 1956 this television tower was the world's first to be built entirely from ferro-concrete. It is 217 m (712 ft) high and stands on top of a wooded hill, Hoher Bopser. Its observation platform provides splendid views over Schwäbische Alb, Schwarzwald and, on a clear day, even the Alps.

🏛 Porsche-Museum

Porscheplatz 1. **Tel** (01805) 356 911. **Open** 9am–6pm Tue–Sun.

The Porsche museum was revamped and reopened in 2009. The exhibition area is made up of a steel structure resting on

House designed by Le Corbusier in Weißenhofsiedlung

For hotels and restaurants in this area see pp492–503 and pp510–33

just three concrete cores, giving it the appearance of hovering in space. More than 80 cars are on display, ranging from the Lohner-Porsche, the world's first hybrid automobile built in 1900, to the latest generation of the Porsche 911. There are also historical archives, an open workshop, a restaurant and café.

🖩 Markthalle

Dorotheenstraße 4. **Open** 7am–6:30pm Mon–Fri, 7am–5pm Sat.

Stuttgart's market hall, built in 1912–14 in Art Nouveau style on the site of an earlier vegetable market, is one of the finest in Europe. Built as a food exchange, it has magnificent frescos. Today it still sells fresh fruit and vegetables to the general public, and also houses a small restaurant and café.

🏛 Schloss Solitude

Solitude 1. **Tel** (0711) 69 66 99. **Open** Apr–Oct: 10am–noon, 1:30–5pm Tue–Sat, 10am–5pm Sun; Nov–Mar: 1:30–4pm Tue–Sat, 10am–4pm Sun. 🎟 obligatory. 🖼 garden free.

This exquisite small palace, standing on the slopes of a hill, was built for Prince Karl Eugene in 1763–67. The Prince not only commissioned the residence, but also took an active part in its design, which is the work of Pierre Louis Philippe de la Guêpière, who introduced the Louis XVI-style to Germany. Many consider this palace to be his masterpiece.

Following its full restoration in 1990, and the provision of 45 residential studio apartments, the palace now serves art students on scholarships from all over the world. A 15-km (9-mile) long, straight road connects Schloss Solitude with Ludwigsburg.

🖩 Bad Cannstatt

Once an independent health resort, Bad Cannstatt is now a district of Stuttgart. Set in a beautiful park, it has a late-Gothic parish hall-church, a Neo-Classical town hall and a Kursaal (spa-house), built in 1825–42. One of its attractions is the Neo-Classical Schloss Rosenstein, built in 1824–29 at the request of King Wilhelm I, based on amended designs by John Papworth. The King was also the initiator of the beautiful "Wilhelm's complex". This includes a Moorish-style villa located in a symmetrically laid-out park, with many Oriental-style pavilions and other decorative elements. Completed in the 1840s, its main designer was Karl Ludwig Wilhelm von Zanth. The park has now been transformed into a botanical-zoological garden.

Environs

Stuttgart provides a convenient base for exploring the surroundings. In **Sindelfingen**, 15 km (9 miles) southwest, it is worth visiting the Romanesque Church of St Martin Canons, which was founded in 1083. While you are there, take a stroll along Lange Straße to the old town hall, which dates from 1478 and is joined with the Salt House (1592). The two buildings, both half-timbered in their upper sections, now house the town museum.

A little further to the west, **Weil der Stadt** is the birthplace of the astronomer Johannes Kepler and the reformer Johannes Brenz. The town's late-Gothic church of St Peter and St Paul was completed in 1492 by Aberlin Jörg. Inside is a beautiful Renaissance sacrarium, dating from 1611. The Marktplatz, with a statue of Kepler at its centre, has a Renaissance town hall (1582). Nearby, at Keplergasse 2, stands the house in which the famous astronomer was born and which now houses a small museum, the Kepler-Museum.

Another place worthy of a visit is **Waiblingen**, 10 km (6 miles) to the northeast of Stuttgart. It features a Romanesque church, the vaults of which are decorated with some splendid wall paintings dating from 1515.

The façade of the Schloss Solitude, in the hills to the west of Stuttgart's centre

Staatsgalerie

The Staatsgalerie grew from the museum of fine arts founded in 1843 by King Wilhelm I and containing the king's private collection. Now it ranks among the finest of German galleries. As well as its own magnificent collection of old masters and modern artists, the gallery has an extensive collection of graphics. In 1984 the art gallery acquired an extension designed by James Stirling.

The Mourning of Christ (c.1490)
This subtle depiction of Christ is the work of the Venetian artist Giovanni Bellini.

Spring Fields (1887)
One of the leading members of the French Impressionist movement, Claude Monet was unsurpassed in his rendition of iridescent light.

Entrance to Alte Staatsgalerie

Mother and Child (1905)
This painting by Pablo Picasso represents his "pink period", which preceded the famous Cubist experiments of this great Spanish artist.

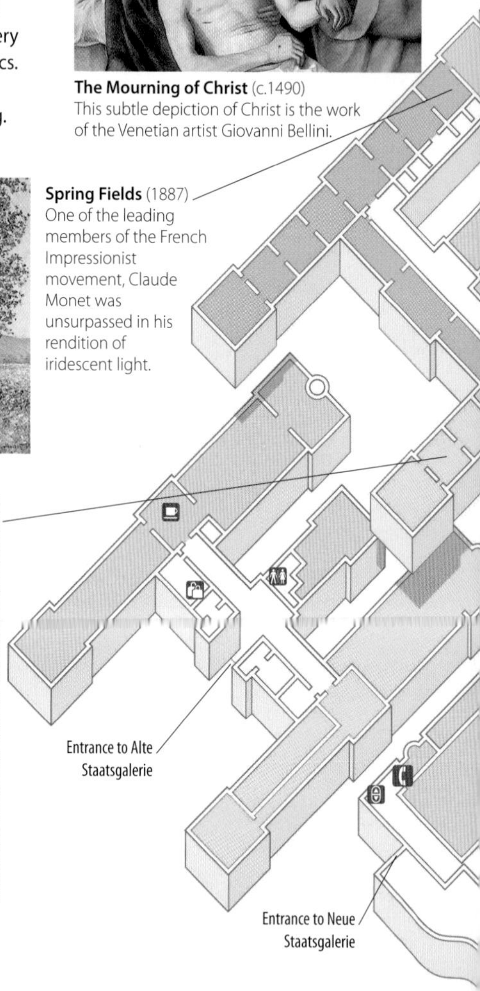

Entrance to Neue Staatsgalerie

Key

- ☐ 14th–19th-century Art
- ▨ 19th-century Art
- ☐ 20th-century Art
- ☐ Contemporary Art
- ☐ Temporary exhibitions
- ▨ Non-exhibition rooms

Female Nude Reclining on a White Pillow (1917)
Amadeo Modigliani became famous for his idiosyncratic portraits and female nudes.

★ **Iphigenie** (1871)
Anselm Feuerbach's painting was inspired by a play by Goethe, Iphigenie on Tauris.

VISITORS' CHECKLIST

Konrad-Adenauer-Straße 30–32.
Tel (0711) 47 04 00.
Open 10am–6pm Wed, Fri–Sun, 10am–8pm Tue, Thu.
W staatsgalerie.de

Crossing of the Rhine near Rhenen (1642)
The Dutch painter Jan van Goyen became famous for his evocative landscapes, which were often executed in uniform tones of lead-grey or brown-green.

★ **St Paul in Prison** (1627)
In this, one of his earliest works, Rembrandt depicted the Apostle Paul awaiting death in a humble cell.

Bathsheba at her Toilet
(c.1485)
In this painting, which is a fragment of a lost triptych illustrating Justice, Hans Memling uses the Old Testament story of Bathsheba to exemplify the abuse of power, intervention by God and the reformation of a sinner.

First floor

Ground floor

Gallery Guide
Permanent exhibitions are located over the first floor of the two buildings. In the Neue Staatsgalerie are works by the old masters and from the 19th-century. The Alte Staatsgalerie holds 20th-century art.

㉑ Schwäbische Alb

The mountain range of Schwäbische Alb (the Swabian Jura) extends like an arc, 220 km (137 miles) long and 40 km (25 miles) wide, from the area around Tuttlingen and Sigmaringen, in southwest Germany, to Nördlinger Ries, at the border between the federal counties of Baden-Württemberg and Bavaria. The highest peak in the range is Lemberg (1,015 m/ 3,330 ft). Beech woods and scented juniper shrubs dominate the mellow landscape, whose whole system of interconnected stalagmitic caves was carved from the sedimentary limestone rocks.

Hechingen
On the outskirts of Hechingen, the remains of a 1st–3rd-century AD Roman villa are open to the public.

Haigerloch
In the vaults of this castle is a vast bunker that was used as an atomic research laboratory towards the end of World War II.

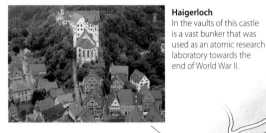

★ **Burg Hohenzollern**
The ancestral seat of the Hohenzollern family was remodelled in 1850–67. Only the 15th-century St Michaelkapelle survives from the original fortress.

★ **Beuron**
Beuron's magnificent Benedictine Abbey was founded in the 11th century. Its subsequent remodelling resulted in a Baroque structure, which survives to this day.

Key

 Motorway

Main road

Secondary road

River

☀ Viewpoint

For hotels and restaurants in this area see pp492–503 and pp510–33

Swabian Jura Landscape
The gentle hills and enchanting villages attract hikers and tourists from all over the world.

VISITORS' CHECKLIST

Practical Information
ℹ Schwäbische Alb
Tourismusverband, Marktplatz 1,
Bad Urach (07125-94 81 06).
🌐 **schwaebischealb.de**

Hohenneuffen
A massive castle dominates the tiny town of Neuffen. It is the most impressive ruin in the Swabian Jura.

Lichtenstein
This romantic castle was immortalized in a novel by Wilhelm Hauff.

★ Sigmaringen
The town's skyline is dominated by the castle, which was reconstructed following a fire in 1893. Only the towers of the medieval fortress remain.

0 km   5
0 miles   5

㉒ Tübingen

Road map C6. 🏔 85,000. 🚌 ℹ️ An der Neckarbrücke 1 (07071-913 60). 🏛 Mon, Wed, Fri. 🌐 **tuebingen. info.de**

Along with Heidelberg and Freiburg im Breisgau, Tübingen is the home of one of southern Germany's three most famous universities. It was founded in 1477 by Count Eberhard the Bearded.

The first records of the fortress that later gave rise to a settlement on this site date from 1078. By around 1231, the settlement had become a town. In 1342, Tübingen passed to the counts of Württemberg, having previously belonged to the counts Palatinate.

Schloss Hohentübingen, which towers over the town, has a magnificent gateway (Unteres Tor). Built in 1606, it is richly adorned with the coat of arms of the House of Württemberg. The walled castle complex, with its central courtyard and long approach, was built in stages during 1507–15, 1534–42 and 1606.

A walk along the Burgsteige takes you to the picturesque old town. Here, at the centre of Marktplatz, is the Neptune Fountain, the work of Heinrich Schickhard, dating from 1617. In the western corner of the square is a lovely Renaissance town hall,

Tübingen's Gothic-Renaissance town hall

built in 1435 and extended in the 16th century. It features an astronomical clock, which dates from 1511. *Sgraffiti* on the western façade dates from 1876; those on the elevations facing Haaggasse date from the 16th century.

The collegiate church of St George (**Stiftskirche St Georg**), built in 1440–1529, is a triple-nave hall with rows of side chapels, galleries and a single tower. Of particular note are the ducal tombs, the late-Gothic reading-room and the stained-glass windows of the choir, dating from 1475. Magnificent stalls, adorned with carved figures of the Prophets, date from the late 15th century.

The bookstore in Holzmarkt (*Buchhandlung Heckenhauer*)

is where Hermann Hesse once served as an apprentice bookseller. On the banks of the Neckar stands the **Hölderlinturm**, in which the German poet Hölderlin lived from 1807 until his death. Not far from here stands the large building of the Alte Burse, which was built in 1478–80 and later remodelled in 1803–1805. The building was once used to accommodate students and as a lecture hall. Martin Luther's close associate, Philipp Melanchthon, lectured here between 1514 and 1518.

The Protestant seminary in Neckarhalde was founded by Prince Ulrich in 1536. Its graduates include the poets Hölderlin, Mörike and Schiller and the philosophers Hegel and Schelling.

The **Kunsthalle** is famous throughout Germany not only for its temporary exhibitions, but also for its fine collection of modern art. Other popular attractions in Tübingen include the **Stadtmuseum**, which is devoted to the town's history, and the **Auto- und Spielzeugmuseum**.

🏛 **Museum Schloss Hohentübingen**
Burgsteige 11. **Tel** (07071) 297 73 84. **Open** 10am–5pm Wed–Sun (to 7pm Thu). 📷

🔺 **Stiftskirche St Georg**
Tel (07071) 525 83. **Open** Apr–Sep: 9am–5pm daily, Oct–Mar: 9am–4pm daily. 📷

🏛 **Hölderlinturm**
Bursagasse 6. **Tel** (07071) 220 40. **Open** 10am–noon, 3–5pm Tue–Fri, 2– 5pm Sat, Sun & public hols. 📷

🏛 **Kunsthalle**
Philosophenweg 76. **Tel** (07071) 969 10. **Open** 11am–6pm Wed–Sun, 11am–7pm Tue (during exhibitions). 🌐 **kunsthalle-tuebingen.de**

🏛 **Statdtmuseum**
Kornhausstraße 10. **Tel** (07071) 204 17 11 or 94 54 60. **Open** 11am–5pm Tue–Sun. 📷

🏛 **Auto-und Spielzeugmuseum**
Brunnenstraße 18. **Tel** (07071) 55 11 22. **Open** Jan–Oct: 10am–noon, 2–5pm Wed–Fri, 10am–5pm Sun; Nov–Dec: hours vary. 📷
🌐 **boxenstop-tuebingen.de**

Unteres Tor leading to Schloss Hohentübingen

For hotels and restaurants in this area see pp492–503 and pp510–33

㉓ Rottweil

Road map C7. ⌂ 24,000. ⌂
ℹ Hauptstraße 21–23 (0741-49 42
80). Fasnet (last Mon of Carnival),
Jazzfest (May), Klassikfestival (Jun),
Ferienzauber (Aug).

Situated on the banks of the
river Neckar, Rottweil is one
of the oldest towns in Baden-
Württemberg. It grew from a
Roman settlement that was
established on a hilltop here
in AD 73. In 1234 Rottweil
was granted town status and,
by 1401, it had become a
free town of the Holy Roman
Empire. Between 1463 and
1802 it belonged to the
Swiss Confederation, which
was founded in 1291 by the
cantons of Uri, Schwyz and
Unterwalden. In 1802, the
town passed into the rule of
the dukes of Württemberg.

Rottweil has many historic
remains, including sections of
the fortified city walls, with
several well-preserved turrets.

The parish church of St Cross
(Heilig-Kreuz-Münster), built in
1230–1534, has a triple-nave
basilica with stellar and network
vaults. Late-Gothic altars,
including St Bartholomew's, by
Michael Wolgemut and a crucifix
attributed to Veit Stoss, are
among its features.

To the south of the church
stands the late-Gothic town hall
(1521). On the opposite side of
the street, at Hauptstraße 20,
the **Stadtmuseum** has an
outstanding collection of

Crucifixion attributed to Veit Stoss in
Heilig-Kreuz-Münster, Rottweil

Fountain and "Black Gate" in Rottweil's main street, Hauptstraße

prehistoric remains. The
Dominikanermuseum has
an interesting exhibition of
Roman relics. These include the
famous Orpheus mosaic,
dating from the 2nd century
AD, and an outstanding
collection of late-Gothic
sculpture, including the
statue of St Barbara by
Multscher (c.1450).

The Hauptstraße is lined
with burghers' houses,
displaying characteristic
oriel windows. One of the
most beautiful historic
buildings in Rottweil is
the Kapellenkirche, built in
1330–1478. Its 70-metre (230-ft)
tower and three portals are
adorned with carved ornaments
reminiscent of the French Gothic
style. The Baroque interior
features frescos by Josef
Fiertmayer, who was a pupil of
renowned painter and architect
Cosmas Damian Asam. The
Gothic Dominican church,
built in 1266–82 and remodelled
in the 18th century, has
some frescos by Joseph
Wannenmacher (1755). Roman

Kapellenturm,
Rottweil

baths dating from the 2nd
century AD have been excavated
at the corner of what is now
the cemetery.

Rottweil is famous for
its carnival processions
(Fasnet), a tradition that goes
back to the Middle Ages.
A collection of carnival
costumes can be seen
in the Stadtmuseum.

The **Puppen- und
Spielzeugmuseum** has a
fine collection of historic
dolls and toys which is
perfect for keeping the
children entertained.

🏛 **Stadtmuseum**
Hauptstraße 20. **Tel** (0741) 494
330. **Open** 10am–noon, 2–4pm Tue–
Sun.

🏛 **Dominikanermuseum**
Am Kriegsdamm. **Tel** (0741) 7662.
Open 10am–5pm Tue–Sun.
Closed public holidays.

🏛 **Puppen- und
Spielzeugmuseum**
Hauptstraße 49. **Tel** (0741) 942 21 77.
Open 10am–12:30pm, 2pm–5:30pm
Wed–Fri, 10am–12:30pm Sat, 2–5pm
Sun.

㉔ Ulm

Road map B6. ![icon] 115,000. ![icon]
ⓘ Münsterplatz 50 (0731-161 28 30.
![icon] Fischerstechen (every 4th year in
Jul, next is 2017), Schwörmontag (3rd
Mon in Jul), Stadtfest (Jun). **W** **ulm.de**

Lying on the river Danube, Ulm
dates back to 854. It became a
town in 1165 then, in 1274, a
free town of the Holy Roman
Empire. During the 15th century
Ulm was one of the richest
towns in Europe but the Thirty
Years' War put an end to its
rapid development. In 1810
Ulm came under the rule of the
Württemberg kings. The town is
renowned as the birthplace of
Albert Einstein.
During World
War II, most of the
old town was
destroyed during
bombing raids.

The Münster is
a true masterpiece
of European Gothic
architecture. A vast,
five-nave basilica, its
161-m (530-ft) high
west tower is the
highest church
tower in the world.
The cathedral's
construction from

Gothic font in Ulm Cathedral

1377 until 1545, was overseen
by the greatest builders
of the German Gothic –
Heinrich and Michael Parler,
Urlich von Ensingen, Hans Kun
and Matthäus Böblinger. The
unfinished cathedral was
extended in 1844–90, based
on the original medieval
design. The interior contains
many outstanding features,
including the altar by Hans
Multscher (1443),
the famous stalls with
figures of philosophers,
poets, prophets and
apostles carved by
Jörg Syrlin the Elder,
15th-century stained-
glass windows, and the
font, by Jörg Syrlin
the Younger.

The town has many
fine historic buildings,
including the Gothic-
Renaissance town hall,
which is decorated with brightly
coloured frescos and features
an astronomical clock. Other
features of Marktplatz include
the Gothic fountain *Fischkasten*
(Fish Crate), dating
from 1482, and the
Reichenauer Hof,
which dates from
1370–1535.

The **Ulmer
Museum**, which is
housed in a number of
historic 16th- and
17th-century buildings,
has a collection of art
spanning a period from
the Middle Ages up to
the present day. The
collection includes
the work of local
artists, such as
Hans Multscher. The **Deutsches
Brotmuseum** specializes in
artifacts related to bread and
bread-making, including items
depicting bread in art and
graphic designs.

🏛 **Ulmer Museum**
Marktplatz 9. **Tel** (0731) 161 43 12.
Open 11am–5pm Tue–Sun, 11am–
8pm Thu (during exhibitions). ![icon]

🏛 **Museum der Brotkultur**
Salzstadelgasse 10. **Tel** (0731) 699 55.
Open 10am–5pm daily. ![icon]
W **museum-brotkultur.de**

㉕ Ravensburg

Road map: C7. ![icon] 45,000. ![icon]
ⓘ Kirchstraße 16 (0751-828 00).
![icon] Fasnet (Feb), Rutenfest (Jul).
W **stadt-ravensburg.de**

The first historic records of the
"Ravespurc" fortress date from
1088, when it was one of the
seats of the Welf family. It is
believed to be the birthplace of

**Main altar by Hans Multscher in
Ravensburg's Liebfrauenkirche**

Henry the Lion, the powerful
Duke of Saxony and Bavaria,
born in 1129. The settlement
that sprang up at the foot of
the castle became a free
imperial city in 1276. From 1395,
paper was produced here and,
during the 15th century, the
town became one of the richest
in Germany from its involvement
in the linen trade.

Standing in Kirchstraße is the
14th-century parish church of
Liebfrauenkirche, which retains
original 15th-century features,
including the main altar and
some fine stained-glass windows.

In Marienplatz stands the
late-Gothic town hall (14th–
15th century), with its lovely
Renaissance bay window. Also
in Marienplatz is the Waaghaus
(1498), which housed the
weigh-house and mint on the
ground floor, with a trading hall
upstairs, when Ravensburg was
engaged in coin production.
The watchtower *(Blaserturm)* is
crowned by a Renaissance
octagon that has become the
symbol of the town. Another
attractive building here is the
Lederhaus, which dates from
1513–14. Near the town hall is
the old 14th–15th century
granary *(Kornhaus)*.

Marktstraße features many
old burgher houses. No. 59, the
oldest house in town, dates
from 1179. The neighbouring
house was built in 1446. The
tall white cylindrical tower that
can be seen from here is
known as the "sack of flour"
(Mehlsack). It was erected in the
16th century. A magnificent
view of the town can be
obtained from Veitsburg,
which occupies the site of
the original Welf castle.

**Astronomical clock on Ulm's
Gothic-Renaissance town hall**

For hotels and restaurants in this area see pp492–503 and pp510–33

Former Cistercian abbey complex in Salem, now a secular building

㉖ Weingarten

Road map: C7. 🚹 24,500. 🚉
🛈 Münsterplatz 1 (0751-40 52 32).
🎭 Blutritt (day after Ascension).

The House of Welf founded a Benedictine abbey in Weingarten in 1056. During the Romanesque period, around 1190, the monks of the abbey produced a chronicle of the House of Welfs, known as the *Welfenchronik*.

Ambitious plans, drawn up in the 18th century at the initiative of Abbot Sebastian Hyller, provided for an extension of the abbey and the construction of another vast complex of buildings. Two side courtyards and four external courtyards, encircled with curved galleries with smaller pavilions, were planned to be grouped around the church. These were designed by Casper Moosbrugger, Franz Beer, Donato Giuseppe Frisoni and others, and built in 1715–24.

The church is reminiscent of the Basilica of St Peter's in Rome. Although it is half the size of the latter, it is nevertheless an immense structure. Inside are some magnificent ceiling frescos by Cosmas Damian Asam, while the carved and inlaid choir stalls are the work of Joseph Anton Feuchtmayer. Also of note is the organ by Josef Gabler. In an ingenious design, the organ pipes are concealed within a series of towers to avoid obscuring the windows of the façade. The **Alamannenmuseum** has a fascinating exhibition of

relics that have been found in graves dating from the Merovingian period.

🏛 **Alamannenmuseum**
Karlstr. 28. **Tel** (0751) 40 52 55.
Open 2–5pm Tue–Sun. 📷

㉗ Salem

Road map: C7. 🚹 8,500.

The first Cistercian monks arrived in Salmansweiler (now known as Salem) in 1134. Between 1299 and 1414 they built a church according to the rules of their order, which espoused poverty and banned any decoration of the monastic buildings.

The abbey is a triple-nave basilica with transept and straight-end choir. Its austere façade is relieved by blind windows, some of which have attractive traceries. In later years the restraints of poverty were

relaxed to the extent that the abbey now has an interesting tabernacle (1500), stalls (1594) and early-Renaissance altars (dating from the 18th century).

The new abbey buildings were built between 1700 and 1710 and constitute **Schloss Salem**. The buildings include some richly decorated abbot's apartments and the extremely impressive Emperor's room *(Kaisersaal)*, which was built between 1708 and 1710.

Since its secularization in 1802, the abbey has been the private property of the Baden margraves who keep some of their art collection here. The west wing houses a private boarding school founded by Kurt Hahn, who also founded Gordonstoun in Scotland.

🏠 **Schloss Salem**
Tel (07553) 814 37. **Open** Apr–Oct: 9:30am–6pm Mon–Sat, 10:30am–6pm Sun. 📷

Ceiling fresco in Weingarten's abbey

㉘ The Bodensee

Sometimes known as Lake Constance, the Bodensee lies on the border of Germany, Switzerland and Austria. The area surrounding the lake is one of the most attractive in Germany, in terms of both natural beauty and cultural heritage. Towns and villages around the shores feature countless reminders of past times and cultures. The best time for a visit is summer, when local fishermen stage colourful fairs and water sports are possible.

The Bodensee
The lake is 15 km (9 miles) across at its widest point and 63 km (39 miles) long. It lies at an altitude of 395 m (1,295 ft) and reaches 252 m (826 ft) in depth.

Reichenau
The greatest attraction of this island is the Benedictine abbey, which was famed during the era of Otto the Great (10th century) for its illuminated manuscripts. It has a beautiful Romanesque-Gothic church and an intoxicating herb garden.

★ Mainau
Mainau is known as the "Island of Flowers". The most beautiful displays are in the park surrounding the Baroque palace, which was built in 1739–46. It is currently owned by the Lennart Bernadotte family.

KEY

① **Friedrichshafen** is best known for its Zeppelin-Museum. The first Zeppelin airships were tested here in 1900.

② **Langenargen** has an enchanting, small Moorish-style palace named Montfort.

★ Konstanz (Constance) The largest town in the region, its main attraction is the magnificent 11th-century Romanesque cathedral. The vaults over the central aisle were built between 1679 and 1683.

Map labels: Stockach, Ludwigshafen, ÜBERLINGER SE, Überl, Singen, Radolfzell, M., Gottmadingen, ZELLERSEE, Reichenau, Konsta, UNTERSEE, Kreuzlingen

Meersburg
The exquisite Baroque town of Meersburg has two residences – the Baroque Neues Schloss and the Altes Schloss. The latter is a 16th-century structure built on top of a hill. It contains within its walls an old Carolingian palace.

VISITORS' CHECKLIST

Practical Information
Map 7 C. 🛈 Bahnhofplatz 43, Konstanz (07531-13 30 30).
Ⓦ **konstanz-tourismus.de**
Sea Life Centre: Hafenstr. 9, Konstanz **Tel** (07531)-12 82 70.
Open Sep–Jun: 10am–5pm daily; Jul & Aug: 10am–6pm daily. 🅿
Museum Reichenau: Ergat 1–3.
Tel (07534) 99 93 21. **Open** Apr–Oct: 10:30am–4:30pm daily (Jul & Aug: to 5:30pm); Nov–Mar: 2–5pm Sat, Sun & hols. 🅿

★ Wasserburg
This charming church, with a tower crowned with an onion-shaped dome, is one of the most frequently photographed sights in this region.

Lindau
This island town has so many historic buildings that the whole area has been listed as a historic monument (see p288).

Meersburg

GERMANY

①

②

Romanshorn

BODENSEE

Wasserburg

Lindau

SWITZERLAND

AUSTRIA

• Arbon

• Bregenz

• Rorschach

Key

▬ Motorway

▬ Major road

▬ Minor road

▭ River

🚢 Ferry or catamaran route

– – International border

0 km ⌶⌶⌶⌶⌶ 5

0 miles 5

❷⁹ Freiburg im Breisgau

The dukes of Zähringen first established Freiburg in 1120. The town, which later belonged to the counts von Urach, became so rich over the years that, in 1368, it bought its freedom and voluntarily placed itself under the protection of the Habsburgs. Marshal Vauban fortified the town in the 17th century, when Freiburg briefly belonged to France. Since 1805 it has been part of Baden. Situated between Kaiserstuhl and Feldberg, it is a natural gateway to the southern Schwarzwald (Black Forest).

Freiburg University
Freiburg University occupies a Baroque post-Jesuit complex. In the main entrance stands this statue of the pensive Aristotle.

This former Jesuit church belongs to the university complex.

0 metres   50
0 yards   50

Railway station

Tourist information

RATHAUS–PLATZ

RATHAUSGASSE

BERTOLDSTRASSE

Fischerau
Fischerau and, parallel to it, Gerberau are picturesque streets in the old town, running along the Gewerbebach stream.

Key

— Suggested route

Bertoldsbrunnen
(Bertold's fountain) stands a the intersection of Bertholdstraße and Kaiser-Joseph-Straße, known as "Ka

Martinstor
St Martin's Gate was part of the 13th-century town fortifications. Its present appearance is the result of work carried out in 1900.

◄ An example of the beautiful stained glass windows in Freiburg im Breisgau's Münster

Haus zum Walfisch
The façade of the Whale House in Franziskanergasse, with its lovely bay window, is a magnificent example of late-Gothic style.

Münsterplatz
The picturesque square at the foot of the cathedral, lined by houses of various periods, from Gothic to Rococo, is still used for markets.

VISITORS' CHECKLIST

Practical Information
Road map B7. 197,000.
ℹ️ Rathausplatz 2–4 (0761-388 18 80). 🎭 Fasnet (end of carnival), Frühlingsmesse (May), Internationales Zeltmusikfest (Jun), Weintage (Jun), Weinkost (Jun), Herbstmesse (Oct), Umwelt-Film-Festival (Oct).
Ⓦ **freiburg.de**

Transport
🚉

KAISER–JOSEPH–STRASSE

SCHUSTERSTRASSE

SALZSTRASSE

MÜNSTER PLATZ

★ Bächle
From the Middle Ages, fast-flowing canals have been running along the streets, draining excess surface waters, and providing the water needed to extinguish the frequent fires.

Augustiner Museum

★ Münster – the Main Altar
The cathedral, which started in c.1200 as a Romanesque basilica, was completed by 1513 in the French Gothic style. Inside is the original main altar by Hans Baldung Grien.

★ Kaufhaus
Completed in 1520, with ground-floor arcades and richly adorned gables, the Kaufhaus (literally buying house) was used by local merchants for meetings, conferences and lively festivities.

⓾ Schwarzwald (Black Forest)

Covered with tall fir trees and spruces, the Schwarzwald is one of Germany's most picturesque regions. The area is famous not just for its cuckoo clocks, *Kirschwasser* (schnaps) and *Schwarzwälder Kirschtorte* (Black Forest Gâteau); in the past, Celts and later the Romans came to appreciate the therapeutic qualities of the local spring waters. (The sources of the rivers Donau and Neckar are here.) The area is also a paradise for skiers, climbers, ramblers, hang-glider pilots and sailors.

★ Staufen im Breisgau
The town is also known as Fauststadt: Dr Faustus, who had resided here, died in 1539 – he is variously reputed to have blown himself up, to have been strangled or to have had his neck broken.

Todtnau
Todtnau is not only a sports centre and a base for hikers and cyclists: it also has a fanstastic annual festival devoted entirely to *Schwarzwälder Kirschtorte* (Black Forest Gateau).

Todtmoos
The heart of this resort is the Baroque pilgrimage church, which dates from the 17th–18th centuries. Popular dog-sleigh races are held annually in the town.

Friesenheim
Lahr
Herbolzheim
Emmendir
Teningen
Denzlingen
Freiburg im Breisg
Bad Krozingen
Staufen im Breisgau
Müllheim
SCHWARZWALD
Kandern
Todtmc
Wiese
Wehr
Lörrach
Rheinfelden
Basel

Gutach

In the open-air museum near the
small town of Gutach visitors can
see the Schwarzwald's oldest house
– the Vogtsbauernhof – which
dates from the 16th century.

★ Furtwangen

The main attraction of Furtwangen is its clock museum
(Uhrenmuseum), which houses a collection of more than
8,000 varied chronometers.

Hangloch-Wasserfall

This magnificent mountain
waterfall near Todtnau is one of the
most beautiful in the Black Forest.

★ St Blasien

In the beautiful health resort of St
Blasien is a Benedictine Abbey,
founded in the 9th century. Crowned
with a vast dome, its church (1783)
is an excellent example of early
Neo-Classical style.

0 km 10
0 miles 10

Key

Motorway

Main road

Secondary road

River

☀ Viewpoint

WESTERN GERMANY

Introducing Western
  Germany   334–339

Rhineland-Palatinate
  and Saarland   340–363

Hesse   364–385

North Rhine-Westphalia   386–419

Western Germany at a Glance

Famed for its excellent wines and the festivities of Cologne's annual carnival, Western Germany is the country's wealthiest and most heavily industrialized region. The Ruhr district still harbours enormous industrial potential, while Frankfurt am Main is Germany's largest financial centre. The region is also rich in tourist attractions – visitors are drawn to the romantic castles which line the Rhine and Mosel valleys, to Cologne with its majestic twin-towered cathedral, the spa town of Aachen, the museums of Frankfurt and Kassel and the imposing Romanesque cathedrals of Speyer, Worms and Mainz.

Locator Map

Cologne Cathedral *(see pp406–7)*, which was not completed until the 19th century, is generally considered one of the most outstanding Gothic buildings in Germany.

0 kilometres   100

0 miles   100

Rhein

Gronau

Coesfeld   Münster

Kleve

**NORTH RHINE-
WESTPHALIA**
(See pp386–419)   Ham

Duisburg   Essen   Dortr

Düsseldorf   Hag

Wuppertal

Solingen

Köln

Aachen

Bonn   Hennef

Kol

Prüm

Wittlich

B
Kreuzna

Trier   **RHINELAND-
PALATINATE &
SAARLAND**
(See pp340–63)

Kaiserslautern

Saarbrücken

Pirmas

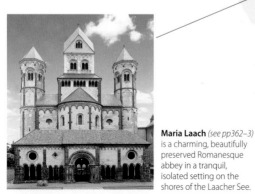

Maria Laach *(see pp362–3)* is a charming, beautifully preserved Romanesque abbey in a tranquil, isolated setting on the shores of the Laacher See.

◀ The Saar river bend, near Mettlach, Saarland

Detmold is best known for its magnificent castle *(see p419)* – one of the most beautiful examples of the "Weser Renaissance" style of architecture.

The Museum Fridericianum in Kassel *(see pp368–9)*, originally built to house Friederich II's art collection, has hosted the *documenta*, an exhibition of contemporary art that has achieved international acclaim, every four to five years since 1955.

Fulda Cathedral *(see p372)* is one of the finest Baroque churches in Hesse. It was built on the site of the previous Romanesque church and follows the original layout.

The old town in Frankfurt am Main *(see p379)* is centred around the Römerberg – a square surrounded by attractive half-timbered houses, with the Fountain of Justice as a focal point.

Minden

Bielefeld

Wiedenbrück

Paderborn

Warburg

Meschede

Kassel

HESSE
(See pp364–85)

Marburg

Alsfeld

Bad Hersfeld

Wetzlar

Giessen

Fulda

Frankfurt am Main

sbaden

Mainz

Darmstadt

Ludwigshafen

Wine in Western Germany

Of the great European vineyards, Germany's are the farthest north. There are 13 wine-growing regions in Germany, but the most famous German vineyards are those in the western part of the country, especially the Rheingau, Pfalz, Rheinhessen and Mosel regions. The most widely drunk alcoholic beverage in Germany is beer – unlike in France, Italy or Spain – and therefore the wines produced here are mainly high-quality wines of named vineyards, with a relatively low production of table wine.

Vineyards in Edenkoben, in the southern part of the Weinstraße *(see p351)*, in the Palatinate

The Mosel region produces superb white wines from the Riesling grape. The highest quality wines are those labelled Prädikatswein.

NORTH RHI
WESTPHAL

Coesfeld

Duisburg
Essen
Hag
Düsseldorf
Wup

Dortmu

Köln

Aachen
H
Bonn

Koble

Wittlich

Trier

RHINELAND-
PALATINATE &
SAARLAND

Saarbrücken

Important Facts About German Wine

Region and climate
Gentle, rocky hills stretching along the river bends – perfect for Rieslings – are typical of the Mosel and Rheingau regions. Clay and limestone soil, appropriate for the Müller-Thurgau variety, are found in Hesse on the Rhine. The German climate is considerably more severe than that of southern countries, which gives the wines a slightly sharp, refreshing taste.

Typical grape varieties
The most popular red variety is the Spätburgunder, known in France as Pinot Noir, which produces a heavy wine with a strong flavour. White grapes are much more popular, especially the famous Rieslings, from which the best white wines are produced, the Müller-Thurgau, which gives a light wine with a fruity bouquet, the Grauburgunder (Pinot Grigio) and the Weißburgunder (Pinot Blanc). Less well-known are: Silvaner, Gewürztraminer and Gutedel. Rosé wines are produced from the Portugieser variety, cultivated in the Rhineland–Palatinate (Pfalz) and Rheinhessen.

Famous wine producers
Mosel-Saar-Ruwer: Fritz Haag, Heymann-Löwenstein, Karthäuserhof, Dr. Loosen, Egon Müller, J.J. Prüm, C. von Schubert, Willi Schaefer; Rheingau: Georg Breuer, Robert Weil; Rheinhessen: Gunderloch, Keller; Pfalz: Müller-Catoir, Georg Mosbacher, Dr. Bürklin-Wolf, Reichsrat von Buhl.

The Nahe is famous for its white wines, produced from Silvaner as well as Riesling and Müller-Thurgau grapes.

The Rheingau, where the "Rhine" wines are made, is well known for its Rieslings, particularly the Johannisberger Riesling. A famous vineyard is Prinz von Hessen.

The fountain of the "Wine Witch" in the small town of Winningen, in the Mosel region

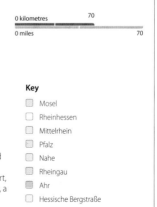

Wine cellars in the former Cistercian monastery at Eberbach in the Rheingau region

Wine Regions

Two well-known wine regions are the Mosel and the Rheingau. Exceptional Rieslings are produced here as well as smaller amounts of other wines. The Rheingau produces a full-bodied red wine in addition to the dominant Rieslings. Rheinhessen produces not only several types of white and red wines, but also a rosé, as does the Palatinate.

0 kilometres   70

0 miles   70

Key

☐ Mosel
☐ Rheinhessen
☐ Mittelrhein
☐ Pfalz
☐ Nahe
☐ Rheingau
☐ Ahr
☐ Hessische Bergstraße

Liebfrauenmilch has been produced in the Rheinhessen region for over 40 years. Originally designed for export, it is a sweetish, medium-class of wine, a blend of several grape varieties.

Romanesque Architecture

Western Germany boasts some of the most interesting examples of Romanesque architecture in the whole of Europe. Charlemagne's famous chapel in Aachen was erected as early as the Carolingian period. The cathedral in Trier and the church of St Maria im Kapitol in Cologne are among the most outstanding creations of early-Romanesque architecture of the Frankish dynasty. In the 12th century, the most important German centres of art were Cologne and the towns of the central Rhineland, with three magnificent cathedrals in Speyer, Mainz and Worms, and the monastery in Maria Laach, preserved to this day.

The choir of St Martin in the Dom in Mainz is an example of the spaciousness that is typical of the late-Romanesque style.

The front elevation of the St Gotthard-Kapelle in Mainz has upper galleries with arcades decorated with friezes. This is a common feature of Romanesque architecture.

Twin western towers

Gallery above the vestibule

The northern portal of the Dom in Worms is framed by an offset architrave and flanked by pairs of columns, as are the portals of many other Romanesque cathedrals.

Lavishly decorated main portal

The monastery in Maria Laach has many capitals with intricate decorations, such as these carvings with human faces.

Cross-vaulting (or cross-ribbed vaulting)

Tower at the intersection of the nave and transept

The portal of the Dom in Trier has a magnificent tympanum, depicting Christ with the Virgin Mary and St Peter.

Romanesque Cathedrals

Cathedrals of the type shown here were built with a basilica-type internal arrangement, including a transept and presbytery, and a double choir usually ending in a semicircular apse. The Dom in Speyer has a massive twin-towered west front, as shown here. The other pair of towers rises above the presbytery, and the intersection of the nave and transept has a lower, broad fifth tower.

The system of vaults also acts as support.

Twin eastern towers

Romanesque Capitals

Romanesque churches in the Rhine Valley feature exquisite stone sculptures. The capitals, with their extraordinary variety of form, ranging from simple blocks to fine figurative or animal-decorated compositions, are of particular interest.

Water-leaf capital of a bonded column

Simplified Corinthian capital

The St Gotthard-Kapelle in Mainz, next to the Dom, was the archbishop's personal chapel for private prayer. It is comparable to similar private buildings in secular palaces.

Cushion (or block or cube) capital

Zoömorphic (animal-decorated) capital

RHINELAND–PALATINATE AND SAARLAND

The Rhineland-Palatinate is one of Germany's most romantic regions, attracting visitors with its vineyards, gentle hills and fairy-tale castles along the Rhine and Mosel valleys. Several towns, such as Trier, have kept reminders of their Roman heritage.

These two states, which border France in the west, did not emerge in their present form until after World War II. The Rhineland-Palatinate was created from the previously independent Bavarian Palatinate and the southern part of the Central Rhineland, making it a true jigsaw-puzzle of territories without a coherent history. The Saarland was under French rule until 1956. Today, it forms a bridge between France and Germany, the two driving forces of European unity.

The turbulent history of the region has left many traces. The picturesque Mosel Valley is lined with grand Medieval fortresses, such as Burg Eltz, while Worms on the Rhine is the setting for most of the Nibelungen legend as well as the residence of the mythical king of Burgundy, Gunther. The Nibelung treasure is still said to lie at the bottom of the Rhine. The impressive cathedral in Worms, along with the Romanesque cathedrals of Speyer and Mainz, is a fascinating example of Medieval sacral architecture.

The "Deutsches Eck" in Koblenz is the strategic spot where the Mosel flows into the Rhine, and Koblenz also marks the beginning of the romantic Rhine Valley. A boat trip upriver, justifiably popular with visitors, will pass some spectacular rocky scenery, including the famous Lorelei Rock and countless castles set among vineyards on either side of the gorge.

The famous ironworks complex in Völklingen is a reminder of a bygone era, when most of the Saarland's inhabitants were active in mining, steelworks and other heavy industries.

Panorama of Saarbrücken, with the Saar river in the foreground

◄ The majestic ceiling in the Hall of Banners, in Burg Eltz

Exploring Rhineland-Palatinate and Saarland

White wine enthusiasts come here, attracted by the beautiful, picturesque valleys of the Rhine and Mosel rivers, with their Medieval castles and small towns. Travelling along the Deutsche Weinstraße (German wine route), Germany's oldest tourist route, visitors can see fascinating historic buildings and taste the different types of wine made by the numerous small vineyards scattered throughout the entire region. Speyer and Mainz have monumental Romanesque cathedrals, while Trier boasts many interesting Roman relics. The huge ironworks in Völklingen is a surprising sight, transporting visitors back to a time when heavy industry ruled much of the region.

The imposing red-sandstone building of the Dom in Mainz

0 kilometres 20

0 miles 20

The proud complex of Schloss Stolzenfels near Koblenz, designed by Karl Friedrich Schinkel

For additional map symbols *see back flap*

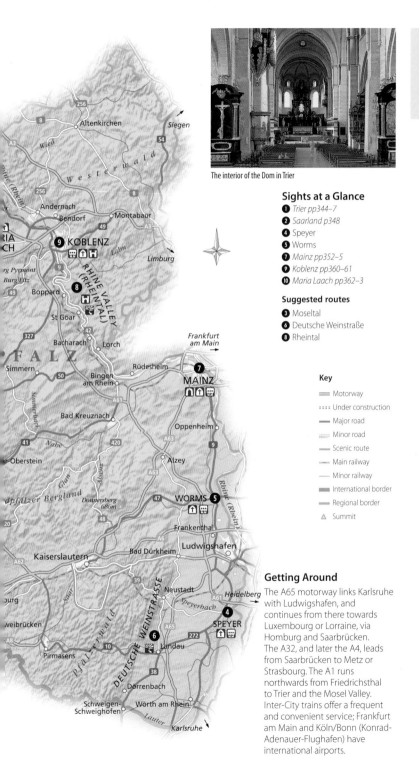

The interior of the Dom in Trier

Sights at a Glance

1 Trier *pp344–7*
2 Saarland *p348*
4 Speyer
5 Worms
7 *Mainz pp352–5*
9 *Koblenz pp360–61*
10 *Maria Laach pp362–3*

Suggested routes

3 Moseltal
6 Deutsche Weinstraße
8 Rheintal

Key

═══ Motorway
∷∷∷∷ Under construction
─── Major road
▭▭▭ Minor road
─── Scenic route
─── Main railway
─── Minor railway
▬▬▬ International border
─── Regional border
△ Summit

Getting Around

The A65 motorway links Karlsruhe with Ludwigshafen, and continues from there towards Luxembourg or Lorraine, via Homburg and Saarbrücken. The A32, and later the A4, leads from Saarbrücken to Metz or Strasbourg. The A1 runs northwards from Friedrichsthal to Trier and the Mosel Valley. Inter-City trains offer a frequent and convenient service; Frankfurt am Main and Köln/Bonn (Konrad-Adenauer-Flughafen) have international airports.

❶ Trier

One of Germany's oldest towns, Trier was founded in 17 BC as *Augusta Treverorum*, supposedly by the Emperor Augustus himself. In the 3rd and 4th centuries it was an imperial seat and the capital of the *Belgica prima* province. In the 5th century the town, which now numbered 70,000 inhabitants, was conquered and destroyed by Germanic tribes. Trier never returned to its former importance – in the 17th century it had a mere 3,600 inhabitants, and 100 years later they still numbered fewer than 4,000. The town, which is also the birthplace of Karl Marx, has a rich architectural heritage.

🏛 Porta Nigra
Tel (0651) 754 24. **Open** Mar & Oct: 9am–5pm daily; Apr–Sep: 9am–6pm daily; Nov–Feb: 9am–4pm daily. 🅿

This town gate, named *Porta Nigra* (black gate) in the Middle Ages because of the colour of its weathered stone, was erected in the 2nd century (a similar gate would have stood at the town's southern entrance). The oldest German defensive structure, it still impresses with its colossal size: 36 m (118 ft) long, 21.5 m (70.5 ft) wide and 30 m (27 ft) high. Two gateways lead onto a small inner courtyard, and there are two tiers of defence galleries with large open windows. It is flanked by the four-storey western tower and the three-storey unfinished eastern tower.

In the 12th century, the building was transformed into the two-storey church of St Simeon and served as such until the early 19th century. Porta Nigra is a UNESCO World Heritage Site.

Petrusbrunnen (fountain of St Peter) in Hauptmarkt

🏛 Hauptmarkt
Trier's main market square, one of the most attractive in Germany, dates back to the 10th century. The Marktkreuz (market cross) erected around the same time symbolized the town's right to hold markets. Today a copy of the original cross is mounted on a granite Roman column, with a relief of the Lamb of God. On the southeastern side of the square is the Petrusbrunnen (St Peter's fountain), from 1595, with sculptures of St Peter and the Four Virtues. On the southwestern side stands the 15th-century Steipe, with a steep gabled roof. Originally it was used by the town councillors as a guesthouse and banqueting hall. The Baroque Rotes Haus (red house) next door dates from 1683. Löwen-apotheke, in a 17th-century building on the southeastern side of the square, is Germany's oldest pharmacy, its records dating back to the 13th century.

🏛 Museum am Dom Trier
Bischof-Stein-Platz 1. **Tel** (0651) 710 52 55. **Open** 9am–5pm Tue–Sat; 1–5pm Sun. **Closed** 1 Jan, 24–26, 31 Dec & public hols. 🅿

A 19th-century former Prussian prison near the cathedral now houses the art collection of the Diocese, including early Christian works of art. Its most prized possession is a 3rd-century ceiling painting from the imperial palace that once stood on the site of the cathedral. Rediscovered in 1945, the fresco painstakingly reassembled over the following decades. Another exhibit is the reconstructed crypt of the Benedictine church of St Maximin, which has 9th-century Carolingian wall paintings.

⛪ Dom St Peter
Tel (0651) 979 07 90. **Open** 6:30am–6pm daily (Nov–Mar to 5:30pm). 🅿

The present cathedral, a UNESCO World Heritage Site, incorporates the remains of an older 4th-century church. The oldest cathedral in Germany, it was constructed in stages – in the early 11th century, late 12th century, mid-13th century and 14th century. It is a triple-nave, two-choir basilica with transept and six towers, and its furnishings include several outstanding objects, such as the tomb of the papal envoy Ivo (1144).

⛪ Liebfrauenkirche
Liebfrauenstr. **Tel** (0651) 979 07 90. **Open** 10am–7pm daily. 🅿

Adjoining the cathedral is the Liebfrauenkirche (Church of Our Dear Lady), built in 1235–60 and also a UNESCO World Heritage Site. Along with the cathedral in Marburg, this is one of the earliest examples of German

The magnificent *Porta Nigra*, gigantic Roman gateway into Trier

For hotels and restaurants in this area see pp492–503 and pp510–33

The Liebfrauenkirche – one of the country's earliest Gothic churches

Gothic architecture. Its ground plan is based on the Greek cross, and the tower above the dome accentuates the intersection of the naves. Its western portal is richly decorated with carved ornaments and iconographic symbols. The interior features many outstanding relics, including 15th-century wall paintings on 12 columns, which symbolize the apostles. There are also some important tombs, including that of a local nobleman, Karl von Metternich (1636), which is in the northeast chapel.

Aula Palatina (Konstantin-Basilika)

Konstantinplatz. **Tel** (0651) 42 570. **Open** Apr–Oct: 10am–6pm Mon–Sat, noon–6pm Sun; Nov–Mar: 11am–noon & 3–4pm Tue–Sat, noon–1pm Sun.

Another UNESCO World Heritage Site, the *Aula Palatina* (Palatinate hall) dates from AD 310. An elongated, rectangular brick building 67 m (220 ft) long, 27.5 m (90 ft) wide and 30 m (98 ft) high with a vast semicircular apse, it served as the throne hall of the Roman emperor or his representative. Following the town's sacking by Germanic tribes, the building was reduced to rubble. In the 12th century the apse was converted into a tower, to accommodate the archbishop. In the 17th century,

VISITORS' CHECKLIST

Road map A5. 99,000. An der Porta Nigra (0651-97 80 80). **w** trier-info.de

Transport An der Porta Nigra.

the *Aula Palatina* was integrated into the newly built palace and its eastern wall partly demolished. During Napoleonic and Prussian times, the hall served as army barracks. The Prussian king Friedrich Wilhelm IV eventually ordered its reconstruction. From 1856 it has served as the Protestant church of St Saviour. Restored after bombing in 1944, its giant size still seems remarkable.

The monumental, austere exterior of the Aula Palatina

Trier City Centre

① Porta Nigra
② Hauptmarkt
③ Museum am Dom Trier
④ Dom St Peter
⑤ Liebfrauenkirche
⑥ Kurfürstliches Palais
⑦ *Aula Palatina*
⑧ Rheinisches Landesmuseum
⑨ Stadtbibliothek
⑩ Kaiserthermen
⑪ Viehmarktthermen

0 metres   400
0 yards   400

Portal of the Kurfürstliches Palais

🏛 Kurfürstliches Palais

Konstantinplatz. **Tel** (0651) 949 42 02.
Open only by appointment.

The Kurfürstliches Palais is considered to be one of the most beautiful Rococo palaces in the world. It has undergone several transformations over the centuries and remains of the earlier buildings can still be seen. The present building was designed by Johannes Seiz and built in 1756–62 for Archbishop Johann Phillipp von Walderdorff. The sculptures were created by Ferdinand Tietz. The central tympanum shows Pomona, Venus, Apollo and a group of angels. The stairs, which lead from the garden to the inner staircase, were designed in the 18th century, but not built until 1981. They have beautiful handrails with typical Rococo motifs. The gardens are equally beautiful and include a miniature garden, a landscape garden and a mother-and-child area.

🏛 Rheinisches Landesmuseum

Weimarer Allee 1. **Tel** (0651) 977 40.
Open 10am–5pm Tue–Sun.
Closed 1 Jan, 24, 25 & 26 Dec.

Only a few steps separate the electoral palace from the Rhine regional museum founded in 1877. Its collections are grouped into four sections: prehistoric, Roman, Franconian-Merovingian, and medieval to contemporary.

The largest space is devoted to Roman relics. Among the star exhibits are a magnificent mosaic depicting Bacchus, from the dining room of a Roman villa, and the lovely statuette of a nymph, undoubtedly the work of a major artist. Also on display is the largest treasure of gold coins from the Roman imperial age. Equally impressive is a stone carving showing a ship loaded with four giant barrels, sailing on the Mosel River. Dating from AD 220, the carving decorated the tomb of a local wine-merchant.

📖 Stadtbibliothek

Weberbach 25.

The municipal library contains a number of important collections that were assembled here in the early 19th century, when many monastic libraries closed down. Among its treasures the library holds 74 full-page miniatures of the famous Trier Apocalypse (c.000), as well as one of the few surviving copies of the first Bible printed by Gutenberg.

🏛 Kaiserthermen

Weimarer Allee/Kaiserstr. **Tel** (0651) 442 62. **Open** Apr–Sep: 9am–6pm; Oct & Mar: 9am–5pm; Nov–Feb: 9am–4pm daily.

Not far from the Rheinisches Landesmuseum are the remains of the vast imperial baths. Built in the early 4th century, during

Nymph in Rheinisches Landesmuseum

the reign of Constantine, they were the third largest bathing complex in the Roman world. The remaining sections of the walls and foundations indicate the former layout. Best preserved are the walls of the *caldarium*, the room with the hot water pool. Next to it is the round *tepidarium*, the warm baths. The spacious *frigidarium* was used for cold baths. Considerable room was given to the *palaestra*, an outdoor exercise area.

🏛 Viehmarktthermen

Viehmarktplatz. **Tel** (0651) 994 10 57.
Open 9am–5pm Tue–Sun.

Following excavations completed in 1994, the remains of these Roman baths, along with those of medieval refuse pits and the cellars of a Capucin monastery, are now on display to the pubic under a large glass canopy.

📖 Jesuitenkirche

Jesuitenstr. 13. **Open** 8:30am–6pm daily.

The Gothic Church of the Holy Trinity was built for Franciscan friars, who settled in Trier before 1238. The surviving church, from the late 13th century, went to the Jesuits in 1570. The college (1610–14) was transferred to the university following the dissolution of the Jesuit Order. It now houses a theological seminary. In the church, the tomb of Friedrich von Spee (1591–1635) is worth a visit.

Vast complex of the Kaiserthermen (imperial baths)

⌂ Amphitheater

Petrisberg. **Tel** (0651) 730 10. **Open** Apr–Sep: 9am–6pm; Oct & Mar: 9am–5pm; Nov–Feb: 9am–4pm daily.

Near the imperial baths are the ruins of the Roman amphitheatre, dating from the 1st century AD. This was the scene of gladiatorial fights and animal contests. The entire structure, consisting of an elliptical arena and a stepped auditorium, was surrounded by a high wall, divided into individual storeys by colonnaded arcades. The complex was designed to seat up to 20,000 people. In the 5th century the inhabitants of Trier used the amphitheatre as a place of refuge from the increasingly frequent raids by Germanic tribes.

⌂ Heiligkreuzkapelle

Arnulfstraße/Rotbachstraße.

The Chapel of the Holy Cross, in a secluded spot, is one of Trier's more interesting historic buildings. Built in the Romanesque style in the second half of the 11th century, at the initiative of the parson of Arnulfa Cathedral, it is a small building with a ground plan in the shape of the Greek cross and an octagonal tower set within the cross. Although it suffered serious damage during World War II, it was meticulously restored to its original state in the years 1957–8.

⌂ Basilika St Matthias

Matthiasstraße 85. **Tel** (0651) 170 90. **Open** 8am–7pm daily.

This church's history dates back to the 5th century, when it became the burial place of St Eucharius, the first bishop of Trier. From the 8th century, the church was run by Benedictine monks. In the 10th–11th centuries a new church was erected as burial site of the relics of the apostle, St Matthew. It was twice remodelled at the turn of the 15th to 16th centuries, when it acquired its rich Gothic vaults. The present abbey dates from the 16th century. The shrine holding the apostle's relics ensured that the church became one of the most important destinations for pilgrims in the region.

The ruins of Barbaratherme, ancient Roman baths

⌂ Barbaratherme

Südallee. **Tel** (0651) 994 10 57. **Closed** until further notice (dilapidated).

Not far from the Roman bridge across the Mosel River are the ruins of the Barbara baths, dating from the 2nd century AD. Although above ground not much has been preserved, the extensive system of underground heating channels, the *hypocaustum*, clearly demonstrates the original size of this public bath complex. In the Middle Ages, Patrician and aristocratic families transformed the baths into their residences. In the 17th century Jesuit monks dismantled the remaining structures, and used the recovered building materials to construct their own college.

⌂ Kirche St Maximin

Maximinstraße. **Tel** (0651) 979 07 90. obligatory.

In the Middle Ages there were as many as four abbeys in Trier. St. Maximin Abbey was founded on the burial site of its patron saint, who died in AD 325. The surviving church was built in the 13th century, on the foundations of the previous buildings. Its Romanesque–Gothic forms were partly obscured by the remodelling work carried out in 1580–1698. Now deconsecrated, the church is used as a music venue. It is possible to book guided tours of the atmospheric crypt. The Carolingian wall paintings that originally adorned the crypt are now in the Museum am Dom Trier *(see p344)*.

⌂ Kirche St Paulin

Thebäerstraße. **Tel** (0651) 270 850. **Open** Mar–Sep: 9am–6pm Mon, Wed–Sat, 11am–6pm Tue, 10am–6pm Sun; Oct–Feb: 9am–5pm Mon, Wed–Sat, 11am–5pm Tue, 10am–5pm Sun.

This church was built in the 12th century, on the foundations of an older Christian chapel. In 1674 it was blown up by the French army. St Paulin, its patron saint and bishop in Trier, was one of the few to voice his opposition to the Aryan credo of Emperor Constantine II, in which he rejected the divinity of Christ and proclaimed himself alone to be made in God's image. Paulin did not meet with a martyr's death, but was exiled to Phrygia (now Turkey), where he died in 358. The present church, a true gem of Rococo architecture, was designed by Balthasar Neumann, who also created the main altar.

Baroque ceiling paintings in the Rococo Kirche St Paulinus

❷ Saarland

This German state, bordered by Luxembourg and France, was long disputed between France and Germany, but has now been firmly integrated into the Federal Republic. Almost forgotten are its coal and steel industries, which declined in the 1960s and 70s. The region has seen a turbulent history – it was ruled in turn by Celts, Romans and Franks. In the 17th century, on the order of Louis XIV, Vauban built the town-fortress of Saarlouis. Saarbrücken, an 18th-century town, is famous for its Baroque architecture, mostly created by Friedrich Joachim Stengel.

Von Nassau-Saarbrücken family tombs in Saarbrücken

Saarbrücken

Road map B6. 190,000.
Rathaus St Johann, main entrance (0681-194 33 or 93 80 90). Max Ophüls-Preis (Jan), Perspectives du Théâtre (May), Saar Spektakel (Aug).
w saarbruecken.de

The capital of Saarland Saarbrücken was first built as the Franconian fortress of *Sarabrucca*. The town, on the Saar River, flourished in the 17th and 18th century, under the rule of Duke Wilhelm Heinrich von Nassau-Saarbrücken.

The churches and other prestigious buildings are largely the work of Friedrich Joachim Stengel, court architect to the von Nassau-Saarbrücken family. He designed the Catholic **Basilika St Johann** (1754–8) in the market square, as well as the monumental **Schloss**, the palace on the opposite bank of the Saar (1739–48). Its original, modern façade, created in 1989 after damage in World War II, is the work of the architect Gottfried Böhm.

Opposite the Schloss stands the **Altes Rathaus** (old town hall), dating from 1748–50, which today houses an interesting museum of ethnography. The Protestant

Ludwigskirche (1762–75) is one of the last works completed by Stengel. A true architectural gem, it is laid out in the shape of a Greek cross. The **Stiftskirche St Arnual**, in the southwestern part of the town, contains the splendid Gothic and Renaissance tombs of the von Nassau-Saarbrücken family. Since 1960 it has also featured a "German–French Garden". One of the garden's entrances leads to Gulliver-Miniwelt (miniature world of Gulliver), where small versions of the world's most famous buildings are exhibited.

Völklinger Hütte, the historic steelworks in Völklingen

Völklingen

Road map B6. 43,500.
Rathausstr. 57 (06898-132 800).

About 10 km (6 miles) west of Saarbrücken lies the small industrial town of Völklingen, which was granted town status in 1937. In 1881, Carl Röchling, a native of Saarbrücken, bought a small steel mill, the **Völklinger Hütte**, which he soon developed as the heart of his family's industrial empire. The steel mill still exists, and in 1994 it became a UNESCO World Heritage Site, listed as a historical object of international importance. Another attraction is an original, early 20th-century housing estate.

Homburg

Road map B6. 42,000. Rathaus, Am Forum 5 (06 841-10 11 66).

This town grew up around the Hohenburg castle, which now is just a picturesque ruin. In the Schlossberg nearby were unearthed the remains of a fortress, which was built in 1680–92 by Sébastien Le Preste Vauban on the orders of the French King Louis XIV. The greatest attraction of Homburg, however, is its Schlossberg caves, the largest man-made caves in Europe, cut into the red sandstone.

Ottweiler

Road map B5. 16,000.
Schlosshof 5 (06 824-35 11).

The small picturesque town of Ottweiler has a beautifully preserved old town. The Alter Turm (old tower), which in the 15th century formed part of the town's fortifications, now serves as a belfry to the parish church, whose origins go back to the 15th century. Its present Baroque form was the work of Friedrich Joachim Stengel from 1756–7.

Rathausplatz is a beautifully proportioned complex of historic houses, mostly the homes of wealthy citizens, dating from the 17th and 18th centuries. Many have half-timbered upper halves. The Altes Rathaus (old town hall, 1714) combines two different building methods – the base is stone, the top half-timbered. In Schlossplatz is the Renaissance Hesse Haus (c.1590).

❸ Moseltal

The Mosel river, 545 km (338 miles) long, is one of the longest tributaries of the Rhine. The Mosel valley between Trier and Koblenz, where the Mosel flows into the Rhine, is one of the most beautiful parts of Germany. On both sides of the river, romantic castles tower over endless vineyards, where excellent white grapes are grown – both are typical features of the charming landscape.

② **Burg Thurant** Near the town of Alken stands Thurant castle, which was built in the 13th century. It is the only twin-towered castle along the Mosel.

① **Matthias-Kapelle** This late-Romanesque chapel was once used to house the remains of the Apostle Matthew. These were later transferred to the Matthiaskirche in Trier.

⑤ **Burg Pyrmont** Pyrmont's grim 13th-century medieval castle was remodelled and extended several times during the Baroque era.

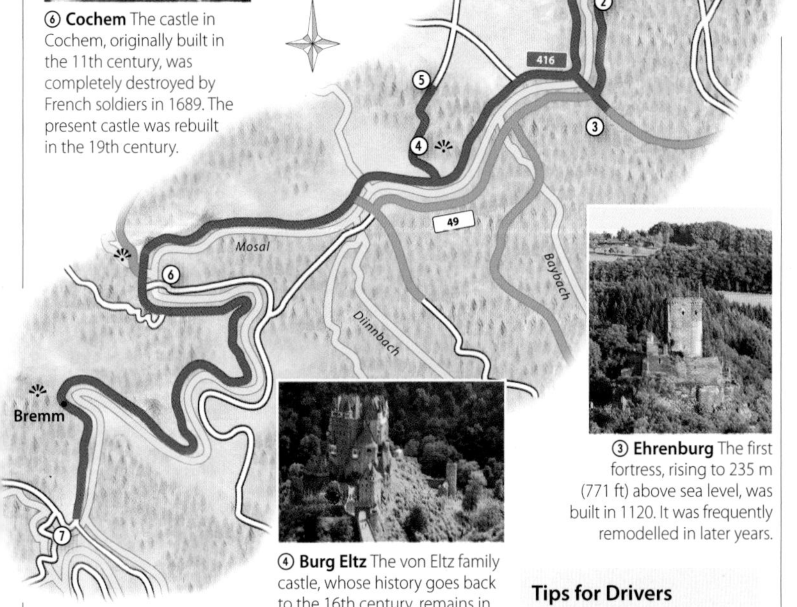

⑥ **Cochem** The castle in Cochem, originally built in the 11th century, was completely destroyed by French soldiers in 1689. The present castle was rebuilt in the 19th century.

Mosal

Dünnbach

Baybach

Bremm

③ **Ehrenburg** The first fortress, rising to 235 m (771 ft) above sea level, was built in 1120. It was frequently remodelled in later years.

④ **Burg Eltz** The von Eltz family castle, whose history goes back to the 16th century, remains in private hands to this day, but it is open to visitors.

⑦ **Burg Arras** This fortress was built around 900–950 as part of the fortifications against frequent pillaging raids by Normans.

Key

▬ Suggested route
▬ Scenic route
— Other road
═ River, lake
☆ Viewpoint

Tips for Drivers

Length of the route: about 75 km (46 miles).
Stopping-off points: there are numerous restaurants and cafes in Cochem; small pubs can be found along the entire route.
Additional attractions: a boat trip on the Mosel River, from Koblenz to Cochem or Trier.

0 km 5
0 miles 5

Altar in the Dreifaltigkeitskirche, in Speyer

❹ Speyer

Road map B6. 🏙 47,000. 🚇
ℹ️ Maximilianstraße 13 (06232-14 23
92). 🎭 Brezelfest (Jul), Kaisertafel (Aug),
Altstadtfest (Sep), Bauernmarkt (Sep).

In the 7th century, Speyer was
the seat of a diocese. As a free
city of the Holy Roman Empire
from 1294 until 1779, 50 sessions
of the imperial parliament took
place here. The most famous
session was in 1529, when the
Protestant states of the Holy
Roman Empire lodged a
protest (hence "Protestant")
against the decisions of the
Catholic majority.

The most important historic
building in Speyer is the
Romanesque **Kaiserdom** (St
Maria und St Stephan), a World
Heritage Site. For a time, before
being superseded by the
gigantic abbey of Cluny in
Burgundy, this was the largest
monumental Romanesque
building in Europe. The Dom,
built in 1025–61 on the initiative
of Conrad II, is a triple-nave,
cross-vaulted basilica with
transept, vestibule, choir,
apse and several towers. Its
magnificent triple-nave crypt,
the burial place of Salian
emperors, has stunning stone
carvings, some worked by
Lombard stonemasons. **St
Afra's**, dating from around 1100,
has some interesting sculptures,
including *Christ Bearing His Cross*
and *Annunciation* (c.1470). The
Domnapf, a vast stone bowl seen
at the forecourt of the cathedral,
dates from 1490. It was used
during enthroning ceremonies,

when the newly anointed bishop
would order it to be filled with
wine right to the brim in order
to win the hearts of his flock.

Another 11th-century
interesting building is the **Mikwe**
in Judenbadgasse, a ritual
Jewish bath for women, and
the remains of a synagogue
nearby. To the west of the
Dom stand the remains of the
medieval fortifications including
the **Altpörtel**, a 14th- to
16th-century town gate. The
late-Baroque **Dreifaltigkeitskirche** (church of the Holy
Trinity), built in 1701–17, is an
architectural masterpiece with
marvellous interiors.

❺ Worms

Road map B5. 🏙 83,000. 🚇
ℹ️ Neumarkt 14 (06241-250 45).

Worms is one of the oldest
towns in Germany. In the Middle
Ages it was the home of the
Reich's Parliament, hosting more
than 100 sessions. The **Dom St
Peter** is one of the largest
late-Romanesque
cathedrals in
Germany, along
with the cathedrals
in Mainz and
Speyer. It was built
in 1171–1230 as a
two-choir basilica,
with eastern
transept, four
towers and two
domes. Its northern nave
includes five beautiful sandstone reliefs from a Gothic
cloister, which no longer exists.
The interior furnishings date
mainly from modern times.
Particularly noteworthy is the
high altar designed in
the 18th century
by Balthasar

Tombstones in the Heiliger Sand Jewish
cemetery in Worms

Neumann, and the stalls dating
from 1760. A short distance from
the cathedral is the Marktplatz
(market square), with the
interesting **Dreifaltigkeitskirche** church of the Holy
Trinity (1709–25). Northeast of the
square stands the **Stiftskirche
St Paul** (church of St Paul), built
in the 11th–12th centuries and
completed in the 18th century,
with original 13th century wall
paintings. Nearby is the only
surviving Renaissance
residential building in
Worms, the **Rotes
Haus** (red house).

In the western part
of the old town is the
Heiliger Sand (holy
sands), the oldest
Jewish cemetery in
Europe; the earliest
tombstones date
from the 11th and
12th centuries. Also
worth a visit is the 14th-century
Liebfrauenkirche (Church of Our
Dear Lady). The most noteworthy
feature of the **Magnuskirche**
(11th–12th centuries) is its
crypt, from around AD 800,
while the **Stiftskirche
St Martin** (late 11th
century) has some
interesting portals.

A relief from 1488, in the
Dom in Worms

The vast Romanesque Dom St. Peter in Worms

❻ Deutsche Weinstraße

The "German Wine Route" starts in Bockenheim and ends in Schweigen, near the Alsatian town of Weißenburg. The tour suggested here includes the most interesting sections of this route. This is one of the most beautiful parts of Germany, where visitors will encounter aspects of German and European historical and cultural heritage at every step, set among the picturesque scenery of the endless vineyards covering the sun-drenched slopes of the Pfälzer Wald.

⑧ Bad Dürkheim
This famous resort is best known for its annual Wurstmarkt, held in September. Despite its name, it celebrates the wine harvest, and sausages take second place.

⑥ St Martin
Not much remains of the Romanesque church of St Martin, but the 16–18th-century buildings surviving in the town continue to enchant visitors.

⑦ Hambacher Schloss
The castle's fame is based on the Hambacher Fest when, on 27 May 1832, students protested against the fragmentation of Germany. It was restored and is now a national monument and museum.

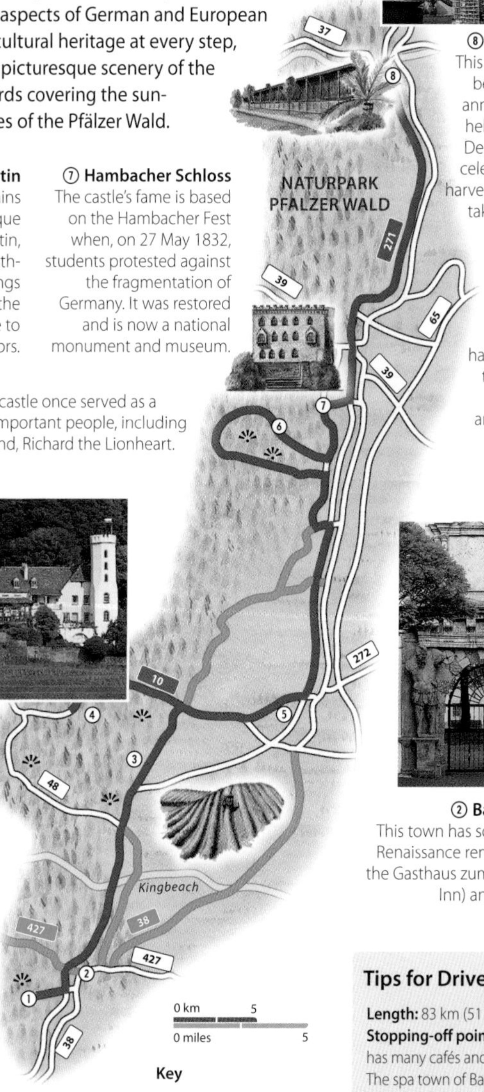

NATURPARK PFÄLZER WALD

⑤ Landau
This little town has the remains of the fortress built by Vauban, and an extraordinarily beautiful post-Augustinian church.

④ Trifels
This grim, ruined castle once served as a prison for many important people, including the King of England, Richard the Lionheart.

③ Leinsweiler
Hilltop Hof Neukastel was once the home of the German impressionist artist Max Slevogt, and to this day, wall paintings by the artist can be seen here.

② Bad Bergzabern
This town has some interesting Renaissance remains, including the Gasthaus zum Engel (Angel's Inn) and a royal castle.

Kingbeach

① Dörrenbach
The star attractions in this small town are the half- timbered town hall and the Gothic church surrounded by fortifications.

0 km 5
0 miles 5

Key

▬▬▬ Suggested route
▬▬▬ Scenic route
═══ Other road
──── River, lake
🔆 Viewpoint

Tips for Drivers

Length: 83 km (51 miles).
Stopping-off points: Landau has many cafés and restaurants. The spa town of Bad Dürkheim, with its cafés and wine bars, is also a good place to stop.
Signs: Look for signposts showing a bunch of grapes or a wine jug.

● Mainz

The town, which grew out of the Roman military camp *Moguntiacum* established in 39 BC, is today the capital of the Rhineland-Palatinate. Mainz is the home of an important German television station (ZDF). It is also the main centre of trade for the popular Rhine wines. Its splendid late-Romanesque cathedral symbolizes the power of the Kurfürsten, the prince-electors, who used to crown German kings. Indisputably the town's most famous son is Johannes Gutenberg – the inventor of printing.

🏛 Kurfürstliches Schloss
Peter-Altmeier-Allee.
Römisch-Germanisches
Zentralmuseum.
Tel (06131) 91 240.
Open 10am–6pm
Tue–Sun.

Construction of the Baroque electoral palace, which began in 1627 during the rule of Archbishop Georg von Greifenclau, was completed more than a century later, in 1775–6, under Johann Friedrich Carl Joseph von Erthal. Today the palace houses the fascinating museum of Roman and Germanic history.

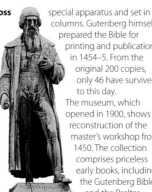
Statue of Gutenberg
in Gutenbergplatz

special apparatus and set in columns. Gutenberg himself prepared the Bible for printing and publication in 1454–5. From the original 200 copies, only 46 have survived to this day.

The museum, which opened in 1900, shows a reconstruction of the master's workshop from 1450. The collection comprises priceless early books, including the Gutenberg Bible and the Psalter published in 1457 by Fust & Schöffer, Gutenberg's erstwhile partners and latterday creditors. The Psalter was the first work to be printed using three different colours of inks.

🏛 Gutenberg-Museum
Liebfrauenplatz 5. **Tel** (06131) 12 26 40.
Open 9am–5pm Tue–Sat, 11am–3pm
Sun. **Closed** public holidays.

Johannes Gensfleisch zum Gutenberg became famous as the inventor of the printing process using movable metal type. The letters were cast in a

🏛 Kaiserdom
See pp354–5.

🏛 Gutenbergplatz
A short distance from the Protestant parish church of St John is Gutenbergplatz, a

pleasant square with a statue of the inventor. Set in its paving stones is a line marking the 50th parallel. The Staatstheater (state theatre) in the square is a late Neo-Classical building (1829–33).

Historic half-timbered houses
in Kirschgarten

🏛 Kirschgarten
Near the Baroque hospital of St Roch, built in 1721 and now an old people's home, runs a street called Kirschgarten (cherry orchard). This is one of the loveliest parts of old Mainz, which suffered serious damage in World War II. The well-preserved complex of historic half-timbered houses, dating from the 16th–18th centuries, makes this district worth visiting and a pleasant place for a stroll.

🏛 Kirche St Stephan
Kleine Weißgasse 12. **Tel** (06131) 23 16 40. **Open** Mar–Oct: 10am–5pm Mon–Sat, noon–4:30pm Sun; Nov–Feb: 10am–4:30pm Mon–Sat, noon–4:30pm Sun.

This Gothic parish church was built in stages on the site of an edifice dating from the 10th century. Construction began in the mid-13th century and continued until the end of the 15th century. The resulting church is a triple-nave hall with eastern transept and a single-nave choir. The adjacent late 15th-century cloisters are a true gem of late-Gothic design. The original stained-glass windows in the presbytery, destroyed in World War II, were replaced by six new ones in 1978–81, designed and partly made by Marc Chagall. Set against a

The Baroque Kurfürstliches Schloss and museum

Landing stage for boats on the Rhine

VISITORS' CHECKLIST

Practical Information
Road map B5. [N] 190,000.
[i] Im Brückenturm am Rathaus
(06131-28 62 10). [N] Mainzer
Fastnacht (Jan/Feb), Johannis-
nacht (Jun), OpenOhr Festival
(Whitsun), Mainzer Zeltfestival
(end of Jun/early Jul) Weinforum
Rheinhessen (last weekend in
Oct). [W] **mainz.de**

Transport
[N]

beautiful blue background,
they depict biblical scenes,
including Abraham with the
three travellers, the Patriarch
pleading to God to spare the
righteous in Sodom and
Gomorrah, Jacob's dream, and
Moses with the Tablets of the
Ten Commandments.

The church interior contains
many other interesting original
features. The four large brass
candelabra were cast in Mainz
in 1509. The small polyptych
depicting the Crucifixion dates
from around 1400, while its
movable wings were made
some 100 years later. The niche
below the tower contains the
Holy Tomb (c.1450).

[N] Römersteine

Southeast of the University
campus are the impressive
remains of the Roman aqueduct,
dating from the 1st century AD.
The Zahlbach valley was a
vantage point for the
southwestern flank of the Roman
camp, *Castrum Moguntiacum*,
but it presented a major
technical problem of supplying
the camp with drinking water.
The aqueduct was built by
Roman engineers. Although
some of its pillars were 23 m
(75 ft) high, the present remains
only reach up to 10 m (32 ft).

Environs

The pride of **Oppenheim**, a
centre of the wine trade 20 km
(12 miles) to the south, is its
Gothic Katharinenkirche, a
church built of red sandstone
in the 13th–14th centuries.
The neighbouring hill and the
ruins of Landskron castle
provide the most spectacular
view over the Rhine valley. The
Weinbaumuseum, museum of
viticulture, is also worth visiting.

Mainz City Centre

① Kurfürstliches Schloss
② Gutenberg-Museum
③ Kaiserdom
④ Gutenbergplatz
⑤ Kirschgarten
⑥ Kirche St Stephan

Kaiserdom

The greatest attraction of Mainz is its superb cathedral, gleaming red in the sunshine. Together with those of Speyer and Worms it is one of the only three Romanesque imperial cathedrals to have survived almost intact to this day. Its basic framework was laid out in 1081–1137 and 1183–1239, but its oldest parts date from the early 11th century, with the rows of Gothic side chapels added during the 13th and 14th centuries. Although neither the Gothic altars nor the magnificent choir screen have survived to this day, it is still possible to see the large group of bishops' monuments from the 13th to the 19th century.

Portal of the "Memorie" Burial Chapel
The late-Gothic portal, leading to the Romanesque burial chapel of the cathedral canons, was made by Madern Gerthener, after 1425.

Pulpit
This Neo-Gothic pulpit was made in 1834 by Joseph Scholl.

St Stephen's Choir
The Romanesque eastern choir, one of the first parts to be built, is simpler in style than other parts of the cathedral.

KEY

① **Round staircase towers** are from the previous building, built in the early 11th century.

② **Two large and two small towers** are symmetrically positioned on the ends of the cathedral.

★ **Monument of Heinrich Ferdinand von der Leyen**
This Baroque monument of the Dom rector, the work of Johann Mauritz Gröninger, was erected during his lifetime, in 1706.

VISITORS' CHECKLIST

Practical Information
Bischöfliches Dom- und Diözesanmuseum: Domstr. 3.
Tel (06131) 25 33 44. **Open** 10am–5pm Tue–Sun (to 7pm Thu).
W **dommuseum-mainz.de**

St Martin's Choir
The late-Romanesque western choir with its trefoil closing is an early 13th-century addition.

Main entrance

★ **Stalls**
These superb Rococo oak stalls encircle almost the entire presbytery. They were created by Franz Anton Hermann, who completed them in 1767.

Tomb of Jakob von Liebenstein
The late-Gothic tomb of the archbishop von Liebenstein, who died in 1508, is the work of an unknown artist. It depicts the deceased in draped robes, lying under an ornate canopy.

⑥ Rhine Valley (Rheintal)

The Celts called it *Renos*, the Romans *Rhenus*, while to Germanic tribes it was the Rhein, or *Vater Rhein* ("Father Rhine"), as it is known today. The source of this mighty, 1320-km (825-mile) long river is in Switzerland, from where it flows through Liechtenstein, Germany, Luxembourg and Holland, yet the Germans regard it as "their" river. The Rhine is steeped in many legends – it was into this river that Hagen von Tronje, faithful follower of King Gunther and slayer of Siegfried, threw the treasure of the Nibelungs, and Lohengrin's swan is said to appear near the town of Kleve *(see p392)* to this day.

Bonn

Bendorf

Rhein

Siegen

Kobl

Trier

Saarbrücken

① **Stolzenfels** The existing castle complex has little in common with the original 13th-century fortress, which burned down in 1688. In the early 19th century, the ruins were bought by the future king Friedrich Wilhelm IV. The castle, designed by the famous Prussian architect Karl Friedrich Schinkel, was built in 1833–45.

| 0 kilometres | 5 |
| 0 miles | 5 |

Saarbrücken

② **Boppard** Boppard's most famous sights are the remains of the Roman military camp of Bodobrica, the church of St Severus (12th–13th centuries), famous for its wall paintings, and the Medieval market square, built on the site of Roman hot baths. Michael Thonet, the creator of famous chairs made from bent wood, was born here in 1796.

Tips for Walkers

Length of the route: about 125 km (78 miles).
Stopping-off points: the best places to stop are Boppard or Bacharach, offering the widest choice of bars and restaurants.
Further attractions: a boat trip on the Rhine river, from Koblenz to Mainz.

③ **Burg Rheinfels** This castle ruin was begun in 1245 by Count Diether V of Katzenelnbogen, and was partially destroyed by French Revolutionary army troops in 1797. Some of the outer buildings are a luxury hotel, wellness centre and restaurant.

◀ The River Mosel near Trittenheim, Rheinland-Palatinate

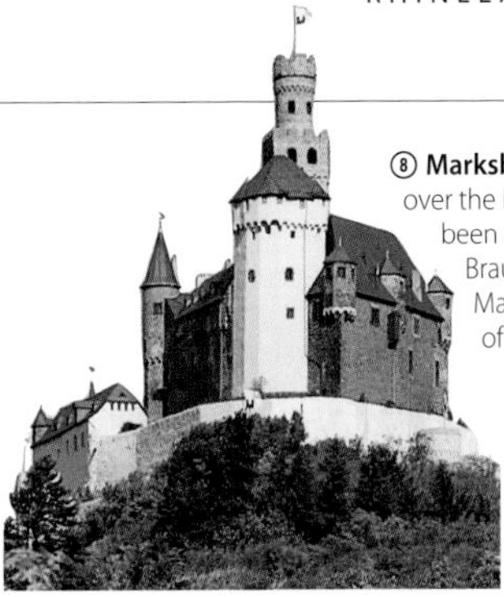

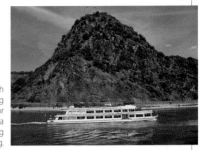

⑧ **Marksburg** From 1117 this castle, which towers over the Rhine and the small town of Braubach, has been owned at different times by the von Braubachs and the powerful Epstein family. The Marksburg is the only castle along this stretch of the Rhine which has never been damaged.

⑦ **Loreley** The Loreley Rock, onto which many boats have been smashed by the strong currents, has been a source of inspiration for many poets. A 19th-century legend tells of a beautiful blonde combing her hair and luring unlucky sailors to their deaths with her song.

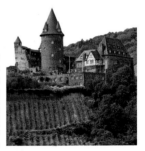

④ **Pfalzgrafenstein** In the middle of the Rhine River stands the proud and mighty fortress of Pfalzgrafenstein – one of the most beautifully situated castles in the Rhineland. Its origins date back to 1326, but its present shape is the result of Baroque refurbishments in the 17th–18th centuries.

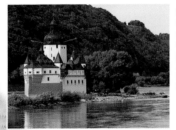

⑤ **Bacharach** The town has a unique complex of historic buildings, with fortified town walls, the church of St Peter, the ruins of the Gothic chapel of St Werner, and Burg Stahleck – the castle towering over the town which today houses a youth hostel.

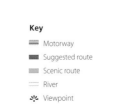

⑥ **Burg Sooneck** In the 13th century, Sooneck castle was the home of various robber knights. The fortress fell into ruin in the late 17th century, due to frequent raids by the French. In the 19th century it was bought by the Hohenzollerns, who rebuilt the castle in its original form.

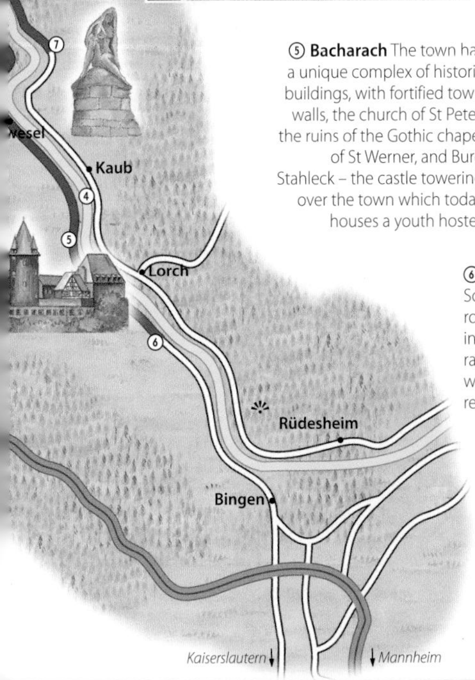

Limburg
7
wesel
Kaub
4
5
Lorch
6
Rüdesheim
Bingen
Kaiserslautern
Mannheim

Key

- Motorway
- Suggested route
- Scenic route
- River
- Viewpoint

For hotels and restaurants in this area see pp492–503 and pp510–33

⑨ Koblenz

The name which the Romans gave to their camp in 9 BC – *castrum ad confluentas,* meaning the "camp at the confluence" – reflects the town's strategic importance, for it is here that the Mosel flows into the Rhine. From the Middle Ages until the 19th century, Koblenz was the seat of the powerful archbishop–electors of Trier. It was also the birthplace of Prince von Metternich, the 19th-century Austrian statesman. Today it is a modern metropolis which attracts many visitors, and is the main centre of the region's cultural life.

Romanesque twin-tower façade of the Basilika St Castor

🏛 Deutsches Eck

Ludwig-Museum im Deutschherrenhaus: Danziger Freiheit 1. **Tel** (0261) 30 40 40. **Open** 9am–6pm daily.

The "German corner" is the place where the Mosel flows into the Rhine. Here stands the enormous equestrian statue of Emperor Wilhelm I. Designed by Bruno Schmitz, it was erected in 1897, destroyed in World War II and replaced with a copy in 1993. The name refers to the complex of buildings known as Deutschherrenhaus belonging to the Order of Teutonic Knights. Only part of the three-wing residence of the Order's Commander, built in the early 14th century, has survived to this day. The building now houses the Ludwig-Museum, with a collection of modern art (mainly German and French post-1945 artists) donated by Peter and Irene Ludwig.

🏛 Basilika St Castor

Kastorstraße 7.

The collegial church of St Castor was built in 817–36 on the initiative of the archbishop of Trier, on a site previously occupied by an early Christian church. The treaty of Verdun, which divided the Carolingian Empire between the three sons of Ludwig I the Pious, was signed here in 843. The present appearance of the church is the result of extensions from the 11th–13th centuries. Inside are beautiful wall epitaphs of the Trier archbishops Kuno von Falkenstein (1388) and Werner von Königstein (1418). Also noteworthy is the pulpit dating from 1625.

🏛 Florinsmarkt

Mittelrhein-Museum: Florinsmarkt 15–17. **Tel** (0261) 129 25 20. **Open** 10:30am–5pm Tue–Sat, 11am–6pm Sun.

This square takes its name from the Romanesque-Gothic church of St Florin, which dates from the 12th and 14th centuries. The Mittelrheinisches Museum, with its collection of archaeology and medieval art of the Central Rhine region, occupies three historic buildings. The Kaufhaus, in the centre, dates from 1419–25 and 1724. The image of a horse-rider shows the robber baron Johann von Kobem, beheaded in 1536, who now sticks his tongue out at passers-by every half hour. To its right stands the late-Gothic Schöffenhaus, and to its left is the Baroque Bürresheimer Hof, from 1659–60.

The Renaissance Alte Burg, now housing archives and a library

🏛 Alte Burg

Burgstraße 1.

In the Middle Ages, the powerful von Arken family had a fortified residence built for themselves in the northwestern section of the Roman fortifications. In 1277 the building was taken over by Heinrich von Finstingen, the archbishop of Trier, who ordered its extension. The fortress was to protect him from the citizens of Koblenz who were striving for independence. Successive archbishops continued with the conversion of the building, which acquired its final shape in the 17th century. The eastern Renaissance façade of the complex is particularly attractive. Today it houses the municipal archives and parts of the library.

The spur between the Mosel and the Rhine, called Deutsches Eck

⛪ Liebfrauenkirche

Florinspfaffengasse 14.
Tel (0261) 315 50.
Open 8am–6pm Mon–Sat, 9am–12:30pm Sun.

At the highest point in the old town stands the Romanesque church of Our Dear Lady. Its history dates back to early Christian times, but its present form is the result of remodelling work carried out in 1182–1250. A triple-nave basilica with galleries, it has a twin-tower western façade. The beautiful, elongated Gothic choir was added in 1404–30.

⛪ Kurfürstliches Schloss

Neustadt.
Not far from the bridge across the Rhine stands the electoral palace, an example of the Rhineland's early Neo-Classical architecture. It was built, and for a short time occupied, by Clemens Wenzeslaus von Sachsen, the last of Trier's electors. Construction of the castle began in 1777, to a design prepared by Michael d'Ixnard, and continued until 1786, overseen by Antoine François Peyère the Younger.

Statue of the Madonna in Liebfrauenkirche

🏰 Festung Ehrenbreitstein

Landesmuseum Koblenz
Tel (0261) 66 75 40 00.
Open 15 Mar–mid-Nov: 9:30am–5pm daily.

On the opposite side of the Rhine stands the mighty fortress of Ehrenbreitstein, one of the largest in the world and barely changed since Prussian days. A smaller fortress was erected on this site in 1000, and extended in subsequent years by the archbishops and electors of Trier, who lived in it from 1648 to 1786. Trier's holiest relic, the Rock Christi (vestments of Christ) was kept here. The fortress offers splendid views over Koblenz, the Rhine and the Mosel. Today, it is home to the **Landesmuseum**

Koblenz (regional museum) with an interesting collection on the development of technology, and to the **Rhein-Museum** with hydrological collections. At Wambachstraße 204, in the same district, is the house of Beethoven's mother.

The Classical façade of the Kurfürstliches Schloss

Koblenz City Centre

① Deutsches Eck
② Basilika St Castor
③ Florinsmarkt
④ Alte Burg
⑤ Liebfrauenkirche
⑥ Kurfürstliches Schloss
⑦ Festung Ehrenbreitstein

0 metres 250
0 yards 250

⑩ Maria Laach

A true masterpiece of German and European Romanesque architecture, the Maria Laach Abbey stands next to the Laacher See, a lake formed in the crater of an extinct volcano. Its construction started in 1093 at the behest of Heinrich II, who also lies buried here. Building continued from 1093 until 1220. Until secularization in 1802, the Abbey was the home of the Benedictines. Since 1892 the church has once again been resounding with Gregorian chants, which are sung here several times a day.

View from the West
The monumental western façade of the abbey consists of a semicircular apse, a massive, square 43-m (141-ft) tall central tower, and two slim 35-m (115-ft) tall flanking towers.

★ Tomb of Heinrich II
The tomb of the Count Palatine Heinrich II, who died in 1095, dates from about 1280. His effigy has been reproduced in a magnificent walnut wood block, which to this day has kept its original colours.

Löwenbrunnen
The lion fountain, which adorns the atrium, was made in 1928. It was modelled on the famous Alhambra fountain in Granada, Spain.

Detail from a Column Capital
The western entrance is surrounded by columns with interesting capitals. Carved figures can be seen, including that of a devil recording the sins of each entrant and others which are pulling each other's hair out.

Church entrance

Main entrance

Mosaics

The interior is decorated with paintings and mosaics created over centuries by artists of the Beuronese School. In the main eastern apse is a mosaic of Christ the Ruler dating from 1911.

VISITORS' CHECKLIST

Practical Information
Road map B5. **Tel** (02652) 59350.
Open Easter–Oct: 9:30–11:15am, 1:15–4:45pm Mon–Sat, 1:45–4:45pm Sun & hols; Nov–Easter: 2:30–4:45pm Mon–Sat, Sun as above. Crypt: video show.

🖉 ▢ 📷

Transport
🚌 6032 from Niedermendig, 6031 from Andernach.

Stained-glass Windows

Three vast stained-glass windows in the main eastern apse were made by a contemporary artist, W. Rupprecht, in 1956.

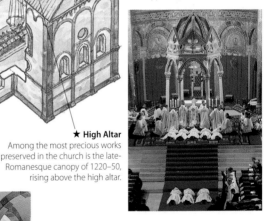

★ High Altar

Among the most precious works preserved in the church is the late-Romanesque canopy of 1220–50, rising above the high altar.

★ Crypt

The vaults of the exquisite early-Romanesque crypt are supported by austere square capitals. This is also the resting-place of Gilbert, the first abbot at Maria Laach.

KEY

① **The "Paradise"**, the courtyard, is meant to symbolize the Garden of Eden.

② **The church towers** have arcaded galleries, typical of Romanesque style.

HESSE

Hesse lies in the very heart of present-day Germany. Scattered over the region are reminders of its former glory: Roman camps, Carolingian buildings, Romanesque churches and Gothic cathedrals with lofty spires. Territorial partitions, so typical of the former German Reich, brought about the blossoming of art and architecture during the Renaissance and the Baroque eras.

A post-World War II creation, the borders of this federal state roughly approximate those of its 13th-century forerunner. For most of its history, Hesse was divided between Hesse-Darmstadt and Hesse-Kassel.

Today, when admiring the distinctive panorama of Frankfurt am Main – its towering banks and skyscrapers more reminiscent of New York's Manhattan than of a European metropolis – it is hard to believe that this was the birthplace of Goethe. The importance of this city extends far beyond Hesse: it is the financial centre of the European Union, and its annual Book Fair is the largest event of its kind in the world.

Darmstadt became famous as a centre for Jugendstil (Art Nouveau) early in the

20th century. Wiesbaden is the seat of Hesse's state government, and Marburg is one of the best-known university towns. In the 16th century, at the times of fierce religious feuds, the first Protestant university was built here. The Church of St Elizabeth is one of the earliest examples of Gothic architecture in the region. Lovers of modern art will know of Kassel – every five years it hosts the *documenta*, an exciting exhibition of artistic developments.

He sse has much more to offer. The Waldecker Land, near Kassel, boasts the Eder lake and attractive health resorts. Eberbach in the picturesque Rheingau, the wine-growing area around Eltville, has a well-preserved former Cistercian abbey, which has been used as a film setting.

Park and Baroque Orangery of the palace complex in Fulda

◀ The dramatic juxtaposition of old and new buildings in Frankfurt am Main

Exploring Hesse

Eltville, situated in the Rheingau, one of Germany's most important wine-producing regions, is famous for its Riesling wine. Frankfurt am Main, known around the world as a great financial and commercial centre, also has fantastic museums, drawing visitors with their outstanding art collections, while the International Book Fair is a true paradise for readers and bookworms. In the 19th century, wealthy socialites chose Bad Homburg as their favourite spa, while the romantic town of Marburg still has the lively atmosphere of a university town.

The Dom in Limburg, overlooking the Lahn river

The giant Niederwalddenkmal near Rüdesheim

Sights at a Glance

1. *Kassel pp368–9*
2. Fritzlar
4. Fulda
5. Alsfeld
6. Marburg
7. Gießen
8. Wetzlar
9. Weilburg
10. Limburg
11. Bad Homburg
12. Eltville
13. Wiesbaden
14. Kiedrich
15. Rüdesheim
16. *Frankfurt am Main pp378–9*
17. Darmstadt
18. Lorsch
19. Michelstadt

Excursions

3. Waldecker Land

For additional map symbols *see back flap*

The Messeturm in the Frankfurt fairgrounds, designed by Helmut Jahn

Getting Around

The A7 motorway, cutting across Hesse in a north–south direction, provides a fast transport link. Starting from Hannover, it runs through Göttingen, Kassel and Fulda to Würzburg in Bavaria. The A4 runs from Dresden, via Weimar, to Bad Hersfeld. From there visitors can take the A7 or the A5, towards Gießen, Bad Homburg, Frankfurt am Main and onwards to Darmstadt and Heidelberg. The fast ICE railway connects Kassel and Frankfurt am Main with Basel (in Switzerland), Stuttgart, Berlin and Munich. Frankfurt am Main has one of Europe's largest airports.

| 0 kilometres | 20 |
| 0 miles | 20 |

Key

- ▭ Motorway
- ▭ ▭ Motorway under construction
- ▬ Major road
- ▭ Minor road
- ▬·▬ Main railway
- ▬ Minor railway
- ▬ Regional border
- △ Summit

Statue of the Brothers Grimm in Hanau

❶ Kassel

The cultural, scientific and commercial centre of northern Hesse, Kassel suffered severe damage during World War II due to the armaments industries based here, and much of the town has been rebuilt in functional 1950s style. Today, Kassel has become synonymous with one of the most important shows of contemporary art – *documenta* – held here every five years (the 13th documenta is scheduled for 2017). The town is equally famous for its outstanding collection of European art, housed in the splendid Schloss Wilhelmshöhe, as well as for its parks and gardens, especially the large forest-park adjoining the castle.

17th-century cameo-decorated tureen in the Landesmuseum

🏛 Hessisches Landesmuseum

Brüder-Grimm-Platz 5. **Tel** (0561) 316 800. **Closed** until further notice.

Outstanding items in the Neo-Baroque Hesse Regional Museum, built in 1910–13, are the astronomical instruments, originally installed in 1560 in a landgrave's castle, which no longer exists. The ethnographic section has displays of Hessian folk costumes and regional craft items.

The Landesmuseum also houses the Tapetenmuseum (wallpaper museum). Established in 1923, the museum presents the history of wallpaper and the methods of its production

Wallpaper (1670–80), in the Tapetenmuseum

around the world. The collection includes examples of leather wall coverings (cordovans) and wallpapers representing Secession and Art-Deco styles. *Vues de Suisse* (views of Switzerland), dating from 1802, is one of the earliest examples of scenic wallpaper. It was printed using 95 different inks and 1,024 wooden blocks. Equally famous is the panoramic *Rénaud et Armide*, from the workshop of Joseph Dufours, printed in 1828 using 2,386 wooden blocks.

During renovation, some displays are held in the nearby Torwache building.

🏛 Neue Galerie

Schöne Aussicht 1. **Tel** (0561) 316 80 400. **Open** 10am–5pm Tue–Sun.

The New Gallery, founded in 1976 and devoted to 19th- and 20th-century art, occupies a Neo-Classicist building from 1871–74. The gallery's collection includes a number of canvases by artists such as Carl Schuch, Max Slevogt and Lovis Corinth. The splendid collection of 20th-century paintings focuses on German Expressionism. An entire room is also devoted to the installations of the controversial sculptor and performance artist Joseph Beuys.

🏛 Brüder-Grimm-Museum

Schöne Aussicht 2. **Tel** (0561) 787 20 33. **Open** 10am–5pm daily (8pm Wed). **Closed** 1 Jan, Good Friday, 24, 25, 31 Dec. 🗪

Next to the New Gallery is the small Schloss Bellevue, built in 1714 by Paul du Ry. Although brothers Jacob and Wilhelm Grimm were born in Hanau, they lived in Kassel from 1798 until 1830, and in 1960 a museum devoted to the lives and work of the famous fairy-tale tellers and philologers was opened, containing many first editions.

An illustration for Cinderella, one of the Grimm fairy-tales

🏛 Kunsthalle Fridericianum

Friedrichsplatz 18. **Tel** (0561) 707 27 86. **Open** 11am–6pm Wed–Sun. **Closed** Mon–Tue. 🗪

Königsplatz and Friedrichsplatz were designed by the court architect, Simon Louis du Ry. The northwestern side of the latter is occupied by the Neo-Classical Fridericianum, built by du Ry in 1769–76. Its founder, Landgrave Friedrich II, had always intended it to be a museum, and it became the second public museum (after the British Museum in London) to be built in Europe, and the first one on the European mainland. Since 1955, the Fridricianum has been the main venue for Kassel's multi-media contemporary art show – the *documenta*, which every five years takes over the entire city. An additional exhibition hall, the Documentahalle, was opened in 1992, in the nearby Staatstheater.

🏛 Ottoneum

Steinweg 2. Naturkundemuseum **Tel** (0561) 787 40 66. **Open** 10am–5pm Tue–Sun (to 8pm Wed, 6pm Sun). 🗪

For hotels and restaurants in this area see pp492–503 and pp510–33

The Ottoneum, home of the first permanent theatre in Germany

The Ottoneum (1604–5), built for Landgrave Maurice the Learned, was Germany's first permanent theatre. Designed by Wilhelm Vernukken and remodelled in the late 17th century by Paul du Ry, it was converted into a natural history museum in 1885.

Orangerie

An der Karlsaue 20c. **Tel** (0561) 316 80 500. Museum für Astronomie und Techniksgeschichte: **Open** 10am–5pm Tue–Sun (until 8pm Thu). **Closed** 24, 25, 31 Dec. Zeiss-Planetarium: 2pm Tue, Sat, 3pm Wed, Fri, Sun, 2 & 7pm Thu. (free Fri.)

The southern part of Kassel is home to Karlsaue, a vast palace and garden complex named after its founder, Landgrave Karl. The site was earlier occupied by a small Renaissance Schloss (1568), surrounded by a garden. In 1702–10 Pierre-Etienne Monnot built the large Orangery, which now houses a museum of astronomy and technology. Monnot is also the creator of Marmorbad, a bath pavilion from 1722, while the kitchen pavilion was designed by Simon Louis du Ry in 1765.

Wilhelmshöhe

Gemäldegalerie Alter Meister. Schloss Wilhelmshöhe. **Tel** (0561) 31 68 00. **Open** 10am–5pm Tue–Sun (until 8pm Thu). **Closed** 1 May, 24, 25, 31 Dec.

At the top of Wilhelmshöher Allee, designed in 1781, stands Wilhelmshöhe, a magnificent palace and park. The palace is situated along the axis of the avenue that runs up the hill, through a long forest glade. The original intention was to fill it with a series of cascades, but only a few of these were ever built. At the top of the hill is the Octogon, crowned with the statue of Hercules, the symbol of the town. The palace was designed by Simon Louis du Ry and Heinrich Christoph Jussow and built in 1793–1801 for the Elector Wilhelm. Now it houses the Gemäldegalerie Alte Meister with its outstanding collection of European masters including paintings by Rubens, Titian, Rembrandt, Dürer and Poussin. There is a large and attractive park.

Cascades, with Octogon and Hercules statue, in Wilhelmshöhe

VISITORS' CHECKLIST

Practical Information
Road map C4. 195,000. Hauptbahnhof, Bahnhof Wilhelmshöhe. Obere Königsstraße 8 (0561-707 71 64). documenta (every 5 years, next to be held in 2017), Zissel (Aug), Museumsnacht (Sep), Kasseler Musiktage (Nov). **kassel.de**

Transport

Kassel City Centre

① Hessisches Landesmuseum and Deutsches Tapetenmuseum
② Neue Galerie
③ Brüder-Grimm-Museum
④ Fridericianum
⑤ Ottoneum
⑥ Orangerie

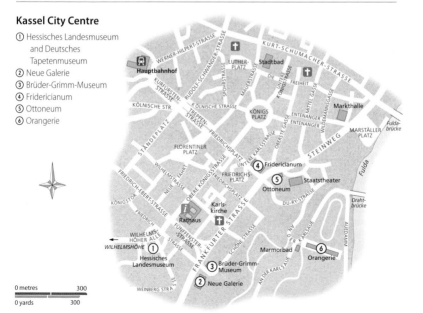

0 metres 300
0 yards 300

➋ Fritzlar

Road map C4. 15,500. Kasseler Straße. *i* Rathaus, Zwischen den Krämen 5 (05622-98 86 43). Pferdemarkt (Jul), Stadtfest (Aug).

The beautiful town of Fritzlar has preserved its original, nearly complete ring of medieval walls with watch-towers, bastions and over 450 half-timbered houses from various periods. In the early 8th century, St Boniface, the apostle of Germany, had the holy oak of the Germanic god Donar, which grew here, cut down to build a Christian chapel. In 724 he founded the Benedictine **Dom** (abbey of St Peter). In 1118 the original church was replaced by a cruciform, vaulted basilica with a triple-nave crypt, and this was remodelled in the 13th and 14th centuries. Adjacent to the church is a lovely 14th-century ambulatory. The church interior is rich in historic treasures. The east wall of the transept is decorated with wall paintings from c.1320, and the south nave includes a Pietà (1300). The 14th-century **parish church** of the Franciscan Order nearby has a lovely painting of the Madonna, on the northern wall of the choir.

In Fritzlar's picturesque old town stands the **Rathaus** (town hall), whose lower floors date from the 12th century, while the upper ones were added in the 15th century. The exquisite **Hochzeitshaus** (wedding house), in the street of the same name, is a Renaissance half-timbered house, built in 1580–90, which now houses a museum. Another interesting sight is the **Alte Brücke**, a 13th-century stone bridge spanning the Eder River.

Relief of St Martin, on the walls of the Rathaus in Fritzlar

➌ Waldecker Land

The Waldecker Land, situated west of Kassel, was once an independent county and later, until 1929, a free state within the German Reich. Today this region, with its Eder-Stausee (reservoir), is one of the most attractive tourist regions in Germany. The wooded hills provide a perfect setting for long rambles, the roads and tracks are ideally suited for cycling tours and the rivers and lakes permit visitors to practise a wide variety of watersports.

② **Korbach**
Korbach is a beautiful old town with many half-timbered houses. Worth seeing are the Gothic church of St Kilian with its interesting 14th-century pulpit, and the church of St Nicholas, with the Baroque tomb of Georg Friedrich von Waldeck (1692).

⑤ **Frankenberg**
This small town is brimming with half-timbered houses. The town hall (1509), also half-timbered, has humorous polychrome wood-carvings. The Gothic Marienkirche with its 15th-century wall paintings is also worth visiting.

Padert

Key

━━ Motorway
━━ Suggested route
━━ Scenic road
━━ Other road
┄┄ River, lake
✳ Viewpoint

0 kilometres   10
0 miles   10

For hotels and restaurants in this area see pp492–503 and pp510–33

① Bad Arolsen

Both the sculptor Christian Daniel Rauch and the painter Wilhelm von Kaulbach were born in this spa town, and they are commemorated in two museums. The star attraction, however, is the Baroque castle (1713–28) of the von Waldeck family, designed by Julius Ludwig Rothweil.

③ Waldeck

The old fortress of Waldeck is now a hotel. It offers superb views over the Eder-Stausee reservoir and the small town of Waldeck with its 18th-century half-timbered houses. The Gothic town church has a high altar (c.1500), devoted to the Virgin Mary.

Tips for Visitors

Length of route: 110 km (68 miles).
Stopping-off points: There are many good cafés and restaurants in every town along the route.
Further attractions: Cruises and ferries run on the Edersee. A viewing platform on top of the Peterskopf hill, near Hemfurth, can be reached by electric train.

④ Bad Wildungen

This popular spa town has many charming half-timbered houses. The church has a priceless altar painted with scenes of the Passion by Konrad von Soest (1403).

Projecting gate of the Baroque Stadtschloss in Fulda

The Brothers Grimm

The two brothers are known around the world as collectors of German folk-tales, which were first published in 1812 and subsequently translated into most languages. Fairy-tales such as *Hänsel and Gretel*, *Cinderella* and *Little Red Riding Hood* have been favourites for generations of children. Above all, however, the brothers were scholars. In his *German Grammar*, published in 1819, Jacob Grimm proved that all German dialects sprang from a common origin, and thus laid the foundations of German philology. The Grimm Brothers also initiated the publication of the *Dictionary of the German Language*.

❹ Fulda

Road map C5. ⚏ 65,000. 🚉
ℹ️ Bonifatiusplatz 1 (0661-1 02 18 12).

Fulda's history began in March 744, when Sturmius, a pupil of St Boniface, laid the foundation stone for the Benedictine abbey. Ten years later the body of St Boniface, who had been killed by Frisian pagans, was laid to rest here. The town, which grew around the abbey, experienced its heyday during the Baroque period, and a new Baroque building, designed by Johann Dientzenhofer, was built in 1704–12 on the foundations of the old abbey. The **Dom St Salvator und Bonifatius** is a triple-nave basilica with a dome above the nave intersection, a monumental eastern façade and a shrine with the saint's relics under the high altar, in the western section.

Opposite the cathedral stands the **Stadtschloss** (former episcopal palace), a shoe-shaped edifice, built by Johann Dientzenhofer and Andreas Gallasini, with richly decorated Baroque and Rococo interiors. Particularly noteworthy are the Kaisersaal (imperial hall) on the ground floor, the magnificent Fürstensaal (hall of princes) and the charming Rococo-style Spiegelsaal (chamber of mirrors) on the first floor. Today, some of the palace chambers hold an impressive collection of porcelain. The palace complex includes a large landscaped garden. To the north of the Dom stands the round **Michaels-kirche**, a Carolingian chapel dating from 822, one of the

oldest church buildings in Germany. Inside the church has a ring of eight columns and a crypt supported by a single column. The circular gallery, the long side nave and the western tower are 11th-century additions.

Other interesting sights in Fulda are the Baroque **Heilig-Geist-Kirche** (church of the Holy Spirit; closed to the public), built in 1729–33 by Andreas Gallasini, and the late 18th-century parish church of St Blasius. In the 8th century, five abbeys were established on the four hills surrounding the town. On Petersberg stands the former Benedictine **Propsteikirche St Peter (Liobakirche)**, from the 9th–15th centuries, with a Carolingian crypt. Inside the church is one of Germany's oldest wall paintings, dating from 836–47.

❺ Alsfeld

Road map C4. ⚏ 18,000. 🚉
ℹ️ Am Markt 12 (06631-9 11 02 43).
🎭 Pfingstfest (Whitsun), Historischer Markt (Jun), Fairy-Tale Day (Jun), Stadt- und Heimatfest (Aug), Historischer Markt (Sep).

The first historic records of Alsfeld date from the late 9th century. Today the town attracts visitors with its pretty old town with numerous 16th–17th century half-timbered houses. On the eastern side of the town square stands a grand late-Gothic **Rathaus** (town hall), built in 1512–16, and one of the finest examples of half-timbered structures anywhere in Germany. Other interesting features in the market square are the stone **Weinhaus**, with its distinctive stepped gable (1538), and the Renaissance **Hochzeitshaus** (wedding

Half-timbered houses in Alsfeld

house), dating from 1565. Opposite the town hall stands the **Stumpfhaus** (1609), its façade beautifully decorated with wood carvings and paintings. From the town hall runs the picturesque Fulder Gasse, with the Gothic parish church **Walpurgiskirche** (13th–15th centuries), which has 15th-century wall paintings. In Rossmarkt stands the former Augustian **Dreifaltigkeits-kirche** (church of the Holy Trinity), from the 13th–15th centuries. It was from here that in 1522 the monk Tilemann Schnabel began to spread the Reformation in Alsfeld.

The **Märchenhaus** (Fairy-Tale House) on Markt has several rooms devoted to the tales of the Brothers Grimm and a collection of puppets. The 18th-century **castle** in Altenburg, 2 km (1 mile) from Alsfeld, enjoys a hilltop position.

❻ Marburg

Road map C4. 🏔 80,000. 🚉
ℹ️ Pilgrimstein 26 (06421-991 20).
📅 Maieinsingen (30 Apr), 3-Tage Marburg (Jul), Elisabethmarkt (Oct), Weihnachtsmarkt (Dec).
🌐 **marburg.de**

When in 1248 the county of Hesse broke away from Thuringia, Marburg became one of the most important seats of the landgraves. The first landgrave, Heinrich II, lived in the castle that towers over the town. The town's history is inseparably linked with the 13th-century figure of Elisabeth of Thuringia, wife of Ludwig IV, who devoted her life to the poor and died here. In 1527, Philipp the Magnanimous founded the first Protestant university in the Reich at Marburg. He also instigated the first Marburg Colloquy in 1529, to unify the Protestant faith. The "articles" presented by Martin Luther to Melanchthon and Zwingli later formed the basis for the Augsburg Creed. Today, Marburg is a picturesque university town. A tour of the

town should start from the **Elisabethkirche**, at the bottom of the hill. Built in 1235–83, it is (after Trier) Germany's second purely Gothic church. There is a large set of Gothic altars from the early 16th century, including the altars of St Elisabeth (1513) and of the Holy Family (1511). Next to the north choir entrance stands the statue of St Elisabeth with a model of the church (1480).

The Gothic portal of the Elisabethkirche in Marburg

The choir contains the tomb of the Saint, positioned under the baldachin (c.1280). The vestry houses the greatest treasure, the reliquary of St Elisabeth (1235–49). In the south choir is an interesting group of monuments to the Hessian landgraves, from the 13th–16th centuries.

Detail on the Rathaus, in Marburg

The **Universitäts-museum für Bildende Kunst** holds a collection of paintings produced after 1500, with a predominance of 19th- and 20th-century German artists. Around the market square stands a group of historic, half-timbered houses from the 14th–17th centuries. Particularly pretty are the Sonne (sun, No. 14), the Stiefel (boot, No. 17) and the house at No. 19. The Steinernes Haus (stone house, No. 18), built in 1318, is the oldest in Marburg, along with that at No. 13 Hirschgasse. At No. 16 Markt is the Renaissance Künstlerhaus (artists' house). High above the town towers

the **Landgrafenschloss**, the landgraves' castle dating from the 10th–16th centuries. The two-storey Fürstenbau (dukes' building) has a large ducal chamber, dating from 1330. The Wilhelmsbau was built in 1492–8. It houses a museum of sacral art with mementos of the debate between Luther, Zwingli and Melanchthon.

🏛 **Elisabethkirche**
Elisabethstraße. **Tel** (06421) 655 73.
Open Apr–Oct: 9am–5pm Tue–Sun; Nov–Mar: 10am–4pm Tue–Sun.

🏛 **Universitätsmuseum für Bildende Kunst**
Biegenstraße 11. **Tel** (06421) 282 21 66.
Open 11am–1pm & 2–5pm Tue–Sun.

🏛 **Landgrafenschloss und Universitätsmuseum für Kulturgeschichte im Wilhelmsbau**
Schloss 1. **Tel** (06421) 282 21 66.
Open 10am–6pm Tue–Sun (Nov–Mar: to 4pm).

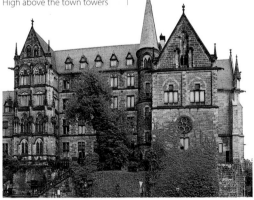

The Alte Universität (old university) in Marburg

❼ Gießen

Road map C4. 🚊 72,000. 🚉
ℹ️ Berliner Platz 2 (0641-194 33).

Giessen was granted town status in 1248, and in 1607 it acquired its university. In Brandplatz stands the partially reconstructed **Altes Schloss** (old palace), dating from the 14th–15th centuries. Now the home of the Oberhessisches Museum, it holds a large collection of art dating from the Gothic period to today.

The **Botanischer Garten** is one of Germany's oldest botanical gardens, established in 1609 for the purposes of scientific research. To the north of it stands the **Neues Schloss** (new palace), built in 1533–9 for Landgrave Philipp the Magnanimous. It miraculously escaped damage when the town was bombed in 1944. The Wallenfelssches Haus nearby houses interesting ethnological collections. The only remaining part of the Gothic **Pfarrkirche St Pankratius**, which was almost completely destroyed in 1944, is its tower, dating from 1500.

At No. 2 Georg-Schlosser-Straße is the **Burgmannenhaus**, an attractive half-timbered mansion dating from the 14th century.

Portal of the Altes Schloss in Gießen

Along with the old stable block in Dammstraße, it is the only half-timbered building that has survived to this day.

❽ Wetzlar

Road map C5. 🚊 52,000. 🚉
ℹ️ Domplatz 8 (06441-997 755).

Occupying a picturesque spot on the banks of the Lahn river, Wetzlar is overlooked by the ruins of the 12th-century **Kalsmunt** fortress. It was built for the Emperor Friedrich I Barbarossa (1122–90). Only parts of the tower remain intact. The **Dom** (Collegiate Church of St Mary) was begun in 897 but by the late 15th century had only been partly completed. The splendid western double portal has remained unusable for the last 500 years – although the iconography of the tympanum was finished, the stairs leading to the entrance were never built. If they had been built, they would have led not to the church's nave, but to a courtyard. Wetzlar's Dom is a rare, perhaps even unique surviving example of the typical appearance of most European churches in the mid-15th century. Inside the church are several interesting historic artifacts, including the statue of the *Madonna on the Moon Crescent* (mid-15th century) and a late-Renaissance *Crucifixion*.

In 1772, the young Johann Wolfgang Goethe spent three months in Wetzlar working as an apprentice at the court of appeal. During this time he fell in love with Charlotte Buff, called Lotte, who was engaged to one of Goethe's friends. The **Lottehaus**, her former home, has a collection of items relating to Goethe and Lotte. It was the suicide of a friend, Karl Wilhelm Jerusalem, who lived in the 18th-century **Jerusalemhaus** at No. 5 Schillerplatz, that

inspired Goethe to write his tragic novel, *The Sorrows of Young Werther* (1774). Jerusalem had suffered unrequited love, just like Goethe. The novel, which was published two years later, made Goethe famous around Europe, but it also unwittingly led many young men to commit suicide.

The Gothic south tower of the Dom in Wetzlar

❾ Weilburg

Road map B5. 🚊 13,500. 🚉
ℹ️ Mauerstraße 6 (06471-76 71).

Weilburg enjoys a particularly scenic location in a bend of the Lahn river. The town is dominated by the Renaissance–Baroque **Schloss** of the Nassau-Weilburg family. The monumental castle complex was created in stages. Its main section dates from the Renaissance era; the east wing was built in 1533–9, the south and west wings in 1540–48 and the west tower in 1567. The northern part of the palace was completed in 1570–73. In the late-17th century, various Baroque additions were made, mainly to the interior of the castle. The 16th-century furnishings show the rich ornamentation typical of the German Renaissance. The **Obere Orangerie** (upper orangery), built in 1703–5 and today used for temporary exhibitions, and the **Hofkirche** (castle church), dating from 1707–13, are the work of Ludwig Rothweil. Terraces lead from the castle to the Lahn river, which is crossed by an 18th-century stone bridge. In Frankfurtstraße stands the **Heiliggrabkapelle** (Chapel of the Holy Sepulchre), dating from 1505.

⑩ Limburg

Road map B5. 🚶 31,000. 🚆
ℹ️ Bahnhofsplatz 2 (06431-61 66).

Limburg's history dates back to the 8th century. In 1821, the town became the see of a newly created diocese.

The **Dom** (collegiate cathedral church of St George) towers high above the Lahn river. This monumental building, whose style combines late-Romanesque and early French-Gothic, was erected in 1190–1250. Its well-proportioned interior contains a rich variety of historic artifacts, including some 13th-century wall paintings in the presbytery and the transept, a font dating from the same period and the tombstone of Konrad Kurzbold, who founded the first church on this site.

To the south of the Dom stands the **Burg** (castle), an irregular structure built in the 13th–16th centuries. It houses the interesting **Diözesan-museum** (Diocese museum).

Limburg has many original examples of beautiful half-timbered buildings. The houses at No. 1 Römerstraße, No. 6 Kolpingstraße, No. 4 Kleine Rütsche and No. 11 Kornmarkt date from the last decade of

Romanesque–Gothic wall paintings in the Dom in Limburg

the 13th century. Near the 14th-century **Alte Lahnbrücke** (old Lahn bridge), with its defensive towers, stands a mansion belonging to the Cistercians of Eberbach. The post-Franciscan Sebastiankirche (church of St Sebastian) dates from the 14th and 18th centuries.

⑪ Bad Homburg

Road map C5. 🚶 52,000. 🚆
ℹ️ Kurhaus, Louisenstraße 58 (06172-178 37 10). 🎭 Fugato (Sep every two years – 2014, 2016), Laternenfest (Sep yearly).

Bad Homburg grew up around a fortress whose earliest records date back to 1180. Friedrich II von Hessen-Homburg initiated the conversion of the medieval castle into the **Schloss**, a

Baroque palace built in 1678–86. It features a magnificent Festsaal (ballroom) and Spiegelkabinett (hall of mirrors). The only part of the former complex remaining today is the 14th-century Weißer Turm (white tower). Following the annexation of Hesse-Homburg by Prussia in 1866, the palace became the favourite summer residence of the royal then (from 1871) imperial family.

Along with Baden-Baden and Wiesbaden, Homburg was one of Germany's most fashionable spas, and today the town reflects its former splendour. The **Kurpark**, a landscaped park established in 1854–67, was designed by Peter Joseph Lenné.

The **Spielbank** (1838), in Brunnenallee claims to be the oldest casino in the world. Built in 1887–90, the **Kaiser-Wilhelm-Bad** is still used as the main bath complex for therapeutic treatments. An Orthodox chapel, designed by Leonti Nikolayevich Benois for the Russian Orthodox nobility, was finished in 1899.

Environs
Saalburg, 7 km (4 miles) to the northwest, has a Roman fortress, which was completely reconstructed in 1898–1901. The fortress formed part of the *limes*, the fortified border that separated the Roman Empire from its Germanic neighbours in the 1st to 3rd century AD.

The grand edifice of the Kaiser-Wilhelm-Bad in the Kurpark, Bad Homburg

⑫ Eltville

Road map B5. 🚩 17,000. 🚊
ℹ️ Rheingauer Str. 28 (06123-90 98 0).
🎭 Biedermeier- und Sektfest (Jul).

In the 2nd century, the area that is now the old town was a Roman *latifundium*, a large agricultural estate. In 1332, Eltville was granted town status. Part of the Mainz diocese, it is today known for its excellent sparkling wine.

In 1337–45 the **Burg** (castle) was extended at the request of Archbishop Heinrich von Virneburg. The east wing of the castle was added in 1682–3 by Giovanni Angelo Barell. The only part of it remaining today is the five-storey residential tower; the rest of the building is a picturesque ruin. In the tower are original 14th-century wall paintings and friezes.

The twin-naved **Pfarrkirche St Peter und St Paul** (parish church) was built in 1350–1430. The vestibule has well-preserved wall paintings (1405) showing scenes from the Last Judgement. The town boasts several attractive mansions, including Hof Langenwerth von Simmern (1773), Stockheimer Hof (1550) and Gräflich-Eltzscher Hof (16th–17th century).

Crest of the Hessische Staatsweingüter-Vinothek, in Eltville

⑬ Wiesbaden

Road map C5. 🚩 280,000. 🚊
ℹ️ Marktplatz 1 (0611-17 29 930).
🎭 Internationale Maifestspiele (May), Theatrium (Jun), Rheingau Wine Festival (Aug), Christmas Market (Nov–Dec).

Wiesbaden is the modern capital of Hesse. Highly valued as a spa by the Romans, who exploited the healing properties of its waters, the town grew from a small settlement known as *aquae mattiacorum* after the Germanic tribe of the Mattiacs. In 1774 the Nassau-Usingen family chose Wiesbaden as their residence. This, as well as the

The Baroque Biebrich Palace, south of Wiesbaden

subsequent rapid growth of the town as a spa resort in the 19th century, laid the foundations for its lasting prosperity. Today, the town is still dominated by large-scale developments carried out in the spirit and style of Classicism and Historicism.

The **Stadtschloss** (municipal castle), today the seat of the state parliament, was built in 1835–41. In Schlossplatz the Neo-Renaissance **Marktkirche**, built in 1853–62, soars above the town's other buildings. In front of the church stands a statue of Wilhelm I the Great von Nassau-Oranien. The oldest building in the town is the **Altes Rathaus** (old town hall), dating from 1610. In Wilhelmstraße is the imposing Neo-Renaissance and Neo-Baroque **Hessisches Staatstheater** (state theatre). It was built in 1892–4 for Kaiser

Wilhelm II to the designs of the theatre architects Fellner and Helmer. Adjacent to the Marktkirche is the attractive Kurhauskolonnade (spa house colonnade). It was erected in 1825 and is the longest colonnade in Europe. The early 20th-century **Kurhaus** (spa house) itself, with its grand façade and portico, is the work of Friedrich Thiersch. Inside is the original **Spielbank** (casino), where Fyodor Dostoyevsky and Richard Wagner tried their luck at the tables.

To the south of the town centre stands **Schloss Biebrich**, where the counts von Nassau-Usingen resided until the early 19th century. The Schloss was built in stages during the 18th century. The north pavilion was built first, in 1700, followed nine years later by the south pavilion. The wings, which join the two pavilions, and the central rotunda were added during the first two decades of the 18th century. Finally, the two external wings were added in 1734–44, creating an overall horseshoe layout. The interior is richly furnished, predominantly in Baroque-Rococo style.

On the northern outskirts of the town is a large hill, the Neroberg, whose summit can be reached by funicular railway. At the top is the so-called **Griechische Kapelle** (Greek chapel). Built in 1847–55 by Philipp Hoffmann, it served as a mausoleum for Princess Elisabeth von Nassau, the niece of Alexander I Tsar of Russia, who died young.

The attractive façade of Hessisches Staatstheater in Wiesbaden

The ornate Gothic portal of Basilika St Valentin, in Kiedrich

⑭ Kiedrich

Road map B5. ⛰ 3,400. 🚉
ℹ️ Marktstr. 27 (06123-90 50 10).

The earliest recorded mention of Kiedrich was in the mid-10th century, in a document produced by the Archbishop Friedrich of Mainz. One of the town's main attractions is the **Basilika St Valentin**, a gem of Gothic architecture. The church was built in stages, beginning with the main hall (1380–90). The west tower was added in the early 15th century and the light, lofty choir in 1451–81. Some time later the central nave was raised to the level of the choir, creating a row of galleries above the aisles, and at the same time the magnificent star vaults were created. The whole project was financed from donations made by countless pilgrims who came to pray to the relics of St Valentine, kept here since 1454. A statue of the saint adorns the western portal. The early 15th-century tympanum depicts the *Annunciation* (on the left) and the *Coronation of the Virgin Mary* (on the right); above is an image of *God the Father giving His Blessing,* with two archangels playing musical instruments. Inside, the church harbours an incredible wealth of ancient art treasures. The high altar and St Catherine's altar in the south aisle date from the late-Renaissance period. The magnificent Gothic stalls were created in 1510, while the church organ is one of the oldest in Germany, with pipes made in 1310. Next to the parish church stands a late-Gothic, two-storey funeral chapel built in 1445.

Kiedrich has several interesting old mansion houses, such as the Schwalbacher Hof (1732). The **Rathaus** (town hall) is evocative of the late-Gothic style, although it was built much later (1585–6).

Environs

Five km (3 miles) west of Kiedrich, in Oestrich, is **Kloster Eberbach**, a former Cistercian abbey. This vast complex, built between the 12th and 14th centuries, was once home to nearly 300 monks and is one of the best-preserved medieval monasteries in Germany. The church interior provided the setting for some of the scenes in the film *The Name of the Rose*, based on the novel by Umberto Eco. The Cistercians used to have their own vineyards here, and today the abbey buildings are used by the Hessian Wine Co-operative to press, ferment, store and sell Eberbacher Steinberg, a famous white Rheingau wine.

A short way to the west, in **Winkel**, stands the Baroque castle of Reichardshausen, which in the early 19th century was the home of Princess Luise von Nassau.

🏠 **Kloster Eberbach**
Tel (06723) 91 78 115. **Open** Apr–Oct: 10am–6pm daily; Nov–Mar: 11am–5pm daily. **Closed** Carnival Mon, 24, 25, 31 Dec. ♿

⑮ Rüdesheim

Road map B5. ⛰ 10,000. 🚉
ℹ️ Rheinstraße 29 (06722-906 150).
🎆 Fireworks (Jul), Weinfest (Aug).

Rüdesheim, enjoying a picturesque location on the banks of the Rhine, has a long history going back to Roman times. The town is famous for the **Drosselgasse**, a street lined with countless wine bars and shops. There are also the remains of two castles: the **Boosenburg** and the 12th-century **Brömserburg**, which also houses a wine museum.

Rüdesheim also has several historic mansions, including the half-timbered Brömserhof (1559) with a collection of musical instruments, and the early 16th-century Klunkhardshof. Above the town towers the **Niederwalddenkmal**, a statue of Germania, 10.5 m (34 ft) high, built to commemorate victory in the Franco-Prussian War of 1870–71, which resulted in German unification. The monument can be reached by a cable-car ride over the vineyards and affords excellent views of Rüdesheim and the Rhine valley.

Gabled and half-timbered houses in Drosselgasse, in Rüdesheim

⑯ Frankfurt am Main

Frankfurt, nicknamed "Mainhattan" and "Chicago am Main" because of its skyscrapers, is one of the main economic and cultural centres of both Germany and Europe. The headquarters of many major banks and newspaper publishers are based here, including those of the *Frankfurter Allgemeine Zeitung*, one of Europe's most influential newspapers. The city's International Book Fair is the world's largest event of its kind. Goethe was born in Frankfurt, and the Johann-Wolfgang-Goethe-Universität is one of Germany's most famous universities. The city also boasts magnificent art collections.

The Neo-Renaissance façade of the Alte Oper

🎭 Alte Oper

Opernplatz 8. **Tel** (069) 134 00.

The monumental old opera house stands near the Stock Exchange. Built in 1872–80, it was completely burned down during World War II. Subsequently rebuilt, it is today used as a conference centre. Its façade and decorations are a fine imitation of the Italian Renaissance style.

🏛 Eschenheimer Turm

Große Eschenheimer Straße.
The Eschenheimer Turm, at the corner of Hochstraße, presents a silhouette typical of old Frankfurt. A relic of the medieval town's fortifications, it was designed by Klaus Mengoz; construction began in 1400 and was completed in 1428 by Madern Gerthener. The façade of the tower features many attractive

bay windows; it also has two reliefs depicting eagles, the symbol of the German empire and the city of Frankfurt.

🏛 Börse

Börsenplatz.
According to historical records, local merchants founded the town's first Stock Exchange in 1558. The new building, designed by Heinrich Burnitz and Oskar Sommer, was erected in 1864–79. It has been used again by stockbrokers since 1957, and is open to the public. Like the old opera house, the stock exchange is designed in Neo-Renaissance style.

Putti with model ship, at the front of the Börse

🏛 Hauptwache

An der Hauptwache.
Built in 1730, the Hauptwache was originally a guardhouse. Later it was turned into a prison.

Dismantled stone by stone during the construction of the town's underground system, it was reassembled in its original form following the completion of the project. Since 1904 the Hauptwache has been a chic café and a popular meeting place.

🏛 Goethehaus

Großer Hirschgraben 23. **Tel** (069) 13 88 00. **Open** 10am–6pm Mon–Sat, 10am–5:30pm Sun. 🌐
🌐 **goethehaus-frankfurt.de**

Southwest of the Hauptwache is Johann Wolfgang Goethe's family home. The great German poet, novelist and dramatist was born here on 28 August 1749. The house, along with many other buildings in Frankfurt, was totally destroyed in World War II, but later lovingly restored. Its interior was reconstructed to represent the style typical of the mid- to late 18th century. Goethe lived in this house until 1775, when he moved to Weimar. The desk at which he wrote his early works, including the first versions of *Götz von Berlichingen* (1771) and *Egmont* (1774), has been preserved.

The adjacent building now houses the Goethemuseum. Opened in 1997, the museum recreates the atmosphere of the 1750–1830 period, and holds a collection of items related to the writer. There is an excellent library, which contains some of his writings.

The distinctive Neo-Classical rotunda of the Paulskirche

Portal of the Goethehaus, with the ancestral family crest

⛪ Paulskirche

Paulsplatz. **Tel** (069) 21 23 85 26.
Open 10am–5pm daily.

The distinctive Neo-Classical rotunda of the church was begun in 1786 but not completed until 1833, due to continuous hostilities with France. Today, however, this building is no longer thought of, or indeed used as, a church. After the first, albeit ill-fated, German National Assembly met here following the revolutionary upheavals of 1848–9, the church became a symbol of republican and liberal Germany. The Paulskirche now serves as a venue for many important events. Each year the awards ceremony for the prestigious German Publishers' Peace Prize takes place here.

🏛 Römerberg

Located in the centre of Frankfurt's old town, this square contains the Gerechtigkeits-brunnen (fountain of justice). Its highlight, however, is the **Römer** (literally the Roman). So-called after the remains of ancient settlements, it is a complex of 15th- to 18th-century houses, including the Altes Rathaus (old town hall), which were rebuilt after World War II. Opposite is a group of half-timbered houses, commonly referred to as Ostzeile. The Steinernes Haus (stone house) was originally built in

1464 for a Cologne silk merchant. It has been reconstructed and is now the home of the Frankfurter Kunstverein (artists' league).

The Ostzeile on the Römerberg, one of the symbols of Frankfurt

Frankfurt City Centre

① Alte Oper
② Eschenheimer Turm
③ Börse
④ Hauptwache
⑤ Goethehaus
⑥ Paulskirche
⑦ Römerberg
⑧ St Leonhardskirche
⑨ Historisches Museum
⑩ Nikolaikirche
⑪ Kunsthalle Schirn
⑫ Kaiserdom
⑬ Museum für Moderne Kunst
⑭ Ikonen-Museum
⑮ Museum für Angewandte Kunst
⑯ Deutsches Architekturmuseum
⑰ Jüdisches Museum
⑱ Städelsches Kunstinstitut

0 metres   400
0 yards   400

For additional map symbols *see back flap*

🏛 Jüdisches Museum

Untermainkai 14–15. **Tel** (069) 21 23 50 00. **Open** 10am–5pm Tue–Sun (to 8pm Wed). 🅿

The Jewish community of Frankfurt was the second largest in Germany, after that of Berlin. This museum, in the former Rothschild Palace, documents the rich cultural heritage of Frankfurt's Jews.

⛪ St Leonhardskirche

Alte Mainzer Gasse.

Close to the banks of the Main stands the church of St Leonhard, a fine example of Gothic and Romanesque architecture. A five-naved hall-church with an elongated choir, it was built in stages in the 13th and 15th centuries. Inside are many treasures, including at the front of the main nave a copy of Leonardo da Vinci's *Last Supper* by Hans Holbein the Elder, from 1501. Next to it is St Mary's altar, created by master craftsmen from Antwerp in 1515–20. On the north wall of the choir visitors can see a fresco depicting the *Tree of Life and the Apostles* (1536) by Hans Dietz.

🏛 Historisches Museum

Saalgasse 19. **Tel** (069) 21 23 55 99. **Open** 10am–6pm Tue, Thu–Sun, 10am–9pm Wed. 🅿

The building housing the history museum was finished in 1972. The museum has an interesting display of items relating to Frankfurt's history, including a fascinating model of the medieval town, a collection of

The early-Gothic Alte Nikolaikirche, in Frankfurt's Römerberg

local prehistoric finds and several decorative architectural fragments from buildings that were destroyed during World War II.

The adjacent building is the Saalhof, which dates back to the time of the Emperor Friedrich I Barbarossa (1122–90). In 1333, the building passed into private hands and from then on it frequently changed its appearance.

⛪ Alte Nikolaikirche

Römerberg.

This twin-naved church was consecrated in 1290. Used as a court church until the late 15th century, it now serves a Lutheran congregation. Popular attractions are its many statues of St Nicholas (Santa Claus) and the 40-bell carillon, which twice a day plays German folk songs.

🏛 Kunsthalle Schirn

Römerberg 6. **Tel** (069) 299 88 20. **Open** 10am–7pm Tue, Fri–Sun, 10am–10pm Wed & Thu. 🅿

One of Europe's most prestigious exhibition buildings, the Kunsthalle opened in 1986. It hosts temporary art exhibitions featuring archaeological themes and the work of old masters and contemporary artists.

⛪ Kaiserdom

Domplatz 14. **Tel** (069) 297 03 20. **Open** 8am–8pm daily (from noon Fri; from 9am Sat & Sun). Dommuseum: **Tel** (069) 13 37 61 84. **Open** 10am–5pm Tue–Fri, 11am–5pm Sat & Sun.

Near the archaeological park, where the ruins of a Carolingian fortress have been unearthed, stands the imperial cathedral, used for the coronation of German kings from 1356, and of Holy Roman Emperors from 1562. The cathedral, dedicated to St Bartholomew and Charlemagne, was built between the 13th and 15th centuries on the site of a Carolingian chapel. It has several priceless masterpieces of Gothic art, including the magnificent 15th-century Maria-Schlaf-Altar and a high altar dating from the second half of the 15th century. The choir has original 14th-century stalls; above these there is a fresco painted in 1427 which depicts scenes from the life of the cathedral's patron saint, Bartholomew.

The Dom's huge tower affords some magnificent views of the town. While in the cloisters is the Dommuseum which has an interesting collection of liturgical objects, sacred art and precious artifacts.

🏛 Museum für Moderne Kunst (MMK)

Domstraße 10. **Tel** (069) 21 23 04 47. **Open** 10am–6pm Tue & Thu–Sun, 10am–8pm Wed. 🅿

The modern art museum occupies a building that looks like a slice of cake. It was designed by Hans Hollein in 1989–92. The museum's collection represents all the major artistic trends from the 1960s until the present day, and includes works by Roy

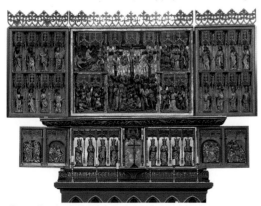

The magnificent late-Gothic high altar in the Kaiserdom

Hollein's modern design, housing the Museum für Moderne Kunst

Lichtenstein, Andy Warhol and Claes Oldenburg. Temporary exhibitions held here focus on multimedia shows, incorporating photography and video art.

Ikonen-Museum

Brückenstraße 3–7. **Tel** (069) 21 23 62 62. **Open** 10am–5pm Tue–Sun, 10am–8pm Wed.

The museum of icons holds an extensive collection of Russian-Orthodox icons from the 16th–19th centuries. It is housed in the Deutschordens-haus, originally built in 1709–15 by Maximilian von Welsch for the Order of the Teutonic Knights. The present building is a faithful copy of the earlier Baroque three-wing structure destroyed in World War II. Inside is the 14th-century Teutonic Church of St Mary, with original altars and 14th- to 17th-century wall paintings.

Museum für Angewandte Kunst

Schaumainkai 17. **Tel** (069) 21 23 40 37. **Open** 10am–6pm Tue–Sun (to 8pm Wed).

The Museum of Applied Arts was opened in 1983, in a building designed by Richard Meier. He used a Biedermeier house, the Villa Metzler, and added a modern wing. The museum has a collection of some 30,000 objects of applied art from Europe and Asia.

Nearby, in a villa with a large garden in Schaumainkai, is the small but fascinating Museum der Weltkulturen (ethnography museum), which is well worth a visit.

Deutsches Architekturmuseum

Schaumainkai 43. **Tel** (069) 21 23 88 44. **Open** 11am–6pm Tue–Sun (to 8pm Wed).

One of the most interesting museums in the Schaumainkai complex is undoubtedly the museum of architecture, opened in 1984 in an avant-garde building designed by Oswald Mathias Ungers. The museum has a permanent collection as well as temporary exhibitions concentrating mainly on developments in 20th-century architecture.

Nearby, at No 41 Schaumainkai, is the Deutsches Filmmuseum, which holds documents and objects relating to the art of filmmaking and the development of film technology. The museum has its own cinema, which shows old and often long-forgotten films.

Liebieghaus

Schaumainkai 71. **Tel** (069) 650 04 90. **Open** 10am–6pm Tue–Sun (to 9pm Wed & Thu).

Built for the Czech industrialist Baron Heinrich Liebieg in 1896, today this building houses a museum of sculpture, with works ranging from antiquity through to Mannerism, Baroque and Rococo. The museum also has superb examples of ancient Egyptian and Far Eastern art, as well as works from the Middle Ages and the Renaissance. Its highlights are the works of Neo-Classical masters such as Antonio Canova, Bertel Thorwaldsen and Johann Heinrich Dannecker.

The Liebieghaus, home of the museum of sculpture

Naturmuseum Senckenberg

Senckenberganlage 25. **Tel** (069) 754 20. **Open** 9am–5pm Mon, Tue, Thu & Fri, 9am–8pm Wed, 9am–6pm Sat & Sun.

This museum, situated near the university, is one of the best natural history museums in Germany. Besides a vast collection of plants and animals, including dinosaur skeletons, it contains human and animal mummies from Egypt.

Environs

Hanau, 30 km (19 miles) east of Frankfurt, is the birth-place of the Grimm brothers. An exhibition devoted to their lives and work is held at the local history museum, in Philippsruhe, a Baroque palace.

The Deutsches Architekturmuseum, in Schaumainkai

Frankfurt – Städelsches Kunstinstitut

The founder of this excellent museum, banker Johann Friedrich Städel, left his art collection to the town in 1815. Since then, the museum has grown through acquisitions and donations, and now contains many masterpieces from seven centuries of European art. It moved to a Neo-Renaissance building in 1878, on the picturesque "museum embankment" by the Main. In the 1920s it acquired the Hohenzollern collection from Sigmaringen. The museum is undergoing renovation and new buildings are under construction, including a subterranean exhibition hall for contemporary art.

Ideal Portrait of a Woman (c.1480)
Simonetta Vespucci, mistress of Giuliano Medici, is the subject of this painting by Sandro Botticelli. Her pendant belonged at the time to the Medici collection.

Ecce Homo
Members of the family who commissioned this painting from Hieronymus Bosch also originally figured in it, but they were later painted over and now only a few figures are partially visible.

First floor

★ **Lucca Madonna**
This small painting by Jan van Eyck, which evokes an intimate and intensely private atmosphere, takes its name from its former owner, Charles Ludwig de Bourbon, Duke of Lucca.

Around 100,000 prints and drawings, dating from the 14th century to the present day and making up one of Germany's most valuable collections, are exhibited in this exhibition hall.

Main entrance

Library

★ **The Geographer** (1669)
Although the signature on the painting is not genuine, there is no doubt that this picture, depicting a scholar at work, is the work of Jan Vermeer van Delft.

VISITORS' CHECKLIST

Practical Information
Schaumainkai 63. **Tel** (069) 605 09 80. **Open** 10am–6pm Tue–Sun (to 9pm Wed & Thu). free Tue.
w staedelmuseum.de

Second floor

★ **Blinding of Samson** (1636)
Rembrandt's dramatic painting depicts the violent blinding of Samson by the Philistines after Delilah cut off his hair.

Gallery Guide

The ground floor is used for changing exhibitions of prints and drawings, as well as a book store and a museum shop. The first floor is devoted to 19th- and 20th-century art and the second floor to the Old Masters.

Pilgrimage to the Isle of Cythera (c.1710)
Jean-Antoine Watteau painted three pictures on this theme, inspired by Dancourt's play *The Three Sisters*. The museum holds the earliest of the three, which shows a Flemish influence.

Ground floor

Orchestra Players (1870–74)
Edgar Degas, not completely satisfied with his painting, retrieved it from its owner. In 1874, he cropped it on three sides, added a bit at the top and repainted the entire painting.

Key

- 19th-century paintings
- 20th-century paintings
- German, Dutch and Flemish 17th- and 18th-century paintings
- Italian, French and Spanish 17th- and 18th-century paintings
- German and Dutch 14th–16th-century paintings
- Italian 14th–16th-century paintings

⑰ Darmstadt

Road map C5. 🗺 138,000. 🚂
ℹ Luisencenter, Luisenplatz 5 (06151-
134 513); for tickets only (06151-134
535). 🎭 Days of Art Nouveau (May),
Schlossgrabenfest (May), Heinerfest
(early Jul), Herbstfest (Oct).
ⓦ darmstadt.de

The earliest historical records of
Darmstadt, which was probably
named after Darimund, a
Frankonian settler, date from the
12th century. Until 1479, the
castle and the town belonged to
the Counts von Katzenelnbogen,
and later to Hessian landgraves.
In 1567, the Landgraves von
Hessen-Darmstadt chose
Darmstadt as their residence,
and they continued to live
here until 1918.

To the north of the old town
stands the **Residenzschloss**,
initially a ducal palace, and
from 1806 residence of the
Landgraves von Hessen-
Darmstadt. The Renaissance-
Baroque complex is centred
around three courtyards. The
earlier medieval castle, which
stood on the same site, burned
down in 1546. The present
palace was created in stages,
with its earliest parts, the
Renaissance wings, dating from
1567–97. The Glockenbau has a
35-bell carillon which can be
heard every half hour; it was
completed in 1663. Further
modifications, planned in 1715–
30, were never completed. Two
Baroque wings, the so-called

Neubau or Neuschloss (new
castle), surround older buildings
to the south and west. The
Schloss was bombed in World
War II and subsequently rebuilt.
Today it houses part of the
Technical University, while the
Glockenbau is home to the
fascinating **Schlossmuseum**
(castle museum). As well as
a splendid collection of
coaches and furniture,
it contains the famous
Darmstädter Madonna
(1526), by Holbein.

Also worth seeing,
the late-Renaissance
Rathaus (town hall),
built in 1588–90,
survived World War II.
The 15th-century choir
of the **Stadtkirche**
has an enormous
monument (1587) to
Magdalena zur Lippe,
first wife of Landgrave
Georg I the Pious. To
the southwest of the
Stadtkirche stands the
Altes Pädagog, built in
1629 as an educational
establishment.

To the north of the Schloss is
the **Hessisches Landesmuseum**
(regional museum of Hesse),
erected in 1892–1905. Its
collection includes artifacts
dating from the Roman era to
the 20th century. The museum
also has an excellent natural
history section, whose exhibits
include the impressive skeleton
of a mammoth as well as birds

Statue on the door
of the Behrens-Haus
in Darmstadt

of every species native to
southern Hesse. Set in the park
behind the museum is the
Baroque Prinz-Georg-Palais
(1710), which houses the
**Großherzoglich-Hessische
Porzellansammlung**, an
extensive porcelain collection.

The last Grand Duke of Hesse,
Ernst Ludwig, was an
important patron of the
Jugendstil, the German Art
Nouveau movement. He
initiated the building of
an exhibition and
residential complex,
the **Mathildenhöhe**,
which was established
in 1901 in the grounds
of the former ducal park,
to serve the existing
artists' colony led by
Joseph Maria Olbrich.
Olbrich designed the
Ernst-Ludwig-Haus,
which now houses
the **Museum
Künstlerkolonie**, an
exhibition space for
the colony's artists,
as well as the famous
Hochzeitsturm
(wedding tower), erected in
1907–8 to celebrate the
Grand Duke's wedding. The
Behrens-Haus, designed by
the Hamburg architect Peter
Behrens, is sober in contrast.
The Orthodox church of **St
Mary Magdalene** was built
in 1897–9 by the Russian
architect Leonti Nikolayevich
Benois, in honour of Alice, wife
of the last tsar of Russia and
sister of Ernst Ludwig.

🏛 **Schlossmuseum**
Residenzschloss, Marktplatz 15.
Tel (06151) 240 35. **Open** 10am–5pm
Fri–Sun. 📷 obligatory.

🏛 **Hessisches Landesmuseum**
Friedensplatz 1. **Tel** (06151) 16 57 03.
Open 10am–6pm Tue, Thu & Fri,
10am–8pm Wed, 11am–5pm Sat
& Sun. 📷

🏛 **Museum Künstlerkolonie**
Olbrichweg 15/Mathildenhöhe.
Tel (06151) 13 33 85.
Open 11am–6pm Tue–Sun. 📷

🏛 **Großherzoglich-Hessische
Porzellansammlung**
Schlossgartenstr. 10. **Tel** (06151) 71 32
33. **Open** 10am–5pm Fri–Sun.

Hochzeitsturm and Orthodox Church in Mathildenhöhe, Darmstadt

For hotels and restaurants in this area see pp492–503 and pp510–33

The Carolingian Torhalle (gate-house) of the Kloster (abbey) in Lorsch

⓲ Lorsch

Road map B5. 🚊 10,700.
ℹ Marktplatz 1 (06251-175 26 0).

This small town is mainly known for the **Kloster**, a Benedictine abbey first founded in 764 by Chrodegang of Metz and one of the most important cultural and intellectual centres in Europe in the Carolingian era. It reached the peak of its power in the 8th–13th centuries, before being sold to the Archbishop of Mainz in 1232. The Benedictines were forced to leave, and in their place the Cistercians arrived. The monastery was dissolved during the Reformation, and in 1621 the Spanish Army destroyed and plundered the greater part of the complex.

Fragments of the 13th-century nave, the towers and the gate-house, dating from c.790, are all that has survived. The original 8th-century church, a basilica without transept, burned down in 1090 and was rebuilt in the 12th century. The original crypt is the burial place of Ludwig II the German, the first ruler of the Eastern Franks. The **Torhalle** (gate-house) is one of the most important architectural remains of the Carolingian period, and it was listed as a UNESCO World Heritage site in 1991. Its lower section is made up of three arcades, equal in height and width, modelled on Roman triumphal arches. The first-floor quarters above were probably used as a guest room

or courtroom, and from the 14th century they served as a chapel. Remains of the original wall paintings are still visible here. The façade is decorated with red and white stone mosaics inspired by Franco-Merovingian art. The vertical divides, created by pilasters and entablature, are copies of ancient designs – an architectural feature typical of the Carolingian Renaissance. The chapel's high roof and vaults date from the 14th century.

⓳ Michelstadt

Road map B5. 🚊 16,000.
ℹ Marktplatz 1 (06061-979 41 10).
🎪 Bienenmarkt (Whitsun), Christmas Market (Dec).

Michelstadt, set among the hills of the Odenwald, is first mentioned in historical records in 741. From the 13th century the town belonged to the von Erbach family (the future Counts von Erbach).

The town has preserved many historic half-timbered houses and presents a typical image of medieval Germany. The 16th-century **Kellerei** is built around the remains of an earlier castle dating from 970. It now houses a regional museum. The sight most popular with photographers is the half-timbered **Rathaus** (town hall), dating from 1484, with its three towers and an open ground-floor gallery.

Nearby stands the late-Gothic, 15th-century **Pfarrkirche St Michael** (parish church of St Michael). Inside are some interesting epitaphs including the double tombstone of Philipp I and Georg I, dating from the late 15th century. A true rarity is the 18th-century **synagogue**, which escaped being burned by the National Socialists in 1938.

In the Steinbach district of Michelstadt stands the **Einhardsbasilika**, a church dating from around 821. The first church built on this site, at the initiative of Einhard, a courtier of Charlemagne, was a small, pillared and vaulted basilica with a short choir ending with a rounded apse. Under the eastern section is a crypt. The parts which remain to this day include the main nave, the north aisle with an apse and the crypt which holds precious religious relics.

Environs
In **Fürstenau**, situated about 1 km (0.6 mile) northwest of Michelstadt, is a beautiful complex including the Altschloss (old palace), remodelled from a medieval castle, the Neuschloss (new palace), dating from 1810, the park and its garden pavilions.

Erbach, 3 km (2 miles) south of Michelstadt, became famous as a centre for the art of ivory carving. In No. 1 Otto-Glenz-Straße is the Deutsches Elfenbeinmuseum (German ivory museum), which is devoted to this craft. Other attractions in this town include the Baroque Schloss (castle) and its interesting art collection.

The Carolingian Einhardsbasilika in Michelstadt-Steinbach

NORTH RHINE– WESTPHALIA

Originally consisting of two distinct provinces with somewhat diverging histories, the region of North Rhine-Westphalia today has its own strong identity. It encompasses the vast valley of the Ruhr river, rich in mineral deposits, where over the past 200 years huge conurbations have developed, comprising dozens of industrial cities that are gradually merging into one another.

As a province, the North Rhineland, situated along the lower Rhine valley, goes back to Roman times. In the Middle Ages most of this area was ruled by the Bishops of Köln. The North Rhineland cities grew and prospered thanks to their trade links, and in the 19th century they became major centres of mining and heavy industry.

Westphalia forms the eastern part of the land. Once a Saxon territory, its history was often intertwined with that of the Rhineland. Only its western end has been heavily industrialized.

North Rhine-Westphalia is not the largest of the German regions, but with a population of nearly 18 million it is the most heavily populated one. It is often thought that the region, and in particular the heavily industrialized Ruhr valley, has little to offer to its visitors, but this is a mistaken belief. Its splendid past has left many priceless historic monuments and

more recently, thanks to great investment, its industrial cities have transformed themselves into attractive cultural centres.

The history of towns such as Bonn, Aachen, Cologne (Köln) and Xanten goes back to Roman times, and they have preserved much of their ancient heritage to this day. Evidence of Romanesque art, which flourished in the Rhineland, is today apparent in numerous impressive abbeys dotted throughout the region and in the churches of Cologne, which also boasts the colossal Gothic Dom.

Much of North Rhine-Westphalia is rural, and the region offers thousands of kilometres of tracks for walking in the Teutoburg Forest and in the Northern Eifel mountains, as well as splendid conditions for watersports and fishing in the Sauerland. It also has surprisingly good ski slopes, such as in the Rothaar Mountains.

A typical lowland landscape near Xanten, in the Rhineland

◀ The historic town of Freudenberg, in the Siegerland region, is filled with half-timbered houses

Exploring North Rhine-Westphalia

Despite being heavily industrialized, the land of North Rhine-Westphalia has many attractions for visitors. At least two days should be set aside to admire the historic treasures in Cologne, while those who prefer museums – or shopping – might allocate more time for Düsseldorf. The towns of Bonn, Aachen and Münster should also feature on every visitor's schedule. The best areas for rest and relaxation are the mountain ranges of the Eifel and the Teutoburg Forest, ideally suited for walking and cycling holidays.

Burg Altena in the Sauerland

Sights at a Glance

1. Münster pp390–91
3. Kleve
4. Xanten
5. Dortmund
6. Essen
7. Duisburg
8. Wuppertal
9. Düsseldorf pp396–7
10. Neuss
11. Dormagen
12. Solingen
13. Altenberg
14. Cologne (Köln) pp402–9
15. Aachen pp398–9
16. Northern Eifel
17. Brühl
18. Bonn pp412–13
19. Königswinter
20. Siegen
21. Hagen
22. Sauerland
23. Soest
24. Paderborn
25. Höxter
26. Lemgo
27. Teutoburger Wald (Teutoburg Forest)
28. Bielefeld
29. Minden

Tours

2. Münsterland

For additional map symbols see back flap

0 kilometres 20
0 miles 20

Getting Around

There are international airports at Düsseldorf, Köln–Bonn (Konrad-Adenauer-Flughafen) and at Münster–Osnabrück. North Rhine-Westphalia has the highest density of motorways anywhere in Germany, making it easy to travel between cities, and providing links with other German regions, Belgium and the Netherlands.

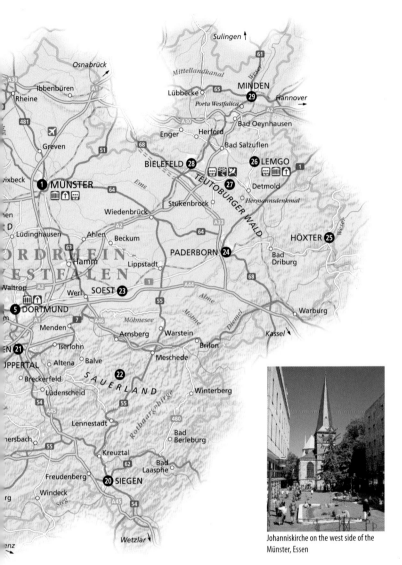

Sulingen ↑

61

Mittellandkanal · Weser

MINDEN
29

Lübbecke · 65 · Hannover →

Porta Westfalica

A30 · Bad Oeynhausen

Enger · Herford

Bad Salzuflen

BIELEFELD · 28 · 26 · LEMGO
1

27

TEUTOBURGER WALD · Detmold

Ibbenbüren
Rheine
A30
A1
A33

481

Greven

51

68

MÜNSTER · 1

64

Ems

Wiedenbrück · Stukenbrock

Hermannsdenkmal

Lüdinghausen · Ahlen · Beckum

Waltrop

A2

64

PADERBORN · 24

Bad Driburg

HÖXTER · 25

Weser

NORDRHEIN

WESTFALEN

Hamm · Lippstadt

Werl · SOEST · 23

1

A44 · Alme

68

Warburg

DORTMUND · 5

A1

7 · A46 · Möhnesee

55

Möhne · Diemel

Kassel ↙

Menden

Arnsberg · Warstein

Iserlohn

Briton

EN · 21

Altena · Balve

Meschede

UPPERTAL

Breckerfeld

SAUERLAND

Lüdenscheid

55

Winterberg

54

Rothaargebirge

A45

Lennestadt

480

ersbach

55

Bad Berleburg

Kreuztal

62

Bad Laasphe

Freudenberg

20 · SIEGEN

Windeck

Sieg

A45

54

Wetzlar

Johanniskirche on the west side of the Münster, Essen

Roman amphitheatre in the Archäologischer Park in Xanten

Key

═══ Motorway

━━━ Major road

┄┄┄ Minor road

= = Under construction

───── Main railway

───── Minor railway

━━━ International border

━━━ Regional border

❶ Münster

Münster and its surroundings were already inhabited in Roman times, but its history proper started in the 9th century, with the establishment of a bishopric. Town status was granted in 1137, and in the 13th century Münster joined the Hanseatic League. In 1648 the Westphalian Peace Treaty was signed here, ending the Thirty Years' War. Münster's Westfälische Wilhelms-Universität (1773) is one of Germany's largest universities. World War II saw 90 percent of the old town laid to ruins, but most of it has now been rebuilt.

🏛 Erbdrostenhof

Salzstraße 38.
Closed to the public.

This beautiful mansion was skilfully positioned diagonally across a corner site. Designed by Johann Conrad Schlaun, it was built in 1753–7, and despite destruction in World War II it still enchants with its "wavy", late-Baroque façade.

🏛 Rathaus

Prinzipalmarkt. Friedenssaal: **Tel** (0251) 492 27 24. **Open** 10am–5pm Tue–Fri, 10am–4pm Sat & Sun. **Closed** 25 Dec. 🅿

The imposing Gothic town hall, the pride of Münster, was almost completely destroyed during World War II. After its splendid reconstruction, it is again a major draw for visitors. The only parts that had escaped destruction were the furnishings of the main council chamber, which have been returned to their rightful place after the rebuilding work. It was here that on 15 May 1648

Houses on Prinzipalmarkt, reconstructed in the medieval style

part of the Westphalian Treaty was signed, ending the Thirty Years' War.

🏛 Lambertikirche

Prinzipalmarkt.

St Lamberti is an excellent example of the hall-churches characteristic of Westphalia. It was built in 1375–1450, but the openwork finial of the tower dates from 1887. The cages hanging on the tower held the bodies of the leading Anabaptists, following the crushing of their commune in 1536. It is also worth taking a look at the relief depicting the *Tree of Jesse*, above the southwest entrance, and the figures of the apostles (c.1600) by Johann Koess.

🏛 Dom St Paulus

Domkammer: Domplatz.
Tel (0251) 495 333.
Open 6:30am–7pm daily (to 7:30pm Sun and hols). 🅿

The most precious historic relic in Münster is undeniably its massive St Paulus' cathedral, built in

1225–65 and representing a transitional style between late Romanesque and early-Gothic. The vast basilica has two transepts, two choirs and two massive towers. The northern cloister was added in the 14th century, and in the 16th–17th centuries the passage that runs around the presbytery acquired a ring of chapels. In the vestibule stands a group of 13th-century sculptures. Especially worth seeing are the two altars by Gerhard Gröninger (1st half of the 17th century), the early 16th-century stained-glass windows brought here from Marienfeland monuments of many bishops. The cathedral's best-known treasure is the astronomical clock (1540), with paintings by Ludger tom Ring the Elder and sculptures by Johann Brabender. At noon, figures show the Magi paying tribute to the infant Jesus to the sounds of the carillon.

🏛 LWL Museum für Kunst und Kultur

Domplatz 10. **Tel** (0251) 590 701.
Closed due to relocation; reopening in Autumn 2014.

The Westphalian regional museum specializes mainly in Gothic art, with a large collection of sculptures and altars rescued in World War II. Its most noteworthy exhibits include the works by Heinrich and Johann Brabender. The upstairs galleries show works by Conrad von Soest and the tom Ring family. Contemporary art is represented by, among others, August Macke's work. The museum is moving to a new building in Autumn 2014, which will have increased exhibition space and facilities.

Figure of a saint in Dom St Paulus

🏛 Überwasserkirche

Überwasserkirchplatz.
The Liebfrauenkirche (Church of Our Lady) is popularly named Überwasserkirche (church above

The beautifully restored façade of the late-Gothic Rathaus

The Baroque-Classical Schloss, residence of Münster's prince-bishops

the water), after the district on the banks of the tiny Aa river. This Gothic edifice was built in c.1340–46, on the site of a Romanesque Benedictine church. Inside are 16th-century votive paintings by Ludger and Hermann tom Ring.

🏠 Residenzschloss
Schlossplatz 2.
This beautiful Baroque residence was built in 1767–87, by Prince-Bishop Maximilian Friedrich. It was designed by Johann Conrad Schlaun, a local master of Baroque architecture. Maximilian Friedrich started the redevelopment of Münster in the northern Baroque style. On his initiative the town acquired a large park, part of which was transformed into a botanical garden in 1803. After World War II, the castle was rebuilt

and became the headquarters of Münster university.

🏛 Museum für Lackkunst
Windthorststraße 26. **Tel** (0251) 41 85 10. **Open** noon–8pm Tue, noon–6pm Wed–Sun & public holidays. 🖼
This unique museum, devoted to lacquer ware, has a good collection with items from different eras and from across the world, making a visit to the museum a treat for those interested in this craft.

Watermill in the open-air museum in Mühlenhof

🏠 Mühlenhof
Theo-Breider-Weg 1. **Tel** (0251) 98 12 00. **Open** Mar–Oct: 10am–6pm daily; Nov–Feb: 11am–4pm Mon–Fri. 🖼
This small but interesting open-air museum is situated on the banks of the picturesque Aasee, Münster's lake and main recreation area. Displayed are a number of rural dwellings with authentic furnishings and two mills (17th and 18th centuries).

🏠 Drostenhof
Wolbeck, Am Steintor 5.
Southeast of the town, in Wolbeck, is an original Renaissance mansion from the mid-16th century. Its exquisite gate-house leads into the courtyard of the mansion, which has original fireplaces and ceiling paintings.

Münster City Centre

① Erbdrostenhof
② Rathaus
③ Lambertikirche
④ Dom St Paulus
⑤ LWL Museum für Kunst und Kultur
⑥ Überwasserkirche
⑦ Museum für Lackkunst

0 metres 300
0 yards 300

For map symbols see back flap

❷ Münsterland

The region stretching in a narrow strip to the north of Münster is the land of horses and Wasserburgen (moated castles). The castles were surrounded by moats or built on islands to give their owners protection in the surrounding lowlands. Almost 50 Wasserburgen have survived, some converted into residences. Not all are open to visitors as most remain to this day in the hands of the family of the original owners. The best way to tour the flat Münsterland region is by car or bicycle.

② **Vischering** The magnificent Burg Vischering is one of the oldest and best-preserved castles in Westphalia. Founded in 1270, it was extended in the 16th and 17th centuries.

⑤ **Schloss Raesfeld** The beautiful 17th-century castle has some original 14th-century elements. Particularly worth seeing is the castle chapel with its Baroque altar.

① **Havixbeck** Two interesting castles are near this small town: the Renaissance Haus Havixbeck and the Renaissance-Baroque Burg Hülshoff, birthplace of and museum to the 19thcentury writer Annette von Droste-Hülshoff.

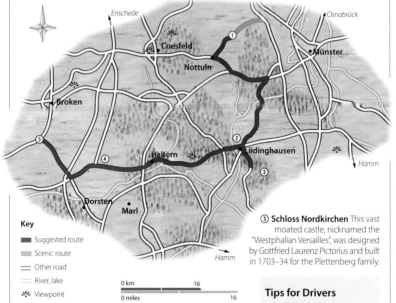

Enschede
Osnabrück
Coesfeld
Münster
Nottuln
Broken
Haltern
Lüdinghausen
Hamm
Dorsten
Marl

③ **Schloss Nordkirchen** This vast moated castle, nicknamed the "Westphalian Versailles", was designed by Gottfried Laurenz Pictorius and built in 1703–34 for the Plettenberg family.

Key

▬ Suggested route
▬ Scenic route
═ Other road
┈ River, lake
❄ Viewpoint

Hamm

0 km   16
0 miles   16

④ **Schloss Lembeck** In its present shape, the Lembeck castle complex is the result of Baroque remodelling, under the direction of Johann Conrad Schlaun. Nearby is a nature reserve.

Tips for Drivers

Tour length: 97 km (58 miles).
Stopping-off points: Every town has inns, and there is a hotel in Schloss Lembeck.
Suggestions: All castles are open to visitors Tuesday to Sunday, with the exception of Nordkirchen, which opens only at weekends.

❸ Kleve (Cleves)

Road map A3. 🏠 50,000. 🚉 🚌
ℹ️ Opschlag 11–13 (02821-89 50 90).

The town of Kleve is named after the high cliff, on which a castle was built in the 10th century. Around it, a settlement developed, which became a town in 1242. It was ruled by the dukes of Kleve, whose ambitions reached their peak in 1539, when Anne of Cleves married the English King Henry VIII.

During World War II Kleve lost most of its historic buildings. One that has survived is the imposing Gothic church of the Assumption of the Virgin Mary, **St Mariä Himmelfahrt** (1341–1426). It has remains of the high altar, dating from 1510–13, with reliefs by Henrik Douvermann and Jakob Dericks, as well as beautiful monuments to the von Kleve dukes. The former Franciscan **St Mariä Empfängnis**, a Gothic twin-nave hall-church from the first half of the 15th century, includes noteworthy features such as the Gothic stalls (1474) and a Baroque pulpit (1698). The well-preserved ducal castle of **Schwanenburg** was remodelled twice: in Gothic style in the late 15th century and in Baroque style in 1636–66. Testifying to former splendour are the parks established in the mid-17th century by Johann Moritz von Nassau. The most beautiful of these is the **Neuer Tiergarten** (new animal garden). **Haus Koekkoek** once belonged to the Romantic painter Barend Cornalis Koekkoek, after whom it was named. The **Museum Kurhaus Kleve – Ewald Mataré-Sammlung** presents interesting and diverse art exhibitions.

The Gothic Dom St Victor in Xanten

🏰 **Schwanenburg**
Am Schlossberg. **Tel** (02821) 22 884.
Open Apr–Oct: 11am–5pm Mon–Fri, 10am–5pm Sat & Sun; Nov–Mar: 11am–5pm Sat & Sun. 📷

🏛️ **Museum Kurhaus Kleve – Ewald Mataré-Sammlung**
Tiergartenstraße 41. **Tel** (02821) 750 10. **Open** 11am–5pm Tue–Sun. 📷

Environs
The suspension bridge across the Rhine – at 1,228 m (4,028 ft) the longest such structure in Germany – connects Kleve with **Emmerich**. Worth a visit here is the Martinskirche, with its exquisite, late-10th-century shrine of St Willibrod.

Twelve km (7 miles) to the southeast of Kleve lies the charming town of **Kalkar** which, in around 1500, was home to the famous Kalkar School specializing in woodcarving. The church of St Nicolai has superb furnishings dating from the same period.

Six km (4 miles) southeast is the moated castle of **Moyland**. It houses a modern art collection, which belongs to the brothers von der Grinten and includes over 4,000 works by the artist Joseph Beuys.

❹ Xanten

Road map B4. 🏠 21,500. 🚉 🚌
ℹ️ Kurfürstenstr. 9 (02801-772 200).

The history of Xanten goes back to the Romans, who founded the settlement of

The Hafentempel in the Archäologischer Park in Xanten

Colonia Ulpia Traiana near the local garrison. The present town, however, did not rise out of the ruins of the Roman town. It was established nearby, around the memorial church built on top of the grave of the martyr St Viktor. It was named *ad sanctos* (by the saints), later shortened to Xanten. A powerful town in the Middle Ages, Xanten also features in the Nibelung myth, and was said to be the birthplace of Siegfried.

The most important historic building in the town is the **Dom St Viktor**, which, according to legend, was built on the graves of St Viktor and members of the Thebian Legion. The surviving Gothic cathedral (1263–1517) holds the shrine of St Viktor (1129), the early-Gothic stalls (1228) and, above all, the exquisite Marienaltar by Henrik Douvermann. There are also Gothic sculptures by the pillars of the main nave. Equally fascinating are the collegial buildings and the cloister holding the tombs of the canons.

Another sight worth visiting is the **Klever Tor**, a magnificent double town-gate, dating from the late 14th century, in the northwest of the town. The **Archäologischer Park**, on the site of the Roman town, and the **Römer Museum** display many reconstructed Roman public buildings including the impressive Hafentempel (harbour temple).

🏛️ **Archäologischer Park & Römer Museum**
Wardter Str. **Tel** (02801) 29 99. **Open** 9am–6pm daily (Nov: 9am–5pm; Dec–Feb: 10am–4pm). 📷

The picturesque exterior of Palace Haus Rodenberg in Dortmund-Aplerbeck

❺ Dortmund

Road map: B4. �︎ 600,000. 🚌 🚆
ℹ️ Königswall 18A (0231-18999222).
🎭 Dortmund à la carte (Jun), Dortmund aller art (Aug), Hansetage (Nov).

The large city of Dortmund is famous not only for its excellent beer and highly developed industry, but also for its more than 1,000 years of history. In the Middle Ages, the town grew rich through trade and joined the Hanseatic League; after a period of decline it flourished again in the 19th century.

A walk through the small old town will take visitors to the **Museum für Kunst-und Kulturgeschichte** (museum for art and cultural history) with displays of interiors from various periods, including Secessionist designs by Joseph Maria Olbrich. A short distance from here is the **Petrikirche**, a Gothic 14th-century hall-church, whose greatest attraction is its high altar (1521), the work of Gilles, a master from Antwerp. Also noteworthy is the former Dominican **Propsteikirche**, with its exquisite late-Gothic main altar. A shortcut across the market square and along Ostenhellweg takes the visitor to two more churches: the **Reinoldikirche** and the **Marienkirche**. The former,

Statue on Alter Markt, in Dortmund

dedicated to St Reinold, the patron saint of Dortmund, has an early-Gothic 13th-century main body and a late-Gothic, 15th-century presbytery. It includes many Gothic sculptures and furnishings. The second one, the church of St Mary, is a 12th-century Romanesque structure. It has a magnificent main altar, by Conrad von Soest (1415–20) and a statue of the Madonna (c.1230).

The **Museum am Ostwall** has an excellent modern art collection.

🏛 **Museum für Kunst-und Kulturgeschichte**
Hansastr. 3. **Tel** (0231) 502 55 22.
Open 10am–5pm Tue–Sun (to 8pm Thu, from noon Sat). 🔾

🏛 **Museum am Ostwall**
Ostwall 7. **Tel** (0231) 502 32 47.
Open 10am–6pm Tue, Wed; 10am–8pm Thu, Fri; 11am–6pm Sat & Sun.

Environs
Ten km (6 miles) northwest, in Waltrop, on the Dortmund-Ems Canal, is the Schiffshebewerk Henrichenburg, a hoist built in 1899 to lift ships.

❻ Essen

Road map B4. 🚏 600,000. 🚌 🚆 ℹ️
Im Handelshof (am Hauptbahnhof 2)
(0201-194 33). 🎭 Essen Original (Aug).

It is hard to believe that this vast industrial metropolis has grown from a monastery, established in 852. The town owes its

growth and prominence to the Krupp family, who, over several generations from the mid-19th century, created the powerful German steel and arms industry.

The most important historic building in the town is the **Münster**, the former collegiate church of the canonesses. This unusual edifice consists of the 15th-century Gothic church of St John, an 11th-century atrium and the main church, which in turn has a Romanesque 11th-century frontage and a Gothic 14th-century main body. Without doubt the most precious object held by the church is the *Goldene Madonna*, a statue of the Virgin Mary with the Infant, made from sheet gold, probably c.980. The treasury has an outstanding collection of gold items from the Ottonian period.

Another important sight in Essen is the **Synagogue** built by Edmund Körner in 1911–13. The largest synagogue in Germany, it managed to outlast the Third Reich and is now a place of commemoration.

Visitors who are interested in 20th-century architecture should see the church of **St Engelbert in Fischerstraße**, designed by Dominikus Metzendorf (1934–6), the town-garden in **Margarethenhöhe** built from 1909 to a design by Georg Metzendorf, and the opera house designed by the Finnish architect, Alvar Aalto.

Essen has much to offer to modern art enthusiasts. The **Museum Folkwang** boasts an excellent collection of 20th-century paintings, mainly German Expressionists. It also has a graphic arts section.

The **Grugapark** is a large green area with botanical gardens, zoo and the Grugahalle, where major concerts are held. To the south of the centre, on the banks of the Baldeneysee, stands **Villa Hügel**, which belonged to the Krupp family until 1945. Today interesting art exhibitions are frequently hosted here. Further south, in **Werden**, is the former Benedictine church of St Ludger, consisting of a 13th-century body preceded by a

The grand Villa Hügel, former home of the Krupp family in Essen

10th-century imperial frontage. The treasury holds many precious objects including a bronze crucifix from around 1060.

🏛 **Museum Folkwang**
Goethestr. 41. **Tel** (0201) 884 53 14. **Open** 10am–6pm Tue–Thu, Sat & Sun, 10am–10:30pm Fri. **Closed** 1 Jan, Easter, 1 May, 24 & 31 Dec. 🅿

Environs
Visitors interested in technology should visit **Bochum**, which is also the seat of the excellent Ruhr-Universität. There are two excellent museums: the **Deutsches Bergbau-Museum** devoted to mining, and the **Eisenbahnmuseum** (railway museum) in Dahlhausen. Both have world-class exhibits.

❼ Duisburg

Road map B4. 🅰 540,000. 🚆 🚌
🅸 Königstr. 86 (0203-285 44 11).

Duisburg, on the edge of the Ruhr region, underwent a period of rapid development in the 19th and 20th centuries. Once a small town, it became the world's largest inland harbour thanks to its location at the spot where the Ruhr flows into the Rhine.

The small old town was almost totally destroyed in World War II, but the 15th-century Gothic **Salvatorkirche** (church of St Saviour) has been rebuilt. Some of the town's greatest attractions are its museums. The **Wilhelm-Lehmbruck-Museum** focuses on the work of the sculptor Lehmbruck, who was born in Duisburg. The museum has an interesting collection of

20th-century sculptures, including works by famous artists such as Salvador Dali, Henry Moore, Max Ernst, Emil Nolde and Joseph Beuys. Also worth visiting is the **Museum der Deutschen Binnenschifffahrt** with its collection of barges and inland waterway vessels. In the 16th century, Duisburg was the home of the famous geographer and cartographer Gerhard Mercator, whose collection of globes, maps and charts can now be seen in the **Kulture- und Stadthistorisches Museum**.

🏛 **Wilhelm-Lehmbruck-Museum**
Friedrich-Wilhelm-Str. 40. **Tel** (0203) 283 76 30. **Open** noon–7pm Wed, Fri, Sat; noon–9pm Thu; 11am–7pm Sun. 🅿

Environs
CentrO in **Oberhausen**, 14 km (9 miles) north of Duisburg, is the largest shopping and leisure complex in Europe.
Krefeld, 6 km (4 miles) south-west of Duisburg, has been a centre of silk fabric production from the 17th century, and the Deutsches Textilmuseum has over 20,000 exhibits, ranging from antiquity to the present day.

❽ Wuppertal

Road map B4. 🅰 380,000. 🚆
🅸 Elberfeld, Informationszentrum am Döppersberg (0202-194 33); Rathaus Barmen (0202-563 66 88).

Wuppertal, capital of the Bergisches Land area, was created in 1929 by combining six towns strung along a 20-km (12-mile) stretch of the Wupper river. The towns are joined by the **Schwebebahn**, a monorail constructed in 1900. Carriages are suspended from a single rail, which rests on tall pillars.

The most interesting of the former towns is Elberfeld, with a museum of clocks, and the **Von-der-Heydt–Museum** of 19th- and 20th-century German art. The museum in the Friedrich-Engels-Haus in Barmen (Engelsstr. 10) is worth seeing, and Neviges has a Baroque pilgrimage church, with a much-visited miraculous picture of the Virgin Mary.

🏛 **Von-der-Heydt-Museum**
Elberfeld, Turmhof 8. **Tel** (0202) 563 62 31. **Open** 11am–6pm Tue, Wed, Fri–Sun, 11am–8pm Thu. 🅿 🅿 🅿

The unusual monorail, linking Wuppertal's six constituent towns

❾ Düsseldorf

Düsseldorf, the administrative capital of North Rhine-Westphalia, received its municipal rights in 1288. From the late 14th century it was the capital of the Duchy of Berg, and from 1614 that of the Palatine. The town owes much to Duke Johann Wilhelm (called Jan Wellem), who lived here in 1690–1716. One of the most important industrial and cultural centres in the Rhine Valley, this European metropolis has a renowned university, superb museums and theatres and, as the German capital of fashion, many excellent shops.

🏛 Museum Kunst Palast

Ehrenhof 4–5. **Tel** (0211) 899 02 00.
Open 11am–6pm Tue–Sun (until 9pm Thu). 🔲 📷 🛍 🔳

This art museum is one of the most interesting in Germany, with a collection of paintings dating from the 16th to the 20th centuries, including works by Rubens, Cranach and Dutch masters of the 17th century. It also holds a large collection of paintings by the Düsseldorf Academy, active in the first half of the 19th century, whose best known artists were Peter von Cornelius and Friedrich Wilhelm Schadow.

🏠 Altstadt

The small old town area suffered severe damage during World War II. Among the surviving monuments it is worth seeing some of the beautiful town houses and the late-Gothic **Rathaus** (town hall), built in the years 1570–73. In front of it stands a famous equestrian statue of the Elector Jan Wellem, built in 1703–11 by Gabriel Grupello. The Düsseldorf castle, burned down in 1872, only has the **Schlossturm** (castle tower) remaining, which now houses a museum of navigation. Another building worth visiting is the Baroque, post-Jesuit **Pfarrkirche St Andreas** (parish church of St Andrew), from the years 1622–9. It has a central ducal mausoleum complex situated behind the presbytery, where the remains of Jan Wellem and others are kept. The **Lambertuskirche**, the former collegiate church of St Lambertus, is a Gothic hall-church with a tall front tower, built in 1288–1394. Some valuable furnishings have survived, including the Gothic sacramentarium and important Gothic ducal tombs, such as that of Duke Wilhelm V, from 1595–9.

Detail from the façade of the Lambertuskirche

🏛 Kunstsammlung Nordrhein-Westfalen

K20: Grabbeplatz 5.
Tel (0211) 838 11 30.
Open 10am–6pm Tue–Fri, 11am–6pm Sat & Sun.
10am–10pm 1st Wed of the month. K21: Ständehausstr. 1. **Tel** (0211) 838 18 30.
Open As for K20. **Closed** 24, 25 & 31 Dec. 🔲 🖥 📷 🛍

The art collection of the state of North Rhine-Westphalia is enormous, featuring mainly the work of 20th-century artists. Particularly valuable are 88 paintings by Paul Klee, which were acquired in 1960. There are also works by Wassily Kandinsky, Marcel Duchamp, Piet Mondrian and Pablo Picasso. The gallery at Grabbeplatz is known as K20, and a second building at Ständehaüsstr. 1, where contemporary art is exhibited, is known as K21. Temporary exhibitions are held nearby, at Kunsthalle Düsseldorf, which is at No. 4 Grabbeplatz.

🏛 Hetjens-Museum

Schulstraße 4. **Tel** (0211) 899 42 10.
Open 11am–5pm Tue & Thu–Sun, 11am– 9pm Wed. 🔲

This museum, in the Nesselrode Palace, is the oldest German museum devoted to ceramics. Visitors can learn about techniques for producing faïence and porcelain, and see global exhibits from prehistory to the present day.

🏛 Königsallee

The "kings' avenue", often just referred to as Kö, was laid out at the beginning of the 19th century, along the edge of the old city moat. The Kö is lined with expensive shops. Luxurious galleries, exclusive boutiques, department stores, fashion houses and shopping malls are interspersed with bars and restaurants. Particularly noteworthy is the Art Nouveau Warenhaus Tietz (now housing the Kaufhof-Galleria department store), which was built in 1907–9, to a design by Joseph Maria Olbrich.

🏵 Hofgarten

Schloss Jägerhof. Goethemuseum:
Jacobistraße 2. **Tel** (0211) 899 62 62.
Open 11am–5pm Tue–Fri & Sun, 1–5pm Sat. 🔲

This charming park, originally laid out in 1769 for Elector Karl Theodor, was recreated in the English style at the beginning of the 19th century. The park is a marvellous setting for Schloss Jägerhof, a Baroque hunting lodge dating from the years 1752–63 and built according

Interior of the Pfarrkirche St Andreas

The late-Baroque Schloss Benrath

to a design by Johann Josef
Couven and Nicolas de Pigage.
The castle was rebuilt after
World War II. It now houses the
Goethe-Museum, holding
memorabilia and documents
related to the writer's life, and a
collection of 18th-century art,
funded by Ernst Schneider.

Heinrich-Heine-Institut
Bilker Str. 12–14. **Tel** (0211) 899 55 71.
Open 11am–5pm Tue–Fri & Sun,
1–5pm Sat.

The former city moat which runs
alongside Königsallee

The celebrated German poet
Heinrich Heine was born in
Düsseldorf in 1797. This institute
was established to preserve his
legacy, to conduct research
nto his work and to organize
exhibitions. Düsseldorf's university
and a number of streets have
also been named after Heine.

Schloss Benrath
Benrather Schlossallee. **Tel** (0211) 899
38 32. **Open** 11am–5pm Tue–Sun.

Part of Düsseldorf since 1929,
Benrath is home to this beautiful
Neo-Classical hunting palace,
built for the electors of the
Palatine in 1755–73 by Nicolas
de Pigage. Decor, beautiful
furnishings and an extensive
park and gardens have survived.

Kaiserswerth
Today a part of Düsseldorf,
this area prides itself on a

history dating back to the
8th century. Its Pfarrkirche
St Suitbertus, a Romanesque
basilica from the 12th century,
has the magnificent 13th-
century golden relic of its
patron saint. There are also
the ruins of a palace, built
in the 12th century for
Friedrich I Barbarossa.

Environs
The "Neanderthal" part of the
Düssel valley was originally
named after the poet Joachim
Neander. It became famous in
1856, when the remains of ape-
like creatures were uncovered
in a cave. A museum dedicated
to these "Neanderthal Men" is
located in Mettman, 17 km
(11 miles) east of Düsseldorf.

Dusseldorf City Centre

① Museum Kunst Palast
② Altstadt
③ Kunstsammlung Nordrhein-
 Westfalen
④ Hetjens-Museum
⑤ Königsallee
⑥ Hofgarten

For key to symbols *see back flap*

⑩ Neuss

Road map B4. 🔼 150,000. 🚃 🚌
ℹ️ Rathausarkaden, Büchel 6 (02131-403 77 95).

The history of Neuss goes back to Roman days. The town developed around a Bernhardine monastery, which became a girls' boarding school in the 12th century. The most famous building is the magnificent 13th-century Romanesque **Münster St Quirinus**. After a fire in 1741, a Baroque dome with a statue of St Quirin, the patron saint, was added to the eastern tower of the church. Also worth seeing is the Obertor (upper gate), built in 1200, one of the mightiest gates in the Rhineland.

⑪ Dormagen

Road map B4. 🔼 62,000. 🚃 🚌
ℹ️ Dormagen, Schlossstraße 2–4 (02133-276 28 15). 🎭 Freilichtspiele in Zons (Jun–Sep).

This medium-sized town, which principally relies on its chemical industry, would not be found in a guide book were it not for two remarkable historic monuments within the city limits. On the banks of the Rhine lies the fortified customs town of **Zons**, established around 1373–1400 at the instigation of archbishop Friedrich von Saarwerden. This small regular, four-sided fortress has survived in excellent condition. The buildings in the settlement are mainly from a later time, but the walls and gates, as well as the ruined castle **Schloss Friedestrom** are among the most fascinating examples of Medieval fortifications in the Rhine Valley.

Equally interesting is an excursion to **Knechtsteden**, west of Dormagen, where an amazing monastery was built for the Norbertines in the 12th century. Set amid woods and orchards, the vast twin-choired basilica has mighty towers in the eastern section. There are impressive murals, including a 12th-century mural of Christ in the western apsis, as well as attractive cloisters.

The Gothic post-Cistercian Bergischer Dom in Altenberg

⑫ Solingen

Road map B4. 🔼 165,000. 🚃 🚌 ℹ️
Clemens-Galerien Mummstr. 10 (0212-290 36 01). 🎭 Frühjahrskirmes (Mar).

Solingen is almost synonymous with its famous factory where quality scissors and knives are produced. The main attraction in town is the **Klingenmuseum**, which shows cutting tools from the Stone Age to the present day.

Environs
Remscheid, 7 km (4 miles) east of Solingen has the Röntgen-Museum, dedicated to the German Nobel Prize winner Wilhelm Röntgen, who was born here and discovered

Baroque façade of the local Heimatmuseum in Remscheid

the X-ray. One of the most beautiful buildings is the Heimatmuseum with displays of typical regional interiors.

Schloss Burg, on the Wupper river, is the 12th-century fortress of the von Berg family. Many times rebuilt, it now houses a museum.

⑬ Altenberg

Road map B4. 🔼 5,745. 🚃 🚌
ℹ️ Bergisch-Gladbacher-Str. 2, 51519 Odenthal (02202-71 01 31).

Altenberg near Odenthal has preserved its **Bergischer Dom**, a former Cistercian cathedral and one of the most important destinations for pilgrims. Built in 1259–1379, it is also one of the most beautiful Gothic buildings in Germany. In accordance with their rules, the Cistercians built the church without a tower. The interior is furnished with Gothic works of art and has stunningly beautiful stained-glass windows, the altar of the *Coronation of the Blessed Virgin Mary* from the late 15th century, a beautiful 14th-century *Annunciation* and a sacrarium (1490). After the dissolution of the Order in 1803, the cathedral suffered a turbulent history. It now serves as a church for both Catholics and Protestants.

Children also enjoy a visit to Altenberg because of its **Märchenwald** (fairy-tale wood), an enchanted forest, with interactive scenes and statues representing all the most popular fairy tales.

⓮ Köln (Cologne)

See pp402–3.

⓯ Aachen

Road map A4. 247,000.
Elisenbrunnen (0241-180 29 60).
Frühjahrsbend (Apr), horse-riding competitions CHIO (Jul), Europamarkt der Kunsthandwerker (Sep).

Aachen owes its fame to its hot springs, whose healing powers were already highly rated by the Romans when they established baths here in the 1st–2nd centuries AD. The name of the town, *aquae grani* or Aquisgrani, also relates to the source.

The settlement grew mainly in the 8th century, when Charlemagne chose it as his principal residence in 768. He built a huge palace complex with chapel, cloistered courtyard and hall for himself.

When Charlemagne was crowned emperor in 800, Aachen became the capital of the Holy Roman Empire. Although the town soon lost this title, it remained an important destination for pilgrims because of the valuable relics brought here by Charlemagne. From the 10th to the 16th centuries, all German kings were crowned in the palace chapel.

In the 18th and 19th centuries, Aachen gained great importance as a spa. Many magnificent buildings dating from this splendid era have long since vanished. Further destruction was inflicted by World War II,

yet some historic monuments have survived. The most important of these, in the centre of the old town, is the **Pfalz** (*see pp400–1*), a complex of buildings belonging to Charlemagne's former palace. They include a cathedral with a palace chapel and a hall which was rebuilt as the **Rathaus**.

In the old town, not far from the cathedral complex, is the church of St Folian, where a Gothic Madonna dating from 1411 has survived. A short distance south from here stands the Elisenbrunnen (fountain of Elizabeth), an exceptionally beautiful building where mineral water can be taken. It was built in 1822–7 according to designs by Johann Peter Cremer and Karl Friedrich Schinkel.

After admiring the attractive houses around the central market square visitors can enjoy the **Couven-Museum**. Based in an historic middle-class town house, it has an interesting collection dedicated to the life of the bourgeoisie in the 18th and 19th centuries. There is also a collection of ceramic tiles from the 16th–19th centuries.

The house where Israel Berr Josaphat Reuter established the first-ever news agency in 1850 (transferred to London a year later) now houses the

Internationales Zeitungs-museum, devoted to the history of the press, with over 200,000 newspapers from the 16th century to today. The building has undergone an extensive renovation to house a temporary exhibition space and lecture halls.

It is also worth visiting the **Suermondt-Ludwig-Museum**, a short distance beyond the town centre, which has a great collection of art from the Middle Ages until the present day, including some beautiful sculptures and paintings from the 17th century.

To the northeast of the old town extends the spa district of Aachen. Here, visitors can stroll through the spa park or spend an evening at the casino. Aachen also has much to offer lovers of modern art: the Ludwig-Forum für Internationale Kunst hosts interesting exhibitions.

Statue of David Hansemann

🏛 **Internationales Zeitungsmuseum**
Pontstr. 13. **Tel** (0241) 432 49 10.
Open 10am–6pm Tue–Sun.

🏛 **Suermondt-Ludwig-Museum**
Wilhelmstr. 18. **Tel** (0241) 47 98 00.
Open noon–6pm Tue–Sun (to 8pm Wed).

🏛 **Couven-Museum**
Hühnermarkt 17. **Tel** (0241) 432 44 21.
Open 10am–6pm Tue–Sun.
Closed public holidays.

Environs
Kornelimünster, 6 km (4 miles) southeast of the centre, is a beautiful place with a well-preserved old town and churches. The most important of these is the Propsteikirche St Kornelius, a former Benedictine monastery which dates from the early 9th century. The surviving building is a 14th-century Gothic basilica, extended by the early 16th century to an imposing five-nave structure. In the 18th century the octagonal chapel of St Kornelius was added at the axis of the presbytery.

The Neo-Classical building which houses the casino in Aachen's spa park

The Pfalz in Aachen

The original palace of Charlemagne in Aachen did not survive; of his vast construction only the Pfalzkapelle (palatine chapel) remains. Modelled on the church of San Vitale in Ravenna, Italy, it was built by Odo von Metz in 786–800. In the mid-14th century a front tower was added, and in the years 1355–1414 a new presbytery was built. Side chapels were added later, and in the 17th century the central section was covered by a dome.

Charlemagne's Throne
This modest throne, fashioned from marbled tiles, served as the coronation throne for successive German leaders.

Candelabra
This copper candelabra, a masterpiece of Romanesque craftsmanship, was a gift from Emperor Friedrich I Barbarossa.

KEY

① **Ungarnkapelle**

② **Antique Columns** The arcaded ambulatory is divided by beautiful columns, made from red marble and porphyry which had been brought from Ravenna and Rome.

③ **Hubertus- and Karls-kapelle**

④ **The Gothic presbytery** was modelled on Sainte-Chapelle in Paris.

⑤ **Matthiaskapelle**

⑥ **Annakapelle**

Main entrance

Bronze doors
The doors, dating from the time of Charlemagne, are the oldest historic monument of their kind in Germany.

★ Lotharkreuz

This magnificent cross (c.1000), decorated with a cameo showing a portrait of Emperor Augustus, is one of the most valuable exhibits in the Schatzkammer.

VISITORS' CHECKLIST

Practical Information
Cathedral: Münsterplatz.
Tel (0241) 47 70 90. **Open** 7am–7pm (6pm winter). 🎧 from 10:45am Mon–Fri, from 1pm Sat & Sun. Treasury: Klosterplatz 2.
Tel (0241) 47 70 91 27. **Open** 10am–1pm Mon, 10am–5pm Tue–Sun (6pm Apr–Dec), 10am–9pm first Thu of month.

★ The Shrine of Charlemagne

The Emperor Charlemagne was canonized as a saint in 1165 and in 1215 his remains were placed in this gold and silver casket by Friedrich II. It is on display in the presbytery.

★ Pala d'Oro

The front of the main altar is adorned with valuable gold sheets from c.1020, which were funded by Heinrich II.

Proserpina's Sarcophagus

This sarcophagus, in the Schatzkammer (treasury), is a beautiful example of early 3rd-century Roman sculpture. It is thought that the body of Charlemagne rested in this coffin until he was canonized.

Ambo

The ambo, a pulpit fashioned from gold-plated copper and inlaid with precious stones and ivories, was donated by Heinrich II in 1014.

⑭ Köln (Cologne)

Originally founded by the Romans, Köln is one of the oldest towns in Germany. The Franks ruled the town from the end of the 5th century, and Charlemagne raised its status to that of an archbishopric. Köln has remained a powerful ecclesiastical centre – it boasts 12 Romanesque churches as well as the famous Gothic cathedral. In the Middle Ages the city also played a significant role in the Hanseatic League. Present-day Köln is known for its trade fairs and as an important centre for art and culture, with excellent museums, historic buildings and art galleries. The highest number of visitors today come for the five days preceding Ash Wednesday, to watch the grand carnival processions.

⛪ St Andreas

Komödienstraße 4–8.
This late-Romanesque basilica was founded c.1200, with a presbytery added in 1414–20. Particularly noteworthy are the beautiful capitals, which link the pillars between the naves, and the stalls (c.1420–30).

Picturesque houses on Fischmarkt

⛪ Pfarrkirche St Mariä Himmelfahrt

Marzellenstraße 32–40.
The parish church of the Assumption of Mary is one of the few Baroque buildings in Köln. It was built for the Jesuit Order in 1618–89. Its Romanesque and Gothic elements are not surviving parts of an earlier building, but a consciously created link with earlier styles.

⛪ Dom St Peter und Santa Maria

See *pp406–7.*

🏛 Museum Ludwig

Bischofsgartenstraße 1. **Tel** (0221) 22 12 61 65. **Open** 10am–6pm Tue–Sun, 10am–10pm first Thu of month. 🖼

This museum has one of Europe's best collections of modern art. There are paintings by Picasso, German Expressionists, Surrealists, American Pop Artists and the Russian Avantgarde as well as many sculptures.

⛪ Groß St Martin

An Groß St Martin 9. **Tel** (0221) 16 42 56 50. **Open** 8:30am–7.30pm Tue–Sat, 1–7:15pm Sun.

This church, with its attractive triangular presbytery and vast tower dominating Fischmarkt, was founded for the Benedictine Order in the late 12th century. The Romans built a sports arena on this site with a swimming pool, remains of which have been uncovered under the crypt. The houses in the surrounding Martins-viertel are post-World War II, however they were built to historic designs with a medieval street layout.

🏛 Römisch-Germanisches Museum

Roncalliplatz 4. **Tel** (0221) 22 12 45 90. **Open** 10am–5pm Tue–Sun (until 10pm first Thu of month).

This building houses a number of Roman and pre-Roman archaeological finds unearthed in Köln and the Rhine Valley. On display are weapons, ornamental and artistic objects, the superb Dionysus mosaic and the monument to Poblicius.

🏛 Farina Haus

Obenmarspforten 21. **Tel** (0221) 399 88 94. **Open** 10am–6pm Mon–Sat, 11am–4pm Sun. 🖼

Farina Haus traces the history of fragrance. Tours lead to the over 300-year-old cellar where the Italian perfumier Johann Maria Farina first began producing Eau de Cologne, now a generic brand recognized world-wide.

Panorama with the Rathaus, Groß St Martin and the Dom, with the Rhine in the foreground

For hotels and restaurants in this area see pp492–503 and pp510–33

A detail of the Gothic section of the Rathaus façade

🏛 Rathaus

Alter Markt. ℹ️ (0221) 22 10. **Open** 9am–3pm Mon–Thu, 9am–noon Fri. Jewish Baths: **Open** 10am–5pm Tue–Sun (keys available from ticket counter). Praetorium: Kleine Budengasse. **Open** 10am–5pm Tue–Sun.

The town hall is an irregular shape created by successive modifications. In the first phase, around 1330, a wing with a Hanseatic Hall was built, decorated with Gothic sculptures of heroes and prophets. In 1407–14 a vast Gothic tower was added, and in the 16th century the arcaded Renaissance Lions Courtyard

and a magnificent front lodge were built. In front of the town hall, under a glass pyramid, are the remains of 12th-century ritual Jewish baths that were destroyed after the expulsion of the Jews in 1424. From Kleine Budengasse an entrance leads to the *Praetorium*, the remains of a Roman town hall.

🏛 Wallraf-Richartz-Museum – Fondation Corboud

See *pp408–9*.

🏛 Gürzenich

Gürzenichstraße.
This Gothic building has a huge celebration hall (1437–44), which occupies the entire first floor. Next to it are the ruins of the Romanesque church Alt St Alban. It has a copy of the sculpture *Parents* by Käthe Kollwitz.

⛪ Minoritenkirche Mariä Empfängnis

Minoritenstraße.
This modest Gothic Franciscan church was established in the 13th–14th centuries. It is an elegant three-naved basilica without a tower,

modelled on the Elisabethkirche in Marburg. There are historic furnishings and a 14th-century shrine with the remains of Johannes Duns Scotus, a Scottish Minorite.

Place of remembrance, in Alt St Alban, near the Gürzenich

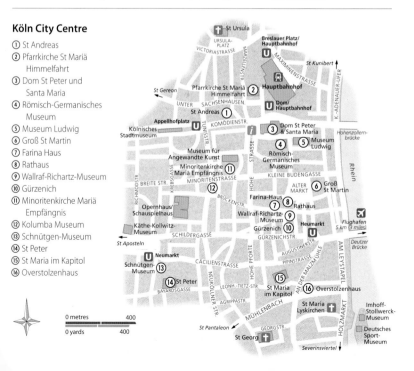

Köln City Centre

① St Andreas
② Pfarrkirche St Mariä Himmelfahrt
③ Dom St Peter und Santa Maria
④ Römisch-Germanisches Museum
⑤ Museum Ludwig
⑥ Groß St Martin
⑦ Farina Haus
⑧ Rathaus
⑨ Wallraf-Richartz-Museum
⑩ Gürzenich
⑪ Minoritenkirche Mariä Empfängnis
⑫ Kolumba Museum
⑬ Schnütgen-Museum
⑭ St Peter
⑮ St Maria im Kapitol
⑯ Overstolzenhaus

0 metres 400
0 yards 400

Exploring Köln (Cologne)

🏛 Kolumba Museum

Kolumbastraße 4. **Tel** (0221) 933 19 30.
Open noon–5pm Wed–Mon. 🔲

Designed by Swiss architect
Peter Zumthor to much critical
acclaim, this museum houses
the archbishopric of Köln's
collection of religious art.
The building, which opened in
2007, accommodates the ruins
of the late Gothic church St
Kolumba; a chapel built in the
1950s to house a statue of the
Madonna which miraculously
escaped bombing during
World War II; and a unique
archaeological excavation that
was made in the 1970s.

🏛 Schnütgen-Museum

Cäcilienstraße 29. **Tel** (0221) 22 12 23
10. **Open** 10am–6pm Tue–Sun (to
8pm Thu). 🔲

The Romanesque church of St
Cecilia, built in 1130–60 as a
nunnery, was taken over in 1479
by the Augustinian Sisters;
today it houses the Schnütgen-

The Romanesque church of St Gereon,
with its vast dome

Museum. Destroyed during
World War II and subsequently
rebuilt, this museum specializes
in religious art, mainly from the
Middle Ages. Its collection
includes magnificient
sculptures, gold and ivory
items and sacral objects.

🏠 St Peter

Leonhard-Tietz-Straße 6.

The late-Gothic church of St
Peter is a galleried basilica, built
in 1515–39. Following its
destruction in World
War II, the former
vaulting was
replaced by a
ceiling. The
church's greatest
attractions include
its Renaissance
stained-glass

Detail from Stadtmuseum

windows (1528–30) and the
magnificent *Crucifixion of St
Peter*, painted after 1637 by
Peter Paul Rubens, who spent
his childhood here and whose
father lies buried in the church.

🏠 St Maria im Kapitol

Marienplatz 19.

Originally built in the early part
of the 11th century as a
convent, the church's extension
and remodelling took until the
early 13th century. Noteworthy
among the furnishings are its
extensive crypt and the mid-
11th-century wooden door in
the west closure, richly carved
with reliefs depicting scenes
from the life of Christ. It also
has a superb Renaissance
rood screen, and is the only
church in Köln with cloisters.

🏠 Overstolzenhaus

Rheingasse 8.

World War II deprived Köln of
many of its historic residential
buildings, but this one has
been lovingly restored. Built
for a prosperous patrician
family in the 13th century,
it is regarded as one of the
town's finest Gothic houses.

🏠 St Maria Lyskirchen

An Lyskirchen 12.

This, the smallest Romanesque
church in Köln, was built around
1220 and slightly remodelled in
the 17th century. Its
greatest attractions are
magnificent frescos
depicting scenes
from the Bible and
the lives of the
saints, which
adorn the vaults
(c.1250), as well as
the *Schöne Madonna*, a huge
statue of the Virgin with the
Infant Christ (c.1420).

🏛 Imhoff-Stollwerck-Museum (Schokoladen Museum)

Rheinauhafen 1a. **Tel** (0221) 931 88
80. **Open** 10am–6pm Tue–Fri,
11am–7pm Sat & Sun. 🔲

This fantastic museum of
chocolate explains the history
of cocoa bean cultivation as
well as the cultural significance,
use and marketing of chocolate.
It also shows the production
process, and lets visitors sample
the product.

🏠 St Georg

Georgsplatz 17.

This church was built around
the middle of the 11th century,

Romanesque Churches

Köln has 12 surviving Romanesque
churches, bearing testimony to the
importance of the Church in the town's
development. Built on the graves of
martyrs and early bishops of Köln, the
forms of the churches influenced the
development of Romanesque
architecture well beyond the Rhineland.
Almost all the churches were damaged in
World War II. Some, such as the church of
St Kolumba, have not been restored, but
most were returned to their former glory.

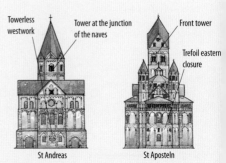

Towerless
westwork

Tower at the junction
of the naves

Front tower

Trefoil eastern
closure

St Andreas

St Aposteln

The attractive Romanesque church of St Kunibert, seen from the Rhine

originally as a transept basilica with two choirs. In the mid-12th century the west choir was replaced by a massive frontage (westwork), but the towers were never added.

St Pantaleon
Am Pantaleonsberg 2.

A little way from the centre is this exquisite church, a former Benedictine monastery founded c.950 by Archbishop Bruno, brother of Emperor Otto I. The archbishop and the Empress Theophanu, who completed the building, are both buried here. The church has a superb late-Gothic choir screen with richly carved ornamentation. From the crypt, the remains of a Roman villa are accessible.

Severinsviertel

The Severin Quarter, a district on the southern edge of the old town, owes its name to the 13th-century Romanesque church of St Severinus. The church, largely remodelled in the Gothic style in the 15th and 16th centuries, features rich original furnishings and has a mid-10th-century crypt.

St Aposteln
Neumarkt 30.

The vast 12th-century church of the Apostles, which towers over Neumarkt, is one of the most interesting Romanesque churches in the Rhineland. The original basilica has a trefoil eastern closure, a low tower at the junction of the naves and a tall front tower. It was given two further slim turrets flanking the apse of the presbytery.

From Neumarkt, Hahnen-strasse leads to Rudolfplatz and the Hahnentor, perhaps the most beautiful of all surviving medieval gates.

St Gereon
Gereonsdriesch 2–4.

This church must be the most unusual edifice not only in the Rhineland, but in all of Germany. Its oldest part, an oval building surrounded by small conchas, was built in the late 4th century on the graves of martyrs and – according to legend – founded by St Helen. The Romanesque presbytery is an 11th-century addition and, in 1219–27, the oval was encircled with a ten-sided, four-storey structure in early-Gothic style. This is topped with a massive dome, 48 m (157 ft) in diameter, with ribbed vault.

St Ursula
Ursulaplatz 24.

This church was built in the 12th century, on the site of an earlier church probably dating from c.400. In the late 13th century the presbytery was rebuilt in Gothic style. The Baroque golden chamber at the southern end, added in the 17th century, is lined with many shrines. According to legend, these hold the remains of St Ursula and 11,000 virgins, all of whom were reputedly killed at the hands of the Huns. The town insignia of Köln also testify to the veneration of the virgins.

St Kunibert
Kunibertskloster 2.

Bishop Kunibert was buried in a church on this site in 663. The present Romanesque church (1215–47) has precious Romanesque stained-glass windows (c.1220–30).

The medieval Hahnentor, exit from Köln towards Aachen

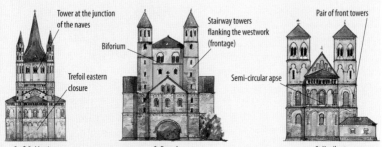

Tower at the junction of the naves

Biforium

Trefoil eastern closure

Groß St Martin

Stairway towers flanking the westwork (frontage)

St Pantaleon

Pair of front towers

Semi-circular apse

St Kunibert

Cologne Cathedral (Kölner Dom)

The most famous Gothic structure in Germany, the Kölner Dom is also unusually complex, whether in terms of its splendour, its size or even simply the date of its construction. The foundation stone was laid on 15th August 1248, the presbytery consecrated in 1322. The cathedral was built gradually until c.1520. It then remained unfinished until the 19th century, when Romanticists revived interest in it. The building was finally completed in 1842–80, according to the rediscovered, original Gothic designs.

Pinnacles
Elaborately decorated pinnacles top the supporting pillars.

Cathedral Interior
The presbytery, the ambulatory and the chapels retain a large number of Gothic, mainly early-14th-century, stained-glass windows.

KEY

① **Petrusportal**, or the portal of St Peter, the only one built in the second half of the 14th century, has five Gothic figures.

② **Buttresses** support the entire bulk of the cathedral.

③ **Semicircular arches** transfer the thrust of the vaults onto the buttresses.

④ **The contemporary German artist** Gerhard Richter created an abstract stained-glass collage in 2007.

Main entrance

Engelbert Reliquary (c.1630)
The cathedral treasury is famous for its large collection of golden objects, vestments and the fine ornamentation of its liturgical books.

★ **Gothic Stalls**
The massive oak stalls, built in 1308–11, were the largest that have ever been made in Germany.

VISITORS' CHECKLIST

Practical Information
Cathedral: **Open** 6am–7:30pm daily. Treasury: Domkloster 4. **Tel** (0221) 17 94 05 55. **Open** 10am–6pm daily. 🔲 📷 Viewing platform: **Open** Jan, Feb & Nov, Dec: 9am–4pm; Mar, Apr & Oct: 9am–5pm; May–Sep: 9am–6pm. 📷 Organ recitals: Jun–Aug: 8pm Tue. Exhibition of Rubens tapestries: Whit Sunday until Corpus Christi.

High Altar
The Gothic altar slab, which dates back to the consecration of the presbytery, depicts the Coronation of the Virgin Mary, flanked by the twelve apostles.

★ **Shrine of the Three Kings**
This huge Romanesque reliquary was made by Nikolaus von Verdun in 1190–1220, to hold the relics of the Three Kings, which were brought to Köln in 1164 for Emperor Friedrich I Barbarossa. It is decorated with scenes from the Salvation History.

★ **Altar of the Magi**
This splendid altar (c.1442), the work of Stephan Lochner, is dedicated to the Three Kings, the patrons of Köln.

Mailänder Madonna
This fine early-Gothic carving of the Milan Madonna and Child dates from around 1290. It is currently displayed in the Marienkapelle.

Wallraf-Richartz-Museum & Fondation Corboud

This museum was named after Ferdinand Franz Wallraf, who bequeathed his art collection to the city in 1824, and Johann Heinrich Richartz, who funded the first building. Medieval and early modern paintings (1250 to 1550) form the core of the collection. There are also works by Rubens and Rembrandt, as well as examples from Impressionism, Realism and Symbolism. In 2001 the Wallraf-Richartz-Museum moved to a new building, incorporting many new works from the collection of Gérard Corboud.

Bleaching the Linen (1882)
Max Liebermann created this painting in the early stages of his career, when his work was largely concerned with Realism.

★ Stigmatization of St Francis (c.1616)
This dark and mysterious painting, originally created by Peter Paul Rubens for the Capuchin church in Köln, is untypical of the artist's work.

Second floor

Reclining Girl (1751)
This young nude, arranged on her bed in a provocative pose, is an example of the light-hearted works of so-called "boudoir art" that François Boucher specialized in.

Foyer

★ Fifer and Drummer (1502–4)
This subtle painting, the wing of an altarpiece, is the work of Albrecht Dürer, who included himself in the scene – the drummer is a self-portrait of Dürer himself.

Main entrance

For hotels and restaurants in this area see pp492–503 and pp510–33

Gallery Guide

Each floor in the museum displays paintings belonging to one era. On the second floor, the exhibition begins with the collection of 13th-century art; the third floor holds 16th–18th century art, and on the fifth floor works of art from the 19th century are displayed, organized by the schools of art they represent.

VISITORS' CHECKLIST

Practical Information
Wallraf-Richartz-Museum &
Fondation Corboud:
Obermarspforten.
Tel (0221) 22 12 11 19.
Open 10am–6pm Tue–Sun &
hols (to 9pm Thu). 🏛 🚻 📷 🅿
W wallraf.museum

Girls on a Bridge (1905)
Edvard Munch covered the same subject several times *(see p441)*. The version held in Köln is one of the earliest, and features an urbanized landscape.

Fourth floor

Jacob accuses Laban of giving him Lai instead of Rachel as a wife (1628)
This biblical scene was painted by one of the most outstanding Dutch masters, Hendrick ter Brugghen.

First floor

Old Woman and Boy
(c.1650–60)
This scene was painted by Bartolome Esteban Murillo. The artist excelled not only as the master of charmingly sentimental depictions of the Madonna, but was also an excellent observer of every-day life in 17th-century Spain.

Madonna and Child (1325–30)
This central panel of a polyptych by Simone Martini is thought to have originated from the San Agostino church in San Giminiano.

Key
- ☐ Medieval paintings
- ☐ 17th- and 18th-century paintings
- ☐ 19th-century paintings
- ☐ Non-exhibition space

One of the artificial reservoirs in the northern Eifel

⑯ Northern Eifel

Road map A4. 🛈 Kalvarienbergstr. 1, 54595 Prüm (0180) 500 22 83. 🎪 Bad Münstereifel: Burg in Flammen (Jul).

Barely 20 per cent of the Eifel mountain range is in North Rhine-Westphalia. Low, forested mountains line the valley of the Rur river, which has been dammed in several places. The resulting artificial lakes provide a perfect opportunity for relaxation and sporting activities. There are also many attractive towns and fascinating monuments.

Blankenheim is famed for its picturesque half-timbered houses, the late-Gothic church and the frequently modified 12th-century castle of the counts von Manderscheid-Blankenheim, which today is a youth hostel. The source of the Ahr river can also be seen here – a house was built over the top of it in 1726.

In **Schleiden**, the castle, built in the 12th century and frequently rebuilt up until the 18th century, is worth visiting. There is also a late-Gothic church with valuable stained-glass windows and an impressive organ dating from 1770.

Probably the most beautiful town in this region is **Monschau**, which until 1919 was called Montjoie. It is known also for the Montjoier Düttchen (croissants) and an excellent mustard. The ruin of a 13th-century castle towers on a hill. At its foot, the Rur river runs through a narrow valley, with attractive small towns, narrow, steep streets and timber-frame houses from various eras. In Hasenfeld visitors can see a dam dating from 1904, and an amazing hydro-electric

building, decorated in a way that reflects its purpose. One of the most interesting monuments of this region is the Steinfeld monastery, with a history dating from the 10th century. In 1121 the Augustinians settled here, and in 1126 they accepted the rule of St Norbert of Xanten, and this became the first monastery on German territory. A beautiful Romanesque basilica was built in the second half of the 12th century. It has retained wall paintings from the 12th and 14th centuries, and vaulted ceilings from the 16th century. The **Rheinisches Freilichtmuseum Kommern** is an open-air museum with examples of the building styles typical of the Northern Eifel. It is also worth visiting the town of **Euskirchen**, which

Merry-go-round at the Phantasialand in Brühl

has an attractive Gothic church with superb furnishings, and the moated castle of Veynau (14–15th centuries). The spa town of **Bad Münstereifel** dates

Picturesque half-timbered houses in Monschau

back to 830, when a Benedictine monastery was established here. The present church is a 12th-century Romanesque basilica with impressive 11th-century frontage. Also worth seeing are the Gothic town hall and a Romanesque house, now housing a museum.

🏛 **Rheinisches Freilichtmuseum Kommern**
Auf dem Kahlenbusch. Mechernich-Kommern. **Tel** (02443) 998 00.
Open Apr–Oct: 9am–6pm; Nov–Mar: 10am–4pm. 🎭

⑰ Brühl

Road map B4. 🗻 42,000. 🚉 🚌 🛈 Uhlstr. 1 (02232-793 45). 🎪 Hubertusmarkt (Oct).

The small town of Brühl has one of the most beautiful residential complexes, since 1984 a UNESCO World Heritage Site. As early as the 13th century, a palace was established here for the archbishops of nearby Köln, but this was destroyed in 1689. A Baroque palace, **Augustusburg**, was built on its foundations in 1725–8, according to a design by Johann Conrad Schlaun. It was named after the instigator of the building, Elector Klemens August. The building was almost immediately refurbished, with a new façade and furnishings, the work of François Cuvilliés, and in the 1940s a new staircase was completed to a design by Balthasar Neumann. After devastation in World War II, the palace was carefully restored, and the magnificently furnished late-Baroque and Rococo interior, especially a stunning dining room designed by Cuvilliés, can now be seen again. A path leads from the orangery to a Gothic church built for the Franciscans in the 15th century. The *Annunciation* on the high altar is the work of Johann Wolfgang van der Auwer, while the magnificent canopy above was designed

Phantasialand, one of the largest theme parks in Germany, near Brühl

by Balthasar Neumann. The castle is surrounded by a Baroque park, designed by Dominique Girard.

About 2 km (1 mile) east of the main residence is another castle, **Falkenlust**, built in 1729–40, to a design by Cuvilliés. Its captivating interior includes a lacquered and a mirror cabinet. Nearby stands an octagonal chapel, its interior decoration modelled on a secluded grotto.

It is also worth visiting the small villa near Augustusburg where the great Surrealist artist Max Ernst was born. It now houses a small display commemorating his work.

Another attraction, which draws a large number of visitors is **Phantasialand**, Germany's largest theme park. Visitors will need several days to see all the attractions of this vast fairground with its roller-coaster, water-rides and numerous merry-go-rounds.

Augustusburg
Tel (02232) 440 00. **Open** Feb–Nov: 9am–noon & 1:30–4pm Tue–Fri, 10am–5pm Sat & Sun.

Falkenlust
Tel (02232) 440 00. **Open** Feb–Nov: 9am–noon & 1:30–4pm Tue–Fri, 10am–5pm Sat & Sun.

Phantasialand
Berggeiststr. 31–41. **Tel** (02232) 362 00. **Open** Apr–Oct: 9am–6pm daily, later in summer.

Environs
Two moated houses await the visitor at **Kerpen**, 27 km (17 miles) to the north: the small 16th-century castle of Lörsfeld, and the Baroque palace of Türnich, built in 1756–66.

In **Pulheim-Brauweiler**, 30 km (19 miles) to the north, is an extremely beautiful Benedictine monastery, founded in 1024. Building began in 1048, funded by Rycheza, the wife of the Polish King Boleslav Chrobry.

From here it is worth travelling another 23 km (14 miles) west to **Bedburg**, where the moated castle is worth seeing. This is a vast brick structure with four wings, which was established in stages over 300 years, starting in around 1300.

⑱ Bonn

See p412.

⑲ Königswinter

Road map B4. 35,000. Drachenfelsstr. 51 (02223-91 77 11).

Königswinter lies in the centre of the Siebengebirge, an attractive range of small, wooded mountains (the "seven mountains"), excellently suited for walking. The most popular mountain is the Drachenfels (dragon's rock). The oldest mountain railway in Germany, built in 1883, takes visitors to the top (321 m/1,053 ft). During the ascent visitors can see the Neo-Gothic Drachenburg, a palace dating from 1879–84, and on the top are the ruins of the Gothic Drachenburg, dating from the 12th century. The "dragon" in the name relates to the myth of the Nibelungs – the dragon slain by Siegfried was supposed to have lived here.

The little town of Königswinter, at the foot of the mountains, has picturesque 17th-century half-timbered houses, town houses and late 19th-century hotels.

Environs
Bad Honnef, 6 km (4 miles) to the south, is a charming spa town known as "Nice on the Rhine", where the former chancellor Konrad Adenauer lived until his death. A museum commemorates this great politician.

Situated 15 km (9 miles) to the north is **Siegburg**, home to a Benedictine monastery from 1064 (closed to the public). The present church is a 17th-century building, reconstructed after World War II. The Anno-Schrein is a magnificent Romanesque reliquary box dating from 1183.

The Baroque Schloss Augustusburg in Brühl

⑱ Bonn

Bonn was founded by the Romans in 11 BC, and flourished thanks to the archbishops of Cologne. It gained fame because of Ludwig van Beethoven, who was born here in 1770, and Robert Schumann, who spent the final years of his life here. The world heard of Bonn when, on 10 May 1949, it was elevated to the status of capital of the Federal Republic of Germany. When parliament decided in 1991 to make Berlin the capital of the newly unified country, Bonn was deprived of its role, although six ministries stayed on.

The Baroque portal of the Beethovenhaus in Bonn

🏛 Beethovenhaus
Bonngasse 20. **Tel** (0228) 981 75 25.
Open Apr–Oct: 10am–6pm Mon–Sat, 11am–6pm Sun; Nov–Mar: 10am–5pm Mon–Sat, 11am–7pm Sun. 🏛

The museum is housed in the Baroque 18th-century house where the composer Ludwig van Beethoven was born and lived until the age of 22. He never returned to his home town, but there is a large and impressive collection of memorabilia from his entire life.

🏛 Markt
The central market square in Bonn, shaped like a triangle, owes its present appearance to a mixture of modern and

Baroque architecture. Its most outstanding feature is the late-Baroque **Rathaus** (town hall), built in 1737–8, to a design by Michel Leveilly. The centre of the market square is decorated with the Marktbrunnen, a fountain in the shape of an obelisk, erected in 1777 in honour of the Elector Maximilian Friedrich.

Not far from the Markt are some churches worth seeing. The first is the Gothic **Remigius-kirche**, built for the Franciscans in the years 1274–1317, and the second is the Baroque **Namen-Jesu-Kirche** built for the Jesuits according to a design by Jacob de Candreal in the years 1686–1717.

🏛 Rheinufer
The Rhine embankment, which changes its name several times along its course, runs along the western bank of the Rhine. Many of Bonn's attractions are grouped along this street. To the north of Kennedybrücke (Kennedy bridge) lies the Beethovenhalle, a vast concert and congress hall, and

to the south of the bridge is the Bonn opera house. Next to the opera is the Alter Zoll, the former customs house, based in one of the bastions that were part of the 17th-century city defences.

🏛 Universität
Am Hofgarten.
Founded in 1818, the university is based in what is probably the most beautiful home for an educational institution anywhere in Germany. The stunningly attractive Baroque castle was built for the Elector Joseph Klemens in 1607–1705, to a design by Enrico Zuccalli, and extended after 1715 by Robert de Cotte.

🏛 Münster St Martin
Münsterplatz.
Bonn's cathedral is a magnificent example of Romanesque architecture in the Rhine Valley. The church was built in around 1150–1230, on the site of an earlier 11th-century cathedral, of which a three-naved crypt has survived. South of it, the romantic 12th-century Romanesque cloister is also worth seeing.

Gold clasps in the Rheinisches Landesmuseum

🏛 Rheinisches Landesmuseum
Colmantstraße 14–16.
Tel (0228) 20 700. **Open** 10am–6pm Tue–Sun, 10am–9pm Wed. 🌐 **rlmb.lvr.de**

This interesting regional museum has a vast collection of excavated items dating back to Roman times, as well as medieval and modern art. The skull of a Neanderthal Man is also exhibited here.

The Baroque Elector's palace, housing Bonn University

▦ Regierungsviertel

Until 1999 this was the central authority of one of the most powerful countries in Europe. Now it creates a somewhat desolate impression. Some ministries and offices have remained in Bonn, and the transfer to Berlin is under discussion, but the town is definitely changing.

The former Bundestag building, in the Regierungsviertel

▦ Haus der Geschichte der BR Deutschland

Willy-Brandt-Allee 14. **Tel** (0228) 916 50. **Open** 9am–7pm Tue–Fri, 10am–6pm Sat & Sun.

This excellent museum details the history of Germany after World War II, with fascinating multi-media displays. It is one of the architecturally impressive buildings which form Bonn's "Museums Mile".

▥ Kunstmuseum Bonn

Friedrich-Ebert-Allee 2. **Tel** (0228) 77 62 60. **Open** 11am–6pm Tue–Sun, 11am–9pm Wed. **Closed** 24, 25 & 31 Dec; Sat, Sun & Mon in carnival.

This superb museum of 20th-century art, in an interesting building designed by Axel Schultes, has a great collection of Expressionist paintings, including many works by August Macke. Next to the museum is the Kunst- und Ausstellungshalle, which opened in 1992 as a venue for temporary exhibitions.

▨ Bad Godesberg

The small spa town of Bad Godesberg was incorporated into Bonn in 1969. An elegant neighbourhood, its villas line the spa park. On top of the hill is the Godesburg, a ruined 13th-century castle.

⛪ Poppelsdorf

This leafy southwestern suburb is home to the Baroque Schloss Clemensruhe (1715–18). Both the castle and its extensive park with an attractive botanical garden belong to the university. The Baroque pilgrimage church on the Kreuzberg, a low hill, houses the chapel of the Holy Steps, attributed to Balthasar Neumann.

The Baroque Schloss Clemensruhe, in Poppelsdorf

Bonn City Centre

① Beethovenhaus
② Markt
③ Rheinufer
④ Universität
⑤ Münster St Martin

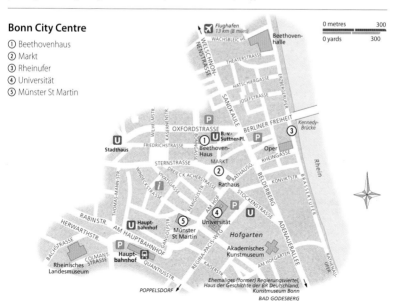

For keys to symbols see back flap

The medieval Oberes Schloss in Siegen

⑳ Siegen

Road map B4. 👥 100,000. 🚇 🚌
ℹ️ Markt 2 (0271-404 13 16).
🎭 Kultur Pur (May/Jun), Rubensfest
(Jun/Jul), Weihnachtsmarkt (Dec).

Beautifully located amid the
hills on the high banks of the
Sieg river, Siegen is the largest
town in the Siegerland region.
For centuries the city was the
residence of the dukes of
Nassau. Religious divisions in the
family resulted in two castles
being built in Siegen. The
Oberes Schloss (upper castle) is
a medieval building, frequently
refurbished in the 16th, 17th and
18th centuries. The museum,
which has been opened inside
the castle, has some paintings
by Peter Paul Rubens, who was
born in Siegen. The lower
Unteres Schloss is a Baroque
palace, which replaced an
earlier building. In the centre of
Siegen it is also worth visiting
the **Nicolaikirche**, a 13th-
century hexagonal church

with a presbytery and tower,
which served as the ducal
family mausoleum.

Environs
In **Freudenberg**, 10 km
(6 miles) northwest of Siegen,
is the small settlement of Alter
Flecken, which is reproduced
in virtually all German guidebooks. Founded in 1666 at the
instigation of Duke Johann
Moritz von Nassau, the village
consists of identical half-
timbered houses.

㉑ Hagen

Road map B4. 👥 210,950. 🚇 🚌
ℹ️ Rathausstr. 13 (02331-207 58 94).
🎭 Marktschreiertage (Jan).

Hagen would probably not
feature in the guidebooks, were
it not for Karl Ernst Osthaus,
who created an artists' colony
here at the beginning of the
20th century, inviting Art
Nouveau designers such as
Peter Behrens and Henry van
der Velde. The magnificent
Hohenhof, Osthaus' home, was
created by van der Velde. It
houses the **Karl-Ernst-Osthaus-
Museum**, with a collection of
modern art. Behrens designed
the crematorium in the suburb
of Delstern and the beautiful
villas **Haus Cuno** (Haßleyer Str.
35) and **Haus Goedeke**
(Amselgasse). In the south of
the town is the Westfälisches

Freilichtmuseum, a popular
open-air museum, which
displays many historic
workshops and factories with
reconstructed equipment.

㉒ Sauerland

Road map B4. ℹ️ Sauerland-Touristik,
Johannes-Hummel-Weg 1, 57392
Schmallenberg (02974-96 980).

The Sauerland is the region to
the south and east of the Ruhr
coalfields, making an obvious
holiday destination for the
inhabitants of this large,
industrialized conurbation.
Embracing the northern part
of the Rhenish slate massif, its
densely wooded mountains are
not high – the highest peak is
Hegekopf at 843 m (2,766 ft).
Crossed by rivers teeming with
fish and full of artificial lakes,
the area is perfect for walking,
cycling and fishing.
    Enjoyable days can be had on
an excursion to one of the caves
such as **Attahöhle, Dechenhöhle** and **Heinrichshöhle** near
Iserlohn. There are charming
towns, too, and in **Breckerfeld**,
the Gothic parish church has
preserved a superb altar, from
around 1520. The main attraction
in **Altena** is the superb, gigantic
Burg (castle), built in the 12th
century and restored in the
early 20th century. In 1910 the
world's first youth hostel for
tourists was created here. The

One of the charming villages, nestling in the hilly landscape of the Sauerland

Timber-frame house, typical of the Sauerland landscape

14th-century Schloss Wocklum in **Balve** was rebuilt in the 18th century. One of the greatest tourist draws in the Sauerland is the **Möhnesee**, a lake with a huge dam, built in 1908–12 and bombed by Allied "dambusters" in 1943 with catastrophic consequences. **Arnsberg** has a regional museum and the lovely Neo-Gothic moated castle Herdringen with assorted furnishings from other castles.

In the south extend the Rot-haargebirge (red-haired mountains). Their most beautiful town is the spa resort of Bad Berleburg, while the Kahler Asten mountain and the town of Winterberg are popular winter sports areas.

㉓ Soest

Road map B4. 🏙 50,000. 🚪 🚌
ℹ️ Teichsmühlengasse 3 (02921-66 35 00 50). 🎪 Bördetag (May), Gauklertag (Sep), Jahrmarkt Allerheiligenkirmes (Nov).

The Westphalian town of Soest made its mark in history when, in about 1100, the town's civic rights were formulated and subsequently adopted by 65 other towns. Today the town captivates visitors with its well-preserved old town, its historic churches, and the almost completely intact walls which surround the town. The focus of the old town is the Romanesque **Propsteikirche St Patrokli**, founded in 965 by Bruno, archbishop of Cologne, and built in stages until the 13th century. Further historic buildings are grouped around the church: the 18th-century, Baroque **Rathaus** (town hall), the 12th-century Romanesque

Petrikirche with its Gothic presbytery, and the 12th-century **Nicolaikapelle**, a chapel with 13th-century wall paintings and an altar painted by Konrad von Soest.

In the northern part of the old town, two churches are worth seeing: the **Hohnekirche** with beautiful Gothic and early Baroque furnishings, and the **Wiesenkirche** with a magnificent group of stained-glass windows from the 14th and 15th centuries. The window above the northern portal shows the so-called Westphalian Last Supper, depicting a table laden with plentiful Westphalian smoked ham and local pumpernickel bread.

A 'Three Hares' window, an emblem of Paderborn

Environ

In **Lippstadt**, 23 km (14 miles) east of Soest, it is worth visiting the Gothic Marienkirche. In the suburb of Bökenförde is the 18th-century Baroque moated palace Schwarzenraben, and there is an early-Baroque castle in Overhagen.

㉔ Paderborn

Road map C3. 🏙 140,000. 🚪 🚌
ℹ️ Marienplatz 2 (05251-88 29 80). 🎪 Puppenfestspiele (Feb), Schützenfest (Jul), Liborifest (Jul–Aug), Liborikirmes (Oct).

Paderborn has featured on the historical map for over 1,000 years. In the 8th century Charlemagne built a palace here, and in about AD 800, a bishopric was established. The town's most important monument is the beautiful **Dom St Maria, St Kilian und St Liborius**, a Romanesque-Gothic cathedral. This enormous hall-church with two transepts and tall front tower suffered greatly during World War II, but it continues to captivate visitors with its magnificent decor on the richly carved portal, the great Romanesque crypt, interesting plaques and richly

decorated bishops' tombs and epitaphs. The diocesan museum holds the Imad-Madonna, funded by Bishop Imad, an outstanding figure of the Madonna and Child dating from 1051–8. On the northern side of the cathedral a section of the foundations of the emperor's palace can be seen, together with the **Bartholomäuskapelle** (chapel of St Bartholomew), the oldest hall-church in Germany, completed in 1017. To the south of the cathedral complex, on Rathausplatz, is the exceptionally beautiful **Rathaus** (town hall) dating from 1613–20. An example of the Weser-Renaissance style, it is crowned with richly ornamented gables. The **Heinz-Nixdorf-Museumsforum** provides a pleasant break from the past – this museum is dedicated to the history of computers.

Environs

Near **Stukenbrock**, 15 km (9 miles) north of Paderborn, is the theme park Hollywood-Park and the fascinating Safariland, where more than 500 African animals roam freely.

Tower of the Romanesque-Gothic Dom in Paderborn

Front of the early-Romanesque Abtei Corvey in Höxter

㉕ Höxter

Road map C3. 🗺 35,000. 🚌 🚏
ℹ Weserstraße 11 (05271-194 33).
🎭 Corveyer Musikwochen (May–Jun), Huxorimarkt (Sep), Kirchenmusiktage (Nov–Dec).

In a picturesque spot on the Weser river, Höxter can pride itself on its beautiful old town with many timber-frame houses, fragments of the city walls, a Renaissance **Rathaus** (town hall) from 1610, and important churches. The history of **Kilianikirche**, in the centre of the old town, goes back to the late 8th century, although in its present form it is a Romanesque building from the 11th–12th centuries. Also in the centre of Höxter is a

Gothic church built for the Franciscans in 1248–1320.

The city's greatest attraction, however, is the magnificent **Abtei Corvey**, a monastery founded in 822. It was originally built as the church of St Stephen and St Vitus, but only the grandiose two-storey frontage completed in 885 survived. It became the model for several other churches built in Westphalia, while the main body of the church was rebuilt in the 17th century.

㉖ Lemgo

Road map C3. 🗺 42,000. 🚌 🚏
ℹ Kramerstr 1. (05261-988 70).

This exceptionally pretty town was founded in 1190 by Bernhard II von Lippe. It was a member of the Hanseatic League, and had its heyday during the witch hunts of the 17th century. Today, Lemgo has numerous Renaissance monuments – it was spared during World War II, and the Gothic Nicolaikirche and Marienkirche, with Gothic wall paintings and a Renaissance organ by Georg Slegel, have survived. The pearl of the city is the beautiful **Rathaus** (town hall), built in the 15th–17th centuries. It contains an original pharmacy that is still in use.

Many timber-frame houses have also survived, the best ones in Papen-, Mittel- and Echternstraße. The most beautiful house in Lemgo

Façade of a Renaissance pharmacy inside the Rathaus in Lemgo

is the **Hexenbürgermeisterhaus**. This "witches' mayor's house" (1571), an excellent example of Weser Renaissance, belonged to the mayor, Hermann Cothmann, who started the witch hunt. It now houses a town museum. Also worth visiting are the **Junkerhaus** (1891), the architect's home, and **Schloss Brake** (13th-16th centuries), a castle which now houses the **Weserrenaissance-Museum**.

🏛 **Weserrenaissance-Museum**
Schloss Brake. **Tel** (05261) 945 00.
Open 10am–6pm Tue–Sun.

㉗ Teutoburger Wald (Teutoburg Forest)

Road map C3. ℹ Detmold, Rathaus Am Markt 5 (05231-97 73 28).
🎭 Sommerbühne (Aug), Andreas-Messe in Detmold (Nov).

A range of low mountains extending from Osnabrück through Bielefeld right up to Paderborn, the Teutoburg Forest is one of the most attractive tourist regions in Westphalia. The best base for walking and cycling holidays is **Detmold**, which has a very attractive old town with well-preserved timber-frame buildings from various periods, and the elegant Residenzschloss, the castle of the zur Lippe family. Originally medieval, the palace was rebuilt in the 16th century in the Weser-Renaissance style. The interior is composed of 17th and 19th

The picturesque Renaissance Rathaus in Höxter

◀ The Beethoven Monument on the Munsterplatz, Bonn

century furnishings. The star feature is a set of eight gobelins crafted in a Brussels workshop around 1670, showing scenes of Alexander the Great's triumphs. Furnishings from the 19th century include designs by Charles Le Brun.

Three km (2 miles) south of Detmold is the spot where in the year AD 9 Cherusko Arminius, known as Hermann, leader of the Germanic tribes, triumphed against the Roman army led by Varus. At the top of the mountain, the **Hermannsdenkmal**, a huge monument designed by Ernst von Bandel, was erected in 1838–75. It was supposed to symbolize the German struggle for unification.

Two fascinating attractions near Detmold are the **Adlerwarte Berlebeck**, an ornithological research station, where eagles and many other birds of prey can be observed, and the **Vogelpark Heiligenkirchen**, a bird park with over 2,000 varieties of birds in all shapes and sizes from around the world.

㉘ Bielefeld

Road map C3. 325,000.
Niederwall 23 (0521-51 69 99).
Hermannslauf (Apr), Leinenweber-Markt (May), Bielefelder Kultur-Sommer (May–Sep), Sparrenburgfest (Jul), Weinmarkt (Sep), Weihnachtsmarkt (Dec).

On the edge of the Teutoburg Forest, Bielefeld owes its evolution to the production of and trading in linen. The old town is dominated by the **Sparrenburg** castle, built in the 13th century for the von Ravensberg family. In the 1500s the castle was surrounded by new fortifications including new bastions, and in the 19th century the residential part of the city was greatly extended.

The central feature of the old town is Alter Markt (old market), on which stands the

Nicolaikirche. This Gothic church suffered heavily in World War II, although the marvellous Antwerp altar (c.1520) was preserved. Nearby, on Obernstraße, stands the **Crüwell-Haus**, an interesting late-Gothic town house from the early 16th century. The street leads to **St Jodokus-Kirche**, a late-Gothic church, whose greatest treasure is the amazing figure of the Black Madonna (c.1220). Further south is the **Kunsthalle**, a modern building with a significant collection of 20th-century art. It is also worth visiting the **Marienkirche** in the new town. Built in 1280–1330, this Gothic church holds the tomb of one of the von Ravensberg dukes (c.1320) and a high altar (c.1400) with a central Gothic section.

Environs

Picturesque **Herford**, 17 km (11 miles) north of Bielefeld, has timber-frame houses, beautiful Gothic churches and **MARTa Herford**, an art and design museum by Frank O. Gehry. In **Enger**, 21 km (13 miles) to the north, in the former church of the canons, a tomb dating from 1100 holds the remains of the Saxon Duke Widukind, buried in 807.

The spa town of **Bad Salzuflen**, with its pretty old town and spa, is ideal for relaxation.

An observation tower in the Sparrenburg complex in Bielefeld

The Wasserstraßenkreuzung (waterway junction) in Minden

㉙ Minden

Road map C3. 85,000.
Domstraße 2 (0571-829 06 59).
Klassik-Open-Air (Jul/Aug).

Charlemagne created a bishopric here as early as 798. The town evolved thanks to its strategic location on the Weser river. The city's most important monument is the cathedral, **Dompfarrkirche St Petrus und St Gorgonius**. It has a Romanesque presbytery, transept and monumental frontage built in the 11th–12th centuries, although the body of the church is an example of early-Gothic style from the 13th century. It is worth visiting the church treasury with its 11th-century crucifix.

The **Rathaus** (town hall), with 13th-century lower sections, is worth seeing, as are Minden's many charming houses around the market square. A great attraction is the **Wasserstraßenkreuz** (waterway junction), where a 375-m (1,230-ft) long bridge takes the Mittellandkanal across the Weser river.

Environs

On top of a hill in **Porta Westfalica**, 6 km (4 miles) south of Minden, is a giant monument to Kaiser Wilhelm (1892–6) by Bruno Schmitz.

The **Westfälische Mühlenstraße**, (Westphalian mill route), signposted around Minden, takes visitors past 42 different mills and windmills.

Hermannsdenkmal, near Detmold

NORTHERN GERMANY

Introducing
  Northern Germany   422–427

Lower Saxony,
  Hamburg and Bremen   428–457

Schleswig-Holstein   458–469

Mecklenburg–
  Lower Pomerania   470–485

RATS ∴ APOTHEKE

Northern Germany at a Glance

Northern Germany has very varied landscapes, ranging
from the sandy beaches on the Baltic and North Sea
coasts to the moraine hills of Schleswig-Holstein and the
moorlands of the Lüneburger Heide. Nature-lovers are
enchanted by the countless lakes in Mecklenburg and
the Harz mountains, while those interested in history
or architecture enjoy the Renaissance castles along the
Weser River and the Gothic brick architecture in former
Hanseatic towns. Historic buildings in Goslar and
Hildesheim testify to the importance of these two towns.

Locator Map

Helgoland is a popular
tourist destination. Red cliffs
as high as skyscrapers, a
picturesque town and the
sea aquarium are the star
attractions of this island.

Niebüll

Flensburg

Schleswig

SCHLESWIG-
HOLSTEIN
(See pp458–69)

Neumünst

Itzehoe

Cuxhaven

Elmshorn

Wilhelmshaven

Bremerhaven

Hamb

Emden

Leer

Oldenburg

Bremen

Soltau

Cloppenburg

LOWER SAXONY,
HAMBURG AND
BREMEN
(See pp428–57)

Meppen

Nienburg

Lingen

Bramsche

Hannover

Osnabrück

Hildeshei

Oldenburg, symbolized by its
heraldic shield, is famous for its large
collection of paintings and interiors
in its Kunstmuseum (art museum).

Göttinge

Bremen, a historic harbour town,
draws visitors with its many historic
buildings and monuments, including
a Renaissance-Gothic town hall.

◀ Handsome period buildings in Neuer Markt, Rostock

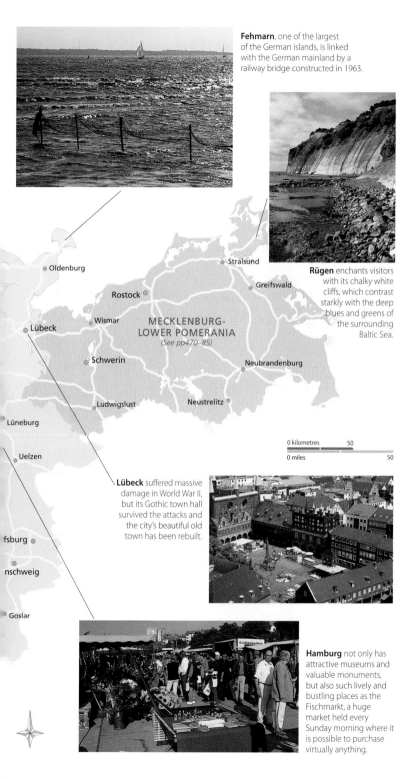

Fehmarn, one of the largest of the German islands, is linked with the German mainland by a railway bridge constructed in 1963.

Rügen enchants visitors with its chalky white cliffs, which contrast starkly with the deep blues and greens of the surrounding Baltic Sea.

Stralsund

Oldenburg

Greifswald

Rostock

Wismar

MECKLENBURG-LOWER POMERANIA
(See pp470–85)

Lübeck

Schwerin

Neubrandenburg

Ludwigslust

Neustrelitz

Lüneburg

Uelzen

0 kilometres   50

0 miles   50

Lübeck suffered massive damage in World War II, but its Gothic town hall survived the attacks and the city's beautiful old town has been rebuilt.

fsburg

nschweig

Goslar

Hamburg not only has attractive museums and valuable monuments, but also such lively and bustling places as the Fischmarkt, a huge market held every Sunday morning where it is possible to purchase virtually anything.

Gothic Brick Architecture

Brick was used as a building material in many parts of medieval Europe, but in Northern Germany it gave rise to the distinctive style of *Backsteingotik* (brick Gothic). Brick technology was introduced in the mid-12th century by Norbertine monks arriving from Lombardy. The style is characterized by a rich variety of vaults, the use of buttresses instead of supporting arches, and colourful designs achieved by using glazed bricks. Through trade and the activities of religious orders these forms spread throughout the Baltic region.

The storeys are divided by friezes.

The eastern façade of many churches, such as the Marienkirche in Prenzlau *(above)* was often crowned by an elaborate, ornamental gable.

Marienkirche in Lübeck

Considered the crowning achievement of Backsteingotik, this church, built from around 1260, became the model for countless others, including the cathedral in Schwerin. It is a triple-naved basilica, with a twin-towered façade, braced with buttresses.

A pointed arched portal, decorated with ceramic borders, was a typical feature of many village churches.

Main portal

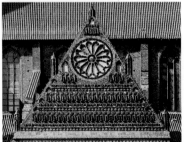

Gables with tiled decorations and intricate openwork, such as this gable of the south chapel of the Nikolaikirche in Wismar, are a feature of many Lower Pomeranian churches.

The vast twin-towered façade symbolizes the power of its founders – wealthy Lübeck patricians.

Terracotta tiles with raised decorative motifs were used in brick architecture in place of stone bas-reliefs.

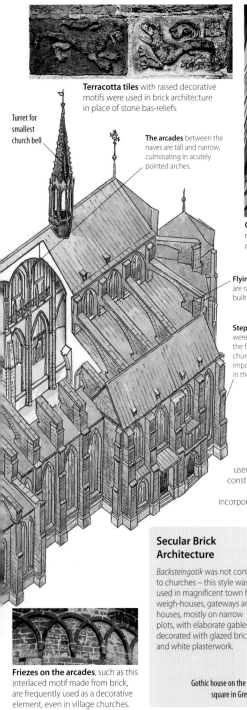

Turret for smallest church bell

The arcades between the naves are tall and narrow, culminating in acutely pointed arches.

Complex star vaulting with intricate ribbing replaced the earlier cross-ribbed vaulting.

Flying buttresses are rare in brick-built churches.

Stepped walls were used to dress the façades of the church. They were an important element in the construction.

Beam openings indicate that a robust type of scaffolding was used in the course of construction. The ends of the beams are incorporated in the walls.

Secular Brick Architecture

Backsteingotik was not confined to churches – this style was used in magnificent town halls, weigh-houses, gateways and houses, mostly on narrow plots, with elaborate gables decorated with glazed bricks and white plasterwork.

Gothic house on the market square in Greifswald

Friezes on the arcades, such as this interlaced motif made from brick, are frequently used as a decorative element, even in village churches.

The German Coastline

The waters of two seas – the North Sea and the Baltic Sea – lap on northern Germany's shores, linked by the Kiel Canal, which cuts across the base of the Jutland peninsula. The cool climate on the coast makes for short summers yet, on a sunny day, the beaches are packed with holidaymakers, and a holiday here can have alot to offer. Heiligendamm was the first seaside resort to be established in Germany, in 1783 by a duke of Mecklenburg. By the end of the 19th century, spas with elegant villas, promenades and piers were springing up everywhere. A popular attraction are the *Strandkörbe* – huge wickerwork beach chairs.

The sand dunes form part of a nature reserve in the northern part of Sylt, the largest of the North Frisian islands.

The Cliffs of Helgoland have a characteristic reddish hue indicating the red sandstone from which they are composed.

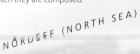

Borkum, one of the East Frisian islands, was once inhabited by whalers. Garden fences were often constructed from whale bones, and some have survived to the present day.

The Kiel Canal, known in Germany as the Nord-Ostsee-Kanal, was constructed in 1887–95. Around 40,000 vessels pass through the canal every year.

Bremerhaven is a vast port at the mouth of the Weser river. It was constructed from 1827 to support the port of Bremen, which is located farther inland, away from the sea.

Stralsund, a Hanseatic harbour town with a medieval layout, has a large number of well-preserved historic monuments.

On the small, flat island of Hiddensee all car traffic is banned. The island was much loved by the writer Gerhart Hauptmann, who lies buried here in the local cemetery.

The Coastline

The hinterland of the Baltic region is generally flat and sandy, but in some areas it is steep and rocky. For visitors the greatest draw are the islands: Rügen with its steep chalky cliffs, Usedom with its wide, sandy beaches and Hiddensee. Off the lowlands and the marshy coastal region in the hinterland of the North Sea coast extends the chain of Frisian islands.

The beach at Ahlbeck and the pier with its restaurant are the greatest attractions on the island of Usedom, at the mouth of the Oder river.

207

OSTSEE (BALTIC SEA)

•Bergen
RÜGEN

Stralsund

ODERBUCHT

Ribnitz-
- Damgarten
96

LÜBECKER
BUCHT
105
•Rostock
103
•Greifswald

Wismar
20
E251/96
109

Gustrow
•Anklam
104

Schwerin
Ueckermünde•

Rügen, famous for its unusual chalky cliff formations, was immortalized by Caspar David Friedrich and continues to inspire artists.

0 km   60

0 miles   60

Cross-Section of Watt (North Sea)

The Watt is a flat, boggy stretch of coastline, up to several kilometres wide, that is covered by the sea as the tide comes in, and laid bare as it goes out again. The Watt landscape is fairly monotonous, but it is fascinating to observe the rich flora and fauna, which has adapted to cope with life both underwater and exposed to the air.

Winkles and other small snails live in the coastal zone by the sea.

Starfish   Lugworm and sand cast   Sand gaper (mussel)

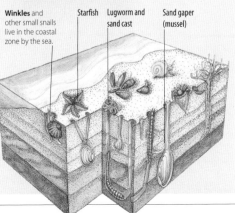

LOWER SAXONY, HAMBURG AND BREMEN

Three federal states – Lower Saxony and the independent city states of Hamburg and Bremen – cover an enormous terrain, embracing the whole of northwestern Germany. For the visitor they provide a series of memorable snapshots: the mighty cosmopolitan port of Hamburg, enchanting towns and villages with half-timbered houses and the blooming heather of the Lüneburger Heide.

Lower Saxony was formed in the 19th century through the merging of the kingdom of Hannover with the duchy of Brunswick, Oldenburg and Schaumburg-Lippe and other parts of northern Germany. The second-largest German state after Bavaria, it only ranks fourth in terms of the number of its inhabitants, being less densely populated than other states.

Lower Saxony is characterized by lowlands that become hillier in the south, culminating in the Harz Mountains. The only large cities are Hannover, a modern centre renowned for its trade fairs and for hosting Expo 2000, and Braunschweig, a venerable town that cherishes its link with the Saxon king Heinrich der Löwe, its first important ruler. The Romanesque splendour of Hildesheim is a magnet for visitors, as are the Renaissance centres along the Weser River including Hameln, the charming towns of Celle, Lüneburg and Einbeck, and Wolfenbüttel, Stadthagen and Bückeburg which contain some remarkable Mannerist works of art.

Nature lovers will enjoy excursions to the Lüneburger Heide or paddling in the endless expanses of mud-flats in the North Sea. Tourists are also attracted by the sandy beaches of the East Frisian islands, as well as the solitary rock of the island of Helgoland.

The "free and Hanseatic" towns of Hamburg and Bremen rejoice in a different atmosphere, urban and urbane, tolerant and multicultural, based on centuries of trade with the world.

The glorious moorlands of the Lüneburger Heide, with tall juniper bushes and flowering heathers

◀ Statue of Roland in front of the town hall in Bremen

Exploring Lower Saxony, Hamburg and Bremen

Hamburg and Bremen, the region's largest cities, are also the most convenient bases for tourists, offering accommodation in every price category. The most attractive area in this region is the south-eastern section, extending to the foothills of the Harz Mountains with picturesque towns, such as the university town of Göttingen, Romanesque Hildesheim or the stunningly beautiful merchant town of Goslar. A visit to the seaside and an excursion to the islands are also enjoyable.

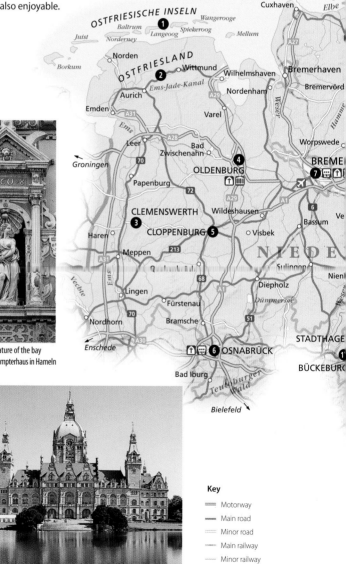

The crowning feature of the bay window of the Dempterhaus in Hameln

The massive edifice of the Neues Rathaus in Hannover

Key

- ═══ Motorway
- ── Main road
- ┈┈ Minor road
- ▪▪▪ Main railway
- ── Minor railway
- ▓▓ National border
- ▬▬ Regional border

For additional map symbols *see back flap*

Getting Around

There are international airports in Hamburg, Bremen and Hannover. A network of motorways links Lower Saxony with Scandinavia (via Schleswig-Holstein), and with the rest of western Europe (via the Netherlands or southern Germany). An extensive rail network makes the entire state accessible, although bus connections are limited.

The Grosse Wallanlagen Park in Hamburg, laid out along the city's former fortifications

Sights at a Glance

1. Ostfriesische Inseln (East Frisian Islands)
2. Ostfriesland (Eastern Frisia)
3. Clemenswerth
4. Oldenburg
5. Cloppenburg
7. *Bremen pp434–7*
6. Osnabrück
8. *Hamburg pp438–43*
9. Altes Land
10. Stade
11. Lüneburg
12. Lüneburger Heide
13. Soltau
14. Celle
15. Wolfsburg
16. Stadthagen
17. Bückeburg
18. Braunschweig (Brunswick)
19. Wolfenbüttel
20. *Hannover (Hanover) pp448–9*
21. *Hildesheim pp452–3*
22. *Goslar pp454–5*
23. Einbeck
24. Göttingen
25. Duderstadt

Tours

26. The Weser Renaissance Trail

0 kilometres 40

0 miles 40

❶ Ostfriesische Inseln (East Frisian Islands)

Road map B2. 🚢 Emden-Borkum, Norden-Norddeich to Juist and Norderney, Nessmersiel-Baltrum, Benfersiel-Langeoog, Neuharlingersiel-Spiekeroog, Harlesiel-Wangerooge. 🛈 Leer, Ledastr. 10. (0491) 91 96 96 60. 🌐 ostfriesland.de

Along the North Sea Coast extends the belt of East Frisian Islands consisting of, from west to east: Borkum, Juist, Norderney, Baltrum, Langeoog, Spiekeroog and Wangerooge. All around them is the **Nationalpark Niedersächsisches Wattenmeer**, a large national park established to protect the unique ecosystem of the shallow seas. At low tide it turns into vast mud-flats, extending to the horizon. This is the time to tour the Watt, as it is known locally, either by horse-drawn carriage or barefoot – always making sure to return before the tide comes in!

The islands themselves, with their beautiful sandy beaches, sand dunes and healthy climate, are among the most popular holiday destinations in Germany.

The car-free island Juist, a 17-km (11-mile) strip of land less than 500 m (1,640 ft) wide, and Norderney with its main town of the same name are the most interesting islands. Neo-Classical villas recall the days when such figures as Heinrich Heine and Otto von Bismarck spent their holidays here. It is also worth

Moormuseum in Elisabethfehn, Ostfriesland

visiting Wangerooge, another island where cars are banned. Three lighthouses – Westturm, Alter Leuchtturm and Neuer Leuchtturm – indicate the island's role in the navigation of the Weser River estuary.

❷ Ostfriesland (East Frisia)

Road map B2. 🚉 Emden, Leer, Norden. 🛈 (0491) 91 96 96 60. 🎭 Kiewittmarkt (Jever, end Mar); Altstadtfest (Jever, Aug). 🌐 ostfriesland.de

East Frisia is a peninsula near the border with the Netherlands and the Jadebusen bay, at Wilhelmshaven. This is a land of flat meadows, grazing cows and windmills.

Emden, the region's capital, has an attractive town hall resembling that in Antwerp, and a town centre crossed by many canals. The **Kunsthalle Emden**, founded in the early 1990s by Henri Nannen, publisher of the magazine *Stern*, holds a remarkable collection of 19th-century paintings, including the works of many German Expressionists such as Emil Nolde, Max Beckmann and Oskar Kokoschka.

Another attraction is the **Moor- und Fehnmuseum** (moor and fen museum) in Elisabethfehn, which is dedicated to the extraction of peat. Its exhibits include the world's largest plough, as well as the story of Jever, the local beer. Also worth visiting are the Renaissance palace whose reception hall

has a ceiling with sunken panels, and next to the parish church the wood and stone tomb of the Frisian leader Edo Wiemken, made in 1561–4 by master craftsmen from Antwerp.

🏛 Kunsthalle Emden
Hinter dem Rahmen 13. **Tel** (04921) 975 00. **Open** 10am–5pm Tue–Fri, 11am–5pm Sat & Sun; 10am–9pm first Tue of month. 🅿

🏛 Moor- und Fehnmuseum
Oldenburger-Str. 1. **Tel** (04499) 22 22. **Open** Apr–Oct: 10am–5pm Tue–Sun.

❸ Clemenswerth

Road map B3. 🚉 Sögel or Lathen. 🛈 Papenburg, Rathausstr. 2 (04961-839 60). Schloss: **Tel** 05952-93 23 25. **Open** Apr–Oct: 10am–6pm Tue–Sun. **Closed** winter.

Emsland, to the south of East Frisia, extends along the Dutch border, a poor area since time immemorial, with moors and boglands. Only the discovery of oil in the 20th century engineered its progress. Sögel, 33 km (21 miles) south of Greater Papenburg, has the region's greatest attraction, the palatial hunting lodge or Schloss Clemenswerth, built from 1737–49. In search of solitude, the elector and archbishop of Cologne Clemens August commissioned the lodge from Johan Conrad Schlaun. The design was modelled on the pavilion-pagoda of Nymphenburg in Munich. Altogether it comprises seven pavilions with mansard roofs and a chapel. All the brick buildings were laid out on a green lawn, creating a star shape around the palace. Inside there is a museum of the region.

Nationalpark Niedersächsisches Wattenmeer in the Greefsiel area

❹ Oldenburg

Road map B2. 🚌 160,000. 🚊
ℹ️ Kleine Kirchenstr. 10 (0441 36 16
13 66). 🎪 Hafenfest (7 days after
Whitsun); Altstadtfest (end Aug);
Kramermarkt (Sep/Oct).
ⓦ **oldenburg.de**

A thousand years old, and
once part of Denmark, this
town remained the seat of
a duchy until 1918.

The **Lambertikirche**, in the
central market square, is a late-
Gothic hall-church with a Neo-
Classical rotunda added in
1797. The **Schloss**, the ducal
residence, displays a similar
marriage of styles, particularly
Baroque and Neo-Classical. The
**Landesmuseum für Kunst und
Kulturgeschichte** (state
museum of art and culture),
based in the castle, is known
mainly for its collection of
paintings assembled by Wilhelm
Tischbein, who lived here for 25
years. The affiliated **Augusteum**,
a Neo-Renaissance building in
a picturesque spot, holds the
museum's modern collection.

🏛️ **Landesmuseum für Kunst und
Kulturgeschichte**
Damm 1. **Tel** (0441) 220 73 00.
Open 10am–6pm Tue–Sun.
Closed 1 Jan, Good Friday, Easter,
1 May, 24, 25 & 31 Dec. 🅿️

Environs

The town of **Bad Zwischenahn**
is worth a visit. Its star attraction
is the Gothic St Johanniskirche
with frescoes from 1512.

A windmill in the open-air museum in
Cloppenburg

❺ Cloppenburg

Road map B2. 🚌 29,000. ℹ️ Eschstr.
29 (04471-152 56). 🎪 Mariä
Geburtsmarkt (Sep).

The small market town of
Cloppenburg boasts the
Museumsdorf, the oldest
open-air museum in
Germany, established
in 1934. On a vast site,
50 architectural
monuments from all
over Lower Saxony
have been assembled.
There are houses,
including charming
examples of the half-
timbered style of
Wehlburg, windmills
and a small
17th-century church
from Klein-Escherde
near Hildesheim.

To the east of
Cloppenburg lies Visbek. Here
the visitor is taken back to the
Stone Age, with megalithic
graves from 3,500 to 1,800 BC,
including the 80-m (262-ft) long
grave known as "Visbeker
Bräutigam" (bridegroom) and
the even larger, 100-m (321-ft)
long "Visbeker Braut" (bride).

🏛️ **Museumsdorf Cloppenburg**
Bether Straße 6. **Tel** (04471) 948 40.
Open Mar–Oct: 9am–6pm daily,
Nov–Feb: 9am–4:30pm daily. 🅿️

❻ Osnabrück

Road map B3. 🚌 157,000. 🚊
ℹ️ Bierstr. 22–23 (0541-32 32 202).
🎪 Herbstjahrmarkt (early Nov).
ⓦ **osnabrueck.de**

This Westphalian town has
been a bishop's see since the
time of Charlemagne. In 1648,
negotiations took place here
between representatives of
Sweden and the
Protestant duchies of
the Reich. The signing
of the Peace of
Westphalia in 1648,
which ended the
Thirty Years' War, was
announced from the
town hall steps. It was
also the birthplace of
the writer Erich Maria
Remarque in 1899.

Despite damage in
World War II, **Dom St
Peter**, Osnabrück's
13th-century
cathedral, is worth
visiting. It has a bronze baptismal
font and enormous triumphal
cross, and the late-Gothic
Snetlage-Altar of the Crucifixion.
From here a short walk takes
the visitor to the market square,
Marienkirche and the Gothic
Rathaus (town hall), with a
sculpture of Charlemagne.

Epitaph for Albert von
Bevessen in the Dom in
Osnabrück

Environs

South of Osnabrück is the
western part of the Teutoburger
Wald (Teutoburg Forest). The spa
town of **Bad Iburg**, 12 km (8
miles) to the south of Osnabrück,
has a monumental Benedictine
monastery and bishop's palace.
The Rittersaal (knights' hall) has
a giant ceiling fresco depicting
an architectural fantasy of
foreshortened perspectives.

The Schloss in Oldenburg, featuring Baroque and Neo-Classical styles

❼ Bremen

Bremen, together with its deep-water port Bremerhaven, constitutes a separate town state. Not so much a bustling modern metropolis as a peaceful country town, it is conscious of its historical origins dating back to Charlemagne. The townscape is not dominated by the port as in Hamburg, but by the old town with its magnificent cathedral and town hall. Bremen enjoyed prosperity from 1358 when it joined the Hanseatic League, its wealth based on the coffee and wool trade. Today, Bremen still benefits from its port, which ships around 700,000 cars a year.

Statue of the Bremen Town Musicians, by Gerhard Marcks

Gabled houses and the statue of Roland in the Marktplatz

Exploring Bremen

Most of Bremen's tourist attractions are in the old town, on the east bank of the Weser River. The area is easy to pick out on a map as it is surrounded by a green belt, established when the town's fortifications were demolished. The Übersemuseum (ethnography museum) is close to the old town, and trams run to Schwachhausen, where the Focke-Museum is based.

🏛 Marktplatz

On the main square of Medieval Bremen stand the town hall and the cathedral, and, on the west side, several gabled houses. This lovely view is slightly marred by the unattractive 1960s Haus der Bürgerschaft, the state parliament building.

In front of the town hall stands a 10-m (32-ft) statue of Roland, dating from 1404. It is the largest of many similar statues in German towns, and the prototype for others. A nephew of Charlemagne, Roland symbolizes a town's independence. His gaze is directed toward the cathedral, the residence of the bishop, who frequently sought to restrict Bremen's autonomy. Roland's sword of justice symbolizes the judiciary's independence, and the engraved motto confirms the emperor's edict, conferring town rights onto Bremen.

The second, more recent (1953) monument in the square is dedicated to the Bremen Town Musicians – a donkey, dog, cat and cockerel, who according to the Grimm fairy tale trekked to Bremen.

🏛 Rathaus

Marktplatz. **Tel** (0421) 30 80 00.
🕐 11am, noon, 3pm, 4pm Mon–Sat, 11am–noon Sun. 🖼

The original Gothic building dating from 1405–10 was clad with a magnificent façade, one of the finest examples of Weser Renaissance architecture in northern Germany, designed by Lüder von Bentheim. He masterfully incorporated the Gothic figures of Charlemagne and seven Electors, as well as four prophets and four wise men. In the 40-m (131-ft) Große Halle (great hall) new laws were passed, as symbolized by the fresco (1932) of Solomon's court. Other Rathaus treasures include the Renaissance spiral staircase. On the western side of the town hall is the entrance to the "Ratskeller" where you can sample 600 different wines, and delight in the murals from 1927, by the Impressionist Max Slevogt.

🏛 Schütting

Marktplatz.
On the southwestern side of Marktplatz stands this mansion used by the Merchants' Guild

The late-Renaissance façade of Bremen's Rathaus

for their conventions. It was built in 1537–9 by the Antwerp architect Johann der Buschener in Dutch Mannerist style. The eastern gable, more classically Renaissance in style, is the work of the local builder Carsten Husmann.

🏛 Dom

Tower and "Bleikeller": **Tel** (0421) 36 50 40. **Open** Easter–1 Nov: 10am–5pm Mon–Fri, 10am–2pm Sat, 2–5pm Sun.

This magnificent Romanesque cathedral, with its vast twin-towered façade, dates from the 11th century and has been extensively refurbished. At the end of the 19th century, while the southern tower was rebuilt, the façade was also reconstructed and a tower

The Mannerist Schütting, a meeting place for merchants

was added. Inside, it is worth looking at the sandstone bas-reliefs which divide the western choir stalls as well as fragments of Gothic stalls that were destroyed in the 19th century, with scenes of the Passion and the battle of Judas Machabeus. There is also a Baroque pulpit paid for by Christina the Queen of Sweden in 1638, and numerous

VISITORS' CHECKLIST

Practical Information
Road map: C2. 🚇 556,000. ℹ Hauptbahnhof & Obernstraße (01805 10 10 30). 🚢 Port tours (0421-33 89 89). Cruises: May–Sep: 10 & 11:30am, 1:30 & 3:15pm daily. 🚃 🚌 Sat & Sun. 🎭 6 Tage Rennen (Jan); Osterwiese (Apr); Vegesack Harbour Festival (Jun); Bremer Freimarkt (late Oct/early Nov); Christmas market (1–23 Dec). 🅆 bremen-turismus.de

Transport
🚈

multi-coloured memorials, including one to Segebad Clüver by the entrance to the north tower (1457). The larger eastern crypt has interesting Romanesque capitals, while in the second eastern crypt visitors can admire the oldest Bremen sculpture of Christ the Omnipotent (1050) as well as the baptismal font. The latter has 38 bas-reliefs, and a bowl supported by four lions with riders. In the so-called "Bleikeller" (lead cellar) underneath the former church cloisters, eight perfectly preserved mummies are on show.

Bas-reliefs on the western choir stalls in the Dom

Bremen Town Centre

① Marktplatz
② Rathaus
③ Dom
④ Schütting
⑤ Böttcherstraße
⑥ Schnoorviertel
⑦ Kunsthalle
⑧ Übersemuseum

0 metres 500
0 yards 500

For keys to symbols see back flap

Kunstsammlungen Böttcherstraße
Paula-Modersohn-Becker-Museum and Roseliushaus

Böttcherstr. 6–10. **Tel** (0421) 338 8222. **Open** 11am–6pm Tue–Sun. **W** pmbm.de

This once insignificant lane where coopers lived was transformed into Art Deco style in 1926–30 by Ludwig Roselius, a wealthy coffee merchant. The National Socialists pre- served the street as an example of degenerate art. At the entrance to the street is a bas-relief by Bernhard Hoetger from 1920, of the Archangel Michael fighting a dragon.

The **Paula-Modersohn-Becker-Museum**, built in the Expressionist style, contains an art museum, while in the neighbouring 16th-century **Roseliushaus** the original period interiors can be admired. The street's other attraction is a carillon which chimes tuneful melodies every day at noon, 3pm and 6pm.

Archangel Michael fighting a dragon, on a bas-relief in Böttcherstrasse

Schnoorviertel
Spielzeugmuseum: Schnoor 24. **Tel** (0421) 32 03 82. **Open** 10am–6pm daily

This historic district of small houses dates from the 15th–18th centuries. One of Bremen's poorest areas before World War II, it miraculously escaped destruction. It has been restored gradually since 1958 and now teems with restaurants, cafés, souvenir shops and tourists. In the centre of the district is the Gothic **Johanniskirche**, which once belonged to the Franciscans. In accordance with the order's rules it has no tower, although this is compensated for by a decorative gable on the western façade, and three levels of arched alcoves and herringbone brickwork. The **Spielzeugmuseum** (toy museum) nearby is also worth visiting.

Kunsthalle
Am Wall 207. **Tel** (0421) 32 90 80. **Open** 10am–9pm Tue, 10am–6pm Wed–Sun.

This art gallery on the edge of the old town lost most of its collection to Russia during World War II. The pieces that remained, as well as works subsequently acquired, make the collection of great importance. There are works by Dürer, Altdorfer, Rubens, Jan Breughel, van Dyck and Rembrandt. There is also an excellent French section, with works by Delacroix, Denis, Monet and Manet, as well as 19th- and 20th-century German painters such as Beckmann and Kirchner. At the heart of the collection are about 40 paintings by Paula Modersohn-Becker.

Übersee-Museum
Bahnhofplatz 13. **Tel** (0421) 160 38 101. **Open** 9am–6pm Tue–Fri, 10am–6pm Sat & Sun.

This museum of overseas countries transports the visitor to faraway destinations. Founded in 1891, it was originally a museum of German colonialism and is now dedicated to the culture of non- European nations. Of special interest are exhibits on Pacific cultures, with life-sized models of houses and boats from the Solomon Islands.

Focke-Museum
Schwachhauser-Heerstr. 240. **Tel** (0421) 699 60 00. **Open** 10am–9pm Tue, 10am–5pm Wed–Sun.

The excellent collections of this museum compensate for its distant location. Founded in 1918, when the history museum was amalgamated with the decorative arts museum, it presents Bremen's art and culture from the Middle Ages to the present day. Exhibits from patrician houses and original sculptures from the façade of the town hall testify to the wealth of the Hanseatic town. Other sections are devoted to the archaeology of the region as well as to whaling and emigration to the US in the 19th and 20th centuries.

The nearby Rhododendronpark offers a pleasant respite from the museums. It includes 1,600 varieties of rhododendron which become a sea of flowers from late April to June.

Environs
Three places in the Bremen area are particularly worth a detour. About 50 km (31 miles) to the north lies Bremen's deep-sea harbour **Bremerhaven**, with the **Deutsches Schifffahrtsmuseum**. This wonderful marine museum,

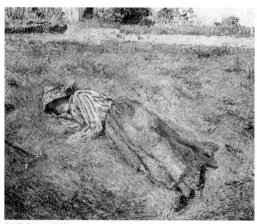
Camille Pissarro, *Girl lying on a grassy slope*, Kunsthalle

For hotels and restaurants in this area see pp492–503 and pp510–33

Paula Modersohn-Becker (1876–1907)

A pupil of Fritz Mackensen and wife of Otto Modersohn, Paula Modersohn-Becker was the most significant artistic figure in Worpswede. She learned about the Impressionist use of colour

during visits to Paris, and her own unique sensibility made her a precursor of Expressionism. She became famous for her naturalistic paintings of poor, starving and even dying country folk. She died in childbirth, aged only 31, and this is how she was commemorated on her tombstone, in the peaceful village cemetery in Worpswede, by the sculptor Bernhard Hoetger.

Girl playing a flute in birch woods (1905)

Exhibits in the Große Kunstschau in Worpswede near Bremen

designed by the renowned architect Hans Scharoun, displays both originals and models of a wide range of ships, dating from the Roman Empire to the present day. A special hall displays the *Hanse Kogge,* a merchant ship dredged from the bottom of the Weser River in 1962. Displayed outside, in the open-air part of the museum, are the last great German sailing boat *Seute Deern*, the polar ship *Grönland* and *Wilhelm Bauer*, a U-boat from World War II.

The small village of **Worpswede**, northeast of Bremen, takes the visitor into the world of art. From 1889 until the end of World War II it was a famous artists' colony, situated in the middle of peat bogs. Apart from poets, such as Rainer Maria Rilke, and such architects as Bernhard Hoetger, the fame of this village rested principally on the painters: Fritz

Mackensen, Otto Modersohn, Hans am Ende, Fritz Overbeck and Heinrich Vogeler. Unquestionably the greatest artist in Worpswede was Paula Modersohn-Becker, whose sad fairy-tale world of rustic subjects cannot be defined within one style. Work by the founding members is on display in the **Große Kunstschau and the Worpsweder Kunsthalle**.

Verden an der Aller, the picturesque bishops' residence and once a free town of the Reich, is known to sports enthusiasts thanks to its horse-racing tracks, training centres and stadiums, and the **Deutsches Pferdemuseum** (horse museum), with a large collection of equestrian artifacts. Seven horse auctions are held in the town each year, the main ones being in April and October.

Above the town rises the Dom with a large, steep roof. The hall of this cathedral, a modification of earlier basilicas, is architecturally interesting, with a multi-sided presbytery, a passageway dating from 1268–1311 and Romanesque cloisters and a tower. North of the cathedral is the Domherrenhaus, housing the Historisches Museum, with exhibits on regional history and archaeological and ethnographic departments.

The **Deutsches Auswandererhaus Bremerhaven** traces the history of more than 7 million Germans who emigrated via Bremerhaven, especially to the United States. A database of records is available.

🏛 **Deutsches Schifffahrtsmuseum**
Bremerhaven, Hans-Scharoun-Platz 1. **Tel** (0471) 482 070. **Open** 10am–6pm daily (Nov–Feb: Tue–Sun only). 📷

🏛 **Große Kunstschau**
Worpswede. Lindenallee 3 & 5. **Tel** (04792) 13 02. **Open** 10am–6pm daily (closed Mon in Nov–Mar). 📷

🏛 **Worpsweder Kunsthalle**
Bergstr. 17. **Tel** (04792) 12 77. **Open** Apr–Oct: 10am–6pm daily; Nov–Mar: 11am–6pm daily. 📷

🏛 **Deutsches Pferdemuseum**
Holzmarkt 9. **Tel** (04231) 80 71 40. **Open** 10am–5pm Tue–Sun.

🏛 **Deutsches Auswandererhaus Bremerhaven**
Columbusstr. 65. **Tel** (0471) 90220-0. **Open** Mar–Oct: 10am–6pm daily; Nov–Feb: 10am–5pm daily.
🌐 dah-bremerhaven.de

The Dom in Verden an der Aller, with its unusually large roof

❽ Hamburg

Germany's second largest city, Ham- burg has an openness to the world and a variety of architectural styles in its districts, making it a fascinating place to visit. For many years, Hamburg was a leading member of the Hanseatic League and an independent trading town, and in 1945 it became a city-state of the Federal Republic. Visitors are attracted by Hamburg's enormous port, situated right in the centre of the city, colourful entertainments in the red-light district St Pauli, many attractive parks and lakes as well as the warm welcome extended by the locals who, on first encounter, may seem a little cool.

A fountain in the Neo-Renaissance Rathausmarkt

Exploring Hamburg

The best way to get around Hamburg is by metro (U-Bahn and S-Bahn), using an all-day ticket (Tageskarte). The city centre can be explored on foot, including the area between the main railway station and the lake, along with the rest of the old town, the port and Hamburg's two largest museums.

🏛 Rathausmarkt

The symbol of Hamburg is the enormous Neo-Renaissance town hall, the fifth in the city's history. Previous town halls were destroyed by wars as well as a catastrophic fire in 1842. Little remains of the old town. The city's current appearance is characterized by 19th-century style as well as Modernism. The town hall itself, with its ornamental halls, is worth visiting.

The town hall square is enclosed on one side by Alster-fleet. Originally a small river, it is today one of numerous canals which have given Hamburg the name "Venice of the North". A monument in memory of the victims of World War I is the work of the artist Ernst Barlach. Between Rathausmarkt and Gänsemarkt runs a network of elegantly roofed shopping arcades. These were built in the 19th century, and have since been continually extended.

🏛 Alster

Elegant arcades lead from the Rathausmarkt to Binnenalster, a large lake in the middle of the city. Like the much larger Außenalster lake further north, it was created by damming the Alster River. On a sunny day, the Jungfernstieg, an elegant boulevard running the length of the Alster, is a pleasant place for a walk. Great views of the city can be had from the café in the Alsterpavilion. There is a small quay from which boats depart for the "Alster-rundfahrt", an excursion that takes the visitor all the way to the Außen-alster and to smaller canals with views of the villas in the north of Hamburg and the cityscape of the centre with its five main towers.

Door knocker on St Petrikirche

⛪ St Petrikirche

Mönckebergstr. **Tel** (040) 325 74 00.
Open 10am–6:30pm Mon, Tue, Thu, Fri; 10am–7pm Wed; 10am–5pm Sat; 9am–9pm Sun.

The church of St Petri, originally Gothic, was extensively rebuilt in the Neo-Gothic style after the Great Fire of 1842. The Grabower Altar that once belonged to the church has been transferred to the Kunsthalle (see pp440–41). Tourists can still admire the Gothic sculpture of the Madonna, dating from 1470.

🏛 Jakobikirche

Jakobikirchhof 22. **Tel** (040) 303 73 70.
Open Oct–Mar: 11am–5pm Mon–Sat; Apr–Sep 10am–5pm Mon–Sat.

The church of St Jacobi, from 1340, was bombed during World War II, and subsequently rebuilt in its original style. Its captivating interior includes the largest Baroque organ in northern Germany, the work

The main altar in Jakobikirche

of Arp Schnitger. The triptych of St Luke in the presbytery of the southern nave, a magnificent example of late-Gothic art, was originally created in 1499 for Hamburg's cathedral, which was pulled down in 1804.

🏛 Kontorhausviertel

Deichtorhallen: Deichtorstr. 1–2. **Tel** (040) 32 10 30. **Open** 11am–6pm Tue–Sun (during exhibitions).
After World War I, a district of commercial offices known as Kontorhausviertel was built between Steinstraße and Messberg. The **Chilehaus**, built by Fritz Höger in 1922–4, was an experiment in creating a traditional brick building with a Modernist design. This ten-storey building, with its pointed eastern façade resembling a ship's bow, became internationally famous as a symbol of Expressionist architecture.

Nearby are the enormous **Deichtorhallen**, market halls of the port built in 1911–12. Turned into dramatic exhibition halls in 1997, they are now used for major art exhibitions.

The Expressionist Chilehaus in Kontorhausviertel

🏛 Speicherstadt

Deutsches Zollmuseum: Alter Wandrahm 16a. **Tel** (040) 30 08 76 11. **Open** 10am–5pm Tue–Sun.
The atmosphere of the giant warehouse district by the port will seem depressing to some, charming to others. Located within the toll-free area of the port, this district is reached after crossing the customs post. It is the largest complex of ware-houses in the world. The Neo-Gothic buildings, dating from the end of the 19th century, are separated by canals. They still serve as storerooms for coffee, tea and carpets. Listed as one of

VISITORS' CHECKLIST

Practical Information
Road map C2. 🗺 1.7 million.
ℹ️ Hauptbahnhof, Kirchenallee (040-30 05 12 00) **Open** 9am–7pm Mon–Sat, 10am–6pm Sun & hols; in the port, Landungsbrücken (040-30 05 12 03). 🌐 **hamburg-tourism.de** Hafenrundfahrten (harbour tours): **Tel** (040) 311 70 70 & 31 31 40. **Open** Apr–Oct: once every 1.5 hrs,10:30am–4:30pm; Nov–Mar: call for times. 🎉 Hafengeburtstag (anniversary of the port, around 7 May).

Transport
✈️ in Fuhlsbüttel, U1 or S1 to Ohlsdorf, then Airport Express (40 min). 🚃 Kirchenallee.

the city's historic monuments, Speicherstadt now houses the Speicherstadt Museum and is part of Hafen City, a residential and office development. The **Deutsches Zollmuseum** (German customs museum) located by Kornhausbrücke, (corn house bridge), tells the story of customs and excise from the Roman Empire to the present day.

Hamburg City Centre

① Rathausmarkt
② Alster
③ St Petrikirche
④ Jakobikirche
⑤ Kontorhausviertel
⑥ Speicherstadt
⑦ Kunsthalle
⑧ Altstadt (Old Town)

For keys to symbols *see back flap*

Kunsthalle

The most interesting art gallery in northern Germany, the Kunsthalle in Hamburg has a tradition dating back to 1817, when the Kunstverein (friends of the fine arts), proud of its middle-class, non-aristocratic background, was established. The museum opened to the public in 1869. The collection has a standard chronological review of European art movements, with an emphasis on 19th-century German Romantics, with works by Caspar David Friedrich and Philipp Otto Runge. A four-storey extension, the Galerie der Gegenwart (contemporary gallery), was built in 1996 to a design by the architect O M Ungers. The building is reached by an underground link from the basement of the main gallery.

The Polar Sea (1823–4)
Caspar David Friedrich's dramatic seascape, with a sinking ship in the background behind the rising flow, is loaded with symbolism.

★ **Hannah and Simeon in the Temple** (c.1627) Thanks to his mastery of a sense of drama, Rembrandt succeeded in depicting the psychological make-up of his elderly subjects, who have recognized the Saviour in an unspoken message conveyed to the temple by Mary and Joseph.

High Altar of St Peter in Hamburg (1383)
This panelled painting, displaying a stunning wealth of detail, was produced by Master Bertram of Minden, the first artist in Germany to be identified by his name.

★ **Morning** (1808)
This painting by Philipp Otto Runge centres around Aurora, goddess of dawn, and was intended to be part of a series called "Times of the Day". The other works were never completed due to the artist's untimely death aged 33.

Main entrance

Ground floor

Self-Portrait with Model
(1910 and 1926) Sixteen years after first painting this picture, Ernst Ludwig Kirchner repainted areas, in order to emphasize the distance between model and artist.

VISITORS' CHECKLIST

Practical Information
Glockengießerwall.
Tel (040) 428 131 200. **Open** 10am–6pm Tue–Sun (to 9pm Thu). Library: **Open** 11am–5pm Tue–Fri (to 9pm Thu). Café: **Open** 10am–6pm Tue–Sun (to 9pm Thu).
w **hamburger-kunsthalle.de**

142
141
139
138
140
143
144
145
147
135/136
148

First floor

134
133
132
131
130

18
19

★ **Girls on the Pier** (1901) This painting is one of six variations on the same theme painted by Edvard Munch. The painter omitted the landscape, concentrating on the relationship and tensions between the girls.

Gallery Guide

On the ground floor, Rooms 2–10 and 16–19 contain works of art from the first half of the 20th century. On the first floor, Rooms 101–116 display the works of old masters. In Rooms 117–136 paintings from the 19th century are exhibited, and more works from the first half of the 20th century are shown in Rooms 137–148.

Stairs down to underground link to Galerie der Gegenwart

10
9
8
7
6
5
4

Stairs to basement and Hubertus-Wald-Forum with temporary exhibitions

Nana (1877) The subject of Édouard Manet's painting was the heroine of a Zola novel. Manet was not allowed to exhibit the painting in the Paris Salon because Nana was known as a Parisian courtesan.

Key
- Gallery of old masters
- 19th-century paintings
- 20th-century paintings (first half)
- Gallery of drawings
- Non-exhibition space

⊞ Altstadt (Old Town)

Hamburg's old town extends to the south of the Rathaus (town hall) but, following the Great Fire of 1842 and bombing during World War II, only a few original buildings remain. **Katharinenkirche** (St Catherine's), with its characteristic tower, was begun in the 13th century and completed in the 17th century. It has been restored after damage in World War II. Of the neighbouring Neo-Gothic **Nikolaikirche** only a single tower remained after 1945, the Nikolaiturm, which is the third tallest in Germany. It serves as a monument to the tragic consequences of war.

Deichstrasse is one of a few surviving streets in the old town, with the original façades still visible from both the road and the canal (the best view can be had from the Hohe Brücke bridge). One of the many famous local restaurants is "Zum Brandanfang", at No. 25. It is here that the Great Fire of 1842, which eventually destroyed most of the city, was said to have broken out.

Ornate Baroque pulpit in Hamburg's Michaeliskirche

⛪ Michaeliskirche

Observation tower: **Tel** (040) 37 67 80. **Open** May–Oct: 9am–7:30pm daily, Nov–Apr: 10am–5:30pm daily.

The massive Baroque church of St Michaelis, visible from afar with its 132-m (433-ft) tower (the "Michel"), is the main symbol of Hamburg.

The neon-lit Reeperbahn in St Pauli

The interior is preserved in a white, grey and gold colour scheme, and some of the fittings are made from tropical wood. The observation platform offers splendid views of the city and its extensive harbour.

⊞ Krameramtswohnungen

Krayenkamp 10. **Tel** (040) 37 50 19 88. **Open** 31 Mar–29 Nov: 10am–5pm Tue–Sun; 30 Nov–30 Mar: 10am–5pm Sat & Sun.

Near the Michaeliskirche, a section of the old town, the Krameramtswohnungen, has miraculously survived. These half-timbered houses were funded by the merchants' guild and built to house the widows of shopkeepers. Today they are occupied by tourist shops, cafés and restaurants.

⚓ The Port

Cap San Diego **Tel** (040) 36 42 09. **Open** 10am–6pm daily. Rickmer Rickmers **Tel** (040) 319 59 59. **Open** 10am–8pm daily.

Situated 104 km (62 miles) inland along the Elbe River, Hamburg is Europe's second largest port after Rotterdam, and the port dominates the panorama. Every year 12,000 ships dock here from 90 countries. From the U3 Baumwall metro station it is best to walk to **Landungs-brücken**, past the museum ships moored here: the freighter *Cap San Diego* and the sailing boat *Rickmer Rickmers* (1896). Landungsbrücken is a 200-m (656-ft) long building from where the passenger ferries depart. A tour of the harbour is highly recommended. Near Landungsbrücken, in a copper-domed building, is the entrance to Alter Elbtunnel (the old tunnel under the Elbe) where people and cars are lowered in a giant lift.

⊞ St Pauli

Infamous around the world, this area is also known as **Reeperbahn**, after the main street. It is a world of nightclubs and bars, pubs and theatres, sex clubs and brothels. It is here, in Hamburg's red light district, that some teenage seasonal workers from Liverpool, the Beatles, started their careers. On Herbertstrasse, scantily clad women offer their services

Fischmarkt – A Market for Everything

This is an attraction for early risers or for those who never get to bed at all. From 5am (7am in winter) on Sundays the Auktionshalle (auction hall) and the nearby waterside turn into a colourful market place. Fishermen returning from the sea with their freshly caught fish compete with noisy greengrocers offering their wares and bric-à-brac merchants setting out stalls. Thousands of tourists mingle with sailors and ladies of the night relaxing with a cup of steaming mulled wine after a hard night's work in St Pauli. Here and there you can hear Plattdeutsch being spoken, the northern patois. Morning mass at 10am used to mark the end of this colourful spectacle, but today's public lingers on and then hurries off to bed instead of church.

Bric-à-brac on sale at a market stall in Fischmarkt

For hotels and restaurants in this area see pp492–503 and pp510–33

behind a metal barrier – women and those under 18 are forbidden entrance. St Pauli even has an Erotic-Museum, where next to the exhibits are reproductions of works by artists from Rembrandt to Picasso, which are said to "prove" that everything revolves around the female posterior.

Environs
The magnificent palace in **Ahrensburg** (1595), 23 km (14 miles) to the northeast, has Baroque and Rococo interiors open to visitors.

Façade of Schloss Ahrensburg, flanked by towers

❾ Altes Land

Road map C2.

On the flood plains stretching for more than 30 km (19 miles) between Hamburg and Stade, along the Lower Elbe River, is the Altes Land (old land).

This area is fertile and has the largest number of orchards in Germany. Many visitors come here in May, when cherry and apple tree blossom turns everything into a sea of white and pink. In this riot of colour stand sturdy red-brick houses with white half-timbered panels, thatched roofs and carved gates. The most beautiful villages are **Neuenfelde**, **Jork**, **Borstel**, **Steinkirchen** and **Hollern**, with their richly furnished Baroque churches.

❿ Stade

Road map C2. 47,000.
U3 to Neugraben, then by train or catamaran from Landungsbrücken.
Hansestrasse 16 (04141-40 91 70).
stade-tourismus.de

This medieval Hanseatic town has retained most of its half-timbered buildings, with the most attractive in the **Alter Hafen** (old harbour). There is a also a quaint crane and the **Schwedenspeicher** (Swedish granary) dating from the Swedish occupation during the Thirty Years' War (1692–1705). It is now home to the **Schwedenspeicher-Museum**, a museum with exhibits on the town's history and defence system, including wheels from 700 BC, which were part of a Bronze-Age cart. Nearby, an interesting building at Am Wasser West 7 houses the **Kaufmann Collection**, with works by Worpswede artists. The

The Baroque portal of the Dutch-influenced Rathaus in Stade

entire old town is surrounded by preserved modern fortifications. Other attractions are the **Bürgermeister-Hintze-Haus** at Am Wasser West 23, a house built for the mayor, Hintze, in 1617–46, and the exquisite Baroque **Rathaus** (town hall) from 1667, its design revealing Dutch influence.

The 14th-century Gothic church of **St Wilhadi** boasts an interesting Gothic hall and a leaning tower, while **St Cosmas and Damiani**, founded after the Great Fire of 1659, features marvellous Baroque furnishings.

🏛 **Schwedenspeicher-Museum**
Am Wasser West 39. **Tel** (04141) 79 77 30. **Open** 10am–5pm Tue–Fri, 10am–6pm Sat & Sun.

The half-timbered houses along the waterside of Alter Hafen in Stade

⓫ Lüneburg

Road map D2. 70,000.
Rathaus; Am Markt (04131-
207 66 20). lueneburg.de

It is hard to believe
that this small, former
Hanseatic town was once
one of the wealthiest in
Germany. Its prosperity
was founded on salt
mines. Opened in 956,
they provided work for
more than 2,000 people by the
late Middle Ages and were the
largest industry in Europe.

Lüneburg's most important
monument is the **Rathaus** (town
hall). The interior is even more
intriguing than the frequently
rebuilt façade, in particular the
Großer Ratssaal (the main hall)
with its Gothic stained-glass
windows and 16th-century
frescoes of the Last Judgement,
as well as the Große Ratsstube
(council chamber) with
Renaissance woodwork by
Albert von Soest. A remarkable
collection of municipal
silverware can be found in
Ostpreußisches Landesmuseum.

Johnniskirche, one of
Lüneburg's three Gothic churches, stands on Am Sande. It
has a 108-m (354-ft) west tower
which leans more than 2 m (6 ft)
from the perpendicular. In one
of its five naves there is a
panelled painting dating from
1482–5, the masterful work of
the German painter Hinrik
Funhof. Also interesting is the
soaring basilica of **Michaeliskirche**, consecrated in 1409.

Not far from here is the old
port on the Ilmenau River.

A typical farmstead in Lüneburger Heide

On Lüner Straße stands the **Altes
Kaufhaus**, a former herring
warehouse with a Baroque
façade. The 14th-century
wooden crane was rebuilt in
the 1700s. It was used to load
salt onto ships. The decorative
wavy brick lines *(Taustäbe)* on
many of the old buildings are
characteristic of the town.

🏛 **Rathaus**
Am Markt. **Tel** (04131) 30 92 30.
11am, 12:30pm, 2:30pm, 4pm
Tue–Sat; 11am, 2pm Sun.

⓬ Lüneburger Heide

Road map D2. Wallstr. 4,
Lüneburg (04131-30 99 60).
lueneburger-heide.de

South of Hamburg, between
the rivers Elbe and Aller, is a
sprawling area of heathland,
grazed by heifers and sheep
and buzzing with bees in the
heathers and pine forests.
Until the Middle Ages, this area
was covered by dense mixed
forests, but these were felled
to satisfy demand for wood
in the saltworks of Lüneburg.
The half-stepped terrain

provides grazing land for
Heidschnucken, the local
breed of sheep. The heather
moors are best seen at the
**Naturschutzpark Lüneburger
Heide**, a large area of nature
reserve founded in 1921.
From the village of Undeloh
it is best to continue by foot,
bike or carriage to the
traditional village of Wilsede.
From Wilsede it is not far to
Wilseder Berg, the highest peak
of this moraine region. The view
of the surrounding countryside
is particularly beautiful at the
end of August, when the
purple heather is blooming.

⓭ Soltau

Road map C3. 23,000. Am
Alten Stadtgraben 3 (05191-82 82 82).
soltau.de

The main attraction of the
town of Soltau is **Heidepark
Soltau**, a vast funfair with
trains, water rides and a
genuine Mississippi steamboat.
For nature lovers, there is the
Vogelpark Walsrode, 20 km
(12 miles) southwest of Soltau.
It holds about 1,000 species of
birds, from penguins to birds
of paradise. Aviaries, some
12-m (40-ft) tall, simulate the
birds' natural environment.

🎡 **Heidepark Soltau**
Tel (01805) 92 91 01. **Open** Apr–Oct:
9am–6pm daily (admission till 4pm).

🎡 **Vogelpark Walsrode**
Tel (05161) 604 40. **Open** Apr–Oct:
9am–7pm daily, Nov–Mar 10am–4pm
daily. weltvogelpark.de

Environs
In grim contrast to both
parks stands **Bergen-Belsen**,
a concentration camp
constructed in the moorland
of Osterheide, about 30 km
(19 miles) south of Soltau.
A monument and small
museum commemorate
the place where 50,000
people were murdered,
among them Anne Frank.

🏛 **Gedenkstätte Bergen-Belsen**
Lohheide. **Tel** (05051) 47 59 200.
Open Apr–Sep: 10am–6pm;
Oct–Mar: 10am–5pm daily.

Eighteenth-century wooden crane in Lüneburg

Vogelpark Walsrode – a paradise with 1,000 different bird species

❶ Celle

Road map C3. 74,000.
Schlossplatz. Markt 14–6 (05141-
12 12). Kunsthandwerkermarkt
(Whitsun). **celle-tourismus.de**

Between 1378 and 1705, Celle
was the seat of distant relations
of the Welf family, the reigning
dynasty in the Duchy of
Brunswick-Lüneburg. The
Schloss (castle), rebuilt in
Renaissance style after 1533, has
a façade with octagonal towers,
gables and bay windows. It is one
of the main early-Renaissance
buildings in Germany. The
Gothic chapel was rebuilt in
Mannerist style to a design by
Martin de Vos, who created 76
of its paintings, including the
famous *Crucifixion* (late 1500s).

Celle prides itself on 500 half-
timbered houses, with the most
interesting ones in picturesque
Kalandgasse and Zöllnerstrasse.
Hoppner Haus, at Poststrasse 8,
is richly decorated with reliefs
of mythological beasts. Equally
interesting is the painted
decoration of the **Rathaus** (town

hall), a great example of Weser
Renaissance *(see p457)* from 1579.
From the **Stadtkirche** church
tower great views unfold. The
Baroque **Synagoge**, beyond
the old town, is the only one
surviving in northern Germany.

🏰 Schloss
Tel (05141) 12 454. **Open** Apr–Oct:
11am, noon, 1, 2 & 3pm Tue–Sun;
Nov–Mar: 11am & 3pm Tue–Sun.

🏛 Stadtkirche
Tel (05141) 7735. **Open** 10am–6pm
Tue–Sat. Tower: Apr–Oct: 10–11:45am
2–4:45pm Tue–Sat.

🔯 Synagoge
Im Kreise 24. **Tel** (05141) 12 12.
Open noon–5pm Mon–Thu, Sun;
10am–3pm Fri.

Environs
The town of **Wietze**, 11 km
(7 miles) west of Celle, has
been a centre of petroleum
since 1858. The **Deutsches
Erdölmuseum Wietze** provides
a very interesting overview on
the history of oil extraction.

The neighbouring village of
Wienhausen has a Cistercian

Kloster (monastery) with a
beautiful 13th–14th century
church. Worth seeing are its
Gothic frescoes, the presbytery
vaults and the 14th- and
15th-century tapestries.

🏛 Deutsches Erdölmuseum
Schwarzer Weg 7–9. **Tel** (05146) 92
340. **Open** Mar–Nov: 10am–5pm
Tue–Sun; Jun–Aug: 10am–6pm
Tue–Sun.

🏛 Kloster Wienhausen
Tel (05149) 18 660. Apr–Oct: 10 &
11am, 2–5pm Tue–Sat, noon–5pm
Sun.

❶ Wolfsburg

Road map D3. 123,000.
Willy-Brandt-Platz 3 (05361-89
99 30). **wolfsburg.de**

During the 1930s, this small
village began to develop into a
sizeable town, based around
the Volkswagen car works.
Production of the "people's car"
was conceived by Hitler – every
German was to be able to afford
this inexpensive car, designed
by Ferdinand Porsche. The
model reached its peak during
the post-war economic boom
years. The **Volkswagenwerk**
factory is open to visitors.

Wolfsburg also has some
outstanding examples of
modern architecture: a cultural
centre designed by Alvar Aalto,
a city theatre designed by Hans
Scharoun and a planetarium.

🚗 Volkswagenwerk Autostadt
Stadtbrücke. **Tel** (0800) 28 86 78 238.
Open 9am–6pm daily. every 30
mins. **autostadt.de**

The façade of the Schloss with octagonal towers at the corners, in Celle

The Renaissance Schloss in Stadthagen

⑯ Stadthagen

Road map C3. 🖼 23,800. 🚉 ℹ Am
Markt 1 (05721-92 50 65).
🆆 stadthagen.de

The counts of Schaumburg-
Lippe used the Renaissance
Schloss (castle) as their private
residence. Apart from this and
the town hall, the main attraction
is the church of **St Martini**, with
an early Baroque mausoleum,
and a masterful bronze
monument by Adrian de Vries,
court artist to Rudolf II in Prague.

🏠 St Martini
Schulstr.18. **Tel** (05721) 78 070.
Open 9am–noon, 2–4pm Mon–Thu,
9am–noon Fri.

Environs
A gem of Romanesque
architecture can be found at
Idensen near Wunsdorf, 22 km
(14 miles) from Stadthagen.
The church interior of Alte
Kirche (1120) is entirely painted
with scenes from the Old and
New testaments, and there is
a vast Byzantine-style image
of Christ's Enthronement on
a vaulted ceiling.

⑰ Bückeburg

Road map C3. 🖼 21,000. 🚉
ℹ Schlossplatz 5 (05722-89 31 81).

In the 16th century this town
became the capital of the
principality of Schaumburg-
Lippe. The philosopher Johann
Gottfried von Herder was the
preacher here. The **Stadtkirche**
(town church), one of the first
Protestant churches in Germany,
is a pinnacle of Mannerism with
its fantasy façade. Another

attraction is the **Schloss** with
its enchanting chapel. The
Goldener Saal (golden hall),
from 1605, has a Götterpforte
(portal of the divinities) and a
beautiful panelled ceiling.

🏠 Stadtkirche
Lange Str. **Tel** (05722) 957 70.
Open 15 Apr–14 Oct: 10:30am–noon
Tue–Fri, 2:30–4:30pm Tue–Sun, 15
Oct–14 Apr: 2:30–4:30pm Fri–Sun.

🏠 Schloss
Tel (05722) 50 39. **Open** Apr–Sep:
9:30am–6pm; Oct–Mar: 9:30am–5pm.

The opulent Goldener Saal in Schloss
Bückeburg

⑱ Braunschweig (Brunswick)

Road map E3. 🖼 240,000. 🚉
ℹ Vor der Burg 1 (0531-470 20 40).
🎵 Festival of Chamber Music (May);
Medieval Fair (May/Jun).

An important commercial and
political centre from the early
Middle Ages, Braunschweig
was chosen as town of
residence by Heinrich der
Löwe (Henry the Lion), ruler
of Saxony and Bavaria. A

member of the Welf family, he
eventually lost in his struggle
against the German emperor.

Very different in character
but equally famous was Till
Eulenspiegel, an ordinary man
who poked fun at dim-witted
citizens, the aristocracy and
the clergy. His exploits were
fictionalized in the 16th century,
and he was immortalized with a
fountain on Bäckerklint Square.

Braunschweig's continued
decline culminated in the almost
total destruction of the town in
1944. During reconstruction, the
concept of the "Traditionsinsel"
was developed: small islands
of reconstructed historic
monuments adrift in a sea
of modernism.

A tour of the town is best
started from Burgplatz (castle
square). Here is the **Burglöwe**,
the monument of a lion funded
by Heinrich in 1166 (the original
is in a museum). Symbolizing
Heinrich's rule, it was the first
such sculpture to be erected
since Roman days. The **Dom**
(cathedral) is well worth seeing.
In the north nave, an extension,
are unusual turned pillars, and in
the transept and presbytery
are 13th-century frescoes. Its
marvellous treasures include
a gigantic seven-armed
bronze candlestick, the tomb of
Heinrich and his wife Mathilde,
the Crucifix of Imerward and a
wooden cross with the figure
of Christ modelled on the
sculpture of *Voltosanto* in Lucca.
Visitors can also see the column
of the Passion with the figure of
Christ, the work of Hans Witten.

To the west of the cathedral
lies the **Altstadtmarkt** (old town
market). Here are the L-shaped
Rathaus (town hall), with a
cloister, and the Gothic church
of **St Martini**. The beautiful
Gewandhaus (cloth hall)
is also worth seeing.

The Burglöwe, Heinrich der Löwe's monument
in Braunschweig

East of the cathedral is the **Herzog-Anton-Ulrich-Museum**, the oldest in Germany. It was opened to the public as a gallery by Duke Anton Ulrich and holds a variety of gems such as Rembrandt's *Family Portrait*, a Giorgioni self-portrait and Vermeer van Delft's *Girl with a Glass of Wine*.

⬆ Dom
Burgplatz. **Tel** (0531) 24 33 50.
Open 10am–5pm daily.

⬆ St Martini
Altstadtmarkt. **Tel** (0531) 161 21.
Open Jan–Apr: 10am–1:30pm Tue–Sat, May–Dec: 10am–1pm, 3–5pm Tue–Fri, 10am–5pm Sat, 10am–noon, 3–5pm Sun.

⬛ Herzog-Anton-Ulrich-Museum
Museumsstr. 1. **Tel** (0531) 122 50.
Closed for renovation.

The richly decorated portal of the Gewandhaus in Braunschweig

Environs
In **Königslutter**, 35 km (22 miles) east of Braunschweig, Emperor Lothar initiated the building of the Benedictine **Kaiserdom**, a monastery church and later his burial place. The portal with figures of lions, a frieze with figures of fishermen, and the cloisters reflect the taste of the times and the northern Italian origin of architects and sculptors; only the frescoes are late 19th-century additions.

Helmstedt, 45 km (28 miles) to the east, is unjustifiably only associated with the former border crossing between East and West Germany. In 1576,

The Marienbrunnen fountain on Altstadtmarkt in Braunschweig

Duke Julius of Brunswick founded the Julius Academy, one of Germany's most popular Protestant universities, where the Italian philosopher Giordano Bruno taught. Juleum (1592–7), the main building, has a central tower and two decorative gables. It is now home to the **Kreis- und Universitäts-museum**, a regional museum and library.

⬆ Kaiserdom
Königslutter. **Tel** (05353) 91 21 29.
Open 9am–6pm daily, in winter to 5pm.

⬛ Kreis- und Universitäts-museum
Collegienplatz 1. **Tel** (05351) 121 11 32. **Open** 10am–noon, 3–5pm Tue–Fri, 3–5pm Sat & Sun.

⑩ Wolfenbüttel

Road map E3. 🏠 53,000. 🚍
🛈 Stadtmarkt 7 (05331-86 280).
🎭 Ostereiermark (Easter); Altstadtfest (Aug).

This small town has a turbulent past. From 1432 until 1753 the Welf dukes moved their seat here from Braunschweig. In the 16th century, innovative town design introduced wide avenues and spacious squares. Largely unscathed by World War II, the town has 500 historic half-timbered houses, and a magnificent library. The **Herzog-August-Bibliothek** holds 130,000 volumes, including the

most valuable book in the world, Heinrich der Löwe's Gospel book. Associated with the town are the philosopher Gottfried Wilhelm Leibniz and writer Gotthold Ephraim Lessing. The **Lessinghaus** houses a literature museum.

The centre of the town is dominated by the **Schloss**, the largest castle in Lower Saxony, refurbished in the Baroque style in 1714–16. It houses the **Schlossmuseum** with regional items such as furniture and tapestries. The Venussaal (hall of Venus) has beautiful Baroque ceiling frescoes. Opposite the castle is the **Zeughaus** (armoury), built in 1613–19 to a design by Paul Francke.

Continuing eastwards the visitor will get to the **Hauptkirche**, the 16th-century church dedicated to *Beatae Mariae Virginis*, the ducal pantheon and the leading example of Protestant Mannerist architecture. Begun in 1608, the church's façade has delicate reliefs, while the interior has an unusual combination of styles.

🔲 Schloss and Schlossmuseum
Schlossplatz 13. **Tel** (05331) 924 60.
Open 10am–5pm Tue–Sun.

Lessinghaus, Museum & Zeughaus:
Tel (05331) 80 82 14. **Open** 11am–5pm Tue–Sun. Herzog-August-Bibliothek: **Open** 10am–5pm Tue–Sun.

⬆ Hauptkirche
Michael-Praetorius-Platz 9. **Tel** (05331) 72 055. **Open** 10am–noon, 2–4pm Tue–Sat.

Baroque façade of Schloss Wolfenbüttel

⑳ Hannover (Hanover)

The capital of Lower Saxony, Hannover does not at first glance seem particularly exciting, but appearances can be deceptive: the town boasts interesting architecture in the historic centre, magnificent Baroque gardens and one of Europe's most important museums of modern art. Hannover's past was marked by its dynastic links with England, sharing the same ruler during the years 1714–1837. Annual industrial trade fairs have earned the town an international reputation, and in 2000 Hannover hosted the international exhibition Expo 2000 which attracted 18 million visitors.

Exploring Hannover

After the near-total destruction of the old town in 1944, many historic monuments have been rebuilt, and large green spaces encourage the visitor to explore the town on foot. It is best to follow an extensive circuit, starting from and returning to the railway station. The Baroque gardens at Herrenhausen in the northwest of the town are reached by metro (U-Bahn 4, 5).

🎭 Opernhaus

Opernplatz 1. **Tel** (0511) 99 99 11 11.
The opera house was built in 1845–57 by George Ludwig Friedrich Laves, Hannover's most important architect, to a fine Neo-Classical design. Particularly charming is the façade with portico columns.

🏛 Niedersächsisches Landesmuseum

Willy-Brandt-Allee 5. **Tel** (0511) 980 76 86. **Open** 10am–5pm Tue–Sun, 10am–7pm Thu. 🖼

The most interesting part of the state museum of Lower Saxony is the picture gallery, which holds excellent German medieval and Renaissance paintings (Dürer, Spranger, Cranach), a good section with Dutch and Flemish paintings (Rubens, Rembrandt, van Dyck) as well as German paintings of the 19th and 20th centuries, with fine examples of Romanticism and Impressionism (Friedrich, Corinth, Liebermann).

🏛 Sprengel Museum

Kurt-Schwitters-Platz 1. **Tel** (0511) 16 84 38 75. **Open** 10am–8pm Tue, 10am–6pm Wed–Sun. 🖼

One of Europe's finest museums of modern art, the Sprengel-Museum reflects the city's role as an artists' mecca in the 1920s before the National Socialists destroyed works of art that they designated as "degenerate". Hannover's controversial artist Kurt Schwitters worked here, as did El Lissitzky, whose *Kabinett der Abstrakten* (school of abstraction, 1928, reconstructed) is worth seeing. Funded by Bernhard Sprengel, a chocolate magnate, the museum was built in 1979, and holds works by Munch, Chagall and Picasso, as well as many more recent artists, including Christo.

The museum is located by Maschsee, a large artifical lake created in the centre of the city in 1936. During the summer it teems with motor and sailing boats, while Hanoverians stroll around its banks.

Mueller's *The Lovers* (1920), in the Sprengel-Museum

🏛 Neues Rathaus

Trammplatz 2. **Tel** (0511) 168 45 333. Dome **Open** 9:30am–6pm Mon–Fri; 10am–6pm Sat & Sun.

The gigantic town hall symbolizes the lofty ambitions of the wealthier citizens at the beginning of the 20th century. It was built from 1901–13, on more than 6,000 beech pillars, modelled on a Baroque palace with a central dome, and decorated with Neo-Gothic and Secessionist detail. The Swiss artist Ferdinand Hodler created a vast painting en- titled *Einigkeit* (unity) for the Debating Hall, which depicts the arrival of Protestantism in the town in 1533. A unique oblique lift takes you up to the dome from where there are wonderful views.

🏛 Leineschloss

Hinrich-Wilhelm-Kopf-Platz.
In the historic city centre by the Leine River stands the Leineschloss, a 17th-century palace completely rebuilt by the local architect Laves between 1817 and 1842. It had to be rebuilt again after destruction

Façade of the vast Neues Rathaus, with its central dome

For hotels and restaurants in this area see pp492–503 and pp510–33

Interior of the church of St Georg und
St Jacobus, in Marktplatz

in World War II, and now
serves as headquarters for
the Niedersächsischer Landtag
(Lower Saxony state parliament).
The porticos on the façade
were modelled on ancient
Greek temples.

Marktplatz
Although the houses on this
square had to be almost
completely rebuilt after World
War II, this is one of the best
examples of 15th-century red-
brick architecture, with amazing
gables with projections as well
as figurative friezes of glazed
terracotta. Nearby, the

Marktkirche St Georg und St
Jacobus (church of St George
and St Jacob) features a
14th-century nave with a
characteristic four-pinnacled
tower. The most valuable
object among its furnishings
is the Gothic altar, with scenes
of the Passion and copper
engravings by the renowned
artist Martin Schongauer.

Herrenhäuser Gärten
Despite having been razed to
the ground during World War II,
the gardens in Hannover's
Herrenhausen district are among
the most beautiful Baroque
gardens in Germany. They were
established by Duchess Sophie
von der Pfalz, daughter of
Elizabeth Stuart and mother of
England's George I. The Großer

Garten, the most important of
the four gardens, has a formal
layout modelled on 17th- and
18th-century Dutch parks. It is a
botanical garden with fountains,
including the Große Fontäne,
the tallest in Europe with a 82-m
(269-ft) water spout. There are
grottoes, mazes, sculptures and
decorative urns, and the hedges
are some 21 km (13 miles) long.

VISITORS' CHECKLIST

Practical Information
Road map: C3. 522,000.
Ernst-August-Platz 8 (0511-123
45-111). Sat. Schützenfest
(Jun/Jul), Maschseefest (Jul/Aug).
w hannover.de

Transport
Ernst-August-Platz.

The stunningly beautiful Baroque gardens in Herrenhausen

Hannover City Centre
1 Opernhaus
2 Niedersächsisches Landesmuseum
3 Sprengel Museum
4 Neues Rathaus
5 Leineschloss
6 Marktplatz

㉑ Hildesheim

The undisputed capital of Romanesque culture, the old town of Hildesheim was transformed into a heap of rubble by heavy bombing on 22 March 1945. The most important monuments have now been recreated, with mixed results, surrounded by modern developments. Two churches, the Michaeliskirche and the Dom St. Mariä, are UNESCO World Heritage sites, and the Roemer-Pelizaeus-Museum of Egyptian Culture also makes a visit to Hildesheim worthwhile.

Wedekindhaus, a beautiful half-timbered house on Marktplatz

Exploring Hildesheim

Contrary to received wisdom, the city is best visited on foot. Visitors can park in the centre, for example near the Church of St Michael, and then explore the main sights from here. A round tour, including the museums, should not take longer than around 4–5 hours. It is also possible to follow the Rosenroute (rose trail) around town which is marked on the pavements by white roses.

🏛 Marktplatz

Since gaining civic rights in the 11th century, the heart of the bishopric town has been its market square. Every detail has now been faithfully reconstructed, and it is easy to forget that the square looked totally different only a few years ago. In 1987, the Knochenhaueramtshaus (butchers' guild hall) was rebuilt, the largest and most famous half-timbered house in Germany, dating from 1529. Opposite are the Gothic town hall and the Tempelhaus, an original 15th-century building with round turrets and a half-timbered annexe, added in 1591. Reliefs depict the story of the Prodigal Son.

🏠 Andreaskirche

Andreasplatz. **Open** Apr–Sep: 9am–6pm Mon–Fri, 9am–4pm Sat, 11:30am–4pm Sun; Oct–Mar: 10am–4pm Mon–Sat, 11:30–4pm Sun. Tower May–Oct: 11am–4pm Mon–Sat, noon–4pm Sun. **Closed** Nov–Apr.

The reconstructed Gothic church of St Andrew is notable for the brightness and the quality of the light that passes through its vast windows, as well as its soaring proportions. The 115-m (377-ft) tower was added in the 19th century.

Bas-relief on the façade of Andreaskirche

🏠 Michaeliskirche

Michaelisplatz. **Tel** (05121) 34 410. **Open** Apr–Oct: 8am–6pm daily; Nov–Mar: 9am–4pm daily.

Built on the instructions of Bishop Bernward, the church is a textbook example of what became known as the Ottonian style, the early Romanesque culture of the Otto dynasty. Its characteristic feature is the streamlined simplicity of interior and exterior, with square pillars intersecting with the naves. The sarcophagus of the founder, St Bernward, is in the crypt in the western part of the church.

Luckily, a rare painted 12th-century ceiling was removed during World War II and thus largely survived. It depicts the story of Redemption, from Adam and Eve through to Mary and the Saviour.

🏛 Roemer-Pelizaeus Museum

Am Steine 1. **Tel** (05121) 93 690. **Open** 10am–6pm Tue–Sun.

The pride of this museum is the Ancient Egyptian collection, one of the best in Europe, which includes the burial figures of Hem Om and the writer Heti from the Old Kingdom (c.2600 BC). It also has fine collections of Chinese porcelain and Inca artifacts, and it is famed for its temporary exhibitions on ancient cultures.

🏠 Dom St Mariä

Domhof. **Tel** (05121) 179 17 60. **Closed** for renovation; scheduled to reopen in Aug 2014.

During a hunting expedition in 815, Ludwig der Fromme (the devout), son of Charlemagne, allegedly hung relics of the Virgin Mary on a tree. When he tried to remove them they would not budge – which he took to be a heavenly sign that a church should be founded on this site and a town alongside it.

The picturesque Presbytery of Michaeliskirche, Hildesheim

◄ A church towers over a row of houses in Kramer Street, Hannover

The Bernwardsäule in the Dom St. Mariä
– a huge bronze column

The Tausendjähriger Rosenstock (1,000-year-old rose) of this legend grows to this day in the cathedral's apse, and even survived bombing. The cathedral was reconstructed after World War II, using a model of the church's 11th-century appearance.

Original works of art bear witness to the cathedral's foundry which flourished under bishop Bernward. Bronze double doors depict the Old Testament version of the Creation on one side, and the life of Christ according to

the New Testament on the other. The Bernwardsäule, a huge bronze column from 1022, was once topped by a crucifix. The column, with scenes from the life of Christ arranged as a spiralling picture story, recalls the column of Emperor Trajan in Rome. Two further important works of art are a chandelier from 1060, with a diameter of 3 m (10 ft), and a baptismal font (c.1225) based on the personifications of the four rivers of the Garden of Eden.

🏠 Godehardkirche

Godehardsplatz. **Tel** (05121) 34578.
Open 9am–6pm daily.

This church is dedicated to Bernward's successor, bishop Godehard, who like him has been included in the canon of saints. Built in 1133–72, it is typical of local architecture, and also recalls the earlier church of St Michaelis. It has interesting carved capitals as well as a northern doorway with the Blessed Jesus Christ accompanied by St Godehard and St Epiphany.

🏠 Mauritiuskirche

Moritzberg.

Another Romanesque church worth visiting is the church of St Maurice, west of the centre.

Founded by bishop Hezilo and built in the years 1058–68, the church has enchanting cloisters, dating from the 12th century, and the sarcophagus of the founder of the church.

Presbytery of the massive Godehardkirche, flanked by towers

Hildesheim City Centre

1. Marktplatz
2. Andreaskirche
3. Michaeliskirche
4. Roemer-Pelizaeus-Museum
5. Dom St. Mariä
6. Godehardkirche

0 metres   300
0 yards   300

㉔ Street-by-Street: Goslar

Goslar, at the foot of the Harz mountains, is a captivating town with 1,500 charming, half-timbered houses, the largest number in Germany. For 300 years the Holy Roman Emperors of Germany resided in Goslar, a member of the Hanseatic League also known as "the treasure chest of the North". Goslar's main source of wealth was the nearby mine in Rammelsberg, where zinc, copper and especially silver were mined. The townscape has remained largely unchanged, making it a great tourist attraction as well as a UNESCO World Heritage Site.

Guildhouse (Hotel Kaiserworth)

Jakobikirche ↑

MARKT

HOHER WEG

★ **Rathaus**
On the western side of the market square stands the 15th-century town hall. Its beautiful Huldigungssaal (hall of homage) has a ceiling and walls with Gothic frescos.

Siemens-haus

KAISERBLEEK

DOM PLATZ

★ **Marktkirche**
The Gothic Church of Saints Cosmas and Damian has Romanesque stained-glass windows and a bronze Renaissance baptismal font.

Statue of the Emperor Barbarossa

Key

— Suggested route

The Kaiserpfalz
The Emperors' palace is a stone building (1005–15), largely rebuilt in the 19th century. The chapel and the Emperors' hall with its superb paintings are worth seeing.

For hotels and restaurants in this area see pp492–503 and pp510–33

VISITORS' CHECKLIST

Practical Information
Road map: D3.  46,000.
i Markt 7 (05321-780 60).
Goslarer Tag der Kleinkunst (Jun);
Internationales Musikfest (Aug).

Transport

★ **Historic Half-Timbered Houses**
Many charming half-timbered buildings
from various periods
have survived in Goslar,
creating compact rows
of houses in the streets
of the city centre.

St Annen Stift

| 0 metres | 50 |
| 0 yards | 50 |

🏠 Siemenshaus
Schreiberstraße 12. **Tel** (05321) 780
620. **Closed** to the public; call for
a tour.

This half-timbered house, one of
the most attractive, was once
owned by the Siemens family
who have their roots in Goslar.
Hans Siemens built it in 1693.

⛪ St Peter and Paul
Frankenberger Platz.

Located in the Frankenberg
neighbourhood, this was one of
47 churches which once stood in
the town. It was built in the 12th
century, and the tympanum of
the south portal dates from this
period. Extensively refurbished,
the church prides itself on its
magnificent Baroque furnishings.

⛪ St Jakobi
Jakobi-Kirchhof. **Tel** (05321) 303 672.
Open 9:30am–4pm daily.

The present appearance of this
church, the only Catholic one in
Goslar, is the result of Gothic
additions, although the structure
of the walls remains Romanesque.
The famous work of art in the
church is the *Pietà* by Hans von
Witten, but it is also worth
looking at the wall paintings, the
organ and the baptismal font.

⛪ Neuwerkkirche
Rosentorstraße 27a. **Tel** (05321) 228 39.
Open Mar–Oct: 10am–noon & 2:30–
4:30pm Mon–Sat; 2:30–4:30pm Sun.

This impressive late-Romanesque
church was built in the 12th–13th
centuries for the Cistercian Order,
although the surviving monastic
buildings date from the early 18th
century. Inside, the wall paintings
and the choir partition are of
interest. The church is surrounded
by a peaceful garden.

The train in the Bergbaumuseum in
Rammelsberg

🏛 Breites Tor
Breite Straße.

Some parts of the defensive
system, dating mainly from
c.1500, are well preserved. This
"wide gate", which can be seen
on the eastern approach of the
town, is the most imposing part.

🏛 St Annen-Stift
Glockengießerstraße 65. **Tel** (05321)
398 700. **Open** 10am–noon Mon,
Thu, Fri.

The hospice of St Anna for
orphans, the elderly and infirm
was founded in 1494 and is the
oldest preserved half-timbered
house in Germany. Behind its
picturesque façade is a beautiful
small chapel with superb
paintings on a wooden ceiling.

🏛 Bergbaumuseum Rammelsberg
Bergtal 19. **Tel** (05321) 750 122.
Open 9am–6pm daily

Goslar's mining museum is
based in the 10th-century
silver mine. One of the oldest
industrial structures in the
world, it is a UNESCO World
Heritage Site. On display are
mining tools and utensils used
in various periods. Visitors can
take a train ride through the
mine and learn about the
history of mining.

The above-ground buildings of the silver mine in Rammelsberg

㉓ Einbeck

Road map C3. 🚗 29,400. 🚉
ℹ️ Rathaus, Markt Str. 13 (05561-313
19 10). 🌐 einbeck.de

In the Middle Ages, this town
had 600 breweries – more than
houses – and today it is still
known for its beers; Bockbier,
the famous German strong
beer, was invented here. Burned
down in 1540 and 1549, the
town subsequently rebuilt
in a uniformly Renaissance style.
The historic town centre is
enclosed by the city walls. More
than 100 half-timbered houses
have survived to this day.
Eickesches Haus (Marktstraße
13) is particularly eye-
catching, with a
sculpted façade based on
biblical and Classical
stories. Other
picturesque houses
can be found in
Tiedexer Straße and
in **Marktplatz**. The
latter boasts the **Rathaus**
(town hall) and the **Ratswaage** (municipal
weigh house) and
Ratsapotheke
(chemist). The tower of the
neighbouring **Pfarrkirche St
Jakobi** (parish church) leans 1.5
m (5 ft) from the perpendicular.
In 1741, a Baroque façade was
added to hide this.

Environs
15 km (9 miles) from Einbeck
is the spa town of **Bad
Gandersheim**. It grew up
around a Benedictine
monastery established here
in 852, which in the 10th
century was the home of
Roswitha von Gandersheim, the
first known German dramatist.

㉔ Göttingen

Road map C4. 🚗 129,000. 🚉
ℹ️ Altes Rathaus, Markt 9 (0551-499
800). 🎭 Händel-Festspiele (Jun);
Literaturherbst (Oct), Jazzfestival
(Nov); student festivals, such as
Stiftungsfest. 🌐 goettingen.de

Along with Tübingen, Marburg
and Heidelberg, Göttingen is one
of the most renowned German
university towns. Established in

1737 by the English King
George II, who was also the
ruler of Hannover, the university
taught the sons of wealthy
German, English and Russian
aristocrats. Important cultural
figures worked here, including
the writer Heinrich Heine, the
brothers Grimm and the explorer
Alexander von Humboldt.
Göttingen's reputation as an
educational centre continues
today, partly due to the establishment of the Max Planck
Institute, named after the scientist
who was born in the city and
developed the quantum theory.
Göttingen is a lively town
thanks to its student population, with dozens of cafés,
cosmopolitan restaurants
and bars. University
buildings are scattered
all over town, and the
Aula, a Neo-Classical
Assembly Hall, is
worth a visit. On
the Marktplatz in
the town centre stands
the **Rathaus** (town
hall) with a Gothic
stone façade. The
**Gänseliesel-
brunnen**, the goose girl
fountain, in front dates from
1901. It is kissed by students
who have passed their exams,
and much loved by tourists.
From the southeastern end of
the market square, Göttingen's
four main churches can be seen:
St Michael to the south, St Jakobi
to the north, St Johannis to the
west and St Albani to the east.
The latter two boast late-Gothic
altars worth visiting. Together,
they testify to Göttingen's
early importance
in the Middle
Ages.

*Stone crest on
Göttingen's Rathaus*

The twin-towered Gothic façade of
St Cyriakus in Duderstadt

㉕ Duderstadt

Road map C4. 🚗 24,500. 🚉
ℹ️ Marktstr. 66 (05527-84 12 00).

To the south of the Harz
mountains, not far from the
former border with East
Germany, lies this often
overlooked gem. A walk around
the medieval town is best
started on **Obermarkt** (upper
market). Here stands the half-
timbered **Rathaus** (town hall),
with an interesting façade and
spiky towers. Inside it has
exhibition halls and a cultural
centre. East of the town hall
rises the Catholic **Probsteikir-
che St Cyriakus** with its rich
interior of altars and 15 Baroque
statues. **St Servatius**, its
Protestant counterpart,
combines Gothic architecture
with a Secessionist interior.
Nearby is the **Westerturm**,
the only surviving town gate.
Its strangely spiralling finial
is not a decorative feature,
but the consequence of a
weakness in its design.

The Gothic Rathaus on Marktplatz in Göttingen

㉖ The Weser Renaissance Trail

The Weser Renaissance is an architectural and decorative style of northern Germany, dating from the mid-16th to the mid-17th century. Its tall roofs and gables were inspired by Dutch architecture, although it has many original features: the *Zwerchhäuser* (bay windows, one or more storeys high), the *Utlucht* (protruding sections of the façade), lavish decorations and multi-wing castles, some with spiral staircases in their towers.

① Hameln
Rattenfängerhaus (rat catcher's house), Hochzeitshaus (wedding house) and Dempstersches Haus (Dempsters' house) are good examples of the Weser Renaissance style. The Romanesque-Gothic Münster (collegiate church) is also worth seeing.

③ Bevern
Another gem of the Weser Renaissance style, the castle in Bevern, near Holzminden, was built from Prussian stone in the years 1602–12. It has four wings as well as two towers in the corners of its courtyard.

② Hämelschenburg
The castle, built in 1588–1612, is a three-winged building, surrounded by a moat. It has an impressive exterior with towers and decorative gables; its original interiors are also preserved.

④ Münden
The principal buildings that exemplify the Weser Renaissance style are the town hall and the castle, now a regional museum with a collection of ceramics. Fragments of a Renaissance fresco of Duke Eryk II of Calenberg can also be admired here.

0 km   20

0 miles   20

Tips for Drivers
Starting point: Hameln.
Length: 112 km (70 miles).
Stopping-off places: good restaurants and bistros can be found in all the towns and villages along the route.

SCHLESWIG-HOLSTEIN

Schleswig-Holstein is the northernmost German state, situated between the Baltic and the North Sea and bordered by the Elbe River and Denmark. Weather-beaten by the unstable marine climate, the Gothic brick buildings of Lübeck, queen of the Baltic coast, testify equally to the turbulent history of this region. Today, tourists visit Schleswig-Holstein for its wide sandy beaches and impressive lakes.

Originally, this state comprised two territories: Schleswig in the north, which was inhabited by Germanic tribes (Angles, Saxons, Vikings and Danes) in the Middle Ages, and Holstein in the south, mainly populated by Slavs, who converted to Christianity as late as the 12th century. Its more recent history was characterized by struggles between the Hanseatic towns and the rulers of Denmark. In the 18th century, the entire region, from Altona in the south (now part of Hamburg) to Kolding in the north, belonged to Denmark, but in 1866 it was annexed to Bismarck's Prussia. In 1920, the political borders that exist today were established when Denmark regained the northern part of Schleswig after a plebiscite, leaving a significant Danish minority on the German side.

Schleswig-Holstein is principally an agricultural region, and less densely populated than any other state in Germany. Art lovers are mainly drawn to Lübeck, the most powerful Hanseatic town in the Baltic during the Middle Ages. Lübeck's old town, an architectural gem, has now been listed as a UNESCO World Heritage Site. Other places offer surprises aplenty – the visitor will be captivated by the Romanesque churches around Flensburg, while the magnificent countryside more than compensates for the lack of major cultural monuments. A walk through the national park of Schleswig-Holsteinisches Wattenmeer, the moving sand dunes of the elegant island of Sylt, or a romantic sunset on the lake shores in Plön will leave lasting impressions.

The moated Renaissance Wasserschloss in Glücksburg

◀ Aerial view of a mudflat on Süderoogsand, one of the North Frisian islands

Exploring Schleswig-Holstein

Undoubtedly the greatest attraction in this two-part state is Lübeck, and at least one day should be set aside to visit this town. Kiel is a popular destination during the annual Kieler Woche, the world's largest sailing festival. The sun-kissed island of Sylt invites the visitor to linger for a few days, while the stunning scenery of Helgoland is best explored in a one-day trip from Cuxhaven or Büsum. Hotels in the larger towns, such as Schleswig, Kiel or Flensburg, and many provincial boarding houses, provide a good base for excursions.

Traditional buildings in Plön, the main town in the Holstein Switzerland Nature Reserve

Getting Around

The nearest international airport is Hamburg. Two motorways bisect Schleswig-Holstein: leaving Hamburg and the long queues for the Elbe Tunnel behind, the E47 (No 7) takes the visitor to Kiel and via Flensburg on to the Danish peninsula of Jutland, while the E22 (turning off the E47) leads via Lübeck to the Danish capital, Copenhagen.

Esbjerg

Westerland
4 SYLT
Seebüll
5
Niebüll
Leck
Föhr
Wyk auf Föhr
Amrum
Halligen   Bredstedt
Pellworm
Husum
Nordstrand
St Peter-Ording   Tonning
Eider
5
Heide
Büsum
Hemmingstedt
1 HELGOLAND   Trischen   MELDORF **3**
Friedrichskoog
Scharhörn
Neuwerk
Brunsbüttel
Elbe

NORTH   SEA
Nordfriesland

The lake at Westensee Nature Reserve, where visitors can experience the captivating nature and wildlife close up

For additional map symbols *see back flap*

Sights at a Glance

1 *Helgoland p462*
2 Glückstadt
3 Meldorf
4 Sylt
5 Flensburg
6 Schleswig
7 Kiel
8 Naturpark Holsteinische Schweiz (Holstein Switzerland Nature Reserve)
10 Lübeck
9 Ratzeburg

Ferries departing for excursions from the harbour in Kiel

Key

≡ Motorway

— Main road

— Minor road

— Main railway

— Minor railway

▬ National border

— Regional border

Glücksburg

5 FLENSBURG

Kappeln

A7

201 *Schlei*

6 SCHLESWIG

201

Eckernförde

76

Gettorf

Owschlag

Altenholz

Rendsburg

A210

7 KIEL

A7

A215

Preetz

205

Bordesholm

76

Plön

Nortorf

Grosser Plöner See

Eutin

4

Bosau

8

Neumünster

Selenter See

Kieler Bucht

Puttgarden

Fehmarn

Burg

Heiligenhafen

207

Oldenburg

202

A1

HOLSTEINISCHE SCHWEIZ

Neustadt

Lübecker Bucht

SCHLESWIG-HOLSTEIN

Itzehoe

206

Bad Segeberg

A21

Bad Schwartau

Bad Oldesloe

A20

10 LÜBECK

A20

Kaltenkirchen

Nord-Ostsee Kanal

77

Stör

2 GLÜCKSTADT

Elmshorn

A23

A7

Norderstedt

Pinneberg

Ahrensburg

Wedel

Hamburg

A1

Trittau

Schaalsee

Ratzeburger See

RATZEBURG 9

A24

Berlin

Reinbek

Schwarzenbek

Geesthacht

Boizenburg

Lüneburg

0 kilometres 20

0 miles 20

● Helgoland

For lovers of spices in Germany, it may have seemed a bad deal when in 1890 Germany received Helgoland from Britain in return for Zanzibar, but the island is nevertheless worth a visit. Farthest out in the open sea (50 km/31 miles from the mainland), the island always had great strategic importance, and after 1945, Britain used it as a bombing target before it was returned to Germany in 1952. Today its fresh air and spectacular red cliffs attract thousands of tourists.

VISITORS' CHECKLIST

Practical Information
Road map B1. 🖾 1,900.
ℹ Lung Wai 28 (04725-20 67 99).
🅦 helgoland.de

Transport
🚢 Hamburg and Büsum.

③ **Lange Anna**
Tall Anna, measuring about 40 m (131ft) high, is the best known red sandstone cliff. Nearby is the Lummenfelsen, which is the smallest nature reserve in Germany.

① **Port**
On the flat part of the island is Unterland, a small town with 1,300 inhabitants and a port. Fishermen store their nets in the colourful little houses, referred to as Hummerbuden (lobster huts).

② **Oberland**
In the upper part of the island stands the Nikolaikirche, dating from 1959. Close by, and worth a visit, are 16th-century tombs.

0 metres   100
0 yards   100

Key

— Suggested route

Tips for Tourists

Starting point: the port of Helgoland.
Length: 1.7 km (1.1 miles).
Stopping places: there are numerous restaurants, bars and cafés all over the island.

❷ Glückstadt

Road map C2. 🏘 12,000. 🚉 🅸
Große Nübelstraße 31 (04124-93 75
85). 🆆 **glueckstadt-tourismus.de**

The Danish king, Christian IV,
founded this little town in 1617
and although less impressive
than Hamburg, the town is
worth a visit for its layout –
roads radiate out from the
hexagonal market square, once
surrounded by fortifications.
On the square stands the
reconstructed 17th-century
town hall as well as the Baroque
Stadtkirche (town church). In
1648, parts of the duchy of
Holstein were transferred to
Glückstadt. Most of the palaces
built to house the Dukes
survived, for example the Palais
Werner with its amazing
ballroom. The regional **museum**
is now in Brockdorf-Palais,
another palace from 1632.

🏛 **Detlefsen-Museum**
Am Fleth 43. **Tel** (04124) 93 76 30.
Open 2–5pm Wed (to 6pm Jun–Aug),
2–6pm Thu–Sat, 2–5pm Sun.

❸ Meldorf

Road map C1. 🏘 7,500. 🚉
🅸 Nordermarkt 10 (04832-97 800).
🆆 **meldorf-nordsee.de**

Meldorf has preserved the
Dithmarscher Dom, its
cathedral, a 13th-century
basilica with an exterior
rebuilt in the 19th century.
The vaulting in the transept is
decorated with Gothic frescos,
depicting the legends of saints
Catherine, Christopher and
Nicholas. There is a richly
decorated dividing wall (1603)
and a grand triptych of the
Crucifixion (c.1520).

The port and waterfront of Flensburg

❹ Sylt

Road map B1. 🏘 50,000. 🚉 in
Westerland. 🅸 Westerland, Stephan-
straße 6 (04651-820 20). 🆆 **sylt.de**

The island of Sylt, the largest of
the North Frisian islands, has
long attracted wealthy German
visitors. The 50-km (31-mile)
long island offers a rich variety
of landscapes: white, sandy
beaches, shifting sand dunes
near List, towering up to 25 m
(82ft) high, steep shorelines,
the Rotes Kliff (red cliff) near
Kampen and the Watt, the
endless expanse of mudflats in
the national park, Schleswig-
Holsteinisches Wattenmeer.
Westerland is Sylt's main
town, and its promenade,
Friedrichstraße, is "the" place
to be seen. There is also an
interesting casino in a former
Secessionist spa building.

❺ Flensburg

Road map C1. 🏘 84,500. 🚉
🅸 Rathausstraße 1 (0461-909 09 20).
🎏 Rum-Regatta in Flensburger Förde
(May/Jun).

The most northerly town in
Germany, Flensburg was an
important trading centre in the
16th century with 200 ships,
although at times it belonged
to Denmark. The **Nordertor**

(northern gate), dating from
1595, is an emblem of the city.
The shipping museum is
fascinating while the
Marienkirche has a Renaissance
altar, sculptures and the
painting *The Last Supper* (1598).
Nearby is the **Heilig-Geist-
Kirche** (church of the Holy
Ghost), which has belonged to
the town's Danish community
since 1588. Other interesting
churches are **Nikolaikirche**
which boasts a magnificent
Renaissance organ, and
Johanniskirche with a vaulted
ceiling dating from around
1500. Its painted scenes show
people disguised as animals,
which was a covert way of
criticizing the church and the
system of indulgences.

Environs
Schloss Glücksburg, 9 km
(6 miles) northeast of Flensburg,
a square castle with massive
corner towers on a granite base,
was built from 1582–7. Visit its
captivating castle chapel, the
Roter Saal (red hall) with its
low vaulting, and the valuable
collection of 18th-century
tapestries from Brussels. The
artist Emil Nolde lived and
worked in **Seebüll**, west of
Flensburg, from the age of
20 until his death in 1956.

The sandy beaches of the North Frisian island of Sylt, extending far to the horizon

For hotels and restaurants in this area see pp492–503 and pp510–33

The inner courtyard of Schloss Gottorf in Schleswig

❻ Schleswig

Road map C1. 👥 27,000. 🚉
ℹ️ Plessenstr. 7 (04621-85 00 56).
🎭 Schleswig-Holstein Musik Festival throughout the region (Jul/Aug); Wikinger-Tage (Aug every other year).
🌐 **schleswig.de**

The main seat of the Vikings, Schleswig became a bishop's see as early as 947, and from 1544 to 1713 it was the residence of the dukes of Schleswig-Holstein-Gottorf, once related to the rulers of Denmark and Russia. They resided in **Schloss Gottorf**, a castle, which now houses the **Schleswig-Holsteinisches Landes- museum** (regional museum) as well as northern Germany's most famous archaeological museum, the **Archäologisches**

Landesmuseum, exhibiting the *Moorleichen*, prehistoric corpses preserved in peat. It is also worth seeing the two-storey chapel (1590).

The **Dom** (cathedral) was built in stages between the 12th and 15th centuries. Its largest treasure is the Bordesholmer Altar, a triptych altar carved by Hans Brüggemann in 1514–21. A masterpiece of Gothic carving, it is 12 m (39 ft) high and comprises 392 figures; the only one to look straight at the visitor is the sculptor himself, bearded and hat askew (in the house of Abraham and Melchisede).

Visitors can also walk around the historic fishermen's district of **Holm**, and visit the **Wikinger-Museum Haithabu**, about 4 km (2 miles) from the town centre.

The fortifications have survived in the grounds of this historic Viking settlement. The museum is housed in a modern building, which looks like an upturned boat. Exhibits include the depiction of Viking life, models of boats, jewellery and everyday items.

🏛️ **Schloss Gottorf/ Schleswig-Holsteinisches Landesmuseum/ Archäologisches Landesmuseum**
Tel (04621) 81 30. **Open** Apr–Oct: 10am–6pm daily; Nov–Mar: 10am–4pm Tue–Fri (to 5pm Sat & Sun).

🏛️ **Wikinger-Museum Haithabu**
Tel (04621) 81 32 22. **Open** Apr–Oct: 9am–5pm daily; Nov–Mar: 10am–4pm Tue–Sun.

❼ Kiel

Road map C1. 👥 245,000. 🚉
ℹ️ Andreas-Gayk-Straße 31 (0431-67 91 00). Town hall: **Open** 9am–6pm Mon–Fri, 9am–1pm Sat. 🚢 🚲
🎭 Kieler Woche (end Jun).

Located at the end of the Kieler Förde inlet, Kiel marks the beginning of the Nord-Ostsee-Kanal (Kiel Canal), in service since 1895, with two giant locks. Ferries depart from Kiel for Scandinavia, and in the summer the "Kieler Woche" turns the town into a mecca for yachtsmen from around the world.

A walk along the Schweden-Kai (embankment) and surroundings will take visitors to the vast **Rathaus** (town hall), dating from the beginning of the 20th century, and the **Nikolaikirche** (church of St Nicholas) which was rebuilt after the devastation of World War II, with its baptismal font and Gothic altar. Ernst Barlach

A house in Kiel's Schleswig-Holsteinisches Freilichtmuseum

Romanesque Baptismal Fonts

There are few places in the world where visitors can see as many Romanesque baptismal fonts as in Angeln. Generally fashioned from granite, they have been preserved in enchanting 12th-century churches, which can be visited by following a 63-km (39-mile) route along the roads linking Flensburg and Schleswig, Munkbrarup, Sörup, Norderbrarup, Süderbrarup and finally Ulsnis.

Font in the church in Borbry

Font in the church in Munkbrarup

Font in the church in Sörup

For hotels and restaurants in this area see pp492–503 and pp510–33

created *Geistkämpfer*, the sculpture outside the church, which symbolizes the triumph of mind over matter. Pieces of the sculpture, which had been cut up by the National Socialists, were found and reassembled after the war.

The most interesting of Kiel's many museums is the **Schleswig-Holsteinisches Freilichtmuseum**, an open-air museum in Molfsee, 6 km (4 miles) from the centre of Kiel, where German rural architecture from the 16th–19th centuries is on show. Pottery, basket-making and baking are demonstrated, and the products are sold here.

🏛 **Schleswig-Holsteinisches Freilichtmuseum**
Hamburger Landstraße 97. **Tel** (0431) 65 96 60. **Open** Apr–Oct: 9am–6pm daily; Nov–Mar: 11am–4pm Sun. 🅿

❽ Holsteinische Schweiz (Holstein's Switzerland)

Road map D1. 🚌 ℹ Bahnhofstr. 3, Malente (0800 20 20 080). 🎷 Jazz-Festival in Plön (May); open-air opera during Sommerspiele in Eutin.

The moraine hills, which reach a height of 164 m (538 ft), and 140 lakes are the reasons why this area is known as Holstein's Switzerland. The best means of transport here is the bicycle, allowing visitors to appreciate the beauty of nature and the wealth of the fauna – ornithologists have counted 200 species of birds. The main centre of this holiday area is

Plön on the Großer Plöner See (large Plön lake). Nearby is **Preetz**, an old shoemakers' town, which has a towerless Gothic church that belonged to a former Benedictine monastery. Older still is the Romanesque church in **Bosau**, a small town in a picturesque location on the Großer Plöner See. It was the first bishopric in this area, and home to Vizelin – the apostle of the Slavs.

It is also worth visiting **Eutin**, a small town full of picturesque buildings, which is sometimes referred to as the "Weimar of the north". The original Schloss, a brick structure with four wings, was built in the Middle Ages as the residence of the Lübeck bishops, but it was substantially altered in the years 1716–27. Worth seeing inside are the palace chapel, the Blauer Salon (blue salon) with Rococo stucco work, as well as paintings by Johann Heinrich Wilhelm Tischbein, which were inspired by the *Iliad* and the *Odyssey*, epic poems written by Homer.

The Dom in Ratzeburg

❾ Ratzeburg

Road map D2. 🚗 12,500. 🚌 ℹ Unter den Linden 1 (04541-80 00 886). 🎪 Drachenbootfest (Jun).

Ratzeburg, situated on an island in the Großer Ratzeburger See, is linked with the mainland by three causeways. The town was named after Ratibor, the duke of the Elbe River area. Henry the Lion established a missionary bishopric here in 1154, and later it became the residence of the Lauenburg dukes.

The **Dom** (cathedral) is one of the earliest examples of brick architecture, a style that was imported from Lombardy. The southern vestibule of the Romanesque basilica is particularly impressive – with herringbone-pattern brickwork and lines of black tiles as interior decoration. The Romanesque stalls, a 13th-century crucifix in a rainbow arch, the ducal gallery above the nave and the Baroque altar in the southern transept are some of its treasures.

The 17th-century Schloss in Plön, in Holstein's Switzerland

⑩ Street-by-Street: Lübeck

This "specific nest", as Lübeck was described by its most famous resident, Thomas Mann, is well worth a visit. The most important town in the Baltic basin by the end of the Middle Ages, it is now a magnet for fans of Backsteingotik, Gothic brick architecture which has been elevated to a national style. In Lübeck it is easy to see why: church interiors, the façades of buildings, the city gates, the unique town hall and even the Medieval hospital resemble pictures from an illustrated history of architecture brought to life. Despite a few blunders, the city has been beautifully rebuilt after World War II and enjoys a positive revival.

Rathaus
Germany's most famous brick town hall, dating from 1226, has unusual walls and turrets.

Buddenbrookhaus
This beautiful Gothic building was once the home of Nobel-prize-winning author Thomas Mann's grandparents. It is now a museum dedicated to the Mann family.

Heiligen-Geist-Hospital

BREITE STRASSE

SCHLÜSSELBUDEN

HOLSTENSTRASSE

★ **Marienkirche**
St Mary's Church, larger than the cathedral and situated behind the town hall, holds great art treasures.

Key

— Suggested route

Holstentor
This gate, once the only entrance into Lübeck, was built by Hinrich Helmstede in the years 1466–78, based on Flemish designs. It has become the emblem of the town.

Petrikirche
The church of St Peter, from the first half of the 14th century, is Lübeck's only five-naved church.

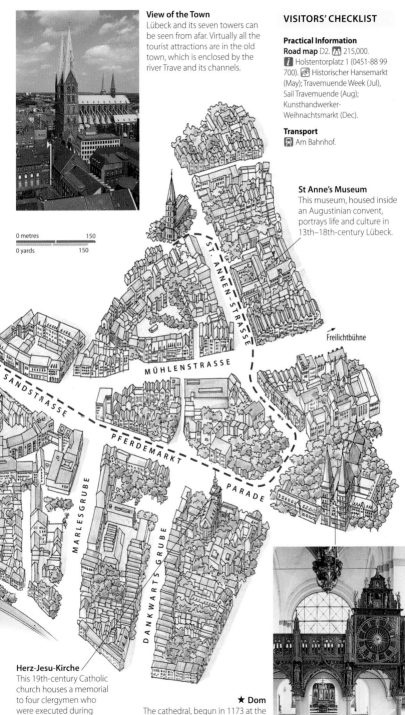

View of the Town
Lübeck and its seven towers can be seen from afar. Virtually all the tourist attractions are in the old town, which is enclosed by the river Trave and its channels.

VISITORS' CHECKLIST

Practical Information
Road map D2. 215,000.
Holstentorplatz 1 (0451-88 99 700). Historischer Hansemarkt (May); Travemuende Week (Jul), Sail Travemuende (Aug); Kunsthandwerker-Weihnachtsmarkt (Dec).

Transport
Am Bahnhof.

St Anne's Museum
This museum, housed inside an Augustinian convent, portrays life and culture in 13th–18th-century Lübeck.

Freilichtbühne

0 metres 150
0 yards 150

ST. ANNEN STRASSE

MÜHLENSTRASSE

SANDSTRASSE

PFERDEMARKT

PARADE

MARLESGRUBE

DANKWARTSGRUBE

Herz-Jesu-Kirche
This 19th-century Catholic church houses a memorial to four clergymen who were executed during the Third Reich for their opposition to the war.

★ Dom
The cathedral, begun in 1173 at the time of Henry the Lion and completed in 1230, is 130 m (426 ft) long.

Marzipan From Lübeck

A favourite present from Lübeck is marzipan, which has been popular throughout Europe since the 19th century. The sweets are made from two-thirds sweet almonds imported from Venice and one-third sugar and aromatic oils. The Persians referred to it as *marsaban*, and in 1530 its name was recorded for the first time in Lübeck as *Martzapaen*. From 1806, the Niederegger patisserie perfected the recipe; they established a patisserie on Breite Strasse which operates to this day.

Exploring Lübeck

All the most important monuments, with the exception of the Holstentor, are situated within the old town, which is best explored on foot.

🏠 Marienkirche

Schüsselbuden 13. **Tel** (0451) 88 99 700. **Open** 9am–5pm daily, in winter to 4pm.

St Mary's church was constructed by the Lübeckers as a monument to themselves. The twin-towered basilica with transept and a passage-way around the polygon-shaped presbytery is the brick modification of a Neo-Classical French cathedral.

Its vast interior boasts the highest vaulted brick ceiling in the world (40 m (131 ft)) which dominates the other interior features. These include a 10 m (32 ft) bronze Holy Sacrament (1476–9); a baptismal font in the main nave dating from 1337; the altar dedicated to the Virgin Mary in the Sängerkapelle (singers' chapel) made in Antwerp in 1518; and the main, late-Gothic Swarte-Altar

with the Madonna. The Brief-kapelle, the southwestern side chapel built around 1310, is one of the earliest examples of star vaulting in Europe.

In one of the towers, the shattered fragments of the church bells have been left embedded in the floor where they fell during the bombing in 1942; the present bells are from St Catherine's in Gdansk.

🏠 Buddenbrook-Haus

Heinrich- und Thomas-Mann-Zentrum, Mengstr. 4. **Tel** (0451) 122 42 43. **Open** Jan–Mar: 11am–5pm daily; Apr–Dec: 10am–6pm daily. **Closed** 24, 25, 31 Dec. 🛇

Literature lovers will wish to visit the Buddenbrook house. Behind its Rococo façade from 1758 is a museum devoted to the Mann family, the great writers who lived here in 1841–91. It is here that Thomas Mann wrote the family saga of the Buddenbrooks, after whom the house is named, and for which he was awarded the Nobel Prize in 1929. The centre exhibits documents relating to this famous family, in particular to Thomas and Heinrich Mann, concentrating on their time in Lübeck and their emigration and exile after 1933.

🏠 Schabbelhaus

Mengstraße 48 & 52.

Originally the western, wealthier half of Lübeck had many patrician houses, facing the streets with their ornate brick gables. Many of these were damaged in the bombing raids of March 1942, but after World War II they were carefully restored. The most interesting buildings survived in Mengstrasse, in particular the famous Schabbelhaus at No. 48. Built in 1558, this house gained a magnificent Baroque hall in the 18th century. Today it is an attraction in its own right as well as a restaurant.

Stepped gables of the Haus der Schiffergesellschaft

🏠 Haus der Schiffergesellschaft

Breite Straße 2.

The house of the Marine Guild, which dates from 1535, has a splendid interior and now houses one of the city's most elegant restaurants. The façade has stepped gables and terraces/forecourts, typical of Lübeck.

🏠 Füchtingshof

Glockengießerstr. 23.

The eastern part of the town is of an entirely different character: narrow streets link charming

The multi-storey Burgtor, crowned by a Baroque cupola

For hotels and restaurants in this area see pp492–503 and pp510–33

The façade of the Gothic Heiliger-Geist-Hospital, with its spiky towers

Höfe (courtyards) and small, modest houses. The most interesting Höfe can be found at numbers 23 and 39. The Baroque portal of the Füchtingshof, at No. 23, leads to houses which, from 1639, were built for the widows of merchants and captains.

🏛 Günter-Grass-Haus
Glockengießerstr. 21. **Tel** (0451) 122 42 30. **Open** Apr–Dec: 10am–5pm daily; Jan–Mar: 11am–5pm Tue–Sun. 🗒

More than 1,100 exhibits (including drawings and manuscripts) here give an insight into the life and work of Nobel Prize-winning author and artist Günter Grass.

🏛 Burgtor
On the northern limits of the old town stands the castle gate, a second surviving gate of the historic fortifications. A Baroque finial was added to the gate in 1685. The tower's five storeys are decorated with uniform rows of windows and windbreaks.

✚ Heiligen-Geist-Hospital
Große Burgstr. **Tel** (0451) 79 07-841. **Open** Apr–Sep: 10am–5pm Tue–Sun; Oct–Mar: 10am–4pm Tue–Sun.

The Holy Ghost hospital is the best preserved Medieval building of its type in central Europe. Built in the shape of the letter T, it has a shorter western section with a twin-aisled hall-church (c.1286), containing frescos of *Christ and the Madonna on Solomon's Throne* and *Majestas Domini*. The second section contains the actual hospice. In 1820, small cubicles were created for the elderly, who lived here until 1970.

🏛 Jakobikirche
This 15th-century church, which suffered only insignificant damage during World War II, has preserved its original, mainly Baroque features. Of particular note are the main altar as well as the side altar in the south chapel. The latter was established around 1500 by the mayor, Heinrich Brömbse, and depicts a scene of the Crucifixion carved in sandstone. Both the small and the large organ originate from the 15th century.

🏛 Katharinenkirche
Königstraße. Museumskirche St. Katharinen **Tel** (0451) 122 41 37. **Open** 15 Apr–30 Sep: 10am–5pm Fri–Sun.

St Catherine's, the only surviving monastic church, was built by the Franciscans, as is apparent from the absence of a tower and its monastic gallery in the presbytery of the main nave. The western façade, with its glazed

The bright interior of the Gothic Dom

brickwork, is of a high artistic quality. In the 20th century, sculptures carved by Ernst Barlach were added (*Woman in the Wind, Beggar on Crutches* and *The Singing Novitiate*). On the western side hangs the painting of *The Resurrection of Lazarus* by Jacopo Tintoretto, bought by a wealthy patrician; the sculpture of St George and the dragon is a copy of the famous original by the Lübeck artist Bernt Notke, which is now in Stockholm.

🏛 St Annen-Museum
St-Annen-str. 15. **Tel** (0451) 122 41 37. **Open** Jan–May: 11am–5pm Tue–Sun, Apr–Dec: 10am–5pm Tue–Sun. **Closed** Easter, 24, 25, 31 Dec. 🗒

The Augustinian convent houses unusual Lübeck art treasures. There is an impressive number of wooden Gothic altars, commissioned by wealthy families for their private chapels in one of the five churches. The altars were supposed to bring them eternal salvation after death, and to symbolize the wealth and prestige of the family during their lifetime. Gems of the collection are the Hans Memling altar with Christ's Passion, and the external side wings of the Schonenfahrer Altar by Bernt Notke.

🏛 Dom
Tel (0451) 747 04. **Open** Apr–Oct: 10am–6pm daily; Nov–Mar: 10am–4pm daily.

The cathedral, completed in 1341, takes the form of a Gothic hall-church. Its most precious possession is the Triumphal Cross sculpted from a 17-m (55-ft) oak tree by Bernt Notke, a celebrated local artist. The giant figures, resplendent with emotion, include Adam and Eve, as well as the founder, bishop Albert Krummedick. Among numerous memorials, that dedicated to bishop Heinrich Bocholt, made from bronze, stands out. Additionally, two valuable sculptures can be seen; *Holy Mary Mother of God* with a crown composed of stars, as well as the *Beautiful Madonna* in the southern nave (1509). Note the bronze baptismal font by Lorenz Grove from 1455, with its three kneeling angels.

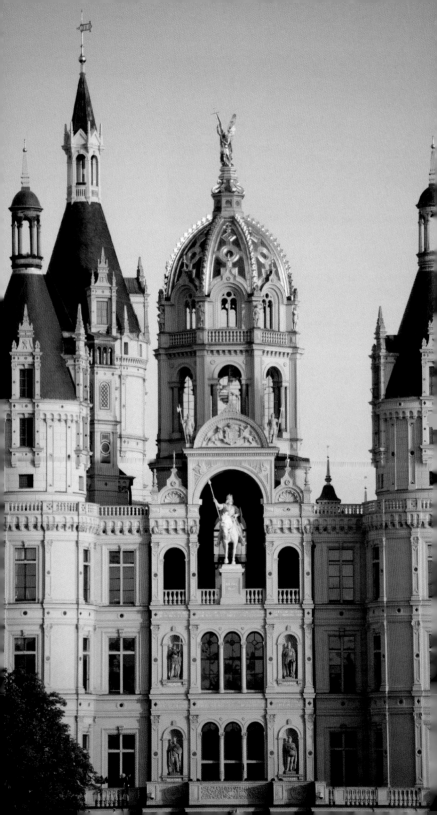

MECKLENBURG-LOWER POMERANIA

The medieval towns of Schwerin, Wismar, Rostock and Stralsund, as well as several magnificent architectural monuments, provide reason enough to visit this part of Germany, yet it also offers a largely untouched landscape of forests and lakes. Along the Baltic coastline, tourists delight in the beautiful sandy beaches of Darß or Usedom, but above all they head for the island of Rügen, with its famous white cliffs.

Mecklenburg-Vorpommern (Lower Pomerania), a mosaic of regions, can look back on an eventful history. In the 12th century, indigenous Slav tribes were colonized and converted to Christianity. The region became part of the Holy Roman Empire and German colonialism resulted in the Slavs' rapid assimilation. In the Middle Ages, several towns became rich trading centres and joined the Hanseatic League. From the 18th century, the Swedish Empire was the most powerful political force in this part of Europe. It ruled Wismar, Rügen and Stralsund until 1803 and 1815 respectively, when the territories became part of Prussia, and later the German Reich. During World War II the Baltic towns suffered terrible destruction and then from neglect under the German Democratic Republic: in 1953 all the hotels were nationalized and the unique buildings in the Hanseatic towns were left to decay or were destroyed.

After reunification, although still one of the poorest states in Germany, Mecklenburg-Lower Pomerania today has become an idyllic holiday destination. Improvements in the infrastructure, new hotels and restaurants have brought positive change, and it has much to offer. Nature lovers, walkers and cyclists, for example, can enjoy the Mecklenburg lake district and the island of Rügen. Fans of architecture will find a wealth of interest in the palace in Ludwigslust and the castle of Güstrow, as well as the Gothic brick architecture in town halls, churches and smaller buildings.

The beautiful white chalk cliffs on the island of Rügen sweep down to the blue Baltic Sea

◄ The superb Schloss of Schwerin, on an island in the middle of Schwerin lake

Exploring Mecklenburg-Lower Pomerania

This is a large region with mostly minor roads so visitors are well advised to allow extra time to explore it. The area can be divided into three: the west, stopping off in pretty Wismar or charming Schwerin with its fairy-tale castle; the centre, with the major port of Rostock as a base, and the east, which can be explored from Stralsund or Greifswald. In the central Mecklenburger Seenplatte is Müritz National Park, a vast area of lakes and forests that is ideal for camping, walking and sailing. It is also a good plan to set aside a few days for relaxation on the sandy beaches of Darß, Zingst, Usedom or Rügen.

Mecklenburg's glorious beaches

Sights at a Glance

1. Schwerin *pp474–75*
2. Ludwigslust
3. Gadebusch
4. Wismar
5. Bad Doberan
6. Güstrow
7. Neubrandenburg
9. *Rostock p480*
10. *Stralsund p481*
11. *Rügen pp482–3*
12. Greifswald
13. Wolgast
14. Anklam
15. Usedom
16. Peenemünde

Excursions

8. Nationalpark Müritz

Neuer Markt, surrounded by charming gabled buildings, Rostock

For additional map symbols *see back flap*

Key

═══ Motorway
─── Main road
∷∷∷ Minor road
─·─ Main railway
─── Minor railway
▭▭▭ National border
═══ Regional border

Getting Around

International flights land at Hamburg and Berlin, domestic flights at Rostock and Heringsdorf on Usedom. Ferries go from Denmark, Sweden and Lithuania to Sassnitz and Rostock, and the E55/A19 motorway runs from the south to Schwerin and Rostock.

Rügen, lit by dawn sunlight

The attractive cloisters of Schloss Güstrow

0 kilometres   30

0 miles   30

❶ Schwerin

Despite protests from Rostock, the smaller town of Schwerin was chosen as the capital of the newly united state of Mecklenburg-Lower Pomerania. This was an inspired choice as the town is picturesquely situated amid several lakes, with a fairy-tale castle on an island, and an enchanting old town with many Neo-Classical and historic buildings that survived World War II largely unscathed. Apart from a brief spell, the Mecklenburg dukes resided in Schwerin from 1318–1918. Intellectual life flourished here in the 16th century and so the city is known as "Florence of the North".

The Neo-Renaissance Schloss on an island in Schweriner See

Exploring Schwerin
The old town of Schwerin is situated between Pfaffenteich railway station and Schweriner See, a vast 65-sq km (25-sq mile) lake. All its major attractions can easily be visited on foot. Close by to the north is Schelf, which was once a separate town.

🏠 Schloss
Schlossinsel. **Tel** (0385) 52 52 920.
Open 15 Apr–14 Oct: 10am–6pm daily; 15 Oct–14 Apr: 10am–5pm Tue–Sun.
Situated on Burg Island, this castle is often referred to as the "Neuschwanstein of Mecklenburg", after the famous Bavarian castle. It was, in fact, largely built earlier (1843–57) to an eclectic design by Georg Adolph Demmler and Friedrich August Stüler, who were inspired by the turrets of Château Chambord in France. Major refurbishment tried to re-create some of the castle's original Renaissance features, of which only the ceramic decorations have remained. Inside, the castle

chapel built by Johan Batista Parr in 1560–63 has survived. The elegant rooms in the castle – Thronsaal (throne chamber), Ahnengalerie (ancestral gallery), Rote Audienz (red auditorium), Speisesaal (dining chamber) – are decorated with gilded stucco work. Despite the proliferation of their styles these rooms delight visitors, transporting them back to the 19th century.

🔵 Burg- und Schlossgarten
The remaining part of the island is occupied by the Burggarten (fortress garden), which has an orangery and an artificial grotto, built from granite around 1850. A bridge leads to the larger Schlossgarten (castle garden), a favourite place for the town's inhabitants to relax. The Kreuzkanal, a canal built in 1748–56, one of the garden's axes, is lined with copies of Baroque statues including the *Four Seasons*, created by the renowned sculptor of the Dresden Zwinger, Balthasar Permoser.

🏛 Staatliches Museum
Am Alten Garten 3. **Tel** (0385) 595 80.
Open Apr–Oct: 10am–8pm Tue, 10am–6pm Wed–Sun; Oct–Apr: 10am–5pm Tue–Sun.
The state art museum stands in Alter Garten, one of the most attractive squares in Germany, where the waters reflect the castle and Neo-Renaissance theatre. The museum, which features lions on its façade and a portico with Ionic columns, houses an art collection based on that of Duke Christian Ludwig II, a testimony to his taste and erudition. As well as works by German artists such as Cranach, Liebermann and Corinth, and the Dutch painters Hals and Fabritius, it holds works by many French artists. This includes 34 paintings by Jean-Baptiste Oudry, who was court painter to Ludwig XIV, as well as paintings by Dadaist artist Marcel Duchamp and sculptures by expressionist artist Ernst Barlach.

🟦 Marktplatz
The town hall square is surrounded by the homes of wealthy citizens, often with 19th-century façades concealing older walls. This is true of the Gothic town hall, which is hidden under an English mock-Tudor-style façade. Demmler was the architect who is responsible for numerous Neo-Renaissance and Neo-Gothic buildings, the showpieces of Schwerin. One of the outstanding buildings in the market square is Neues

Venus and Amor (1527) by Lucas Cranach in the Staatliches Museum

The Dom and houses in Schwerin

Gebäude on the north side. This "new building" is a covered market from 1783–5, with a showpiece façade comprising 12 Doric columns.

⛪ Dom St Maria und St Johannes

Am Dom 4. **Tel** (0385) 56 50 14. Tower **Open** Apr–Oct: 10am–5pm Mon–Sat, noon–5pm Sun; Nov–Mar: 11am–2pm Mon–Fri, 11am–4pm Sat, noon–3pm Sun.

This cathedral is regarded as the most important work of Gothic brick architecture in the Baltic region, in spite of its Neo-Gothic tower, which affords a marvellous view of the entire town. The basilica, dating from 1240–1416, with its wide transept and passageway around the presbytery and its wreath of chapels, is reminiscent of the design of French cathedrals. A number of outstanding original features compare well with the finest works from Antwerp during this time. They include the wooden late-Gothic multi-panelled Crucifixion worked in sandstone, the 14th-century baptismal font, a memorial to Duchess Helen of Mecklenburg created by the Vischer workshop in Nuremberg and the tombstones of Duke Christopher and his wife (1595).

🏛 Freilichtmuseum Schwerin-Mueß

Alte Crivitzer Landstraße 13. **Tel** (0385) 208 41-0. **Open** late Apr–late Sep: 10am–6pm Tue–Sun; late Sep–Oct: 10am–5pm Tue–Sun.

The museum contains a collection of Mecklenburg folk architecture, including 17 houses of the 17th–19th centuries, which strive to recreate the look of an original village. Combine a visit with a leisurely day on the beach in Zippendorf.

Houses of an earlier era in open-air Freilichtmuseum in Schwerin-Mueß

Schwerin City Centre

1 Schloss
2 Burg- und Schlossgarten
3 Staatliches Museum
4 Marktplatz
5 Dom St Maria und St Johannes

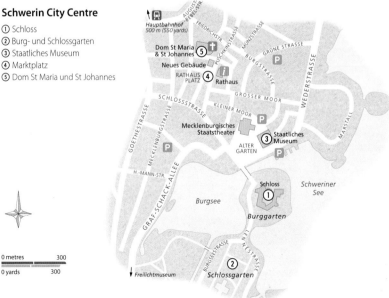

0 metres   300
0 yards   300

One of 24 waterfalls in Ludwigslust Park

❷ Ludwigslust

Road map D2. 🚍 12,600. 🚌 north of centre, 15 min. walk. ℹ️ Schlossstr. 36 (03874-52 62 51).
🌐 stadtludwigslust.de

At the beginning of the 18th century, the small village of Klenow was founded here; from 1765 it grew into a town. The town was laid out around the **Schloss**, residence of the dukes of Mecklenburg-Schwerin until 1837. The "Versailles of Mecklenburg" is quite different from its French namesake. The Baroque palace was built entirely in brick, concealed beneath sandstone from the Ruda hills. The ornate interior, particularly the elegant Goldener Saal (gold hall), was decorated in Ludwigsluster Carton, a type of papier-mâché, in order to cut costs.

In the mid-19th century, the vast **Schlosspark** was redesigned by Peter Joseph Lenné as an English-style landscaped garden. On a scenic walk round the garden, the visitor can discover some 24 waterfalls, a canal, artificial ruins, a stone bridge and the mausoleum of Helena Pavlovna,

daughter of Tsar Peter I, who died tragically young. In the town you will find the Protestant **Stadtkirche**, built in 1765–70 to look like an antique temple. In the presbytery is a giant mural, *The Adoration of the Shepherds*.

🏛 **Schloss**
Tel (03874) 57 19 0. **Open** 15 Apr–14 Oct: 10am–6pm daily; 15 Oct–14 Apr: 10am–5pm Tue–Sun. **Closed** 24, 31 Dec. 🅿️

🏛 **Stadtkirche**
Tel (03874) 21 968. **Open** varies, call ahead.

❸ Gadebusch

Road map D2. 🚍 6,600. 🚌
ℹ️ Mühlenstr. 19 (03886-21 21 10).
🌐 gadebusch.de

This small town, next to the former East–West border, has two interesting historic monuments. The **Stadtkirche**, which dates from 1220, is the oldest brick church in Mecklenburg. Its cross vaulting, chunky pillars and goblet-shaped capitals are Romanesque in style. One of its most precious pieces is the bronze baptismal font (1450). Angels hold the bowl, on which 22 scenes of

Baptismal font in the Stadtkirche in Gadebusch

the Passion were sculpted by an unknown artist.

In the 16th and 17th centuries, the **Schloss** was the residence of distant relations of the dukes of Mecklenburg. Resembling the castle in Wismar, it is decorated with glazed reliefs and pilasters. It is not open to visitors.

❹ Wismar

Road map D2. 🚍 55,000. 🚌
ℹ️ Am Markt 11 (03841-19 433).

Wismar is undoubtedly one of the most attractive towns in Mecklenburg. During the Middle Ages, it was an important Hanseatic centre, as evidenced by the monumental brick church, which is completely out of proportion with the provincial town of today. After the Thirty Years' War, in 1648, the Swedes were established in the town, and rebuilt it as the strongest fortress in Europe. In 1803 they leased Wismar to Mecklenburg, but never claimed it back.

The town centre has a grand market square measuring 100 x 100 m (328 x 328 ft), with **Wasserspiele** (well-house), a Dutch-Renaissance pavilion from 1602 in the centre. Water was piped here from a source 4 km (2 miles) away, until 1897, to supply 220 private and

The Baroque residence of the dukes of Mecklenburg-Schwerin in Ludwigslust

Alter Schwede and Wasserspiele in the market square in Wismar

16 public buildings. The most beautiful house on the square is the **Alter Schwede** (old Swede), built about 1380, with a protruding Gothic brick gable. To the west of the market there are two churches, which act as sad examples of the GDR's neglect of its historical legacy. The reconstruction of the **Georgenkirche**, badly damaged in World War II, was begun in 1989, and it will soon be returned to its former glory. The **Marienkirche** has only one surviving tower – the ruined nave was blown up in 1960. Nearby lies the **Fürstenhof**, residence of the dukes of Wismar. The north wing is the most interesting – its Mannerist style was inspired by the Italian town of Ferrari and northern European ceramic traditions (such as Lübeck workshop). The magnificent sandstone portal is flanked by pairs of intertwined fauns. **Nikolaikirche** is a gem of Wismar architecture. Spared in World War II, the façade of this late-Gothic basilica from the 14th and 15th centuries is decorated with glazed friezes of mythological creatures, saints and, at the peak of the transept,

pair of fauns from the portal of rstenhof in Wismar

a huge rose window. The proportions of the interior and the height of the vaulted main nave measuring 37 m (121 ft) are captivating. Some of the interior fixtures and fittings came from other churches in the city, which were either ruined or no longer exist, including the so-called Krämeraltar with a sculpture of the *Beautiful Madonna and Child* (c.1420). The room by the tower has the most complete cycle of frescos in the region (c.1450).

5 Bad Doberan

Road map D1. 🎟 11,900. 🚌
ℹ Severinstr 6 (038203-621 54).

When Duke Henry Borwin was hunting deer, a passing swan reportedly shouted "*Dobr Dobr*" (a good location) as the deer fell. Borwin duly founded the most important Cistercian monastery of the Baltic region here. The **Münster** was built in 1295–1368, with a severe interior and a small bell, in accordance with the order's rules which stipulate that no tower should be built. The interior is fascinating, its walls surfaced in red, with white plasterwork and colourful ribbing. Most of the original fixtures and fittings have survived almost intact. Among the treasures are a vast, gilded panelled painting, produced in Lübeck in 1310, a 12-m (39-ft) Holy Sacrament made from oak, a small cupboard holding the chalice and relics from an earlier

Romanesque building, as well as a statue of the Virgin Mary. Beautiful tombs mark the resting places of the rulers of Mecklenburg, of the Danish Queen Margaret, and Albrecht, King of Sweden, who died in 1412. Visitors can walk around the outside of the church which has a pleasant lawn. Beyond you can find a small octagonal building, beautifully decorated with glazed brickwork – this lovely piece of 13th-century architecture is the morgue.

A stroll around the health spa is also recommended. Right in its centre it has two early 19th-century pavilions with Chinese features – an ideal place for a coffee break.

Environs
Another adventure the visitor could try is a trip on the "Molli", a narrow-gauge railway that links Bad Doberan with Heiligendamm and Kühlungsborn, where there is a 4-km (2-mile) long beach. On the way, a little gem of 13th-century country architecture, the church in **Stefenshagen**, calls for a visit. On its south portal, see the terracotta figures of the Apostles. Across the presbytery runs a brickwork relief with mythological creatures.

🏛 Doberaner Münster
Klosterstraße 2. **Tel** (038203) 627 16.
Open May–Sep: 9am–6pm daily (from 11am Sun); Mar, Apr, Oct: 10am–5pm daily (from 11am Sun); Nov–Feb: 10am–4pm daily (from 11am Sun). 📷 daily.

The monumental Cistercian Münster in Bad Doberan

The imposing Schloss, dominating the skyline of Güstrow

➏ Güstrow

Road map D2. 🚇 32,500. 🚋
ℹ️ Franz-Parr-Platz 10 (03843-68 10 23). 🌐 **guestrow.de**

Güstrow is one of the most harmonious towns of the former German Democratic Republic, with an attractive old town, unmarred by pre-fabricated tower blocks. All the most important monuments are within easy reach. The town is dominated by the **Schloss**, built from 1558 by Franz Parr, a member of a renowned family of sculptors and architects from northern Italy. German, Italian and Dutch elements come together here, including fantastical chimneys and two-storey arcades in the courtyards. The architect's brother decorated the Festsaal (ballroom) with a hunting frieze – the stucco heads of the deer have real antlers.

In the nearby **Dom**, a brick cathedral of the 13th and 14th centuries, there is a fascinating Gothic altar (c.1500). Look for the vast figures of the Apostles on the pillars of the nave and the 16th-century tomb of Duke Ulrich and his two wives, with a large genealogical family tree of all three of them. In the north nave hangs the burly *Schwebende* (Hovering Angel), a remarkable work by Ernst Barlach, who lived here from 1910 until his death in 1938. He described his works to Bertolt Brecht as: "beautiful without beautifying, sizeable without enlarging, harmonious without smoothness, and full of vitality without brutality". Barlach's work bore the brunt of National Socialist condemnation – the original *Schwebende* was melted down and made into cannons but the copy that replaced it was made from the original plaster cast. Other works by Barlach can be seen in the museum dedicated to him.

It is worth concluding a visit to this town in the market, near which rises the **Pfarrkirche St Marien**. This church has a magnificent high altar, a panelled work of art with painted wings by Belgian artists (c.1522).

Environs
The open-air museum in **Groß-Raden**, near Sternberg, is popular with tourists as well as archaeology students. A village has been re-created with houses, workshops and a system of fortifications.

🏛 **Archäologisches Freilichtmuseum**
Groß-Raden. **Tel** (03847) 22 52.
Open Apr–Oct: 10am–5:30pm daily; Nov–Mar: 10am–4:30pm Tue–Sun. **Closed** 24 Dec, 31 Dec.

➐ Neubrandenburg

Road map E2. 🚇 75 000. 🚋
ℹ️ Stargader Str. 17 (01805-17 03 30).
🌐 **neubrandenburg.de**

Founded in 1248 as a sister town to Brandenburg on the Havel, the town was laid out in the form of a regular oval. It prospered as a trading centre until the Thirty Years' War, after which it fell into disrepair. As a result it now has what is probably the only example of post-World War II concrete tower blocks surrounded by medieval town walls, which have survived virtually intact. The walls extend for 2.3 km (2515 yds), originally with a keep open to the interior, and subsequently interspersed with half-timbered houses, known as **Wiekhäuser** (there were once 58, of which 24 survive). Of the four city gates the most interesting are **Friedländer Tor** (begun in 1300), with inner and outer gateways and a tower, as well as Neues and Stargarder Tor, decorated on the town side with mysterious terracotta figures of women with raised hands (c.1350).

In the town centre stands the Medieval **Marienkirche**, which was damaged during World War II and is now restored as a concert hall.

Environs
The castle in **Stargard**, some 10 km (6 miles) to the south, is the oldest secular building in Mecklenburg. Its 4 m (13 ft) walls were begun in 1200; the residence in 1236. Today it houses a youth hostel.

A typical half-timbered Wiekhaus in the town wall in Neubrandenburg

❽ Nationalpark Müritz

There are about a thousand lakes between Schwerin and Neubrandenburg; the largest of these is Müritzsee, to the east of which a national park was established in 1990. A particularly attractive part of the lake district is the so-called Mecklenburgische Schweiz (Swiss Mecklenburg), with its hilly moraines, such as Ostberg, 115 m (377 ft) above sea level. Tourists are attracted by the breathtaking scenery, perfect conditions for water sports and fascinating castles and palaces.

VISITORS' CHECKLIST

Practical Information
Road map: E2. ℹ Waren, Neuer Markt 21. (03991-66 61 83); Neustrelitz, Strelitzerstr. 1 (03981-25 31 19).

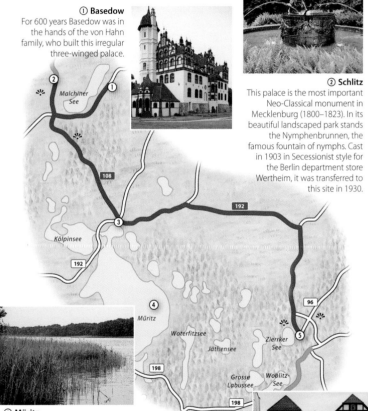

① **Basedow**
For 600 years Basedow was in the hands of the von Hahn family, who built this irregular three-winged palace.

② **Schlitz**
This palace is the most important Neo-Classical monument in Mecklenburg (1800–1823). In its beautiful landscaped park stands the Nymphenbrunnen, the famous fountain of nymphs. Cast in 1903 in Secessionist style for the Berlin department store Wertheim, it was transferred to this site in 1930.

④ **Müritz**
Müritz (meaning "small sea") is, at 115 sq km (44 sq miles), the second largest lake in Germany after Lake Constance.

⑤ **Neustrelitz**
The palace (1712) was the seat of distant relations of the Mecklenburg-Strelitz dukes who established the town and its church, and after 1733 resided here.

③ **Waren**
Waren, an ideal base for tourists, is close to Binnenmüritz with its beaches and shops with watersports equipment for sale or hire.

Key

▬ Tour route
▨ Scenic route
— Minor road
= River, lake
🔆 Viewpoint

0 km　　　　　　　15
0 miles　　　　　　15

❾ Rostock

The history of the most important German port in the Baltic has been turbulent. This prosperous Hanseatic town had established trade links with distant ports such as Bergen (Norway), Riga (Latvia) and Bruges (Belgium) as early as the 15th century. In 1419 the first university in northern Europe was founded here, and it flourished again in the 19th century. After it suffered heavy damage in the Allied air raids of 1942, Rostock was rebuilt on a grand scale as the GDR's showpiece.

VISITORS' CHECKLIST

Practical Information
Road map D1. 🚆 200,000. 🛈
Neuer Markt 3. (0381-381 22 22).
🅦 rostock.de 🎭 Warnemünder
Woche (Jul), Hansesail (Aug).

Transport
🚆

Kröpelinerstraße – a promenade with
17th century houses

Exploring Rostock
A visit to the town is best started from the Neuer Markt (new market), from where the most important monuments can easily be reached on foot.

🏛 Rathaus
The town hall, on Neuer Markt, has a Baroque façade (added in 1727–9), from which seven Gothic towers of the original building emerge. At the rear of the building, in Große Wasserstraße, it is worth seeking out Kerkoffhaus, the best preserved Gothic house in Rostock with a splendidly ornate façade featuring glazed brickwork, dating from 1470.

🏛 Steintor
A few minutes south of Neuer Markt is the Steintor, the best known of the gates in the old city wall. One of only three surviving gates of the original fortifications (at one time with 22 gates), it received its characteristic crowning feature during the Renaissance.

🏛 Marienkirche
Am Ziegenmarkt 4. **Tel** (0381) 492 33 96. **Open** phone to check times.
This church, meant to exceed the height of its Lübeck counterpart, was completed in the mid-15th century, after almost 250 years of construction. The nave, built after the original roof had collapsed, has an untypical, short body, while the massive western tower is as wide as three naves. Interconnected swathes of glazing decorate the exterior of the church, while much of the white-washed interior features star vaulting. The main attraction is the astronomical clock, built in 1472 by maestro Düringer of Nuremberg. Its mechanism will show the correct

Baptismal font in the
Marienkirche

The richly decorated pulpit in
the Marienkirche

time and date until 2017. Every afternoon its clockwork apostles parade before the tourists.

🏛 Kröpelinerstraße
The most popular street in the city is lined by houses from the 17th to the 19th centuries. In summer students congregate around the "Brunnen der Lebensfreude" (fountain of happiness) on the Universitätsplatz (university square). The main university building was built in the years 1867–70 in Neo-Renaissance style. The southern part of the square is occupied by a palace with a beautiful Baroque hall where concerts are performed. A Neo-Classical annexe with a Doric colonnade (1823) stands nearby. A statue on the square commemorates the town's most famous resident, Field Marshal Blücher, who helped defeat Napoleon at Waterloo.

Environs
Between Rostock and Stralsund lies a delightful coastal area. The peninsula, with the three former islands of **Fischland**, **Darß** and **Zingst**, attracts visitors to its quiet, beautiful beaches and splendid natural scenery. Particularly attractive are the villages of **Ahrenshoop**, which was originally an artists' colony, **Prerow**, which has traditional fishermen's houses and churches, and **Wieck**, with its charming thatched houses. A national park has been established here, and includes Darß and its magnificent forest, Zingst, the west coast of Rügen and the island of Hiddensee.

⑩ Stralsund

After Lübeck, Stralsund is the most interesting Hanseatic town in northern Germany. During its history, it has had to defend its independence against Lübeck, Denmark, Holland and Sweden. In the Thirty Years' War, General Wallenstein vowed that he would take the town even if it was chained to heaven – but he failed. Subsequently, Lower Pomerania stayed under Swedish rule for 200 years until 1815, when it became Prussian. Despite its turbulent history, 811 protected buildings survived in the old town, among them some truly remarkable examples of architecture.

The Rathaus with its small turrets

Exploring Stralsund

The town centre of Stralsund is surrounded by water on all sides – in the north by the Strelasund bay, and on the other sides by lakes formed in the moats of the former bastions, Knieperteich and Frankenteich. All the most interesting historic monuments are easily accessible on foot from here.

🏛 Alter Markt

The old market square affords the best view of the filigree façade of the town hall, beyond which stands the vast edifice of St Michael's church. It is surrounded by houses from various eras, of which the two most important are the Gothic Wulflamhaus, and the Commandantenhaus, Baroque headquarters of the town's former Swedish commandant. The Rathaus dates from the 13th century with a 14th-century façade and ground-floor arcades, and resembles the one in Lübeck. In 1370 the Hanseatic League and the defeated

Portal of the Nikolaikirche

Danish king signed a peace treaty here.

The Nikolaikirche, built from 1270–1360, was inspired by French Gothic cathedrals as well as the Marienkirche in Lübeck. It has rare free-standing flying buttresses in brick, which are much more unusual than in stone. Inside there are several intriguing furnishings, for example, the statue of St Anna (c.1290), an astronomical clock (1394), as well as fragments of the Novgorod stall with various fascinating scenes including one of hunting for sables. The Baroque main altar was designed in 1798 by renowned Berlin architect and sculptor Andreas Schlüter.

🏛 Kulturhistorisches Museum

Mönchstr. 25/27.
Tel (0381) 12 87 90.
Open Feb–Nov:
10am–5pm daily. 📷

The Katharinenkloster, a former 15th-century Dominican abbey, now houses two museums. Its abbey rooms provide an appropriate setting for historic exhibitions – the refectory has vaults supported by stylish columns – including copies of the famous Viking treasure from Hiddensee and a collection of 18th- and 19th-century toys and dolls' houses. A branch of the Museum, in Böttcherstraße, has a collection devoted to village life, folklore and costumes of the Baltic region.

🏛 Deutsches Meeresmuseum

Katharinenberg 14. **Tel** (03831) 265 0210. **Open** 10am–5pm daily (Jun–Sep: to 6pm). **Closed** 24, 31 Dec. 📷

Highlights of this museum of the sea, based in a former Dominican convent and the Ozeanum building, include almost 100 aquariums stocked with sharks, seahorses, coral fish and giant turtles, and a 16-m (52-ft) long skeleton of a fin whale. It is also a scientific establishment researching the life of sea organisms.

⛪ Marienkirche

Tower **Open** 10am–noon, 2–4pm Mon–Fri, 10am–noon Sat. Organ concerts: summer: 11am Mon–Wed, Fri–Sun. 📷

Dominating the Neuer Mark is the town's largest church, St Mary's, built in 1383–1473, with an octagonal tower (with good views of Stralsund). Star vaulting lightens the impact of the monu-mental 99-m (325-ft) high interior. Main attractions are Gothic frescos, carved wooden figures of saints and a late-Gothic baptismal font. The huge Baroque organ is used for concerts in summer.

Marienkirche with its dominant, octagonal tower

⓫ Rügen

The largest of Germany's islands at 926 sq km (357 sq miles), Rügen is also the most beautiful and diverse, boasting steep cliffs next to sandy beaches and a hilly hinterland with forests and peat bogs. The island is only 50 km (31 miles) across, yet its rugged coastline extends for hundreds of miles. The Huns once ruled here, and their tombs can still be seen. It was fortified by the Slavs, then ruled by Danes and Swedes. In 1815 Rügen came under Prussian rule, and in 1936 it was linked to the mainland by the 1 km- (0.6 mile-) long Rügendamm.

Kap Arkona
There are two lighthouses on Kap Arkona. The smaller was built in 1827 and is now a museum. The larger was built in 1902 and is still in use.

Key

■ Motorway
= Main road
🚢 Ferry crossing
🌿 Viewpoint

★ **Waase**
At this typical fishing village on the island of Ummanz, an unusual work of art has survived: an altarpiece from Antwerp, from around 1520.

0 km — 5
0 miles — 5

KEY

① **Hiddensee** is a small island is accessible from Stralsund or Schaprode on Rügen. Horse-drawn carts and bikes replace cars in this oasis of tranquillity.

Jasmund Peninsula
The northeast of the peninsula is occupied by the Stubnitz forest of beech trees, which continues down to the sea, interrupted by dazzling white chalk cliffs. The symbol of Rügen, they inspired artists like Caspar David Friedrich.

VISITORS' CHECKLIST

Practical Information
Road map E1. *i* Bergen, Markt 23 (03838-811 206). Binz, Heinrich-Heine-Str. 7 (038393-148 148); Hiddensee, Norderende 162, Vitte (038300-642 26); Putbus, Alleestr. 35 (038301-4 31). In Ralswiek (near Bergen) open-air performances take place under the title of "Festival of Klaus Störtebeker" (Jun–Sep). **W** ruegen.de

Transport

★ Nationalpark Jasmund
An attractive walk starts at the viewpoint of Königsstuhl (king's seat; 119 m/390 ft), continues along the Hochuferweg (cliff-top walk), past Victoriasicht and Wissower Klinken viewpoints, to end at Sassnitz.

Ostseebad Binz
Rügen's largest and most popular seaside resort, Binz has a beautiful white beach, grand early 20th-century villas and a pier.

★ Putbus
This elegant late Neo-Classical town was planned after 1807 on the model of Bad Doberan. Its centrepiece is the theatre, which was built in 1819 to a design by Wilhelm Steinbach.

⓬ Greifswald

Road map E1. 🚖 54,000. 🚉
ℹ️ Rathaus Am Markt (03834-52 13
80). 🎵 Musical concerts "Greifswalder
Bachwochen" (Jun); Jazz Evenings in
Eldena (Jul); Fischerfest (Jul).
W **greifswald.de**

This former Hanseatic town is
situated 5 km (3 miles) from the
Bay of Greifswald. From afar the
picturesque silhouette of the
town with its three church
towers, nicknamed Fat Mary,
Little Jakob and Long Michael,
appears like a painting by
Caspar David Friedrich – the
town's most famous resident –
come to life. Charm pervades
the old town, its architectural
mix resulting from 40 years of
East German rule. Greifswald, an
important academic centre and
market town, has geared up
more for tourism since 1989. It is
certainly worth a visit – a short
walk from east to west enables
visitors to see all the most
important monuments in town.

The 14th-century **Marienkirche** has a vast square tower,
giving it a rather squat
appearance and its nickname,
Fat Mary. Inside, the church
contains the remains of frescos
and an amazing Renaissance
pulpit depicting the Reformation figures of Luther,
Bugenhagen and Melanchthon.
The Gemäldegalerie has a
collection of paintings by

Caspar David Friedrich,
including his famous landscapes
of the ruined monastery of
Eldena, *Ruined Eldena in the
Riesengebirge*, which he
transposed to the mountains
of present-day Poland and
Czech Republic.

The market square with
its Baroque town hall is
surrounded by patrician houses,
with exemplary rich brickwork
façades (particularly numbers
11 and 13). Nearby rises the vast
Dom St Nikolai. The cathedral's
octagonal tower, topped with
a Baroque helm, affords
extensive views of the town.
The Rubenow-Bild (1460), one
of the paintings inside, depicts
the founding professor of
Greifswald's university in front
of Mary, Mother of God.

Environs

Wieck, an attractive working
fishing village, is now
incorporated into Greifswald. It
has a drawbridge dating from
1887, reminiscent of typical
Dutch bridges. The Cistercian
monastery of **Eldena**, just 1 km
(0.6 mile) south of Wieck district,
was made famous by the
Romantic paintings of Caspar
David Friedrich. The monastery
was founded in 1199 and
plundered by the Swedes in
1637. Its ruined red walls amid
the green grass and trees look
wildly romantic.

Alter Speicher – the half-timbered
granary in Wolgast

⓭ Wolgast

Road map E1. 🚖 15,000. 🚉 ℹ️
Rathausplatz 10 (03836-60 01 18). 🎵
Hafenfest (Jul). W **stadt-wolgast.de**

From 1295 the seat of the
Pomeranian-Wolgast dukes,
Wolgast castle was destroyed in
1713, when Peter the Great
ordered the town to be burned.
A notable surviving building is
the 12-sided cemetery chapel
with star vaulting, supported
by a single column. The most
valuable work of art can now
be seen in **Pfarrkirche St Petri**,
a 14th-century parish church.
Dating from the turn of the
17th to the 18th century, the
Totentanz frieze is an imitation

Renovated houses around the Fischmarkt in Greifswald

of the famous *Dance of Death* by Hans Holbein in Basle. Another notable artifact is the epitaph of Duke Philip I, crafted in 1560 by the Saxon artist Wolf Hilinger.

Other attractions in the town are the **Alter Speicher**, an 80 m- (262 ft-) long half-timbered granary (Burgstraße, 1836), and the family home of Philipp Otto Runge, famous romantic painter and adopted son of Hamburg.

Philipp-Otto-Runge-Gedenkstätte
Kronwieckstraße 45. **Tel** (03836) 20 30 41. **Open** May–Oct: 11am–6pm Tue–Fri, 11am–4pm Sat & Sun.

One of the models in the Otto Lilienthal-Museum in Anklam

Anklam

Road map E2. 16,400.
Markt 3, Rathaus (03971-835 154).
anklam.de

A former Hanseatic town, Anklam's erstwhile importance is revealed by its vast defensive walls, in which is set the mid-15th-century city gate, **Steintor**. It is worth visiting the Gothic **Marienkirche**. Inside, the church's octagonal pillars and the arches of its arcades are painted with graceful figures, which reveal a Lübeck influence. A museum recalls the life and inventions of Otto Lilienthal, born here in 1848. After observing storks, he built a flying machine and completed his first flight in 1891. In total he created 2000 machines, none of which flew further than 350 m (1148 ft).

Otto-Lilienthal-Museum
Ellbogenstraße 1. **Tel** (03971) 24 55 00. **Open** Jun–Sep: 10am–5pm

Fishing boat on the beach at Usedom

daily; Oct & May: 10am–5pm Tue–Fri, 1pm–5pm Sat & Sun; Nov–Apr: 11am–3:30pm Wed–Fri, 1pm–3:30pm Sun.

Usedom

Road map E1. Heringsdorf, Kurverwaltung, Waldstr. 1 (038378-477 10); Ahlbeck, Kurverwaltung, Dünenstr. 45 (038378-244 14).

The island, named after the village of Usedom and separated from the mainland by the Peenestrom, is the second largest in Germany at 445 sq km (172 sq miles). A small corner in the east was incorporated into Poland after 1945. Usedom is almost as attractive as Rügen, possessing white beaches, forests, peat bogs and bays overgrown with rushes in the south. It is linked with the mainland by two drawbridges (near Anklam and Wolgast). The resorts follow one another like pearls on a string: Bansin, Heringsdorf and Ahlbeck, known as the "three sisters", are connected by a wide beach. At the beginning of the 20th century they evolved into elegant holiday resorts, with white villas, hotels and boarding houses, as typical of seaside resorts. Worth a visit is the industrialist Oechler's house in Heringsdorf (Delbrückstr. 5), which has an antique appearance with mosaics on its

façade. During the past few years, the early 20th-century piers in all three spas have been rebuilt and restored. The longest, in Heringsdorf, is also the second largest in Europe, after one in Poland. The Marienkirche, one of the island's main attractions, was erected in the 19th century.

Peenemünde

Road map E1. 650.

Historically, the most interesting spot on the island of Usedom is the **museum** at Peenemünde, which is located on military territory. It demonstrates the evolution of space travel, pioneered at this research station since 1936. During World War II, long-distance rockets, powered by liquid fuel and known as V-2 (*Vergeltungswaffe;* retaliatory weapon), were produced here, which inflicted heavy damage on the cities of London and Antwerp in 1944. After the war, the chief engineer, Wernher von Braun, worked for NASA and helped develop the Apollo rockets.

Historisch-technisches Museum
Im Kraftwerk. **Tel** (038371) 50 50. **Open** Apr–Sep: 10am–6pm; Oct–Mar: 10am–4pm. **Closed** Mon (Nov–Mar).
peenemuende.de

V-2 rocket in Peenemünde

TRAVELLERS' NEEDS

Where to Stay   **488–503**

Where to Eat and Drink   **504–533**

Shopping in Germany   **534–535**

Outdoor Activities and
Specialist Holidays   **536–539**

WHERE TO STAY

It is relatively easy to find a room in a hotel or a pension in Germany, even in small towns or large villages. The range of prices for a night's accommodation is wide, depending on the standard of services offered and the location of the establishment. In smaller towns located in attractive tourist areas, it is also possible to find rooms to rent at a reasonable rate in private homes. In large towns and cities it is harder to find inexpensive accommodation. If cost is a consideration, it may be necessary to take a room in a hotel that is some distance from the city centre. Within the list of hotels provided on pages 492–503 there is a large range of hotels and pensions, which represent various price categories and a high standard of services. Tourist offices supply lists of accommodation options and may be able to find a room for you. Information on types of accommodation can be found on pages 490–91.

The spacious lobby of the Hotel Palace, Berlin

The Range of Hotels

German hotels are rated according to a star system that is also used in many other countries. The number of stars awarded to an establishment depends on the facilities offered rather than the standard of service. As a result, it may be possible to enjoy a more pleasant stay in a small hotel that has only one star than in a three-star hotel that offers lifts, a restaurant, swimming pool and business centre, but where refurbishment is long overdue.

The word *"Garni"* in the name of the hotel indicates that there is not a restaurant on the premises, but only a dining room where breakfast is served. *"Apartmenthotel"* means that the establishment is comprised of suites that include equipped kitchens or a kitchen annexe. The price of suites is such that it is not worth booking them for just one night, although a booking of several days for a family or group of friends can turn out to be very economical.

Standards vary enormously between hotels. In large cities visitors will have no difficulty in finding a deluxe (and, of course, expensive) hotel, which will typically be part of an international chain. The choice of less expensive accommodation usually, though not necessarily always, entails accepting a lower standard of service or a less convenient location.

Away from the larger cities, high prices generally apply to rooms in comfortable hotels in particularly peaceful and beautiful locations, or to those located within historic palaces or villas. Smaller hotels in such areas usually offer good accommodation at affordable prices, and visitors can enjoy their stay in small, but cosy and comfortable rooms.

How to Book

As with many European destinations, hotel accommodation in Germany can be booked directly by telephone, email or through the hotel's website. Reservations can also be made through a local tourist office or a third party provider, such as Expedia or Hotels.com.

Hotels may request written confirmation of the booking and will almost certainly ask for a credit card number to guarantee the reservation. Give an indication of expected time of arrival especially if it's likely to be late at night. This will ensure that the room is held for you.

For those who have not pre-booked, the local tourist office can usually find a hotel room or provide information about rooms in private homes.

Entrance of the Opéra Hotel, Munich

◀ The shopping centre Quartier 206, on Berlin's Friedrichstrasse

The deluxe Fairmont Hotel Vier Jahreszeiten in Hamburg *(see p502)*

International and German Chain Hotels

Virtually all the well-known international hotel chains are present in Germany, and there are also hotels belonging to German chains. Many towns in Germany have an Ibis, which can be relied on to provide inexpensive, usually two-star accommodation. In season, they offer a double room for little more than €100.

Somewhat more expensive, and of a higher standard, are the hotels belonging to the Best Western chain. Their excellent standard of service, combined with an affordable price, ensures their popularity with visitors. Hotels belonging to the Sorat group have a similar standard to Best Western establishments and are also recommended. They can be two-, three- or even four-star, and their premises always have interesting interiors, often designed by renowned architects. Many hotels belonging to chains are, in fact, four- or deluxe five-star. Among the finest are the Kempinski and Vier Jahreszeiten hotels. In addition to these, there is no shortage of hotels belonging to chains such as Hilton, Holiday Inn, InterContinental, Mercure, Ramada and Hyatt Regency.

Hotels in Historic Buildings

Germany has numerous palaces, castles and other historic buildings that have been converted into hotels. Often the name *Schlosshotel* is used to indicate that an establishment is a hotel within a palace. Many of these hotels are members of international organizations, such as **European Castle Hotels and Restaurants** or **Romantik Hotels & Restaurants**, which can provide further information.

Hotel Prices

A complicated hotel categorization system operates in Germany, with a diverse range of prices depending on the season, as well as on various events that are taking place. In resort areas, hotels are obviously most expensive during the summer, while in large cities visited frequently for business the most expensive seasons are spring and autumn. In cities where commercial fairs are held, prices may double during the most popular fairs – for example, in Berlin during the tourist fair ITB, in Hanover during the information-computer fair CeBIT and in Frankfurt during the car and publishing fairs. The same is true in Munich during the October beer festival.

Many hotels offer significant reductions at weekends, and often there is the opportunity of a discount for those who turn up without a reservation. Prices can also sometimes be negotiated for longer bookings, especially during periods when business is slack.

Additional Costs

Tax is included in the basic price of a hotel room, but tips should be given for additional services such as having your baggage taken to your room or having theatre tickets reserved for you. Additional costs can come as a surprise when you settle your bill. In the most expensive hotels, for example, breakfast is not included in the cost of the room. Most hotels have their own parking facilities, but the cost may be unacceptably high. Check in advance the cost of making direct-dialled telephone calls from your room, as well as the commission charged by the hotel for cashing travellers' cheques and the rate offered when exchanging currency. Using the mini-bar and pay-to-view TV channels in your room can also prove to be expensive.

The elegant spa in the Hotel de Rome, Berlin *(see p492)*

The picturesque Alter Wirt Hotel in Bernau

Gasthöfe and Pensionen

A *Gasthöf* is a traditional inn with a restaurant on the ground floor and rooms to rent on the upper floor. Be aware, however, that this simple description covers a wide range of establishments – from small, inexpensive, family-run hotels with modestly equipped rooms, to luxurious and elegant accommodation in an exquisitely restored country inn.

Pensionen are less formal establishments than hotels and are typically run by a family. They usually provide modest sleeping quarters, breakfast and a pleasant family atmosphere. They are always comfortable and very clean, at affordable prices.

Inexpensive Accommodation

Germany has a well-established and widely developed chain of youth hostels (*Jugendherberge*), and these provide the most affordable option for an overnight stay. A youth hostel can be found in every large town, as well as in small holiday centres. The most attractive are those that are located in old castles, beautiful villas or other historic buildings. Most hostels are of a high standard. Accommodation may be provided in double and triple rooms, as well as in dormitories.

In order to be eligible to use youth hostels, you must be in possession of a valid membership card issued by the Youth Hostels Association (YHA). This can be obtained from the YHA in your own country. Although overnight accommodation is open to anyone in possession of a valid membership card, things are slightly different in Bavaria. In this region, young people are given priority, but older people can stay, too (although for an additional charge), as can families with young children.

The cost for a one-night stay with breakfast is around €13.50–25. Unless you have a sheet sleeping bag, you must hire one at the hostel, for which an additional charge will be made.

The hostels are usually closed during the day, so you must ensure that all arrangements connected with your stay are in place before 9am or after 4–4:30pm. In large cities during the high season, when demand for beds

Guesthouse near Neuschwanstein

is particularly heavy, your stay may be limited to 2–3 nights.

Private accommodation provides another inexpensive option. In attractive tourist areas, it is quite common for owners of large villas and private houses to rent rooms to tourists, often offering breakfast as well. Houses with rooms available to rent are indicated by the sign *Fremdenzimmer* or *Zimmer frei*. Details of such accommodation can be obtained and booked in tourist information offices.

During the summer months in university towns, students may also benefit from accommodation in hotels that house university students during term times. Again, information about such accommodation may be found at tourist offices.

Agrotourism

Agrotourism, a type of farm holiday, is very popular in Germany as an attractive, low-cost and eco-friendly accommodation choice, particularly for families with children. The rooms that are available are of a perfectly acceptable standard, and meals are often also provided.

For younger children, and especially those from urban areas, it is a great thrill to observe the daily work on a farm. In addition, farmers who take holiday-makers often keep a number of different animals on the farm – an extra bonus for children. They may also offer the possibility of horse-riding, or of hiring bicycles, a boat or fishing tackle. Agrotourist holidays can be booked through **Zentrale für den Landurlaub Landschriften** and **AG Urlaub & Freizeit auf dem Lande**. For more information on eco-friendly accommodation, *see p545*.

Mountain Hostels

Mountainous regions of Germany are generally well prepared to accommodate walkers. Shelters, hostels and mountain hotels can be found not only along Alpine trails, but also in the Thuringian Forest, the Black Forest and the Harz Mountains. Details about such accommodation can be obtained from local tourist information offices.

Camping and Caravanning

Travelling with a camping trailer, camper van or just a tent is very popular in Germany, which has a highly developed network of more than 2,000 camping sites. Of a generally high standard, sites have washrooms and kitchens. There is usually a shop and café, and some even have swimming pools.

Disabled Travellers

Virtually all hotels of a higher standard are equipped to accommodate disabled guests. At least one entrance will have ramp access, and a few rooms will have bathrooms adapted to the needs of those who are confined to a wheelchair. In lower-category hotels, though, specially adapted fixtures and fittings tend to be rarer. In such hotels, you may have to negotiate steep stairs, as many rooms are located on the upper floors of buildings.

In order to receive additional help and advice during their trip, disabled travellers can contact the **Bundes-arbeits-gemeinschaft Selbsthilfe e.V.,** or the **Bundesverband Selbsthilfe Körper-behinderter e.V.**

Travelling with Children

Travelling with children through Germany should not present any problems. In most hotels, accessories such as cots and high chairs can be easily obtained, and there is often no additional accommodation charge for a young child. In better hotels, a few hours of babysitting can usually be booked. For older children, expect to pay a supplement for placing an extra bed in the room.

A mountain shelter in Oybin, Saxony

Recommended Hotels

The hotels recommended in the following listings have been chosen because they represent the best that German accommodation has to offer in service, hospitality, location and value. Entries highlighted as DK Choice are those that stand out. They may have an enviable location, offer an incredible service or be particularly charming. Whatever the reason, they guarantee a memorable stay.

DIRECTORY

Information on Accommodation & Reservations

European Castle Hotels and Restaurants
w european-castle.com

Hotel-Agentur
Lange Str. 67,
31552 Rodenberg.
Tel (05723) 989 70.
w hotel-agentur.de

Hotel Reservation Service (HRS)
Blaubach 32, 50676
Cologne.
Tel (0221) 207 76 00.
w hrs.com

Romantik Hotels & Restaurants
w romantikhotels.com

Youth Hostels

Deutsches Jugend-herbergswerk DJH Service GmbH
Im Gildepark,
Leonardo-da-Vinci-Weg 1,
32760 Detmold.
Tel (05231) 993 60.
w jugendherberge.de

Agrotourism

AG Urlaub & Freizeit auf dem Lande
Lindhooper Str. 63, 27283
Verden. **Tel** (04231) 966 50.
w bauernhofferien.de

Zentrale für den Landurlaub Landschriften – Verlag GmbH
Maarstr. 96, 53227 Bonn.
Tel (0228) 96 30 20. w
bauernhofurlaub.com

Mountain Shelters

DAV Summit Club
Am Perlacher Forst 186,
81545 Munich.
Tel (089) 64 24 00.
w dav-summit-club.de

Verband Deutscher Gebirgs- und Wandervereine e.V.
Wilhelmshöher Allee
157–159, 34121 Kassel.
Tel (0561) 93 87 30.
w wanderverband.de

Camping and Caravanning

Deutscher Camping-Club e.V.
Mandlstr. 28, 80802
Munich. **Tel** (089) 380 14
20. w camping-club.de

Disabled Travellers

Bundesarbeits-gemeinschaft Selbsthilfe e.V.
Kirchfeldstr. 149,
40215 Düsseldorf.
Tel (0211) 31 00 60.
w bag-selbsthilfe.de

Bundesverband Selbsthilfe Körper-behinderter e.V. (BSK)
Altkrautheimerstr. 20,
74238 Krautheim.
Tel (06 294) 428 10.
w bsk-ev.org

Club Behinderter und ihrer Freunde (CBF)
Pallaswiesenstr. 123a,
64293 Darmstadt.
Tel (06151) 812 20.
w cbf-da.de

Where to Stay

Berlin

Eastern Centre

City Hostel Berlin €
Budget   **Map** 4 B3
Glinkastraße 5, 10117
Tel *238 866 85*
W cityhostel-berlin.com
Modern rooms with en suite
bathrooms. Free breakfast and
Wi-Fi. Great terrace bar.

Three Little Pigs Hostel Berlin €
Budget   **Map** 4 B4
Stresemannstraße 66, 10963
Tel *263 958 80*
W three-little-pigs.de
Set in an old convent building
in a vibrant, multicultural area.
Free parking.

Cosmo €€
Boutique
Spittelmarkt 13, 10117
Tel *585 822 22*   **Map** 5 D3
W designhotels.com
A haven of tranquility amid the
bustle of the Mitte. Sleek rooms.

Maritim proArte Hotel €€
Business   **Map** 1 F4
Friedrichstraße 151, 10117
Tel *203 344 10*
W maritim.de
Large, contemporary hotel with
clean and generous-sized rooms.

DK Choice

Adlon Kempinski €€€
Luxury   **Map** 1 F4
Unter den Linden 77, 10117
Tel *226 115 55*
W kempinski.com
The Adlon has won numerous
plaudits, both for its impeccable
standards of service and for
being the final word in opulence.
The hotel has exquisite

bedrooms, and facilities such
as Michelin-starred gourmet
dining and an enormous spa.

Hotel de Rome €€€
Luxury   **Map** 4 C2
Behrenstraße 37, 10117
Tel *460 60 90*
W hotelderome.com
Classy furnishings and alfresco
dining on a rooftop terrace at
this lavish hotel.

Western Centre

Hotel am Schloss Bellevue €
Design   **Map** 3 E1
Paulstraße 3, 10557
Tel *391 12 27*
W hotelamschlossbellevue.de
Small, intimate hotel with
innovative rooms decorated by
a young local grafitti artist.

Altberlin €€
Historic   **Map** 3 F4
Potsdamer Straße 67, 10785
Tel *26 06 70*
W altberlin-hotel.de
Converted from a town house,
the well-located Altberlin is fur-
nished in authentic period style.

Grand Hotel Esplanade €€
Luxury   **Map** 3 E4
Lützowufer 15, 10785
Tel *25 47 80*
W esplanade.de
Excellent amenities at this plush
hotel. Convenient location.

Q Hotel €€
Boutique   **Map** 2 A4
Knesebeckstraße 67, 10623
Tel *810 06 60*
W designhotels.com
Surprisingly affordable designer
hotel aimed mainly at corporate
travellers. Futuristic decor.

Price Guide

Prices are based on one night's stay in
high season for a standard double room,
inclusive of service charges and taxes.

€	up to €75
€€	€75 to €125
€€€	over €125

Savoy €€
Luxury   **Map** 2 A4
Fasanenstraße 9–10, 10623
Tel *31 10 30*
W hotel-savoy.com
Historic hotel famous for its
refined decor. Well-stocked bar.

Concorde €€€
Luxury   **Map** 2 B4
Augsburger Straße 41, 10789
Tel *800 99 90*
W berlin.concorde-hotels.com
Sleek high rise in a great location.
Unwind at the wellness centre,
which has a sauna and solariums.

Further Afield

DK Choice

Circus €
Budget
Rosenthaler Straße 1, 10119
Tel *200 039 39*
W circus-berlin.de
This fun hotel, located close to
the city's night-life, has high
standards of service and great
value. Numerous extras on offer,
from bike rentals to rickshaw
tours and baby-sitting. Enjoy
the elaborate breakfast spread,
or a coffee at the Circus Café.

Ackselhaus €€
Boutique
Belforter Straße 21, 10405
Tel *443 376 33*
W ackselhaus.de
A restored 19th-century property
with a lovely garden. Individually
designed rooms.

Andel's €€
Business
Landsberger Allee 106, 10369
Tel *453 05 30*
W vi-hotels.com
Award-winning hotel with great
views. Chic and spacious rooms.

Riehmers Hofgarten €€
Historic
Yorckstraße 83, 10965
Tel *780 988 00*
W riehmers-hofgarten.de
A grand mansion with elegant
decor set in a 19th-century
courtyard. All modern amenities.

Luxurious suite at the acclaimed Adlon Kempinski

The decadent Hotel Schloss Lübbenau is set in Schloss Park

Villa Kastania €€€
Boutique
Kastanienallee 20, 14052
Tel *300 00 20*
Ⓦ villakastania.com
Rooms are decorated with great attention to detail. Spa facilities available. Impeccable service.

Brandenburg

BRANDENBURG/HAVEL: Sorat Hotel Brandenburg €€€
Business Map E3
Altstädtische Markt 1, 14770
Tel *(03381) 5970*
Ⓦ sorat-hotels.com
Good for people travelling for work as facilities include free Wi-Fi and a fitness centre.

CHORIN: Waldsee Hotel €€
Gasthöfe and Pensionen Map E2
Neue Klosterallee 12, 16230
Tel *(03336) 65310*
Ⓦ waldseehotel-frenz.de
Family-run hotel in beautiful woods by an old monastery. Simple rooms with floral decor.

FRANKFURT AN DER ODER: Palais am Kleistpark €€
Boutique Map F3
Fürstenwalder St 47, 15234
Tel *(0335) 56150*
Ⓦ hotel-gallus.com
Sleek lodgings with Art Nouveau rooms oozing timeless elegance.

LÜBBENAU: Hotel Schloss Lübbenau €€€
Historic Map E3
Schlossbezirk 6, 03222
Tel *(03542) 8730*
Ⓦ schloss-luebbenau.de
Former palace with elegant *fin-de-siècle* rooms and a spa with pretty mosaics and vaulted ceilings.

POTSDAM: Froschkasten €
Gasthöfe and Pensionen Map E3
Kiezstr 4, 14467
Tel *(0331) 291315*
Ⓦ froschkasten.de
Simple pine-furnished rooms above one of Potsdam's oldest and most authentic inns.

POTSDAM: Hotel am Luisenplatz €€€
Gasthöfe and Pensionen Map E3
Luisenplatz 5, 14471
Tel *(0331) 971900*
Ⓦ hotel-luisenplatz.de
Early 18th-century town house with antique furnishings. Rates include a superb breakfast.

POTSDAM: Schloss Cecilienhof €€€
Historic Map E3
Im neuen Garten, 14469
Tel *(0331) 292498*
Ⓦ relexa-hotels.de
Old-fashioned luxury. World War II agreements were signed here.

DK Choice

RHEINSBERG: Pension Holländermühle €
Historic Map E2
Holländer Mühle 01, 16831
Tel *(033931) 2332*
Ⓦ hollaender-muehle.de
This family-run pension has a novel setting in a windmill built in 1894. The bright and simple rooms are all individually decorated. There is also a good restaurant serving regional food.

RHEINSBERG: Der Seehof €€
Gasthöfe and Pensionen Map E2
Seestraße 18, 16831
Tel *(033931) 4030*
Ⓦ seehof-rheinsberg.de
Mid-18th-century farmhouse. The bright and cheerful rooms have balconies and lake views.

Saxony-Anhalt

DESSAU: An den 7 Säulen €
Gasthöfe and Pensionen Map E3
Ebertallee 66, 06846
Tel *(0340) 61 96 20*
Ⓦ pension7saeulen.de
Friendly family-run place in the Bauhaus district. Bright, modern rooms and sauna facilities.

DESSAU: Prellerhaus €
Boutique Map E3
Gropiusallee 38, 06846
Tel *(0340) 6508318*
Ⓦ bauhaus-dessau.de
Stay in the minimalist former Bauhaus student rooms within

an iconic school building. Communal bathrooms, and a gorgeous dining room.

EISLEBEN: Graf von Mansfeld €€
Historic Map D4
Markt 56, 06295
Tel *(03475) 250722*
Ⓦ hotel-eisleben.de
Venerable hotel in the bustling main square. Good rooms, some with four-poster beds. Excellent restaurant.

HALLE: Apart-Hotel Halle €€
Boutique Map D4
Kohlschütter St 5–6, 06114
Tel *(0345) 52590*
Ⓦ apart-halle.de
Art Nouveau place with themed rooms based on German cultural figures. Sauna and whirlpool tubs.

MAGDEBURG: Grüne Zitadelle €€
Boutique Map D3
Breiter Weg 9, 39104
Tel *(0391) 620780*
Ⓦ hotel-zitadelle.de
Designed by the Austrian artist Hundertwasser, the exterior is fantastical while the rooms are furnished with colourful decor.

MAGDEBURG: Hotel Ratswaage €€
Modern Map D3
Ratswaageplatz 1, 39104
Tel *(0391) 59260*
Ⓦ ratswaage.de
Dependable and centrally located four-star hotel with a sauna and fabulous breakfast buffet. Good weekend discounts.

NAUMBURG: Hotel Stadt Aachen €€
Historic Map D4
Markt 11, 06618
Tel *(03445) 2470*
Ⓦ hotel-stadt-aachen.de
Vine-covered lodgings on the market square with dark-wood antiques and floral touches.

QUEDLINBURG: Hotel garni Im Propstei Vorwerk €
Historic Map D4
Im Wasserwinkel 1a, 06484
Tel *(03946) 811386*
Ⓦ hotel-propstei-vorwerk.de
Snug, pine-furnished rooms and good breakfast buffet in a half-timbered building.

QUEDLINBURG: Theophano €€
Historic Map D4
Markt 13–14, 06484
Tel *(03946) 96300*
Ⓦ hoteltheophano.de
Traditional, half-timbered rustic hotel in an unbeatable central location. Many rooms have canopied beds.

For more information on types of hotels *see page 491*

TANGERMÜNDE:
Schloss Tangermünde €€
Historic Map D3
Amt 1, 39590
Tel *(0393) 22 7373*
W schloss-tangermuende.de
Prestigious hotel with attentive
service, dark-beamed rooms,
sauna and fantastic restaurant.

WITTENBERG: Pension
am Schwanenteich €
Gasthöfe and Pensionen Map E3
Töpferstr 1, 06886
Tel *(03491) 402807*
W wittenberg-schwanenteich.de
Small, centrally located pension
with bright and airy en suite
rooms and great half-board deals
in its traditional restaurant.

WITTENBERG: Alte Canzley €€
Historic Map E3
Schloßplatz 3, 06886
Tel *(03491) 429190*
W alte-canzley.de
Stay in an old Chancellery
building with neutral decor and
upmarket dark-wood furniture.

Saxony

BAUTZEN: Schloss Schaenke €
Gasthöfe and Pensionen Map F4
Burgplatz 5, 02625
Tel *(03591) 30*
W schloss-schaenke.net
This family-run hotel opposite
the Schloss Ortenburg castle
has simple, elegant rooms and
a fantastic breakfast buffet.

BAUTZEN: Villa Antonia €€
Historic Map F4
Lessingstraße 1, 02625
Tel *(03591) 5010*
W hotel-villa-antonia.de
Late-1890s villa in a quiet part of
town. Elegantly renovated, with
big, comfortable rooms.

CHEMNITZ: Schlosshotel
Klaffenbach €
Historic Map E4
Wasserschloßweg 6, 09123
Tel *(0371) 26110*
W schlosshotel-chemnitz.de
A spectacular moated castle in
the centre of Chemnitz. The
rooms are large and simply
furnished. Great value for money.

CHEMNITZ: Hotel an der Oper €€
Modern Map E4
Straße der Nationen 56, 09111
Tel *(0371) 6810*
W hoteloper-chemnitz.de
Elegant and stylish hotel close to
the opera house. The rooms are
contemporary, with particularly
impressive bathrooms.

The imposing façade of the Steigenberger Grandhotel Handelshof, Leipzig

DRESDEN: Innside by Melia €€
Modern Map E4
Salzgasse 4, 01067
Tel *(0351) 795150*
W innside.com
Chic accommodation in a central
location. Rooms have avant-garde
decor and there is a rooftop bar.

DRESDEN: Schloss Eckberg €€
Historic Map E4
Bautzner Straße 134, 01099
Tel *(0351) 80990*
W schloss-eckberg.de
A 19th-century castle with stylish
furnishings, elegant grounds and
a superb restaurant.

DRESDEN: Taschenbergpalais
Kempinski €€€
Luxury Map E4
Taschenberg 3, 01067
Tel *(0351) 49120*
W kempinski.com
Renowned hotel, right next to
the Royal Palace. Most rooms
have views of the river or Altmarkt.

FREIBERG: Alekto €
Historic Map E4
Am Bahnhof 3, 09599
Tel *(03731) 79 40*
W alekto.de
An elegant Art Nouveau building.
Some rooms are a little old-
fashioned, but all offer great value.

GÖRLITZ: Romantik Hotel
Tuchmacher €€
Historic Map E4
Peterstraße 8, 02826
Tel *(03581) 4731*
W tuchmacher.de
Dating back to the 16th century,
the Romantik offers individually
decorated rooms.

DK Choice

LEIPZIG: Steigenberger
Grandhotel Handelshof €€€
Luxury Map E4
Salzgäßchen 6, 04109
Tel *(0341) 3505810*
W steigenberger.com
A modern, elegant hotel on
Leipzig's historic Naschmarkt.

The huge rooms are decorated
in avant-garde style and there
are two superb restaurants and
a brasserie to choose from.
Unusual for Germany's five-star
hotels, Wi-Fi here is free.

MORITZBURG:
Landhaus Moritzburg €
Gasthöfe and Pensionen Map E4
Schloßallee 37, 01468
Tel *(035207) 8969*
W landhaus-moritzburg.de
A good countryside escape close
to Moritzburg. Snug rooms and a
restaurant with a lovely terrace.

ZITTAU: Schwarzer Bär €
Gasthöfe and Pensionen Map E4
Ottokarplatz 12, 02763
Tel *(03583) 551*
W hotel-schwarzer-baer.de
Simple hotel offering large, good
value rooms perfect for families.

Thuringia

ALTENBURG: Engel €
Gasthöfe and Pensionen Map E4
Johannisstraße 27, 04600
Tel *(03447) 5651*
W hotel-engel-altenburg.de
Family-run pension in the heart
of old Altenburg with individually
decorated rooms and a cellar bar.

EISENACH: Steigenberger
Hotel Thuringer Hof €
Modern Map C4
Karlsplatz 11, 99817
Tel *(03691) 280*
W steigenberger.com
Excellent value hotel with an
extravagant lobby. Comfortable
rooms and a fine restaurant.

ERFURT: Pullman Erfurt
am Dom €€
Luxury Map D4
Theaterplatz 2, 99084
Tel *(0361) 64450*
W pullmanhotels.coml
Centrally located accommodation
with spacious rooms and

extravagant bathrooms. Opulence at an affordable price.

ERFURT: Zumnorde am Anger €€
Historic   **Map** D4
Anger 50–51, 99084
Tel *(0361) 568 00*
W hotel-zumnorde.de
Historic building offering refined rooms with period furniture. Good beer garden.

GOTHA: Augustinerkloster €
Historic   **Map** D4
Jüdenstraße 27, 99867
Tel *(03621) 3029*
W augustinerkloster-gotha.de
Augustinerkloster, a former monastery, has a historic façade but with contemporary interiors.

JENA: Steigenberger Esplanade Jena €
Modern   **Map** D4
Carl-Zeiß-Platz 4, 07743
Tel *(03641) 800*
W steigenberger.com
Situated next to Jena University, this hotel boasts imaginative design and big, bright rooms.

OBERHOF: Hotel Haus Saarland €
Gasthöfe and Pensionen   **Map** D4
Zellaer Straße 13, 98559
Tel *(036842) 52117*
W haus-saarland.de
Lovely family-owned and run inn. Simple but comfortable rooms. Great buffet breakfast.

DK Choice

WEIMAR: Villa Hentzel €
Boutique   **Map** D4
Bauhausstraße 12, 99423
Tel *(03643) 86580*
W hotel-villa-hentzel.de
The elegant 19th-century Villa Hentzel has been home to numerous writers and also played host to the Chilean

Embassy in the past. The beautifully renovated large rooms are individually furnished and have historic features from the building's distinguished past. Within walking distance of central Weimar, the hotel is wonderful value for money.

WEIMAR: Best Western Premier Grand Hotel Russischer Hof €€
Historic   **Map** D4
Goetheplatz 2, 99423
Tel *(03643) 7740*
W russischerhof-weimar.de
The over 200-year-old Russischer Hof is a luxurious, elegant hotel with modern amenities.

WEIMAR: Romantik Hotel Dorotheenhof Weimar €€
Luxury   **Map** D4
Dorotheenhof 1, 99427
Tel *(03643) 4590*
W dorotheenhof.com
Reasonably priced luxury in superb surroundings. Choose from a range of spacious rooms.

Munich

Carat Hotel €
Budget   **Map** 1 F5
Lindwurmstraße 13, 80337
Tel *(089) 230380*
W carat-hotel-muenchen.de
Centrally located hotel with simple, bright rooms and a large and healthy breakfast buffet.

Ibis München City West €
Budget
Westendstraße 181, 80686
Tel *(089) 5794970*
W ibishotel.com
International chain hotel for those who want simple and functional lodgings at low prices.

DK Choice

Motel One München Sendlinger Tor €
Budget   **Map** 1 F5
Herzog-Wilhelm-Straße 28, 80331
Tel *(089) 51777250*
W motel-one.com
This reliable budget chain has really taken off in Germany in recent history, and for good reason. München offers excellent value rooms with bright tourquoise features that lend a certain minimalist elegance. There is also a great café-bar and lounge on site.

Pension Seibel €
Gasthöfe and Pensionen
Reichenbachstraße 8, 80469
Tel *(089) 2319180*
W seibel-hotels-munich.de
Simple family-run pension with traditional Bavarian decor and fresh buffet breakfasts.

Amalienburg €€
Boutique
Amalienburgstraße 24–26, 81247
Tel *(089) 8911550*
W amalienburg.de
In a tranquil corner of Munich, with artistic design touches in its attractive modern rooms.

Hotel Bavaria €€
Modern
Gollierstraße 9, 80339
Tel *(089) 5080790*
W hotel-bavaria.de
Long-standing family-run hotel. Bright rooms with boutique touches. Good breakfast buffet.

Hotel Laimer Hof €€
Historic
Laimer Straße 40, 80639
Tel *(089) 1780380*
W laimerhof.de
Neo-Renaissance villa with classically furnished rooms. Free bikes provided to explore the tranquil surroundings.

Louis Hotel €€
Modern   **Map** 2 B5
Viktualienmarkt 6, 80331
Tel *(089) 41119080*
W louis-hotel.com
Lovely, airy rooms with natural stone tiles and wooden floors, complemented by Italian fabrics.

Charles Hotel €€€
Luxury   **Map** 1 F3
Sophienstraße 28, 80333
Tel *(089) 5445550*
W charleshotel.de
This fantastic hotel has huge rooms with good views over the nearby botanical gardens.

The spacious lounge at Motel One München Sendlinger Tor, Munich

For more information on types of hotels *see page 491*

Spa facilities at InterContinental Berchtesgaden Resort

Cortiina €€€
Boutique Map 2 C4
Ledererstraße 8, 80331
Tel *(089) 2422490*
🅦 designhotels.com
Elegant hotel whose individually decorated rooms and cocktail bar ooze boutique opulence.

Platzl €€€
Modern Map 2 B4
Sparkassenstraße 10, 80331
Tel *(089) 237030*
🅦 platzl.de
Warm, modern accommodation, a stylish spa and a fantastic 16th-century restaurant and pub.

Vier Jahreszeiten Kempinski €€€
Luxury Map 2 C4
Maximilianstraße 17, 80539
Tel *(089) 21250*
🅦 kempinski.com
Prestigious hotel with boutique-style rooms and a variety of five-star facilities.

Bavaria

AUGSBURG: Dom Hotel €€
Modern Map D6
Frauentorstraße 8, 86152
Tel *(0821) 343930*
🅦 domhotel-augsburg.de
Centrally located in the cathedral district, but quiet hotel with a spa.

AUGSBURG: Villa Arborea €€
Modern Map D6
Goggingerstraße 124, 86199
Tel *(0821) 90739199*
🅦 hotel-villa-arborea.de
Villa Arborea offers large country-style pastel rooms, some with views over a lovely guest garden.

BAMBERG: Barockhotel am Dom €
Historic Map D5
Vorderer Bach 4, 96049
Tel *(0951) 54031*
🅦 barockhotel.de
Baroque features are dotted around this standard but smart hotel. Lovely breakfast buffet.

BAMBERG: National €€
Historic Map D5
Luitpoldstraße 37, 96052
Tel *(0951) 509980*
🅦 hotel-national-bamberg.de
Grand 19th-century building with modern, brightly decorated rooms and a bar.

BAMBERG: St Nepomuk €€
Gasthöfe and Pensionen Map D5
Obere Mülbrücke 9, 96049
Tel *(0951) 98420*
🅦 hotel-nepomuk.de
Old timber-framed hotel with an exceptional location next to the river. Rooms have modern facilities.

BAYREUTH: Ramada Hotel Residenzschloss Bayreuth €€
Modern Map D5
Erlanger Straße 37, 95444
Tel *(0921) 75850*
🅦 ramada.de
Standard chain hotel with comfortable modern rooms, a sauna and a good restaurant.

BERCHTESGADEN: Berghotel Edelweiß €
Gasthöfe and Pensionen Map E7
Kehotelhweg 2, 83471
Tel *(08652) 5559*
🅦 berghotel-edelweiss.de
Traditional Bavarian inn with mountain views from most rooms. Sauna and table tennis.

BERCHTESGADEN: Vier Jahreszeiten €
Budget Map E7
Maximilianstraße 20, 83471
Tel *(08652) 9520*
🅦 hotel-vierjahreszeiten-berchtesgaden.de
Family-run hotel with traditional Bavarian decor throughout and alpine views from many rooms.

DK Choice

BERCHTESGADEN: InterContinental Berchtesgaden Resort €€€
Luxury Map E7
Hintereck 1, 83471
Tel *(08652) 97550*
🅦 intercontinental.com
This exclusive five-star establishment has immaculate views of the Alps from almost every part of the hotel, including the minimalist bedrooms and the luxurious spa and pools. The gourmet restaurants on site specialize in regional cuisine.

FÜSSEN: Hotel Hirsch €€
Boutique Map D7
Kaiser-Maximilian-Ptaz 7, 87629
Tel *(08652) 5559*
🅦 berghotel-edelweiss.de
Bavarian antiques meet modern amenities in one of many successful combinations of new and old at this boutique hotel.

GARMISCH-PARTENKIRCHEN: Hotel Edelweiss €€
Gasthöfe and Pensionen Map D7
Martinswinkelstraße 15–17, 82467
Tel *(08821) 2454*
🅦 hoteledelweiss.de
Romantic family-run guesthouse with spotless and spacious country-style rooms.

DK Choice

GARMISCH-PARTENKIRCHEN: Gasthof Frandorfer €
Gasthöfe and Pensionen Map D7
Ludwigstraße 24, 82467
Tel *(08821) 9270*
🅦 gasthof-fraundorfer.de
As much a celebration of Bavarian culture as a guesthouse, Gasthof Frandorfer has beautiful murals, individually decorated rooms with regional themes and nightly dancing and yodeling in the restaurant and bar.

INGOLSTADT: Altstadthotel Guesthouse Die Galerie €€
Boutique Map D6
Gymnasiumstraße, 985049
Tel *(0841) 88690*
🅦 altstadthotel-ingolstadt.de
Angluar design dominates in this spotless mid-range hotel with a café, sauna and hot tub.

INGOLSTADT: Hotel Ammerland Garni €€
Boutique Map D6
Hermann-Paul-Müller-Straße 15, 85055
Tel *(0841) 953450*
🅦 hotel-ammerland.de
Great choice away from the town centre, with creatively-styled rooms, two saunas and a bar.

LINDAU: Spiegel-Garni €
Gasthöfe and Pensionen Map C7
In der Grub 1, 88131
Tel *(08382) 94930*
🅦 hotel-spiegel-garni.de
Rooms at Spiegel-Garni range from simple to extravagantly

alpine, with wood-clad interiors, iron stoves and floral drapes.

LINDAU: Reutemann €€
Modern **Map** C7
Ludwigstraße, 2388131
Tel *(08382) 9150*
W reutemann-lindau.de
Stylish hotel with an extraordinary harborside location, airy rooms, a spa and an excellent restaurant.

LINDAU: Bayerischer Hof €€€
Luxury **Map** C7
Bahnhofplatz 2,88131
Tel *(08382) 9150*
W bayerischerhof-lindau.de
Neo-Classical building in a prime lakefront location. Spacious rooms with 19th-century furnishings.

NÜRNBURG: Elch €
Gasthöfe and Pensionen **Map** D6
Irrerstr 9, 90403
Tel *(0911) 2492980*
W hotel-elch.de
Clean and simple family-run lodging in a historic 14th-century house with exposed beams.

NÜRNBURG: Dürer Hotel €€
Modern **Map** D6
Neutormauer 32, 90403
Tel *(0911) 2146650*
W duerer-hotel.de
Dürer features spacious rooms decorated in rich colours. Sauna and steam room on site.

NÜRNBURG: Hotel Drei Raben €€
Boutique **Map** D6
Königstraße 63, 90402
Tel *(0911) 274380*
W hoteldreiraben.de
Modern trendy accommodation with bold colour schemes, a bar and tasty breakfast buffet.

NÜRNBURG: Hotel Victoria €€
Modern **Map** D6
Königstraße 80, 90402
Tel *(0911) 24050*
W hotelvictoria.de
Lovely and clean three-star hotel with a café serving delicious cakes.

NÜRNBURG: Le Méridien Grand €€
Boutique **Map** D6
Bahnhofstraße 1, 90402
Tel *(0911) 23220*
W lemeridiennuernberg.com
Elegant hotel with sleek Art Deco and Art Nouveau furnishings. Excellent regional brasserie.

DK Choice

OBERAMMERGAU: Hotel Maximilian €€
Gasthöfe and Pensionen **Map** D7
Ettaler Straße 5, 82487
Tel *(08822) 948740*
W maximilian-oberammergau.de
This alpine hotel features a striking array of boutique rooms, along with a luxurious spa with a sauna, steam room, massages and beauty treatments. There is also a fantastic Mediterranean restaurant and a beer garden to sample the hotel's own brews.

OBERSTDORF: Saschas Kachelofen €
Gasthöfe and Pensionen **Map** C7
Kirchstraße 3, 87561
Tel *(08322) 97750*
W saschas-kachelofen.de
Traitional inn with standard rooms above a rustic restaurant.

PASSAU: Wilder Mann €
Historic **Map** E6
Rathausplatz, 94032
Tel *(0851) 35071*
W wilder-mann.com
Central hotel that sports heavy traditional furniture including one royal wedding bed.

PASSAU: Hotel Schloss Ort €€
Modern **Map** E6
Im Ort 11, 94032
Tel *(0851) 34072*
W schlosshotel-passau.de
Pleasant rooms, but the picturesque location at the confluence of the Ilz and Danube rivers is the highlight.

REGENSBURG: Goldenes Kreuz €€
Gasthöfe and Pensionen **Map** D6
Haidplatz 7, 93047
Tel *(0941) 55812*
W hotel-goldeneskreuz.de
Lovely collection of small suites in a centrally located historic building. Wonderful café.

REGENSBURG: Goliath €€
Boutique **Map** D6
Goliathstraße 10, 93047
Tel *(0941) 2000900*
W hotel-goliath.de
Goliath promises bold colours and modern design along with great views from the rooftop terrace.

ROTHENBURG: Roter Hahn €
Historic **Map** C6
Obere Schiedgasse 21, 91541
Tel *(09861) 9740*
W roterhahn.com
Standard rooms in a 14th-century building on a quiet street.

ROTHENBURG: Gerberhaus €€
Historic **Map** C6
Sptialgasse 25, 91541
Tel *(09861) 94900*
W hotel-gerberhaus.de
Attractive country-style rooms in a beautiful converted 16th-century tannery.

ROTHENBURG: Burg Hotel €€€
Historic **Map** C6
Klostergasse 1, 91541
Tel *(09861) 94890*
W burghotel.eu
Hotel combining a 12th-century structure with trendy designs. Sauna and spa facilities.

WÜRZBURG: Central Hotel Garni €
Budget **Map** C5
Koelikerstraße 1, 97070
Tel *(0931) 4608840*
W centralhotel-wuerzburg.de
Centrally located good-value hotel with basic but good rooms and buffet breakfasts.

WÜRZBURG: Hotel Gruener Baum €€
Gasthöfe and Pensionen **Map** C5
Zeller Straße 35, 97082
Tel *(0931) 450680*
W gruener-baum-wuerzburg.de
Small rooms in a traditional Franconian inn. Breakfast buffet.

WÜRZBURG: Hotel Würzburger Hof €€
Modern **Map** C5
Barbarossaplatz 2, 97070
Tel *(0931) 53814*
W hotel-wuerzburgerhof.de
Würzburger Hof features richly decorated rooms in wide variety of styles and price ranges.

Stylishly designed room at Le Méridien Grand, Nürnburg

For more information on types of hotels *see page 491*

Traditionally-styled room at Graf Zeppelin, Stuttgart

Baden-Württemberg

BADEN-BADEN: Am Markt €
Gasthöfe and Pensionen **Map** B6
Marktplatz 18, 76530
Tel *(07221) 27040*
w hotel-am-markt-baden.de
Friendly, family-run pension
with basic rooms. Views over
the charming marketplace.

BADEN-BADEN: Bad-Hotel Zum Hirsch €€
Historic **Map** B6
Hirschstraße 1, 76530
Tel *(07221) 9390*
w heliopark-hirsch.de
Thermal spring water flows from
the taps in this Old Town hotel.
Also boasts a splendid ballroom.

BADEN-BADEN: Brenners Park Hotel €€€
Luxury **Map** B6
Schillerstraße 4–6, 76530
Tel *(07221) 9000*
w brenners.com
Effortlessly elegant hotel with
extravagant antique furnishings
in the rooms and lounges.

FREIBURG IM BREISGAU: Schemmer €
Budget **Map** B7
Eschholzstraße 63, 79106
Tel *(0761) 207490*
w hotel-schemmer.de
Tidy little town house with modest
accommodation, some rooms
have shared baths.

DK Choice

FREIBURG IM BREISGAU: Zum Roten Bären €€€
Historic **Map** B7
Oberlinden 12, 79098
Tel *(0761) 87870*
w roter-baeren.de
Germany's oldest hotel, Zum
Roten Bären opened in 1120
and became part of the city

gate in 1250. The contemporary
rooms have the occasional
antique providing a sense of
history. First-class breakfasts.

HEIDELBERG: Der Europäischer Hof €€€
Luxury **Map** C6
Friedrich-Ebert-Anlage 1, 69117
Tel *(06221) 5150*
w europaeischerhof.com
One of Heidelberg's premier hotels
with individually decorated rooms,
several great restaurants and a bar.

HEIDELBERG: Hirschgasse €€€
Luxury **Map** C6
Hirschgasse 3, 69120
Tel *(06221) 4550*
w hirschgasse.de
The former lodgings of Mark Twain
and Otto von Bismarck. Has a
country feel with four-poster beds.

KARLSRUHE: Hotelwelt Kübler €
Boutique **Map** B6
Bismarckstraße 37–43, 76133
Tel *(0721) 1440*
w hotel-kuebler.de
Variety of rooms from standard
mid-range to themed suites.
On-site microbrewery.

KONSTANZ: Barbarossa €€
Historic **Map** C7
Overmarkt 8–12, 78462
Tel *(07531) 22021*
w barbarossa-hotel.com
Mid-range hotel with a frescoes
covering the walls. This building
was host to Friedrich I when he
signed an 1183 treaty here.

KONSTANZ: Steigenberger Inselhotel €€€
Luxury **Map** C7
Auf der Insel 1, 78462
Tel *(07531) 1250*
w steigenberger.com
Prestigious establishment in a
medieval Dominican monastery.
Located on its own island.

LUDWIGSBURG: Hotel Favorit €€
Business **Map** C6
Gartenstraße 18, 71638
Tel *(07141) 976770*
w hotel-favorit.de
Great hotel with cheerful pine-
furnished pastel rooms. Sauna
and an extensive breakfast buffet.

MAULBRONN: Hotel Klosterpost €€
Historic **Map** C6
Klosterstraße 2, 75433
Tel *(07043) 1080*
w hotel-klosterpost.de
Traditional half-timbered 13th-
century inn with bright rooms
and a good regional restaurant.

MEERSBURG: Hotel Löwen €€
Historic **Map** C7
Marktplatz 2, 88709
Tel *(07532) 43040*
w hotel-loewen-meersburg.de
Romantic medieval building with
beautiful geranium-filled
windows and snug rooms.

STUTTGART: Hotel Espenlaub €
Boutique **Map** C6
Charlottenstraße 27, 70182
Tel *(0711) 210910*
w hansa-stuttgart.de
Basic hotel with small, bright
and simple rooms and a modest
complimentary breakfast buffet.

STUTTGART: Der Zauberlehrling €€€
Boutique **Map** C6
Rosenstraße 38, 70182
Tel *(0711) 2377770*
w zauberlehrling.de
Located in the hip Bohnenviertel
district. Tasteful themed rooms,
from Japanese to faded *fin de siècle*.

STUTTGART: Graf Zeppelin €€€
Luxury **Map** C6
Arnulf-Klett-Platz 7, 70173
Tel *(0711) 20480*
w steigenberger.com
This five-star hotel promises 19th-
century elegance. Classical as
well as avant-garde rooms.

TÜBINGEN: Hotel am Schloss €€
Historic **Map** C6
Burgsteige 18, 72070
Tel *(07071) 92940*
w hotelamschloss.de
Half-timbered place with colour-
ful window boxes and fine town
views from below the castle.

TÜBINGEN: Hotel Krone €€€
Luxury **Map** C6
Uhlandstraße 1, 72072
Tel *(07071) 13310*
w krone-tuebingen.de
Prestigious riverside hotel with
bright rooms, a sophisticated
gourmet restaurant and chic bar.

ULM: Hotel Bäumle €€
Gasthöfe and Pensionen Map C6
Kohlgasse 6, 89073
Tel *(0731) 62287*
W hotel-baeumle.de
Housed in a renovated over
500-year-old building with
good-value standard rooms.

DK Choice

ULM: Hotel Schiefes Haus€€€
Historic Map C6
Schwörhausgasse 6, 89073
Tel *(0731) 967930*
W hotelschiefeshausulm.de
This famous half-timbered
establishment built in 1443 has
wood-beam ceilings and floors
so crooked that the bed legs
are of different lengths. The
property's rustic nature has been
well-preserved, with plush
additions such as bathrooms
with spacious tubs.

Rhineland-Palatinate and Saarland

DK Choice

BACHARACH: Rhein Hotel €€
Gasthöfe and
Pensionen Map B5
Langstraße 50, 55422
Tel *(06743) 1243*
W rhein-hotel-bacharach.de
Rhein is a fine family-run,
half-timbered hotel in an
atmospheric location between
the town ramparts and the
Rhine. On offer are spotless
rooms, a superb regional
restaurant, an extensive breakfast
buffet and free bike rental.

The Modernist exterior of the Hyatt
Regency Mainz

BOPPARD: Bellevue €€
Gasthöfe and Pensionen Map B5
Rheinallee 41, 56154
Tel *(06742) 1020*
W bellevue-boppard.de
Grand 19th-century waterfront
hotel with antique-decorated
rooms overlooking the Rhine.

MAINZ: Stadt Coblenz €
Gasthöfe and Pensionen Map B5
Rheinstraße 49, 55116
Tel *(06131) 6290444*
W stadtcoblenz.de
Old, centrally located inn with
bargain rates, though the rooms
are small and sometimes noisy.

MAINZ: Hof Ehrenfels €€
Historic Map B5
Grebenstraße 5–7, 55116
Tel *(06131) 9712340*
W hof-ehrenfels.de
Smart hotel in a 15th-century
convent overlooking the Dom.

**MAINZ: Hyatt
Regency Mainz**
Luxury Map B5
Malakoff-Terrasse 1, 55116
Tel *(06131) 731234*
W mainz.regency.hyatt.com
Sophisticated five-star hotel
in a striking modern building
overlooking the Rhine.

**OBERWESEL: Hotel
Römerkrug** €€
Historic Map B5
Marktplatz 1, 55430
Tel *(06744) 8176*
W hotel-roemerkrug.rhine
castles.com
This dignified half-timbered
guesthouse has old-fashioned
rooms with modern amenities.

**OBERWESEL: Burghotel Auf
Schönburg** €€€
Historic Map B5
Auf Schönburg, 55430
Tel *(06744) 939 30*
W burghotel-schoenburg.de
A castle dating back to 1914 with
10th-century foundations. Lovely
interiors and terrace restaurant.

SAARBRÜCKEN: Madeleine €
Budget Map B6
Cecilienstraße 5, 66111
Tel *0681 32228*
W hotel-madeleine.de
A family-run hotel with small
and bright rooms, free bike rental
and bargain mid-week rates.

SPEYER: Domhof €€
Historic Map B6
Im Bauhof 3, 67346
Tel *(06232) 13290*
W domhof.de
Stay in this ivy-clad hotel with
spacious antique-furnished

rooms overlooking a cobbled
courtyard. There is also a superb
breakfast buffet.

**ST MARTIN: St Martiner
Castell** €€
Historic Map B5
Maikammererstraße 2, 67487
Tel *(06323) 9510*
W hotelcastell.de
St Martiner is an attractive castle
hotel with well-priced rooms in
an exceptionally pretty village.

TRIER: Becker's €€
Boutique Map A5
Olewiger Straße 206, 54295
Tel *(0651) 938080*
W weinhaus-becker.de
Stylish vineyard guesthouse in a
wine-producing suburb of Trier.
Room decor reminiscent of
Japanese minimalism.

TRIER: Casa Chiara €€
Gasthöfe and Pensionen Map A5
Engelstraße 8, 54292
Tel *(0651) 270730*
W casa-chiara.de
Friendly place with good breakfasts
and spotless rooms, some with
views of a Roman city gate.

TRIER: Villa Hügel €€€
Luxury Map A5
Bernhardstraße 14, 54295
Tel *(0651) 937100*
W hotel-villa-huegel.de
Upmarket Art Nouveau villa
sporting cheerful rooms and a
terrace with lovely valley views.

WORMS: Parkhotel Prinz Carl €€
Historic Map B5
Carl Prinz-Carl-Anlage 10–14, 67547
Tel *(06241) 3080*
W parkhotel-prinzcarl.de
Located in a 19th-century
barracks with large, cheerful
rooms. On site bar and restaurant.

Hesse

ALSFELD: Zum Schwalbennest €
Gasthöfe and Pensionen Map C4
Pfarrwiesenweg 12–14, 36304
Tel *(06631) 911440*
W hotel-schwalbennest.de
Serene and cheerful hotel with
comfortable rooms, a rustic
restaurant and a beer garden.

**BAD HOMBURG: Maritim
Kurhaushotel** €€€
Modern Map C5
Ludwigstraße 3, 61348
Tel *(06172) 6600*
W maritim.de
Impeccably decorated rooms
with balconies overlooking a
park. Pool and golfing facilities.

For more information on types of hotels *see page 491*

**DARMSTADT: Jagdschloss
Kranichstein** €€€
Historic Map C5
Kranichsteiner Straße 261, 64289
Tel *(06151) 977 90*
[W] hotel-jagdschloss-kranichstein.de
Fabulous luxury accommodation
in a beautiful Renaissance castle.

**ELTVILLE AM RHEIN:
Kronenschlösschen** €€
Luxury Map B5
Rheinallee, 65347
Tel *(06723) 640*
[W] kronenschloesschen.de
Stylish rooms with individual
furnishings and lovely bathrooms.
Fine-dining restaurant on site.

**FRANKFURT AM MAIN:
Hamburger Hof** €€
Business Map C5
Poststraße 10-12, 60329
Tel *(069) 271 396 90*
[W] hamburgerhof.com
Modern hotel with sleek design
and a breakfast buffet.

**FRANKFURT AM MAIN:
Hessischer Hof** €€€
Luxury Map C5
Friedrich-Ebert-Anlage 40, 60325
Tel *(069) 754 00*
[W] hessischer-hof.de
Exquisitely styled building with
well-equipped classic rooms,
some furnished with antiques.

**FULDA: Maritim Hotel
am Schlossgarten** €€
Modern Map C5
Pauluspromenade 2, 36037
Tel *(0661) 28 20*
[W] maritim.de
Ostentatious yet elegant lodgings
with a pool and spacious rooms,
some with balconies.

DK Choice

**KASSEL: Schlosshotel Bad
Wilhelmshöhe** €€
Luxury Map C4
Schlosspark 8, 34131
Tel *(0561) 308 80*
[W] schlosshotel-kassel.de
A refined hotel in the
magnificent Wilhelmshöhe
Bergpark. Rooms are large and
stylish; ask for the superior
rooms or suites for the best
views over Kassel. Good
wellness and spa facilities.

**LIMBURG: Romantik Hotel
Zimmermann** €€
Gasthöfe and Pensionen Map B5
Blumenröder Straße 1, 65549
Tel *(06431) 46 11*
[W] romantikhotel-zimmermann.de
Relaxed vibe, with ornate rooms
and marble-clad bathrooms.

**MARBURG: Vila Vita Hotel &
Residenz Rosenpark** €€€
Luxury Map C4
Rosenstraße 18–28, 35037
Tel *(06421) 600 50*
[W] vilavitahotels.com
Elegant hotel with a glass-domed
lobby, impeccable service, several
apartments and three restaurants.

**MICHELSTADT: Zum
Grünen Baum** €
Gasthöfe and Pensionen Map C5
Große Gasse 17, 64720
Tel *(06061) 24 09*
[W] gruenerbaum-michelstadt.com
A charming half-timbered inn
with inviting rooms and an
award-winning restaurant.

**RÜDESHEIM AM RHEIN:
Jagdschloss Niederwald** €€
Historic Map B5
Am Niederwald 1, 65385
Tel *(06722) 710 60*
[W] niederwald.de
Historic hunting castle with a
tennis court, swimming pool and
a restaurant with panoramic views.

**WEILBURG: Schlosshotel
Weilburg** €€
Historic Map B5
Langgasse 25, 35781
Tel *(06471) 509 00*
[W] schlosshotel-weilburg.de
Set in a luxurious Renaissance
castle with tastefully decorated
rooms and a good restaurant.

**WETZLAR: Landhotel
Naunheimer Mühle** €€
Gasthöfe and Pensionen Map C5
Mühle 2, 35584
Tel *(06441) 935 30*
[W] naunheimer-muehle.de
Traditional to modern rooms and
a rustic restaurant located right
next to the Lahn River.

WIESBADEN: Nassauer Hof €€€
Luxury Map B5
Kaiser-Friedrich-Platz 3, 65183
Tel *(0611) 13 30*
[W] nassauer-hof.de
Exclusive, opulent hotel with
superb rooms, an acclaimed
restaurant and a wellness area.

North Rhine-
Westphalia

**AACHEN: Best Western
Hotel Royal** €
Modern Map A4
Jülicher Straße 1, 52070
Tel *(0241) 182 280*
[W] royal.bestwestern.de
This city-centre hotel has
gorgeous minimalist rooms done

in beautiful soft colours. The
suites are equipped with private
terraces and kitchenettes.

**AACHEN: Pullman
Aachen Quellenhof** €€€
Luxury Map A4
Monheimsallee 52, 52062
Tel *(0241) 913 20*
[W] sofitel.com
A grand establishment with
elegant rooms and suites, a
wellness area and a fantastic
on-site brasserie.

BIELEFELD: Brenner Hotel €
Gasthöfe and Pensionen Map C3
Otto-Brenner-Straße 133, 33607
Tel *(0521) 299 90*
[W] brenner-hotel.de
Small bowling alley, a restaurant
and a quirky bar at this quaint
little hotel.

BONN: Kaiser Karl €
Gasthöfe and Pensionen Map B4
Vorgebirgsstraße 56, 53119
Tel *(0228) 985 570*
[W] kaiser-karl-hotel-bonn.de
Choose from exquisitely decorated
rooms and enjoy the wonderful,
old-fashioned bar.

**BONN: Schlosshotel
Kommende Ramersdorf** €€
Historic Map B4
Oberkasselerstraße 10, 53227
Tel *(0228) 440 734*
[W] schlosshotel-kommende-
ramersdorf.de
This beautiful castle has antique-
filled hallways, individually styled
rooms and a superb restaurant.

**DORTMUND:
Cityhotel Dortmund** €
Modern Map B4
Grafenhof/Silberstraße 37, 44137
Tel *(0231) 477 96 60*
[W] cityhotel-dortmund.de
Efficient hotel with comfortable
rooms. Terrific breakfast buffet.

A glimpse of a luxurious suite at the Vila Vita
Hotel & Residenz Rosenpark, Marburg

**DÜSSELDORF: Madison Novum
Düsseldorf City Center** €
Gasthöfe and Pensionen   Map B4
Graf-Adolf-Straße 94, 40210
Tel *(0211) 168 50*
W novum-hotels.de
Range of tasteful, inviting rooms
along with a terrace bistro and
an extensive fitness centre.

**DÜSSELDORF: Steigenberger
Parkhotel** €€€
Luxury   Map B4
Königsallee 1a, 40212
Tel *(0211) 138 10*
W steigenberger.com
Well-styled rooms and a fantastic
restaurant with a diverse menu.

ESSEN: Welcome Hotel €
Modern   Map B4
Schützenbahn 58, 45127
Tel *(0201) 177 90*
W welcome-to-essen.de
Colourful place with well-
equipped rooms and a great
garden restaurant.

**HÖXTER: Ringhotel
Niedersachsen** €€
Modern   Map C3
Grubestraße 3–7, 37671
Tel *(05271) 68 80*
W hotelniedersachsen.de
Airy rooms, some with large
wooden beams. Four restaurants,
a wellness spa and a pool.

KÖLN: NH Köln City €
Modern   Map B4
Holzmarkt 47, 50676
Tel *(0221) 272 20 00*
W nh-hotels.com
This centrally located hotel
houses comfortable rooms and a
good Mediterranean restaurant.

KÖLN: Hotel im Wasserturm €€
Boutique   Map B4
Kaygasse 2, 50676
Tel *(0221) 200 80*
W hotel-im-wasserturm.de
Stay in an interestedly-shaped
room fitted with all the amenities
in this former water tower.

DK Choice

**KÖLN: Excelsior
Hotel Ernst** €€€
Luxury   Map B4
Trankgasse 1–5, 50667
Tel *(0221) 27 01*
W excelsiorhotelernst.com
A historic and truly grand hotel
beside Cologne's magnificent
cathedral, with rooms and
suites that are contemporary
but retain classical features.
The several restaurants here
include the world-renowned,
Michelin-starred Taku.

LEMGO: Im Borke €
Gasthöfe and Pensionen   Map C3
Salzufler Straße 132, 32657
Tel *(05266) 16 91*
W hotel-im-borke.de
Peaceful, family-friendly hotel
with a popular restaurant.

**MÜNSTER: Romantik Hotel
Hof zur Linde**
Gasthöfe and Pensionen   Map B3
Handorfer Werseufer 1, 48157
Tel *(0251) 327 50*
W hof-zur-linde.de
A lovely farm cottage hotel with
magnificent river views and fire-
places in the suites and cottages.

**MÜNSTER: Schloss
Wilkinghege** €€
Historic   Map B3
Steinfurter Straße 374, 48159
Tel *(0251) 144 270*
W schloss-wilkinghege.de
Castle with modern comfort and
historic charm, as well as a
refined on-site French restaurant.

**SIEGEN: Best Western
Parkhotel Siegen** €€
Modern   Map B4
Koblenzer Straße 135, 57072
Tel *(0271) 338 10*
W parkhotel-siegen.bestwestern.de
Stylishly furnished rooms and
a sauna in a serene location.

**WUPPERTAL: Art Fabrik
& Hotel** €
Boutique   Map B4
Bockmühle 16-24, 42289
Tel *(0202) 283 70*
W art-fabrik-hotel.de
A former property of Friedrich
Engels with spacious rooms,
saunas and an artistic touch.

XANTEN: Fürstenberger Hof €€
Gasthöfe and Pensionen   Map B3
Fürstenberg 11, 46509
Tel *(02801) 16 13*
W fuerstenbergerhof-xanten.de
A castle-like building in a nature
reserve. Rooms furnished with
chandeliers and antiques.

The magnificently lake-front façade of the Dorint Park Hotel, Bremen

---

Lower Saxony, Hamburg and Bremen

BREMEN: Heldt €
Gasthöfe and Pensionen   Map C2
Friedhofstraße 41, 28213
Tel *(0421) 213 051*
W hotel-heldt.de
Small establishment with
tastefully furnished rooms and
apartments. Free bike rental.

BREMEN: Dorint Park Hotel €€
Luxury   Map C2
Im Bürgerpark, 28209
Tel *(0421) 340 80*
W hotel-bremen.dorint.com
Stay in this opulent hotel located
in a lovely area in Bremen.
Comfortable rooms and several
good bars and restaurants.

**BREMEN: Landhaus
Höpken's Ruh** €€
Gasthöfe and Pensionen   Map C2
Oberneulander Landstraße 69, 28355
Tel *(0421) 205 853*
W hoepkens-ruh.de
Stylish, small hotel set in parkland,
with individually furnished rooms
and a commendable restaurant.

**CELLE: Hotel am
Braunen Hirsch** €
Modern   Map C3
Münzstraße 9c, 29223
Tel *(05141) 939 30*
W hotel-ambraunenhirsch.de
Bright and comfortable rooms
with modern design. There is also
a historic restaurant next door.

CELLE: Fürstenhof Celle €€
Luxury   Map C3
Hannoversche Straße 55–56, 29221
Tel *(05141) 20 10*
W fuerstenhof-celle.de
Fürstenhof Celle offers fabulous
accommodation, with English
country-style rooms, an
impressive fitness area and
a gourmet restaurant.

For more information on types of hotels *see page 491*

CLOPPENBURG: Park Hotel €
Gasthöfe and Pensionen   Map B3
Burgstraße 8, 49661
Tel *(04471) 66 14*
w parkhotel-cloppenburg.de
Lovely, quiet hotel by the Soeste
river. Stylish rooms, sauna, golf
and tennis facilities.

DUDERSTADT: Zum Löwen €€
Modern   **Map** C4
Marktstraße 30, 37115
Tel *(05527) 30 72*
w hotelzumloewen.de
Zum Löwen features sleek rooms,
a beautiful pool and a famous
regional restaurant.

GOSLAR: Brusttuch €€
Historic   **Map** D3
Hoher Weg 1, 38640
Tel *(05321) 346 00*
w brusttuch.de
Located in a medieval Old Town
building with quaint rooms and
all modern amenities.

GOSLAR: Der Achtermann €€
Boutique   **Map** D3
Rosentorstraße 20, 38640
Tel *(05321) 700 00*
w der-achtermann.de
This Art-Deco-style hotel has
a large pool and sauna area as
well as a good restaurant.

GÖTTINGEN: Gebhards €€€
Luxury   **Map** C4
Goetheallee 22–23, 37073
Tel *(0551) 496 80*
w gebhardshotel.de
Beautifully furnished rooms,
sauna and whirpool facilities and
a traditional German restaurant.

**HAMBURG: Gastwerk
Hotel Hamburg** €€
Historic   **Map** C2
Beim Alten Gaswerk 3, 22761
Tel *(040) 890 624 24*
w gastwerk.com
An impressive renovated
gasworks plant with industrial-

styled rooms and lofts fitted with
all modern amenities, along with
an exceptional spa.

HAMBURG: The George Hotel €€
Gasthöfe and Pensionen   **Map** C2
Barcastraße 3, 220 87
Tel *(040) 280030*
w thegeorge-hotel.de
British-style inspired hotel with
dark wood in the traditional rooms
and a fantastic Italian restaurant.

DK Choice

**HAMBURG: Fairmont Hotel
Vier Jahreszeiten** €€€
Historic   **Map** C2
Neuer Jungfernstieg 9–14, 20354
Tel *(040) 349 40*
w fairmont-hvj.com
A large, elegant hotel with great
views of the Alster from most
rooms. With its subdued design,
excellent service, an award-
winning restaurant and a great
spa and fitness club, Fairmont
never ceases to impress. Come
here for the subtle luxury.

**HAMBURG: Le Royal
Meridien** €€€
Luxury   **Map** C2
An Der Auster 52–56, 200 99
Tel *(040) 210 00*
w leroyalmeridienhamburg.com
Minimalist rooms, an excellent
spa and great views of Hamburg
along the banks of the Alster.

**HANNOVER: Central-Hotel
Kaiserhof** €€
Historic   **Map** C3
Ernst-August-Platz 4, 301 59
Tel *(0511) 36830*
w centralhotel.de
Classically furnished rooms in a
historic building. The acclaimed
restaurant serves trout sourced
from the courtyard fountain.

**HANNOVER: Kastens Hotel
Luisenhof** €€
Gasthöfe and Pensionen   **Map** C3
Luisenstraße 1-3, 30159
Tel *(0511) 304 40*
w kastens-luisenhof.de
Kastens is an elegant mansion
with large and quiet rooms, and
good spa and fitness facilities.
Great views.

**HILDESHEIM: Parkhotel
Berghölzchen** €
Historic   **Map** C3
Am Berghölzchen 1, 31139
Tel *(05121) 97 90*
w berghoelzchen.de
An old hotel with comfortable
rooms. Do not forget to try the
delicious regional food that has
been served here since 1770.

**KÖNIGSLUTTER: Avalon
Hotelpark Königshof** €
Modern   **Map** D3
Braunschweigerstraße 21a, 38154
Tel *(05353) 50 30*
w hotelpark-koenigshof.de
Large hotel with cheerful rooms,
various sports amenities and a
good restaurant.

LÜNEBURG: Bremer Hof €
Gasthöfe and Pensionen   **Map** D2
Lüner Straße 12, 21335
Tel *(04131) 22 40*
w bremer-hof.de
Comfortable rooms, some with
old wooden beams, in a family-
run hotel dating to 1889. The
restaurant serves local cuisine.

**OLDENBURG: Best Western
Hotel Heide** €€
Modern   **Map** B2
Melkbrink 49–51, 26121
Tel *(0441) 80 40*
w hotel-heide.de
Conveniently located, this chain
hotel has large rooms and an
elegant restaurant.

**OSNABRÜCK: Romantik
Hotel Walhalla** €
Historic   **Map** B3
Bierstraße 24, 49074
Tel *(0541) 349 10*
w hotel-walhalla.de
This museum-like hotel, dating
back to 1690, has spacious rooms
and suites. Beer garden, lounge
bar and restaurant too.

**WOLFENBÜTTEL: Parkhotel
Altes Kaffeehaus** €
Gasthöfe and Pensionen   **Map** D3
Harztorwall 18, 38300
Tel *(05331) 88 80*
w parkhotel-wolfenbuettel.de
Comfortable, quiet, parkside
hotel with good-sized rooms
and a great French restaurant.

**WOLFSBURG: Brackstedter
Mühle** €€
Gasthöfe and Pensionen   **Map** D3
Zum Kühlen Grunde 2, 38448
Tel *(05366) 900*
w brackstedter-muehle.de
Peaceful hotel in an old millhouse
with simple rooms, a restaurant
and a beautiful winter garden.

Schleswig-Holstein

KIEL: Kieler Kaufmann €€€
Luxury   **Map** C1
Niemannsweg 102, 24105
Tel *(0431) 881 10*
w kieler-kaufmann.de
Kieler Kaufman is a stylish old
villa with richly decorated rooms
befitting an English country house.

Spacious, elegant suite at Fairmont Hotel Vier
Jahreszeiten, Hamburg

Comfortable room with splashes of colour at the Dorint Hotel Söl'ring Hof, Sylt

LÜBECK: Kaiserhof €
Historic **Map** D2
Kronsforder Allee 11–13, 23560
Tel *(0451) 703 301*
w kaiserhof-luebeck.de
A grand hotel with impressive rooms and a fish restaurant.

RATZEBURG: Der Seehof €
Gasthöfe and Pensionen **Map** D2
Lüneburger Damm 1–3, 23909
Tel *(04541) 860 100*
w derseehof.de
Set between two lakes, this hotel's rooms have lovely balcony views. Good seafood restaurant.

SCHLESWIG: Waldschlösschen €€
Modern **Map** C1
Kolonnenweg 152, 24837
Tel *(04621) 38 30*
w hotel-waldschloesschen.de
Well-located, with bright rooms, great food and a swimming pool.

SYLT: Aarnhoog €€€
Luxury **Map** C1
Gaat 13, Keitum, 25980
Tel *(04651) 39 90*
w faehrhaus-hotel-collection.de
Excellent traditional hotel amidst the dunes and forests. Rooms with antique furniture.

DK Choice

SYLT: Dorint Hotel Söl'ring Hof €€€
Luxury **Map** C1
Am Sandwall 1, 25980
Tel *(04651) 83 62 00*
w soelring-hof.de
Peeking out over the dunes to a wide view of the sea, this wonderful thatch-roofed building is a destination in itself. The rooms are first-class and often booked weeks in advance. Enjoy the outstanding spa facilities and world-class cuisine by acclaimed chefs.

Mecklenburg-Lower Pomerania

BAD DOBERAN: Grand Hotel Heiligendamm €€€
Luxury **Map** D1
Prof-Dr-Vogel-Straße 16–18, 18209
Tel *(038203) 74 00*
w grandhotel-heiligendamm.com
A stately seaside hotel in a castle with classy rooms, several quality restaurants and a spa.

GREIFSWALD: Kronprinz €€
Gasthöfe and Pensionen **Map** E1
22 Lange Straße, 17489
Tel *(03834) 79 00*
w hotelkronprinz.de
Kronprinz features lovely, uncluttered rooms and a rustic German brasserie downstairs.

GÜSTROW: Kurhaus am Inselsee €€
Gasthöfe and Pensionen **Map** D2
Heidburg 1, 18273
Tel *(03843) 85 00*
w kurhaus-guestrow.de
Peaceful accommodation by a lake with comfortable rooms with all the amenities.

NEUBRANDENBURG: Landhotel Broda €
Gasthöfe and Pensionen **Map** E2
Oelmühlenstraße 29, 17033
Tel *(0395) 56 91 70*
w landhotel-broda.de
Located in a forest near a lake, this small hotel has quiet rooms and a wellness centre.

ROSTOCK: GreifenNest €
Gasthöfe and Pensionen **Map** D1
August-Bebel-Straße 49b, 18055
Tel *(0381) 877 56 18*
w greifennest.de
Affordable, basic lodging in rooms with clean private facilities and a communal lounge.

Suite with sea views at Dorint Strandhotel Binz, Rügen

ROSTOCK: Neptun Hotel €€€
Luxury **Map** D1
Seestraße 19, 18119
Tel *(0381) 77 78 71*
w hotel-neptun.de
This luxury resort on the beach promises guests fantastic panoramic seaviews.

RÜGEN: Herrenhaus Bohlendorf €
Gasthöfe and Pensionen **Map** E1
Bohlendorf bei Wiek, 18556
Tel *(038391) 770*
w bohlendorf.de
Pretty villa with bright rooms, a terrace café and a reading room.

DK Choice

RÜGEN: Dorint Strandhotel Binz €€€
Luxury **Map** E1
Strandpromenade 58, 18609
Tel *(038393) 430*
w hotel-ruegen.dorint.com
Dorint is a fabulous seaside resort where the rooms have a nautical theme, crisp linen and big windows that overlook the sea. Choose between two fantastic restaurants, one serving gourmet Mediterranean and the other regional seafood.

RÜGEN: Hotel Vier Jahreszeiten Binz €€€
Luxury **Map** E1
Zeppelinstraße 8, 18609
Tel *(038393) 500*
w vier-jahreszeiten.de
A classy spa hotel near the town and beach. Modern, bright rooms.

SCHWERIN: Schloss Basthorst €€€
Historic **Map** D2
Schlossstraße 18, 19089
Tel *(03863) 52 50*
w schloss-basthorst.de
Stay in a beautiful 18th century manor house with renovated rooms and a wellness centre.

STRALSUND: Radisson Blu Stralsund €
Modern **Map** E1
Grünhufer 18-20, 18437
Tel *(03831) 377 30*
w radissonblu.com
Scandinavian-style hotel with an attached spa and water park.

WARNEMÜNDE: KurPark Hotel €€€
Luxury **Map** E1
Kurhausstraße 4, 18119
Tel *(0381) 440 29 90*
w kurparkhotel-warnemuende.de
This lovely old resort has airy rooms, some with balconies, and an impressive restaurant.

For more information on types of hotels *see page 491*

WHERE TO EAT AND DRINK

While German cuisine may not enjoy the same reputation as that of, say, France, visitors can nevertheless eat very well here. A large number of establishments specialize in regional cuisine, which, although often heavy, is always very appetizing. It is also fairly easy to find good restaurants serving ethnic cuisine such as Italian, Greek, Indian, Chinese, Thai or Turkish. In past years, many fine eateries, owned and run by renowned master chefs, have opened in Germany. Not surprisingly, the cuisine served here is of the highest European standards.

From the many thousands of restaurants in Germany, we have listed the finest on pages 510–33. These have been chosen across a range of price categories for their variety, service and good value.

Types of Restaurants

The term restaurant in Germany includes both eateries offering exquisite cuisine and excellent service, at steep prices, as well as popular local establishments with affordable prices. A *Gasthaus* is a traditional inn specializing in straightforward regional cuisine. Similar food is served in a *Ratskeller* located in the town hall cellar. These usually have atmospheric, stylized interiors that are well adapted to the vaulted, dark spaces of the historic cellars. A *Weinstube* is a wine bar on the lines of an old-fashioned tavern. Here, good, usually local, wine is served along with a limited menu of quality food. A *Bierstube* is similar, except that the beverage is beer.

While the term café has a variety of connotations in Germany, it is usually a good choice for breakfast and lunch. However, guests are welcome to stop in at any time of day for a cup of coffee, ice cream, a slice of cake, a beer or wine. There is often music in the evenings.

A *Kneipe*, which has a similar atmosphere to an English pub, is a great place to spend an evening. Patrons generally come here to drink, but there are usually a few hot dishes on offer too. Self-service venues offering snacks are known as *Imbiss*. These can have a very varied character, from a stall serving baked sausages and cans of drink to elegant kiosks offering a large choice of salads and fast food. These kiosks are often run by Germans with immigrant backgrounds, so Greek, Arabic, Turkish and Thai food tends to be well represented. Many larger shops, particularly department stores, will also have a cafeteria for weary shoppers.

What and When to Eat

Breakfast is usually a hearty affair and involves several types of bread, cheeses, sausages and jam. On Sundays, brunch buffets are offered in many places until 2pm. Otherwise lunch is generally

Entrance to a *Gasthaus* near the cathedral in Köln (Cologne)

served between noon and 2pm, when most establishments offer an excellent salad or a bowl of filling soup. Many restaurants serve a special fixed-price menu for lunch that is significantly cheaper than in the evening. Restaurants start to fill up after 6pm, although dinner is most usually eaten after 8pm.

Opening Hours

Cafés generally open from 9am, while restaurants are open from noon, sometimes with a break from 3 to 6pm. The most expensive places only open for dinner and are frequently closed one day in the week.

Menu

In all restaurants and cafés, a menu with prices should be displayed at the door. Many of the better establishments will have a menu in English as well as in German, and where they do not, staff

The cheerful interior of Der Butt in Rostock (see p533)

Elegant dining room of the highly acclaimed Fahrhaus in Sylt *(see p532)*

should be able to help with a translation. In several less expensive places, there is an additional daily menu with attractive seasonal dishes – often written on a blackboard.

Reservations

Making an advance reservation is essential in the best restaurants and advisable in many good and popular standard restaurants as well, particularly on weekend nights. Those who have not made any reservations can try one of the popular restaurant complexes for a table.

Prices and Tips

The cost of a restaurant -meal in Germany depends massively on the location. A three-course meal without alcohol might typically cost €20, but in the centre of larger cities a minimum of €30 would be more usual. In a luxury restaurant, the bill for a six-course meal, without drinks, can cost in excess of €80. The price of alcoholic drinks also varies, but beer is usually cheapest.

Prices include service and tax, but it is usual to leave a tip – around 10 per cent of the total bill. Credit cards are not as widely accepted in Germany, but restaurants and cafés that accept credit cards usually display the l ogos of acceptable cards near the entrance.

Visitors with Disabilities

If a table with wheelchair access is required, it is best to specify this when making the reservation. It is also a good idea to check if toilets are disabled-friendly at the time of making bookings.

Dress Code

Germans usually dress casually, comfortably and practically, preferring a sporty style to a more formal attire. When going out in the evenings, many women – regardless of their age – wear trousers and comfortable low-heeled shoes, though some prefer elegant dresses. Men generally wear jackets and ties only during office hours. Going to a restaurant does not require dressing up. However, guests will not look or feel out of place in formal clothes in the more expensive, gourmet restaurants.

Children

Restaurants usually provide high chairs for toddlers and, particularly during lunch, offer light dishes for children. In places that do not have such arrangements, it is always possible to order small portions for kids.

Vegetarians

Vegetarianism is increasingly popular in Germany, but the number of vegetarian restaurants is still very limited. Restaurants serving only German food will have the most limited selection, though there should be at least one or two vegetarian dishes. Italian restaurants – very common

A street stall serving snacks of freshly cooked sausages

and usually very good – are a better choice for vegetarians, as are Indian or Thai establishments.

Recommended Restaurants

The restaurants recommended on the following pages have been chosen for their quality food, good value and decent service, and include a broad range of cuisines from Persian to Mediterranean, and North African to Chinese.

In a restaurant offering traditional German food expect to see a lot of hearty dishes, stews and breads on the menu. Regional German restaurants will specialize in dishes of the region, usually with locally sourced ingredients. Modern German food tends to take its influences from the traditional menu but add innovative twists and more delicate flavours.

Entries highlighted as DK Choice are those that offer something extra special. This may be their superb location, romantic atmosphere, particularly creative dishes, sensational cuisine or impeccable service. Book in advance and expect to enjoy a memorable meal.

Dine with splendid fjord views at Hotel Bellevue's seafood restaurant in Kiel *(see p531)*

The Flavours of Germany

Germany is famous for its hearty sausages, meats, breads, beer and wine. But German cuisine is much more regionally varied than many visitors might imagine. In addition to standard high-calorie plates, young chefs are coming up with creative new versions of German classics and old regional recipes. The key to this new trend is the fresh German produce found at colourful farmers' markets and old-world stores in quaint little towns around the country. Locally grown vegetables, pork, poultry and game, as well as freshwater and ocean fish, freshly made breads, cakes and dumplings are usually of a very high standard.

Harzer Roller and Emmentaler cheeses

Coffee and cakes at a typical city *Konditorei* (café)

Northern and Eastern Germany

The frugality and hardships of life in the northern and East German lowlands and coast are reflected in the hearty fish- and game-based dishes found in this region. Ocean fish like halibut, sea bass, cod, herring or plaice feature in local dishes like Hamburg's *Finkenwerder*

Scholle (plaice fried with North Sea shrimps and bacon), as do freshwater fish such as pike-perch (a Berlin-Brandenburg favourite) or trout, served as *Grüne Forelle* or *Forelle Müllerin Art*, two herb-oriented recipes for roasted trout. Warming winter soups and stews such as lentil or potato soup or *Pichelsteiner Eintopf* (a one-pot dish with meat, potatoes and

vegetables cooked in broth) are omnipresent – as is the famous potato salad, which is served in numerous ways. In East Germany, Thuringian and Saxonian cuisines have made a stunning comeback with *Thüringer Bratwurst* (spicy, roasted sausage served with hot mustard), *Sauerbraten* (roast beef marinated in vinegar) and some of

Mehrkornbrötchen (mixed grain roll)

Laugenbrötchen (salty sourdough rolls)

Berliner Landbrot (mild rye bread)

Grau-oder Mischbrot (wholewheat)

Semmel (milk-dough roll)

Selection of typical German loaves and bread rolls

Classic German Food

Many of the classic German dishes revolve around meat, particularly pork and poultry. Berliners and North Germans love *Kasseler Nacken*, a salted and dried slice of pork, served with mashed potatoes and *Sauerkraut*, while Bavarians prefer roast pork knuckle. There are delicious fish recipes, too, with Hamburg and Northern Germany leading the way. Ocean fish dishes like *Matjes* (salted herring with onions and cream served with baked potatoes) are now enjoyed throughout the country, as are freshwater fish and even sweet river crabs. German pasta and dumplings, along with soups, and a great selection of desserts and cakes round up any classic German menu.

Pork salamis

Maultaschen, large pasta parcels, are stuffed with a meat or vegetable filling and served in soup or with butter.

Display of traditional German sausages in a Berlin butcher's shop

Germany's best cakes, such as *Dresdner Christstollen* (Christmas cake with raisins, nuts and marzipan) or *Baumkuchen* (a very sweet, multi-layered pyramid cake covered in chocolate glaze).

Western and Southern Germany

This part of Germany, and in particular the German wine regions around the rivers Rhine, Mosel and Neckar, has always had a love of superb, often French-influenced, gourmet feasts. Alsace- Lorraine is a fascinating hotch-potch of French and German cooking. Regions such as the Pfalz, Schwaben, Franken, the Black Forest and many others, have also developed their own, very distinctive, delicious and often very hearty cuisines. The Pfalz, for example, is famous for its *Pfälzer Saumagen*, a sow's stomach filled with sausage, herbs and potatoes; the Schwaben are known for their *Maultaschen* and an endless varieties of *Spätzle*

A selection of fresh vegetables from the Brandenburg region

(curly pasta); and the Franken for their *Nürnberger Rostbratwürstchen* (little spicy roast sausages), various fish dishes, using rare types such as sheatfish, and perhaps the best gingerbread found anywhere in the country. In the far southeast, Austrian and Eastern European influences are evident in great goulash and dumpling dishes. But pride of place possibly goes to the Bavarians, whose hearty, no-nonsense dishes are what the world considers to be German cuisine. Here, *Weißwürste* (white sausages with a beer pretzel) are enjoyed in the morning, often with a beer, while dinner might be soup with liver dumplings, roast pork, *Sauerkraut* and a pile of potato dumplings.

NEW GERMAN CUISINE

In the early 1970s, chefs like Eckart Witzigmann broke free of the high-carb diet of postwar times, and cooked light, delicate "nouvelle" German dishes with superb ingredients in innovative combinations. Witzigmann, still Germany's most popular chef, won the first three German Michelin stars in 1979. A new generation of chefs calling themselves "Junge Wilde" (young wild) are still enjoying the shock waves today: healthy, international cooking is the norm in restaurants and homes, and almost no traditional recipe is sacrosanct.

Zanderfilet, or Havel-Zander, is delicious pan-fried pike-perch served with a vegetable sauce, onions and potatoes.

Schweinshaxe is roast pork knuckle, best accompanied by Sauerkraut, potato dumplings and a good, strong beer.

Rote Grütze mixes summer berries with spices and red wine, which is set into a jelly and topped with cream.

What to Drink

Throughout Germany, beer is undoubtedly the most popular drink, and each region has its own beer-brewing traditions. However, the country is also renowned for excellent wines, which are produced in the south. The most well known are Mosel and Rhine wines, although these are not necessarily better than Franconian wines. Stronger spirits and liqueurs are also available, as are some very pleasant non-alcoholic cold drinks.

Shop in Eberbach stocked with wine from the adjoining monastery

Hot Drinks

In German establishments there is no difficulty in getting a cup of tea *(Tee)*, but don't be surprised if the waiter asks whether you mean mint tea *(Pfefferminztee)* or camomile *(Kamillentee)*, since herbal infusions are popular in Germany. To be sure of being served Indian tea, it is advisable to specify *Schwarztee* when placing the order. Coffee is another popular drink. In general, filter coffee, which is fairly mild, is served. For customers who prefer a stronger coffee, it is best to order an espresso.

Herbal infusions include mint and camomile tea

Non-Alcoholic Cold Drinks

Various types of carbonated drinks and fruit juices – ubiquitous throughout Europe and the US – are popular, and an extensive choice is available in every café and restaurant in Germany. A refreshing non-alcoholic drink is *Apfelschorle*, which is apple juice mixed with equal proportions of sparkling mineral water. (The alcoholic version is *Weinschorle*, which is wine mixed with mineral water.) Another popular non-alcoholic drink is *Spezi*, which is a mixture of cola and Fanta.

Although tap water is generally safe to drink, it is not usually served with restaurant meals. To order a bottle of mineral water, ask for *Mineralwasser*, adding the phrase *"stilles Wasser"* if still water is preferred.

Mineralwasser (Mineral water)

Limonade (Lemonade)

Apfelschorle

Spirits and Liqueurs

Strong spirits are often drunk after heavy meals, particularly pork dishes. It is best to order one of the popular drinks distilled from rye or wheat, such as *Doppelkorn*. Brandy (known as *Weinbrand*) is also produced in Germany. Liqueurs are also popular, as is a spirit flavoured with herbs and roots (known as bitters). Among the most popular are *Kümmerling* and *Jägermeister* while, in Berlin, *Kaulsdorfer Kräuterlikör* is served. In many restaurants various kinds of whisky can be ordered, including well-known Scottish and Irish brands and popular American bourbons, but connoisseurs may miss their personal favourites. Italian restaurants often serve grappa, a grape spirit, after a meal, while in Greek restaurants ouzo – an aniseed spirit – may be offered.

Bitter-sweet spirit, Jägermeister

Herbal/root-flavour spirit, Kümmerling

Weizen Doppelkorn (rye spirit)

Wines

Germany is renowned for its excellent white wines, particularly those made from the Riesling grape. Among the most highly prized wines are those from the Rheingau region. Lovers of red wine might like to try Assmannshausen Spätburgunder wine, which is produced from the Pinot Noir grape.

Germany has a system of classifying wines into three groups according to their quality: the lowest quality is *Tafelwein*, then *Qualitätswein* and the highest quality *Qualitätswein mit Prädikat*. The latter includes wines produced from appropriately selected grapes, which is always confirmed on the bottle label. The term *Trocken* indicates a dry style, *Halbtrocken*, semi-dry and *Süß* means sweet. Very good sparkling wines, known as *Sekt*, are also produced in Germany.

Mainstockheimer Hofstück Spätburgunder

Spätburgunder from the Rheingau region

Riesling Schloss Vollrads

Beers

Beermat with brewery logo

Each region of Germany has its own beer-brewing tradition: the most popular breweries in the north are Jever in Freesia and Beck's in Bremen, along with Bitburger, Warsteiner and Karlsberg. In the Rhine region, the biggest producers are DAB from Dortmund and König in Duisburg. In Berlin, Schultheiss, Berliner Kindl and Engelhardt compete for the primary position, while in Dresden the main beers are produced by a brewery in Radeberg. Bavaria is by far the major brewing centre – the names of the breweries Löwenbräu, Hofbräu and Paulaner are known to beer lovers around the world. The oldest brewery in the world, Weihenstephan, is also in Bavaria. The most commonly drunk beer is Pils, a bottom-fermented lager of the pilsner type. Brown ales are also popular, particularly in the south. Schwarzbier, a bottom-fermented brown ale of over 4 per cent alcohol, is increasingly popular. Weizenbier, a bitter top-fermented beer, also has many fans, as has Bock, which is strong, at around 6 per cent alcohol.

Löwenbräu beer

König Ludwig Dunkel beer

Schultheiss beer

Wheat beer mixed with fruit juice, Berliner Weiße mit Schuss – speciality of Berlin

Franziskaner Hefe Weissbier beer

A tankard of beer with the essential head of foam

Where to Eat and Drink

Berlin

Eastern Centre

12 Apostel €
Italian **Map** 4 C1
Georgenstraße 2, 10117
Tel *(030) 201 02 22*
Located under the railway arches
near Friedrichstrasse station, this
eatery serves 12 types of pizza,
named after the apostles, cooked
to perfection in a stone oven.

Hasir Ocakbasi €
Turkish **Map** 5 F5
Adalbertstraße 12, 10999
Tel *(030) 615 070 80*
Berlin's love affair with the *döner
kebab* began here in 1971. Large
selection of chargrilled meat and
fish dishes, delicious *mezes* and
home-made desserts.

Max und Moritz €
Traditional German **Map** 5 F5
Oranienstraße 162, 10969
Tel *(030) 695 159 11* **Closed** *Sun;
dinner daily*
A bustling over 100-year-old
eatery serving generous helpings
of traditional German fare, such
as Schnitzel and meatballs. Large
selection of beers, too.

Nante Eck €
Traditional German **Map** 4 C2
Unter den Linden 35, 10117
Tel *(030) 22 48 72 57*
Berlin-style cheap eats are on
offer at this casual pub. Fill up
on calf's liver with port sauce or
meatballs with mustard, washed
down with good local beer.

**Augustiner am
Gendarmenmarkt** €€
Regional **Map** 4 C2
Charlottenstraße 55, 10117
Tel *(030) 204 540 20*
Decorated with oak barrels and
wooden panelling, this Bavarian
pub serves hearty German fare,

including baked *Eisbein* (knuckle
of pork) with *sauerkraut* and beef
goulash in a beer sauce.

Gambrinus €€
Traditional German **Map** 4 C1
Krausnickstraße 1, 10115
Tel *(030) 282 60 43*
A traditional *kneipe* (pub) with
dark-wood furnishings, old-
fashioned tiles and framed posters
of Old Berlin. Massive portions.

Zum Nussbaum €€
Traditional German **Map** 5 E2
Am Nussbaum 3, 10178
Tel *(030) 242 30 95*
This reconstructed country inn
serves traditional Berlin cuisine –
rollmops, vegetable and fish
pancakes, *bouletten* (spicy meatballs) – along with local beers.

Zur Letzten Instanz €€
Traditional German **Map** 5 F2
Waisenstraße 14–16, 10179
Tel *(030) 242 55 28* **Closed** *Sun*
Berlin's oldest pub, dating from
1621, serves classic German fare,
including *Eisbein* (pork knuckle)
and *Rinderroulade* (beef olive),
in a wood-panelled room with
a majolica-tiled stove.

Borchardt €€€
French/German **Map** 4 C2
Französische Straße 47,10117
Tel *(030) 81 88 62 30*
Politicians and celebrities flock to
this restaurant with retro decor
from early 1900s. Schnitzel is the
mainstay of an ever-changing
menu. Reserve ahead.

Facil €€€
Modern Fusion **Map** 4 A3
Potsdamer Straße 3, 10785
Tel *(030) 590 051 234*
A glass-roofed pavilion is the
backdrop for Berlin master chef
Michael Kempf's inspired cuisine,
which uses the freshest market
produce and subtly exotic spices.

DK Choice
Fischers Fritz €€€
French **Map** 4 C3
Charlottenstraße 49, 10117
Tel *(030) 203 363 63*
The creative flair of the chef has
turned Fischers Fritz into an
award-winning restaurant. The
meat dishes are tempting, but it
is the seafood dishes that get
most accolades. Try the Breton
lobster roasted with salt, chilli
and coriander, or the fillet of
Mediterranean red mullet with
mashed potatoes, Nyons olives
and tomatoes. The two-course
lunch menu is good value.

Käfers Dachgarten €€€
Modern German **Map** 1 E4
Platz der Republik, 11011
Tel *(030) 226 29 90*
A lovely roof-garden restaurant
with spectacular views. Sample
sophisticated German dishes
made with fresh regional
produce and accompanied by
choice wines. Book in advance.

Vau €€€
French **Map** 4 C2
Jägerstraße 54–55, 10117
Tel *(030) 202 97 30*
Celebrity TV chef Kolja Kleeberg
won this classy restaurant a
Michelin star with his inspired
take on French cooking. The
striking interior is best described
as modern meets Art Nouveau.

Western Centre
Café am Neuen See €
German/Italian **Map** 2 C3
Lichtensteinallee 2, 10787
Tel *(030) 254 49 30*
This café with a lakeside terrace
offers Bavarian snacks and
draught beers, as well as Italian
mains such as pizzas. There are
boats to rent and a sandpit for
kids. Warm seating in winter.

Dicke Wirtin €
Traditional German **Map** 2 A4
Carmerstraße 9, 10623
Tel *(030) 312 49 52*
This authentic Berlin *kneipe* (pub)
serves a menu of hearty food.
Select the *Eintopf* (a steaming hot

Al fresco dining at Zum Nussbaum, a traditional inn

pot), and the Berliner Kindl, one of the nine draught beers available.

Gaststätte Ambrosius €
Traditional German Map 3 E4
Einemstraße 14, 10785
Tel *(030) 264 05 26*
Nourishing home cooking, with specialities such as tasty potato soup and Berlin-style liver served with onions and apple sauce.

Café-Restaurant Wintergarten im Literaturhaus €€
German/International Map 2 A5
Fasanenstraße 23, 10719
Tel *(030) 882 54 14*
Take a break from shopping on Ku'damm and visit this café-restaurant favoured by artists and intellectuals. Breakfast and international dishes are served in Art Nouveau interiors.

DK Choice

Esswein am Fasanenplatz €€
Modern German Map 2 A5
Fasanenstraße 40, 10719
Tel *(030) 889 292 88*
Esswein is making waves within Berlin's culinary scene thanks to its contemporary German cooking. The seasonal menu may feature *Pfälzer Wurstsalat* (Rhineland sausage with cheese and bread) and *Ochsen Fetzen* (ox slices baked in a ragout of mushrooms, chestnuts and grapes). Choose from a selection of more than 40 Mosel wines to accompany the meal.

Florian €€
Traditional German Map 2 A4
Grolmanstraße 52, 10623
Tel *(030) 313 91 84*
A small restaurant with an understated charm that attracts celebrities. Excellent South-Western German cuisine with a modern twist is prepared with organic produce.

Grüne Lampe €€
Russian Map 2 A5
Uhlandstraße 51, 10719
Tel *(030) 887 193 93*
Popular with Russian expats, who love the authentic food on offer. Large selection of *zakuski* (starters) and *blini* (buckwheat pancakes). Vegetarian options available, too.

La Mano Verde €€
Vegan Map 2 A4
Kempinski Plaza, Uhlandstraße 181–183, 10623
Tel *(030) 827 031 20*
A treat for non meat-eaters: this strictly vegan restaurant uses

The homely dining room at Pasternak

only plant-based ingredients and has several gluten-free dishes on its menu. Choose one of the inspired daily specials.

Belmondo €€€
French Map 2 A3
Knesebeckstraße 93, 10623
Tel *(030) 362 872 61*
Red leather banquettes and photos of the actor Jean-Paul Belmondo lend a touch of French elegance to this bistro. Excellent fish and seafood dishes, including a sensational *bouillabaisse*.

Die Quadriga €€€
European Map 2 B5
Eislebener Straße 14, 10789
Tel *(030) 214 056 51*
French and other European creations are served at this restaurant located inside the Hotel Brandenburger Hof.

Further Afield

Baraka €
North African
Lausitzer Platz 6, 10997
Tel *(030) 612 63 30*
Baraka serves an appetizing range of Moroccan and Egyptian specialities, including tagines, couscous and vegetarian dishes.

DK Choice

Blockhaus Nikolskoe €€
German
Nikolskoer Weg 15, 14109
Tel *(030) 805 29 14*
Idyllically located with the Grunewald forest as a backdrop and the broad expanse of Havel and Peacock Island ahead, this restaurant is set in a wooden *dacha* (country house) built in 1819 for the heir to the Russian throne. The food, especially the fresh fish and local game, suits the spectacular setting.

Gugelhof €€
French
Knaackstraße 37, 10435
Tel *(030) 442 92 29*
Lively restaurant offering Alsatian specialities such as tarte flambé and lamb cassoulet.

Ming Dynastie €€
Chinese Map 5 F1
Brückenstraße 6, 10179
Tel *(030) 308 756 80*
This excellent Chinese restaurant serves an extensive menu that includes regional dishes, dim sum and Peking duck.

DK Choice

Pasternak €€
Russian
Knaackstraße 22/24, 10405
Tel *(030) 41 33 99*
A long-time favourite with the city's Russian community, Pasternak prides itself on its authentic cuisine. Focus on the rich assortment of *zakuski* (starters), but do not overlook the *blini*. The warm dining room is adorned with traditional wallpaper, lamps and candles.

E.T.A. Hoffmann €€€
Modern Austrian/German
Yorckstraße 83, 10965
Tel *(030) 780 988 09*
Here the menu sports a creative spin on traditional Austrian and German recipes. The cushion of Brandenburg venison with Gatow radish and potato noodles is a definite highlight.

Horváth €€€
Modern German
Paul Lincke Ufer 44A, 10999
Tel *(030) 612 899 92* **Closed** *Mon*
This award-winning restaurant offers creatively constructed, sophisticated cuisine. The desserts are also a highlight.

For more information on types of restaurants *see page 505*

Brandenburg

BRANDENBURG:
Bismarck Terrassen €
Regional Map E3
Bergstraße 20, 14770
Tel *(03381) 30 09 39*
Huge helpings of dishes such
as duck with red cabbage and
dumplings can be enjoyed at this
earthy local pub cluttered with
kitsch 19th-century memorabilia.

BUCKOW: Fischerkehle €€
Modern German Map E4
Fischerberg 7, 15377
Tel *(033433) 374*
Enjoy lovely lakeside dining at
this fish and game specialist.
Delicacies include rosefish with
boiled potatoes, and game
ragout with *spätzle* (regional
noodles) and cranberries.

CHORIN: Alte Klosterschänke €€
Regional Map E2
Am Amt 9, 16230
Tel *(033366) 53 01 00*
Traditional restaurant located
in an exquisite 18th century
half-timbered building. Fresh,
seasonal, organic food.

CHORIN: Immenstube
at Hotel Haus Chorin €€
Regional Map E2
Neue Klosterallee 10, 16230
Tel *(033366) 500* **Closed** *Wed*
Honey makes an appearance in
every dish at this largely organic
restaurant that relies on local
produce. The delicious honey-
marinated pork roast is a must.

COTTBUS: Mosquito €
South American Map F3
Altmarkt 22, 3046
Tel *(0355) 288 904 44*
This cocktail bar pulls in droves
of locals for both its great Cajun
jerk chicken and the delightful
Sunday brunch buffet.

Tastefully decorated restaurant at Hotel
Schloss Lübbenau

Frankfurt an der
ODER: Nirwana €
Indian Map F3
Marktplatz 3, 15230
Tel *(0335) 53 45 21*
Delicious North Indian food
comes with quick and friendly
service here. Well-priced lunch-
time specials are on offer as well.

LEHNIN: Markgraf €€
Austrian/German Map E3
Friedenstraße 13, 14797
Tel *(03382) 76 50*
A small menu of tasty Austrian
and German dishes is available
at this smart hotel restaurant.

LEHNIN: Rittergut Krahne €€
Traditional German Map E3
Krahner Hauptstraße 6A, 14797
Tel *(033835) 60 88 91* **Closed** *Tue–Thu*
This eatery in a converted barn
serves traditional food based on
seasonal ingredients – expect
asparagus in spring, mushrooms
in summer and goose in winter.

LÜBBEN: Schlossrestaurant
Lübben €€
Modern German Map E3
Ernst-von-Houwald-Damm 14, 15907
Tel *(03546) 40 78* **Closed** *Mon*
Contemporary versions of
regional dishes are on offer at this
elegant old palace. The business
lunch is a genuine bargain.

LÜBBENAU: Saloon Santa Fe €
International Map E3
Robert Koch Straße 45, 03222
Tel *(03542) 88 87 70*
Steaks, burgers and Tex-Mex fare
are served in mock-Western
surroundings here. There is even
a table in a covered wagon.

LÜBBENAU: Hotel Schloss
Lübbenau €€€
International Map E3
Schloßbezirk 6, 3222
Tel *(03542) 87 30*
This high-end hotel restaurant
relies on fresh local ingredients to
create a variety of contemporary
fish and meat dishes.

ORANIENBURG: Gasthaus
Charlottenhof €€
Regional Map E3
Neulöwenberger Straße 26, 16775
Tel *(033094) 504 17*
Regional dishes, particularly pork
and fish, dominate the menu at
this quiet hotel restaurant. Do
not miss the home-made soups.

POTSDAM: Babette €
International/German Map E3
Brandenburger Straße 71, 14467
Tel *(0331) 29 16 48*
After trekking around Potsdam's
parks, take the weight off your

Inviting café atmosphere at Drachenhaus
in Potsdam

feet at this pleasant pavement
café, a handy stop for a rich
cake or a simple snack.

POTSDAM: Drachenhaus €
Regional Map E3
Maulbeerallee 4a, 14469
Tel *(0331) 505 38 08* **Closed** *Nov–*
Feb: Mon
This elegant little café in a
pagoda-style building serves
hearty Brandenburg specialities.
Try the creamy gateaux.

POTSDAM: Froschkasten €
Regional Map E3
Kiezstraße 3–4, 14467
Tel *(0331) 291315*
An old Prussian eatery in a
traditional inn serving basic
regional cuisine, including
several scrumptious fish dishes.

POTSDAM: Hafthorn €
Modern German Map E3
Friedrich Ebert Straße 90, 14467
Tel *(0331) 280 08 20*
This hip pub is often packed with
a fashionable crowd. Simple but
good snacks – superb burgers
and *rösti* (potato pancakes).

POTSDAM: La Madeleine €
Crêperie Map E3
Lindenstraße 9, 14467
Tel *(0331) 270 54 00*
Small crêperie serving more than
30 variations of crêpes, ranging
from delicious buckwheat with
goat's cheese salad to the more
unusual chicken curry.

POTSDAM: Arco €€
Italian Map E3
Nauener Tor, Friedrich Ebert
Straße, 14467
Tel *(0331) 270 16 90*
A stylish little Italian restaurant
that also serves international
dishes and a scrumptious
Sunday brunch buffet.

POTSDAM: Indian Garden €€
Indian Map E3
Kurfürstenstraße 35, 14467
Tel *(0331) 585 71 85*
Enjoy excellent home-made
Indian food in smart
surroundings at this fantastic
restaurant. Attentive service.

**POTSDAM: Friedrich Wilhelm
at Hotel Bayrisches Haus** €€€
Modern German Map E3
Elisenweg 2, 14471
Tel *(0331) 550 50* **Closed** *Sun & Mon*
The premier address for
neue Deutsche Küche (German
nouvelle cuisine), this charming
hotel restaurant features
inventive gourmet delights.

DK Choice

POTSDAM: Juliette €€€
French Map E3
Jägerstraße 39, 14467
Tel *(0331) 270 17 91* **Closed** *Tue*
A classy, romantic place with
candles, white tablecloths and
a crackling fire. The changing
menu oozes French flair and
may include dishes such as
loach with couscous and
avocado, or steak with truffles
and *foie gras*. Come here for the
superb *crème brûlée* and the
exemplary wine list. Vegetarians
are well catered for, too.

**POTSDAM: Speckers
Landhaus** €€€
French Map E3
Jägerallee 13, 14469
Tel *(0331) 280 43 11* **Closed** *Sun
& Mon*
This modern, family-run
restaurant is as unpretentious
as it is high-class. Fresh local
produce dominates the creative
menu. Good-value set lunch.

The beautifully-styled dining room of Friedrich Wilhelm at Hotel Bayrisches Haus in Potsdam

**RHEINSBERG: Steakhaus at
Schloss Hotel Rheinsberg** €€
Traditional German Map E2
Seestraße 13, 16831
Tel *(033931) 390 59*
Diners build their own dishes
using South American cuts of
meat and a selection of sides
at this great steakhouse.

Saxony-Anhalt

DESSAU: Mensa €
German Map E3
Gropiusallee 38, 06846
Tel *(0340) 650 84 21* **Closed** *Sat
& Sun*
Mensa offers a basic cafeteria
experience, with fresh daily
dishes served in a stylishly
minimalist Bauhaus interior.

DESSAU: Goa €€
Indian Map E3
Albrechtstraße 26, 06844
Tel *(0340) 870 56 26*
Relish authentic Indian food at
this restaurant as well as the
comprehensive cocktail menu.

DESSAU: Kornhaus €€
International Map E3
Kornhausstraße 146, 06846
Tel *(0340) 650 199 63*
A genuine Bauhaus restaurant,
with a graceful riverside balcony
and contemporary cuisine. The
fish dishes are a cornerstone of
the well-priced daily menu.

EISLEBEN: Lutherschenke €€
Traditional German Map D4
Lutherstraße 19, 06295
Tel *(03475) 61 47 75*
This traditional-style inn cooks
hearty dishes dating back to
medieval times. Expect lots of
deer, pork liver and turkey.

The modern-styled exterior of Kornhaus
in Dessau.

HALLE: Bella Donna €
Italian Map D4
Große Ulrichstraße 47, 06108
Tel *(0345) 682 53 50*
This popular, tiny Italian joint
with a cheerful atmosphere and
an open kitchen serves generous
portions. Reserve ahead.

HALLE: Hallesches Brauhaus €€
Traditional German Map D4
Große Nikolaistraße 2, 06108
Tel *(0345) 212 57*
An Old Town microbrewery with
good beers and hearty regional
favourites, such as goulash with
dumplings and dark beer sauce.

HALLE: Ökoase €€
International Map D4
Kleine Ulrichstraße 2, 06108
Tel *(0345) 290 16 04* **Closed** *Sun*
Vegetarian cuisine with bargain
canteen lunches and table
service in the evenings, when
dishes such as pumpkin-seed
rösti (potato pancakes) with pears
and Roquefort are served.

MAGDEBURG: Le Frog €€
International Map D3
Heinrich Heine Platz 1, 39114
Tel *(0391) 531 35 56*
Highlights of Le Frog's extensive
menu include local game and
wild mushrooms. There is also a
great weekend brunch. Regular
live music in the beer garden.

MAGDEBURG: Liebig €€
International Map D3
Liebigstraße 3, 39104
Tel *(0391) 555 67 54*
Trendy bar, café and restaurant
with appetizing international
food, ranging from curries to
steaks and Mediterranean dishes.

For more information on types of restaurants *see page 505*

MAGDEBURG: Petriförder €€
International   Map D3
Petriförder 1, 39104
Tel *(0391) 597 96 00*
The eclectic menu at this large
riverside restaurant features
many Italian dishes, as well as
Schnitzel and Argentinian steaks.
Children's menu available.

**MAGDEBURG: Wenzel
Prager Bierstuben**   €€
Czech   Map D3
Leiterstraße 3C, 39104
Tel *(0391) 544 66 16*
This relaxed, informal restaurant
is part of a dependable regional
chain of rustic Czech pubs that
specializes in good beers and
hearty meat dishes.

**NAUMBURG: Mohrencafé
am Dom**   €€
German   Map D4
Steinweg 16, 06618
Tel *(03445) 20 45 65*
A little café with a small but
delicious lunch menu. The rabbit
or duck served with red cabbage
and dumplings is a must-try.

NAUMBURG: Toscana   €€
Regional   Map D4
Topfmarkt 16, 06618
Tel *(03445) 28920*
Look out for scrumptious
traditional local dishes here, such
as *Naumburger Rahmtöpfchen* (a
pork chop smothered in a
creamy onion sauce).

**QUEDLINBURG: Brauhaus
Lüdde**   €€
Traditional German   Map D4
Blasiistraße 14, 06484
Tel *(03946) 70 52 06*
A barn-sized microbrewery with
a beautiful, bustling beer garden.
On offer are solid, traditional
meals and a wide range of beers.

QUEDLINBURG: Theopano €€€
Modern German   Map D4
Markt 13, 06484
Tel *(03946) 96 30*   **Closed** *Sun
& Mon*
Contemporary regional cuisine
in an old half-timbered house.
Highlights on the menu include
cod and veal, and the handmade
truffles make for a great finale.
Friendly staff.

TANGERMÜNDE: Exempel €
Regional   Map D3
Kirchstraße 40, 39590
Tel *(039322) 44899*
Situated in a former schoolhouse
and featuring many original
furnishings, this restaurant
serves old-fashioned dishes
such as pea soup, along with
the local Kuhschwanz beer.

The picturesque setting of Schloss Tangermünde

DK Choice

**TANGERMÜNDE: Schloss
Tangermünde**   €€€
Traditional German   Map D3
Amt 1, 39590
Tel *(039322) 73 73*
This elegant restaurant, in an
atmospheric 17th-century
castle, offers wonderful river
views from its outdoor terrace.
The menu includes high-end
versions of rustic, traditional
dishes such as wild boar, *Eisbein*
(pickled ham) and zander, but it
is the gourmet set meals that
really tantalize the taste buds.

**WITTENBERG: Brauhaus
Wittenberg**   €
Regional   Map E3
Markt 6, 06886
Tel *(03491) 43 31 30*
A lively pub with an attractive
courtyard serving large portions
of hearty staples, including ribs
and *Bratwurst*, and a refreshing
variety of beers.

**WITTENBERG: Zum
Schwarzen Baer**   €
Traditional German   Map E3
Schlossstraße 2, 06886
Tel *(03491) 420 43 44*
The menu at this old-fashioned
dark-wood pub is a homage to
the humble potato, which appears
in salads, and is fried, grilled or *au
gratin* as an accompaniment to
meat and fish dishes. Potato also
features in the dessert cakes.

WITTENBERG: Alte Canzley €€
International   Map E3
Schloßplatz 3, 06886
Tel *(03491) 42*   **Closed** *Nov–
Mar: Mon*
An excellent organic restaurant
in a 14th-century building. The

experimental menu features
some innovative choices: orange
and ginger soup, beef in black
beer and asparagus ice cream.

WITTENBERG: Tante Emmas €€
Traditional German   Map E3
Markt 9, 06886
Tel *(03491) 41 97 57*   **Closed** *Mon*
This quirky, traditional
establishment furnished with
curios, whips up refined German
standards such as *Schnitzel*.

**WÖRLITZ: Gastwirtschaft
im Küchengebäude**   €€€
International   Map E3
Schloßstraße, 06786
Tel *(034905) 22 5 30*
A beer garden and restaurant in
the old palace kitchens. Sample
such fare ranging from goose,
deer, gnocchi to steaks.

Saxony

**AUGUSTUSBURG: Café
Freidrich**   €
Bistro   Map E4
Hans-Planer-Straße 1, 09573
Tel *(037291) 66 66*
This lovely bistro in a picturesque
part of the town relies on more
than 100 years of family tradition
and is good for light meals as
well as dinners. The cakes are a
must-try. Amazing castle views.

**BAD MUSKAU:
Am Schlossbrunnen**   €€
Regional   Map F4
Köbelner Straße 68, 02953
Tel *(035771) 52 30*
A delightful family-run restaurant
offering typical dishes based on
local produce, including fish from
the nearby lakes. Do not miss the
home-made ice creams.

BAUTZEN: Bautzener Brauhaus €
Traditional German   Map F4
Thomas-Mann-Straße 7, 02625
Tel *(03591) 49 14 56*
Choose from several beers, including Schwarzbier and the original Pilsner, at this brewery. The menu offers scrumptious German fare at affordable prices.

CHEMNITZ: Antica Roma €
Italian   Map E4
Hartmannstraße 7, 09111
Tel *(0371) 466 07 37*
A little nondescript from the outside, Antica Roma offers good-value Italian food – big, freshly made pizzas and pasta dishes, as well as more sophisticated main courses.

CHEMNITZ: Gasthaus an der Schlossmuhle €€
Traditional German   Map E4
Schloßberg 3, 09113
Tel *(0371) 335 25 33*
Historic hotel restaurant in a splendid location above the lake, with superb views. The simple yet delicious food has made it a popular neighbourhood haunt.

CHEMNITZ: Villa Esche €€
International   Map E4
Parkstraße 58, 09120
Tel *(0371) 236 13 63*
Set in gorgeous surroundings, this wonderful restaurant serves modern European dishes – with a focus on German fare. Good-value set lunches and cookery courses on offer. Lovely garden.

DK Choice

DRESDEN: Schillergarten €
Regional   Map E4
Schillerplatz 9, 01309
Tel *(0351) 81 19 90*
Located in a historic building next to the Blaus Wunder bridge, this fine restaurant and pub is the perfect place to eat well and at a reasonable price in the city centre. Sample great local food, including first-class *Bratwurst*, as well as an extensive range of beers. There is also a wonderful, lovely summer terrace on the embankment of the Elbe River. Reserve ahead.

DRESDEN: Cuchi €€
Asian   Map E4
Wallgäßchen 5, 01097
Tel *(0351) 862 75 80*
Chinese, Japanese and Vietnamese cuisines are fused together to create outstanding, inventive dishes here. For the purists, there is sushi.

Bright and modern dinning area of Café Restaurant in Meissen

DRESDEN: Ogura €€€
Japanese   Map E4
An der Frauenkirche 5, 01067
Tel *(0351) 864 29 75*
One of Germany's best sushi restaurants, Ogura also serves soups, *tempura* and Kirin beer. Good-value set menus.

DRESDEN: Sternerestaurant Caroussel €€€
Fine dining   Map E4
Königstraße 14, 01097
Tel *(0351) 80 03*
Expect only the finest food in the luxurious surroundings of this proud award winning restaurant.

KAMENZ: Goldner Hirsch €
Italian/German   Map F4
Markt 10, 01917
Tel *(035787) 835*
This stylish restaurant offers mainly Italian food, while the rustic Ratskeller downstairs serves classic German fare.

LEIPZIG: Zest €
Fusion   Map E4
Bornaische Straße 54, 04277
Tel *(0341) 231 91 26*   **Closed** *Tue*
A fresh and creative take on modern European cuisine, with plenty of vegetarian dishes on the menu. The great-value fare and an extensive wine list make Zest worth the trip from the city centre.

LEIPZIG: Michaelis €€
International   Map E4
Paul-Gruner-Straße 44, 04107
Tel *(0341) 267 80*   **Closed** *Sun*
Set in a building that dates back more than 100 years, Michaelis offers imaginative food in an intimate atmosphere. There is a nice terrace, too.

LEIPZIG: Auerbachs Keller €€€
Regional   Map E4
Grimmaische Straße 2–4, 04109
Tel *(0341) 21 61 00*
One of the town's oldest eateries, Auerbachs Keller serves first-class German cuisine, including a variety of game dishes. There is also a great selection of beer to help wash it all down. Reserve in advance.

LEIPZIG: Niemanns Tresor €€€
Fine Dining   Map E4
Thomaskirchhof 20, 04109
Tel *(0341) 9800947*   **Closed** *Sun & Mon*
Enjoy outstanding food and wine in the elegantly renovated Art Nouveau interiors of a former private bank.

MEISSEN: Café Restaurant Meissen €
Bistro   Map E4
Talstraße 9, 01662
Tel *(03521) 46 87 30*
Terrific, inventive bistro food is served in a bright, modern setting by cheerful staff. A great value option.

One of Leipzig's oldest restaurants, the Auerbachs Keller is dramatically decorated

For more information on types of restaurants *see page 505*

MEISSEN: Domkeller €€
Traditional German **Map** E4
Domplatz 9, 01662
Tel *(03521) 45 76 76*
Founded in 1470, Domkeller is
the oldest restaurant in town.
Savour generous portions of
German food and great beer
in a warm, friendly atmosphere.

**MORITZBURG: Churfürstliche
Waldschaenke** €
Regional **Map** E4
Grosse Fasanenstraße, 01468
Tel *(035207) 86 00*
Serving mainly food from the
Saxony region, this place boasts
an enviable location, surrounded
as it is by woods on all sides. It
also has one of the best wine
cellars in the region.

PIRNA: Escobar €
South American **Map** F4
Obere Burgstraße 1, 01796
Tel *(03501) 58 27 73*
A treat for those looking for a
break from German cuisine,
this café, bar and restaurant
has decor reminiscent of 1950s
Latin America. Friendly staff.

PIRNA: Deutsches Haus €€
Modern German **Map** F4
Niedere Burgstraße 1, 01796
Tel *(03501) 468 80*
Popular with locals, this place
specializes in modern cuisine
from around the region. Superb
selection of beers and wine.

TORGAU: Central Hotel €
Regional **Map** E4
Friedrichplatz 8, 04860
Tel *(03421) 73 28*
A simple yet elegant restaurant
inside a gorgeous 1908 building.
The food is great value and just
about the best in town.

ZWICKAU: Drei Schwäne €€
French **Map** E4
Tonstraße 1, 08056
Tel *(0375) 204 76 50*
Fresh flowers on the tables
create the perfect ambience
for intimate, first-class dining
at this lovely restaurant with
an exemplary wine list.
Reservations recommended.

Thuringia

ALTENBURG: Altenburger Hof €€
International **Map** E4
Schmöllnsche Landstraße 8, 04600
Tel *(03447) 584*
Altenburger Hof's restaurant
offers good food at decent prices.
There is both a casual café and
a smart restaurant on site.

**EISENACH: Café Lackner &
Julian's Restaurant** €
Bistro **Map** C4
Johannisstraße 22, 99817
Tel *(03691) 78 45 50*
A bright café and bistro where
smartly dressed staff serve
delicious regional food. There
is also a streetside terrace.

EISENACH: Lutherstuben €€
Traditional German **Map** C4
Katharinenstraße 13, 99817
Tel *(03691) 293 90*
This historic restaurant in the
Eisenacher Hof Hotel specializes
in the favourite dishes of Martin
Luther. The bar has an excellent
selection of beers and wine.

ERFURT: Feuerkugel €
Regional **Map** D4
Michaelisstraße 3–4, 99084
Tel *(0361) 789 12 56*
In the heart of Erfurt, this
restaurant offers an authentic
Thuringian experience. Divine
food served in huge portions
and top-quality beer, both best
enjoyed in the pretty courtyard.

**ERFURT: Haus zum
Naumburgischen Keller** €€
Regional **Map** D4
Michaelisstraße 49, 99084
Tel *(0361) 540 24 50*
Located in a 19th century half-
timbered building, this restaurant
serves excellent food and beer.
Try the *Rostbratel* (roasted meat
with braised onions).

ERFURT: Zum alten Schwan €€
Bistro **Map** D4
Gotthardtstraße 27, 99084
Tel *(0361) 67 40*
A good-value bistro with a wide
range of light salads and soups, as
well as more filling main courses.

**ERFURT: Clara Alboth's
Restaurant im Kaisersaal** €€€
International **Map** D4
Futterstraße 15/16, 99084
Tel *(0361) 568 82 07*
One of the best restaurants in the
city, Clara Alboth offers inventive,
contemporary cusine using high-
quality, fresh, local ingredients.

**ERFURT: Köstritzer Zum
güldenen Rade** €€€
International **Map** D4
Marktstraße 50, 99084
Tel *(0361) 561 35 06*
There is something here for
everyone: from typical local
fare to innovative modern Italian
and French creations, plus a
range of vegetarian dishes.

GERA: Goldener Drachen €€
Chinese **Map** D4
Altenburger Straße 4, 07546
Tel *(0365) 269 51*
In a part of Germany not known
for exotic cuisine, this excellent
Chinese restaurant is well worth
a visit. Nice covered courtyard.

GOTHA: Hotel am Schlosspark €
Regional **Map** D4
Lindenauallee 20, 99867
Tel *(03621) 442*
The indoor plants and sunny
outdoor surroundings add to
the casual atmosphere at this
hotel restaurant with a fantastic
menu and selection of beers.

JENA: Schwarzer Bär €€
Regional **Map** D4
Lutherplatz 2, 07743
Tel *(03641) 406*
Housed in a historic building,
close to the university. Sample
culinary delights such as the
Goethe set menu (potato soup,
lamb and sausages).

The colourful Clara Alboth's Restaurant im Kaisersaal in Erfurt

Key to Price Guide *see page 510*

The elegantly decorated Ratskeller set in Munich's old town hall

JENA: Scala €€€
International Map D4
Leutragraben 1, 07743
Tel *(03641) 35 66 66*
Wonderful restaurant on the
27th floor of the former Car
Zeiss Jena tower. Delight in
fantastic food while enjoying
panaromic city views.

**MÜHLHAUSEN: Brauhaus
zum Löwen** €€
Traditional German Map D4
Felchtaer Straße 2–4, 99974
Tel *(036014) 710*
This local brewery serves its
own beer in the pub and
restaurant. Most of the food is
traditional German fare – the
sausages, in particular, are
worth a try.

SCHMÖLLN: Bellevue €€
Fine Dining Map E4
Am Pfefferberg 7, 04626
Tel *(034491) 70 00*
Inventive food is complemented
by a terrific wine list at this
refined hotel restaurant. There is
also a beautiful garden terrace.

**WEIMAR: Zum Schwarzen
Bären** €
Regional Map D4
Markt 20, 99423
Tel *(03643) 85 38 47*
One of Weimar's oldest
restaurants, Zum Schwarzen
Bären offers a Thuringian
gastropub experience right
in the centre of town. Simple,
tasty food includes delicious
Bratwursts, and zander with
sauerkraut.

**WEIMAR: Café und
Restaurant Frauentor** €€
Bistro Map D4
Schillerstraße 2, 99423
Tel *(03643) 51*
A charming bistro with a bakery
that makes some of the best
cakes in town. Excellent-value
food and a fine street terrace.

**WEIMAR: Scharfe
Ecke Weimar** €€
Traditional German Map D4
Eisfeld 2, 99423
Tel *(03643) 20 24 30*
Great-value local food – large
portions of Thuringian sausages
and potato dumplings – is served
inside an old guesthouse. There
is delicious beer, too.

DK Choice

WEIMAR: Anna Amalia €€€
Fine dining Map D4
Geleitstraße 8, 99423
Tel *(03643) 495 60*
Located in Hotel Elephant, this
award-winning gourmet
restaurant offers contemporary
dining in a historic 17th-century
building. The tasting menu is
an eight course extravaganza
featuring outstanding food as
well as a range of fine wines.
Visit the Anna Bistro, on the
charming garden terrace, for
a simpler, cheaper option.

Munich

Cohen's €
Kosher Map 2 A1
Theresienstraße 31, 80333
Tel *(089) 280 95 45* **Closed** *Sun*
This hip gastropub draws an arty
crowd and students with its
stews and regional dishes, mostly
with a kosher Jewish twist.

Milagros €
Mexican Map 2 B5
Frauenstraße 9, 80469
Tel *(089) 2323 872 929* **Closed** *Mon–
Wed lunch*
The authentic and zesty Mexican
food here includes scrumptious
tamales (steamed masa which
can be filled with meat, vegetables,
cheese or fruit) and a wonderfully
rich chocolate Kahlúa dessert flan.

Ratskeller €
Regional Map 2 B4
Marienplatz 8, 80331
Tel *(089) 219 98 90*
Set in the charming old town-hall
cellars, this large and touristy
restaurant serves good-quality
local specialities.

Sushi Sano €
Japanese Map 1 F5
Josephspitalstraße 4, 80331
Tel *(089) 26 74 90* **Closed** *Sun lunch*
Dine on authentic sushi and
noodle dishes at this popular
restaurant. Takeaway boxes
are available for picnics.

DK Choice

Wirtshaus in der Au €
Regional
Lilienstraße 51, 81669
Tel *(089) 448 14 00*
Waitresses at this lovely Bavarian
inn sport traditional *dirndl*
dresses. The special experimental dumplings on offer
include spinach and beetroot
versions. They have also published a cookbook, and run a
dumpling restaurant, Münchner
Knödelei, on the Oktoberfest
grounds during the festival.

Augustiner Bräustuben €€
Regional
Landsberger Straße 19, 80339
Tel *(089) 50 70 47*
Jolly beer hall with long benches
to sit on. Dumplings are served
with duck, pork knuckle or simply
smothered in mushroom sauce.

Café Glockenspiel €€
International Map 2 B4
Marienplatz 28, 80331
Tel *(089) 26 42* **Closed** *Sun dinner*
Café/restaurant with magnificent
rooftop views from its terrace.
Highlights on the menu include
seafood glass noodles and
salmon on saffron spinach.

For more information on types of restaurants *see page 505*

The lively bar at seafood restaurant Bar München

Due Passi €€
Italian Map 2 C4
Ledererstraße 11, 80331
Tel *(089) 22 42 71* Closed *Sat & Sun*
Unpretentious pasta bistro with authentic recipes and cheerful service. Cash only.

Fisch Poseidon €€
Seafood Map 2 C5
Westenriederstraße 13, 80331
Tel *(089) 29 92 96* Closed *Sun*
Diners come to this basic, no-frills restaurant specializing in fresh fish dishes for the brilliant *bouillabaisse* and the superb seafood spaghetti. Self-service.

Goa €€
Indian Map 3 D5
Müllerstraße 6, 80336
Tel *(089) 211 117 89*
A small and friendly restaurant with a wide variety of Indian food – from chicken and lamb curries to *biryani* and *tandoori*.

Kulisse €€
International Map 2 C4
Maximilianstraße 26, 80539
Tel *(089) 29 47 28*
The Kammerspiele theatre's restaurant offers a wide choice of dishes ranging from Asian to Bavarian. The outside tables are good for people-watching.

Le Stollberg €€
French Map 2 C4
Stollbergstraße 2, 80539
Tel *(089) 242 434 50* Closed *Sun*
Excellent, carefully prepared French-inspired food is made with high-quality ingredients at this bright and airy restaurant.

Riva Tal €€
Italian Map 2 C5
Tal 44, 80331
Tel *(089) 22 22 40*
This pizzeria and espresso bar is a popular spot for after-work

drinks, but you can stop by at any time of the day for standard Italian dishes. Cheerful service.

Sababa €€
Middle Eastern Map 2 C5
Westenriederstraße 9, 80331
Tel *(089) 232 378 81* Closed *Sun*
A simple and smart Persian eatery renowned for its excellent *falafel* and friendly service.

Stadtkantine €€
Mediterranean Map 2 A4
Neuhauser Straße 15a, 80331
Tel *(089) 242 936 99* Closed *Sun*
Tucked down an alleyway, this sleek and stylish bistro serves a creative *antipasti* platter and phenomenal spare ribs. Good wine selection, too.

Tavernetta €€
Italian Map 2 C4
Hildegardstraße 9, 80539
Tel *(089) 212 694 24* Closed *Sun*
Quality fare includes fine seafood pasta dishes and satisfying *antipasti* such as courgette and wild mushroom *carpaccio*. Leave some room for the tiramisu.

Traditional English-inspired decor and at The Victorian House

Viktus €€
International Map 2 B5
Frauenstraße 2, 80331
Tel *(089) 230 776 45*
With superb salads and soups including a flavourful Asian chicken soup, this bistro proves that fast food can also be healthy.

Weisses Bräuhaus €€
Traditional German Map 2 C5
Tal 7, 80331
Tel *(089) 290 13 80*
A well-established beer hall with a touristy yet authentic feel. Try the appetizing liver dumplings with *sauerkraut*.

Bar München €€€
International Map 2 C4
Maximilianstraße 36, 80539
Tel *(089) 22 90 90*
A chic and upmarket place with mouthwatering seafood on an oft-changing menu. Good-value set business lunches and amazing cocktails.

Restaurant Pfistermühle €€€
International Map 2 C4
Pfisterstraße 4, 80331
Tel *(089) 237 038 65* Closed *Sun*
A small, seasonal and regionally inspired menu is served under elegant 16th-century arches here. Impeccable service. Reserve in advance.

The Victorian House €€€
British Map 2 B5
Frauenstraße 14, 80469
Tel *(089) 233 489 47*
One of a local chain of English-themed cafés. Good for breakfast and sandwich lunches. For afternoon tea, try the Earl Grey with scones.

DK Choice

Trader Vic's €€€
Polynesian Map 2 A3
Promenadenplatz 2–6, 80333
Tel *(089) 212 09 95*
Creative Polynesian food and exotic cocktails are served in the relaxed, colourful cellar-bar of the plush Hotel Bayerischer Hof. Popular with locals and visitors alike, not to mention celebrities such as Tina Turner.

Weinhaus Neuner €€€
International/Regional Map 1 F4
Herzogspitalstraße 8, 80331
Tel *(089) 260 39 54* Closed *Sun*
The menu at this smart wine bar presents strong Mediterranean influences. There are piquant Bavarian mustard sauces as well.

Key to Price Guide *see page 510*

Bavaria

ANSBACH: Madame Thu Trang €
Japanese/Indochina **Map** D6
Platenstraße 2, 91522
Tel *(0981) 972 33 99* **Closed** *Tue*
Hidden in a little passage in the shopping district, this incongruous little eatery's menu includes sushi and Vietnamese rice paper rools and Indonesian curries worth going out of the way for.

AUGSBURG: Berghof €€
Traditional German **Map** D6
Bergstraße 12, 86199
Tel *(0821) 998 43 22*
Bright, country-style inn offering traditional German food – such as grilled chicken with roasted potatoes – cooked to perfection.

AUGSBURG: Drei Königinnen €€
Regional **Map** D6
Meister-Veits-Gäßchen 32, 86152
Tel *(0821) 15 84 05*
Highly regarded for its bustling upmarket beer garden, this pub/ restaurant also serves pleasing *Spätzle* (egg noodles) and other pasta dishes.

AUGSBURG: Manyo €€€
Japanese **Map** D6
Schertlinstaße 12a, 86159
Tel *(0821) 57 11 19*
Watch teppanyaki being prepared on an iron griddle at this restaurant with a convivial ambience. Book ahead.

BAMBERG: Poseidon €
Greek **Map** D5
Habergasse 11, 96047
Tel *(0951) 254 22* **Closed** *Tue*
A cheerful, family-run Greek restaurant featuring dark wooden

The minimalist and authentic interior of Japanese restaurant Manyo in Augsburg

Spectacular views from the terrace at Restaurant 360° in Berchtesgaden

beams. On the menu are traditional dishes such as octopus salad, baked feta and *gyros* (pita filled with meat, tomato, onion and tzatziki sauce).

BAMBERG: Hofbräu €€
Traditional German **Map** D5
Karolinenstraße 7, 96049
Tel *(0951) 533 21*
A classy restaurant with good *Schnitzel*, warm and friendly service, and live piano music on Mondays. Reservations advised for this popular spot.

BAMBERG: Fellini €€€
Italian **Map** D5
Urbanstraße 6, 96047
Tel *(0951) 208 61 03* **Closed** *Sun*
Fresh, simple and beautifully presented Italian cuisine is served by enthusiastic waiters here. Fine drinks menu, too. Book ahead on weekend nights.

BAMBERG: Hoffmanns Steak & Fish €€€
International **Map** D5
Schillerplatz 7, 96047
Tel *(0951) 700 08 85* **Closed** *Sun*
Renowned for its incredible steaks, Hoffmanns is also widely credited with intoducing *nouvelle cuisine* to Bamberg. Choose from a range of innovative dishes served in an elegant environment.

BAYREUTH: Hansl's Holzofen Pizzeria €
Italian **Map** D5
Friedrichstraße 15, 95444
Tel *(0921) 543 44*
The thin and crunchy pizzas topped with fresh produce, served straight from the wood-fired oven, are as delicious as they are misshapen. This tiny eatery has only three tables; however, takeaway is available.

BERCHTESGADEN: Am Luitpoldpark €€
Regional/International **Map** E7
Kälbersteinstraße 2, 83471
Tel *(08652) 96 45 55* **Closed** *Mon*
The flavourful menu at this café/ restaurant includes both regional cooking and international fare, such as tapas, pasta dishes and burgers. Superb mountain views.

DK Choice

BERCHTESGADEN:
Restaurant 360° €€€
International **Map** E7
Hintereck 1, 83471
Tel *(08652) 975 50*
The premier dining spot in the InterContinental Resort, Restaurant 360° is named after the spectacular mountain views from its panoramic windows. Watch delicious local ingredients being transformed into exquisite regional and international dishes in the open kitchen. Many of the choices on the menu are rich and meaty, but there are also several nutritious and health-conscious options.

BURGHAUSEN: Chillis €
International **Map** E7
Marktler Straße 5, 84489
Tel *(08677) 87 75 50*
Come here for an extensive range of Asian and Indian dishes, as well as steaks and fresh fish. The house speciality is baked potatoes. Good-value set lunches

CHIEMSEE: Fritzi's Biergarten €
Regional **Map** E7
Chiemsee 39, 83256
Tel *(08054) 90 29 36*
This lakeside beer garden is a great place to watch the sunset while sampling fresh Chiemsee fish and other regional specialities.

FÜSSEN: Michelangelo €€
Italian **Map** D7
Lechhalde 1, 87629
Tel *(08362) 92 49 24* **Closed** *Mon*
Giant pizzas and home-made pasta dishes are served up in bright and airy interiors or on the terrace of this delightful café.

GARMISCH-PARTENKIRCHEN:
Café Restaurant Vaun €€
Modern German **Map** D7
Zugspitzstraße 2, 82467
Tel *(08821) 730 81 87* **Closed** *Sun*
Striking modern interiors with flavours to match. Delicacies include lime and sweet potato soup and smoked cod with radish. Booking recommended.

For more information on types of restaurants *see page 505*

GARMISCH-PARTENKIRCHEN:
Colosseo €€
Italian **Map** D7
Klammstraße 7, 82467
Tel *(08821) 528 09*
Large, crispy pizzas and delicious pasta dishes ensure that this Italian restaurant is always packed, despite its discreet location above a supermarket.

INGOLSTADT: Taj Mahal €
Indian **Map** D6
Beckerstraße 11, 85049
Tel *(0841) 981 46 18*
Decorated with wooden carvings and colourful fabrics, this restaurant offers good-quality North Indian food and popular bargain lunch buffets.

INGOLSTADT: Daniel €€
Traditional German **Map** D6
Roseneckstraße 1, 85049
Tel *(0841) 352 72* **Closed** *Mon*
Excellent-quality traditional food shines through at this popular pub with basic, no-frills decor.

KEMPTEN: Rendez-vous
à Quiberon €€
French **Map** C7
Rathausstraße 2, 87435
Tel *(0831) 520 81 16*
Rendez-vous à Quiberon serves unusually well-priced French cuisine. Go for the smoked salmon and radish *galette* (pancake) for a perfect summer meal.

LANDSHUT: Taverna Delphi €€
Greek **Map** E6
Isargestade 742, 84028
Tel *(0871) 211 59* **Closed** *Mon*
Black-and-white photographs adorn the walls of this modern bistro. Unpretentious food with crisp, fresh flavours includes feta salads, meat skewers and fish.

LINDAU: Alte Post €€
Traditional German **Map** C7
Fischergasse 3, 88131
Tel *(08382) 934 60*
Dark-wood decor at this inn serving *Schnitzels*, boiled beef and home-made *Maultaschen* (giant Swabian ravioli). The cobbled terrace makes for lovely summer dining.

LINDAU: Zum Sünfzen €€
Regional **Map** C7
Maximilianstraße 1, 88131
Tel *(08382) 58 65*
An atmospheric and traditional place in a 14th-century building. The speciality is fresh Bodensee fish, though the venison is also fantastic. Reserve ahead.

LINDAU: Villino €€€
Asian/Italian **Map** C7
Hoyerbergstraße 34, 88131
Tel *(08382) 934 50*
Savour amazing gourmet food inspired by Asian and Italian flavours at this exquisite family-run hotel restaurant with an idyllic garden and terrace.

NÜRNBURG: Padelle d'Italia €
Italian **Map** D6
Theatergasse 17, 90402
Tel *(09112) 74 21 30* **Closed** *Sun*
This smart, family-run *trattoria* serves home-made pasta dishes, thin-crust pizzas, scrumptious *antipasti* platters and delicious seafood. Superb wine list.

NÜRNBURG: Red Curry House €
Indian/Thai **Map** D6
Lorenzer Straße 29, 90402
Tel *(0911) 621 74 17* **Closed** *Sun*
Choose from a variety of mouth-watering Asian curries at this informal restaurant. Vegetarian options and takeaway available.

NÜRNBURG: Schanzenbräu
Schankwirtschaft €
Traditional German **Map** D6
Adam-Klein-Straße 27, 90429
Tel *(0911) 937 767 90*
A tavern with a great beer garden. The small menu changes daily but always includes German classics, such as *Bratwurst*, and vegetarian choices.

> ### DK Choice
>
> **NÜRNBURG: Bratwurst**
> **Herzle** €€
> Regional **Map** D6
> *Brunnengasse 11, 90402*
> **Tel** *(0911) 22 68 10* **Closed** *Sun*
> This unpretentious place in the Old Town has been serving grilled Nürnburg mini-sausages and *sauerkraut* since 1529. Sit at the shared tables in the half-timbered interior or outside on the street. Wide selection of beers and Franconian wines. Reservations recommended.

NÜRNBURG:
Bratwurstglöcklein €€
Regional **Map** D6
Waffenhof 5, 90402
Tel *(0911) 22 76 25*
This historical inn dating back to 1313 serves Franconian set meals consisting of dumpling soup, pork knuckle and sausages simmered in onions and vinegar.

NÜRNBURG: Herr Lenz €€
Organic **Map** D6
Schonhover Straße 18, 90409
Tel *(0911) 598 53 85*
A colourful neighbourhood bistro featuring first-rate daily specials comprising soups, beef *bourguignon* and a glorious chocolate cake.

Dine al fresco at Bratwurst Herzle in Nürnburg

Key to Price Guide *see page 510*

Homely and welcoming dining area of Vinothek Tiepolo in Würzburg

NÜRNBURG: Wittmanns €€
Organic   Map D6
Beckschlagergasse 8, 90403
Tel *(0911) 33 10 88*   **Closed** *Mon*
Bright, modern restaurant
serving nouvelle cuisine. Start
with sweet potato soup, and
continue with wild boar sausages
with pear and red cabbage.

NÜRNBURG: Wonka €€
International   Map D6
Johannisstraße 38, 90419
Tel *(0911) 39 62 15*   **Closed** *Sun*
& Mon
Relatively unpretentious gourmet
gem housed in a former bakery.
The changing menu offers a range
of tasty dishes with an exotic flair
– from soups to seafood and
desserts. Great wine pairings.

NÜRNBURG: Essigbrätlein €€€
International   Map D6
Weinmarkt 3, 90403
Tel *(0911) 221 31*   **Closed** *Sun & Mon*
An intimate little restaurant with
remarkable food, wines and
service. The daily menu often
features fish and exquisite
desserts. Reserve in advance.

**NÜRNBURG: Nassauer
Keller** €€€
Traditional German   Map D6
Karolinenstraße 2, 90402
Tel *(0911) 233 60*
Housed in an atmospheric, vaulted
medieval cellar, this is the place
for a unique dining experience.
The sausages are exemplary.

NÜRNBURG: Würzhaus €€€
Modern German   Map D6
Kirchenweg 3, 90419
Tel *(0911) 937 34 55*   **Closed** *Sun*
The trendy decor at Würzhaus
perfectly complements the
small portions of imaginative
gourmet food accompanied
by fine wine pairings.

**OBERAMMERGAU:
Zauberstub'n** €€
Traditional German   Map D7
Ettaler Straße 58, 82487
Tel *(08822) 46 83*   **Closed** *Tue*
Wood-clad inn with a solid,
traditional menu. The owner
entertains his diners with magic
tricks, making this place a must
for those travelling with kids.

PASSAU: Pizzeria Gallo Nero €€
Italian   Map E6
Schmiedgasse 5, 94032
Tel *(0851) 363 15*   **Closed** *Tue*
Smart bistro offering an extensive
menu of pizzas, pasta dishes and
grilled fish. The mussels in white
wine are recommended.

PASSAU: Heilig Geist €€€
Regional   Map E6
Heilig-Geist-Gasse 4, 94032
Tel *(0851) 26 07*   **Closed** *Wed*
A rustic, wood-panelled wine bar,
with tiled stoves, specializing in
Bavarian food – mostly local fish,
pork and beef. Reserve a table in
the courtyard for a romantic meal.

REGENSBURG: Papageno €€
Mediterranean   Map D6
Keplerstraße 14, 93047
Tel *(0941) 630 81 65*   **Closed** *lunch
Mon–Fri*
Choose from an authentic Italian
menu, including a first-class *osso
buco* (stew made with veal shank
and cooked in a tomato sauce),
and enjoy your food beneath a
whitewashed vaulted ceiling.

REGENSBURG: Steidle Wirt €€
Regional   Map D6
Am Ölberg 13, 93047
Tel *(0941) 56 08 20*
This is a traditional family-run
inn with a small seasonal menu
and lovingly prepared daily
specials. Warm, friendly owners.
Reservations recommended.

**REGENSBURG: Zur geflickten
Trommel** €€€
International   Map D6
Gesandtenstraße 2, 93047
Tel *(0941) 569 964 89*
This medieval-themed tavern
with candles, fur-covered
benches and costumed staff is
just the place to try *Flammkuchen*
(Alsatian pizza).

**ROTHENBURG: Gasthof
Goldener Greifen** €
Traditional German   Map C6
Obere Schmiedgasse 5, 91541
Tel *(09861) 22 81*
Classic German food is served
in the historic setting of a 15th
century house. Specialities
include spicy goulash soup,
Schnitzel and Swabian pot roast.

**ROTHENBURG: Hotel-
Restaurant Kloster-Stüble** €€
Regional   Map C6
Herrngasse 21, 91541
Tel *(09861) 93 88 90*
A popular inn housed in a 1534
farmhouse with town views from
the terrace. Relish traditional
delicacies such as pork roast
with crackling, mushrooms
and bread dumplings.

ROTHENBURG: Eisenhut €€€
German/International   Map C6
Herrngasse 3–5/7, 91541
Tel *(09861) 70 50*
The antique furnishings in the
dining room of this premier
hotel are reminiscent of an
aristocratic country manor. The
varied menu features gourmet
seasonal and international dishes.

STRAUBING: Unterm Rain €
Regional   Map E6
Unterm Rain 15, 94315
Tel *(09421) 227 72*
Basic and cheerful, this traditional
restaurant and beer garden
serves big portions of pan-
German specialities, including
Schnitzel and sausages.

WÜRZBURG: Auflauf €
International   Map C5
Peterplatz 5, 97070
Tel *(0931) 57 13 43*
A charming bistro specializing in
casseroles and noodle gratins.
Guests choose from the menu
or assemble their own creations.

**WÜRZBURG: Vinothek
Tiepolo** €
Regional   Map C5
Innerer Graben 22, 97070
Tel *(0931) 561 63*
Elegant wine bar with lots of fish
on the seasonal menu and some
130 different wines to wash it all
down with.

For more information on types of restaurants *see page 505*

Fabulous views from Schlosshotel Steinburg in Würzburg

WÜRZBURG: Bella Napoli da Luigi €€
Italian   **Map** C5
Neubaustraße 16, 97070
Tel *(0931) 517 06*
A dependable Italian menu and a cheerful vibe ensure that this restaurant is always bustling with regulars. Look out for the interesting daily specials.

WÜRZBURG: Ratskeller €€
Regional   **Map** C5
Langgasse 1, 97070
Tel *(0931) 130 21*
Reliable regional food is served in the impressive cellars of the city's town hall. The cinnamon and *Silvaner* white wine soup, if available, is a must-try.

WÜRZBURG: Schlosshotel Steinburg €€€
International   **Map** C5
Mittlerer Steinbergweg 100, 97080
Tel *(0931) 97 02*
Surrounded by vineyards, this romantic riverside castle is a gourmet's delight. The wonderful selection of Franconian wines is unparalleled. Reserve in advance.

Baden-Wurttemberg

BADEN-BADEN: Le Jardin de France €€€
International   **Map** B6
Lichtentaler Straße 13, 76530
Tel *(07221) 300 78 60*   **Closed** *Sun & Mon*
An elegant gourmet restaurant decorated with antiques. Ingredients that heavily feature are bok choy, morels mushrooms, turbot (flatfish) and Alsatian pigeon.

BADEN-BADEN: Medici €€€
International   **Map** B6
Augustaplatz 8, 76530
Tel *(07221) 20 06*
Former guests at this *belle époque*-style restaurant include

Bill Clinton and Nelson Mandela. Savour culinary delights with the town's most fashionable crowd.

FREIBURG IM BREISGAU: Pizzeria Taormina €
Italian   **Map** B7
Schwabentorring 4, 79098
Tel *(0761) 341 60*
This modest eatery arguably serves the best pizzas in town – and at reasonable prices. Takeaway, too.

FREIBURG IM BREISGAU: Englers Weinkrügle €€
Regional   **Map** B7
Konviktstraße 12, 79098
Tel *(0761) 38 31 15*
Enjoy scrumptious German cuisine at this wood-panelled *Weinstube* (wine bar). The amazing Black Forest dessert (cherries in hot liqueur with vanilla ice cream) is unmissable.

FREIBURG IM BREISGAU: Hausbrauerei Feierling €€
Traditional German   **Map** B7
Gerberau 46, 79098
Tel *(0761) 24 34 80*
First-class pub food, including giant *Schnitzels*, can be had at this cheerful microbrewery with a wood and copper interior and a fantastic beer garden.

FREIBURG IM BREISGAU: Weinstube Oberkirch €€
Regional   **Map** B7
Münsterplatz 22, 79098
Tel *(0761) 202 68 68*
This excellent traditional hotel restaurant offers large portions of regional delicacies, including pheasant and ox.

FRIEDRICHSHAFEN: Glückler €€
German/French   **Map** C7
Olgastraße 23, 88045
Tel *(07541) 221 64*
Small wine tavern with a delightful range of local fish dishes and many

varieties of Breton *galette* (crusty cake) the in-house speciality.

FRIEDRICHSHAFEN: Kurgarten €€
International   **Map** C7
Graf-Zeppelin-Haus, Olgastraße 20, 88045
Tel *(07541) 320 33*
Watch yachts on the marina while enjoying food such as steak, scampi and vegetarian options like spinach-stuffed mushrooms and *ratatouille* at this café-restaurant.

FRIEDRICHSHAFEN: Restaurant im Zeppelin Museum €€
Regional/Seafood   **Map** C7
Adenauerplatz 1, 88045
Tel *(07541) 38 01*
A popular harbourside restaurant with an eclectic menu ranging from well-priced Swabian specials to Norwegian salmon.

HEIDELBERG: Alte Münz Schnitzelhaus €€
German/Austrian   **Map** C6
Neckarmünzgasse 10, 69117
Tel *(06221) 43 46 43*
This traditional place offers 100 varieties of *Schnitzel* dishes, from the classic Viennese to more exotic versions, such as a serving with a spicy chocolate sauce.

HEIDELBERG: Zum Roten Ochsen €€
Traditional German   **Map** C6
Hauptstraße 217, 69117
Tel *(06221) 209 77*
The collectables and sepia photos on the walls at this atmospheric student haunt bear witness to its popularity since the early 19th century.

HEIDELBERG: Simplicissimus €€€
French   **Map** C6
Ingrimstraße 16, 69117
Tel *(06221) 18 33 36*   **Closed** *Sun*
Superb French cuisine, including imaginative beef, veal and

seafood concoctions. Sit in the intimate dining room or in the pretty, flower-filled courtyard.

KARLSRUHE: Casa Aposto €
Italian   **Map** B6
Waldstraße 57, 76133
Tel *(0721) 160 77 73*
Delight in quality Italian cuisine and outstanding ice cream. In good weather, there is outdoor seating in a bustling square.

**KONSTANZ: Brauhaus
Johann Albrecht** €€
Regional   **Map** C7
Konradigasse 2, 78462
Tel *(07531) 250 45*
A charming microbrewery with a good array of beers and well-priced pub food, such as *Schnitzel* and *Flammkuchen* (thin bread base topped with onion, lardons and crème fraîche). Good-value buffet menu.

KONSTANZ: Hafenhalle €€
Regional   **Map** C7
Hafenstraße 10, 78462
Tel *(07531) 211 26*
Large, smart restaurant in an old harbourside warehouse. Simple canteen food is served in the beer garden. Great for breakfast.

KONSTANZ: Staader Fährhaus €€
Regional   **Map** C7
Fischerstraße 30
Tel *(07531) 361 67 63*   **Closed** *Wed*
Off the beaten path, but worth the trek for fresh, creative fish dishes accompanied by organic, local ingredients.

LUDWIGSBURG: Alte Sonne €€€
International   **Map** C6
Bei der Katholischen Kirche 3, 71634
Tel *(07141) 643 64 80*   **Closed** *Mon & Tue*
Innovative cuisine ranging from Pinot Noir risotto to Breton-style lamb goulash. There is a relaxed, informal brasserie as well.

MAINAU: Schwedenschenke €€€
Regional/Swedish   **Map** C7
Insel Mainau 0, 78465
Tel *(07531) 303*
Romantic island restaurant serving great Swedish meatballs for lunch and *haute cuisine* for dinner. Relish the fresh, local perch and trout.

MANNHEIM: C-Five €€€
International   **Map** B5
C5, 68159
Tel *(0621) 122*
A stylish spot serving high-end French and Italian fare, such as calf's liver with confit shallots, in the restaurant, and more basic pasta dishes and salads at the bar.

MAULBRONN: Klosterkatz €€
Italian   **Map** C6
Klosterhof 21, 75433
Tel *(07043) 10 80*
Good, everyday Italian food is served in an atmospheric monastery courtyard.

MEERSBURG: Zum Becher €€
Regional   **Map** C7
Höllgasse 4, 88709
Tel *(07532) 90 09*
This rustic, cluttered wine bar serves fine traditional food and local fish. Extensive wine list.

DK Choice

REICHENAU: Riebel €€
Seafood   **Map** C7
Seestraße 13, 78479
Tel *(07534) 76 03*   **Closed** *Sat dinner; Sun*
Owned and run by fishermen, this basic restaurant does a brisk trade in superbly simple grilled fish served with fresh side salads. The seafood soup is another highlight. Share a long, communal table with the locals who gather here for lunch. Takeaway available.

**ST BLASIEN: Hotel
Klostermeisterhaus** €€
European   **Map** B7
Im Süßen Winkel 2, 79837
Tel *(07672) 848*
Sample slick modern European cuisine – grilled zander with spinach, roast beef and red lentil risotto – in an early 19th-century villa.

STUTTGART: Calwer-Eck-Bräu €€
Regional   **Map** C6
Calwer Straße 31, 70173
Tel *(0711) 222 49 44*
Stuttgart's oldest micro-brewery features organically produced, seasonal beers. Typical local food includes *Maultaschen*.

STUTTGART: Nirvan €€
Persian   **Map** C6
Eberhardstraße 73, 70173
Tel *(0711) 24 05 61*
Authentic Middle Eastern decor and excellent grilled lamb, poultry and veal dishes at this basement restaurant. Belly-dancing on Fridays.

**STUTTGART:
Tauberquelle** €€
Regional   **Map** C6
Torstraße 19, 70173
Tel *(0711) 553 29 33*   **Closed** *Sun*
Good-value Swabian favourites, cooked to perfection, include *Gaisburger Marsch* (beef stew), *Maultaschen*, *Kasespätzle* (noodle with cheese and fried onions) and *Rostbraten* (beef steak).

STUTTGART: Délice €€€
International   **Map** C6
Hauptstätter Straße 61, 70178
Tel *(0711) 640 32 22*
This intimate, six-table restaurant offers inventive high-quality gourmet food and an award-winning, first-class wine list.

The bright and stylish dining room at Schwedenschenke in Mainau

For more information on types of restaurants *see page 505*

TÜBINGEN: Hotel am Schloss €€
Regional   Map C6
Burgsteige 18, 72070
Tel *(07071) 929 40*
The speciality at this half-timbered establishment with overstuffed wondow boxes is *Maultaschen*. Fine views over the town.

TÜBINGEN: Weinstube Forelle €€
Regional   Map C6
Kronenstraße 8, 72070
Tel *(07071) 240 94*
The walls in this traditional wine bar are painted with vines, cherubs and heraldic crests The trout in almond butter and the game dishes are excellent.

ULM: Zunfthaus der Schiffleute €€
Regional   Map C6
Fischergasse 31, 89073
Tel *(0731) 644 11*   **Closed** *Sun*
Set in a 15th-century fishermen's guild house, the menu consists of only seasonal ingredients. Do not miss the exceptional *Spätzle*.

ULM: Zur Forelle €€€
Regional   Map C6
Fischergasse 25, 89073
Tel *(0731) 639 24*
In a snug 1626 house with an original Napoleonic cannonball in one wall, Zur Forelle serves high-end versions of regional dishes such as *Gaisburger Marsch* (beef stew).

Rhineland-Palatinate and Saarland

BACHARACH: Altes Haus €€
Regional   Map B5
Oberstraße 61, 55422
Tel *(06743) 12 09*
There are plenty of options at this archetypal old Rhine inn: trout makes an ideal light meal, while

The elaborate sign to Altes Haus in Bacharach

wild boar in wine sauce is an appealing, substantial main.

BACHARACH: Kurpfälzische Münze €€
Regional   Map B5
Oberstraße 72, 55422
Tel *(06743) 937 77 79*
A warm and inviting place full of character. Superb light meals are accompanied by local wines.

DK Choice

BACHARACH: Rhein Hotel €€
Traditional German   Map B5
Langstraße 50, 55422
Tel *(06743) 12 43*   **Closed** *Tue*
This family-run restaurant is set in a half-timbered building with an elegant dining room and a delightful courtyard terrace. The highlight is the pot roast marinated in wine and mustard. Impeccable service. Reserve in advance.

BOPPARD: Weinhaus Heilig Grab €
Regional   Map B5
Zelkesgasse 12, 56154
Tel *(06742) 23 71*
An over 200-year-old wine tavern with a pretty shaded garden. Try the superb *Flammkuchen* (thin bread base topped with onion, lardons and crème fraîche).

BOPPARD: Severusstube €€
Regional   Map B5
Untere Marktstraße 7, 56154
Tel *(06742) 32 18*   **Closed** *Wed lunch; Thu*
This welcoming, wood-beamed inn offers hearty lamb and pork dishes at reasonable prices.

KOBLENZ: Los Gauchos €€
South American   Map B5
Am Plan 7, 56068
Tel *(0261) 140 06*
Many dishes are *flambéed* (covered in alcohol and set alight) at your table at this excellent steakhouse.

KOBLENZ: Weinhaus Hubertus €€€
Regional   Map B5
Florinsmarkt 6, 56068
Tel *(0261) 311 77*   **Closed** *Tue*
Dating from 1696, this *Weinstube* (wine bar) serves local fish and wine, as well as tasty seasonal treats.

MAINZ: Haus des Deutschen Weines €€
Regional   Map B5
Gutenbergplatz 3–5, 55116
Tel *(06131) 22 13 00*
Good-quality and inexpensive regional food such as marinated

The tastefully decorated dining room at Rhein Hotel in Bacharach

salmon and venison are complemented by an extensive wine list from all over Germany.

MAINZ: Geberts Weinstuben €€€
Regional   Map B5
Frauenlobstraße 94, 55118
Tel *(06131) 61*   **Closed** *Mon*
This elegantly decorated wine tavern is a cut above the rest for its fish and game dishes and fine choice of wines.

SAARBRÜCKEN: Zum Stiefel €€
Regional   Map B6
Am Stiefel 2, 66111
Tel *(0681) 93 64 50*
Hearty portions of provincial food – potato rissoles, and leek, meat and potato casserole – are served in this beerhall.

DK Choice

SPEYER: Zum Alten Engel €€
Regional   Map B6
Mühlturmstraße 5, 67346
Tel *(06232) 709 14*
Set in a brick-vaulted cellar, this atmospheric restaurant is furnished with paintings and antiques. On the menu are meaty, substantial regional classics such as liver dumplings and pig's stomach. Good wine list. Reserve ahead.

SPEYER: Backmulde €€€
Regional/French   Map B6
Karmeliterstraße 11–13, 67346
Tel *(06232) 715 77*   **Closed** *Sun dinner; Mon*
This high-end gourmet restaurant delivers imaginative culinary treats such as quail stuffed with lamb and oysters in champagne.

Refined interiors of Restaurant Villa Rothschild in Frankfurt am Main

made with organic ingredients and packed with flavour. Order the *gyro* (filled pita) wraps, and finish with the tiramisu.

EGELSBACH: Schuhbeck's
Check Inn €€
International **Map** C5
Am Flugplatz, 63329
Tel *(06103)* 485 93 80
Situated in an old hangar overlooking the regional airfield, this eatery serves great local food with Mediterranean and Asian influences. There is also a microbrewery and beer garden.

ELTVILLE: Burg
Schwarzenstein €€€
Gourmet **Map** B5
Rosengasse 32, 65366
Tel *(06722)* 995 00 **Closed** *Mon & Tue*
This wonderful restaurant is housed in a modern pavilion with views of the vineyards on the banks of the Rhine. The ingredients are carefully chosen and meticulously prepared, and accompanied by award-winning wines.

FRANKFURT AM MAIN:
Zum Schwarzen Stern €€
International/German **Map** C5
Römerberg 6, 60311
Tel *(069)* 29 12 79
Well-prepared seasonal and international dishes are served in a medieval building. Try the *Tafelspitz* (boiled beef).

ST GOAR: Zum Goldenen
Löwen €€
Regional **Map** B5
Heerstraße 82, 56329
Tel *06741 16 74*
Top-notch traditional fare in an 18th-century Baroque building. Delicacies include *Pfälzer Saumagen* (cabbage in pig's stomach) and *Spanferkal Braten* (roasted suckling pig).

ST GOAR: Hotel
Schloss Rheinfels €€€
Regional **Map** B5
Schlossberg 47, 56329
Tel *(06741)* 80 20 **Closed** *Mon*
This stunning restaurant is part of a historic castle in a picturesque location. It specializes in local game; try the smoked venison with celery and mango.

ST GOARSHAUSEN:
Rheingold €€
Regional **Map** B5
Professor-Müller-Straße 2, 56346
Tel *(06771)* 450
This riverside restaurant serves great meatball and vegetable stews. There are splendid castle views from the upstairs terrace.

TRIER: Zum Domstein €€
Regional **Map** A5
Hauptmarkt 5, 54290
Tel *(0651)* 744 90
Choose from the recipes of Emperor Tiberius's cook and dine like a Roman. The sauces are delightfully rich.

TRIER: Palais Kesselstatt €€€
International **Map** A5
Liebfrauenstraße 10, 54290
Tel *(0651)* 411 78
A lovely restaurant in the extravagant Baroque residence of a former count – with gourmet food to match.

WORMS: Ambiente €€
Italian **Map** B5
Weckerlingplatz 6, 67547
Tel *(06241)* 304 98 88 **Closed** *Mon*
This quality restaurant with modern decor serves tasty pizzas, as well as dishes with a creative flair, such as venison and chestnut tortellini. For dessert, have tiramisu or ice cream.

Hesse

ALSFELD: Krone €
Regional **Map** C4
Schellengasse 2, 36304
Tel *(06631)* 40 41
Delicious regional food is on offer at this small restaurant. Be sure to leave room for the warm cherries with ice cream. Attentive service.

BAD HOMBURG: Hölderlins €€
Traditional German **Map** C5
Louisenstraße 15, 61348
Tel *(06172)* 680 47 11
A bright and comfortable café offering satisfying breakfasts and Sunday brunches to kick off the day. Tasty national and local dishes are served in the evening.

BAD WILDUNGEN: Waffelhaus €
Regional **Map** C4
Billsteinstraße 67, 34537
Tel *(05621)* 51 90 **Closed** *Mon*
Over 100 varieties of waffles, along with many local dishes, served in generous proportions. Nice terrace and beer garden.

DARMSTADT: Café Habibi €
International **Map** C5
Landwehrstraße 13, 64293
Tel *(06151)* 660 27 60 **Closed** *Mon*
The vegan and vegetarian creations in this old-fashioned café are magical. Excellent food is

DK Choice

FRANKFURT AM MAIN:
Restaurant Villa
Rothschild €€€
French **Map** C5
Im Rothschildpark 1, 61462
Tel *(06174)* 290 80 **Closed** *Sun & Mon*
Situated in a mansion resembling a castle, this award-winning restaurant is one of the best in Germany and a must-visit for gourmands. The chef and his team specializes in imaginative versions of French *haute cuisine*, perfectly complemented by the excellent and extensive selection of wines and champagnes. Reservations recommended.

FULDA: Dachsbau €€
French **Map** C5
Pfandhausstraße 8, 36037
Tel *(0661)* 741 12 **Closed** *Mon & Tue*
An intimate and friendly restaurant serving creatively presented French cuisine. Choose from a large selection of wines. Reserve ahead.

For more information on types of restaurants *see page 505*

The warm and artistic-styled dining room in Käfers Bistro in Wiesbaden

GIESSEN: Ibsen €
International **Map** C5
Westanlage 33–35, 35390
Tel *(0641) 97 99 90*
This small, welcoming restaurant in the Hotel Köhler offers steaks, *Schnitzels*, fish dishes and more – all accompanied by a good selection of wines.

KASSEL: Restaurant Santé €€€
Gourmet **Map** C4
Konrad-Adenauer-Straße 117, 34132
Tel *(0561) 94 04 80*
Located near the magnificent Wilhelmshöhe, with nice views over Kassel, this restaurant at Zum Steinernen Schweinchen offers fine culinary delights. À la carte and set menus and superb wines.

KIEDRICH: Klostermühle €
Traditional German **Map** B5
Eltviller Straße 2, 65399
Tel *(06123) 40 21* **Closed** *Mon*
Enjoy traditional recipes and fruity Rheingau wines at this romantic former monastery. Try the *Tafelspitz* (boiled beef served with horse-radish) with a glass of Riesling.

KLOSTER EBERBACH:
Klosterschänke €€
Regional **Map** B5
Pfortenhaus, 65346
Tel *(06723) 99 30*
Specialities at this atmospheric 12th-century former monastery with a vaulted dining hall include regional Rheingau dishes and wines made from grapes harvested on the property.

LIMBURG: Wirsthaus
Obermühle €€
Modern German **Map** B5
Am Huttig 3, 65549
Tel *(06431) 584 00 84* **Closed** *Mon*
Charming restaurant next to a 12th-century water mill. The amazing *Schnitzels*, steaks and other regional delicacies reflect the ongoing evolution of German cuisine.

LORSCH: Gaststätte Schillereck €
International **Map** B5
Schillerstraße 27, 64653
Tel *(06251) 570 10 27* **Closed** *Fri*
An unexpected find for gastronomes on a budget. Outstanding food and wines, combined with great service, create a memorable dining experience.

MARBURG: Das Kleine
Restaurant €€
French **Map** C4
Barfüssertor 25, 35037
Tel *(06421) 222 93* **Closed** *Mon*
Small restaurant, big on flavour and style. Four-course set menus blend French and German tech-niques with eclectic ingredients and artistic presentation. Superb wine list with over 400 options.

MICHELSTADT: Drei Hasen €€
Regional **Map** C5
Braunstraße 5, 64720
Tel *(06061) 710 17*
The "Three Hares" is renowned for its traditional ambience, as well as its delectable cuisine, especially the fish dishes. The interior has a strong rustic charm, and there is a large beer garden.

OFFENBACH: Markthaus
am Wilhelmsplatz €€
Traditional German **Map** C5
Bieberer Straße 9b, 63065
Tel *(06982) 801 018 83*
Warm restaurant with an outside terrace overlooking the town market. Authentic dishes on the menu include *Handkäse* (sour milk cheese), home-made *Wurst* (sausage) and roast pork.

RÜDESHEIM AM RHEIN:
Kronenstube €€
French/German **Map** B5
Rheinuferstraße 10, 65685
Tel *(06722) 40 30*
Classic French and contemporary German cuisine is served with a variety of regional wines in a rustic setting. In summer, the flower-clad terrace offers lovely, scenic views over the Rhine.

WEILBURG: Alte Reitschule €€
International **Map** B5
Langgasse 25, 35781
Tel *(06471) 509 07 17*
This picturesque restaurant serves a small range of seasonal dishes. The terrace offers wonderful views of the Schloss and the surrounding area.

WETZLAR: Der Postreiter €
Regional **Map** B5
Konrad-Adenauer-Promenade 20, 35578
Tel *(06441) 90 30*
This restaurant in the Bürgerhof Hotel prepares fresh, seasonal local cuisine – trout is the speciality. Ask the staff to help you select from the extensive wine list.

WIESBADEN: Käfers Bistro €€
French **Map** B5
Kurhausplatz 1, 65189
Tel *(0611) 53 62 00*
A spacious and busy bistro combining German portions and produce with French subtlety. There is a good variety of wines from the region, and a large terrace for outside dining.

North Rhine-Westphalia

AACHEN: Schloss Schönau €€
International **Map** A4
Schönauer Allee 20, 52072
Tel *(0241) 17 35 77* **Closed** *Mon*
Gourmet food in an opulent 11th-century castle with breathtaking views of the countryside. The set menus always include a seafood option, and there is a vast array of wines and champagnes.

AACHEN: Sankt Benedikt   €€€
International   **Map** A4
Benediktusplatz 12, 52076
Tel *(02408) 28 88*   **Closed** *Sun & Mon*
Choose from a creative award-winning menu featuring French and international fare. Impressive wine selection.

BIELEFELD: Westfälische Hofstube   €€
Regional   **Map** C3
Niederholz 2, 33699
Tel *(0521) 209 00*
The Oldentruper Hof Hotel's restaurant prepares traditional delicacies from the Westphalia area, though there are a few international dishes on the menu as well. In autumn, ask for the venison specialities.

BONN: Zur Lindenwirtin Aennchen   €€
International   **Map** B4
Aennchenplatz 2, 53173
Tel *(0228) 31 20 51*   **Closed** *Sun*
A romantic restaurant with impeccable service. The kitchen produces international dishes with a strong leaning towards French cuisine. There is a carefully chosen wine list as well.

BONN: Halbedel's Gasthaus   €€€
International   **Map** B4
Rheinallee 47, 53173
Tel *(0228) 35 42 53*   **Closed** *Mon*
First-rate service, innovative cuisine and an impressive list of 700 wines in a villa just a stone's throw from the Rhine. The chef constantly invents new dishes.

BRÜHL: Seerose   €€
International/Regional   **Map** B4
Römerstraße 1, 50321
Tel *(02232) 20 40*
A short walk from the magnificent Brühl castles, Seerose serves international and regional food in a colourful dining area.

DETMOLD: Strate's Brauhaus   €
Traditional German   **Map** C3
Lange Straße 35, 32756
Tel *(05231) 99 99 45*
Set in a historic house filled with brewing paraphernalia. Enjoy specialities such as *Pickert* (crispy fried potato pancakes with raisins) with Strate's home-brewed Pilsner and cloudy wheat beers.

DK Choice

DORTMUND: View   €€
International   **Map** B4
Leonie-Reygers-Terasse, 44137
Tel *(0231) 476 47 80*   **Closed** *Sun–Thu*
Unique "club kitchen" on the top floor of the monumental former Dortmunder U brewery tower. Open only on Friday and Saturday nights, View serves tasty, affordable food, then the whole place converts into a lively club attracting a trendy crowd. Ask for a table by the window and visit the terrace for superb views.

DUISBURG: Walsumer Hof   €€
Seafood   **Map** B4
Rheinstraße 16, 47179
Tel *(0203) 49 14 54*   **Closed** *Mon*
The distinctive nautical decor in this restaurant is the perfect match for the superb seafood. Start with North Sea sprats salad, then try the catch of the day – grilled, steamed or fried to order.

DÜSSELDORF: Brauerei Uerige in der Altstadt   €
Traditional German   **Map** B4
Berger Straße 1, 40213
Tel *(0211) 86 69 90*
The highlight at this legendary brewpub is the renowned *Altbier* (an amber bitter served in little glasses). Savour solid German fare in the unforgettable atmosphere of several dimly lit rooms.

DÜSSELDORF: Libanon   €€
Lebanese   **Map** B4
Berger Straße 19–21, 40213
Tel *(0211) 13 49 17*
Typical Middle Eastern fare is served in generous portions at Libanon. Occasional belly-dancing shows in the evening.

DÜSSELDORF: Im Schiffchen   €€€
French   **Map** B4
Kaiserswerther Markt 9, 40489
Tel *(0211) 40 10 50* **Closed** *Sun & Mon*
Reserve well in advance at this popular restaurant. Well-informed staff advise on the extensive menu and the 900-strong wine list.

ESSEN: Casino Zollverein   €€
International   **Map** B4
Gelsenkirchener Straße 181, 45309
Tel *(0201) 83 02 40*   **Closed** *Mon*
Located in an old mine, the dining hall alone, with its industrial look, is worth the trip. The New World cuisine served is seasonal and original, and retains hints of traditional miners' food.

ESSEN: Tio Pepe   €€
Spanish   **Map** B4
Witteringstraße 92, 45130
Tel *(0201) 878 984 15*   **Closed** *Sun*
Enjoy tasty, fresh Spanish dishes in stylish interiors. There is no real menu – the chef comes up with proposals based on guests' tastes. For dessert, try the delectable *crema catalana flambeado* (similiar to *crème brûlé*).

ESSEN: Résidence   €€€
International   **Map** B4
Auf der Forst 1, 45219
Tel *(02054) 89 11*   **Closed** *Sun & Mon*
The highly acclaimed Résidence attracts patrons from all over Germany. The chef produces irresistible cuisine – particularly seafood dishes – that never fails to impress.

HAGEN: Felsengarten   €
International   **Map** B4
Wasserloses Tal 4, 58093
Tel *(02331) 391 12 00*
A wide variety of international dishes is served in a modern, bright interior. There is a lovely beer garden and terrace as well.

HÖXTER: Bauernstube Schenkenküche   €
Traditional German   **Map** C3
Kapenberg 6, 37671
Tel *(05278) 889*   **Closed** *Mon–Fri*
Set in a massive old country farmhouse; kids can play among the haystacks as their parents savour delicious offerings such as oven-baked ham *flambé* (cooked in flaming alcohol) with wild berry sauce.

The vibrant interior of View in Dortmund

For more information on types of restaurants *see page 505*

Informal outdoor eating area at L'Escalier in Köln

KÖLN: Alcazar €
French/German **Map** B4
Bismarckstraße 39A, 50672
Tel *(0221) 51 57 33*
An institution in Köln's humming nightlife quarter, this appealing little bar/restaurant fuses French and German cuisine. Lunch is the best bet for a table, since evenings are often packed solid.

KÖLN: Engelbät €
Crêperie **Map** B4
Engelbertstraße 7, 50674
Tel *(0221) 24 69 14*
Enjoy delicious crêpes filled with cheese, spinach, fresh garlic and other ingredients (savoury or sweet) at this popular crêperie in the trendy Belgian quarter.

KÖLN: Pöttgen €
Traditional German **Map** B4
Landmannstraße 19, 50825
Tel *(0221) 55 52 46* **Closed** *Mon*
This cheerful restaurant has been in the Pöttgen family for four generations, and several recipes can be traced back to the family's ancestors. Great value.

KÖLN: Il Carpaccio €€
Italian **Map** B4
Lindenstraße 5, 50674
Tel *(0221) 23 64 87* **Closed** *Sun*
Relish fantastic home-made pasta and other classic Italian dishes made with top quality ingredients in a stylish setting. Remarkable wine selection and live music at weekends.

KÖLN: L'Escalier €€€
French **Map** B4
Brüsseler Straße 11, 50674
Tel *(0221) 205 39 98* **Closed** *Sun & Mon*
A restaurant with a passion for innovative French cuisine with German influences. The elegant modern dining area is a great place for lunch or dinner, and there is a terrace, too.

KÖLN: Le Moissonier €€€
French **Map** B4
Krefelder Straße 25, 50670
Tel *(0221) 72 94 79* **Closed** *Sun & Mon*
Fabulous French food made with the finest ingredients and served in a warm interior. Expect dishes such as Icelandic cod, braised rabbit and Australian beef fillet.

KÖLN: Maitre €€€
French **Map** B4
Olympiaweg 2, 50933
Tel *(0221) 48 53 60* **Closed** *Mon & Tue*
The restaurant of the Landhaus Kuckuck hotel has a reputation for its fine cuisine as well as its well-stocked wine cellar. The frequently changing menu uses plenty of seasonal produce.

LEMGO: Im Borke €€
Regional **Map** C3
Salzufler Straße 132, 32657
Tel *(05266) 16 91*
A little restaurant with lots of rustic charm. The menu features regional food, as well as a few international dishes.

MONSCHAU: Wiesenthal €
Modern German **Map** A4
Laufenstraße 82, 52156
Tel *(02472) 860*
The menu at this refined restaurant in the Carat Hotel offers creative food made with seasonal produce from the region.

MÜNSTER: Alter Pulverturm €
Traditional German **Map** B3
Breul 9, 8143
Tel *(0251) 458 30*
This quiet and peaceful spot located along Münster's promenade features a pleasant beer garden. The extensive menu offers a variety of German dishes.

MÜNSTER: Landhaus Eggert €€
International **Map** B3
Zur Haskenau 81, 48157
Tel *(0251) 32 80 40* **Closed** *Mon & Tue*
The varied menu at this fine-dining restaurant in a family-owned country-house hotel explore international cuisine while showcasing the region's best dishes.

MÜNSTER: Villa Medici €€
Italian **Map** B3
Ostmarktstraße 15, 48145
Tel *(0251) 342 18* **Closed** *Sun & Mon*
Dine on well-balanced and wonderfully presented, imaginative food in one of Germany's best Italian restaurants. A monthly changing multicourse set menu is also on offer.

PADERBORN: Balthasar €€€
International **Map** C3
Warburger Straße 28, 33098
Tel *(05251) 244 48* **Closed** *Sun & Mon*
An attractive and modern restaurant that enthusiastically mixes art with food. The chef creates inventive dishes using a variety of interesting ingredients and suggests wines to complement the food.

SIEGBURG: Gaststätte zur Talsperre €
Modern German **Map** B4
Braschosser Straße 55, 53721
Tel *(02241) 38 39 88*
Expect modern takes on classic dishes such as chanterelle mushrooms in cream sauce, pangasius (cat fish) fillet and Holstein steak at this charming restaurant. Wash it all down with a freshly tapped Bitburger (pilsner).

The stylish French exterior of Le Moissonier in Köln

**TROISDORF: Forsthaus
Telegraph** €€
International **Map** B4
Mauspfad 3, 53842
Tel *(02241) 766 49* **Closed** *Mon*
Hidden in a forest, this restaurant
serves international dishes in a
sophisticated setting. The sauces
are rich and diverse, with the
chef combining the best of all
styles and cuisines. Book ahead.

WUPPERTAL: Scarpati €€€
Italian **Map** B4
Scheffelstraße 41, 42327
Tel *(0202) 78 40 74* **Closed** *Mon*
A classic Italian restaurant serving
fresh and flavourful pasta dishes
that are worth the calories. The
dining area has a pleasant view
over the garden.

XANTEN: Hotel van Bebber €€
Regional **Map**
Klever Straße 12, 46509
Tel *(02801) 66 23*
This hotel restaurant serves
excellent regional cuisine in a
traditionally styled dining area
and a unique wine cellar. The
fish dishes are truly special.

Lower Saxony, Hamburg and Bremen

**BRAUNSCHWEIG:
Herrendorf** €€
Regional **Map** D3
Am Magnitor 1, 38100
Tel *(0531) 471 30*
This modern restaurant in a
historic building dating back to
1476 serves tasty seafood and
regional fare, with some French
influences in the sauces.

BREMEN: Das Kleine Lokal €€
International **Map** C2
Besselstraße 40, 28203
Tel *(0421) 794 90 84* **Closed** *Sun
& Mon*
An intimate restaurant offering
everything from regional recipes
to international fare. Small
portions of delicious dishes are
served on beautifully designed
crockery. Friendly service.

**BREMEN: Meierei
Bürgerpark** €€
Mediterranean **Map** C2
Bürgerpark 1, 28209
Tel *(0421) 340 86 19* **Closed** *Mon
& Tue*
This Art Nouveau Swiss chalet in
the middle of a park has been
serving great food since 1881.
The menu features dishes with
Mediterranean flavours, as well
as some seasonal local choices.

BREMEN: Ratskeller €€
Traditional German **Map** C2
Am Markt, 28195
Tel *(0421) 305 98 88*
Housed in Germany's oldest wine
cellar, established over 600 years
ago, Ratskeller has an extensive
wine selection and serves tasty
food in a magnificent setting.

**BREMEN: Schröter's
Leib und Seele** €€
International **Map** C2
Schnoor 13, 28195
Tel *(0421) 32 66 77*
Stylish yet welcoming, this
restaurant is one of the best
places to sample typical Bremen
fare and international cuisine.
There is also a bistro for less
upmarket dining.

BÜCKEBURG: Ambiente €€
International **Map** C3
Herminstraße 11, 31675
Tel *(05722) 96 70*
With high-glass ceilings, lots of
plants and a little summer garden,
this serene place offers mainly
German and Italian cuisine,
served in generous portions.

CELLE: Landhaus Ludewigs €
Regional **Map** C3
Dorfstraße 1A, Oppershausen, 29342
Tel *(05149) 18 58 00* **Closed** *Tue*
Set in a lovely villa surrounded
by greenery, Landhaus Ludewigs
serves seasonal ingredients
including asparagus, mushrooms
and kale. Do not miss the regional
speciality *Roha Roulado* (meat rolls
with bacon, onions and pickles).

CELLE: Endtenfang €€€
French **Map** C3
Hannoversche Straße 55–56, 29221
Tel *(05141) 20 10* **Closed** *Mon & Tue*
This highly acclaimed restaurant
offers fantastic French cuisine, as

well as a few Mediterranean-
inspired dishes. The sommelier
helps select the perfect
accompaniment from more
than 800 wines.

CLOPPENBURG: Margaux €€
International **Map** B3
Lange Straße 66, 49661
Tel *(04471) 24 84* **Closed** *Mon & Tue*
The enthusiastic young chef
at this friendly restaurant
combines different styles and
ingredients to create enjoyable
food. Highlights include lobster
and scallops. Excellent wine list.

GÖTTINGEN: Gaudi €€
Mediterranean **Map** C4
Rote Straße 16, 37073
Tel *(0551) 531 30 01* **Closed** *Sun*
Colourful and unorthodox, this
restaurant is named after the
Catalan architect Antoni Gaudí.
The extensive tapas selection
is perfect for lunch; for dinner,
choose one of the fish dishes.

HAMBURG: Café Paris €
French **Map** C2
Rathausstraße 4, 20095
Tel *(040) 325 277 78*
Enjoy delicious French food, as
well as coffee and cakes, at this
gorgeous former butchery with
Art Nouveau tiled walls and
ceiling. The bistro menu has
oysters, steak tartare and cheeses.

HAMBURG: Au Quai €€
Mediterranean **Map** C2
Grosse Elbstraße 145, 22767
Tel *(040) 380 377 30* **Closed** *Sun*
An old cold-storage depot has
been transformed into a chic,
contemporary restaurant serving
excellent fresh seafood, sushi and
sashimi, as well as meat dishes.
Book a table on the terrace for
great views across the harbour.

The grand former wine cellars that house the dining room at Ratskeller, in Bremen

For more information on types of restaurants *see page 505*

The well-stocked bar at Die Bank, Hamburg

DK Choice

HAMBURG: Die Bank   €€
Modern German   **Map** C2
Hohe Bleichen 17, 20354
Tel *(040) 238 00 30*   **Closed** *Sun*
Inside a magnificent historic
former bank, this elegant dining
hall is always buzzing. The
acclaimed chef creates
unexpected variations of well-
known local dishes with an
emphasis on fresh fish and
vegetables. The wine list is
equally impressive. Expect a
business clientele for lunch
and an arty crowd for dinner.

HAMBURG: Brahms   €€
Seafood   **Map** C2
Kajen 12, 20459
Tel *(040) 36 56 31*   **Closed** *Sun*
Fresh, seasonal fish and seafood
are served in a trendy dining
room decorated with nautical
colours and plenty of flowers. The
crab dishes are especially good,
as is the extensive wine list.

HAMBURG: Fischereihafen   €€
Seafood   **Map** C2
Grosse Elbstraße 143, 22767
Tel *(040) 38 18 16*
Gourmets flock to this charming
restaurant with harbour views for
the delicious seafood. The menu
includes sushi and sashimi as well
as traditional fare, such as smoked
eel fillet on scrambled eggs.

HAMBURG: Fischmarkt   €€
Seafood   **Map** C2
Ditmar-Koel-Straße 1, 20459
Tel *(040) 36 38 09*   **Closed** *Sun*
A bustling, friendly restaurant
inside the popular fish market

hall. The ambience is warm and
informal, and the helpful staff
provide useful suggestions on
food and wine selection.

HAMBURG: Henssler
& Henssler   €€
Fusion   **Map** C2
Grosse Elbstraße 160, 22767
Tel *(040) 386 990 00*   **Closed** *Sun*
Run by renowned German
celebrity chef Steffen Henssler
and his father, this stylish and
well-liked restaurant serves a
fusion of Californian and
Japanese cuisine.

HAMBURG: Jus   €€
International   **Map** C2
Lehmweg 30, Eppendorf, 20251
Tel *(040) 429 496 54*   **Closed** *Sun*
A small restaurant serving modern,
seasonal fare such as zander fillet
with potato *mousseline* (soft, light
mousse). The chef handles traditional ingredients with a balance
of subtlety and confidence.

HAMBURG: Porto   €€
Portuguese   **Map** C2
Ditmar-Koel-Straße 15, 20459
Tel *(040) 317 84 80*
A quaint family-run place serving
delicious tapas, grilled prawns,
swordfish salad and more. Iberian
home-cooking at its best.

HAMBURG: Rach & Ritchy   €€
International   **Map** C2
Holstenkamp 71, 22525
Tel *(040) 89726170*   **Closed** *Sun*
This colourful *Grillhaus* (grill
house) serves fantastic meat and
seafood dishes. The emphasis is
on grilled steaks from both the
local area and afar, prepared in a
special infrared grill oven.

HAMBURG: Jacobs   €€€
International   **Map** C2
Elbchaussee 401–403, 22609
Tel *(040) 82 25 50*   **Closed** *Mon*
& Tue
Housed in the beautiful Louis
C Jacob Hotel, this restaurant
is one of the best in the city.
International cuisine with French
influences is accompanied by a
remarkable wine selection.

HANNOVER: Gallo Nero   €€
Italian   **Map** C3
Gross-Buchholzer Kirchweg
32b, 30655
Tel *(0511) 546 34 34*   **Closed** *Tue;*
Sat lunch
Set in a homely barn with
exposed beams, Gallo Nero
serves top-quality Northern
Italian cuisine, made using simple
ingredients with refined sauces
and spices.

HANNOVER: Hindenburg
Klassik   €€
German/Mediterranean   **Map** C3
Gneisenaustraße 55, 30175
Tel *(0511) 85 85 88*   **Closed** *Sun*
This relaxed, modern restaurant
is renowned for its home-made
pasta, truffles and seafood dishes.
There is a bar serving amazing
cocktails and a lovely outside
seating area.

HANNOVER: Pier 51   €€
International   **Map** C3
Rudolf-von-Bennigsen-Ufer 51, 30173
Tel *(0511) 8071800*
Built on a pier jutting over Lake
Masch, Pier 51 is a stylish, award-
winning restaurant offering light
and scrumptious fish, meat and
pasta dishes. Enjoy a cocktail on
the elegant terrace afterwards.

HANNOVER: Titus   €€
International   Map C3
Wiehbergstraße 98, 30519
Tel *(0511) 83 55 24*   **Closed** *Sun & Mon*
Both the lunch and the dinner menus at this welcoming living room-style restaurant list fabulous creations such as octopus with quail and wild garlic crumble.

HANNOVER: Clichy   €€€
French   Map C3
Weissekreuzstraße 31, 30161
Tel *(0511) 31 24 47*   **Closed** *Sun*
A beautiful, classy restaurant serving modern interpretations of French cuisine, with some German and Italian influences. Try one of their fish specialities.

HANNOVER: Die Insel   €€€
French/Mediterranean   Map C3
Rudolf-von-Bennigsen-Ufer 81, 30519
Tel *(0511) 83 12 14*
Enjoy picturesque views of Lake Masch from the elegant dining room and fantastic terrace. The menu is full of beautifully presented dishes with subtle flavours and spices.

KÖNIGSLUTTER: Merlin   €€
International   Map D3
Braunschweiger Straße 21A, 38154
Tel *(05353) 50 30*
Fantastic seasonal cuisine – including good meat and fish dishes – is on offer in the bright and cheerful dining room of the Königshof Hotel's restaurant. Friendly staff.

OLDENBURG: Kiebitzstube   €€
Traditional German   Map B2
Europaplatz 4–6, 26123
Tel *(0441) 80 80*
Located in the City Club Hotel, Kiebitzstube is a formal, classic-looking place with well-composed set menus and a good wine list.

OSNABRÜCK: VIla Real   €€€
Mediterranean   Map B3
Natruper-Tor-Wall 1, 49076
Tel *(0541) 609 60*   **Closed** *Sun*
An upmarket restaurant combining fresh ingredients with great imagination. Enjoy country-themed dishes – lobster, scallops or one of the other delicious seafood choices.

STADTHAGEN: Blanke   €€
Seafood   Map C3
Rathauspassage 5, 31655
Tel *(05721) 817 86*   **Closed** *Mon*
Blanke has been serving wonderfully fresh seafood since 1924. There is a vast array of fish and shellfish dishes on offer. The ambience is rustic and relaxed.

WOLFENBÜTTEL: Altes Kaffeehaus   €€
International   Map D3
Harztorwall 18, 38300
Tel *(05331) 88 80*
This elegant restaurant in the Park Hotel offers large portions of good-value regional fare. In winter, sit downstairs in the attractive wine grotto with vaulted ceilings. There is a terrace for dining in the summer months.

WOLFSBURG: La Fontaine   €€€
International   Map D3
Gifhorner Straße 25, 38442
Tel *(05362) 94 00*   **Closed** *Sun & Mon*
A charming award-winning restaurant with a lovely terrace. The chefs combine regional and international produce to create innovative dishes.

Schleswig-Holstein

AHRENSBURG: Berlin Milljöh   €
International   Map C2
Große Straße 15, 22926
Tel *(04102) 529 19*
This friendly little tavern is a great place to savour international and local dishes – steak, roast beef, herring – at affordable prices.

AHRENSBURG: Le Marron   €€
International   Map C2
Lübecker Straße 10A, 22926
Tel *(04102) 23 04 00*
Situated in the Park hotel, Le Marron is highly regarded for its diverse cuisine and impeccable service. The Ahrensburg fish platter and the home-made *Lobscouse* (beef or lamb stew) are not to be missed.

BAD MALENTE: Weisser Hof   €
Regional   Map D1
Vossstraße 45, 23714
Tel *(04523) 992 50*
Sample Holstein food accompanied by German and Austrian wines at this welcoming restaurant. In spring, the menu features asparagus specialities.

FLENSBURG: Im Alten Speicher   €€
International   Map C1
Speicherlinie 44, 24937
Tel *(0461) 120 18*
This large, tastefully decorated restaurant with several dining rooms is located in a quirky, former grain warehouse. Enjoy generous portions of delicious seafood and hearty steak.

DK Choice

HUSUM: Eucken   €€€
International   Map C1
Süderstraße 2–10, 25813
Tel *(04841) 83 30*   **Closed** *Mon & Tue*
An intimate hideaway in the romantic, red-brick Altes Gymnasium hotel. This gourmet restaurant is named after Rudolf Eucken, a former teacher who won the 1908 Nobel Prize for Literature. Enjoy imaginative international dishes with regional influences. The set menus combine exotic fish dishes with veal, calf and lamb.

KIEL: Hotel Bellevue   €€
Seafood   Map C1
Bismarckallee 2, 24105
Tel *(0431) 389 40*
Watch ships sail by on Kiel fjord while enjoying consistently delicious seafood. Superb staff.

The informal terrace with superb views at Hotel Bellevue in Kiel

For more information on types of restaurants *see page 505*

LÜBECK: Historischer Weinkeller
International   €   **Map** D2
Koberg 6–8, 23552
Tel *(0451) 762 34*
Located in the wine cellar of an 13th century hospital, this grand restaurant has retained its historic ambience. The extensive menu has an assortment of meat and regional fish dishes.

LÜBECK: Wullenwever
Regional   €€   **Map** D2
Beckergrube 71, 23552
Tel *(0451) 70 43 33*   **Closed** *Sun & Mon*
Innovative regional cuisine is served in this elegant restaurant with a number of communal and private dining rooms. The chef happily gives out his recipes to interested patrons.

RATZEBURG: Hansa
International   €   **Map** D2
Schrangenstraße 25, 23909
Tel *(04541) 20 94*
The Hansa hotel's restaurant bases its menu around seasonal vegetables and fish. Small dining area with a mellow atmosphere.

SCHLESWIG: Schleswig
International/German   €€   **Map** C1
Strandweg 2, 24837
Tel *(04621) 90 90*
A cheerful restaurant with a family friendly atmosphere, welcoming staff and a great range of dishes. The dining room overlooks the Gahlai river.

SIEK: Alte Schule
Modern German   €€   **Map** D2
Hauptstraße 44, 22962
Tel *(04107) 87 73 10*   **Closed** *Mon*
Set in an old schoolhouse, Alte Schule serves excellent regional

dishes with French influences. The set menus are themed "Earth" and "Sea" to reflect the origin of the ingredients.

SYLT: Sansibar
Regional   €€   **Map** C1
Hörnumer Straße 80, 25980
Tel *(04651) 96 46 46*
A boisterous hangout for Germany's high society, this restaurant has a rustic setting and warm service. Fresh fish and meat dishes attract many visitors each day.

SYLT: Fährhaus
International   €€€   **Map** C1
Heefwai 1, 25980
Tel *(04651) 939 70*   **Closed** *Mon; Oct–May: Sun*
This highly regarded and award-winning restaurant boasts incredible sea views. The chef uses contrasting ingredients and flavours to create delicious dishes.

SYLT: Restaurant Jörg Müller
International   €€€   **Map** C1
Süderstraße 8, 25980
Tel *(04651) 277 88*   **Closed** *Tue*
An acclaimed restaurant attracting guests from all over Europe. The chef blends regional produce in imaginative dishes. Great wine list, too.

UETERSEN: La Cuisine
French   €€   **Map** C2
Marktstraße 25, 25436
Tel *(04122) 40 21 32*   **Closed** *Tue*
Gourmet cuisine from southern France and the Mediterranean. The fish dishes – depending on availability – are particularly good, and there is an excellent selection of French wines.

Mecklenburg-Lower Pomerania

AHLBECK: Das Ahlbeck
International/Regional   €€   **Map** E2
Dünenstraße 48, 17419
Tel *(038378) 499 49 21*
With a grand classical interior and a terrace overlooking the beach, this hotel restaurant is a great choice, especially in summer. On the menu is a mix of regional and international fare.

BAD DOBERAN: Friedrich Franz
International   €€€   **Map** D1
Prof-Dr-Vogel-Straße 16–18, Heiligendamm, 18209
Tel *(038203) 74 00*   **Closed** *Mon & Tue*
There are just 10 tables at this cosy gourmet restaurant in the Grand Hotel Heiligendamm. Dine on regional and French-inspired cuisine with fantastic sea views.

DASSOW: Schlossrestaurant 1745
Mediterranean   €€   **Map** D2
Am Park 1, 23942
Tel *(038827) 884 80*
This romantic fine-dining restaurant in Schwansee castle has vaulted ceilings and serves divine food. The terrace offers sea views, while the snug bar has a fireplace.

GREIFSWALD: Wallensteinkeller
Regional   €   **Map** E1
Markt 3, 17489
Tel *(03834) 85 59 45*
A medieval-themed restaurant with good local soups, roast pork and ribs, all best washed down with one of the draught

The homely yet elegant interior of Fährhaus in Sylt

Key to Price Guide *see page 510*

The atmospheric interior of Scheel's, Stralsund

beers. Look out for the authentic suit of armour near the entrance.

GÜSTROW: Marktkrug €
Traditional German **Map** D2
Markt 14, 18273
Tel *(03843) 68 12 82*
Home-cooked regional food in a rustic house with dining on two floors and a large terrace over-looking the main square. Go for the local speciality *Rippenbraten* (roast ribs), served with delicious local plums.

NEUBRANDENBURG: Gasthaus Zur Lohmühle €
Traditional German **Map** E2
Am Stargarder Tor, 17033
Tel *(0395) 544 28 43*
Set in a lovely half-timbered water mill dating back to the 14th century, this restaurant offers home-cooked German cuisine, including game, fish and Mecklenburg specialities.

NEUBRANDENBURG: Zur Alten Münze €€
Regional **Map** E2
Burg 2–3, Burg Stargard, 17094
Tel *(039603) 274 00* **Closed** *Mon*
The restaurant/*Weinstube* (wine bar) at this beautiful castle estate serves flavourful, uncom-plicated regional dishes and crisp *Flammkuchen.* (thin bread base topped with onions, lardons and crème fraîche)Everyone dresses up on the occasional medieval-themed nights.

ROSTOCK: Silo 4 €€
Regional **Map** D1
Am Strande 3D, 18055
Tel *(0381) 458 58 00* **Closed** *Mon*
This seventh-floor restaurant has a huge panoramic window offering breathtaking harbour views, and a nicely lit bar. Choose from the à la carte menu or take advantage of the fantastic buffet, which is full of regional and sea-food dishes.

DK Choice

ROSTOCK: Der Butt €€€
International **Map** D1
Am Yachthafen 1, 18119
Tel *(0381) 504 00* **Closed** *Sun & Mon*
In the Hohe Düne hotel's restaurant, the award-winning chef uses regional, organic ingredients to create superb French-influenced *haute cuisine.* The two set menus offer an amazing range of delicious dishes. The walk through the glass wine cellar is a particular treat for wine connoisseurs. Reservations recommended.

RÜGEN: Brasserie Loev €€
International **Map** E1
Hauptstraße 20–22, 18609
Tel *(038393) 390*
The Loev Hotel's French-style brasserie is enviably located on the town's main boulevard. Hearty meat and fish dishes and several mouthwatering steak choices feature on the menu.

RÜGEN: Orangerie €€
Seafood **Map** E1
Zeppelinstraße 8, Binz,18609
Tel *(038393) 500*
A wonderful restaurant in the Vier Jahreszeiten hotel, Orangerie offers regional specialities with a different theme every day – barbecue nights, Mediterranean, Nordic and "Gala" buffets.

RÜGEN: Schlossrestaurant Ralswiek €€
International **Map** E1
Parkstraße 35, 18528
Tel *(03838) 203 20*
Enjoy dishes such as *Rügener* (creamy fish soup) and roast Baltic flounder at this restaurant with an emphasis on regional and seasonal ingredients. There are also candlelit dinners and barbecue evenings.

SCHWERIN: Alt Schweriner Schankstuben €
Regional **Map** D2
Schlachterstraße 9–13, 19055
Tel *(0385) 592 53 13*
Waitresses in traditional attire serve filling regional fish and meat dishes at this welcoming restaurant. There is a summer terrace beneath the linden trees.

SCHWERIN: Altstadtbrauhaus Zum Stadtkrug €
Regional **Map** D2
Wismarsche Straße 126, 19053
Tel *(0385) 593 66 93*
This atmospheric brewery/restaurant dating back to 1936 still brews excellent beer in huge copper tanks. There are plenty of hearty meat-based dishes, *Schnitzels* and other regional spcialities.

SCHWERIN: Weinhaus Wöhler €
German/Italian **Map** D2
Puschkinstraße 26, 19055
Tel *(0385) 55 58 30*
This historic *Weinstube* (wine bar) built in 1819 features wood-panelled walls, stained-glass windows and an inner courtyard. The tasty food is a combination of regional and Italian fare.

STRALSUND: Tafelfreuden €€
International **Map** E1
Jungfernstieg 5A, 18437
Tel *(03831) 29 99 20* **Closed** *Mon*
Located in a wooden 19th-century Swedish-style summer villa, this restaurant offers delectable German and Mediterranean dishes, accompanied by a selection of superb wines.

STRALSUND: Scheel's €€€
International **Map** E1
Fährstraße 23–25, 18439
Tel *(03831) 2833113* **Closed** *Mon & Tue*
Sophisticated restaurant in the cellar of the Scheelehof hotel. Exquisite regional meat and fish dishes are served by an enthusiastic young team of chefs.

For more information on types of restaurants *see page 505*

SHOPPING IN GERMANY

Germany is known for its regional handicrafts, high quality manufacturing, good wines and beers, as well as wonderful bread, cakes and fresh produce. Make sure you sample some of the various cakes from the Konditorei. Organic food and produce is also big in Germany, more so than elsewhere in Europe. All towns have the usual international brands of clothing and accessories, as do German department stores. The food markets are a real treat for seasonal local produce and are a meeting place for locals once or twice a week. The pedestrian precinct is also common in German town centres where there is usually a department store, a post office, boutiques and a weekly market, as well as cosy cafés and ice-cream parlours. Often it is considered the social hub of the town.

Opening Hours

In 2003 the law was relaxed and shops were allowed to remain open until 8pm on weekdays and Saturdays. As a general rule, shops open between 9 and 10am and close at 8pm. Department stores are also open until 8pm. However, in smaller towns, shops will often close at lunchtime from 12:30 to 2:30pm and in the evening at 6:30pm. On the last four Sundays before Christmas, shops stay open until 6pm. The only other shops opening on Sundays are those in railway stations and some of the bakeries and cake shops (though these only open for a few hours in the morning). Everything shuts on public holidays. Outside these hours the only places open are petrol stations or railway kiosks. Dispensing chemists work on a rota so that there is always one open 24 hours in each town. Each chemist displays a sign in the window saying which one is on duty.

Methods of Payment and VAT Refunds

Cash is widely used for small items and at markets. Large department stores take credit cards, as do international chains of boutiques. Smaller shops will only accept the local E-Card or debit card and no cheques, so visitors are advised to use cash where credit cards are not taken. Cash machines are widely available, though some are inside the bank and only accessible during opening hours.

Visitors from countries outside the EU can claim a VAT refund (*Mehrwertsteuer*) in shops displaying the Tax-Free sign. Ask for a special form to be completed and, on leaving the country, all forms have to be stamped for a refund at the border, which may be given on the spot or sent to your address. Goods bought tax-free must remain unopened in the original packaging for a valid refund at the border.

Sales

End of season goods are sold off at a discounted price during the twice-yearly sales *(Schlussverkauf)* – in summer at the end of July and in winter at the end of January. Depending on trading, discounts of 30 to 70 per cent may be given.

Food market in Munich selling fresh local farmers' produce

Green Shopping

Germans are very ecologically aware when it comes to shopping and recycling. They buy locally when it comes to basics and fresh fruit and vegetables, supporting local farmers and small businesses. Shoppers can be seen all over the country with their wicker shopping baskets at markets and local stores, and any additional bags are reusable cotton totes, rather than plastic bags. Cotton bags are also available to buy at cash desks in every supermarket or department store, and you are always asked if you need a plastic bag or whether you can do without. Organic shopping has boomed. Several organic supermarkets have opened up

One of Germany's very popular organic supermarkets

in the cities, selling fresh and packaged food, cosmetics, clothing and household goods.

Fashion

What Germany does best in the way of clothing and accessories is casualwear, jeanswear, sportswear and outerwear. Typical brands originating in Germany are Esprit, S. Oliver, Hugo Boss, Bogner, Adidas and Puma. German fashion design is classic, purist and discreet.

Although it is not on a par with Italy or France, well-known names on the international scene include Jil Sander, Strenesse, Wolfgang Joop, Escada and the famous couturier Karl Lagerfeld. Classic department store chains are Karstadt and Galeria Kaufhof; there are also independent department stores such as Ludwig Beck in Munich. Speciality stores (*Fachhandel*) are still common in German towns, especially for leather goods and homeware. International chains have a high presence, though mixed brand boutiques are still thriving.

Factory outlets are another way of getting hold of German design, albeit for seconds or reduced goods. Metzingen has a high concentration – Hugo Boss was the first outlet, followed by Bogner, Jil Sander and Escada. Other stores worth trying here are Villeroy & Boch in Mettlach and Puma in Herzogenaurach.

High fashion in the KaDeWe department store in Berlin

Regional Products

There are many high quality regional products on sale throughout Germany which make ideal souvenirs. The most common are glass from Saxony and Bavaria, porcelain and ceramics from Meissen in Saxony, and gourmet products and intricate carved wooden objects, such as cuckoo clocks, from the Black Forest. Traditional toys, dolls and dolls houses are common around the Nürnberg area with its long standing reputation of toy manufacturing and traditional Christmas markets. In terms of food, marzipan is a speciality of Lübeck, gingerbread comes from Nürnberg, jams from the Black Forest, cheese from Allgäu, ham from Westphalia, and each region has its own special sausages.

Traditional beer tankard

Markets

Once or twice a week, local farmers set up their stalls in town centres in the market square or a car park. They sell farm produce from the region,

Gingerbread (*Lebkuchen*) on sale at a market stall

as well as imported goods, such as exotic fruits. It is a colourful, lively sight full of local flavour. Flea markets are also popular all over Germany.

Food and Drink

Wine and beer are readily available at supermarkets. Specialist wine stores are also common in most towns. Germans drink a lot of sparkling water at home, often mixed with sparkling apple juice (*Apfelsaftschorle*), as well as beer, wine and other soft drinks. All these are bought at the wholesaler (*Getränkemarkt*) with a deposit on bottles and crates. Local food is best sought in the markets, though supermarkets and specialist delicatessen offer a good choice as well.

Size Chart

Women's dresses, coats and skirts

European	36	38	40	42	44	46	48
British	10	12	14	16	18	20	22
American	8	10	12	14	16	18	20

Women's shoes

European	36	37	38	39	40	41
British	3	4	5	6	7	8
American	5	6	7	8	9	10

Men's suits

European	44	46	48	50	52	54	56	58 (size)
British	34	36	38	40	42	44	46	48 (inches)
American	34	36	38	40	42	44	46	48 (inches)

Men's shirts (collar size)

European	36	38	39	41	42	43	44	45 (cm)
British	14	15	15½	16	16½	17	17½	18 (inches)
American	14	15	15½	16	16½	17	17½	18 (inches)

Men's shoes

European	39	40	41	42	43	44	45	46
British	6	7	7½	8	9	10	11	12
American	7	7½	8	8½	9½	10½	11	11½

OUTDOOR ACTIVITIES AND SPECIALIST HOLIDAYS

Germany is home to some of the most active holiday- makers in the world, so it is certainly fitting that there is an abundance of leisure activities available throughout the country. Outdoor pursuits of every kind are readily accessible, from mountain sports, such as climbing, skiing and hiking, to water sports, such as sailing, water-skiing and diving. Numerous other, slightly less adventurous activities such as golf, tennis, biking and spas are available and all are thoroughly organized and regulated. Any regional tourist office can provide you with detailed information and advice about planning your outdoor activities.

Walking in the Trettachtal valley in the Bavarian Alps

General Sporting Information

The **Deutscher Sportbund** can provide a great deal of general information about sport in Germany.

Walking and Hiking

Walking trails are everywhere in Germany, from the most demanding of Alpine trails to gentler excursions in the Erzgebirge of Saxony (see p170) and over the hills and mountains of the picturesque Thuringian Forest (see pp194–5) and Black Forest (see pp330–31).

Before setting off on an expedition you should get maps showing the walking trails in your chosen region. Detailed information can be obtained from the **Deutscher Volkssportverband e.V.** (German Sports Federation) or the **Deutscher Wanderverband** (German Hiking Club). Guided walking excursions can also be organized through the local tourist offices or by contacting the **Deutscher Wanderverband**.

The **DAV Summit Club** is also a very useful source of information.

Cycling

Cycling is a great way of enjoying the German countryside. In most towns and tourist areas, bicycles can be hired for just a few days or for a week or more. A bike can easily be transported on trains and on the urban U-Bahn or S-Bahn trains for a minimal fee. You will find that most towns and cities are bike-friendly with cycle lanes and plenty of bike stands. For those interested in mountain biking and more adventurous cycling there are many great places to visit, and the **ADFC (Allgemeiner Deutscher Fahrrad-Club)** (German Cycling Federation) can supply maps, guidebooks and advice.

Water Sports

Germans enjoy all kinds of water sports. Water-skiing and wake-boarding are extremely popular, especially at lakes equipped with static towing lines, where upon payment of an hourly fee you can take as many trips skiing around the lake as you want. The **Deutscher Wasserski- und Wakeboard Verband e.V.** can provide detailed advice on locations and prices.

There are excellent sailing opportunities in the lakeland areas of Mecklenburg (see pp472–3), the coastal regions and on Lake Constance (see pp324–5). As is the case in most countries, you must demonstrate sailing knowledge before being allowed to hire a full-sized boat or small catamaran by showing a valid sailing licence. To find out more about sailing locations, boat hires and regulations, contact the **Deutscher Segler-Verband e.V.** There are also plenty of opportunities for scuba diving. These are mostly centred on the lakes

Cyclists outside a traditional tavern in Rhineland-Palatinate

or the protected coastal regions. The **Verband Deutscher Sporttaucher (VDST) e.V.** (German Divers' Association) can provide up-to-date advice.

Canoe trips can be taken on many of the country's rivers – from calm and picturesque stretches of water and the canals of the Spreewald *(see p145)*, to exhilarating adventures in rapidly flowing Alpine streams that demand professional skill.

Golfing on the Castle Hotel course in Kronberg, Hesse

Golf and Tennis

Over the last decade or so, golf has become hugely popular in Germany and the number of courses has increased. Golf is usually played at a club, however. You usually need to prove a certain level of golfing proficiency before you are allowed onto the course. This can be achieved by showing a membership card from a course or club back home. Alternatively, look for one of the "Pay & Play" courses, which can be found throughout the country and usually have only six holes. For further information contact the **Deutscher Golf Verband e.V.**

Most large German towns have tennis courts that can be hired for a few hours and there is almost always a private tennis club in all the sizeable towns and cities. For more information on how to make a booking, contact the **Deutscher Tennis Bund e.V**.

Canoeing on a stretch of the River Main in Miltenberg

Skiing and Mountain Sports

The most renowned centre for skiing is still Garmisch-Partenkirchen *(see p284)*. Other regions such as the Black Forest *(see pp330–31)* and the Erzgebirge *(see p170)* also offer skiing. Some of the larger cities have indoor skiing halls, though they are a poor substitute for the Alps *(see pp208–9)*. Cross-country skiing is also popular, and there are many well-prepared routes. Information can be obtained from local tourist information offices or contact the **Haus des Ski, Deutscher Skiverband DSV** (German Ski Association).

The Alps are the centre of German climbing. Here you can find sport climbers mixing with Alpinists. The Allgäu region is probably the most well-known place for climbers but challenges can also be found in the Ries basin. The **Verband Deutscher Berg- und Skiführer (VDBS)** (Association of German Mountain and Ski Guides) can help you with hiring a guide.

Interesting rock formations that provide memorable challenges are not only to be found in the Alps, but throughout Germany. Places such as the Harz Forest *(see p151)*, Fichtelgebirge and the Schwäbische Alb *(see pp304–5)* are all outstanding places for sport climbing. Also, you can find indoor climbing gyms in most cities. The **Deutscher Alpenverein (DAV) Bundesgeschäftsstelle** (German Alpine Association) can help with all your climbing requirements.

National Parks

Germany has a richly varied landscape, from mountains to coasts, and has many nature reserves, biosphere reserves and national parks. From the swamp-like Spreewald *(see p145)* to the lush forests and mountain peaks of the Bavarian Forest *(see p261)*, each park has its own spectacular natural characteristics and offers a range of different visitor services and facilities.

All parks have sign-posted trails and most have special maps for walking, biking or jogging tours. These are also excellent locations for observing and enjoying the flora and fauna of Germany's various regions. Many parks have notices posted to inform visitors about the animals and plants indigenous to the area. To find out more about the various locations and holidays available in Germany's national parks and nature reserves contact the **Verband Deutscher Naturparke** or **Europarc Deutschland e.V.**

Mountain sports in the Schildenstein Mangfall mountains

Camping and Caravanning

During the months of July, August and September there are a great many foreign holiday-makers on Germany's Autobahns heading for the camping parks. The word "camping" in Germany means primarily caravanning, not pitching a tent. Most sites are privately owned and offer a lot of extras. The majority have wash facilities, snack stands or restaurants as well as small shops and play-grounds. The more upscale parks will offer electricity as well as group activities, caravans and bungalows for hire. To find out more contact the **Deutscher Camping-Club e.V.** Tent-pitching holidays are also possible and this is strongly regulated in order to avoid misuse of national parks. Tents are often allowed in the camping parks mentioned above and many national parks have places set aside for tents and campfires. **Backpacker Network Germany e.V.** is a good resource for information about camping.

Burgenstraße (Castle Road) scenic route following the Rhine

Spiegelau, the well-known hiking spot in the Bavarian Forest

Historic and Scenic Routes

Germany has over 50 official driving routes. These routes highlight the best features of an individual region. The following are just a few of many excellent drives. The **Burgenstraße e.V.** (Castle Road) is over 1,000 km (620 miles) long, from Mannheim (see p298) through Bavaria to Prague. It offers plenty of romantic castles and

historical sites. The **Deutsche Märchenstraße** (Fairytale Route) covers more than 600 km (370 miles) from Bremen (see pp434–7) to Hanau (see p381), linking more than 70 towns and villages associated with the Brothers Grimm and the realm of fairytales, sagas, myths and legends. The **Deutsche Weinstraße e.V.** (Wine Route) (see p351) is 85 km (52 miles) and runs from Bad Dürkheim to Bad Berzabern. The **Touristik Arbeitsgemeinschaft Romantische Straße** (Romantic Road) is Germany's most famous and popular tourist route. It runs for 350 km (217 miles) through a rich and varied landscape along the River Main to the Alps. The **Tourismusverband Ruppiner Land e.V. "Deutsche Tonstraße"** (Ceramics Route) is a circular route running 215 km (134 miles) through the Ruppiner Land area of northern Brandenburg (see pp134–5).

Specialist Holidays

Language tours offer you the chance to immerse yourself in German culture. Living arrangements range from homes to hotels and hostels, depending upon budget. The **Goethe Institut** is the best place for information on this type of holiday.

Wine holidays are becoming more commonplace because German wines are coming back into popularity. Most winemakers offer tastings and small meals,

but some also offer packaged holidays. To find out more about wine holidays contact **Deutsches Weininstitut GmbH** or **Viniversität – Die Weinschule GmbH**.

There are equestrian centres in many parts of Germany where visitors can ride under supervision or head off on their own. Specialized weekends or week-long riding vacations are available throughout Germany. More information can be obtained from the **Deutsche Reiterliche Vereinigung e. V.**

Spa Vacations

Germany has more than 350 health and spa resorts, as well as numerous hotels and holiday centres, where your wellbeing is the top priority. Cultural delights, culinary experiences, sights of historical importance and physical activites all form part of the German philosophy of looking after yourself, known as "Das Wellness". Health and fitness breaks are available all year round and facilities vary from the minimalist ultra-modern to marble and gold imperial luxury, with everything in between. Each region has something special to offer, though some of the most well-known spas are in the Black Forest (see pp330–31), on the East Frisian Islands (see p432) and in Schleswig-Holstein (see pp459–69). The **Deutscher Heilbäder-verband e. V.** can help you find the right spa and holiday package.

Wine from the Mosel

DIRECTORY

General Sporting Information

Deutscher Sportbund
Otto-Fleck-Schneise 12,
Frankfurt am Main.
Tel (069) 67 000.
w dosb.de

Walking and Hiking

DAV Summit Club
Am Perlacher Forst 186,
81545 München.
Tel (089) 64 24 00.
w dav-summit-club.de

Deutscher Volks-sportverband e.V.
Fabrikstraße 8,
D-84503 Altötting.
Tel (08671) 963 10.
w dvv-wandern.de

Deutscher Wanderverband
Wilhelmshöher Allee
157–159, D-34121 Kassel.
Tel (0561) 938 730.
w wanderverband.de

Cycling

ADFC (Allgemeiner Deutscher Fahrrad-Club)
Bundesgeschäftsstelle,
Postfach 10 77 47,
28077 Bremen.
Tel (0421) 34 62 90.
w adfc.de

Water Sports

Deutscher Segler-Verband e.V.
Gründgensstr. 18,
22309 Hamburg.
Tel (040) 632 00 90.
w dsv.org

Deutscher Wasserski-und Wakeboard Verband e.V.
Am Campingpark 10,
49597 Rieste.
Tel (5464) 969 11 66.
w wasserski-online.de

Verband Deutscher Sporttaucher (VDST) e.V.
Bundesgeschäftsstelle,
Berliner Str. 312,
63067 Offenbach.
Tel (069) 981 90 25.
w vdst.de

Inline Skating

Inline News
Thalkircher Str. 101,
81371 München.
Tel (089) 747 196 33.
w inlinenews.de

Golf and Tennis

Deutscher Golf Verband e.V.
Postfach 21 06,
65189 Wiesbaden.
Tel (0611) 99 02 00.
w golf.de/dgv

Deutscher Tennis Bund e.V.
Hallerstraße 89,
20149 Hamburg.
Tel (040) 41 17 80.
w dtb-tennis.de

Skiing and Mountain Sports

Deutscher Alpenverein (DAV) Bundesgeschäfts-stelle
Von-Kahr-Str. 2–4,
80997 München.
Tel (089) 14 00 30.
w alpenverein.de

Haus des Ski, Deutscher Skiverband DSV
Am Erwin-Himmelseher-Platz Hubertusstraße 1,
D-82152 Planegg.
Tel (089) 85 79 00.
w deutscherskiver band.de

Verband Deutscher Berg- und Skiführer (VDBS)
Bahnhofstr. 25,
83646 Bad Tölz.
Tel (08041) 793 86 06.
w bergfuehrer-verband.de

National Parks

Europarc Deutschland e.V.
Friedrichstraße 60,
D-10117 Berlin.
Tel (030) 288 788 20.
w europarc-deutschland.de

Verband Deutscher Naturparke
Platz der Vereinten
Nationen 9,
53113 Bonn.
Tel (0228) 921 28 60.
w naturparke.de

Camping and Caravanning

Backpacker Network Germany e.V.
Postfach 160138,
60064 Frankfurt.
Tel (040) 43 18 23 10.
w backpacker network.de/home/

Deutscher Camping-Club e.V.
Mandlstraße 28,
80802 München.
Tel (089) 380 14 20.
w camping-club.de

Historic and Scenic Routes

Burgenstraße e.V
(Castle Road) Allee 28,
D-74072 Heilbronn.
Tel (07131) 56 40 28.
w burgenstrasse.de

Deutsche Märchenstraße
(Fairytale Route)
Kurfürstenstr. 9,
34117 Kassel.
Tel (0561) 920 479 10.
w deutsche-maerchenstrasse.de

Deutsche Weinstraße e.V. (Wine Route)
Martin-Luther-Str. 69,
67433 Neustadt an
der Weinstraße.
Tel (06321) 91 23 33.
w deutsche-weinstrasse.de

Tourismusverband Ruppiner Land e.V. "Deutsche Tonstraße" (Ceramics Route)
Fischbänkenstr. 8,
16816 Neuruppin.
Tel (03391) 65 96 30.
w deutscheton strasse.de

Touristik Arbeitsgemeinschaft Romantische Straße (Romantic Road)
Segringer Str. 19,
91550 Dinkelsbühl.
Tel (09851) 55 13 87.
w romantische strasse.de

Specialist Holidays

Deutsche Reiterliche Vereinigung e.V.
Freiherr von Langen-Straße 13,
48231 Warendorf.
Tel (025 81) 636 20.
w pferd-aktuell.de

Deutsches Weininstitut GmbH
Gutenbergplatz 3–5,
55116 Mainz.
Tel (06131) 282 90.
w deutscheweine.de

Goethe Institut
Dachauer Straße 122,
80637 München.
(Postal address: P.O. Box
19 04 19, 80604 München).
Tel (089) 15 92 10.
w goethe.de
50 Princes Gate,
Exhibition Road,
London SW7 2PH.
Tel (020) 7596 4000
or (020) 7594 0240.

Viniversität – Die Weinschule GmbH
Bilker Allee 49,
40219 Düsseldorf.
Tel (0211) 390 026 50.
w viniversitaet.de

Spa Vacations

Deutscher Heilbäderverband e. V.
Reinhardtstr. 46,
10117 Berlin.
Tel (030) 246 369 20.
w deutscher-heilbaederverband.de

SURVIVAL GUIDE

Practical Information   **542–551**

Travel Information   **552–559**

PRACTICAL INFORMATION

Germany is a country that is particularly well prepared to receive visitors. Every town, large or small, has a helpful tourist information centre that can assist with finding accommodation and provide information about local restaurants, attractions and activities. Virtually all the larger cities have websites with up-to-date information on hotels, restaurants, museums and historic monuments. The country is served by an excellent public transport system and a first-rate network of roads and motorways, which makes getting around quick and easy. There is a plentiful supply of comfortable, affordable tourist accommodation in Germany, but it is worth bearing in mind that hotels can become booked up quickly during the festivals and fairs that occur throughout the year in different parts of the country.

When to Go

In Germany, a pleasant vacation can be enjoyed at any time of the year. If you are planning to visit cities and historic monuments, however, it is best to come in the spring or early autumn. July and August are ideal for a restful holiday by the sea, in the lake districts or in the mountains. Arriving in Bavaria in the last half of September offers the chance to take part in Oktoberfest. In December, Christmas markets all over the country enchant shoppers with their old-world charm, while later in the winter, skiing is a popular pursuit in the Black Forest, the Alps, and the Harz Mountains.

Road traffic increases during school holidays, the dates of which may vary between states. Roads can also be quite busy at the start of the "long weekends" that occur at Easter, Whitsun, and around other national holidays.

Visas and Passports

Citizens of EU countries, apart from the UK and Ireland, can enter Germany with a national identity card. Visitors from the UK, Ireland, the US, Canada, Australia and New Zealand will need a full passport. Non-EU citizens may visit Germany for up to 3 months without a visa, after that a residence permit (*Aufenthaltserlaubnis*) is required. For more information and to check the visa requirements visitors should consult the website of their German embassy. Visitors from South Africa need to obtain a valid visa before entering Germany for any length of stay.

Germany is one of the 25 European countries that are part of the Schengen Agreement for shared border control. Once you enter a Schengen country, you may travel continuously between the member countries for up to 90 days. Non-EU visitors require a passport when entering the Schengen Zone and a Schengen visa is required for visitors from most Asian and African states.

Customs Regulations

German regulations prohibit importation of drugs, animals and exotic plants that are under special protection. Importation of cigarettes is also regulated. An adult may bring in 200 cigarettes or 50 cigars, and 250g (9oz) of tobacco, as well as one litre of spirits and two litres of wine. You can also import up to 5 kg (11 lb) of food, but restrictions apply to meat and dairy products. Beyond these limits, goods must be cleared by Customs when entering the country.

Tourist Information

Tourist information centres can be found in all German cities, as well as most of the larger towns. They provide information on accommodation, addresses and opening hours of historic monuments and museums, cruises, organized excursions and city tours, as well as brochures covering the most important tourist information. They sell useful guide books, maps and postcards and may be able to find and book hotel rooms.

The embassies of most countries, including the UK and US, are located in Berlin. Consulates are also based in other major German cities.

Oktoberfest celebrations at the Theresienwiese, Munich

◀ A modern train station in Germany

Tourist information centre in Berlin

Admission Prices

Admission to museums and monuments can be expensive and prices vary. Entry to a small regional museum, for example, may cost as little as €2–5, a large state-run museum around €5–10, while a private venue may charge up to €12. Admission to smaller churches is usually free, but a fee may be charged in some cathedrals, monastic churches and church treasuries.

In many cases, discounted tickets are available for students, seniors and families. Combination tickets, offering entry to multiple sites, are often good value (see p544).

Opening Hours

Opening hours of shops, offices, and other businesses depend on the size of the town. In larger cities, typical opening hours are from 9am–6pm, while large stores are open until 8pm. Banks have shorter hours in smaller towns (see p548). Trading is limited on Saturdays, especially in rural areas and on Sundays and public holidays, only airport and train station shops are open (see pp534–5).

Museums in Germany are generally open from 9am–6pm, in smaller towns from 10am to 4 or 5pm. Some museums open later, on Wednesdays or Thursdays, while on Mondays most museums tend to be closed. Larger churches in major cities are accessible to tourists throughout the day. In smaller places, visits may require prior arrangements.

Language

Although German is spoken nationwide, many areas have dialects that are virtually incomprehensible, even to those from neighbouring regions. Travellers can usually be understood in Germany by speaking English, particularly in larger cities and in places that are frequented by tourists.

Social Customs and Etiquette

Although generally friendly, Germans tend to be very honest and direct, sometimes to the point of seeming rude. However, most people, particularly the older generation, attach great importance to courteous behaviour. You constantly hear "Guten Tag" when entering a shop, and "Auf Wiedersehen" – or the more youthful "Tschüss" – when leaving. Germans are also very punctual and consider even a small delay to be impolite. Arriving slightly early for an engagement is regarded as courteous.

Among younger Germans, however, ideas of politeness are changing. Older people and women are shown less respect and are no longer automatically offered seats on public transport. Another change is the tolerance shown towards unruly children by parents and other adults.

The German dress code, except in a work environment and among the older generation, is rather casual. Formal dress is required in only the most upmarket restaurants. Nudity in parks and at beaches may shock some visitors.

Most traffic rules are strictly observed. Crossing the street on a red light, even if the road is deserted, is considered an offence and can result in an official reprimand.

Accessibility of Public Conveniences

Public toilets (often automatic cubicles) can usually be found without much difficulty in large cities. Instructions on how to use these facilities are given in several languages on the doors. Public toilets can also be found in museums, cafés, restaurants and department stores. Men's toilets are marked Herren and ladies' Damen or Frauen.

Taxes and Tipping

There are no standard rates for tipping in Germany, but taxi drivers are usually tipped €1–2. Service and tax is generally included on restaurant bills, but it is usual to leave a tip of about 10 per cent of the bill.

Exterior of Brandhorst Museum in Munich (see p224)

Kids' Kingdom at the Deutsches Museum in Munich *(see pp232–3)*

Travellers with Special Needs

Germany is relatively well prepared to receive disabled travellers. Large museums and important historic monuments have ramps or lifts for wheelchair access and public toilet facilities are designed to accomodate disabled travellers. The majority of hotels are well equipped for disabled travellers *(see p491)*. A large proportion of public transport vehicles have been adapted for wheelchair users. Public transport companies are also making efforts to accommodate visually impaired people.

A disabled person may, however, still have problems in gaining access to some places, such as the smaller museums, certain historic monuments, and toilets in restaurants, which are often located in the cellar.

Contact **NatKo** for detailed information on travelling with special needs in Germany. Companies such as **Directions Unlimited** (in the US) and **Holiday Care** (in the UK) also offer useful information and advice for disabled travellers.

Travelling with Children

Families travelling in Germany benefit from a range of cost cutting discounts. The majority of hotels and guesthouses offer discounts for children *(see p491)*. Discounts or even free travel for the youngest children are available on various forms of transport and there are similar concessions in most museums. In many German cities it is possible to purchase family tickets that provide substantial discounts on fares and admission fees.

Restaurants can usually provide a high chair for toddlers and offer a special *Kindermenu* (children's menu) with smaller portions. Public toilets in railway stations, airports and motorway service stations, as well as in many museums and stores, usually offer a separate facility for mothers and babies.

An ISIC card (international student identity card)

Gay and Lesbian Travellers

Germans have a very relaxed and welcoming attitude toward gay travellers, especially in Berlin, Cologne, Hamburg, Munich, and Frankfurt, where there is a lively gay scene with a variety of hotels, clubs and bars. Gay pride is celebrated nationwide with Christopher Street Day parades and festivals throughout June and July. The **National Tourist Office** offers detailed information on gay cultural events nationwide.

Travelling on a Budget

You can save on airfare by travelling to Germany off-season and flying with a low-cost carrier *(see p552)*. Cheap hostels can be found in most German cities, providing an option that is increasingly popular with families *(see p490)*. For eating out, try one of the many cheap eateries *(Imbiss)*, for German *wurst* or ethnic food. Some of the larger German cities sell city cards that double as public transport passes and discount cards at museums and events. City cards can be purchased at tourist offices, many hotels, and public transport ticket counters. For several cities, the cards can also be bought online before travel.

For students, an **International Student Identity Card** (ISIC) entitles the holder to a 50 per cent discount to many museums and reductions on some theatre and cinema tickets. It also allows students to get discounts on hostel prices, air tickets, rental cars and bicycles.

Christopher Street Day celebrations, Berlin

Time

Germany uses Central European Time (GMT plus one hour). Clocks move forward one hour on the last Sunday in March and back on the last Sunday in October.

Electricity

UK 220V appliances can be used with an adaptor; US 110V appliances will also need a transformer.

Responsible Tourism

Germany is one of the most environmentally aware countries in Europe, with 17 per cent of the energy used coming from renewable sources. Agrotourism is gaining popularity as a cost effective holiday option *(see p490),* and bicycle tours and walking holidays are increasingly common *(see p559).* An eco-friendly alternative to staying in a hotel is camping, there are over 2,000 camping sites throughout the Germany *(see p491).*

Hostels and hotels are becoming increasingly aware of environmental issues and encourage the responsible use of resources. German eco-tour operator **Viabono** offers a search engine for eco-hotels and lodges across Germany. The **Blaue Schwalbe** ("Blue Swallow") is an eco-award given to hotels meeting certain sustainability standards and offering organic local food. The **Verträglich Reisen** website provides a full list of accredited hotels. In Bavaria, environmentally friendly hotels are awarded the *Umweltsiegel* (eco-label).

Organic and locally grown produce is clearly labelled and widely available at most shops and supermarkets. Many towns hold regular markets selling organic and traditional produce, allowing visitors to give back to the local community.

Information on local green tourism activities and initiatives can be found in tourist offices.

Stall at Oktomarkt, an organic market in Kollwitzplatz, Berlin

DIRECTORY

Embassies

Australia
Wallstraße 76–79,
10179 Berlin.
Tel (030) 880 08 80.
Fax (030) 880 08 8-210.
[w] germany.embassy.gov.au

Canada
Leipziger Platz 17,
10117 Berlin.
Tel (030) 20 31 20.
Fax (030) 20 31 25 90.
[w] kanada-info.de

Republic of Ireland
Jägerstr. 51,
10117 Berlin.
Tel (030) 22 07 20.
Fax (030) 22 07 22 99.
[w] embassyofireland.de

New Zealand
Friedrichstraße 60,
10117 Berlin.
Tel (030) 20 62 10.
Fax (030) 20 62 11 14.
[w] nzembassy.com

South Africa
Tiergartenstraße 18,
10785 Berlin.
Tel (030) 22 07 30.
Fax (030) 22 07 31 90.
[w] suedafrika.org

United Kingdom
Embassy: Wilhelmstraße
70, 10117 Berlin.
Tel (030) 20 45 70.
Fax (030) 20 45 75 49.
[w] britische botschaft.de
Consulate: Harvestehuder
Weg 8a, 20148 Hamburg.
Tel (040) 448 03 20.
Fax (040) 410 72 59.

United States of America
Embassy: Pariser Platz 2,
10117 Berlin.
Tel (030) 8 30 50.
Fax (030) 83 05 10 50.
[w] usembassy.de
Consulates:
Clayallee 170,
40191 Berlin.
Tel (030) 8305-1200.

Königinstraße 5,
80539 Munich.
Tel (089) 288 80.
Gießener Str. 30,
60435 Frankfurt am Main.
Tel (069) 7535-0.

Tourist Offices

National Tourist Office
PO Box 2695, London,
W1A 3TN, UK.
Tel (020) 7317 0908.
[w] germany-tourism.de

Berlin Tourist Information
Tel (030) 25 00 25.
[w] visitberlin.de/en

Travellers with Special Needs

Directions Unlimited
123 Green Lane, Bedford
Hills, NY 10507, USA.
Tel (800) 533 53 43.

Holiday Care
Tel 0845 124 9971.

[w] holidaycare.org or
[w] tourismforall.org.uk

NatKo e.V. (Nationale Koordinationsstelle Tourismus für Alle)
Düsseldorf. **Tel** (0211) 336
80 01. [w] natko.de

Gay and Lesbian Travellers

[w] gay-web.de
[w] gay.de/
[w] cometogermany.com

Travelling on a Budget

ISIC Card
[w] isic.org

Responsible Tourism

Blaue Schwalbe
[w] sanftes-reisen.org.

Viabono
Tel (02205) 919 83 53.
[w] viabono.de

Verträglich Reisen
[w] vertraeglich-reisen.de

Security and Health

Germany is a safe place for visitors, but it is always a good idea to take sensible precautions especially in larger towns and cities. Extra caution should be taken against pickpockets – particularly on public transport or in busy tourist areas. It is worth using a money belt or other means of hiding your money and documents. Taking out medical insurance cover is always advisable when travelling abroad, but for minor health problems that do not require the services of a doctor, pharmacists are a good and easily accessible source of assistance.

Policeman and policewoman

Police

German police can be easily identified by their blue uniforms, except in Bavaria and the Saarland where the traditional green uniforms are still worn. Investigators of criminal offences, *Kriminalpolizei*, are generally dressed in plain clothes. They will produce their identification and badge as necessary.

Municiple officers and traffic wardens also wear the navy-blue uniforms. They are in charge of minor offences such as illegal parking, crossing at a red light, littering or riding a bicycle on the sidewalk and are entitled to check documents and issue fines.

To report a crime, it is necessary to go to a local police station (*Polizeiabschnitt*) and, in event of theft, get a *Bericht*, the report required by insurance. In the case of a traffic accident or an emergency, call 110 or 112.

What to Be Aware of

Violent crime is very rare in Germany and the law is enforced energetically. The most serious threat for a tourist is always the pickpocket. These thieves tend to prowl in crowded places, such as railway platforms, train carriages and buses. They also frequent popular tourist sights and any events where large groups of people are likely to gather. It is best to leave your valuable items and documents in the hotel safe. Park your car in the hotel car park whenever possible and never leave valuable items in the vehicle, especially if it has to be left in the street overnight. Should you become the victim of a crime, the **Crime Victim Hotline** offers a counselling service.

Buying counterfeit items like cigarettes from street vendors is an offence and should be avoided.

Although alcohol is sold at every fuel station, drinking and driving is not a good idea and it is against the law to drive with a blood alcohol level over 50mg/dl, the equivalent of one beer.

It is illegal to use your mobile phone while driving or even sitting in a car with the engine running; doing so can result in a fine of €40.

Be aware of cyclists. They tend to be everywhere but the autobahn, and have right of way in dedicated bike lanes.

A woman travelling on her own will not surprise anyone in Germany and only the usual safety precautions need be taken. However, it is best to avoid certain areas in towns where there is a lively nightlife, particularly in large cities – for example, the Reeperbahn in Hamburg. Hitchhiking is quite popular in Germany, but a better option for single women may be to use the services of *Mitfahrzentrale (see p557)*.

In an Emergency

The national emergency number for medical assistance and the fire brigade is 112. In a medical emergency, call an ambulance, which will take you to the nearest emergency room (*Rettungsstelle*). In large hotels, medical care for minor ailments can often be provided on the premises.

If a road accident or breakdown occurs call for help on your mobile phone (110 or 112 for police and ambulance). Several breakdown companies offer roadside assistance *(see p557)*. If your car breaks down in the middle of nowhere, you can call 0800 6 683 663 on your mobile phone. This automobile emergency service is equipped to track you down.

If you witness a crime on the platform of an underground or commuter railway, a designated emergency alarm button can be used to summon assistance. Special alarm buttons, within small red boxes, also provide a direct connection with the fire brigade (*Feuerwehr*). These alarm buttons are easy to find, usually located in prominent positions on the streets and in large department stores.

In an emergency, consulate officials can help travellers with legal or other advice, locate a translator, or contact family members. In some circumstances they may be able to lend money for a ticket home *(see p545)*.

Alarm button for the fire brigade

Fire engine from the Berlin fire brigade

Ambulance of the paramedic rescue services

Traditionally coloured white and blue police car

Lost and Stolen Property

Before leaving home it is advisable to take out an insurance policy to cover property against loss or theft. Theft and burglaries must be reported to the police immediately and a certificate obtained to confirm that the loss has been reported; this is needed if an insurance claim is submitted.

If property has been lost, it is worth checking at a lost property office (*Fundbüro*). These exist in every German city. The **Deutsche Bahn** has its own lost property offices, as do transport systems in individual towns.

In the event of a lost or stolen mobile phone, inform the service provider immediately to have the account locked and avoid unwanted charges on your bill. They may also be able to trace the phone. You should also report a theft to the nearest police station. The police will need the phone's identification

number (IMEI). To replace lost or stolen passports, visit your local consulate who can issue a replacement. Keep a photocopy of your passport/ID in your luggage to reduce hassle if it gets lost or stolen.

Hospitals and Pharmacies

For a serious illness or injury, visit a hospital (*Krankenhaus*) or call an ambulance. All emergency rooms are part of the public health system, so your EHIC or supplementary insurance will cover you. The symbol for hospitals is a red cross on white background.

Pharmacies in Germany are indicated by a red stylized letter "A" for *Apotheke* and are usually open 8am–6pm; in small towns they may close 1–3pm. In larger towns there is always a rota and this is clearly displayed in the window of each pharmacy with a note of addresses. Information on rota pharmacies may also be obtained from tourist offices, local newspapers or the Internet.

Minor Hazards

Germany poses few serious health hazards for travellers. Tap water is safe to drink throughout the country, there are no prevalent diseases, and the country is well served with

Entrance to a pharmacy in Heidelberg

hospitals and pharmacies. No vaccinations are required when entering Germany. However, ticks are prevalent in forests and rural areas, especially during summer, and visitors should seek medical advice if bitten.

Health Insurance

Citizens of countries within the European Union with a European Health Insurance Card (EHIC) are entitled to free medical care in Germany. It is also advisable to take out some form of supplementary health insurance, as some services, such as repatriation costs, are not covered.

If plans include sporting activities, particularly dangerous sports, make sure the policy covers rescue services (for example, mountain rescue). This type of insurance is usually much more expensive.

Banking and Local Currency

Debit and credit cards are widely accepeted in Germany, but it is still advisable to travel with some cash. Some of the smaller shops, cafés, and bars, do not accept credit cards. Cash can be easily obtained from automatic cash points (ATMs), and bank branches are easy to find. Bureaux de change are located at airports and larger railway stations.

Banks and Bureaux de Change

There are no limits on the amount of foreign currency that can be brought into the country and credit and debit cards are accepted in most of the larger hotels, restaurants and shops. Foreign currency can be exchanged in a bank or exchange bureau (*Wechselstube*). Both offer a similar rate, but usually charge a commission. Be sure to check commission rates and confirm how much you will have to pay before beginning a transaction. Money can also be changed at special ATMs. Some hotel reception desks will change cash, but the exchange rate may be poor.

Most banks are open Monday–Friday 9am–5pm, with a break for lunch, and once a week they are open until 6pm. Opening hours may be a little longer in larger cities and some of the larger branches open until 1pm on Saturdays. It is often more convenient to take advantage of the services offered by branches located in airports and larger railway stations as soon as you arrive.

Cash point machine (*Geldautomat*)

Travellers' cheques are best purchased in euro denominations and can be used to pay for goods and services or hotel bills, but they are not always accepted. It is often better to pay by cash or card.

For wiring money, contact a Western Union branch in a major city. If you hold a bank-issued **Visa** or **MasterCard** credit card, you can transfer money through the **Western Union Bank** website.

For all financial transactions in Germany, decimals are indicated by a comma and thousands by a point.

ATMs

The most convenient way to get cash is at an ATM (*Geldautomat*), found on main streets and in shopping centres, airports and railway stations. Most have multilingual instructions or are self-explanatory and carry logos showing which cards are accepted.

Costs for cash withdrawals vary, so contact your bank for advice before traveling, to avoid any high fees.

Debit and Credit Cards

In Germany, the most popular cards are **Maestro** debit cards. **Visa**, **MasterCard** and **American Express** are widely accepted; **Diner's Club** a little less so. Always check that credit or debit cards are an acceptable method of payment before making a purchase, and watch for minimum charges in restaurants and cafés.

Lost credit cards or travellers' cheques should be reported immediately to the issuing bank or company.

DIRECTORY

Lost Credit Cards/ Travellers' Cheques

All Cards
Tel 116 116
(nationwide free number).

American Express
Tel (069) 97 97 10 00.

Barclaycard
Tel (040) 89 09 98 77.

Diner's Club
Tel 01805 070704.

EC/Maestro and Bank Cards
Tel 01805 021021.

MasterCard
Tel 0800 819 10 40.

VISA
Tel 0800 811 8440.

Wiring Money

Western Union Bank
Tel 0800 33 44 33 55
(free hotline).
Tel (0180) 18 18 123 (English).
w westernunionbank.com

A branch of Sparkasse branch, Berlin

Currency

The euro (€) is the common currency of the European Union. It went into general circulation on 1 January 2002. Germany was one of the 12 original countries taking the euro; the Deutschmark was phased out by mid-2002. EU members using the euro as sole official currency are known as the Eurozone.

Euro notes are identical throughout the Eurozone countries, each one including designs of fictional architectural structures and monuments. The coins, however, have one side identical (the value side), and one side with an image unique to each country. Both notes and coins are accepted in all of the participating EU countries (not all European nations belong to the Eurozone).

Euro Bank Notes

Euro bank notes have seven denominations. The €5 note (grey in colour) is the smallest, followed by the €10 note (pink), €20 note (blue), €50 note (orange), €100 note (green), €200 note (yellow) and €500 note (purple). All notes show the stars of the European Union.

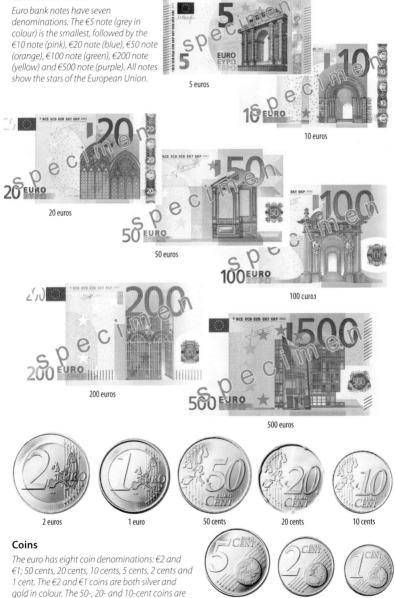

5 euros

10 euros

20 euros

50 euros

100 euros

200 euros

500 euros

2 euros

1 euro

50 cents

20 cents

10 cents

Coins

The euro has eight coin denominations: €2 and €1; 50 cents, 20 cents, 10 cents, 5 cents, 2 cents and 1 cent. The €2 and €1 coins are both silver and gold in colour. The 50-, 20- and 10-cent coins are gold. The 5-, 2- and 1-cent coins are bronze.

5 cents

2 cents

1 cent

Communications and Media

Postal and telecommunications services in Germany work very efficiently. Though it may be necessary to queue for a few minutes for service, letters and postcards are usually delivered within the country in 24 hours. Public phones are simple to use, many with foreign language instructions, but they are becoming rarer due to the popularity of mobile phones. The distinctive yellow mail-boxes are a common sight.

Telekom phones at Frankfurt Hauptbahnhof

International and Local Telephone Calls

Public telephones are serviced by **Deutsche Telekom** and can still be found in busy places like railway stations and malls. Most phones will only accept telephone cards, which can be purchased at Telekom shops, fuel stations and newsstands. Some older telephones however, are coin-operated and require a minimum deposit, which is the cost of a single local call. Travellers can also purchase an international phone card, which is valid in several countries and can be used when calling from a public telephone, a mobile or a hotel phone. The cards offer low rates on calls abroad and have a prepaid balance – ask to see call rates before purchase.

Call shops are common in all major German cities and provide an economical way to make international calls. They usually charge a small initial fee, and then offer a low rate per minute, which is paid at the end of the call. These shops also sell international phone cards and often double as Internet cafés.

Depending on the time and day, different tariffs apply to local, intercity and international calls. The most expensive period to make a call is between 7am and 6pm. Calls cost less between 6pm and 9pm, and later in the evening they are even cheaper. Likewise, calls are cheaper on weekends than on weekdays.

Mobile Phones

Mobile phone coverage is generally good throughout the country, although the signal may be weaker in more remote areas. German mobile phones use standard European frequencies, so UK phones will work provided they have a roaming facility enabled. North American phones will only operate in Germany if they are tri- or quad-band.

Making and receiving calls outside your home country can be very expensive and travellers should check roaming charges before travel. If you are planning to use your phone frequently, it may be economical to buy a local SIM card with a German telephone number from a local provider such as **Base**. Check with your service provider to ensure your phone is SIM-unlocked and compatible with local technology. Anti-terrorism laws have made it more complicated for non-residents to buy a SIM card, as travellers will need a valid ID and a German address (a hotel address should work).

If your phone is Wi-Fi capable, you can save on roaming costs by locating a free Wi-Fi (wireless Internet) network and making calls with **Skype**. Bear in mind that as useful as a smartphone can be overseas, all data use will be charged at a higher rate.

It is wise to carry your mobile provider's contact details so you can deactivate your card if your phone is lost or stolen.

Internet and Email

Many hotels include Internet access in their room rates, but this varies, so be sure to check in advance. Some hotels have Internet terminals allowing guests to check emails and go online for free.

Internet cafés, where online access can be obtained for a small fee (typically €1–2 per hour), can be found in most towns and cities. Usually, the higher the number of terminals,

Useful Telephone Numbers

- Directory enquiries, national numbers: 11 833 or 11 837 (English service).
- National telephone directory (White Pages): www.dastelefonbuch.de
- Directory enquiries, international numbers: 11 834.
- International calls: Dial 00, wait for dialling tone, then dial country code, area code + number, omitting first 0.
- Country codes: UK 44; Eire 353; Canada and US 1; Australia 61; South Africa 27; New Zealand 64.

the better the rates. If you are going to be online for a while, a special multi-hour pass may be the most cost effective option.

Wi-Fi access is increasingly available in Germany. Expect to find Wi-Fi at many cafés, libraries, hostels and hotels. Most networks are password-protected and an access code is required, although it is often provided free of charge to the customer. Free Wi-Fi hotspots are located in public areas around most larger towns and cities.

Postal Services

Dedicated Deutsche Post offices have virtually disappeared and postal services are instead offered by **Postbank Finanzcenter**, newsstands and some other shops, including selected supermarkets. These retailers also sell phone cards, postcards and mailing supplies.

Stamps are sometimes sold with postcards, or can be bought from vending machines. It costs €0.65 to send a postcard anywhere in Europe and €1 to overseas destinations. When posting a letter in a mail-box, be aware that some boxes have two slots – one for local post only, the other for all other destinations.

Germany also has a private mail network, **PIN Mail**, which

Postbank logo

Information plaque indicating the collection times

Opening for local letters

Opening for long-distance mail

The distinctive yellow mail-box of Germany's official postal service

A kiosk selling newspapers and cigarettes

offers competitive prices for mail and package delivery.

For quick delivery of a package, look for one of the courier services. **DHL** is the national parcel delivery service. Packages can be sent via DHL from post offices or DHL-affiliated retailers. **Federal Express** or **UPS** are also available, but they are more business-oriented.

Newspapers and Magazines

Every city or state has its own newspapers and listings magazines. In Berlin the most widely read newspapers are *Berliner Zeitung*, *Der Tagesspiegel* and *Berliner Morgenpost*. In southern Germany it is *Süddeutsche Zeitung*. Popular national newspapers include *Frankfurter Allgemeine Zeitung* and *Bild*. *Der Spiegel*, Germany's leading news magazine, has an English-language version online. Major German cities have a listings magazine called *PRINZ* – where *PRINZ* is not available, ask for the *Stadtmagazin*.

Foreign language publications, such as the *International Herald Tribune*, the *Guardian*, *Le Monde*, *El País*, and *Corriere della Sera*, are available at kiosks, railway stations and airports, as well as in more expensive hotels.

Television and Radio

German television is exclusively in German – all foreign movies are dubbed rather than subtitled. Non-German broadcasts are hard to find, but hotels usually provide some English-language

channels, such as *BBC World*, *CNN* and *NBC Super Channel*.

German sports channels often show soccer highlights, and major sporting events can be watched at most sports bars. Very little English-language radio is available terrestrially, although *BBC World* and *NPR* can be picked up in most parts of Germany.

DIRECTORY

International and Local Calls

Deutsche Telekom
w telekom.com

Mobile Phones

BASE
w base.de

Skype
w skype.com

Internet and Email

Internet cafés
w online-cafes.net

Wi-Fi hotspots
w hotspot-locations.de

Postal Services

DHL Express
Tel (0)1805 34 53 001 (national).
Tel (0)1805 34 53 003 (international).

FedEx
Tel (0)1803 123 800.

PIN Mail
w pin-ag.de.

Postbank Finanzcenter
w postbank.de

UPS
Tel (0)1805 882 663.

TRAVEL INFORMATION

Travelling in Germany is very efficient and easy. All of the big cities have airports, most of which offer international connections. The entire country is linked by a dense network of motorways with convenient facilities for travellers, while main roads are also of a high standard and are well signposted. Rail travel throughout the country is comfortable and reliable; for longer journeys it is worth taking advantage of the fast connections offered by InterCity Express (ICE). Buses are also comfortable and efficient and are particularly useful in rural areas not served by rail. In German cities, trams, buses and sometimes underground rail systems provide reliable services.

The arrival hall of Dusseldorf airport

Arriving by Air

Germany's most important airports are Frankfurt am Main, Munich, Cologne-Bonn and Düsseldorf, from where connecting flights can be made to other German cities. Airport expansion in Berlin will create a major air hub on completion in 2015.

The country's national carrier, **Lufthansa**, operates regular, scheduled flights to most of the world's major destinations. **British Airways** also offers regular flights to Germany from London (Heathrow and Gatwick) as well as from several regional airports in the United Kingdom.

The US is well served, with flights to German cities, particularly to Frankfurt, which is Germany's largest airport and one of the busiest in Europe. Direct flights are usually available from major US cities, including New York (JFK), Washington, DC, Boston, Chicago, San Francisco and Los Angeles. Although Canada does not have many direct flights to Germany, **AirCanada** operates a regular flight from Toronto to Frankfurt.

Among the busiest airports are Düsseldorf, Munich, and Cologne-Bonn. In 2015, Tegal airport in Berlin will close to make way for the Berlin Brandenburg International Airport (BBI) at Schönefeld, a major new airport, which will serve the whole of the capital. Frankfurt am Main is the largest German airport and is comprised of two huge terminals, which are connected by a fast overground railway. The modern Munich airport is somewhat smaller but still very busy. When changing planes, transfers may take longer due to the long walk between two terminals. Düsseldorf is smaller than Frankfurt and Munich Airports and easier to navigate, with a central building connecting the three terminals. Cologne-Bonn, a smaller airport, is usually hassle-free. Leipzig-Halle is an important air-traffic hub in the east of Germany due to its built-in train station that connects to the long-distance railway network.

Control tower at Munich's international airport

Tickets and Fares

The cost of scheduled airfares can vary considerably, so early reservation and online price comparison is a good idea. Cheap Apex tickets work for those who are unlikely to change their travel plans. They are not available for one-way journeys. All Apex airfares must be booked well in advance (usually at least 14 days); some require a 28-day advance booking to qualify for the lowest airline ticket prices.

When buying a ticket it is worth finding out about any price reductions for children, young people and elderly passengers. Students and passengers under the age of 26 are often eligible for discounts. If the journey is going to be undertaken by a large group, it is worth checking whether a group discount on the fare or a free ticket for the group leader is available.

Once booked, it is extremely difficult if not impossible to reschedule discount tickets, so it is wise to take out insurance to cover the loss if travel plans have to be changed.

The exterior of Cologne Bonn airport

The cheapest airfares are often those offered by low-cost, no-frills airlines such as **EasyJet** and **Ryanair**, or by discount agents. The latter offer discounted seats on charter or scheduled flights.

Domestic Flights

In addition to Lufthansa, there are a number of other smaller carriers in Germany including **Air Berlin** and **German Wings**. These carriers provide air links with small airports, such as Augsburg, Dortmund and Erfurt, that would not be economically viable for Lufthansa to operate. Smaller airlines often offer cheaper fares than Lufthansa on internal routes.

On Arrival

Prior to departure, you should check with authorities or online which items cannot be brought to Germany and what the import regulations are *(see p542)*. Normally, clearing customs and immigration is fast and painless in German airports.

All major German airports are served by public transportation. Information on transport into the city centre, tickets and fares can be found in the arrival hall or the lobby. Tickets should be purchased from vending machines before boarding trains or buses.

On most forms of public transport, one or two pieces of luggage may be carried at no extra cost, for two or more items you may be charged extra.

Taxis are available from all of the main city airports. It is best to pre-book a taxi or confirm the cost of the journey before travelling.

DIRECTORY

Airlines

Air Berlin
Tel (01805) 73 78 00.
W airberlin.com

Air Canada
W aircanada.com

British Airways
Tel (01805) 00 34 19.
W britishairways.com

Continental
Tel (01803) 21 26 10.
W continental.com

Delta Air Lines
Tel (01803) 33 78 80.
W delta.com

EasyJet
Tel (01805) 02 92 92.
W easyjet.com

German Wings
Tel (0871) 702 99 87.
W germanwings.com

Lufthansa
Tel (01805) 83 84 26.
W lufthansa.com

Qantas
Tel (01805) 25 06 20.
W qantas.com

Ryanair
W ryanair.com

United Airlines
Tel (069) 50 07 03 87.
W united.com

Airport	Information	Distance from Centre	Journey Time to Centre by Taxi	Journey Time to Centre by Public Transport
Berlin Schönefeld	(0180) 500 01 86	20 km (12 miles)	45 min	S-Bahn: 35 min
Cologne-Bonn	(02203) 40 400 1	Bonn: 28 km (17.5 miles); Cologne: 17 km (10.5 miles)	Bonn: 15 min Cologne: 20 min	Bus to Bonn: 35 min Bus to Cologne: 45 min
Dresden	(0351) 881 33 60	9 km (5.5miles)	25 min	Bus: 30 min
Düsseldorf	(0211) 42 10	8 km (5 miles)	25 min	S-Bahn: 13 min
Frankfurt am Main	(01805) 372 46 36	10 km (6 miles)	20 min	Train: 11 min S-Bahn: 10 min
Hamburg	(040) 50 75 25 57	13 km (8 miles)	30 min	Bus: 30 min
Hannover	(0511) 97 70	12 km (7.5 miles)	20 min	S-Bahn: 13 min
Leipzig-Halle	(0341) 224 11 55	Leipzig: 20 km (12 miles); Halle: 24 km (15 miles)	Leipzig: 30 min Halle: 40 min	S-Bahn to Leipzig: 15 min S-Bahn to Halle: 12 min
Munich	(089) 97 52 13 13	40 km (25 miles)	45 min	S-Bahn: 40 min Bus: 45 min
Nürnberg	(0911) 937 00	6 km (4 miles)	20 min	Bus: 45 min U-Bahn: 12 min

Travelling by Train and Ferry

Travelling around Germany by train is not the cheapest form of transport, but it is undoubtedly one of the most comfortable. German trains are renowned for their punctuality, safety and cleanliness, though in peak travel season, visitors may feel that these are a little overrated. Germany is also well served by ports to which ferries and passenger ships operate.

InterCity Express train

Arriving by Train

There are regular rail services into Germany from most European cities. Travelling by train from the UK usually costs more than flying. The most common routes into Germany are to travel to Brussels by **Eurostar** or take the **Eurotunnel** shuttle to France and continue your journey by road or rail.

Travelling by Train

Germany's fastest trains, InterCity Express (ICE), can travel at more than 200 km/h (125 mph), which means that a journey from Hamburg to Munich takes only a few hours. *ICE* and *ICE Sprinter* trains (even faster) operate on routes linking the largest cities.

Somewhat slower and less expensive are the *InterCity (IC)* trains, which stop only at larger towns and cities. When travelling over shorter distances it is often quicker to take the *Regional Express (RE)* trains. Alternative service providers like **Interconnex** and **Metronom** often have lower fares than **Deutsche Bahn** but run less frequently.

Train aficionados can enjoy a trip on one of the steam-engine trains travelling along the Baltic coast (**Rasender Roland**) or a mountain route (**Brockenbahn**).

Logo of German railways
(Deutsche Bahn)

Railway Stations

In large towns and cities, railway stations are generally located in the centre. They include several shops (often open on Sundays), car rental firms, hotel reservation bureaux, and other services, such as cash points, left luggage provision and public toilets with shower facilities.

Tickets and Fares

Train fares are expensive in Germany and express trains have a surcharge (*Zuschlag*). For multiple train trips, buy a BahnCard, which gives a 25 or 50 per cent discount. Otherwise, discounts are available only if tickets are bought 3 or 7 days ahead and low-price seats have not sold out.

When planning a lengthy stay in Germany and travelling around the country, it is worth acquiring an InterRail card, which is available to every European citizen, regardless of age. Regional tickets, offering unlimited travel within a state for a set period of time, are also available. Each year the variety of discounted fares to which this card entitles the bearer is extended, so it is worth checking out the full range. Schoolchildren and students

DIRECTORY

Travelling by Train

Brockenbahn/Harzer Schmalspurbahn
Tel (03943) 55 80.
w hsb-wr.de

Deutsche Bahn
Tel (01805) 99 66 33.
Tel (08718) 80 80 66 (UK).
w bahn.de
w bahn.co.uk

Eurostar
Tel 08432 186 186.
w eurostar.com

Eurotunnel
Tel 08443 35 35 35.
w eurotunnel.com

Interconnex (Rostock-Berlin-Leipzig)
Tel (01805) 101616.
w interconnex.com

Metronom (Bremen-Hamburg-Hannover-Göttingen)
Tel (0581) 164 164.
w der-metronom.de

Brockenbahn
Tel (03943) 55 80.
w hsb-wr.de

Rasender Roland
Tel (03838) 813 594.
w rasender-roland.de

Tickets and Fares

InterRail
w interrailnet.com

Eurail
w eurail.com

Ferries

Color Lines
Tel (0047) 22 94 42 00 (calling from outside of Germany).
w colorline.com

Scandlines
Tel (0049) 381 543 50 (calling from outside of Germany).
w scandlines.de

Train Routes and Ferry Ports in Germany

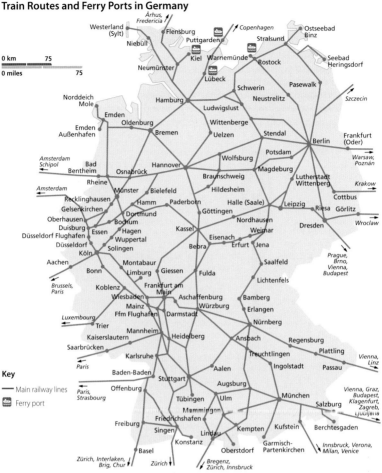

Árhus,
Fredericia
Westerland
(Sylt)
Flensburg
Niebüll
Copenhagen
Ostseebad
Binz
Puttgarden
Stralsund
0 km   75
0 miles   75
Kiel
Warnemünde
Rostock
Seebad
Heringsdorf
Neumünster
Lübeck
Norddeich
Mole
Hamburg
Schwerin
Neustrelitz
Pasewalk
Szczecin
Emden
Ludwigslust
Emden
Außenhafen
Oldenburg
Bremen
Wittenberge
Uelzen
Stendal
Berlin
Frankfurt
(Oder)
Amsterdam
Schipol
Bad
Bentheim
Hannover
Wolfsburg
Potsdam
Magdeburg
Warsaw,
Poznán
Rheine
Osnabrück
Braunschweig
Lutherstadt
Wittenberg
Krakow
Amsterdam
Münster
Bielefeld
Hildesheim
Halle (Saale)
Leipzig
Riesa
Cottbus
Görlitz
Recklinghausen
Hamm
Paderborn
Göttingen
Wroclaw
Gelsenkirchen
Dortmund
Nordhausen
Dresden
Oberhausen
Bochum
Kassel
Weimar
Duisburg
Hagen
Eisenach
Düsseldorf Flughafen
Essen
Wuppertal
Bebra
Erfurt
Jena
Düsseldorf
Solingen
Prague,
Brno,
Vienna,
Budapest
Köln
Aachen
Montabaur
Saalfeld
Bonn
Limburg
Giessen
Fulda
Lichtenfels
Brussels,
Paris
Koblenz
Frankfurt am
Main
Wiesbaden
Aschaffenburg
Bamberg
Mainz
Würzburg
Erlangen
Luxembourg
Ffm Flughafen
Darmstadt
Nürnberg
Trier
Mannheim
Heidelberg
Anspach
Regensburg
Kaiserslautern
Saarbrücken
Karlsruhe
Treuchtlingen
Plattling
Vienna,
Linz
Paris
Baden-Baden
Aalen
Ingolstadt
Passau
Offenburg
Stuttgart
Augsburg
München
Vienna, Graz,
Budapest,
Klagenfurt,
Zagreb,
Ljubljana
Paris,
Strasbourg
Tübingen
Ulm
Salzburg
Freiburg
Memmingen
Friedrichshafen
Singen
Lindau
Kempten
Kufstein
Berchtesgaden
Basel
Konstanz
Oberstdorf
Garmisch-
Partenkirchen
Innsbruck, Verona,
Milan, Venice
Zürich, Interlaken,
Brig, Chur
Zürich
Bregenz,
Zürich, Innsbruck

Key

— Main railway lines

Ferry port

---

are entitled to a reduced-rate card. Non-European residents can buy a Eurail global, regional or country pass.

Train tickets can be bought and reservations made online, at travel agents or at the *Reisezentrum* (travel centre) at railway stations. It is simple to plan your journey yourself using this facility. Reservations cost €5 per person for a return trip if paid online with a ticket purchase, or €9 at a ticket counter.

Advance booking is necessary for ICE Sprinter and Thalys trains (between Cologne and Aachen). The sleeper CityNightLine trains also require reservations. On all other trains, reservations are advisable when travelling at peak times or in a group.

Arriving by Ferry

Visitors travelling to Germany by car from the UK will have to decide which crossing to use (unless using the Channel Tunnel). The crossings from Dover to Ostend, in Belgium, or to Calais, in France, are the shortest, while the Harwich to Hook of Holland route is useful for those travelling from further

north. There are many links between German ports and other countries. The main ferry terminals are Kiel, Lübeck and Rostock on the Baltic Sea coast. Color Lines run a service from Oslo (Norway) to Kiel and Scandlines operate between Trelleborg (Sweden) to Rostock and Sassnitz. Scandlines also run ferries from Denmark.

Ship taking passengers to Helgoland

Travelling by Car and Coach

A fast and comfortable way of travelling around Germany is to use the motorways. The excellent network of toll-free routes guarantees fast progress over longer distances, while a well-maintained system of main roads enables you to reach interesting places throughout the country. Motorways have the advantage of regularly sited service stations, where travellers can stop for fuel and something to eat. On lesser roads and in remote areas, petrol stations may be few and far between.

A selection of traffic signs one might encounter on German roads

Arriving by Car

With the addition of Poland and the Czech Republic to the Schengen Area, border check-points are now largely non-existent. Border stations do occasionally check cars, and trucks. Trains and tourist buses are sometimes stopped for passport checks.

Those wishing to drive to Germany from the UK will need to travel to France with their vehicle either by ferry or on the Eurotunnel shuttle (see p554).

What You Need

When driving in Germany, visitors must carry a valid driving licence as well as their vehicle's registration document and a valid insurance policy. All cars must carry a plate indicating country of origin, a first-aid kit and a red warning triangle for use in case of breakdown.

If you plan to drive in large cities, check whether you need an environmental badge (Umweltplakette, see p558).

Roads and Tolls

The German motorway network is extensive. Roads

Motorway telephone

are toll-free and have regularly spaced petrol stations as well as service areas with parking areas, toilets, restaurants and motels. On the hard shoulder there are yellow poles with emergency buttons, which can be used to call for help in case of breakdown or accident. An Autobahn (motorway) is indicated by the letter "A" and a number – some also have a letter "E" and a number, denoting that the road crosses the German border. A Bundesstraße (main road) is indicated by the letter "B" and a number.

Additional Road Signs

In addition to internationally understood road signs on German roads, there are a few other signs. On motorways, for example, a yellow triangular warning sign with a row of cars is a warning about the possibility of traffic jams, which may be accompanied by the word Stau. On mountain roads, a warning sign showing a car tyre wrapped in a chain, accompanied by the word

Schnee, warns against driving without chains when there is snow.

A diversion is indicated by the colour yellow and the word Umleitung, while the diversion route is indicated by the letter "U" followed by the number of the road. A sign with the word Baustelle always precedes a stretch that is being renovated.

A sign showing a horizontal blue arrow with the word Einbahnstraße indicates a one-way street.

Rules of the Road

Germans on the whole drive in accordance with the regulations. They are generally courteous but can be a little aggressive, particularly on motorways. German drivers hurtle along the outside lane at great speed and get annoyed if they have to slow down because of other drivers. Visitors should be very careful if they are not used to driving on the right.

Seatbelts are compulsory and children under 12 must sit in the back, with babies and toddlers in child seats.

In the event of an accident on the motorway, or if a traffic jam necessitates an abrupt reduction in speed, drivers should turn on their flashing emergency lights to warn drivers behind of the impending danger.

Driving after drinking a glass of beer or wine (50mg/dl) is allowed, but if an accident occurs, the consequences will be more severe if alcohol is found in your blood.

In built-up areas the speed limit is 50 km/h (31 mph); beyond this it is 100 km/h (62 mph), and on motorways there is no limit. When travelling

Fuel station at a motorway service area

Cars in heavy traffic on the Autobahn A3 near Ratingen

with a caravan or trailer outside built-up areas, do not exceed 70 km/h (44 mph), and on motorways 100 km/h (62 mph). Drivers will be fined for speeding, tailgating and parking offences. Note that parking meters may be quite far away from where you park.

Breakdown Services

In the event of a breakdown, turn on your flashing emergency lights and position a warning triangle 100 m (100 yd) behind your vehicle. Roadside assistance is offered by **ADAC** and **AVD** automobile associations – although they may insist you become a member. If you breakdown when lost, use one of the telephones set at intervals along the hard shoulder *(see p556)*. If a road accident occurs, contact the police immediately.

Car Hire

Car-hire firms such as **Avis**, **Hertz** and **Sixt Rent-a-Car** can be found at airports and railway stations. Drivers need to produce their passport and driving licence. Most rental agencies require drivers to be over the age of 21 and to have an international licence.

Hitchhiking

Hitchhiking is popular among young people, but a safer method of finding a lift or a travelling companion is through **Mitfahrzentrale**, a contact agency for drivers who offer spare seats on a journey for an agreed fee. You can even catch a ride from or to other EU countries, (including the UK).

Arriving by Coach

Travelling to Germany by coach from the UK is not a very attractive option, as the journey times are very long and the fares are not particularly cheap. Routes are operated by **Eurolines**, depart at Victoria Coach Station and arrive at Berlin's central coach station at the Funkturm (ZOB). Other routes, also departing from Victoria Station, terminate in Frankfurt, Duesseldorf, Cologne, Dortmund or Munich.

Travelling by Coach

There is a good network of inter-city coach services in Germany, and journeys tend to be cheaper than by express train. Most towns have a central station (*Zentraler Omnibus Bahnhof*) near the train station. It is here that most bus services originate and where timetables can be obtained and tickets purchased. All national bus companies have websites, making ticket purchases easy. Many local coach services also operate from the central bus station, so it is easy to make a connection on arrival. **Reisebus 24** offers a search and reservation portal for bus tours of Germany.

DIRECTORY

Breakdown Services

ADAC
Tel (01802) 22 22 22.

AVD
Tel (0800) 990 99 09.

Car Hire

Avis
Tel (06171) 68 18 00 *or* (01805) 21 77 02.
W avis.com

Hertz
Tel (01805) 33 35 35.
W hertz.com

Sixt Rent-a-Car
Tel (01805) 25 25 25.
W sixt.com

Hitchhiking

Mitfahrzentrale
W mitfahrzentrale.de

Coach Companies

Berlin Linien Bus
Tel (030) 860 96 211.
W bex.de

Eurolines
W touring.de *or*
W touring.com

Reisebus 24
(bus tours across Germany)
Tel (030) 2000 7747.
W reisebus24.de

Comfortable, long-distance, double-decker coaches

Travelling within Cities

Driving around Germany's huge cities is not easy, and the historic centres are best visited on foot. Large towns often suffer from traffic congestion and parking can be hard to find. It is advisable to leave your car in a car park on the outskirts and use the city/suburban railway (S-Bahn), underground (U-Bahn), trams or city buses. The latter operate frequent services and can usually avoid traffic jams as they run in dedicated traffic lanes. All modes of public transport run less frequently on weekends.

Electric car charging station in Berlin

Green Travel

Public transportation in Germany is extensive and reliable within urban areas and there are fast train connections between cities. There is not much need for a car unless you wish to explore the countryside extensively. Some car rental companies offer hybrid or electric cars, and many taxis run on bio fuel.

There is an emphasis on public and alternative transport in Germany. Many cities have introduced low-emission zones, which only allow vehicles with an **Umwelt Permit** (*Umwelt-plakette*). Tourists need to obtain this permit prior to travelling to Germany in their own car (see p559).

Bike rentals are everywhere, and with a good network of bike lanes and paths, Germany is a safe country to ride a bicycle. Drivers are very aware of bikes. Many tour operators offer guided bicycle tours – a good way to start and gather confidence on two wheels. **German Cycling Tours** offers guided bike tours of Germany and **Fahradreise** runs a portal with search engines for bicycle tours and accommodation, arranged by region, price and date.

Bike & Bus is an interesting concept that works like a shuttle for cyclists. You tour Europe by bus while your bike is transported in a trailer and available for use where the shuttle stops.

U-Bahn and S-Bahn

Most big German cities have a network of fast connections by underground railway (U-Bahn) and commuter rail (S-Bahn). The U-Bahn offers frequent services – in peak hours, every 3–5 minutes – and individual stations are quite close to each other. The S-Bahn offers less frequent services, every 10–20 minutes, and connects city centres with the suburbs.

Generally, S- and U-Bahn, buses and trams within a city use the same tickets. Tickets can be bought from machines at the entrance to stations or on platforms; the tickets need to be validated in the red punching machines nearby. Railway stations have no ticket-operated barriers, but tickets are frequently checked and €40 fines are imposed on the spot for those not holding a valid ticket.

U-Bahn stations are indicated by square signs with a white "U" on a dark blue background, while S-Bahn stations have round signs with a white "S" on a green background. On maps of the network, each line of the U- and S-Bahn is marked in a different colour and has its own number. The direction of the route is indicated by the name of the terminus station. On every platform a display shows the destination of the next incoming train. A white circle or oval on the map indicates an interchange station.

Carriage doors on U- and S-Bahn trains are sometimes opened manually, but they close automatically. Passengers are not allowed to board the train after an operator's call of "*Zurückbleiben!*" (the doors are about to close).

Buses

Bus operating hours vary from city to city and are much shorter in rural areas. Timetables can be found online or in ticket or tourist offices. Bus tickets can be purchased from the driver.

During the journey, the driver generally announces the name of the bus stop that the bus is approaching. In the centre of town, this is not so important, as in heavy traffic the bus stops at every bus stop. However, further away from the city centre or when traffic is lighter, you will need to listen for these announcements. At many bus stops, the driver will pull in only on request, so passengers must press the "Halt" button in plenty of time.

A city bus in Munich

A modern type of tram found in Germany

Trams

Trams are comfortable and do not get stuck in traffic jams. They run as frequently as buses and have similar operating hours – check with local tourist offices or online for more details.

Tickets

Large cities are generally divided into public transport zones, with the cost of a ticket depending on which zones are travelled through.

In addition to standard tickets (*Normaltarif*), there are also cheaper tickets (*Kurzstrecke*) that limit you to short distances. In many cities you can buy tickets in the form of a strip, which is punched according to the length of your journey.

Children under 14 travel at a reduced rate, while those under the age of six go free. Other types of tickets include a one-day ticket (*Tageskarte*), a one-day group ticket (*Gruppen-tageskarte*), and a weekly ticket (*7-Tage-Karte*). Some towns issue a WelcomeCard that includes travel, plus discounts at local attractions.

Most U-Bahn and S-Bahn trains permit transportation of bicycles in designated cars with a separate ticket.

Driving

Many cities, including Berlin, Munich and Cologne, have introduced a low-emissions zone, indicated by the word *Umwelt* in a red circle. All vehicles must carry a permit in these zones or incur a fine. Permits can be bought online (*see Directory*). Alternatively, use "Park and Ride" (P+R) facilities near S-Bahn stations.

Watch out for bus lanes marked by round blue signs, which can only be used by taxis and cyclists.

Parking in towns can be difficult, the best option is to find a car park (*Parkhaus*). Cars left in a controlled parking zone must display a ticket bought from a machine nearby. Illegally parked cars can be towed; retrieving them is expensive and difficult.

Cream coloured taxis that operate throughout German cities

Taxis

Taxis are a comfortable though expensive way of getting around. If several people share a cab however, it can be cheaper than using the bus or train. All taxis are cream coloured and have a "TAXI" sign on the roof; this is illuminated if the taxi is free. Taxis can be hailed on the street or booked by telephone. They can also be picked up at taxi ranks, though these are rare.

Cycling

Germany has numerous cycle lanes, making it safe, and many junctions have special lights for cyclists. Bikes can be hired from hostels or at various hire places (*Fahrradverleih*). In some major cities, you can use the **Call-A-Bike** hire system. It is relatively expensive – about €15 a day, unless you hold a BahnCard (*see p554*).

(*see p554*)

DIRECTORY

Green Travel

Bike and Bus
W bike-and-bus.de

Fahrradreisen
W fahrradreisen.de

German Cycling Tours
W germancyclingtours.com

UMWELT Permits
W umwelt-plakette.de

Public Transportation Networks

BVG Berlin
W bvg.de

HVV Hamburg
W hvv.de

MVV Munich
W mvv-muenchen.de

VGF Frankfurt/M.0
W vgf-ffm.de

Taxis

Berlin
Berlin Taxi
Tel (030) 21 01 01.

Frankfurt
Taxis Frankfurt
Tel (069) 23 00 01 or (069) 25 00 01.

Hamburg
Taxi Hamburg
Tel (040) 666 666.

Munich Taxi Central
Tel (089) 21 610.

Cycling

Call-A-Bike
Tel 07000 522 522.
W callabike-interaktiv.de

Bicycles for public hire near the Hofgarten in Munich

General Index

Page numbers in **bold** refer to main entries

A

A-trane (Berlin) 115
Aachen **399–401**
 hotels 500
 Pfalz **400–401**
 restaurants 526–7
Aalto, Alvar 394, 445
Abbeys
 Karmelitenkloster (Bamberg) **252**
 Maria Laach 17, 334, 338, **362–3**
 Maulbronn Abbey 204, **306–7**
 Salem **323**
 Weingarten **323**
Abel, Adolf 314
Abendzeitung Schalterhalle (Munich) 237
Accidents 546
Achtermann, Theodore Wilhelm 73
Ackerkeller (Berlin) 115
Activity holidays **536–9**
ADAC 557
Addresses, postal 551
Adenauer, Konrad 64, 65, 411
ADFC (Allgemeiner Deutscher Fahrrad-Club) 539
Adlerhorst (Eagle's Nest) **280**
Admission charges 543
Agrartour GmbH 491
Agrotourism **490**, 491
Ahlbeck 427
 restaurants 532
Ahrensburg 443
 restaurants 531
Ahrenshoop 480
Air Antik (Munich) 235
Air Berlin 553
Air Canada 553
Air travel **552–3**
Airports 552, 553
Albany Phhee Barssen 133, 137
Albertinum (Dresden) **176**
Albertus Magnus, St 402
Albrecht, King of Sweden 477
Albrecht II, Emperor 56
Albrecht der Bär 133
Albrecht-Dürer-Haus (Nürnberg) 14, **263**
Alcohol
 shopping 535
 What to Drink **508–9**
 see also Beer; Wines
Alexa Centre (Berlin) 111
Alexander I, Tsar 83
Alexanderplatz (Berlin) **83**
Alexandrowka (Potsdam) **138**
Allgäu 288
Allianz Arena (Munich) 237
Alps **208–9**
Alpspitze 209
Alsfeld **372–3**
 hotels 499
 restaurants 525
Alster (Hamburg) **438**
Alster lakes (Hamburg) 13
Altdorfer, Albrecht 264, 436
Alte Brücke (Heidelberg) 300
Alte Burg (Koblenz) **360**
Alte Hofhaltung (Bamberg) **252**
Alte Kapelle (Regensburg) **273**
Alte Mainbrücke (Würzburg) **249**
Alte Nationalgalerie (Berlin) 78, **79**
Alte Nikolaikirche (Frankfurt am Main) **380**

Alte Oper (Frankfurt am Main) **378**
Alte Pinakothek (Munich) 13, **226–7**
Alte Universität (Heidelberg) 301, **303**
Altena 414
Altenberg (North Rhine-Westphalia) **398–9**
Altenburg (Thuringia) **201**
 hotels 494
 restaurants 516
Alter Markt (Stralsund) **481**
Altes Land **443**
Altes Museum (Berlin) **79**
Altes Rathaus (Bamberg) **252–3**
Altes Rathaus (Leipzig) **167**
Altes Rathaus (Munich) 12, 215, **218–19**
Altes Rathaus (Passau) 278
Altes Rathaus (Regensburg) **272**
Altes Schloss (Stuttgart) **312–13**
Altötting **274**
Altstadt (Düsseldorf) **396**
Altstadt (Hamburg) **442**
Amalienburg (Munich) 229
Amberg **258**
Ambulances 546
American Express 548
Amphitheater (Trier) **347**
Andechs **268**
Andechs-Meran, Count von 256
Andreaskirche (Hildesheim) **452**
Angelico, Fra 201
Anger (Erfurt) **197**
Angermuseum (Erfurt) **197**
Anklam **485**
Anna Amalia, Duchess of Weimar 198
Anna Wilhelmina, Princess 158
Annaberg-Buchholz 170
Anne of Cleves 393
Anne Frank Zentrum (Berlin) 105
Ansbach 14, **259**
 restaurants 519
Antik & Trödelmarkt am Ostbahnhof (Berlin) 111
Antique shops
 Berlin **111**
Anton Ulrich, Duke of Brunswick 447
Appiani, Giuseppe 247
Archäologische Staatssammlung (Munich) **223**
Archenhold Sternwarte (Berlin) 107
Architecture
 The Baroque in Southern Germany **206–7**
 Castles **36–7**
 Gothic brick architecture **424–5**
 Romanesque architecture **338–9**
 Romanesque churches in Köln **404–5**
 Weser Renaissance trail **457**
Arminius 51
Arnsberg 415
Arnstadt 16, **194**
Arnstorf 271
Arsenal (Berlin) 117
ART 1900 (Berlin) 111
Art
 German Painting **34–5**
 see also Museums and galleries
Arts House (Berlin) **222–3**
Asam, Cosmas Damian 206, 321
 Asamkirche (Munich) 211, 217
 Aufhausen 271
 Church of St Maria Victoria (Ingolstadt) 269
 Dreifaltigkeitskirche (Munich) 217
 Freising 269
 Schloss Thurn und Taxis (Regensburg) 273

Asam, Cosmas Damian (cont.)
 Weingarten Abbey 323
Asam, Egid Quirin 206
 Asamkirche (Munich) 211, 217
 Aufhausen 271
 Freising 269
 Mannheim 298
 Rohr 206
Asamkirche (Munich) 12, 211, **217**
Aschaffenburg **246**
 restaurants 519
Athletics 42–3
Attahöhle 414
Attlee, Clement 143
Aufhausen 271
Aufsess, Hans von 264
Augsburg 211, **290–91**
 festivals 46
 hotels 496
 restaurants 519
Augustinerbräu (Munich) 214
Augustinerkloster-Augustinerkirche (Erfurt) **196**
Augustus, Emperor 290, 344, 401
Augustus I, Elector 169
Augustus II the Strong, Elector 163, 172
 Gemäldegalerie Alte Meister (Dresden) 180
 Japanisches Palais (Dresden) 177
 Schloss Moritzburg (Moritzburg) 171
 Schloss Pillnitz (Dresden) 177
 statue of 176
 Zwinger (Dresden) 178, 179
Augustus III, Elector 180
Augustusbrunnen (Augsburg) 290
Augustusburg **169**
 restaurants 514
Aula Palatina (Trier) **345**
Australian Embassy 545
Automobile Welt Eisenach **191**
Autumn in Germany **46**
Auwer, Johann Wolfgang von der 250, 410
Avis 557

B

b-flat (Berlin) 115
Babelsberg Film Studio (Potsdam) **143**
Babelsberg Palace (Potsdam) 133
Bach, Carl Philipp Emanuel 32, 144
Bach, Johann Christian 32
Bach, Johann Christoph Friedrich 32
Bach, Johann Sebastian 32, 44, 45
 Altenburg 201
 Arnstadt 194
 Bacharchive und Bachmuseum (Leipzig) 167
 Bachhaus (Eisenach) **191**
 Leipzig 166
 Naumburg 153
 tomb of 166
 Weimar 126
Bach, Wilhelm Friedemann 32
Bacharach 359
 hotels 499
 restaurants 524
Bächle (Freiburg im Breisgau) 329
Backpacker Network Germany 539
Bacon, Francis 298
Bad Arolsen 371
Bad Bergzabern 351
Bad Cannstatt (Stuttgart) **315**
Bad Doberan 15, **477**
 hotels 503
 restaurants 532

Bad Dürkheim 351
Bad Frankenhausen 193
Bad Gandersheim 456
Bad Godesberg **413**
Bad Homburg **375**
  hotels 499
  restaurants 525
Bad Honnef 411
Bad Iburg 433
Bad Malente
  restaurants 531
Bad Mergentheim **296–7**
Bad Münstereifel 410
Bad Muskau **184**
  restaurants 514
Bad Salzuflen 419
Bad Schandau 183
Bad Wildungen 371
  restaurants 525
Bad Wilsnack 136
Bad Wimpfen **308–9**
Bad Zwischenahn 433
Baden-Baden **305**
  hotels 498
  restaurants 522
Baden-Durlach, Karl Wilhelm von 304
Baden-Wurttemberg **293–331**
  Bodensee **324–5**
  climate 48
  hotels 498–9
  map 294–5
  restaurants 522–4
  Schwäbische Alb **318–19**
Badenscher Hof Jazzclub (Berlin) 115
Bähr, Georg 172
Baldung Grien, Hans 264
  Freiburg im Breisgau Cathedral 329
  Neue Residenz und Staatsgalerie
   (Bamberg) 252
  Schloss Johannisberg
   (Aschaffenburg) 246
  Schwäbisch Gmünd 308
Dallenstedt 151
Baltic Sea **426–7**
Baltrum 432
Balve 415
Bamberg 14, **252–5**
  Cathedral **254–5**
  hotels 496
  map 253
  restaurants 519
Bandel, Ernst von 419
Banknotes 549
Banks **548**
Baptismal fonts, Romanesque **464**
Bar jeder Vernunft (Berlin) 117
Barbaratherme (Trier) **347**
Barell, Giovanni Angelo 376
Barelli, Agostino 222, 228
Barlach, Ernst
  Abandoned 59
  Güstrow 478
  Katharinenkirche (Lübeck) 469
  Kiel 464–5
  Lindenau-Museum (Altenburg) 201
  Magdeburg 156
  Rathausmarkt (Hamburg) 438
Baroque in Southern Germany **206–7**
Basedow 479
Basic Bio (Munich) 235
Basilika St Castor (Koblenz) **360**
Basilika St Matthias (Trier) 347
Bastei 163, 182
Bat-Studiotheater (Berlin) 117
Bauer, William 39
Bauhaus 158, 198
  Bauhaus-Archiv (Berlin) **92**

Bauhaus (cont.)
  Bauhaus-Museum (Weimar) **198**
Baumburger Turm (Regensburg) **273**
Bautzen 164, **184**
  hotels 494
  restaurants 515
Bavaria **243–91**
  Bayerischer Wald **275**
  Berchtesgadener Land **280–81**
  Chiemsee **282–3**
  climate 49
  festivals 44, 46
  hotels 496–7
  map 244–5
  restaurants 519–22
  A Week in the Bavarian Alps 15
Bavaria-Filmstadt (Munich) **231**, 237
Bayerische Staatsbibliothek (Munich)
  224
Bayerischer Wald **275**
Bayerisches Nationalmuseum (Munich)
  223
Bayreuth 14, **256–7**
  festivals 45
  hotels 496
  map 257
  restaurants 519
Beaches
  The German Coastline **426–7**
  Strandbad Wannsee (Berlin) **108**
Bebelplatz (Berlin) **74**
  Street-by-Street map 72–3
Beckmann, Max 225, 432, 436
Bedburg 411
Bednortz, Georg 39
Beduzzi, Antonio 278
Beer **40–41, 509**
  Hofbräuhaus (Munich) **219**
  Oktoberfest (Munich) 46, 211, 227,
   231, 237
  Theresienwiese (Munich) **231**
Beer, Franz 323
Boor, Michael 288
Beethoven, Ludwig van 32, 33, 361
  Beethovenhaus (Bonn) **412**
  festivals 46
Begas, Karl 77
Begas, Reinhold 76
Beheim, Hans the Elder 260
Behler, Theobald 285
Behrens, Peter
  Alexanderplatz (Berlin) 83
  Darmstadt 384
  Hagen 414
  Weißenhofsiedlung (Stuttgart) 314
Bellini, Giovanni
  The Mourning of Christ 316
Bendlerblock (Berlin) **92**
Benisch and Partners 230
Benois, Leonti Nikolayevich 375, 384
Bentheim, Lüder von 434
Benz, Karl 38, 39
  Mannheim 298
  Mercedes-Benz-Museum (Stuttgart)
   314
Berching 258
Berchtesgaden 281
  hotels 496
  restaurants 519
Berchtesgadener Land 15, **280–81**
Berg, Claus 136
Berg, Johann Jakob 259
Bergbaumuseum Rammelsberg
  (Goslar) **455**
Bergen-Belsen 444
Berggruen, Heinz 100
Berghain (Berlin) 115

Berlin **67–123**
  airports 553
  climate 49
  Eastern Centre **71–7**
  entertainment **112–17**
  Fernsehturm **83**
  festivals 45–7
  further afield **99–109**
  Gemäldegalerie **94–5**
  hotels 492–3
  Kaiser-Wilhelm-Gedächtnis-Kirche **90**
  map 21, 68–9
  Pergamonmuseum **80–81**
  Potsdamer Platz **96**
  restaurants 510–11
  Schloss Charlottenburg 12, **102–3**
  shopping **110–11**
  Street-by-Street maps
   Bebelplatz 72–3
   Kulturforum 88–9
   Museum Island 78–9
  Street Finder **118–23**
  Two Days in Berlin 12
  Western Centre **87–97**
Berlin Airlift (1948–49) 64, 107
Berlin Wall 64, 65
Berlinale (Berlin) 96
Berliner Bäderbetriebe (Berlin) 115
Berliner Clubnacht 115
Berliner Dom (Berlin) **77**
Berliner Ensemble (Berlin) 117
Berliner Festwochen 115
Berliner Gruselkabinett (Berlin) 115
Berlins Volkstheater Hansa (Berlin) 117
Bernburg **152**
Bernini, Gianlorenzo 82
Bernward, St, Bishop of Hildesheim
  452, 453
Bertoldsbrunnen (Freiburg im
  Breisgau) 328
Bertram of Minden
  High Altar of St Peter 440
Bertsch, Andreas 288
Bertuch, Justin 198
Berwart, Blasius 296
Beuron 318
Beuys, Joseph 368, 393, 395
Bevern 457
Bevessen, Albert von 433
Bible 130
Bicycling *see* Cycling
Bielefeld **419**
  festivals 44
  hotels 500
  restaurants 527
Bildergalerie (Potsdam) **139**, 141
Binder, Mathias 258
Bischöfliches Dom- und
  Diözesanmuseum (Trier) **344**
Bismarck, Otto von 59, **60–61**, 432
Black Forest *see* Schwarzwald
Blankenburg 151
Blankenheim 410
Der Blaue Reiter 225
Blaues Wunder (Dresden) **177**
Blechen, Karl 145
Blobel, Günter 39
Blücher, Field Marshal 480
Boats
  Deutsches Schifffahrtsmuseum
   (Bremerhaven) 437
  ferries and ships **555**
  regattas 45
  water sports 43, **536–7**, 539
Böblinger, Matthäus 322
Bocholt, Heinrich 469
Bochum 395

Böcklin, Arnold 223
Bode, Wilhelm von 82
Bodemuseum (Berlin) 78, **82**
Bodensee 27, 293, **324–5**
Bodt, Jean de 75
Böhm, Gottfried 312, 348
Böhme, Martin Heinrich 77
Böll, Heinrich 30
Boniface, St 51, 296
  Fritzlar 370
  Fulda 372
  Passau 278
  Regensburg 272
Bonn **412–13**
  airport 553
  festivals 46
  hotels 500
  map 413
  restaurants 527
Boppard 358
  hotels 499
  restaurants 524
Bora, Katharina von 131, 159, 168
Borkum 426, 432
Borman, Martin 280
Börse (Frankfurt am Main) **378**
Borstel 443
Bosau 465
Bosch, Hieronymus
  Ecce Homo 382
Bosehaus (Leipzig) 166
Bossi, Antonio 251
Botanical Garden (Munich) 229
Böttcherstraße (Bremen) **436**
Böttger, Johann Friedrich 38, 128
Botticelli, Sandro
  Ideal Portrait of a Woman 382
  Madonna with Child 94
Böttinger, Counsellor 252
Boucher, François
  Reclining Girl 408
Boumann, Johann the Elder 78, 139
Boyen, Leopold Hermann von 58
Brabender, Heinrich 390
Brabender, Johann 390
Brahl, Tj ... [illegible]
Brahms, Johannes 33
  Brahmshaus (Baden-Baden) **305**
Brancas, Alexander von 224
Brand, Hennig 38
Brandenburg **133–45**
  climate 49
  hotels 493
  map 134–5
  restaurants 512–13
Brandenburg Gate (Berlin) *see*
  Brandenburger Tor
Brandenburg/Havel **137**
  hotels 493
Brandenburger Tor (Berlin) 12, 69, **73**
Brandhorst Museum (Munich) 224
Brandt, Willy 65
Braque, Georges 100, 225
Brasch, Bernhard Matthias 136
Braun, Wernher von 485
Braunfels, Stephan 225
Braunschweig (Brunswick) 55, 429,
  446–7
  restaurants 529
Breakfast 504
Brecht, Bertolt 31, 478
  Brecht-Weigel-Gedenkstätte (Berlin)
  105
Breckerfeld 414
Breites Tor (Goslar) **455**
Bremen 422, **434–7**
  airport 553
  festivals 46
  hotels 501
  map 435

Bremen (cont.)
  restaurants 529
Bremerhaven 426, 436–7
Brendel, Johann 109
Brentano, Bettina 296
Brentano, Clemens 296
Brenz, Johannes 315
Breu, Jörg the Elder 57
Breuning, Johann Adam 299, 301, 303
Brick architecture, Gothic **424–5**
Bridges
  Alte Brücke (Heidelberg) 300
  Alte Mainbrücke (Würzburg) **249**
  Berlin **77**
  Blaues Wunder (Dresden) **177**
  Schlossbrücke (Berlin) **76**, 77
  Steinerne Brücke (Regensburg) **272**
British Airways 553
British Embassy 545
Bröhan, Karl H 100
Bröhan-Museum (Berlin) **100**
Brömbse, Heinrich 469
Bronner, Michael 296
Bruchsal 295, **299**
Die Brücke 465
  Brücke-Museum (Berlin) **108**
Brüder-Grimm-Museum (Kassel) **368**
Brueghel, Jan 436
Brueghel, Pieter
  Dutch Proverbs 95
  Land of Cockaigne 227
Brüggemann, Hans 464
Brühl **410–11**
  restaurants 527
Brühl, Heinrich von 176, 178
Brühlsche Terrasse (Dresden) **176**
Bruno, Archbishop of Köln 405, 415
Bruno, Giordano 447
Brunsberg, Heinrich 137, 157
Brunswick *see* Braunschweig
Buchenwald **199**
Buchner, Paul 173
Buchwald (Berlin) 111
Bückeburg **446**
  restaurants 529
Bückeburg ... [illegible]
  restaurants 512
Buddenbrook-Haus (Lübeck) 466, **468**
Buff, Charlotte 374
Bugenhagen, Johannes 131, 484
Bundesarbeitsgemeinschaft Hilfe für
  Behinderte 491
Bundesverband 'Selbsthilfe'
  Körperbehinderter 491
Burckhardt, Johann Ludwig 79
Burg Altena 388
Burg Arras 349
Burg Eltz 37, 341, 349
Burg Falkenstein 151
Burg Hohenzollern 36–7, 318
Burg Hohnstein 183
Burg Kriebstein 163, 168
Burg Pyrmont 349
Burg Rheinfels 358
Burg- und Schlossgarten (Schwerin)
  474
Burg Sooneck 359
Burg Thurant 349
Burgenstraße 539
Bürgersaal (Munich) 12, 214, **216**
Bürgerspital (Würzburg) **248**
Burggarten (Rothenburg ob der
  Tauber) 267
Burghausen **274**
  restaurants 519
Burgtor (Lübeck) **469**
Büring, Johann Gottfried 142, 143
Burnitz, Heinrich 378
Buses 559
Bustelli, Franz Anton 228

Byss, Johann Rudolf 246
Byss, Rudolph 251

C

Café Global (Berlin) 115
Café Moskau (Berlin) 115
Café Swing (Berlin) 115
Calandrelli, Alexander 78
Calder, Alexander 88, 312
Call A Bike 559
Camerarius, Rudolph Jacob 38
Camping 491, **538**, 539
Canadian Embassy 545
Candreal, Jacob de 412
Canova, Antonio 82, 167, 381
Canzler, Carl Adolf 176
Caputh 137
Caravaggio, Michelangelo Merisi da
  Cupid Victorious 94
  Doubting Thomas 139
Caravanning 491, **538**, 539
Carl Augustus, Duke of Weimar 198,
  199
Carlone, Diego 310
Carnival 47
Cars **556–7**
  accidents 546
  Automobile Welt Eisenach **191**
  hiring 557
  historic and scenic routes **538**, 539
  Mercedes-Benz-Museum (Stuttgart)
  314
  motor racing 43
  Porsche-Museum (Stuttgart) **314–15**
Cash machines 548
Castles **36–7**
  Burg Eltz 37
  Burg Hohenzollern 36–7
  Burg Sooneck 359
  Castle in the Rock 283
  Festung Ehrenbreitstein (Koblenz)
  361
  Festung Marienberg (Würzburg) **249**
  Heidelberg 36, 204, **302–3**
  Hohenschwangau **287**
  Kaiserburg (Nürnberg) **263**
  Lichtenstein 37
  Marburg 36
  Marksburg 359
  Pfalzgrafenstein 359
  Raesfeld 37
  Schloss Glücksburg 463
  Schloss Neuschwanstein 15, 205,
  286–7
  Schloss Weimar **198**
  Schloss Wittenberg 158
  Schloss Wolfenbüttel 447
  Schweriner Schloss 37, **474**
  Stolzenfels 358
  Wartburg (Eisenach) 36, 187, **190–91**
  Wernigerode 37
  see also Palaces
Cathedrals
  Bamberg **254–5**
  Berliner Dom (Berlin) **77**
  Bremen **435**
  Deutscher Dom (Berlin) 12, **76**
  Dom of the Holy Virgin (Augsburg) **291**
  Dom St Kilian (Würzburg) **248**
  Dom St Mariä (Hildesheim) **452–3**
  Dom St Marien (Erfurt) **196**
  Dom St Mauritius und St Katharina
  (Magdeburg) **156**
  Dom St Paulus (Münster) **390**
  Dom St Peter (Regensburg) **272–3**
  Dresden **172**
  Französischer Dom (Berlin) 12, **76**
  Fulda 335
  Gothic brick architecture **424–5**

Cathedrals (cont.)
Güstrow 478
Kaiserdom (Frankfurt am Main) **380**
Kaiserdom (Mainz) 338, 342, **354–5**
Köln (Cologne) 334, 387, **406–7**
Lübeck 467, **469**
Münster St Martin (Bonn) **412**
Naumburg Dom **154–5**
Passau 278
Romanesque architecture **338–9**
St-Hedwigs-Kathedrale (Berlin) 73, **74**
Schwerin 475
Trier **344**
Verden an der Aller (Bremen) 437
Caves
Feengrotten (Saalfeld) 201
Pottenstein 247
Rübeland Caves 151
Sauerland 414
Cayart, Louis 76
Cecilienhof (Potsdam) 134, **138**
Celle **445**
hotels 501
restaurants 529
Central (cinema, Berlin) 117
Ceramics, shopping 535
Cézanne, Paul 100
Pipe Smoker 298
Chagall, Marc 352–3, 448
Chamäleon Variété (Berlin) 117
Charlemagne, Emperor 51
Aachen 338, 399, 400–401
Bremen 434
Köln 402
Minden 419
Paderborn 415
statue of 433
Charles II Philip, Elector 298
Charles III Philip, Elector 298
Charles IV, Emperor 157, 262
Charles V, Emperor 226
Charles VI, King of France 274
Charlotte Mathilde, Queen 310
Checkpoint Charlie (Berlin) 12, **84**
Chemnitz **168–9**
hotels 494
restaurants 515
Chiaveri, Gaetano 172
Chieming 283
Chiemsee 15, **282–3**
restaurants 519
Children 544
in Berlin **114**, 115
entertainment in Munich **237**
in hotels 491
in restaurants 505
shopping in Munich **234–5**
Chinesisches Teehaus (Potsdam) **142**
Chirico, Giorgio de 225
Chorin **144**
hotels 493
restaurants 512
Christian IV, King of Denmark 463
Christian Ludwig II, Duke of
Mecklenburg 474
Christina, Queen of Sweden 435
Christmas 47
Christmas markets
Munich **235**
Christo 448
Christoph, Duke of Bavaria 221
Christopher, Duke of Mecklenburg 475
Chrodegang of Metz 385
Churches
The Baroque in Southern Germany
206–7
opening hours 543
Romanesque churches in Köln **404–5**
see also Cathedrals *and individual
towns and cities*

Churchill, Winston 143
Cinema *see* Film
Cinéma Paris (Berlin) 117
CinemaxX (Berlin) 117
Cinestar Sony Center (Berlin) 117
Circus Cabuwazi (Berlin) 115
Circus Krone Bau (Munich) 237
Clausius, Rudolf J E 39
Clemens August, Elector 432
Clemenswerth **432**
Clement II, Pope 254
Cleves *see* Kleve
Climate **48–9**
Climbing **537**
Cloppenburg **433**
hotels 502
restaurants 529
Clothes
in restaurants 505
shopping 535
shopping in Berlin **110–11**
shopping in Munich **234**, 235
size chart 535
Club Behinderter und ihrer Freunde
(CBF) 491
Clüver, Segebad 435
Coach travel **557**
Coastline **426–7**
A Week in Coastal Germany 14–15
Coburg **246–7**
Cochem 46, 349
Coins 549
Colditz 168
Cologne *see* Köln
Columbia Club (Berlin) 115
Communications **550–51**
Concentration camps
Bergen-Belsen 444
Buchenwald **199**
Dachau **268**
Ravensbrück 136
Sachsenhausen 137
Conrad II, Emperor 350
Constance *see* Konstanz
Constance, Lake *see* Bodensee
Constantine I, Emperor 346
Constantine II, Emperor 347
Consulates 543, 545, 546
Copernicus, Nicolaus 262, 315
Corboud, Gérard 408
Corinth, Lovis 176, 368, 448, 474
Lenbachhaus (Munich) 215
Neue Pinakothek (Munich) 224
Cornelius, Peter von 224, 396
The Wise and Foolish Maidens 34
Cosel, Countess 182
Cothmann, Hermann 418
Cottbus 134, **144–5**
restaurants 512
Cotte, Robert de 412
Couven, Johann Josef 397
Crafts 535
Cranach, Lucas the Elder 131, 158, 264,
396
Angermuseum (Erfurt) 197
Cranachhaus (Lutherstadt
Wittenberg) **159**
Kunstsammlung (Gera) 201
Lutherhalle (Lutherstadt Wittenberg)
159
Martin Luther 130
Meissen 171
Museum der Bildenden Künste
(Leipzig) 167
Naumburg 153
Neue Residenz und Staatsgalerie
(Bamberg) 252
Niedersächsisches Landesmuseum
(Hanover) 448
St Peter und St Paul (Weimar) 198

Cranach, Lucas the Elder (cont.)
Schloss Georgium (Dessau) 158
Schloss Johannisbürg
(Aschaffenburg) 246
Schloss Weimar (Weimar) 198
Schneeberg 170
Torgau 168
Venus and Amor 474
Cranach, Lucas the Younger
Augustusburg 169
Cranachhaus (Lutherstadt
Wittenberg) **159**
Cup Bearer Serving at the Table 131
St Peter und St Paul (Weimar) 198
Schloss Weimar (Weimar) 198
Veste Coburg (Coburg) 247
Crane, Walter 224
Credit cards 548
in restaurants 505
in shops 534
Creglingen **297**
Cremer, Johann Peter 399
Crime 546
Cronberg, Walther von 297
Currency **548–9**
Customs regulations 542
Cuvilliés, François 206
Amalienburg (Munich) 229
Augustusburg (Brühl) 410
Bad Mergentheim 296
Cuvilliés-Theater (Munich) 221
Falkenlust (Brühl) 411
Theatinerkirche (Munich) 222
Cuvilliés-Theater (Munich) 221
Cvijanovic, Alexander 92
Cycling 43, 559
cycling tours **536**, 539

D

Dachau **268**
Dahlem (Berlin) 108
Daimler, Gottlieb 38, 39, 314
Dali, Salvador 395
Dallmayr (Munich) 235
Damm, Christian Friedrich 158
Dance
in Berlin **113**, 115
in Munich **236**, 237
d'Angeli, Domenico 278
Dannecker, Johann Heinrich 381
Darmstadt **384**
hotels 500
restaurants 525
Darß 15, 480
Dassow
restaurants 532
Daumier, Honoré 224
DAV Summit Club 491, 539
DDR Museum 77
Dechenhöhle 414
Degas, Edgar 176, 224
Orchestra Players 383
Degler, Hans 268
Dehmel, Hans 39
Dehne, Christopher 157
Delacroix, Eugène 436
Delicious Doughnuts (Berlin) 115
Delta Air Lines 553
Demmler, Georg Adolph 474–5
Denis, Maurice 436
Department stores
Berlin **110**, 111
Munich **234**, 235
Dericks, Jakob 393
Dessau 148, **158**
hotels 493
restaurants 513
Detmold 335, 418–19
restaurants 527

Deutsche Bahn 554
Deutsche Bahn Lost and Found 547
Deutsche Märchenstraße 539
Deutsche Oper (Berlin) 115
Deutsche Reiterliche Vereinigung 539
Deutsche Wanderverband 539
Deutsche Zentrale für Tourismus (DZT)
 491
Deutscher Alpenverein (DAV) 539
Deutscher Camping-Club 491, 539
Deutscher Dom (Berlin) 12, **76**
Deutscher Golf Verband 539
Deutscher Heilbäderverband 539
Deutscher Segler-Verband 539
Deutscher Skiverband 539
Deutscher Sportbund 539
Deutscher Tennis Bund 539
Deutscher Volkssportverband 539
Deutscher Wasserski- und Wakeboard
 Verband 539
Deutscher Weinstraße **351**, 539
Deutsches Architekturmuseum
 (Frankfurt am Main) **381**
Deutsches Auswandererhaus
 Bremerhaven 437
Deutsches Buch- und Schriftmuseum
 (Leipzig) **167**
Deutsches Eck (Koblenz) **360**
Deutsches Jagd- und Fischereimuseum
 (Munich) 215, **217**
Deutsches Jugendherbergswerk DJH
 Service GmbH 491
Deutsches Meeresmuseum (Stralsund)
 481
Deutsches Museum (Munich) 13, **232–3**
Deutsches Nationaltheater (Weimar) **198**
Deutsches Pferdemuseum (Verden an
 der Aller) 437
Deutsches Schifffahrtsmuseum
 (Bremerhaven) 437
Deutsches Technikmuseum Berlin **85**,
 115
Deutsches Theater (Berlin) 117
Deutsches Theater (Munich) 237
Deutsches Weininstitut 539
Dialware Ela
Dientzenhofer, Johann
 Banz Abbey 247
 Fulda 372
 Kirche St Michael (Bamberg) 253
 Neue Residenz (Bamberg) 252
 St Martin's Church (Bamberg) 253
 Schloss Weissenstein
 (Pommersfelden) 246
 Wasserschloss Concordia (Bamberg)
 252
Dientzenhofer, Leonhard 247, 253
Dieter, Fritz 83
Dietrich, Marlene 62, 143
Dietrich, Wendel 216
Dietz, Hans 380
Diez, Wilhelm von 57
Diner's Club 548
Dingolfing **271**
Dinkelsbühl 14, **258**
 festivals 45
Directions Unlimited 545
Disabled visitors 544, 545
 in hotels 491
 in restaurants 505
Distel (Berlin) 117
Dix, Otto 93, 312
 Otto-Dix-Haus (Gera) 201
Döblin, Alfred 83
Dr Seltsam Kabarett (Berlin) 117
Dokumentationszentrum
 Reichsparteitagsgelände (Nürnberg)
 263
Dom see Cathedrals
Domplatz – the Dom (Bamberg) 14

Donatello 82
Donaustauf **259**
Dormagen **398**
Dornburg 200
Dorndorff, Jobst 182
Dörrenbach 351
Dortmund **394**
 hotels 500
 restaurants 527
Dostoevsky, Fyodor 305, 376
Douvermann, Henrik 393
Drachenfels 411
Drais, Karl Freiherr von 39
Drake, Friedrich 159
Drei Gleichen 194
Dreifaltigkeitskirche (Munich) **216–17**
Dresden 17, 163, **172–81**
 airport 553
 festivals 44
 hotels 494
 map 173
 restaurants 515
 World War II 63
 Zwinger 127, **178–9**
Droste-Hülshoff, Annette von 392
Drostenhof (Münster) **391**
Duchamp, Marcel 396, 474
Duderstadt **456**
 hotels 502
Dufours, Joseph 368
Duisburg **395**
 restaurants 527
Duns Scotus 403
Dürer, Albrecht **263**, 264, 369
 Albrecht-Dürer-Haus (Nürnberg) 14,
 263
 Fifer and Drummer 408
 Four Apostles 226
 Kunsthalle (Bremen) 436
 Kupferstichkabinett (Berlin) 88
 Niedersächsisches Landesmuseum
 (Hanover) 448
 Paumgärtners' Altar 35
 Portrait of Hieronymus Holzschuher 94
 Portrait of Michael Wolgemut 265
 tomb of 263
Düringer of Nuremberg 480
Durm, Joseph 303
Düsseldorf 316–17, **396–7**
 airport 553
 hotels 501
 map 397
 restaurants 527
Düsseldorf Academy 396
Duty-free allowances 542

E

Eagle's Nest **280**
East Frisia see Ostfriesland
East Frisian Islands see Ostfriesische
 Inseln
Easter 44
Eastern Germany **125–201**
 Brandenburg **133–45**
 A Cultural Tour of East Germany
 16–17
 map 126–7
 Saxony **163–85**
 Saxony-Anhalt **147–61**
 Thuringia **187–201**
Eberbach 337
Eberhard, Bishop of Bamberg 252
Eberhard the Bearded, Count 320
Eberhard Ludwig, Prince of
 Wurttemberg 310
Ebermannstadt 247
Echter, Julius 248
Eco, Umberto 377

Edenkoben 336
Effner, Joseph 228, 268
EGA and Gartenbaumuseum (Erfurt) **197**
Egell, Paul 301
Egelsbach
 restaurants 525
Eggert, Moritz 33
Egidienkirche (Nürnberg) **263**
Ehrenburg 349
Eichstätt **259**
Eiermann, Egon 68, 90
Eifel mountains 410
Einbeck **456**
Einhard 385
Einstein, Albert 38, 39, 75
 Archenhold Sternwarte (Berlin) 107
 birthplace 322
Einsteinturm (Potsdam) **143**
Eisenach 16, 36, **190–91**
 festivals 44
 hotels 494
 restaurants 516
 Wartburg **190–91**
Eisleben
 hotels 493
 restaurants 513
Eisstadion Berlin Wilmersdorf 115
Ekkehard, Margrave 154
Elbe, River 157, 158
 Altes Land 443
 Blaues Wunder (Dresden) 177
 Elbtalaue **136**
 Sächsische Schweiz tour 182–3
Eldena 484
Electricity 545
Elisabeth of Thuringia, St 190, 191, 247,
 373
Elsheimer, Adam
 The Flight to Egypt 34
Eltville **376**
 hotels 500
 restaurants 525
Email 550–51
Embassies 545
Emden 432
Emergencies 540, 544
Emmerich 393
Encke, Wilhelmine 109
Ende, Hans am 437
Engels, Friedrich 38, 75
Enger 419
Englischer Garten (Munich) **230**
Ensingen, Matthäus von 309
Ensingen, Ulrich von 309, 322
Entertainment
 Berlin **112–17**
 Munich **236–7**
Ephraim, Nathan Veitel Heinrich 84
Erasmus 56
Erbach 385
Erbdrostenhof (Münster) **390**
Erdmannsdorff, Friedrich Wilhelm von
 158, 160
Eremitage (Bayreuth) 244, **256**
Erfurt 16, 126, 188, **196–7**
 hotels 494–5
 map 197
 restaurants 516
Ermisch, Richard 101
Ernst, Max 395, 411
Ernst Ludwig, Grand Duke of Hesse 384
Erthal, J F C J von 352
Eryk II, Duke of Calenberg 457
Erzgebirge 170
Escada (Berlin) 111
Eschenheimer Turm (Frankfurt am
 Main) **378**
Eseler, Nikolaus 258
Essen 389, **394–5**
 hotels 501

Essen (cont.)
restaurants 527
Esslingen **309**
Ethnologisches Museum (Berlin) 108, 115
Etiquette 543
Ettal 15, **284**
Ettenhofer, Georg 217
Ettenhofer, Johann Georg 216
Eucharius, St 347
Eulenspiegel, Till 446
Europa-Center (Berlin) 111
Europarc Deutschland 539
Euskirchen 410
European Castle Hotels and
Restaurants 489
Eutin 465
Expressionism 437
Eyck, Jan van 167
Lucca Madonna 382
Madonna and Infant Triptych 180
Madonna in Church 88
Eyserbeck, Johann August 109
Eyserbeck, Johann Friedrich 160

F

Fabritius, Carel 474
Falkenstein, Kuno von 360
Far Out (Berlin) 115
Farina Haus (Köln) 402
Fashion
shopping in Berlin **110–11**
shopping in Munich **234**, 235
Faustus, Dr 330
FC Bayern Shop (Munich) 237
Federal Republic of Germany 64–5
Feengrotten (Saalfeld) 201
Fehmarn 423
Feininger, Lyonel 158
Gelmeroda IX 35
Feldherrnhalle (Munich) **222**
Felix (Berlin) 115
Fellner 376
Felsentheater (Hollfeld) 257
Ferdinand, Elector 222
Ferdinand II, Emperor 57
Fernsehturm (Berlin) **83**
Fernsehturm (Stuttgart) **314**
Ferries **555**
Festivals **44–7**
Munich **236**, 237
music 32
Oktoberfest (Munich) 46, 211, 227,
231, 237
Theresienwiese (Munich) 231
Festspielhaus (Bayreuth) **257**
Festung Ehrenbreitstein (Koblenz) **361**
Festung Königstein 183
Festung Marienberg (Würzburg) **249**
Feuchtmayer, Joseph Anton 323
Feuchtmayer, F X 247
Feuchtmayr, Johann Michael 289, 299
Feuchtmayr, Lion 31
Feuerbach, Anselm 223, 263
Iphigenie 317
FEZ Wuhlheide (Berlin) 115
Fichte, Johann Gottlieb 200
Fiertmayer, Josef 321
Film
Bavaria-Filmstadt (Munich) **231**, 237
Berlin **116–17**
festivals 44, 46, 47
Munich **236**, 237
Filmpark Babelsberg (Potsdam) **143**
Finsterau 275
Finstingen, Heinrich von 360
Fire Brigade 547
Fischer, Johann Michael 271, 289
Fischer, Theodor 200
Fischerau (Freiburg im Breisgau) 328

Fischland 15, 480
Fischmarkt (Erfurt) **196**, 197
Fischmarkt (Hamburg) **442**
Flavin, Dan 97
Flea markets
Munich **235**
Fleischerei Bachhuber (Berlin) 111
Flensburg **463**
restaurants 531
Flohmarkt Riem (Munich) 235
Flora and Fauna **28–9**
Florinsmarkt (Koblenz) **360**
Flughafen Tempelhof (Berlin) **107**
Focke-Museum (Bremen) **436**
Folk art 535
Fontane, Theodor 31, 136
Food and drink
The Flavours of Germany **506–7**
German beer **40–41**
marzipan from Lübeck **468**
shopping 535
shopping in Berlin **111**
shopping in Munich 235
What to Drink **508–9**
see also Restaurants
Football 42
Formula One motor racing 43
Forschungs- und Gedenkstätte
Normannenstrasse (Berlin) **106**
40 Seconds (Berlin) 115
Foster, Sir Norman 69, 97
Franck, Georg Michael 296
Francke, Master
St Thomas's Altar 34
Francke, Paul 447
Franco-Prussian War (1870–71) 59, 377
Frank, Anne 444
Franke, Günter 83
Frankenberg 370
Frankfurt am Main 17, 26, 335, 365, 367,
378–83
airport 553
festivals 45, 46
hotels 500
map 379
restaurants 525
Städelsches Kunstinstitut **382–3**
Frankfurt an der Oder **144**
hotels 493
restaurants 512
Fränkische Schweiz 14, **247**
Franz, Michael 259
Franz-Liszt Museum (Bayreuth) **256**
Franziskanerkirche (Rothenburg ob der
Tauber) 266
Französischer Dom (Berlin) 12, **76**
Frauenau 275
Fraueninsel 282
Frauenkirche (Dresden) **172**
Frauenkirche (Munich) 12, 205, 215, **217**
Frauenkirche (Nürnberg) **262**
Frauentor (Nürnberg) **260**
Freiberg **169**
hotels 494
Freiburg im Breisgau
hotels 498
restaurants 522
Street-by-Street map 328–9
Freilichtmuseum Schwerin-Mueß
(Schwerin) 475
Freising **269**
Freudenberg 23, 414
Freyung 275
Fridericianum (Kassel) **368**
Friederike, Princess 75
Friedrich, Archbishop of Mainz 377
Friedrich, Caspar David 79, 167, 448
Albertinum (Dresden) 176
Brühlsche Terrasse (Dresden) 176
Eldena 484

Friedrich, Caspar David (cont.)
Greifswald 484
Oybrin 185
The Polar Sea 440
Rügen 427, 483
Traveller above the Sea of Clouds 35
Friedrich I, King of Prussia 58, 77, 107, 133
Friedrich II, Emperor 53, 335
Friedrich II, Landgrave of Hesse 368
Friedrich II the Great, King of Prussia 58,
133, 293
Bildergalerie (Potsdam) 139
equestrian statue of (Berlin) 72
Neues Palais (Potsdam) 143
Rheinsberg 136
Schloss Charlottenburg (Berlin) 102,
103
Schloss Neue Kammern (Potsdam) 142
Schloss Sanssouci (Potsdam) 127,
140, 142
Friedrich II von Hessen-Homburg 375
Friedrich IV the Righteous, Elector 298
Friedrich V, Elector 302
Friedrich Wilhelm I, Great Elector 57,
82, 104, 139
Friedrich Wilhelm II, King of Prussia 101,
109, 138
Friedrich Wilhelm IV, King of Prussia
345, 358
Schloss Charlottenhof (Potsdam) 143
statue of 78
Friedrich the Wise, Great Elector 158
Friedrich Augustus II, Elector 163
Friedrich Barbarossa, Emperor 52–3,
293, 380, 400, 407
Bad Wimpfen 309
Kaiserswerth 397
Kyffhäuser Mountains 193
Wetzlar 374
Friedrichroda 194
Friedrichshafen 325
restaurants 522
Friedrichstadtpalast (Berlin) 117
Frisian Islands *see* Ostfriesische Inseln
Frisoni, Donato 310, 323
Fritzlar **370**
Frohnau 170
Froimont, Johann Clemens 298
Füchtingshof (Lübeck) **468–9**
Fugger, Jacob 290
Fugger, Jacob II 291
Fugger, Ulrich 290
Fuggerei (Augsburg) **291**
Fuggerhäuser (Augsburg) 291
Fulda 335, 365, **372**
hotels 500
restaurants 525
Fünf Höfe (Munich) 235
Funhof, Hinrik 444
Fürstenau 385
Fürstenbau-Museum (Würzburg) 249
Fürstenzug (Dresden) **173**
Furtwangen 331
Füssen 15, **289**
hotels 496
restaurants 519

G

Gabler, Josef 323
Gadebusch **476**
Gaillard, Eugène 100
Galeria Kaufhof (Munich) 235
Galerie Bessenge (Berlin) 111
Galeries Lafayette (Berlin) 111
Galgentor (Rothenburg ob der Tauber)
267
Galileo 232
Gallasini, Andreas 372
Gallé, Emile 100

Galleria (Berlin) 111
Galleries *see* Museums and galleries
Galli Bibiena, Carlo 256
Galli Bibiena, Giuseppe 256
Galli da Bibiena, Alessandro 298, 299
Galopprennbahn Hoppegarten (Berlin) 115
Gandersheim, Roswitha von 456
Gandino, Francesco Chiaramella da 104
Garbo, Greta 143
Gardens *see* Parks and gardens
Garmisch-Partenkirchen 15, 209, **284**
  hotels 496
  restaurants 519–20
Gärtner, Friedrich von 222, 224
Gasteig Culture Center (Munich) 237
Gasthöfe 490
Gauguin, Paul 224
  Two Women on Tahiti 176
Gaupière, Philippe de la 304
Gaupière, Pierre Louis Philippe de la 315
Gedenkstätte Berlin-Hohenschönhausen (Berlin) **106**
Gedenkstätte Deutscher Widerstand (Berlin) **92**
Gedenkstätte Plötzensee (Berlin) **104**
Gemäldegalerie (Berlin) 12, 68, 88, **94–5**
Gemäldegalerie Alte Meister (Dresden) 179, **180–81**
Gentzkow, Charlotte von 140
Georg, Duke of Landshut 270, 274
Georg Wilhelm, Margrave of Bayreuth 256
George I, King of England 449
George II, King of England 456
Gera **201**
  restaurants 516
Gerhard, Hubert 290
German Democratic Republic 64–5
German History Museum (Berlin) 75
German National Tourist Office 545
German Wings 553
Germanisches Nationalmuseum (Nürnberg) **264–5**
Gernrode 151
Gerthener, Madern 354, 378
Gestapo 85
Gesundbrunnencenter (Berlin) 111
Giacometti, Alberto 100
Gießen **374**
  restaurants 526
Giorgione 447
  Sleeping Venus 181
Girard, Dominique 411
Glass shops 535
Glesker, Justus 255
Glücksberg 459
Glückstadt **463**
Glyptothek (Munich) 13, **225**
Goar, St 358
Godehard, Bishop of Hildesheim 453
Godehardkirche (Hildesheim) **453**
Goethe, Johann Wolfgang von 30, 31, 58, **317**
  birthplace 365
  Goethe-Gedenkstätte (Jena) 200
  Goethe-Wanderweg 195
  Goethehaus (Frankfurt am Main) **378**
  Goethes Gartenhaus (Weimar) **199**
  Goethes Wohnhaus and National Museum (Weimar) **199**
  Leipzig 166
  statue of 91
  Weimar 126, 187, 198
  Wetzlar 374
Goethe Institute 539
Goldener Reiter (Dresden) **176**

Golf **537**, 539
Golgotha (Berlin) 115
Gontard, Carl von 106
  Alexanderplatz (Berlin) 83
  Französischer Dom (Berlin) 76
  Marmorpalais (Potsdam) 138
  Neues Palais (Potsdam) 143
Gorbachev, Mikhail 65
Görlitz **185**
  hotels 494
Goslar
  hotels 502
  Street-by-Street map 454–5
Gotha 16, 189, **193**
  hotels 495
  restaurants 516
Göthe, Johann Eosander 102
Gothic brick architecture **424–5**
Göttingen 429, **456**
  hotels 502
  restaurants 529
Gottwalt, Hans 200
Goya, Francisco
  Die Marquesa de Caballero 224
Goyen, Jan van 193
  Crossing of the Rhine near Rhenen 316
Grafenau 275
Graimberg, Count Charles de 303
Grass, Günter 25, 30
Grasser, Erasmus 218, 219
Grassimuseum (Leipzig) **166**
Grävenitz, Countess Wilhelmine von 310
Great Interregnum 53
El Greco
  Disrobing of Christ 227
Green shopping 534–5
Gregory I, Pope 32
Gregory VII, Pope 52
Greifenclau, Georg von 352
Greifensteine 170
Greifswald 425, **484**
  hotels 503
  restaurants 532
Grimm Brothers 30, **372**
  birthplace 381
  Brüder-Grimm-Museum (Kassel) **368**
  Göttingen 456
  Märchenhaus (Alsfeld) 373
  statue of 367
Gröninger, Gerhard 390
Gröninger, Johann Mauritz 355
Gropius, Walter 92, 158
Groß-Raden 478
Groß St Martin (Köln) **402**
Große Wallanlagen Park (Hamburg) 431
Großer Garten (Dresden) **177**
Großedlitz 165, 182
Grove, Lorenz 469
Grünberg, Martin 75, 76
Grünermarkt (Bamberg) **253**
Grünewald, Mathias 297, 304
Grünstein, Baron Anselm von 299
Grupello, Gabriel 396
Guericke, Otto von 38
Guimard, Hector 100
Günter-Grass-Haus (Lübeck) 469
Günther, Ignaz 216
Günther, Matthias 249
Gürzenich (Köln) **403**
Güstrow **478**
  hotels 503
  restaurants 532–3
Gutach 331
Gutbrod, Rolf 314
Gutenberg, Johannes 38, 346, 352
  Gutenberg-Museum (Mainz) **352**
Gutenbergplatz (Mainz) **352**

H

Habrecht, Isaak 308
Habsburg dynasty 53, **56**, 58
Hackesche Höfe Kino (Berlin) 117
Haeften, Werner von 92
Hagen **414**
  restaurants 527
Hahn, Kurt 323
Hahn, Otto 39
Haigerloch 318
Hainleite hills 192
Halberstadt **150**
Haldeburg 158
Halle **152–3**
  hotels 493
  restaurants 513
Halle an der Buttergasse (Magdeburg) **156**
Hals, Frans 474
  Museum der Bildenden Künste (Leipzig) 167
  Schloss Friedenstein (Gotha) 193
  Schloss Georgium (Dessau) 158
Halspach, Jörg von 217, 218
Hamburg 423, 431, **438–43**
  airport 553
  festivals 44
  Hanseatic League **54–5**
  hotels 502
  Kunsthalle **440–41**
  map 439
  restaurants 529–30
  Two Days in Hamburg 13
Hamburger Bahnhof (Berlin) **97**
Hameln 429, 430, 457
Hämelschenburg 457
Hanau 367, 381
Händel, Georg Friedrich 32
  Händel-Haus (Halle) 153
Hangloch-Wasserfall 331
Hannover 429, 430, **448–9**
  airport 553
  festivals 44
  hotels 501
  map 449
  restaurants 530–31
Hanseatic League **54–5**
Hansemann, David 399
Hartenfels Castle (Torgau) 130
Harz Mountains 147, 150, 429
  Harz Mountain trail **151**
Harzgerode 151
Hascher & Jehle 312
Hauberat, Guillaume d'298
Hauberrisser, Georg 219
Hauff, Wilhelm 37, 319
Hauptmann, Gerhart 31, 427
Hauptmarkt (Nürnberg) 14, **262**
Hauptmarkt (Trier) **344**
Hauptwache (Frankfurt am Main) **378**
Haus der Geschichte der BR Deutschland (Bonn) **413**
Haus der Kunst (Munich) **222–3**
Haus der Schiffergesellschaft (Lübeck) **468**
Haus zum Ritter (Heidelberg) 301
Haus zum Walfisch (Freiburg im Breisgau) 329
Hauser, Kaspar 259
Havana (Berlin) 115
Havelberg 148, **157**
Havixbeck 392
Health 547
Hebbel, Christian Friedrich 25
Hebbel Am Ufer (HAU) Theater (Berlin) 115
Hechingen 318
Heckel, Erich 197

Hegel, Georg Wilhelm Friedrich 38, 200, 320
  Hegel-Haus (Stuttgart) **313**
Heidegger, Martin 38
Heidelberg 17, **300–303**
  Castle 36, 204, **302–3**
  festivals 46
  hotels 498
  restaurants 522–3
  Street-by-Street map 300–301
Heilbronn **308**
  festivals 46
Heilig-Geist-Spital (Nürnberg) **261**
Heiligengrabe 136
Heiligenstadt **192**
Heiliger-Geist-Hospital (Lübeck) **469**
Heiliggeistkirche (Heidelberg) 300, **303**
Heiligkreuzkapelle (Trier) **347**
Heilmann & Littmann 198
Heine, Heinrich 74, 75
  Göttingen 456
  Heiligenstadt 192
  Heinrich-Heine-Institut (Düsseldorf) **397**
  Ostfriesische Inseln 432
Heinrich, Prince of Prussia 75
Heinrich I, Emperor 51, 90, 171
Heinrich II, Count Palatine 362
Heinrich II, Emperor 52, 401
  Bamberg Cathedral 254, 255
  statue of 252
Heinrich II, Landgrave of Marburg 373
Heinrich IV, Emperor 52
Heinrich VII, Emperor 53
Heinrich der Löwe (Henry the Lion) 429, 447
  birthplace 322
  Braunschweig 446
  Landsberg am Lech 268
  Munich 214
  Ratzeburg 465
Heinrich-Heine-Institut (Düsseldorf) **397**
Heinrichshöhle 414
Hekticket Theaterkassen (Berlin) 115, 117
Helen, Duchess of Mecklenburg 475
Helen, St 405
Helena Pavlovna, Grand Duchess 476
Helgoland 422, 426, 429, **462**
Heliger, Bernhard 108
Helmer 376
Helmstede, Hinrich 466
Helmstedt 447
Hemmeter, Karl 90
Henrietta Katharine, Princess of Orange 158
Henriette-Adelaide, Electress of Bavaria 222, 228
Henry, Count of Welf 323
Henry the Lion see Heinrich der Löwe
Henry Borwin, Duke of Mecklenburg 477
Henselmann, Hermann 83, 106
Henze, Hans Werner 33
Herder, Johann Gottfried 187
  Bückeburg 446
  Kirms-Krackow-Haus (Weimar) 198
  St Peter und St Paul (Weimar) 198
Herford 419
Herlin, Friedrich 266
Hermann, Franz Anton 355
Hermann (Cherusko Arminius) 419
Hermann II, Margrave of Baden 305
Herrenchiemsee Palace 15, 282
Herrenhäuser Gärten (Hanover) **449**
Hertz 557
Hertz, Heinrich 39
Herz-Jesu-Kirche (Lübeck) 467
Herzogin-Anna-Amalia Bibliothek (Weimar) **199**

Hess, Rudolf 104
Hesse **365–85**
  climate 48
  hotels 499–500
  map 366–7
  restaurants 525–6
  Waldecker Land **370–71**
Hesse, Hermann 320
Hessisches Landesmuseum (Kassel) **368**
Hetjens-Museum (Düsseldorf) **396**
Heuffner, Michael 168
Hexenturm (Heidelberg) 301
Heydrich, Richard 85
Hezilo, Bishop of Hildesheim 453
Hiddensee 427, 482
Hiking **536**, 539
Hildebrandt, Johann Lukas von 250, 251
Hildesheim 429, **452–3**
  hotels 502
  map 453
Hilinger, Wolf 485
Hilmer and Sattler 100
Hindemith, Paul 33
Hindenburg, Paul von 62
Hintersee 280
Hiring cars 557
Historisches Museum (Bamberg) **252**
Historisches Museum (Frankfurt am Main) **380**
History **51–65**
Hitch-hiking 557
Hitchcock, Alfred 231
Hitler, Adolf **62–3**
  Adlerhorst (Eagle's Nest) **280**
  assassination attempt 92, 104
  Hitler-Putsch **222**, 268
  Volkswagenwerk (Wolfsburg) 445
  World War II 63
Hodler, Ferdinand 448
Hoetger, Bernhard 436, 437
Hofbräuhaus (Munich) **219**
Hoffmann, E T A 33
Hoffmann, Joseph 100
Hoffmann, Ludwig 80
Hoffmann, Philipp 376
Hofgarten (Düsseldorf) **396–7**
Hofkirche (Dresden) **172**
Höger, Fritz 439
Hohenlohe, Heinrich von 296
Hohenlohe family 297
Hohenneuffen 319
Hohenschwangau **287**
Hohenstaufen family 52–3, 293, 308
Hohenzollern, Elisabeth von 303
Hohenzollern-Ansbach, Albrecht von 297
Hohenzollern family 58, 293, 359
  Berliner Dom (Berlin) 77
  Burg Hohenzollern 32–3, 318
  Cecilienhof (Potsdam) 138
  Schlossplatz (Berlin) 77
Holbein, Hans the Elder 271, 288, 380
  Adoration of the Magi 226
  Madonna with Child Crowned by Angels 264
Holbein, Hans the Younger 485
  Darmstädter Madonna 384
  Portrait of George Gisze 68
Hölderlin, J C F 320
Holiday Care 545
Holidays, public 47
Holl, Elias 291
Holländisches Viertel (Potsdam) **138–9**
Hollein, Hans 380
Hollern 443
Holocaust Denkmal (Berlin) 12, **74**
Holsteinische Schweiz (Holstein's Switzerland) **465**

Holstentor (Lübeck) 466
Holy Roman Empire 51–3, 58
Holy Trinity Church (Munich) **216–17**
Hölzel, Adolf 312
Homburg **348**
Hoppetose Boat Bar (Berlin) 115
Hörmann, Martin 289
Höroldt, Johann Gregor 128
Horses
  Deutsches Pferdemuseum (Verden an der Aller) 437
  horse riding 42, 538
Hospitals 547
Hotel Reservation Service (HRS) 491
Hotels **488–519**
  Baden-Wurttemberg 498–9
  Bavaria 496–7
  Berlin 492–3
  Brandenburg 493
  Hesse 499–500
  Lower Saxony, Hamburg and Bremen 501–2
  Mecklenburg-Lower Pomerania 503
  Munich 495–6
  North Rhine-Westphalia 500–501
  Rhineland-Palatinate and Saarland 499
  Saxony 494
  Saxony-Anhalt 493–4
  Schleswig-Holstein 502–3
  Thuringia 494–5
Höxter **418**
  hotels 501
  restaurants 527
Hrdlicka, Alfred 312
Huguenots 76, 106
Humboldt, Alexander von 38, **74**, 75, 456
Humboldt, Wilhelm von **74**, 75
Humboldt family 104–5
Humboldt Universität (Berlin) 72, **75**
Hus, Jan 56
Husmann, Carsten 435
Hussite Wars (1419–36) **56**
Husum
  restaurants 531
Hutten, Cardinal Franz Christoph von 299
Huysburg 150
Hyller, Abbot Sebastian 323

I

Idensen 446
Ihne, Ernst von 72, 82
Ikonen-Museum (Frankfurt am Main) **381**
Ilmenau 195
IMAX (Berlin) 117
Imhoff-Stollwerck-Museum (Köln) **404**
Ingolstadt 211, **269**
  hotels 496
  restaurants 520
Die Insel (Berlin) 115
Insurance 547
  cars 556
Internet 550–51
Inventors **38–9**
Irish Embassy 545
Isobel of Bavaria 274
Isozaki, Arata 96
Ixnard, Michael d' 361

J

Jadwiga, Princess 270, 274
Jagdschloss Grunewald (Berlin) **108**
Jahn, Helmut 96, 367
Jakobikirche (Hamburg) 13, **438–9**

Jakobikirche (Lübeck) **469**
Jamnitzer, Wenzel 263
Jan Wellem, Duke 396
Jank, Christian 285, 286
Japanisches Palais (Dresden) **177**
Jasmund Peninsula 483
Jaspers, Karl 38
Jazz 46
  in Berlin **113**, 115
Jazzfest Berlin 115
Jena **200**
  hotels 495
  restaurants 516–17
Jenisch, Philipp 310
Jerichow 157
Jerusalem, Karl Wilhelm 374
Jesuitenkirche (Heidelberg) 301
Jesuitenkirche (Trier) **346**
Jews
  Jüdisches Museum (Berlin) 69, **84–5**
  Jüdisches Museum (Frankfurt am Main) **380**
  Jüdisches Zentrum (Munich) 218
  Neue Synagoge (Berlin) **105**
Joachim II, Elector 108
Johann, King of Saxony 172
Johann der Buschener 435
Johann Casimir, Prince 247
Johann Wilhelm, Elector 298
Jörg, Aberlin 309, 313, 315
Jörg, Hänslin 313
Jork 443
Joseph Klemens, Elector 412
Jüdisches Museum (Berlin) 12, 69, **84–5**
Jüdisches Museum (Frankfurt am Main) **380**
Jüdisches Zentrum (Munich) 218
Juist 432
Julius, Duke of Brunswick 447
Juliusspital (Würzburg) **248**
Junction Bar (Berlin) 115
Jura see Schwäbische Alb
Jussow, Heinrich Christoph 369
Jüterbog **145**

K

KaDeWe (Berlin) 111
Käfer (Munich) 235
Kaiser-Wilhelm-Gedächtnis-Kirche (Berlin) 12, 68, **90**
Kaiserburg (Nürnberg) 14, 245, **263**
Kaiserdom (Frankfurt am Main) **380**
Kaiserpfalz (Goslar) 454
Kaiserswerth (Düsseldorf) **397**
Kaiserthermen (Trier) **346**
Kalkar 393
Kamenz 165, **184**
  restaurants 515
Kammerspiele (Berlin) 117
Kandinsky, Wassily 396
  Bauhaus 92
  Dessau 158
  Lenbachhaus (Munich) 225
Kändler, Johann Joachim 128, 129, 178
Kandlers, Gottlieb David 309
Kant, Immanuel 38
Kap Arkona 482
Käppele (Würzburg) **249**
Karl, Landgrave of Hesse 369
Karl, Prince of Prussia 109
Karl IV, Emperor 53
Karl V, Emperor 56
Karl Albrecht, Prince-Elector 274
Karl Eugene, Prince 315
Karl-Marx-Allee (Berlin) **106**
Karl-May-Museum (Radebeul) **177**
Karl Theodor, Duke 396
Karl Theodor, Elector 214, 230, 298

Karlsaue (Kassel) 369
Karlsruhe **304**
  hotels 498
  restaurants 523
Karlstor (Munich) 214
Karmelitenkloster (Bamberg) **252**
Karstadt (Berlin) 111
Kassel **368–9**
  festivals 45, 46
  hotels 500
  map 369
  restaurants 526
Katharinenkirche (Lübeck) **469**
Käthe-Kollwitz-Museum (Berlin) **91**
Kaufhaus (Freiburg im Breisgau) 329
Kaufmann Collection (Stade) 443
Kaulbach, Wilhelm von 79, 218, 371
Kehlsteinhaus **280**
Keller, Ferdinand 303
Kempten **288**
  restaurants 520
Kennedy, John F 107
Kepler, Johannes 38, **315**
Kerbel, Lew 169
Kern, Michael 296
Kerpen 411
Kiedrich **377**
  restaurants 526
Kiel 461, **464–5**
  festivals 45
  hotels 502
  restaurants 531
Kiel Canal 426, 464
Kilian, St 248
Kinderbauernhof Görlitzer Bauernhof (Berlin) 115
Kinderreich (Munich) 237
Kirche St Maximin (Trier) **347**
Kirche St Michael (Bamberg) **253**
Kirche St Paulin (Trier) **347**
Kirche St Sebald (Nürnberg) 14, **262**
Kirche St Stephan (Mainz) **352–3**
Kircher, Athanasius 38
Kirchner, Ernst Ludwig 436
  Self-Portrait with Model 441
Flusschgüren (Munich) **551**
Klaproth, Martin H 38
Klee, Paul 92, 100, 158, 396
Kleihues, Josef Paul 97
Klein Glienicke (Berlin) **109**
Klein-Venedig (Bamberg) **253**
Kleines Theater (Berlin) 117
Kleist, Ewald G 38
Kleist, Heinrich von 144, 308
Klemens August, Elector 410
Klenze, Leo von 222
  Alte Pinakothek (Munich) 226
  Baden-Baden 305
  Bayerische Staatsbibliothek (Munich) 224
  Glyptothek (Munich) 225
  Monopteros (Munich) 230
  Propyläen (Munich) 225
  Residenz (Munich) 220
  Ruhmeshalle (Munich) 231
  Schack-Galerie (Munich) 223
  Walhalla (Donaustauf) 259
Kleve (Cleves) **393**
Klimt, Gustav 224
Klinger, Max 167
Kloster Eberbach 377
  restaurants 526
Kloster Lichtenthal (Baden-Baden) 305
Kloster Unser Lieben Frauen (Magdeburg) **156**
Kloster Zinna 145
Knights' War (1522) 56, 57
Knobelsdorff, Georg Wenzeslaus von 74, 142, 143
Knoblauch, Eduard 105

Knöffel, Johann Christoph 182, 200
Knoll, Max 39
Knoller, Martin 284
Kobem, Johann von 360
Koblenz 341, **360–61**
  festivals 45
  map 361
  restaurants 524
Koch, Robert 39, 75
Kochelsee, Lake 209
Ködnitz 257
Koekkoek, Barend Cornalis 393
Koess, Johann 390
Kohl, Helmut 65
Köhler, Christian
  Germany's Awakening 51
Kokoschka, Oskar 432
Kollwitz, Käthe 75, 403
  Käthe-Kollwitz-Gedächtstätte (Moritzburg) 171
  Käthe-Kollwitz-Museum (Berlin) **91**
  Mother and Child 91
Köln (Cologne) **402–9**
  airport 553
  Dom 334, 387, **406–7**
  hotels 501
  map 403
  restaurants 528
  Romanesque churches **404–5**
  Wallraf-Richartz-Museum (Köln) **408–9**
Kolumba Musuem (Köln) 404
Kömer, Edmund 394
Komische Oper (Berlin) 115
Königsallee (Düsseldorf) **396**
Königshütte 60
Königslutter 447
  hotels 502
  restaurants 531
Königssee 208, 281
Königstein, Werner von 360
Königswinter **411**
Konrad II, Emperor 52
Konrad III, Emperor 52
Konstanz 324
  hotels 500
  restaurants 523
Kontorhausviertel (Hamburg) **439**
Konzerthaus (Berlin) **76**, 115
Köpenick (Berlin) **106–7**
Korbach 370
Korbinian, St 269
Korn, Arthur 39
Kornelimünster 399
Kosuth, Joseph 312
Krafft, Johann Peter
  Victory Report at the Battle of Leipzig 59
Kraft, Adam 261
Kramer, Simpert 289
Krameramtswohnungen (Hamburg) **442**
Krämerbrücke (Erfurt) **196**
Kraszewski-Museum (Dresden) **177**
Krefeld 395
Kremer, Fritz 83
Kreuzkirche (Dresden) **176**
Krieg, Dieter 312
Krims-Krackow-Haus (Weimar) **198**
Krone, Gottfried Heinrich 200
Kronprinzenpalais (Berlin) 73
Kröpelinerstraße (Rostock) **480**
Krüger, Andreas 82
Krummedick, Albert 469
Krumpper, Hans 217
Krupp family 394
Küchel, Johann Michael von 253
Ku'damm (Berlin) 12, **91**
Kühne, Max 166
Kulmbach 257

Kulmbach, Hans von 262
Kulturbrauerei (Berlin) 115
Kulturforum (Berlin)
  Street-by-Street map 88–9
Kulturhistorisches Museum
  (Magdeburg) **156**
Kulturhistorisches Museum (Stralsund)
  481
Kun, Hans 322
Kunckel, Johannes 109
Kunibert, Bishop of Köln 405
Kunigunde, Empress 252, 254
Kunstbibliothek (Berlin) 88
Kunstgewerbemuseum (Berlin) 12, 88,
  93
Kunsthalle (Bremen) **436**
Kunsthalle (Hamburg) 13, **440–41**
Kunsthalle Fridericianum (Kassel) **368**
Kunsthalle St-Annen (Lübeck) 467, **469**
Kunsthalle Schirn (Frankfurt am Main)
  380
Kunstmuseum Bonn **413**
Kunstmuseum Stuttgart **312**
Kunstsammlung Nordrhein-Westfalen
  (Düsseldorf) **396**
Kupferstichkabinett und
  Kunstbibliothek (Berlin) 88, **92**
Kurfürstliches Palais (Trier) **346**
Kurfürstliches Schloss (Koblenz) **361**
Kurfürstliches Schloss (Mainz) **352**
Kurpfälzisches Museum (Heidelberg)
  303
Kurzbold, Konrad 375
Kyffhäuser Mountains **193**
KZ-Gedenkstätte Dachau 268

L

Läbben 145
Lachenmann, Helmut 33
Lakes 28
Lambertikirche (Münster) **390**
Landau 351
Landau an der Isar 271
Landes, Anton 273
Landsberg am Lech **268**
Landshut **270–71**
  festivals 45
  restaurants 520
Lang, Fritz 25, 143
Lange Anna 462
Langenargen 325
Langeoog 432
Langfield, Rutger van 107
Langhans, Carl Gotthard 82, 101, 102, 138
Languages 544
  language courses 538
Laurens, Henri 100
Laves, George Ludwig Friedrich 448
Le Brun, Charles 419
Le Corbusier 314
Le Geay, Jean Laurent 143
Lehde 46, 145
Lehmbruck, Wilhelm 395
Lehnin **137**
  restaurants 512
Leibl, Wilhelm
  Three Women in a Church 35
Leibniz, Gottfried Wilhelm 38, 447
Leinberger, Hans 271
Leineschloss (Hanover) **448–9**
Leinsweiler 351
Leipzig 16, 127, **166–7**
  airport 553
  festivals 44, 45
  hotels 494
  map 167
  restaurants 515
Lemgo **418**
  hotels 501

Lemgo (cont.)
  restaurants 528
Lenbach, Franz von 223, 270
Lenbachhaus (Munich) **225**
Lenné, Peter Joseph
  Chorin 144
  Klein Glienicke (Berlin) 109
  Kurpark (Bad Homburg) 375
  Pfaueninsel (Berlin) 109
  Schloss Charlottenhof (Potsdam) 143
  Schlosspark (Berlin) 101
  Schlosspark (Ludwigslust) 476
  Tiergarten (Berlin) 68, 91
Leonardo da Vinci 380
Leopold III, Prince 160
Lepsius, Richard 79
Lessing, Gotthold Ephraim 30, 58
  Lessinghaus (Wolfenbüttel) 447
  Lessingmuseum (Kamenz) 184
Leupold, Jacob 38
Leveilly, Michel 412
Leyen, Heinrich Ferdinand von der 341
Libaerts, Eliseus 179
Libeskind, Daniel 69, 84–5
Lichtenstein 37, 319
Lichtenstein, Roy 380
Liebenstein, Jakob von 355
Liebermann, Max 176, 201, 448, 474
  Bleaching the Linen 408
  Dachau 268
  grave of 105
  Man with Parrots 35
Liebfrauenkirche (Koblenz) **361**
Liebfrauenkirche (Trier) **344–5**
Liebieg, Baron Heinrich 381
Liebieghaus (Frankfurt am Main) **381**
Liebig, Justus von 39
Liebknecht, Karl 77, 91, 107
Liederhalle (Stuttgart) **314**
Lilienstein 183
Lilienthal, Otto 39, 485
Limburg 366, **375**
  hotels 500
  restaurants 526
Lindau 15, **288**, 325
  hotels 496–7
  restaurants 520
Linden, Count Karl von 314
Linden-Museum (Stuttgart) **314**
Lindenau-Museum (Altenburg) 201
Linderhof **285**
Linenau, Bernhard von 176
Lippe, Bernhard II von 418
Lippe, Magdalena zur 384
Lippstadt 415
Liqueurs 508
Lissitzky, El 448
Liszt, Franz 33, 46, 198
  Franz-Liszt Museum (Bayreuth) **256**
  Liszt Museum (Weimar) **199**
Literature **30–31**
Littmann, Max 223, 312
Lochner, Stefan
  Altar of the Magi 407
  Madonna of the Rose Arbour 54
Loden-Frey (Munich) 235
Lollobrigida, Gina 231
Lomersheim, Walter von 204
Longuelune, Zacharias 177
Loreley 359
Lorenzer Platz (Nürnberg) **261**
Lorsch **385**
  restaurants 526
Lossow, William 166
Lost property 547, 548
Lothar, Emperor 52, 447
Lotter, Hieronymus 166, 167, 169
Louis XIV, King of France 348
Löwenstein-Wertheim, Count Ludwig I
  von 296

Lower Pomerania see Mecklenburg-
  Lower Pomerania
Lower Saxony, Hamburg and Bremen
  429–57
  climate 48
  hotels 501–2
  map 430–31
  restaurants 529–31
Lübben
  restaurants 512
Lübbenau 145
  hotels 493
  restaurants 512
Lübeck 14, 55, 423, 424–5, 459, **466–9**
  hotels 503
  marzipan **468**
  restaurants 532
  Street-by-Street map 466–7
Luckau 145
Ludwig I, King of Bavaria
  Bayerische Staatsbibliothek (Munich)
    224
  Feldherrnhalle (Munich) 222
  Glyptothek (Munich) 225
  Oktoberfest (Munich) 231
  Pompejanum (Aschaffenburg) 246
  Propyläen (Munich) 225
Ludwig I the Pious, Emperor 360
Ludwig II, King of Bavaria 15
Ludwig II, King of Bavaria 61
  Archäologische Staatssammlung
    (Munich) 223
  Herrenchiemsee Palace 282
  Linderhof 285
  Marstallmuseum (Munich) 228
  Schloss Neuschwanstein 205, 286
  tomb of 216, 274
  and Wagner 256
Ludwig II the German, Emperor 51,
  272, 385
Ludwig II the Severe, Prince 289
Ludwig IV, Emperor 217, 284
Ludwig Beck (Munich) 235
Ludwig der Fromme 452
Ludwig the Jumper 190
Ludwig, Edward 107
Ludwig, Peter and Irene 360, 402
Ludwigsburg 17, 207, 293, **310–11**
  hotels 498
  restaurants 523
Ludwigskirche (Munich) **224**
Ludwigslust 14–15, **476**
Lufthansa 553
Luise, Queen of Prussia 75, 101
Lüneburg **444**
  hotels 502
Lüneburger Heide 429, **444**
Lurago, Carlo 278
Lusatian mountains 182
Lustgarten (Berlin) 79
Luther, Martin 56, 158, 373, 484
  Erfurt 196
  Luther and the Reformation
    130–31
  Lutherhalle (Lutherstadt Wittenberg)
    159
  Magdeburg 156
  monument to 159
  Schlosskirche (Lutherstadt
    Wittenberg) 158
  tomb of 158
  Torgau 168
  Veste Coburg (Coburg) 246–7
  Wartburg (Eisenach) 190, 191
Lutherstadt Wittenberg **158–9**
  hotels 494
  Luther and the Reformation **130–31**
  map 159
  restaurants 514
Luxemburg, Rosa 91, 107

LWL Museum für Kunst und Kultur (Münster) 390
Lynar, Rochus Graf von 104

M

Mächtig, Hermann 107
Macke, August 390, 413
Mackensen, Fritz 437
Maenz, Paul 198
Magdalenenklause (Munich) 229
Magdeburg 126, **156**
  hotels 493
  restaurants 513–14
Magnus, St 289
Maier, Mathias 300
Mainau 324
  restaurants 523
Mainfränkisches Museum 249
Maini, Andrea 289
Mainz 17, 338, 339, **352–5**
  hotels 499
  Kaiserdom 338, 342, **354–5**
  map 353
  restaurants 524
Manet, Édouard 176, 224, 436
  Nana 441
Mann, Heinrich 468
Mann, Thomas 30, 31, 466, 468
Mannheim **298**
  festivals 46
  restaurants 523
Maps
  Augsburg 290–91
  Baden-Württemberg 294–5
  Bamberg 253
  Bavaria 244–5
  Bayerischer Wald 275
  Bayreuth 257
  Berchtesgadener Land 280–81
  Berlin 21, 68–9
  Berlin: Bebelplatz 72–3
  Berlin: Eastern Centre 71
  Berlin: Further afield 99
  Berlin: Kulturforum 88–9
  Berlin: Museum Island 78–9
  Berlin: Potsdamer Platz 96
  Berlin: Street Finder 118–23
  Berlin: West of the Centre 87
  Bodensee 324–5
  Bonn 413
  Brandenburg 134–5
  Bremen 435
  Chiemsee 282–3
  Deutsche Weinstraße 351
  Dresden 173
  Düsseldorf 397
  Eastern Germany 126–7
  Erfurt 197
  Europe 18–19
  Frankfurt am Main 379
  Freiburg im Breisgau 328–9
  German climate 48–9
  German coastline 426–7
  German literature 30–31
  German painting 34–5
  Germany 20–21
  Germany in 1871 60
  Germany 1949–90 64
  Goslar 454–5
  Hamburg 439
  Hannover 449
  Harz Mountain trail 151
  Heidelberg 300–301
  Helgoland 462
  Hesse 366–7
  Hildesheim 453
  Kassel 369
  Koblenz 361
  Köln 403

Maps (cont.)
  Leipzig 167
  Lower Saxony, Hamburg and Bremen 430–31
  Lübeck 466–7
  Lutherstadt Wittenberg 159
  Mainz 353
  Mecklenburg-Lower Pomerania 472–3
  Moseltal 349
  Munich 20, 212–13
  Munich: Marienplatz 214–15
  Munich: Street Finder 238–41
  Münster 391
  Münsterland 392
  Nationalpark Müritz 479
  North Rhine-Westphalia 388–9
  Northern Germany 422–3
  Nürnberg 260–61
  Passau 278–9
  Potsdam 139
  Regensburg 272–3
  Rhine Valley 358–9
  Rhineland-Palatinate and Saarland 342–3
  Rothenburg ob der Tauber 266–7
  Rügen 482–3
  Sächsische Schweiz 182–3
  Sächsische Silberstraße 170
  Saxony 164–5
  Saxony-Anhalt 148–9
  Schleswig-Holstein 460–61
  Schwäbische Alb 318–19
  Schwarzwald (Black Forest) 330–31
  Schwerin 475
  Southern Germany 204–5
  Stuttgart 313
  Thüringer Wald 194–5
  Thuringia 188–9
  train routes 555
  Trier 345
  Waldecker Land 370–71
  Weimar 199
  Weser Renaissance trail 457
  Western Germany 334–5
  Wine in Western Germany 336–7
  Würzburg 248
Marbach **309**
Marburg **373**
  Castle 36
  hotels 500
  restaurants 526
March, Werner 101
March Revolution (1848–49) 59
Marcks, Gerhard 434
Margaret, Queen of Denmark 477
Marggraf, Andreas 38
Maria Laach 17, 334, 338, **362–3**
Marienberg 170
Marienkirche (Berlin) **82**
Marienkirche (Lübeck) **424–5**, 466, **468**
Marienkirche (Lutherstadt Wittenberg) **159**
Marienkirche (Rostock) **480**
Marienkirche (Stralsund) **481**
Markets 535
  Fischmarkt (Hamburg) **442**
  Munich **235**
Markgräfliches Opernhaus (Bayreuth) 14, **256**
Märkisches Museum (Berlin) **84**
Marksburg 359
Markt (Bonn) **412**
Markthalle (Stuttgart) **315**
Marktkirche (Goslar) **454**
Marktplatz (Bremen) **434**
Marktplatz (Hannover) **449**
Marktplatz (Heidelberg) 300
Marktplatz (Hildesheim) **452**
Marktplatz (Schwerin) **474–5**
Marmorpalais (Potsdam) **138**

Marstall (Potsdam) **139**
Marstallmuseum (Munich) 228
Marta Herford Museum (Herford) 419
Marthakirche (Nürnberg) **260**
Martinstor (Freiburg im Breisgau) 328
Marx, Erich 97
Marx, Karl 38, 59, 75
  birthplace 344
  monument to 169
Marzipan from Lübeck **468**
Mathilde, St 152
Matisse, Henri 225
Matthew, St 347, 349
Matthias-Kapelle 349
Matthieu, Daniel 297
Maulbronn 17, 204, **306–7**
  hotels 498
  restaurants 523
Maurice the Learned, Landgrave of Hesse 369
Mauritiuskirche (Hildesheim) **453**
Mauthalle (Nürnberg) **260**
Max-Schmelling-Halle (Berlin) 115
Maxim-Gorki Theater (Berlin) 117
Maximilian I, Elector 243
Maximilian I, Emperor 56, 220, 226
Maximilian I Joseph, King of Bavaria 222
Maximilian II Emanuel, Elector of Bavaria 229, 269
Maximilian II Joseph, King of Bavaria 223, 285, 287
Maximilian Friedrich, Elector 412
Maximilian-Friedrich, Prince-Bishop 391
Maximilianmuseum (Augsburg) 290
Maximin, St 347
May, Karl 31
  Karl-May-Museum (Radebeul) **177**
Mayer, Julius 39
Mayer, Rupert 214, 216
Mecklenburg-Lower Pomerania 14–15, **471–85**
  climate 49
  hotels 503
  map 472–3
  Nationalpark Müritz **479**
  restaurants 532–3
  Rügen **482–3**
Medical assistance 547
Meer, Erhard van der 169
Meersburg 325
  hotels 498
  restaurants 523
Meier, Richard 381
Meissen 16, 165, **171**
  porcelain **128–9**
  restaurants 515–16
Meit, Conrad
  Judith 223
Meitner, Lise 39
Melanchthon, Philipp 130, 131, 158, 373, 484
  Melanchthonhaus (Lutherstadt Wittenberg) **159**
  monument to 159
  tomb of 158
Meldorf **463**
Memhardt, Johann Gregor 137
Memling, Hans 469
  Bathsheba at her Toilet 316
Mendelssohn, Erich 143
Mendelssohn-Bartholdy, Felix 33, 167
Mengoz, Klaus 378
Mengs, Anton Raphael 172
Mente, Heinrich 157
Menus, in restaurants 505
Menzel, Adolf von 60, 79
Mercator, Gerhard 395

Mercedes-Benz-Museum (Stuttgart) **314**
Merkel, Angela 65
Merseburg **153**
Messegelände (Berlin) **101**
Messel, Alfred 80
Metten 243
Metternich, Prince Clemens von 360
Metternich, Karl von 345
Metzendorf, Dominikus 394
Metzendorf, Georg 394
Meyer, Johann Gustav 107
Michaeliskirche (Hamburg) 13, **442**
Michaeliskirche (Hildesheim) **452**
Michaelskirche (Munich) 12, 214, **216**
Michelangelo 224
Michelstadt **385**
  hotels 500
  restaurants 526
Mielke, Erich 106
Mies van der Rohe, Ludwig 88, 92, 314
Miller, Ferdinand von 222, 250
Miller, Oskar von 232
Minden **419**
Minoritenkirche Mariä Empfängnis
  (Köln) **403**
Mittelalterliches Museum (Rothenburg
  ob der Tauber) 266
Mobile phones 550
Modersohn, Otto 437
Modersohn-Becker, Paula 436, **437**
  Girl playing a flute in birch woods 437
  Paula-Modersohn-Becker Museum
  (Bremen) 436
Modigliani, Amedeo
  Female Nude Reclining on a White
  Pillow 317
Möhnesee 415
Molsdorf 197
Moltke, Count Helmut James von 104
Mondrian, Piet 396
Monet, Claude 176, 436
  Spring Fields 317
Money **548–9**
Monnot, Pierre-Etienne 369
Monschau 410
  restaurants 528
Monuments
  Feldherrnhalle (Munich) **222**
  Gedenkstätte Deutscher Widerstand
  (Berlin) **92**
  Gedenkstätte Plötzensee (Berlin) **104**
  Kaiser-Wilhelm-Gedächtnis-Kirche
  (Berlin) 12, 68, **90**
  Neue Wache (Berlin) 72, **75**
  Niederwalddenkmal (Rüdesheim)
  366, 377
  Siegessäule (Berlin) **91**
  Viktoriapark (Berlin) 107
  Völkerschlachtdenkmal (Leipzig) **167**
Moore, Henry 88, 224, 261, 395
Moosbrugger, Casper 323
Moosburg 270–71
Mörike, Eduard 320
Moritz of Saxony 171
Moritzburg **171**, 174–5
  hotels 494
  restaurants 516
Mosel River 336, 341, 356–7
  Moseltal tour **349**
Mosel wines 336
Moseltal 17, **349**
Mosigkau 158
Motor racing 43
Motorways 556
Mount Nebelhornerstdorf 15
Mountains 29
  German Alps **208–9**
  hostels 491
  mountain sports **537**, 539
  Schwäbische Alb 17, **318–19**

Moyland 393
Mozart, Wolfgang Amadeus 221
Mueller
  The Lovers 448
Mühlenhof (Münster) **391**
Mühlhausen **192**
  restaurants 517
Muldetal **168**
Müller, Heinrich 85
Müller, Karl A 39
Müller, Wolfgang 216
Multscher, Hans 268, 321, 322
Munch, Edvard 448
  Girl on a Beach 92
  Girls on a Bridge 409
  Girls on the Pier 441
Münden 450–51, 457
Munich **211–41**
  airport 553
  Alte Pinakothek **226–7**
  climate 49
  Deutsches Museum **232–3**
  entertainment **236–7**
  festivals 46
  hotels 495–6
  map 20, 212–13
  Marienplatz: Street-by-Street map
  214–15
  Oktoberfest 46, 211, 227, **231**, 237
  Residenz **220–21**
  restaurants 517–18
  Schloss Nymphenburg **228–9**
  shopping **234–5**
  Street Finder 238–41
  Two Days in Munich 12–13
Munich Film Festival 237
Munich Tourist Board 237
Münster **390–91**
  hotels 501
  map 391
  restaurants 528
Münster St Martin (Bonn) **412**
Münsterland 392
Münsterplatz (Freiburg im Breisgau)
  329
Müntzer, Thomas 192
Murillo, Bartolomé Esteban
  Old Woman and Boy 409
Museum Island (Berlin) 12
  Street-by-Street map 78–9
Museums and galleries
  opening hours 543
  Albertinum (Dresden) **176**
  Albrecht-Dürer-Haus (Nürnberg) 14,
  263
  Alte Hofhaltung (Bamberg) 252
  Alte Nationalgalerie (Berlin) 78, **79**
  Alte Pinakothek (Munich) 13, **226–7**
  Altes Museum (Berlin) **79**
  Altes Rathaus (Leipzig) **167**
  Altes Schloss (Stuttgart) **312–13**
  Angermuseum (Erfurt) **197**
  Anne Frank Zentrum (Berlin) **105**
  Archäologische Staatssammlung
  (Munich) **223**
  Automobile Welt Eisenach **191**
  Bacharchive und Bachmuseum
  (Leipzig) 167
  Bachhaus (Eisenach) **191**
  Bauhaus-Museum (Weimar) **198**
  Bayerisches Nationalmuseum
  (Munich) **223**
  Beethovenhaus (Bonn) **412**
  Bergbaumuseum Rammelsberg
  (Goslar) **455**
  Bildergalerie (Potsdam) **139**, 141
  Bodemuseum (Berlin) 78, **82**
  Bosehaus (Leipzig) 166
  Brahmshaus (Baden-Baden) **305**

Museums and galleries (cont.)
  Brandhorst (Munich) 224
  Brecht-Weigel-Gedenkstätte (Berlin)
  105
  Bröhan-Museum (Berlin) **100**
  Brücke-Museum (Berlin) **108**
  Brüder-Grimm-Museum (Kassel) **368**
  Buchenwald 199
  in Burghausen 274
  DDR Museum (Berlin) 77
  Deutsches Architekturmuseum
  (Frankfurt am Main) **381**
  Deutsches Buch- und Schriftmuseum
  (Leipzig) **167**
  Deutsches Historisches Museum
  (Berlin) 73
  Deutsches Jagd- und
  Fischereimuseum (Munich) 215, **217**
  Deutsches Meeresmuseum
  (Stralsund) **481**
  Deutsches Museum (Munich) 13,
  232–3
  Deutsches Pferdemuseum (Verden
  an der Aller) 437
  Deutsches Schifffahrtsmuseum
  (Bremerhaven) 437
  Deutsches Technikmuseum Berlin **85**
  EGA and Gartenbaumuseum (Erfurt)
  197
  Ethnologisches Museum (Berlin) 108
  Focke-Museum (Bremen) **436**
  Franz-Liszt Museum (Bayreuth) **256**
  Freilichtmuseum Schwerin-Mueß
  (Schwerin) 475
  Fridericianum (Kassel) 335
  Fuggerei-Museum (Augsburg) **291**
  Fürstenbau-Museum (Würzburg) 249
  Gedenkstätte Berlin
  Hohenschönhausen (Berlin) **106**
  Gemäldegalerie (Berlin) 12, 68, 88,
  94–5
  Gemäldegalerie Alte Meister
  (Dresden) 179, **180–81**
  German History Museum (Berlin) 75
  Germanisches Nationalmuseum
  (Nürnberg) **264–5**
  Glyptothek (Munich) 13, **225**
  Goethehaus (Frankfurt am Main) **378**
  Goethes Wohnhaus and National
  Museum (Weimar) **199**
  Grassimuseum (Leipzig) **166**
  Gutenberg-Museum (Mainz) **352**
  Hamburger Bahnhof (Berlin) **97**
  Haus am Checkpoint Charlie (Berlin)
  84
  Haus der Geschichte der BR
  Deutschland (Bonn) **413**
  Haus der Kunst (Munich) **222–3**
  Hegel-Haus (Stuttgart) **313**
  Heinrich-Heine-Institut (Düsseldorf)
  397
  Hessisches Landesmuseum (Kassel)
  368
  Hetjens-Museum (Düsseldorf) **396**
  Historisches Museum (Frankfurt am
  Main) **380**
  Holocaust Denkmal (Berlin) 12, **74**
  Ikonen-Museum (Frankfurt am Main)
  381
  Imhoff-Stollwerck-Museum (Köln)
  404
  Japanisches Palais (Dresden) **177**
  Jüdisches Museum (Berlin) 12, 69,
  84–5
  Jüdisches Museum (Frankfurt am
  Main) **380**
  Karl-May-Museum (Radebeul) **177**
  Käthe-Kollwitz-Gedenkstätte
  (Moritzburg) 171
  Käthe-Kollwitz-Museum (Berlin) **91**

Museums and galleries (cont.)
Kaufmann Collection (Stade) 443
Kleist-Museum (Frankfurt an der
Oder) 144
Kloster Unser Lieben Frauen
(Magdeburg) **156**
Kolumba Musuem (Köln) 404
Kraszewski-Museum (Dresden) **177**
Krims-Krackow-Haus (Weimar) **198**
Kulturhistorisches Museum
(Magdeburg) **156**
Kulturhistorisches Museum
(Stralsund) **481**
Kunstgewerbemuseum (Berlin) 12,
88, **93**
Kunsthalle (Bremen) **436**
Kunsthalle (Hamburg) 13, **440–41**
Kunsthalle Fridericianum (Kassel) **368**
Kunsthalle Schirn (Frankfurt am Main)
380
Kunstmuseum Bonn **413**
Kunstmuseum Stuttgart **312**
Kunstsammlung Nordrhein-
Westfalen (Düsseldorf) **396**
Kupferstichkabinett und
Kunstbibliothek (Berlin) 88, **92**
Kurpfälzisches Museum (Heidelberg)
303
Landesmuseum für Vorgeschichte
(State Museum of Prehistory) (Halle)
153
Landesmuseum Wurttemberg
(Stuttgart) 312
Lenbachhaus (Munich) **225**
Liebieghaus (Frankfurt am Main) **381**
Linden-Museum (Stuttgart) **314**
Liszt Museum (Weimar) **199**
Lutherhalle (Lutherstadt Wittenberg)
159
LWL Museum für Kunst und Kultur
(Münster) 390
Mainfränkisches Museum (Würzburg)
249
Märkisches Museum (Berlin) **84**
Marstall (Potsdam) **139**
Marstallmuseum (Munich) 229
Marta Herford Museum (Herford) **419**
Maximilianmuseum (Augsburg) 290
Melanchthonhaus (Lutherstadt
Wittenberg) **159**
Mercedes-Benz-Museum (Stuttgart)
314
Mittelalterliches Museum
(Rothenburg ob der Tauber) 266
Museum für Angewandte Kunst
(Frankfurt am Main) **381**
Museum für Asiatische Kunst (Berlin)
108
Museum der Bildenden Künste
(Leipzig) **167**
Museum Brandhorst (Munich) **224**
Museum am Dom Trier (Trier) 344
Museum Europäischer (Berlin) 108
Museum für Kunst Afrikas (Berlin) 108
Museum Kunst Palast (Düsseldorf)
396
Museum Kurhaus Kleve-Ewald
Mataré-Sammlung (Kleve) 393
Museum für Lackkunst (Münster) **391**
Museum Ludwig (Köln) **402**
Museum Mensch und Natur (Munich)
229
Museum für Moderne Kunst
(Frankfurt am Main) **380–81**
Museum für Naturkunde (Berlin) **97**
Museum für Sächsische Volkskunst
(Dresden) **176–7**
Museum Schlösschen im Hofgarten
(Wertheim) 296
Museumsdorf Düppel (Berlin) 115

Museums and galleries (cont.)
Museumszentrum Dahlem (Berlin)
108
Musikinstrumenten-Museum (Berlin)
89, **93**
Naturmuseum Senckenberg
(Frankfurt am Main) **381**
Neue Galerie (Kassel) **368**
Neue Nationalgalerie (Berlin) 88,
92–3
Neue Pinakothek (Munich) 13, **224**
Neue Residenz und Staatsgalerie
(Bamberg) **252**
Neues Museum (Berlin) 78, **79**
Neues Museum (Weimar) **198**
Newton-Sammlung (Berlin) 91
Niedersächsisches Landesmuseum
(Hanover) **448**
Nordamerika Ausstellung (Berlin) 108
Oberammergau Museum 284
Passauer Glasmuseum (Passau) 278
Paula-Modersohn-Becker Museum
(Bremen) 436
Pavilion Museum (Bad
Frankenhausen) 193
Pergamonmuseum (Berlin) 12, 69, 78,
80–81
Pinakothek der Moderne (Munich) 13,
225
Porsche-Museum (Stuttgart) **314–15**
Reichstadtmuseum (Rothenburg ob
der Tauber) 266
Residenz (Munich) **220–21**
Rheinisches Freilichtmuseum
Kommern 410
Rheinisches Landesmuseum (Bonn)
412
Rheinisches Landesmuseum (Trier)
346
Richard-Wagner-Museum (Bayreuth)
256
Roemer-Pelizaeus-Museum
(Hildesheim) **452**
Römisch-Germanisches Museum
(Köln) **402**
Rosgartenmuseum (Konstanz) **464**
St Anne's Museum (Lübeck) 467, **469**
Sammlung Berggruen (Berlin) **100**
Schack-Galerie (Munich) **223**
Schinkel-Museum (Berlin) **75**
Schloss Babelsberg (Potsdam) 143
Schnütgen-Museum (Köln) **404**
Schwedenspeicher-Museum (Stade)
443
Spielzeugmuseum (Bremen) 436
Spielzeugmuseum (Nürnberg) **262**
Sprengel Museum (Hanover) **448**
Staatliche Antikensammlungen
(Munich) 13, **225**
Staatliche Kunsthalle Baden-Baden
305
Staatliche Porzellan-Manufaktur
(Meissen) **171**
Staatliches Museum (Schwerin) **474**
Staatsgalerie (Stuttgart) **316–17**
Städelsches Kunstinstitut (Frankfurt
am Main) **382–3**
Stadtmuseum (Baden-Baden) 305
Stadtmuseum (Erfurt) **197**
Stadtmuseum (Munich) **218**
Stadtmuseum (Weimar) **198**
Stasi-Museum (Berlin) **106**
Topographie des Terrors (Berlin) **85**
Übersee-Museum (Bremen) **436**
Valentin Karlstadt Musäum (Munich)
218
Verkehrsmuseum (Dresden) **173**
Villa Stuck (Munich) **230–31**
Völkerkundemuseum (Munich) **219**
Völkerschlachtdenkmal (Leipzig) **167**

Museums and galleries (cont.)
Wallraf-Richartz-Museum &
Fondation Corboud (Köln) **408–9**
Weissenhofmuseum im Haus Le
Corbusier (Berlin) 314
Wilhelmshöhe (Kassel) **369**
Wittumspalais (Weimar) **198**
Zwinger (Dresden) 17, 127, **178–9**
Music **32–3**
in Berlin **112–13**, 115
festivals 44–7
Munich **236**, 237
Musical Theater Berlin am Potsdamer
Platz 117
Musikinstrumenten-Museum (Berlin)
89, **93**

N

Nahe 336
Nahl, Johann August 142
Nannen, Henri 432
Napoleon I, Emperor 73, 107, 163, 297
Napoleonic Wars 58–9
Nassau, Princess Elisabeth von 376
Nassau, Johann Moritz von 393, 414
Nassau, Princess Luise von 377
Nassau-Oranien, Louisa Henrietta von
136–7
Nassau-Oranien, Wilhelm I the Great
von 376
Nassau-Saarbrücken, Wilhelm Heinrich
von 348
National parks **537**, 539
Nationalpark-Berchtesgaden 280
Nationalpark Jasmund 483
Nationalpark Müritz **479**
Nationaltheater (Munich) 237
NatKo (Nationale Koordinationsstelle
Tourismus für Alle) 545
Naturmuseum Senckenberg (Frankfurt
am Main) **381**
Naturpark Westensee 460
Naumann, Johann Christoph 169
Naumburg **153**
Dom **120, 121–3**
hotels 493
restaurants 514
Naumburger Meister 154
Nazarenes 176
Nazis **62–3**, 74
Bergen-Belsen 444
Buchenwald **199**
Feldherrnhalle (Munich) **222**
Topographie des Terrors (Berlin) **85**
Neander, Joachim 397
Neher, Erwin 39
Nepomuk, St 217
Nering, Johann Arnold 75, 102
Nessler, Karl Ludwig 330
Nette, Johann 310
Neubrandenburg **478**
hotels 503
restaurants 533
Neuburg an der Donau **270**
Neue Bischofsresidenz (Passau) 278
Neue Galerie (Kassel) **368**
Neue Nationalgalerie (Berlin) 88, **92–3**
Neue Pinakothek (Munich) 13, **224**
Neue Residenz und Staatsgalerie
(Bamberg) **252**
Neue Synagoge (Berlin) **105**
Neue Wache (Berlin) 12, 72, **75**
Neuenfelde 443
Neues Museum (Berlin) 78, **79**
Neues Museum (Weimar) **198**
Neues Palais (Potsdam) **143**
Neues Rathaus (Dresden) **176**
Neues Rathaus (Hannover) 430, **448**
Neues Rathaus (Munich) 12, 215, **219**

Neues Schloss (Bayreuth) **256**
Neues Schloss (Schleißheim) 207
Neumann, Balthasar 206
　Augustusburg (Brühl) 410, 411
　Bruchsal 299
　Dom St Kilian (Würzburg) 248
　Käppele (Würzburg) 249
　Karlsruhe 304
　Kirche St Michael (Bamberg) 253
　Kirche St Paulin (Trier) 347
　Poppelsdorf (Bonn) 413
　Residenz (Würzburg) 250
　St Catherine Hospital and Seminary
　　(Bamberg) 253
　Vierzehnheiligen 205, 247
　Worms Cathedral 350
　Würzburg Residenz 204
Neumark, Johann Christian 160
Neumünster-Kirche (Würzburg) **248**
Neuruppin **136**
Neuschwanstein *see* Schloss
　Neuschwanstein
Neuss **398**
Neustrelitz 479
Neuwerkkirche (Goslar) **455**
Neuzelle 144
New Year's Eve 47
New Zealand Embassy 545
Newspapers 551
Newton, Helmut
　Newton-Sammlung (Berlin) 91
Nicholas I, Tsar 109, 142
Niedersächsisches Landesmuseum
　(Hanover) **448**
Niederwalddenkmal (Rüdesheim) 366,
　377
Nietzsche, Friedrich 38, 153, 198
Nightlife, Berlin **114**, 115
Nikolaikirche (Potsdam) **139**
Nikolaiviertel (Berlin) 12, **84**
Nikolskoe (Berlin) **109**
NIX (Berlin) 111
Noemi & Friends (Munich) 235
Nolde, Emil 395, 432, 463, **465**
　North Friesian Landscape 34
　The Young Horses 394
Norbert, St 410
Nordamerika Ausstellung (Berlin) 108
Norddeich 27
Norderney 432
Nordhausen 192
Nördlingen 14, 205, **258–9**
North Frisian islands 463
North Rhine-Westphalia **387–419**
　climate 48
　hotels 500–501
　map 388–9
　Münsterland **392**
　restaurants 526–9
Northern Eifel **410**
Northern Germany **421–85**
　climate 48
　German Coastline **426–7**
　Gothic brick architecture **424–5**
　Lower Saxony, Hamburg and Bremen
　　429–57
　map 422–3
　Mecklenburg-Lower Pomerania
　　471–85
　Schleswig-Holstein **459–69**
Notke, Bernt 54, 469
Nürnberg (Nuremberg) 14, 211,
　260–65
　airport 553
　festivals 46
　Germanisches Nationalmuseum
　　264–5
　hotels 497
　map 260–61
　restaurants 520–21

Nymphenburg *see* Schloss
　Nymphenburg
Nymphenburg porcelain 228

O

O2 World 115
Oberalteich 271
Oberammergau 15, **284**
　hotels 497
　restaurants 521
Oberaudorf 208
Oberhausen 395
Oberhof 187, 195
　hotels 495
Oberland 462
Oberstdorf 15, **289**
　hotels 497
Oberwesel
　hotels 499
Oberwiesenthal 170
Odeon (Berlin) 117
Odo von Metz 400
Oechler 485
Oetken, August 190
Off & Co (Munich) 235
Offenbach
　restaurants 526
Ohlmüller, Joseph Daniel 287
Ohm, Georg S 39
Oktoberfest (Munich) 46, 211, 227, **231**,
　237
Olbrich, Joseph Maria 384, 394, 396
Olbricht, Friedrich 92
Oldenburg 422, **433**
　hotels 502
　restaurants 531
Oldenburg, Claes 381
Olympia Einkaufszentrum (Munich) 235
Olympiahalle and Olympic Stadium
　(Munich) 237
Olympiapark (Munich) **230**
Olympiastadion (Berlin) **101**, 115
Opening hours 543
　banks 548
　museums 543
　restaurants 505
　shops 534
Opera
　Bayreuth **256–7**
　Munich **236**, 237
　Opernhaus (Hannover) **448**
　Richard Wagner **256**
　Sächsische Staatsoper (Dresden) 172
Oppenheim 353
Orangerie (Kassel) **369**
Orangerieschloss (Potsdam) **142**
Oranienbaum 158
Oranienburg **136–7**
　restaurants 512
Orff, Carl 33
Osnabrück **433**
　hotels 502
　restaurants 531
Osterwieck 150
Ostfriesische Inseln (East Frisian
　Islands) 429, **432**
Ostfriesland (East Frisia) **432**
Osthaus, Karl Ernst 414
Ostritz 185
Ostseebad Binz 483
Ottheinrich the Magnanimous 270
Otto I, Emperor 51, 52, 324
　Klosterkirche (Lehnin) 137
　Magdeburg 156
　Quedlinburg 152
　Saxony 163
　tomb of 156
Otto I, King of Bavaria 225
Otto II, Emperor 52

Otto III, Emperor 52
Otto of Meissen 169
Otto, Nikolaus 39
Otto, Paul 75
Ottobeuren 206, **289**
Ottoneum (Kassel) **369**
Ottweiler **348**
Oudry, Jean-Baptiste 474
Overbeck, Friedrich 224, 437
Overstolzenhaus (Köln) **404**
Oybrin 185

P

Pachelbel, Johann 32
Paderborn **415**
　restaurants 528
Painting **34–5**
Palaces
　Altes Schloss (Stuttgart) **312–13**
　Baroque in Southern Germany **207**
　Cecilienhof (Potsdam) **138**
　Jagdschloss Grunewald (Berlin) **108**
　Klein Glienicke (Berlin) **109**
　Leineschloss (Hanover) **448–9**
　Linderhof **285**
　Ludwigsburg **310–11**
　Marmorpalais (Potsdam) **138**
　Neue Residenz und Staatsgalerie
　　(Bamberg) **252**
　Neues Palais (Potsdam) **143**
　Neues Schloss (Bayreuth) **256**
　Orangerieschloss (Potsdam) **142**
　Residenz (Würzburg) 204, **250–51**
　Residenzschloss (Dresden) **172–3**
　Schleißheim **268–9**
　Schloss Babelsberg (Potsdam) **143**
　Schloss Belvedere (Weimar) 187, **199**
　Schloss Benrath (Düsseldorf) **397**
　Schloss Charlottenburg (Berlin) 12,
　　99, **102–3**
　Schloss Charlottenhof (Potsdam) 140,
　　142–3
　Schloss Neue Kammern (Potsdam) **142**
　Schloss Nymphenburg (Munich) 207,
　　220–9
　Schloss Pillnitz (Dresden) **177**
　Schloss Sanssouci (Potsdam) 12, 127,
　　142
　Schloss Solitude (Stuttgart) **315**
　Schloss Tegel (Berlin) **104–5**
　Schloss Thurn und Taxis (Regensburg)
　　273
　Schwetzingen 298–9
　Wasserschloss Concordia (Bamberg)
　　252
　Wilhelmshöhe (Kassel) **369**
　Zwinger (Dresden) 17, 127, **178–9**
　see also Castles
Palatinate *see* Rhineland-Palatinate and
　Saarland
Palm, Gottlieb von 309
Papworth, John 315
Parking 557
Parks and gardens
　Bad Muskau 184
　Botanical Garden (Munich) 229
　Burg- und Schlossgarten (Schwerin)
　　474
　Cecilienhof (Potsdam) 138
　EGA and Gartenbaumuseum (Erfurt)
　　197
　Englischer Garten (Munich) **230**
　Goethes Gartenhaus (Weimar) **199**
　Großer Garten (Dresden) **177**
　Grosse Wallanlagen Park (Hamburg)
　　431
　Herrenhäuser Gärten (Hanover) **449**
　Hofgarten (Düsseldorf) **396–7**
　Klein Glienicke (Berlin) 109

Parks and gardens (cont.)
Ludwigsburg 293, **310–11**
Ludwigslust 14–15, 476
Lustgarten (Berlin) 79
Neue Residenz und Staatsgalerie (Bamberg) 252
Park Sanssouci **140–41**
Römische Bäder (Potsdam) 142
Schleißheim 268–9
Schloss Charlottenhof (Potsdam) 143
Schloss Nymphenburg **228–9**
Schloss Tegel (Berlin) 104
Schlossgarten (Stuttgart) **312**
Schlosspark (Berlin) **100–101**
Tiergarten (Berlin) 68, **91**
Treptower Park (Berlin) **107**
Viktoriapark (Berlin) **107**
Wilhelmshöhe (Kassel) **369**
Wörlitz Park 149, **160–61**
Parler, Peter 308
Parler family 157, 307, 308, 322
Parr, Franz 478
Parra, Johan Batista 474
Pasinger Fabrik (Munich) 237
Passau 207, 245
hotels 497
restaurants 521
Street-by-Street map 278–9
Passauer Glasmuseum (Passau) 278
Passionskirche (Berlin) 115
Passports 542, 547
Patrick Hellmann (Berlin) 111
Paul VI, Pope 314
Paul, Wolfgang 39
Paula-Modersohn-Becker Museum (Bremen) 436
Paulin, St 347
Paulinzelle 195
Paulskirche (Frankfurt am Main) **379**
Peasants' War (1524–25) 56, 57, 192, 193
Pedetti, Mauritio 259, 304
Peenemünde **485**
Pei, I M 73, 75
Peichl, Gustav 382
Pensions 490
Pergamonmuseum (Berlin) 12, 69, 78, **80–81**
Perlacher Einkaufspassage (Munich) 235
Perleberg 136
Permoser, Balthasar
Albertinum (Dresden) 176
Burg- und Schlossgarten (Schwerin) 474
Hofkirche (Dresden) 172
Museum der Bildenden Künste (Leipzig) 167
Schlossplatz (Berlin) 77
Zwinger (Dresden) 178
Perron, Phillip 285
Persius, Ludwig 109, 139, 142
Peter the Great, Tsar 484
Petersberg (Erfurt) 196
Petersen, Wolfgang 231
Petri, Johann Ludwig 299
Petrikirche (Hamburg) 13
Petrikirche (Lübeck) 466
Petrini, Antonio 253
Peyère, Antoine François the Younger 361
Pfalz (Aachen) **400–401**
Pfalz, Sophie, Duchess von der 449
Pfalzgrafenstein 359
Pfarrkirche St Johannis (Magdeburg) **156**
Pfarrkirche St Mariä Himmelfahrt (Köln) **402**
Pfaueninsel (Berlin) **109**
Pfund, Paul 177

Pfunds Molkerei (Dresden) **177**
Pharmacies 547
Philharmonie (Berlin) 89, **93**, 115
Philip I, Duke of Mecklenburg 485
Phillip the Magnanimous, Landgrave 373, 374
Philosophenweg (Heidelberg) 300
Philosophers **38**
Piano, Renzo 96
Picasso, Pablo 225, 396, 402
Mother and Child 317
Sammlung Berggruen (Berlin) 100
Sprengel Museum (Hanover) 448
Woman in a Hat 100
Pictorius, Gottfried Laurenz 392
Pieck, Wilhelm 107
Pigage, Nicolas de 298, 299, 397
Pinakothek der Moderne (Munich) 13, **225**
Pirna **182**
restaurants 516
Pirna, Peter Ulrich von 182
Pisanello, Antonio 217
Pissarro, Camille
Girl lying on a grassy slope 436
Planck, Max 39, 75, 456
Planetarium am Insulaner (Berlin) 115
Plattenburg Castle 136
Playdenwurff, Wilhelm 271
Plön 460, 465
Plötzensee Memorial (Berlin) **104**
Poelzig, Hans 177
Pokrowski, Vladimir 167
Polak, Jan 217, 225
Police 546, 547
Pomerania *see* Mecklenburg-Lower Pomerania
Pommersfelden **246**
Pöppelmann, Matthäus Daniel 171, 177, 178
Poppelsdorf (Bonn) **413**
Porcelain
Meissen **128–9**, 171
Schloss Nymphenburg (Munich) 228
shopping 535
Porsche, Ferdinand 445
Porsche-Museum (Stuttgart) **314–15**
Port (Hamburg) **442**
Porta Nigra (Trier) **344**
Porta Westfalica 419
Postal services 551
Potsdam 12, 133, **138–43**
hotels 493
map 139
restaurants 512–13
Potsdam Conference (1945) **143**
Potsdamer Platz (Berlin) 12, **96**
Potsdamer Platz Arkaden (Berlin) 111
Pott, Johann 38
Pottenstein 247
Poussin, Nicolas 369
Praetorius, Johannes 265
Predigerkirche (Eisenach) **191**
Preetz 465
Prenzlauer Berg (Berlin) 12, **105**
Prerow 480
Prinzregenttheater (Munich) 237
Pritzwalk 136
Propyläen (Munich) **225**
Public conveniences 543
Public holidays 47
Public transport *see* Travel
Pückler-Muskau, Prince Hermann von 145, 184
Pulheim-Brauweiler 411
Die Puppenstube (Munich) 235
Puppentheatermuseum (Berlin) 115
Pürkel, Konrad 283
Putbus 483

Q
Qantas 553
Quaglio, Domenico 287
Quasimodo (Berlin) 115
Quedlinburg 147, **152**
hotels 493
restaurants 514
Querfurt **153**
Quesnay, Abraham 76
Quirnheim, Ritter Mertz von 92

R
Rabe, Martin Friedrich 109
Rabenden, Meister von 217
Radebeul 177
Raesfeld 37
Railways *see* Trains
Ramsau an der Ache 280
Raphael 142
Sistine Madonna 181
Raschdorff, Julius 77
Ratgeb, Jörg 308
Rathaus (Augsburg) 291
Rathaus (Bremen) **434**
Rathaus (Goslar) 454
Rathaus (Hamburg) 13
Rathaus (Köln) **403**
Rathaus (Lübeck) 466
Rathaus (Lutherstadt Wittenberg) **159**
Rathaus (Magdeburg) **156**
Rathaus (Munich) 211
Rathaus (Münster) **390**
Rathaus (Nürnberg) **262**
Rathaus (Rostock) **480**
Rathaus (Rothenburg ob der Tauber) 267
Rathaus (Würzburg) **248**
Rathaus Schöneberg (Berlin) **107**
Rathausmarkt (Hamburg) **438**
Ratibor 465
Ratisbon *see* Regensburg
Ratzeburg **465**
hotels 503
restaurants 523
Rauch, Christian Daniel 104, 107, 371
Ravensbrück 136
Ravensburg **322**
Recklinghausen
festivals 44
Red Army 107
Reeperbahn (Hamburg) 442
Reformation **56–7**, **130–31**, 158
Regensburg **272–3**
hotels 497
map 272–3
restaurants 521
Regierungsviertel (Bonn) **413**
Reichenau 324
restaurants 523
Reichle, Hans
St Michael Overcoming Satan 290
Reichstadtmuseum (Rothenburg ob der Tauber) 266
Reichstag (Berlin) 12, 26, 60, 65, 69, **97**
Reit im Winkl 208
Remarque, Erich Maria 30, 433
Rembrandt 369, 408, 436, 447, 448
Blinding of Samson 383
Deposition from the Cross 227
Hannah and Simeon in the Temple 440
Portrait of Hendrickje Stoffels 95
St Paul in Prison 316
Self-Portrait with Saskia 180
Remscheid 398
Renaissance-Theater (Berlin) 117
Reni, Guido 139
Residenz (Munich) **220–21**
Residenz (Würzburg) 204, **250–51**

Residenzschloss (Dresden) **172–3**
Residenzschloss (Münster) **391**
Restaurants **504–33**
  Baden-Wurttemberg 522–4
  Bavaria 519–22
  Berlin 510–11
  Brandenburg 512–13
  Hesse 525–6
  Lower Saxony, Hamburg and Bremen 529–31
  Mecklenburg-Lower Pomerania 532–3
  Munich 517–18
  North Rhine-Westphalia 526–9
  Rhineland-Palatinate and Saarland 524–5
  Saxony 514–16
  Saxony-Anhalt 513–14
  Schleswig-Holstein 531–2
  Thuringia 516–17
  see also Food and drink
Retti, Leopoldo 304
Retti, Ricardo 310
Reunification 65
Reuter, Israel Berr Josaphat 399
Rheingau 337
Rheinisches Freilichtmuseum Kommern 410
Rheinisches Landesmuseum (Bonn) **412**
Rheinisches Landesmuseum (Trier) **346**
Rheinsberg 133, 136
  hotels 493
  restaurants 513
Rheintal 17, **358–9**
Rheinufer (Bonn) **412**
Rhineland-Palatinate and Saarland **341–63**
  climate 48
  Deutsche Weinstraße **351**
  A Gourmet Tour of South-West Germany 17
  hotels 499
  map 342–3
  Moseltal **349**
  restaurants 524–5
  Rhine Valley (Rheintal) **358–9**
  Saarland **348**
  see also North Rhine-Westphalia
Richard the Lionheart, King of England 351
Richartz, Johann Heinrich 408
Richter, Gerhard 407
Riedel, E 219
Riem Arcaden (Munich) 235
Riemenschneider, Tilman 200, 264
  Bamberg Cathedral 254
  Bayerisches Nationalmuseum (Munich) 223
  Bodemuseum (Berlin) 82
  Creglingen 297
  Dom St Kilian (Würzburg) 248
  Heiligenstadt 192
  Mainfränkisches Museum (Würzburg) 249
  The Stigmatization of St Francis 266
  Wartburg (Eisenach) 191
Rietschel, Ernst 176, 198
Rilke, Rainer Maria 437
Ring, Hermann tom 391
Ring, Ludger tom 390, 391
Roads 556–7
Röchling, Carl 348
Rochlitz 168
Rochsburg 168
Rock music
  Berlin 113, 115
Rode, Christian Bernhard 82
Rödertor (Rothenburg ob der Tauber) 267

Rodin, Auguste 167, 201
Roemer-Pelizaeus-Museum (Hildesheim) **452**
Rohr 206
Rohrer, Michael 299
Roland
  statues of 136, 150, 185, 434
Roman remains
  Trier **344–7**
Romanesque architecture **338–9**
  baptismal fonts **464**
  Köln **404–5**
Römann, Wilhelm 171
Romantik Hotels & Restaurants 489
Römerberg (Frankfurt am Main) **379**
Römersteine (Mainz) **353**
Römisch-Germanisches Museum (Köln) **402**
Römische Bäder (Potsdam) **142**
Röntgen, Wilhelm 39, 398
Roosevelt, Franklin 143
Roselius, Ludwig 436
Roskopf, Wendel 185
Rostock 15, 55, 472, **480**
  hotels 503
  restaurants 533
Rotes Rathaus (Berlin) **82–3**
Roth, Dieter 312
Rothenburg ob der Tauber 14
  hotels 497
  restaurants 521
  Street-by-Street map 266–7
Rothweil, Julius Ludwig 371, 374
Rottaler, Lukas 217, 218
Rottmayer, Michael 246
Rottweil **321**
Rousseau, Jean Jacques 160
Rübeland Caves 151
Rubens, Peter Paul 369, 396
  Bildergalerie (Potsdam) 139
  birthplace 414
  Deutsches Jagd-und Fischereimuseum (Munich) 217
  Diözesanmuseum (Freising) 269
  Jagdschloss Grunewald (Berlin) 108
  Kunsthalle (Bremen) 440
  Museum der Bildenden Künste (Leipzig) 167
  Niedersächsisches Landesmuseum (Hanover) 448
  Rape of the Daughters of Leukippos 227
  St Peter (Köln) 404
Schloss Friedenstein (Gotha) 193
Schloss Georgium (Dessau) 158
Schloss Weimar (Weimar) 198
Stigmatization of St Francis 408
Rüdesheim **377**
  hotels 500
  restaurants 526
Rudolf I, Emperor 53
Rudolstadt **200**
Rügen 15, 423, 427, 471, 473, **482–3**
  hotels 503
  restaurants 533
Ruhr River 387, 395
Rumford, Count von 230
Runge, Philipp Otto 485
  Morning 440
Rupert II, Abbot of Ottobeuren 289
Rupprecht, W 363
Rupprecht, Crown Prince 281
Ruprecht I, Elector 293, 300
Ruprecht III, Elector 303
Ruska, Ernst 39
Russische Kirche (Leipzig) **167**
Ry, Paul du 368, 369
Ry, Simon Louis du 368, 369
Rycheza, Queen of Poland 411
Ryckwaert, Cornelius 158

S
S-Bahn (railways) 558
Saalburg 375
Saalfeld **200–201**
Saarbrücken 341, **348**
  hotels 499
  restaurants 524
Saarland see Rhineland-Palatinate and Saarland
Saarwerden, Friedrich von 398
Sachs, Nelly 30
Sachsen, Clemens Wenzeslaus von 361
Sachsenhausen 137
Sächsische Schweiz (Saxon Switzerland) 17, 163, **182–3**
Sächsische Silberstraße **170**
Sächsische Staatsoper (Dresden) **172**
Sailing 43
St Andreas (Köln) **402**
St Annen-Stift (Goslar) **455**
St Aposteln (Köln) **405**
St Blasien 331
  restaurants 523
St Cajetan (Munich) 222
St Georg (Köln) **404–5**
St Gereon (Köln) **405**
St Goar
  restaurants 525
St Goarshausen
  restaurants 525
St-Hedwigs-Kathedrale (Berlin) 12, 73, **74**
St Jakobi (Goslar) **455**
St Jakobs Kirche (Rothenburg ob der Tauber) 266
St-Johannis-Friedhof (Nürnberg) **263**
St Kunibert (Köln) **405**
St Leonhardskirche (Frankfurt am Main) **380**
St Lorenz-Kirche (Nürnberg) **260–61**
St Ludwig's Church (Munich) **224**
St Maria im Kapitol (Köln) **404**
St Maria Lyskirchen (Köln) **404**
St Martin 351
  hotels 499
St-Matthäus-Kirche (Berlin) 89
St Michael's Church (Munich) **216**
St Pantaleon (Köln) **405**
St Pauli (Hamburg) 13, **442–3**
St Peter (Köln) **404**
St Peter and St Paul (Goslar) **455**
St Peter und St Paul (Weimar) **198**
St Petrikirche (Hamburg) **438**
Saint-Pierre, Joseph 256
St Severi-Kirche (Erfurt) **196**
St Ursula (Köln) **405**
Sakmann, Bert 39
Salem **323**
Saler, J I 298
Sales 534
Sammlung Berggruen (Berlin) **100**
Sanssouci (Potsdam) see Park Sanssouci
Sauerbronn, Baron Karl Friedrich von 298
Sauerland 388, **414–15**
Saxe-Hildburghausen, Thérèse von 231
Saxon Switzerland see Sächsische Schweiz
Saxony **163–85**
  climate 49
  hotels 494
  map 164–5
  restaurants 514–16
  Sächsische Schweiz **182–3**
  Sächsische Silberstraße **170**
  see also Lower Saxony
Saxony-Anhalt **147–61**
  climate 49
  Harz Mountain trail 151

Saxony-Anhalt (cont.)
hotels 493–4
map 148–9
restaurants 513–14
Schabbelhaus (Lübeck) **468**
Schack, Adolf Friedrich von 223
Schack-Galerie (Munich) **223**
Schadow, Friedrich Wilhelm 396
Schadow, Johann Gottfried 75, 79, 159
Quadriga 73
Schaiblingsturm (Passau) 279
Schaper, Hermann 90
Scharoun, Hans
Deutsches Schifffahrtsmuseum
(Bremerhaven) 437
Musikinstrumenten-Museum (Berlin)
93
Philharmonie (Berlin) 88, 93
Staatsbibliothek (Berlin) 89
Weißenhofsiedlung (Stuttgart) 314
Wolfsburg 445
Schedel 262
Scheer, Johann 299
Scheibe, Richard 92, 103
Scheidemann, Philipp 97
Scheinbar (Berlin) 117
Schelling, Friedrich von 320
Scherer, Hans the Younger 157
Schickhard, Heinrich 320
Schiffshebewerk (Chorin) 144
Schiller, Friedrich 30, 58
Jena 200
Marbach 309
monument to 71
Schillerhaus (Weimar) **198**
statue of 76, 313
Tübingen 320
Weimar 126, 187, 198
Schillerplatz (Stuttgart) **313**
Schilling, Johannes 172
Schindler, Oskar 273
Schinkel, Karl Friedrich 59, 79, 106
Altes Museum 79
Elisenbrunnen (Aachen) 399
Johanniskirche (Zittau) 185
Klein Glienicke (Berlin) 109
Konzerthaus (Berlin) 76
Neue Wache (Berlin) 72, 75
Neuruppin 136
Nikolaikirche (Potsdam) 139
Römische Bäder (Potsdam) 142
Schinkel-Museum (Berlin) **75**
Schinkelwache (Dresden) 172
Schloss Babelsberg (Potsdam) 143
Schloss Charlottenhof (Potsdam) 143
Schloss Ehrenburg (Coburg) 247
Schloss Stolzenfels (Koblenz) 342
Schloss Tegel (Berlin) 104
Schlossbrücke (Berlin) 76, 77
Schlosspark (Berlin) 101
Stolzenfels 358
Viktoriapark (Berlin) 107
Schinkelwache (Dresden) **172**
Schlachtberg 193
Schlaun, Johann Conrad
Augustusburg (Brühl) 410
Clemenswerth 432
Münster 390, 391, 392
Schlegel, Johann Gottfried 198
Schleißheim 207, **268–9**
Schleiden 410
Schleswig **464**
festivals 45
hotels 503
restaurants 532
Schleswig-Holstein **459–69**
climate 48
Helgoland **462**
hotels 502–3
map 460–61

Schleswig-Holstein (cont.)
restaurants 531–2
Schlichting (Munich) 235
Schliemann, Heinrich 101
Schliersee 208
Schlitz 479
Schlöndorff, Volker 25
Schlör, Simon 313
Schloss Babelsberg (Potsdam) **143**
Schloss Belvedere (Weimar) 187, **199**
Schloss Benrath (Düsseldorf) **397**
Schloss Burg 398
Schloss Charlottenburg (Berlin) 12, 99,
102–3
Schloss Charlottenhof (Potsdam) 140,
142–3
Schloss Favorite (Ludwigsburg) 207
Schloss Glücksburg 463
Schloss Güstrow 473
Schloss Lembeck 392
Schloss Linderhof 15
Schloss Moritzburg 17
Schloss Mosigkau (Mosigkau) 158
Schloss Neue Kammern (Potsdam) **142**
Schloss Neuschwanstein 15, 205,
286–7
Schloss Nordkirchen 392
Schloss Nymphenburg (Munich) 207,
228–9
Schloss Pfaueninsel (Berlin) 109
Schloss Pillnitz (Dresden) **177**
Schloss Raesfeld 392
Schloss Ranis 201
Schloss Sanssouci (Potsdam) 12, 127,
142
Schloss Seehof (Bamberg) **253**
Schloss Solitude (Stuttgart) **315**
Schloss Stolzenfels (Koblenz) 342
Schloss Tegel (Berlin) **104–5**
Schloss Thurn und Taxis (Regensburg)
273
Schloss Weesenstein 182
Schloss Weimar (Weimar) **198**
Schloss Wittenberg (Lutherstadt
Wittenberg) 158
Schloss Wörlitz 127
Schlossbrücke (Berlin) 12, **76**, 77
Schlossgarten (Stuttgart) **312**
Schlosskirche (Lutherstadt Wittenberg)
158
Schlosspark (Berlin) **100–101**
Schlosspark Theater (Berlin) 117
Schlossplatz (Berlin) **77**
Schlossplatz (Stuttgart) **312**
Schlot (Berlin) 115
Schlüter, Andreas
Marienkirche (Berlin) 82
Schlossplatz (Berlin) 77
statue of Friedrich Wilhelm I 82
Stralsund 481
Zeughaus (Berlin) 75
Schmalkalden 195
Schmalkalden Union 57, 130
Schmidt, Johann Georg 176
Schmidt-Rottluff, Karl 108, 169
Farm in Daugart 93
Schmitz, Bruno 167, 193, 360, 419
Schmölln
restaurants 517
Schmuzer, Franz 284
Schnabel, Tilemann 373
Schnebel, Dieter 33
Schneeberg 170
Schneider, Ernst 397
Schneider, Romy 231
Schnitger, Arp 439
Schnoorviertel (Bremen) **436**
Schnütgen-Museum (Köln) **404**
Schoch, Johann Leopold Ludwig 160
Scholl, Joseph 354

Scholz, Julius
Fighting on the Barricades in May 1848
59
Schonbein, Christian 39
Schönberg, Arnold 33
Schönborn, Damian Hugo von 299
Schönborn, Friedrich Karl von 250
Schönborn, Johann Philipp von 250
Schönborn, Lothar Franz von 246
Schönburg Castle 25
Schongauer, Martin 167, 449
Birth of Christ 94
Schramm, Carl Augustus 185
Schrobenhausen 270
Schröder, Gerhard 65
Schroer, Hans 270
Schuch, Carl 368
Schult, Johann 38
Schultes, Axel 413
Schultze-Naumburg, Paul 138
Schumann, Robert 33, 168
Schumann-Haus (Zwickau) 168
Schütting (Bremen) **435**
Schütz, Heinrich 32
Schwäbisch Gmünd **308**
Schwäbisch Hall **308**
Schwäbische Alb 17, **318–19**
Schwangau 46, 287
Schwanthaler, Ludwig
Bavaria statue 231
Bayerische Staatsbibliothek (Munich)
224
Feldherrnhalle (Munich) 222
Schwarzeck 208
Schwarzwald (Black Forest) 17, 326–7,
330–31
Schwechten, Franz 90
Schwedenspeicher-Museum (Stade) 443
Schwerin 14–15, 471, **474–5**
hotels 503
map 475
restaurants 533
Schweriner Schloss 37, **474**
Schwetzingen **298–9**
Schwind, Moritz von 190, 223, 287
Schwitters, Kurt 448
SchwuZ (Berlin) 115
Scientists and Inventors **38–9**
Sckell, Friedrich Ludwig von 230, 299
Sea Life Olympiapark (Munich) 237
Sebald, St 262
Security **546–7**
Sedlmayr, Helene 228
Seebüll 463, 465
Seeling, Heinrich 201
Seeon Abbey 283
Sehring, Bernhard 145
Seidl, Gabriel von
Bayerisches Nationalmuseum
(Munich) 223
Deutsches Museum (Munich) 232
Lenbachhaus (Munich) 225
Seiz, Johannes 346
Semper, Gottfried
Brühlsche Terrasse (Dresden) 176
Festspielhaus (Bayreuth) 257
Gemäldegalerie Alte Meister
(Dresden) 179, 180
Sächsische Staatsoper (Dresden) 172
Schloss Branitz (Cottbus) 145
Semperoper (Dresden) 172
Serro, Johann 288
Severinsviertel (Köln) **405**
Severinus, St 278
Severus, St 196
Seybold, M 258
Seyffer, Hans 308
Shopping **534–5**
Berlin **110–11**
Munich **234–5**

Show-jumping 42
Siegburg 411
  restaurants 528
Siegen **414**
  hotels 501
Siegessäule (Berlin) **91**
Siek
  restaurants 532
Siemens, Ernest W 39
Siemenshaus (Goslar) **455**
Sigismund, Emperor 56
Sigismund, Prince 217
Sigmaringen 294, 319
Silbermann, Gottfried 169, 172
Silver
  Sächsische Silberstraße 170
Simone Martini 201
  Madonna and Child 409
Simonetti, Giovanni 76
Sindelfingen 315
Sinwellturm (Nürnberg) 14
Sixt Rent-a-Car 557
Skiing 43, **537**, 539
Slegel, Georg 418
Slevogt, Max 351, 368, 434
Slips (Munich) 235
Smids, Michael Matthias 137
Snethlage, Captain 109, 138
Snyders, Frans 217
SO 36 (Berlin) 115
Soest **415**
Soest, Albert von 444
Soest, Conrad von 371, 390, 394, 415
Sögel 432
Solingen **398**
Soltau **444**
Sommer, Oskar 378
Sondershausen **192**
Sophie Charlotte, Electress 102
Sophienclub (Berlin) 115
Sorbs 184, **185**
South African Embassy 545
Southern Germany 203–331
  Baden-Wurttemberg **293–331**
  The Baroque in Southern Germany
    206–7
  Bavaria **243–91**
  German Alps **208–9**
  map 204–5
  Munich **211–41**
Souvenirs, shopping 535
Spa vacations **538**, 539
Spandau **104**
Specialist holidays **538**, 539
Speck, Paul 168
Spee, Friedrich von 346
Speed limits 556, 557
Speicherstadt (Hamburg) 13, **439**
Speyer **350**
  hotels 499
  restaurants 524
Spiegelau 275
Spiekeroog 432
Spielzeugmuseum (Bremen) 436
Spielzeugmuseum (Nürnberg) **262**
Spindler + Klatt (Berlin) 115
Spirits 508
Spitzweg, Carl 223, 225, 271
Sports **42–3**
  activity holidays **536–7**
  Berlin **114**, 115
  Munich **237**
Spranger, Bartholomeus 448
Spree River 77, 78, 184
Spreewald 45, 133, 135, **145**
Sprengel, Bernhard 448
Sprengel Museum (Hannover) **448**
Spring in Germany **44**
Staatliche Antikensammlungen
  (Munich) 13, **225**

Staatliche Kunsthalle Baden-Baden
  305
Staatliche Porzellan-Manufaktur
  (Meissen) **171**
Staatliches Museum (Schwerin) **474**
Staatsbibliothek (Berlin) 72, 89
Staatsgalerie (Stuttgart) **316–17**
Staatsoper Unter den Linden (Berlin)
  115
Staatstheater am Gärtnerplatz
  (Munich) 237
Stachelschweine (Berlin) 117
Stade **443**
Städel, Johann Friedrich 382
Städelsches Kunstinstitut (Frankfurt am
  Main) **382–3**
Stadtbibliothek (Trier) **346**
Stadthagen **446**
  restaurants 531
Stadtmuseum (Baden-Baden) **305**
Stadtmuseum (Erfurt) **197**
Stadtmuseum (Munich) **218**
Stadtmuseum (Weimar) **198**
Stalin, Joseph 143
Starcke, Johann Georg 166, 177
Stargard 478
Stasi-Museum (Berlin) **106**
Staufen im Breisgau 330
Stauffenberg, Claus Schenk von 92, 104
Stefenshagen 477
Steidl, Melchior 252
Steinbach, Erwin von 309
Steinbach, Wilhelm 483
Steiner, Johann 313
Steinerne Brücke (Regensburg) **272**
Steingaden 206
Steinkirchen 443
Steinplatte 208
Steintor (Rostock) **480**
Stendal **157**
Stengel, Friedrich Joachim 348
Steren, Johann von 248
Stiftskirche (Stuttgart) **313**
Stimmer, Tobias 305
Stirling, James 312, 316
Stoß, Andrew 255
Stoß, Veit
  Archangel 264
  Bamberg Cathedral 255
  Kirche St Sebald (Nürnberg) 262
  Rottweil 321
  St Lorenz-Kirche (Nürnberg) 261
  tomb of 263
Stock 282
Stolberg, Anna von 296
Stolpen 182
Stolzenfels 358
The Story of Berlin (Berlin) 115
Strabo 288
Strack, Johann Heinrich 91
Stralsund 15, 427, **481**
  hotels 503
  restaurants 533
Strandbad Wannsee (Berlin) 12, **108**
Straubing 45, **271**
  restaurants 521
Strauss, Richard 32, 33, 172, 198
Stuber, Nicolaus 297
Stuck, Franz von
  Die Sünde 230
  Villa Stuck (Munich) **230–31**
Student discounts 544
Stukenbrock 415
Stüler, Friedrich August
  Alte Nationalgalerie (Berlin) 79
  Neues Museum (Berlin) 79
  Nikolskoe 108
  Orangerie Schloss (Potsdam) 142
  Schweriner Schloss 474
Sturm und Drang 30

Sturmius 372
Stuttgart 17, **312–17**
  airport 553
  festivals 45, 46
  hotels 498
  map 313
  restaurants 523
  Staatsgalerie **316–17**
Suhl 195
Summer in Germany **45**
Sustris, Friedrich 216, 221
Swabian Jura *see* Schwäbische Alb
Swimming 43
Sylt 426, 459, **463**
  hotels 503
  restaurants 532
Synagogues
  Neue Synagoge (Berlin) **105**
Syrlin, Jörg the Elder 322
Syrlin, Jörg the Younger 322

T

Tagebau (Berlin) 111
Tangermünde **157**
  hotels 494
  restaurants 514
Tanzfabrik (Berlin) 115
Tauberbischofsheim **296**
Taxes, VAT refunds 534
Taxis 559
Taylor, Elizabeth 231
Tegernsee 209
Telemann, Georg Philipp 32
Telephones **550**
Television Tower (Munich) 213
Tempodrom (Berlin) 115
Tennis 42, **537**, 539
Ter Brugghen, Hendrick
  *Jacob accuses Laban of giving him Lai
    instead of Rachel as a Wife* 409
Teutoburger Wald (Teutoburg Forest)
  418–19, 433
Teutonic Order **297**
  Bad Mergentheim 296–7
  Koblenz 360
  Pfarrkirche Divi Blasii (Mühlhausen)
    192
Thale 151
Thalhofer, Johann 251
Theater am Potsdamer Platz (Berlin) 96
Theater des Westens (Berlin) 117
Theatinerkirche (Munich) 207, **222**
Theatre
  Berlin **116**, 117
  Deutsches Nationaltheater (Weimar)
    198
  Markgräfliches Opernhaus (Bayreuth)
    256
  Munich **236**, 237
Theft 546, 547
Theresa (Munich) 235
Theresienwiese (Munich) **231**
Thierchen Kindermode (Munich)
  235
Third Reich **62–3**
Thirty Years' War (1618–48) **57**, 243
Thonet, Michael 358
Thorwaldsen, Bertel 105, 313, 381
Thuringia **187–201**
  climate 49
  A Cultural Tour of East Germany
    16–17
  hotels 494–5
  map 188–9
  restaurants 516–17
  Thüringer Wald (Thuringian Forest)
    187, 189, **194–5**
Tickets, travelling in cities 559
Tieck, Friedrich 107

Tiepolo, Giovanni Battista 250, 251
Tiergarten (Berlin) 12, 68, **91**
Tierpark Hellabrunn (Munich) 237
Tietz, Ferdinand 346
Tilly, Johann 222, 274
Time zones 545
Tintoretto 167, 469
Tipping
    in hotels 489
    in restaurants 505
Tischbein, Johann H W 465
    Goethe in the Roman Campagna 58
Tischbein, Wilhelm 433
Titian 369
    Emperor Charles V 226
    Tribute Money 181
Todtmoos 330
Todtnau 330
Toilets, public 547
Tollwood Festival (Munich) 237
Topographie des Terrors
    (Berlin) **85**
Torgau **168**
    restaurants 516
Tourismusverband Ruppiner
    Land 539
Tourist information offices 542–3
Touristik Arbeitsgemeinschaft
    Romantische Straße 539
Tours by car
    Chiemsee **282–3**
    Deutsche Weinstraße **351**
    Moseltal **349**
    Münsterland **392**
    Nationalpark Müritz **479**
    Rhine Valley **358–9**
    Sächsische Silberstraße **170**
    Waldecker Land **370–71**
    Weser Renaissance trail **457**
Trabrennbahn (Berlin) 115
Trains **554–5**, 558
Trams 559
Tränenpalast (Berlin) 115
Travel **552–9**
    air **552–3**
    bicycles 559
    buses 558–9
    cars **556–7**
    in cities **558–9**
    coaches **557**
    ferries and ships **555**
    S-Bahn 558
    taxis 559
    trains **554–5**
    trams 559
    U-Bahn 558
Travellers' cheques 548
Treptower Park (Berlin) **107**
Tresch, Aberlin 312
Tresor (Berlin) 115
Trier 17, 339, 343, **344–7**
    hotels 499
    map 345
    restaurants 525
Trifels 351
Troisdorf
    restaurants 529
Trost, Paul Ludwig 222
Troth, Thilo von 153
Truman, Harry 143
Trusetal 195
Tschirnhaus, Ehrenfried Walther von
    128
Tschudi, Hugo von 224
Tübingen 17, **320**
    hotels 498
    restaurants 524
Turgenev, Ivan 305
Türkenmarkt (Berlin) 111

U

U-Bahn (underground railway) 558
Übelhör, Johann Baptist 284
Übelhör, Johann Georg 284
Übersee-Museum (Bremen) **436**
Überwasserkirche (Münster) **390–91**
Üblher, J G 247
Uetersen
    restaurants 532
Ulm 294, **322**
    festivals 45
    hotels 499
    restaurants 524
Ulrich, Duke of Mecklenburg 478
Ulrich, Prince 320
Umwelt Permits 557
UNESCO World Heritage Sites
    Aula Palatina (Konstantin-Basilika)
        (Trier) 345
    Bad Muskau 184
    Brühl 410
    Dom St Peter (Trier) 344
    Goslar 454, 455
    Hildesheim 452
    Kaiserdom (Speyer) 350
    Liebfrauenkirche (Trier) 344
    Lorsch 385
    Lübeck 459
    Maulbronn Abbey **306–7**
    Regensburg (Ratisbon) 272
    Völklinger Hütte 348
Unger, Georg Christian 142
Ungers, Oswald Mathias 381, 440
United Airlines 553
United States Embassy 545
Universitätsbibliothek (Heidelberg) **303**
Universities
    Bonn **412**
    Göttingen 456
    Heidelberg 301, **303**
    Humboldt Universität (Berlin) 72, **75**
    Jena 200
Unter den Linden (Berlin) 12, 72, **74–5**
Urschalling 282
Urzula, St 169
Usedom 427, **485**

V

Valentin, Karl 218
Valentine, St 377
Van Dyck, Anton
    Bildergalerie (Potsdam) 139
    Jagdschloss Grunewald (Berlin) 108
    Kunsthalle (Bremen) 436
    Niedersächsisches Landesmuseum
        (Hanover) 448
    Schloss Friedenstein (Gotha) 193
Van Gogh, Vincent 100, 176
VAT refunds 534
Vauban, Sébastien Le Prestre 328, 348,
    351
Vegetarian food 505
Velázquez, Diego
    Portrait of a Man 181
Velde, Henri van de 100, 414
Velen, Alexandra II von 37
Verband Deutscher Berg- und Skiführer
    (VDBS) 539
Verband Deutscher Naturparke 539
Verband Deutscher Sporttaucher
    (VDST) 539
Verden an der Aller (Bremen) 437
Verdun, Nikolaus von 407
Verkehrsmuseum (Dresden) **173**
Vermeer, Jan 447
    The Geographer 383
    Girl Reading a Letter 180
    The Glass of Wine 95

Vernukken, Wilhelm 369
Versailles Treaty (1919) 62, 63
Veste Oberhaus (Passau) 279
Victoria, Queen of England 194
Viehmarktthermen (Trier) **346**
Vienna, Congress of (1815) 163
Vierzehnheiligen 205, **247**
Vikings 464
Viktor, St 393
Viktoriapark (Berlin) **107**
Viktualienmarkt (Munich) 12, **218**, 235
Villa Stuck (Munich) **230–31**
Villa Wahnfried (Bayreuth) **256**
Vinache, Jean Joseph 176
Viniculture (Berlin) 111
Viniversität – Die Weinschule GmbH
    539
Virchow, Rudolf 75
Virneburg, Archbishop Heinrich von
    376
VISA (credit cards) 548
Visas 542
Visbek 433
Viscardi, Giovanni Antonio 216, 217,
    222
Vischer, Hans 158
Vischer, Peter the Elder 262
Vischer workshop 475
Vischering 392
Visit Berlin 115
Vogeler, Heinrich 437
Völkerkundemuseum (Munich) **219**
Völkerschlachtdenkmal (Leipzig) **167**
Völklingen **348**
Volksbühne (Berlin) 117
Vos, Martin de 445
Vries, Adrian de 291, 446

W

Waase 482
Waesemann, Hermann Friedrich 82
Wagner, Cosima 256
Wagner, Richard 25, 32, 33, 45, **256**
    Bayreuth **256–7**
    Deutsches Nationaltheater (Weimar)
        198
    Festspielhaus (Bayreuth) 257
    Sächsische Staatsoper (Dresden) 172
    Schloss Neuschwanstein 205
    statue of 91
    Tannhäuser 190
    tomb of 256
    Villa Wahnfried (Bayreuth) **256**
    Wiesbaden 376
Waiblingen 315
Walchensee 209
Waldbühne (Berlin) 117
Waldeck 371
Waldeck, Georg Friedrich von 370
Waldecker Land **370–71**
Walderdorff, Johann Philipp von 346
Waldmüller, Ferdinand Georg 224
Walhalla (Donaustauf) 259
Walking excursions **536**, 539
    Bayerischer Wald **275**
    Harz Mountain trail **151**
    Sächsische Schweiz **182–3**
    Thüringer Wald **194–5**
Wallenstein, General 481
Wallfahrtskirche Maria Gern 281
Wallfahrtskirche Mariahilf (Passau) 279
Wallot, Paul 60, 69, 97
Wallraf, Ferdinand Franz 408
Wallraf-Richartz-Museum & Fondation
    Corboud (Köln) **408–9**
Walther, Wilhelm 173
Walther von der Vogelweide 248
Wamser, Christoph 402
Wangerooge 432

Wannenmacher, Joseph 321
Wannsee 108
Waren 479
Warhol, Andy 380
Warnemünde
    hotels 503
Wartburg (Eisenach) 16, 36, 187, **190–91**
Wasserburg 325
Wasserschloss Concordia (Bamberg) **252**
Water, drinking 547
Water sports **536–7**, 539
Waterfalls
    Hangloch-Wasserfall 331
    Truseltal 195
The Watt 427, 432
Watteau, Jean-Antoine 129
    Feast of Love 180
    Gersaint's Shop Sign 103
    Love in the French Theatre 95
    Pilgrimage to the Isle of Cythera 383
Watzmann 208
Weather **48–9**
Weber, Carl Maria von 33
Wechselburg 168
Weißenhofsiedlung (Stuttgart) **314**
Weigel, Hélène
    Brecht-Weigel-Gedenkstätte (Berlin) 105
Weikersheim **297**
Weil der Stadt 315
Weilburg **374–5**
    hotels 500
    restaurants 526
Weimar 16, 126, 187, **198–9**
    festivals 46
    hotels 495
    map 199
    restaurants 517
Weimar Republic 62, 198
Weinbrenner, Friedrich 304, 305
Weingarten **323**
    festivals 44
Weinhart, Kaspar 305
Weizsäcker, Richard von 65
Welf family 52, 322, 445, 447
Welles, Orson 231
Welsch, Maximilian von 246, 250, 299, 381
Werden 394
Werner, Anton von
    Inauguration of the Reichstag 60–61
Wernigerode 37, **150**
Wertheim **296**
Weser Renaissance trail **457**
Westerland 463
Western Germany **333–419**
    Hesse **365–85**
    map 334–5
    North Rhine-Westphalia **387–419**
    Rhineland-Palatinate and Saarland **341–63**
    Romanesque architecture **338–9**
    Wine in Western Germany **336–7**
Westfalen, Arnold von 171
Westfälische Mühlenstrasse 419
Westpark Spielzone Ost Untersendling (Munich) 237
Westphalia see North Rhine-Westphalia
Wettin, Albrecht 171
Wettin, Ernst 171
Wettin, Friedrich von 156
Wettin dynasty 58, 187
    Coburg 246
    Dresden 172, 180
Wetzlar **374**
    hotels 500
    restaurants 526
Weyden, Rogier van der

St Luke Painting the Madonna 226
Woman in a Bonnet 94
Wheelchair access see Disabled travellers
White Trash (Berlin) 115
Wichmann, Archbishop 156
Wichmann, Ludwig 107
Widmann, Jörg 33
Widukind, Duke 51, 419
Wieck 480, 484
Wieland, Christoph Martin 187, 198
Wiemken, Edo 432
Wienhausen 445
Wiesbaden **376**
    hotels 500
    restaurants 526
Wiesinger, Wolfgang 274
Wietze 445
Wild at Heart (Berlin) 115
Wilder, Billy 231
Wildlife
    Flora and Fauna **28–9**
    German Alps **209**
Wilhelm, Elector of Hesse 369
Wilhelm I, Kaiser 59, 60, 360
    monument to 193
    Schloss Babelsberg (Potsdam) 143
    tomb of 101
Wilhelm I, King of Wurttemberg 312, 315, 316
Wilhelm II, Kaiser 81, 376
    monument to 419
    Reichstag (Berlin) 61
    World War I 62
Wilhelm IV the Steadfast 226
Wilhelm V, Duke of Bavaria 216, 219, 271
Wilhelm V, Prince 269
Wilhelmine, Margravine of Bayreuth 256
Wilhelmshöhe (Kassel) **369**
Willibald 259
Wimbachklamm 208
Windberg 271
Wines **509**
    Deutsche Weinstraße tour **351**
    shopping 535
    Wine in Western Germany **336–7**
Winkel 377
Winningen 337
Winter in Germany **47**
Winterfeldmarkt (Berlin) 111
Wintergarten Variété (Berlin) 117
Wismar 15, **476–7**
Wisniewski, Edgar 93
Wittelsbach dynasty 53, 58
    Bavaria 243
    Heidelberg Castle 302
    Hohenschwangau 287
    Ingolstadt 269
    Munich 214, 216, 220
    Schloss Dachau (Dachau) 268
Witten, Hans von 446, 455
Wittenberg see Lutherstadt Wittenberg
Wittstock **136**
Wittumspalais (Weimar) **198**
Witz, Konrad 264
Wochenmarkt (Berlin) 111
Wölfel, Carl 256
Wolfenbüttel **447**
    hotels 502
    restaurants 531
Wolff, Jakob 262
Wolfsburg **445**
    hotels 502
    restaurants 531
Wolgast **484–5**
Wolgemut, Michael 168, 258, 263, 265, 321
Women travellers 546

World War I **62**
World War II **63**, 64
    Dresden 172
    Hamburg 442
    Peenemünde **485**
    Potsdam 138
    Potsdam Conference **143**
    Würzburg 248
Wörlitz 149
    restaurants 514
Wörlitz Park **160–61**
Worms 338, 341, **350**
    hotels 499
    restaurants 525
Worpswede 437, 443
Wou, Gerhard 196
Wrede, Karl Philipp von 222
Writers **30–31**
Wühlmäuse (Berlin) 117
Wuppertal **395**
    hotels 501
    restaurants 529
Wurstküche (Regensburg) **272**
Wurttemberg see Baden-Wurttemberg
Würzburg 14, **248–51**
    hotels 497
    map 249
    Residenz 204, **250–51**
    restaurants 521–2

X

Xanten 387, 389, **393**
    hotels 501
    restaurants 529

Y

Youth hostels **490**, 491
Yso, Bishop 437

Z

Zanth, Karl Ludwig Wilhelm von 315
Zeiller, Franz Anton 289
Zeiller, Johann Jakob 289
Zeiss-Planetarium (Berlin) 115
Zenith Flohmarkt (Munich) 235
Zenith Kulturhalle (Munich) 237
Zentrale für den Landurlaub Landschriften 491
Zentraler Kartenverkauf (Munich) 237
Zentrales Fundbüro Berlin 547
Zeughaus (Augsburg) 290
Zeughaus (Berlin) 73, **75**
Zick, Januarius 299
Zick, Johann 251, 299
Ziebland, Georg Friedrich 225, 287
Ziegler, Karl 39
Zimmermann, Franz 229
Zimmermann, Johann Baptist 206, 229
Zingst 15, 480
Zittau **185**
    hotels 494
Zoologischer Garten (Berlin) **91**, 115
Zucalli, Enrico 228
    Dreifaltigkeitkirche (Munich) 217
    Ettal 284
    Schleißheim 269
    Universität (Bonn) 412
Zuckmayer, Carl 106
Zugspitze 209
Zuse, Konrad 39
Zwickau **168**
    restaurants 516
Zwiesel 275
Zwinger (Dresden) 17, 127, **178–9**
Zwingli, Huldreich 373

Acknowledgments

Dorling Kindersley and Wiedza i Życie would like to thank the following people for their help in preparing this guide:

Additional Text Michał Jaranowski, Barbara Sudnik-Wójcicka, Grażyna Winiarska, Konrad Gruda, Bożena Steinborn

Additional Photographs Amin Akhtar, Francesca Bondy, Maciej Bronarski, Demetrio Carrasco, Witold Danilkiewicz, Claire Jones Grzegorz Kłosowski, Renata and Marek Kosińscy, Sergiusz Michalski, Nils Meyer, Ian O'Leary, Jürgen Scheunemann, Andrzej Zygmuntowicz and Ireneusz Winnicki, Władysław Wisławski

Publishing Manager Helen Townsend

Managing Art Editor Kate Poole

Consultant Gerhard Bruschke

Factcheckers Joel Dullroy, Claudia Himmelreich, Barbara Sobeck, Jürgen Scheunemann

Director of Publishing Gillian Allan

Revisions Team
Emma Anacootee, Sam Atkinson, Claire Baranowski, Sonal Bhatt, Hilary Bird, Arwen Burnett, Susi Cheshire, Sherry Collins, Lucinda Cooke, Jo Cowen, Surya Deogun, Joel Dullroy, Conrad Van Dyk, Jeremy Gray, Marcus Hardy, Lucinda Hawksley, Kaberi Hazarika, Christine Heilman, Jacky Jackson, Claire Jones, Maite Lantaron, Carly Madden, Hayley Maher, Nicola Malone, Jeroen van Marle, Claire Marsden, Ferdie McDonald, Sam Merrell, Rebecca Milner, Kate Molan, Casper Morris, Sangita Patel, Marianne Petrou, Dave Pugh, Marisa Renzullo, Simon Ryder, Sands Publishing Solutions, Sadie Smith, James Stewart, Andrew Szudek, Rebecca Taylor, Leah Tether, Craig Turp, Karen Villabona, Stewart J. Wild, Christian Williams

Additional Picture Research Rachel Barber, Marta Bescos, Rhiannon Furbear, Ellen Root, Nikhil Verma

The publisher would also like to thank all the people and institutions who allowed photographs belonging to them to be reproduced, as well as granting permission to use photographs from their archives:

Archäologische Staatssammlung in Munich; Arthothek (Jürgen Hinrichsowi); Bavaria Filmstadt; Bayerisches National-museum in Munich; Bildarchiv Preussischer Kulturbesitz in Berlin (Heidrun Klein); Bildvorlagen Römerschatz – Gäubodenmuseum Straubing (Dr. Prammer); Bischöfliches Dom- und Diözesanmuseum Mainz (Dr. Hansowi-Jurgenowi Kotzurowi); Brecht-Weigel-Gedenkstätte in Berlin (Elke Pfeil); Bridgeman Art Library; Bröhan-Museum in Berlin (Ingrid Jagr and Frau Betzker); Brücke-Museum in Berlin; Brüder-Grimm-Museum in Kassel; Corbis; Das Domkapitel (Gertraut Mockel, Büro Dr Georg Minkenberg); Deutsches Apothekenmuseum in Heidelberg; Deutsches Historisches Museum in Berlin (Kathi Rumlow); Deutsche Presse Agentur (dpa) in Berlin (Tanija Teichmann); Deutsches Museum in Munich (Sigrid Schneider and Marlene Schwarz); Deutsches Schifffahrtsmuseum in Bremerhaven (Hansowi-Walterowi Kewelohowi); Deutsches Tapetenmuseum Kassel (Sabine Thümmler); Deutsches Technikmuseum Berlin (Renate Förster); Diözesanmuseum in Bamberg (Birgit Kandora); Dombauverwaltung des Metropolitankapitels Köln (Birgit Lambert); Dresden Museum für Geschichte der Stadt Dresden (Dr. Christel Wünsch); Flash Press Media (Sylwii Wilgockiej); Forschungs- und Gedenkstätte Normannenstraße (Stasi-Museum) in Berlin (Andrei Holland-Moritz); Fürstlich Hohenzollernsche Schlossverwaltung in Sigmaringen (Heldze Boban); Gemäldegalerie Alte Meister (Steffi Reh); Gemäldegalerie Neue Meister (Gisela Mehnert); Germanisches Nationalmuseum in Nuremberg (Hermanowi Maué); Hamburger Bahnhof in Berlin; Hamburger Kunsthalle; Hessisches Landesmuseum Kassel; Käthe-Kollwitz-Museum in Berlin (A. Ingrid Findell); Komische Oper Berlin (Gaby Hofmann); Kunstmuseum Düsseldorf (Anne-Marie Katins); Kunstsammlungen Paula Modersohn in Bremen (Hubertusowi Morgenthalowi); Kunstsammlungen zu Weimar (Angelice Goder); Kunstverlag Maria Laach

(Helmutowi Keipowi); Kurdirektion des Berchtesgadener Landes (Vroni Aigner, Birgit Tica); Landesmuseum Trier (Margot Redwanz); LBB Photo Archives (Dyrektorowi Christophowi Kalischowi); Linden-Museum Stuttgart, Staatliches Museum für Völkerkunde (Dr. Doris Kurelli); Lutherstube in Wittenberg (Jutcie Strehle); Markgräfliches Opernhaus in Bayreuth; Mercedes-Benz-Museum in Stuttgart; Museum am Ostwall in Dortmund; Museum der Bildenden Künste in Leipzig (Roswitha Engel); Museum Folkwang in Essen, Stadt Essen (Mr Hildebrandowi); Museum of the City of Berlin; Porzellansammlung (Ulrike Maltschew); Rheinisches Landesmuseum Bonn (Dr Gerhard Bauchhenß); Rüstkammer (Yvonne Brandt); Schlösserverwaltung in Munich (Frau Gerum); Seebul Ada und Emil Nolde (Dr Andreasowi Fluckowi); Staatliche Graphische Sammlung in Munich (Wiebke Tomaschek); Staatliche Kunstsammlungen Dresden, Albertinum,Grünes Gewölbe; Staatliche Porzellan-Manufaktur Meißen GMBH (Christine Mangold); Staatliche Schlösser und Gärten, Pforzheim (Herr Braunowi); Staatsarchiv Hamburg (Kathrin Berger); Staatsgalerie Stuttgart (Frau Fönnauer); Städelsches Kunstinstitut in Frankfurt am Main (Elisabeth Heinemann); Stadt Köln, Wallraf-Richartz-Museum in Cologne (Dr Roswitha Neu-Kock and Dr Mai); Stadtmuseum in Munich; Stiftung Luthergedenkstätten in Sachsen-Anhalt; Stiftung Preussische Schlösser und Gärten Berlin (Carli Kamarze); Superstock Polska Sp. z.o.o. (Elżbiecie Gajewskiej); Von der Heydt-Museum Wuppertal (Margarecie Janz); Wartburg-Stiftung in Eisenach (Petrze Wilke); Zefa (Ewie Kozłowskiej)

The publisher would also like to thank the following for their assistance on the guide: Joanna Minz for coordinating information, Tamara and Jacek Draber for their help with correspondence and telephone contacts, Jürgen Christoffer of Deutscher Wetterdienst for meteorological information.

Picture Credits

a-above; b-below/bottom; c-centre; f-far; l-left; r-right; t-top.

Works of art have been reproduced with the permission of the following copyright holders: DACS, London 2011: 31c, 35c, 63clb, 91cl, 93tl, © Munch Museum/Munch - Ellingsen Group, BONO, Oslo/DACS, London 2011 92cra, 409cra, 441cra; © Succession Picasso/DACS, 2011 100tl, 317crb.

Aachener Dom. (Copyright: Dornkapitel Aachen – photo. Ann Münchow) 400cla, 400cb, 401t (Skarbiec); 401cra, 401crb, 401br, 401bl; **Hotel Adlon Kempinski:** 492bl; **Alamy Images:** alwaysstock, LLC/Michael Hill 538tr; David Angel 70; archiv-berlin Fotoagentur GmbH/J. Henkelmann 111tl; Arco Images 534cr; Jon Arnold Images/Walter Bibikow 26tr; Michael bennett 428; BL Images Ltd 10tc, 235cr; Caro/Waechter 559c; FAN travelstock/Sabine Lubenow 536br, 537cl; Iconotexc/Ettore Venturini 535tr; imagebroker 202-3, 386, 458, 470; imagebroker/Manfred Bail 235tl, 556bl; imagebroker/Michael Fischer 537br; INTERFOTO 8-9; Andre Jenny 234cra; Yadid Levy 234bl, 506cla; Muhs 86; John Norman 132; PjrTravel 326-7; Gillian Price 536cl; Robert Stainforth 552cla; **Albertinum:** (Dresden) 176tr; **Clara Alboth's Restaurant:** 516br; **Allianz Arena München Stadion GmbH:** 237tl; **Altes Haus:** 524bl; **Amt für Stadtmarketing und Touristik, Limburg:** 366cla; **Archäologische Staatssammlung:** (Munich) 223br; **Artothek:** 34tr, 34bc, 35cra, 35bc, 58tl, 180cla, 180bc, 181tl, 181ca, 181cra, 181bc, 181br, 226cla, 440ca, 440clb, 440bl, 441cra, 441bc, 448t; Joachim Blauel 35crb, 54tr, 226tr, 226bc, 227crb, 298cr; 226cla, 227tl, 227cra, 263tr; Bayer d/Mitko 227br; Sophie-R. Gnamm 230cr; Alexander Koch 35cra; Christoph Sandig 474br; G. Westermann 436bl, 441tc; **Auerbachs Keller Restaurant:** 515br. Basic AG 534bl; **Bavaria Filmstadt:** 231tl; **Hotel Bayrisches Haus:** 513bl; **Bayerische Staatsoper:** Wilfried Hösl 236bl; **Hotel Bellevue:** 505br, 531bl; **Berlin Tourismus Marketing GmbH:** www.berlin-tourist-information.de 101br, 543tl, 545cra; **BerlinerFestspiele:** Bianka Gobel 113tr; **Berliner Sparkasse:** 548bl; **Brecht-Weigel-Gedenkstätte:** (Berlin) 105bc; **Bridgeman Art Library:** 38bl, 107tl; **;Bronarski Maciej:** 338tr, 354tr, 354cla, 354clb, 355tc, 355cra, 355crb, 355bc; **Bröhan-Museum:** (Berlin) 100tl; **Brüder-Grimm-Museum:** (Kassel) 368cra, 372tr (© Staatliche Museum Kassel). **City of Munich – Fire Department:** 547tl; **Congress-und Tourismus-Zentrale Nürnberg:** 261tl; **Corbis:** 33tr, 33clb, 33bl, Annebicque Bernard/ Sygma 507tl; Massimo

Borchi 340; Wolfgang Deuter/zefa 215cr; Werner Dieterich 162, 450-1; Jack Fields 176c, ivoivanov 364; Sylvain Sonnet 486-7; Herbert Spichtinger/zefa 236cra; Michael S.Yamashita 507c; **Danilkiewicz Witold:** 429b, 470, 478tl; **Deutsches Museum, Munich:** 544tl; **Deutsches Postbank:** 551clb; **Deutsches Apothekenmuseum:** (Heidelberg) 302tr; **Deutsches Technikmuseum Berlin:** 85br; **Deutsches Historisches Museum Berlin:** (Zeughaus) 30bc, 32c, 38ca, 38cla, 38clb, 38br, 39cla, 39tl, 39tr, 39clb, 39cb, 39crb, 39cbr (Holz & Kunststoff), 40cla, 50, 56tl (R. Bemke), 56cra (Jurgen Liepe), 56cb, 56b (A.C. Theil), 57tl (R. Boemke), 58br, 59tr, 59cla, 60clb, 64bc, 64br, 130tr, 130bl; **Deutsches Schifffahrtsmuseum Bremerhaven:** 54cla; **Die Bank Brasserie:** 530t; **dpa:** 30ca, 31tl, 31cra, 31crb, 31br, 31bl, 32tr, 39cla, 39cra, 39bl, 40tr, 43cl, 43br, 44cla, 47cr, 64ca, 143cra, 209tl, 465tr; Claus Felix 47bl; Matthias Hiekel 44bc; Wulf Hirschberger 45br; Frank Leonhardt 42tr; Wolfgang Kluge 32bl; Wolfgang Komm 65clb Kay Nietfeld 43tr; Frank Mächler 45tc; Carsten Rehder 42ca; Wulf Pfeiffer 45cl; Martin Schutt 46tc, 185br; Roland Scheidemann 47tl; Ingo Wagner 65tl; Heinz Wieseler 46bl; **DK Images:** Posteritati/Judith Miller 116cl; Dorint Hotels & Resorts: 501tr; **Drachenhaus Restaurant:** 512tr; **Dreamstime.com:** Adoggster 15t; Francesco Carucci 65br; Editor77 547clb; Eixeneize 75tl; Europhotos 394tl; Karelgallas 10tl; Plotnikov 14bl; Dmitry Rozhdestvenskiy 13tr; Rumifaz 72cl; Anibal Trejo 17tr; Wam 1975 14tr; **Dresden Museum für Geschichte der Stadt Dresden:** 59crb. **Eisenach-Wartburg Stiftung:** 190cla, 190clb, 190bc, 191ca; **L'escalier Restaurant:** 528tl. **Hotel Fährhaus Sylt:** 505tl, 532b; **Fairmont Hotels & Resorts:** 502bl, 503bc; **Foto-Thueringen:** Barbara Neumann 126cb; **Fotolia:** draghicich 146; Fotito 540-1; Jörg Hackemann 416-7; take 11tr. **Gäubodenmuseum Straubing:** 110bl; **Germanisches Nationalmuseum:** (Nuremberg) 264-5 (all images); **Getty Images:** AFP 547cla, 559br; Richard l'Anson 292; Danita Delimont 242, 356-7; Sean Gallup 558cla; Oliver Gerhard 186; Tina & Horst Herzig 537tr; LatitudeStock - TTL 420-2; Hans-Peter Merten 22; narvikk 66-7; Popperfoto 31tr; Andreas Rentz 544br; Patrik Stollarz 42bl, 557tl; **Grünes Gewölbe:** (Dresden) 176t.**Gullivers Bus GmnH:** 557bl; **Hamburger Bahnhof:** (Berlin) 97bl; **Hamburger Kunsthalle:** (Hamburg) 34cla, 440tr; **Hessisches Landesmuseum Kassel:** 368cla, 368bl (© Staatliche Museum Kassel Deutsches Tapetenmuseum); **Hohe Duene Hotel:** 504bl; **Hotel Palace, Berlin:** 488cla; **Hyatt Regency Mainz:** 499bl. **Ihr Herzle-Team:** 520b; **Intercontinental Berchtesgaden Resort:** 496tl, 519tc; **KaDeWe store, Berlin:** Quelle 535bl; **Käfers Bistro:** 526t; **Käthe-Kollwitz-Museum:** (Berlin) 91cl; **Kłosowski Grzegorz:** 28cra; **Kloster Maulbronn:** 306bc, 306clb, 307tl, 307ca, 307cra, 307tr; **Köln Bonn Airport:** 553tl; **Kölner Dom:** 406cl, 406br, 407tl, 407cra, 407cb, 407bl, 407br (© Dombauarchiv Köln, Matz und Schenk); **Komische Oper:** (Berlin) Monika Ritterhaus 112br; **Kosińscy, Renata and Marek:** 28clb, 28bra, 28blb, 29cla, 29tlb, 29blb, 209ca, 209tr, 209cl, 209cr, 209crb; **Kunstmuseum Düsseldorf:** 34clb; **Kunstsammlungen Paula Modersohn:** 437tl; **Kunstverlag Maria Laach:** 338br, 362tr, 362cla, 363tl, 363cra, 363crb, 363bl; **Kurdirektion des Berchtesgadener Landes:** Storto, Leonberg 280bl. **Landesmuseum Trier:** Thomas Zühmer 346c; **Linden Museum für Völkerkunde:** (Stuttgart) 314cla; **Lübeck and Travemuende Tourist-Service GmbH:** HLTS 466cla; **Ludwigsburg – Schloss:** 310ca, 310clb, 310bl, 311tc; **Lutherstube:** (Wittenberg) 131tl. **Mainz – Dom:** 339bl (© M. Hankel-Studio); **Manyo Restaurant:** 519bl; **Café Restaurant Meissen:** 515tc; **Mercedes-Benz-Museum:** (Stuttgart) 314tr; **Le Méridien Grand Hotel Nürnburg:** 497bl; **Meyer Nils:** 64crb; **Michalski Sergiusz:** 24t; **Mittelalterliches Museum:** (Rothenburg ob der Tauber) 266br; **mosellandtouristik:** REMET 349cb; **Motel One:** 495bl; **Munich Police:** 546cla; **Museum der Bildenden Künste:**

(Leipzig) 55tl (MdbK, Gerstenberger 1994); **Museum Brandhorst:** 543br; **Museum Folkwang:** (Essen) 35tc; **Museum für Naturkunde:** (Berlin) 97br; **Musikinstrumenten-Museum:** (Berlin) 89cra. **Nationalmuseum:** (Munich) 223clb. **Opernhaus:** (Bayreuth) 256cla. **Panurama:** 527bl; **Pasternak Restaurant:** 511tr; **Philharmonie:** (Berlin) 89tl; **Photolibrary:** imagebroker.net/Martin Moxter 550cla; **Popkomm GmbH:** 113bl; **Presse- und Informationsamt des Landes Berlin** BTM/Drewes 96bl; BTM/Koch 96cla; G. Schneider 47tl. **Ratskeller Bremen:** 529br; **Ratskeller Munich:** 517t; **Restaurant Bar München:** 518tl; **Rhein Hotel Bacharach:** 524tr; **Rheinisches Landesmuseum Bonn:** 412cr; **Ringhotel Schloss Tangermünde:** 514tr; **Rocco Forte Hotel de Rome:** 489br; **Rosas Dance Company, Belgium:** Herman Sorgeloos 111cr. **Schauspielhaus (Konzerthaus Berlin):** 76bc; **Scheel's Restaurant:** 533t; **Hotel Schloss Lübbenau:** 493tl, 512bl; **Schloss Sigmaringen:** 319br; **Karsten Schirmer:** 112cla; **Schlösserverwaltung (Munich):** 250cla, 251tl, 251cra, 251cr, 251br, 286tr, 286cla, 286clb, 286cb, 286br; **Schlosshotel Steinburg:** 522t; **Schwedenschenke Restaurant:** 523b; **Sea Life München:** 237cr; **STA Travel:** 544cra; **Staatsarchiv Hamburg:** 54-5; **Staatliche Museen Preußischer Kulturbesitz:** (Berlin) 52c, 59br, 60–61, 61tl, 61br, 62tc, 62cra, 62bl, 63tr, 63bl, 63clb, 63br, 64tl, 68br, 69cra, 80cla, 81cra, 93tl, 94clb, 95cb, 108tl, 129cb; Hans-Joachim Bartsch 53crb, 53br, 59bl; Jorg P. Anders 88ca, 88clb, 92cra, 94tr, 94cla, 94b, 95tl, 95cra, 95cl; Grammes 52br; Klaus Göken 60br, 80bl, 81d; Erich Lessing 80tr, 81crb; Jurgen Liepe 79c, 80clb; Georg Niedermeister 81tc; Arne Psille 51br, 52tr, 52bl; Steinkopf 88tr; **Staatliche Porzellan-Manufaktur Meißen GMBH:** 38cra, 128tr, 128cra, 128clb, 128br, 129tc, 129c, Klaus Tänzer 129cra; **Staatsgalerie Stuttgart:** 316tr, 316cla, 316clb, 316br, 317tl, 317cra, 317cr, 317br; **Städelsches Kunstinstitut:** (Frankfurt am Main) 382tr, 382cla, 382clb, 383tc, 383cra, 383crb, 383bc; **Stadtmuseum Berlin:** Hans-Joachim Bartsch 57bl; **Stadtmuseum:** (Munich) 218tl; Hans-Joachim Bartsch 54l; Sudnik 29crb; **Stasi-Museum:** (Berlin) 106bc; **Steigenberger Graf Zeppelin:** 498tl; **Steinberger Hotel Group:** 494tr; **Stiftung Preussische Schlösser und Gärten Berlin:** Roland Handrick 103 ca; Roland Handrick 103crb; 58c, 102cl, 102cb, 103br, 139cr, 140b, 142tl, 142cb, 143bl; **Stiftung Topographie des Terrors:** 85tr; **Superstock:** imagebroker.net 174-5, 332-3; MIVA Stock 98, 124-5; Alexander Schnurer/imagebroker.net; Steve Vidler/Prisma 210; Westend61 2-3; **Tourismuszentrale Rügen GmbH:** Dieter Lindemann 482tr; **The Victorian House Restaurant:** 518bc; **Vila Vita Rosenpark:** 500br; **Villa Rothschild Kempinski:** 525tl; **Vinothek Tiepolo:** 521tl; **Wallraf-Richartz-Museum:** (Cologne) 408tr, 408cla, 408clb, 408bl, 409cra, 409cr, 409cb, 409bl (© Rheinisches Bildarchiv); **www.dresden.de:** Christoph Münch 172tr; **Zefa:** 29cl, 206–7c, 391c, 426bra, 426tr, 427cb, 454cla, 455tr, 455b, 457bl; Bloemendal 5t; Damm 25b, 402b, 292, 398bc, 471b; Eckstein 27br, 427tl, 427tr; Freytag 23b, 208tr, 331tc; 37ca, 460bl, 473tr; Kehrer 29cr; Kinne 410tl, 410bc; Kohlhas 413tc; Rossenbach 402c, 414b, 415tl, 463b, 474cla; Rose 415ca; Steeger 427t; Streichan 367tr, 387b; Svenja-Foto 398tr, 407cra; M. Winkel 406tr; **Zwinger:** (Dresden) 178tc, 178br, 179bc; Gemäldegalerie Alte Meister 179crb.

Jacket Front and Spine – **Corbis:** FRb-Rose/imagebroker

Front Endpaper – **Alamy Images:** Michael Bennett Ltl; imagebroker Ltr, Rtr, Lcr; John Norman Rcra; **Corbis:** Massimo Borchi Lbl; Werner Dieterich Rcrb; ivoivanov Lcl; **Getty Images:** Richard l'Anson Lbr; Danita Delimont Rbr; Oliver Gerhard Rclb; **Superstock:** Vidler Steve/Prisma Rbl.

All other images © Dorling Kindersley.
For further information see: www.dkimages.com

Special Editions of DK Travel Guides

DK Travel Guides can be purchased in bulk quantities at discounted prices for use in promotions or as premiums. We are also able to offer special editions and personalized jackets, corporate imprints, and excerpts from all of our books, tailored specifically to meet your own needs.

To find out more, please contact:
in the United States **SpecialSales@dk.com**
in the UK **travelspecialsales@uk.dk.com**
in Canada DK Special Sales at **general@ tourmaline.ca**
in Australia **business.development@pearson. com.au**

Phrasebook

In an Emergency

Where is the telephone?	Wo ist das Telefon?	voh ist duss tel-e-fone?
Help!	Hilfe!	hilf-uh
Please call a doctor	Bitte rufen Sie einen Arzt	bitt-uh roof'n zee ine-en artst
Please call the police	Bitte rufen Sie die Polizei	bitt-uh roof'n zee dee poli-tsy
Please call the fire brigade	Bitte rufen Sie die Feuerwehr	bitt-uh roof'n zee dee foyer-vayr
Stop!	Halt!	hult

Communication Essentials

Yes	Ja	yah
No	Nein	nine
Please	Bitte	bitt-uh
Thank you	Danke	dunk-uh
Excuse me	Verzeihung	fair-tsy-hoong
Hello (good day)	Guten Tag	goot-en tahk
Goodbye	Auf Wiedersehen	owf-veed-er-zay-ern
Good evening	Guten Abend	goot'n ahb'nt
Good night	Gute Nacht	goot-uh nukht
Until tomorrow	Bis morgen	biss morg'n
See you	Tschüss	chooss
What is that?	Was ist das?	voss ist duss
Why?	Warum?	var-room
Where?	Wo?	voh
When?	Wann?	vunn
today	heute	hoyt-uh
tomorrow	morgen	morg'n
month	Monat	mohn-aht
night	Nacht	nukht
afternoon	Nachmittag	nahkh-mit-tahk
morning	Morgen	morg'n
year	Jahr	yar
there	dort	dort
here	hier	hear
week	Woche	vokh-uh
yesterday	gestern	gest'n
evening	Abend	ahb'nt

Useful Phrases

How are you? (informal)	Wie geht's?	vee gayts
Fine, thanks	Danke, es geht mir gut	dunk-uh, es gayt meer goot
Until later	Bis später	biss shpay-ter
Where is/are?	Wo ist/sind…?	voh ist/sind
How far is it to…?	Wie weit ist es…?	vee vite ist ess
Do you speak English?	Sprechen Sie Englisch?	shpresh'n zee eng-glish
I don't understand	Ich verstehe nicht	ish fair-shtay-uh nisht
Could you speak more slowly?	Könnten Sie langsamer sprechen?	kurnt-en zee lung-zam-er shpresh'n

Useful Words

large	gross	grohss
small	klein	kline
hot	heiss	hyce
cold	kalt	kult
good	gut	goot
bad	böse/schlecht	burss-uh/shlesht
open	geöffnet	g'urff-nett
closed	geschlossen	g'shloss'n
left	links	links
right	rechts	reshts
straight ahead	geradeaus	g'rah-der-owss

Making a Telephone Call

I would like to make a phone call	Ich möchte telefonieren	ish mer-shtuh tel-e-fon-eer'n
I'll try again later	Ich versuche es später noch einmal	ish fair-zookh-uh es shpay-ter nokh ine-mull
Can I leave a message?	Kann ich eine Nachricht hinterlassen?	kan ish ine-uh nakh-risht hint-er-lahss-en
answer phone	Anrufbeantworter	an-roof-be-ahnt-vort-er
telephone card	Telefonkarte	tel-e-fohn-kart-uh
receiver	Hörer	hur-er
mobile	Handy	han-dee
engaged (busy)	besetzt	b'zetst
wrong number	Falsche Verbindung	falsh-uh fair-bin-doong

Sightseeing

library	Bibliothek	bib-leo-tek
entrance ticket	Eintrittskarte	ine-tritz-kart-uh
cemetery	Friedhof	freed-hofe
train station	Bahnhof	barn-hofe
gallery	Galerie	gall-er-ree
information	Auskunft	owss-koonft
church	Kirche	keersh-uh
garden	Garten	gart'n
palace/castle	Palast/Schloss	pallast/shloss
place (square)	Platz	plats
bus stop	Haltestelle	hal-te-shtel-uh
national holiday	Nationalfeiertag	nats-yon-ahl-fire-tahk
theatre	Theater	tay-aht-er
free admission	Eintritt frei	ine-tritt fry

Shopping

Do you have/ Is there…?	Gibt es…?	geept ess
How much does it cost?	Was kostet das?	voss kost't duss
When do you open/ close?	Wann öffnen Sie? schließen Sie?	vunn off'n zee shlees'n zee
this	das	duss
expensive	teuer	toy-er
cheap	preiswert	price-vurt
size	Größe	gruhs-uh
number	Nummer	noom-er
colour	Farbe	farb-uh
brown	braun	brown
black	schwarz	shvarts
red	rot	roht
blue	blau	blau
green	grün	groon
yellow	gelb	gelp

Types of Shop

antique shop	Antiquariat	antik-var-yat
chemist (pharmacy)	Apotheke	appo-tay-kuh
bank	Bank	bunk
market	Markt	markt
travel agency	Reisebüro	rye-zer-boo-roe
department store	Warenhaus	vahr'n-hows
chemist's, drugstore	Drogerie	droog-er-ree
hairdresser	Friseur	freezz-er
newspaper kiosk	Zeitungskiosk	tsytoongs-kee-osk

bookshop	**Buchhandlung**	*bookh*-hant-loong
bakery	**Bäckerei**	*beck-er-**eye***
post office	**Post**	*posst*
shop/store	**Geschäft/Laden**	*gush-**eft**/**lard**'n*
film processing shop	**Photogeschäft**	*fo-to-gush-**eft***
self-service shop	**Selbstbedienungs- laden**	*selpst-bed-**ee**-nungs-lard'n*
shoe shop	**Schuhladen**	*shoo-lard'n*
clothes shop	**Kleiderladen, Boutique**	*klyder-lard'n boo-**teek**-uh*
food shop	**Lebensmittel- geschäft**	*lay-bens-mittel-gush-eft*
glass, porcelain	**Glas, Porzellan**	*glars, Port-sellahn*

Staying in a Hotel

Do you have any vacancies?	**Haben Sie noch Zimmer frei?**	*harb'n zee nokh tsimm-er-fry*
with twin beds?	**mit zwei Betten?**	*mitt tsvy bett'n*
with a double bed?	**mit einem Doppelbett?**	*mitt ine'm dopp'l-bet*
with a bath?	**mit Bad?**	*mitt **bart***
with a shower?	**mit Dusche?**	*mitt **doosh**-uh*
I have a reservation	**Ich habe eine Reservierung**	*ish harb-uh ine-uh rez-er-**veer**-oong*
key	**Schlüssel**	*shlooss'l*
porter	**Pförtner**	*pfert-ner*

Eating Out

Do you have a table for…?	**Haben Sie einen Tisch für…?**	*harb'n zee tish foor*
I would like to reserve a table	**Ich möchte eine Reservierung machen**	*ish **mer**-shtuh ine-uh rezer-**veer**-oong makh'n*
I'm a vegetarian	**Ich bin Vegetarier**	*ish bin vegg-er-**tah**-ree-er*
Waiter!	**Herr Ober!**	*hair oh-bare!*
The bill (check), please	**Die Rechnung, bitte**	*dee **resh**-noong bitt-uh*
breakfast	**Frühstück**	*froo-shtock*
lunch	**Mittagessen**	*mit-targ-ess'n*
dinner	**Abendessen**	*arb'nt-ess'n*
bottle	**Flasche**	*flush-uh*
dish of the day	**Tagesgericht**	*tahg-es-gur-isht*
main dish	**Hauptgericht**	*howpt-gur-isht*
dessert	**Nachtisch**	*nahkh-tish*
cup	**Tasse**	*tass-uh*
wine list	**Weinkarte**	*vine-kart-uh*
tankard	**Krug**	*khroog*
glass	**Glas**	*glars*
spoon	**Löffel**	*lerff'l*
teaspoon	**Teelöffel**	*tay-lerff'l*
tip	**Trinkgeld**	*trink-gelt*
knife	**Messer**	*mess-er*
starter (appetizer)	**Vorspeise**	*for-shpize-uh*
the bill	**Rechnung**	*resh-noong*
plate	**Teller**	*tell-er*
fork	**Gabel**	*gahb'l*

Menu Decoder

Aal	*arl*	eel
Apfel	*upf'l*	apple
Apfelschorle	*upf'l-shoorl-uh*	apple juice with sparkling mineral water
Apfelsine	*upf'l-seen-uh*	orange
Aprikose	*upri-**kawz**-uh*	apricot
Artischocke	*arti-**shokh**-uh- uh*	artichoke
Aubergine	*or-ber-jeen-uh*	aubergine (eggplant)
Banane	*bar-**narn**-uh*	banana
Beefsteack	*beef-stayk*	steak
Bier	*beer*	beer
Bockwurst	*bokh-voorst*	a type of sausage
Bohnensuppe	*burn-en-zoop-uh*	bean soup
Branntwein	*brant-vine*	spirits
Bratkartoffeln	*brat-kar-toff'ln*	fried potatoes
Bratwurst	*brat-voorst*	fried sausage
Brötchen	*bret-tchen*	bread roll
Brot	*brot*	bread
Brühe	*bruh-uh*	broth
Butter	*boot-ter*	butter
Champignon	*shum-pin-yong*	mushroom
Currywurst	*kha-ree-voorst*	sausage with curry sauce
Dill	*dill*	dill
Ei	*eye*	egg
Eis	*ice*	ice/ ice cream
Ente	*ent-uh*	duck
Erdbeeren	*ayrt-**beer**'n*	strawberries
Fisch	*fish*	fish
Forelle	*for-**ell**-uh*	trout
Frikadelle	*Frika-dayl-uh*	rissole/hamburger
Gans	*ganns*	goose
Garnele	*gar-nayl-uh*	prawn/shrimp
gebraten	*g'**braat**'n*	fried
gegrillt	*g'grilt*	grilled
gekocht	*g'**kokh**t*	boiled
geräuchert	*g'**rowk**-ert*	smoked
Geflügel	*g'**floog**'l*	poultry
Gemüse	*g'**mooz**-uh*	vegetables
Grütze	*grurt-ser*	groats, gruel
Gulasch	*goo-lush*	goulash
Gurke	*goork-uh*	gherkin
Hammelbraten	*hamm'l-**braat**'n*	roast mutton
Hähnchen	*haynsh'n*	chicken
Hering	*hair-ing*	herring
Himbeeren	*him-beer'n*	raspberries
Honig	*hoe-nikh*	honey
Kaffee	*kaf-**fay***	coffee
Kalbfleisch	*kalp-flysh*	veal
Kaninchen	*ka-**neensh**'n*	rabbit
Karpfen	*karpf'n*	carp
Kartoffelpüree	*kar-toff'l-poor-ay*	mashed potatoes
Käse	*kayz-uh*	cheese
Kaviar	*kar-vee-ar*	caviar
Knoblauch	*k'nob-lowkh*	garlic
Knödel	*k'nerd'l*	noodle
Kohl	*koal*	cabbage
Kopfsalat	*kopf-zal-aat*	lettuce
Krebs	*krayps*	crab
Kuchen	*kookh'n*	cake
Lachs	*lahkhs*	salmon
Leber	*lay-ber*	liver
mariniert	*mari-neert*	marinated
Marmelade	*marmer-**lard**-uh*	marmalade, jam
Meerrettich	*may-re-tish*	horseradish
Milch	*milsh*	milk
Mineralwasser	*minn-er-**arl**-vuss-er*	mineral water
Möhre	*mer-uh*	carrot
Nuss	*nooss*	nut
Öl	*erl*	oil
Olive	*o-**leev**-uh*	olive
Petersilie	*payt-er-**zee**-li-uh*	parsley
Pfeffer	*pfeff-er*	pepper
Pfirsich	*pfir-zish*	peach
Pflaumen	*pflow-men*	plum
Pommes frites	*pomm-**fritt***	chips/ French fries
Quark	*kvark*	soft cheese
Radieschen	*ra-**deesh**'n*	radish
Rinderbraten	*rind-er-brat'n*	joint of beef
Rinderroulade	*rind-er-roo-lard-uh*	beef olive
Rindfleisch	*rint-flysh*	beef
Rippchen	*rip-sh'n*	cured pork rib
Rotkohl	*roht-koal*	red cabbage
Rüben	*rhoob'n*	turnip
Rührei	*rhoo-er-eye*	scrambled eggs
Saft	*zuft*	juice
Salat	*zal-aat*	salad

Salz	*zults*	salt
Salzkartoffeln	*zults-kar-toff'l*	boiled potatoes
Sauerkirschen	*zow-er-keersh'n*	cherries
Sauerkraut	*zow-er-krowt*	sauerkraut
Sekt	*zekt*	sparkling wine
Senf	*zenf*	mustard
scharf	*sharf*	spicy
Schaschlik	*shash-lik*	kebab
Schlagsahne	*shlahgg-zarn-uh*	whipped cream
Schnittlauch	*shnit-lowkh*	chives
Schnitzel	*shnitz'l*	veal or pork cutlet
Schweine-	*shvine-flysh*	pork
fleisch		
Spargel	*shparg'l*	asparagus
Spiegelei	*shpeeg'l-eye*	fried egg
Spinat	*shpin-art*	spinach
Tee	*tay*	tea
Tomate	*tom-art-uh*	tomato
Wassermelone	*vuss-er-me-lohn-uh*	watermelon
Wein	*vine*	wine
Weintrauben	*vine-trowb'n*	grapes
Wiener	*veen-er voorst-sh'n*	frankfurter
Würstchen		
Zander	*tsan-der*	pike-perch
Zitrone	*tsi-trohn-uh*	lemon
Zucker	*tsook-er*	sugar
Zwieback	*tsvee-bak*	rusk
Zwiebel	*tsveeb'l*	onion

Numbers

0	**null**	*nool*
1	**eins**	*eye'ns*
2	**zwei**	*tsvy*
3	**drei**	*dry*
4	**vier**	*feer*
5	**fünf**	*foonf*
6	**sechs**	*zex*
7	**sieben**	*zeeb'n*
8	**acht**	*uhkht*
9	**neun**	*noyn*
10	**zehn**	*tsayn*
11	**elf**	*elf*
12	**zwölf**	*tserlf*
13	**dreizehn**	*dry-tsayn*
14	**vierzehn**	*feer-tsayn*
15	**fünfzehn**	*foonf-tsayn*
16	**sechzehn**	*zex-tsayn*
17	**siebzehn**	*zeep-tsayn*
18	**achtzehn**	*uhkht-tsayn*
19	**neunzehn**	*noyn-tsayn*
20	**zwanzig**	*tsvunn-tsig*
21	**einundzwanzig**	*ine-oont-tsvunn-tsig*
30	**dreißig**	*dry-sig*
40	**vierzig**	*feer-sig*
50	**fünfzig**	*foonf-tsig*
60	**sechzig**	*zex-tsig*
70	**siebzig**	*zeep-tsig*
80	**achtzig**	*uhkht-tsig*
90	**neunzig**	*noyn-tsig*
100	**hundert**	*hoond't*
1000	**tausend**	*towz'nt*
1 000 000	**eine Million**	*ine-uh mill-yon*

Time

one minute	**eine Minute**	*ine-uh min-oot-uh*
one hour	**eine Stunde**	*ine-uh shtoond-uh*
half an hour	**eine halbe Stunde**	*ine-uh hullb-uh shtoond-uh*
Monday	**Montag**	*mohn-targ*
Tuesday	**Dienstag**	*deens-targ*
Wednesday	**Mittwoch**	*mitt-vokh*
Thursday	**Donnerstag**	*donn-ers-targ*
Friday	**Freitag**	*fry-targ*
Saturday	**Samstag/**	*zums-targ*
	Sonnabend	*zonn-ah-bent*
Sunday	**Sonntag**	*zon-targ*
January	**Januar**	*yan-ooar*
February	**Februar**	*fay-brooar*
March	**März**	*mairts*
April	**April**	*april*
May	**Mai**	*my*
June	**Juni**	*yoo-ni*
July	**Juli**	*yoo-lee*
August	**August**	*ow-goost*
September	**September**	*zep-tem-ber*
October	**Oktober**	*ok-toh-ber*
November	**November**	*no-vem-ber*
December	**Dezember**	*day-tsem-ber*
spring	**Frühling**	*froo-ling*
summer	**Sommer**	*zomm-er*
autumn (fall)	**Herbst**	*hairpst*
winter	**Winter**	*vint-er*

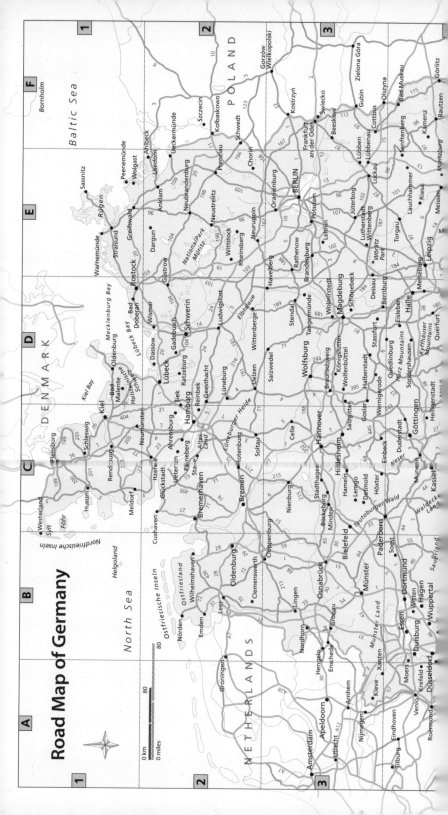